D0163310

An Encyclopedia of
War and Ethics

An Encyclopedia of War and Ethics

Edited by
DONALD A. WELLS

GREENWOOD PRESS
Westport, Connecticut • London

Library of Congress Cataloging-in-Publication Data

An encyclopedia of war and ethics / edited by Donald A. Wells.
    p. cm.
   Includes bibliographical references and index.
   ISBN 0–313–29116–0 (alk. paper)
   1. War—Moral and ethical aspects—Encyclopedias. 2. Just war
doctrine—Encyclopedias. I. Wells, Donald A. (Donald Arthur).
B105.W3E53   1996
172'.42'03—dc20   95–23647

British Library Cataloguing in Publication Data is available.

Library of Congress Catalog Card Number: 95–23647
ISBN: 0–313–29116–0

First published in 1996

Greenwood Press, 88 Post Road West, Westport, CT 06881
An imprint of Greenwood Publishing Group, Inc.

Printed in the United States of America

The paper used in this book complies with the
Permanent Paper Standard issued by the National
Information Standards Organization (Z39.48–1984).

10 9 8 7 6 5 4 3 2 1

CONTENTS

PREFACE

War is an ethical problem because it obligates us to do abroad what would be illegal and immoral at home, namely, to kill strangers, persons whom we have never met and who have personally done us no harm; to hold innocent men, women, and children hostage for putative crimes they did not commit; to lay waste to their environment and plunder their national treasures; and to do all of this in the name of economic, political, and ideological agendas. It was believed at least as far back as Cicero that moral limits existed as to what could be justified in war, and for the past two millennia thinkers have sought for these limits. This search has presupposed two interrelated inviolate premises: killing is prima facie wrong because human beings have a right to life, and the nation-state must be preserved at all costs.

The havoc of war has been encapsulated in myths of national security, evil empires, and crusade language so firmly that opponents rarely see what they are doing when they make war on the innocent by laying siege to civilian centers or napalming villages from the air. Ordinarily, human life is considered an inalienable right. War inverts this elementary right of victims. Persons about to be slain should not be required to prove why this ought not to be done; citizens in cities should not be required to prove why they ought not to be bombed from the air, any more than the inmates of extermination camps should need to justify their survival to the operators of those camps. It is the assassins, the bombardiers, the gas chamber operators who must explain their acts. The judges at Nuremberg saw this clearly. The failure of victims to give a persuasive justification for their survival did not imply that the death camps could continue. Although the Nuremberg judges affirmed that Nazism was unworthy, they left unclear whether the Nazi extermination program could have been justified in the name of democracy. In part, this ambiguity followed from the court's determination that the death camps were militarily unnecessary; it was not clear what the court's conclusion would have been if the camps had been found militarily necessary.

Writers of such documents as the Bhagavad Gita, the Qur'an, and the Old and New Testaments have attempted to explain why, and under what circumstances, what has been forbidden in general might properly be done in some particular circumstance. Augustine (354–430), coming out of a tradition that had tended to reject war altogether, felt compelled to explain why wars could be justified for previously pacifist Christians. His ''just war'' theories were discussed throughout the medieval period, and today most of the language that speaks of the justification or condemnation of war or of the need for war crimes trials comes from these reflections. The problem was divided into two questions: (1) under what conditions is it just to go to war? (*jus ad bellum*), and (2) under what conditions can it be claimed that a war, once justly entered, is being waged justly? (*jus in bello*). Just war theory was designed to judge wars on a case-by-case basis, and it was implied that if some wars were just, others were unjust.

Answers to the first question presupposed that if the proper authority had declared the war, this authority had worthy reasons, and the entry into war was a last resort, then the war was justified. However, in the absence of any authority to assess the reasoning, moral anarchy existed, and nations went to war in defense of their perceived interests. By the 18th century most legal writers had concluded that since sovereign nations had an inviolate right to survival by any means, and since there was no compelling judge to assess their reasons, this question had become irrelevant. The need even to bother with a declaration of war had fallen into desuetude. Between 1770 and 1870, at least eighty wars were fought in Europe alone without any declaration at all, and few of the over 300 wars fought since the end of World War II have been preceded by a formal declaration of war. In spite of the Paris Peace Pact of 1928, few international legalists were persuaded that crimes against the peace existed, notwithstanding the counterclaim of the judges at the Nuremberg and Tokyo war crimes trials.

With regard to the second question, however, efforts continued to try to set limits to the havoc of war using just war notions of proportionality and a combatant–noncombatant distinction. Medieval church councils, and later resolutions at Geneva, St. Petersburg, Brussels, The Hague, and the United Nations General Assembly endeavored to identify forbidden weapons and strategies. All such efforts, however, labored under the limitations of three military axioms: (1) every army has the right to win (the doctrine of military necessity), thus nothing can be prohibited that is required for victory; (2) armies that are illegally attacked have a right of reprisal to respond legally in kind; and (3) since soldiers are obligated to obey the orders of their superiors, neither war crimes nor crimes against humanity can be charged against soldiers acting under superior orders.

The entries that follow deal with efforts both to judge and to justify war. Authorship is noted at the end of each entry. Those not so specified were written by the editor. This volume does not claim to be a moral manual. The contributors do not always agree, and this very disagreement portrays the difficulty faced by war makers who endeavor to show why what prima facie ought not to be done, may now be justifiably defended. International jurists from Hugo Grotius (1583–1645) to the present have sought for the existence of laws either in custom or in supposed natural law, from which laws of war might be deduced. Yet, for every effort to establish that some strategy or weapon ought to be forbidden, another claim has been made that we may "think the unthinkable." The Hague efforts to ban weapons and strategies that caused "superfluous injury" or "unnecessary suffering" foundered on the subjective nature of such assessments. A simple illustration of this may be seen in the current U.S. Army manual, *The Law of Land Warfare,* which bans lances with barbed tips as excessive, while permitting chemicals, incendiaries, fragmentation bombs, and nuclear missiles as not excessive. The entries that follow explore some of the difficulties in relating war to ethics.

Each entry has a bibliography suggesting further reading and contains references at its end to see further related entries in the volume. Asterisks in the body of the texts refer the reader to entries on those topics. Unlike a conventional encyclopedia, this volume contains an index for ease in cross-reference.

This encyclopedia would not have been possible were it not for the scholarly and soul-searching reflection of the forty-five contributors. Obviously, persons of intelligence and good will have disagreed on ethical judgments about war, and the entries printed herein exemplify this disagreement. No book on ethics can serve as a simple *vade mecum,* but it can, hopefully, both sharpen the questions and suggest possible answers. Special acknowledgement is due to Mildred Vasan, Senior Editor at Greenwood Press, whose wise counsel has been of inestimable assistance, and to Nita Romer, Production Editor, whose critical judgment brought the contributions of the many to unity.

—Donald A. Wells
Editor

An Encyclopedia of
War and Ethics

A

ACCIDENTAL NUCLEAR WAR. During the Cold War*, accidental nuclear war was a popular movie topic. In *Dr. Strangelove,* a rogue commander orders a nuclear strike on Russia, irrespective of Washington's wishes. In the movie *Fail Safe,* U.S. military and political leaders are unable to recall a nuclear-armed bomber from attacking Moscow. In *War Games,* U.S. technology brings the world to the brink of destruction as a computer simulates an incoming barrage of Soviet warheads and nearly launches a very real U.S. retaliatory strike. In each of these movies, the world teeters on the brink of a nuclear holocaust. It is misleading, however, to label unauthorized, unwarranted, or unplanned acts as "accidents." No nuclear war* is accidental. Although the timing and target may be accidental, every nation that has the capability to start an accidental nuclear war developed nuclear capabilities mindful that it one day might fight a nuclear war. The country purposefully used its financial and human resources to research, develop, test, evaluate, and procure nuclear weapons and their delivery systems. Nuclear battle plans were drawn, forces were trained, and troops were equipped for the purpose of fighting a nuclear war.

The United States and the former Soviet Union sought to lessen the danger that a nuclear war could be started without proper authorization or by misreading events. Several bilateral and multilateral agreements were reached, aimed at lowering the risk of an unauthorized, unwarranted, or unplanned nuclear war.

The 1963 Hot Line agreement commits the United States and the former Soviet Union to maintain a direct communications link between the two governments for use in a time of crisis. This agreement was spurred by the Cuban Missile Crisis*. The 1971 Hot Line Modernization agreement and the 1984 Hot Line Expansion agreement provided for this U.S.-USSR direct communication link to be updated and improved.

The 1971 Accidents Measures agreement commits the United States and the Soviet Union to notify each other of the detection by missile warning systems of unidentified objects and of any planned missile launches that will extend beyond national territory in the direction of the other country.

The 1972 Incidents at Sea agreement came in response to U.S. and USSR ships and submarines colliding into each other. While this agreement does not seek to limit forces or their deployment, it seeks to enhance mutual knowledge of military activities and to prevent accidental conflict.

The 1973 Prevention of Nuclear War agreement commits the United States and the Soviet Union to enter into urgent consultations with each other when relations between the two countries appear to risk nuclear conflict.

The 1986 Confidence and Security-Building Measures document, also known as the Stockholm agreement, was negotiated under the auspices of the Conference on Security and Cooperation in Europe (CSCE). This important treaty was designed to decrease the chances of war in Europe by increasing openness and predictability about military activities. Signed by all the nations of Europe, the Stockholm agreement, among other things, requires advance notice of military exercises in Europe, provides for international observation of large military activities, and mandates the exchange of annual forecasts of large military activities.

In 1987, Presidents Ronald Reagan and Mikhail Gorbachev agreed to establish Nuclear Risk Reduction centers. Under this agreement, each party agrees to establish a nuclear risk reduction center in its capital and to establish a special communications link between these centers. They became operational on April 1, 1988. The centers have a communications capability that is similar to the modernized Hot Line. Unlike the Hot Line, which is reserved for heads of state, the nuclear risk reduction centers communicate at the government-to-government level. The principal function of the centers is to exchange information and notifications as required by existing arms control and confidence-building agreements such as the 1971 Accidents Measures agreement, the 1972 Incidents at Sea agreement, and the Stockholm agreement.

The 1988 Ballistic Missile Launch Notification agreement builds on the Accidents Measures agreement. This U.S.-USSR agreement requires each party to notify the other through the risk reduction centers in advance of any planned launches of strategic land-based or sea-based ballistic missiles.

The aforementioned agreements coupled with arms control agreements cutting the U.S. and Soviet nuclear weapons stockpiles have helped lessen the threat that nuclear weapons will be used between the United States and Russia. They do not, however, eliminate the threat of a nuclear holocaust. No nuclear arms control treaties to date affect the arsenals of the United Kingdom, France, and China. More importantly, current agreements between the United States and the former Soviet Union only trim the overkill from the nuclear arsenals built up by the superpowers during the Cold War. If all arms control treaties and initiatives are implemented as planned, the United States and Russia will be left with 3,500 and 3,000 strategic nuclear weapons, respectively. In addition, each side plans to maintain upwards of 1,500 battlefield or tactical nuclear weapons. The destructive power of the remaining weapons is very real. Secretary of State Warren Christopher pointed out in congressional testimony (1994) that there was "no question that even the remaining one-third of our strategic forces are extremely powerful and have a capacity to destroy civilization as we know it several times over."

The only way to avoid completely the possibility of nuclear war, planned or not, is to rid the world of the capabilities to launch a nuclear war. Although military planners are taught from day one to analyze capabilities and not focus on intentions, measures undertaken to reduce the risk of unplanned nuclear war fail to address capabilities. No negotiations aimed at eventually eliminating the nuclear threat are planned.

See CAUSES OF WAR; MUTUAL ASSURED DESTRUCTION; NUCLEAR ACCIDENTS; PROPAGANDA.

BIBLIOGRAPHY
"Accidental Nuclear War: A Rising Risk?" *Defense Monitor* 15, no. 7 (Center for Defense Information 1986).
Bundy, McGeorge, William Crowe Jr., and Sidney Drell, *Reducing Nuclear Danger: The Road Away from the Brink* (Council on Foreign Relations, 1993).
Goodpaster, General Andrew, USA (Ret.), *Beyond the Nuclear Peril: The Year in Review and the Years Ahead* (Henry L. Stimson Center, January 1995).

Kathryn R. Schultz

ADDAMS, JANE (1860–1935). Established Hull House (1888) in Chicago, was the first chairperson of the Women's Peace Party (1915), and was the first president of the Women's International League for Peace and Freedom (1920). Born in Cedarville, Illinois on September 6, 1860, the youngest of eight children, Addams received the equivalent of a college education at Rockford Seminary, which became Rockford College. In 1881 she set out to learn medicine at the Women's Medical College in Philadelphia. A chronic spinal condition forced her to drop out in 1882, and although surgery partially helped, she remained ill most of her life, suffering variously from typhoid, tuberculosis of the kidneys, and a heart attack. She had an operation for tumors, and finally died of cancer on May 21, 1935.

Hull House was established to assist poor immigrant women, and in 1891 included a cooperative boarding house for young women. In 1895 Addams was appointed garbage inspector for Chicago's 19th Ward. She was elected to the Daughters of the American Revolution (DAR) in 1901 even though she had defended the anarchist Abraham Isaak. In January 1915, a large convention of women met in the New Willard Hotel in Washington and formed a Women's Peace Party, with Addams as the chairperson. In April 1915 a plan was established to hold a women's peace conference at The Hague, and forty-seven women, with Addams as the leader, sailed for Europe. The conference, attended by 1,136 women, was ridiculed by the press, and President Theodore Roosevelt called the participants "silly and base." The sessions were named the Women's International Committee for Permanent Peace.

At the time of World War I Addams appeared before a congressional subcommittee to ask for a referendum of approval from the American people before any declaration of war was made. Her book, *Peace and Bread in Time of War,* written in 1915, opposed conscription, and she and thirteen other women traveled to fourteen world capitals speaking against the war. The civilian losses in the sinking of the *Lusitania* prompted strong protests against her antiwar stand, and the *New York Times* called her a "silly, vain, impertinent old maid." In the fall of 1915 she persuaded Henry Ford to finance a peace conference in Stockholm.

In 1920 she called a women's conference in Zurich with sixteen delegations. The American and British delegations were shocked at the emaciated condition of the many European delegates, who were so starved that they did not dare eat the banquet foods for fear that they could not digest them. At this meeting the Women's International League for Peace and Freedom (WILPF) was organized, with Jane Addams as president and headquarters in Geneva. One of the league's first declarations was that the Treaty of Versailles had laid the foundation for future wars. The league supported mediation, conscientious objection, racial equality, and peaceful methods for revolutionary movements. In the early 1920s, under the leadership of Emily Greene Balch, who had lost her professorship at Wellesley, in part because of her pacifism*, the league organized a train to travel throughout the midwest speaking against war. The train was attacked by a posse from the DAR, and the Detroit city council declared that the train should be derailed and the women tarred and feathered. In 1929, when Addams resigned as the president of WILPF, she was elected honorary president for life. In 1931 she received the Nobel Peace Prize.

She was not a pacifist and did not oppose war on religious grounds, but considered war a wasteful and ineffective means to solve social problems. She urged eliminating free enterprise in the armaments business and proposed that the need for arms should be determined by the League of Nations, which should also be the sole manufacturer and distributor of arms. She was a pioneer Socialist, inspired in part by her visit with Tolstoy in 1896. She voted for Woodrow Wilson in 1916, Eugene Debs* in 1920, Robert LaFollette in 1924, and Herbert Hoover in 1928 and 1932. She believed that women had a more developed sense of moral obligation than men due to their nurturing and protective functions. She was the author of ten books and many articles.

The Women's International League for Peace and Freedom has remained active, and WILPF lobbyist and executive secretary, Dorothy Detzer, following World War I, prodded Senators Gerald P. Nye (R-ND) and George W. Norris (IR-NE) to conduct the famous investigation of the arms industry ("the merchants of death"), and helped select the chief investigator for the Nye Committee, Stephen Rauschenbush. Although the league had lost two-thirds of its membership by 1946, and it was debated whether the league should be dissolved, WILPF has continued and Emily Balch, as president, received the Nobel Peace Prize that same year.

See CHRISTIANITY AND WAR; DAY, DOROTHY; MUSTE, ABRAHAM JOHANNES; ROYDEN, MAUDE; WOMEN IN THE MILITARY.

BIBLIOGRAPHY

Alonso, Harriet Hyman, *Peace as a Women's Issue: A History of the U.S. Movements for World Peace and Women's Rights* (Syracuse, N.Y.: Syracuse University Press, 1993).

Lasch, Christopher, *The Social Thought of Jane Addams* (New York: Bobbs-Merrill, 1965).

Oldfield, Sybil, *Women Against the Iron Fist: Alternatives to Militarism 1900–1989* (London: Blackwell, 1989).

Tims, Margaret, *Jane Addams of Hull House 1860–1935* (London: George Allen & Unwin, 1961).

AERIAL WARFARE. Before World War II, most commentators believed that the laws of land warfare*—specifically, those that governed the bombardment of unfortified and protected places—would suffice to protect noncombatants from the newly emerging air technology. However, when heavy, multiengine bombers finally became available and were employed in World War II, it quickly became apparent that the existing legal restraints were inadequate.

The conventions against bombing unfortified cities were rendered null and void because there were no unfortified places, at least not after the first attack. Antiaircraft batteries and fighter squadrons were quickly moved into place to defend all possible targets. The conventions protecting medical and other civilian facilities likewise became inoperative for technical reasons. Because of inaccurate bombsights, enemy defensive measures, bombing altitudes, poor weather, and other factors, it was technically impossible for bombers to avoid hitting protected places and persons. This was especially true when all pretense at precision bombing was dropped in favor of area and fire bombing.

However, instead of ordering a stop to the bombing, military and political leaders rationalized these violations of the laws of land warfare in terms of military necessity*, of unavoidable collateral damage*, of the cruelty of total war*, of how the life of each soldier was worth dozens of enemy civilians, of how all our enemies were combatants*, at least in their hearts, and so forth. And so, the destruction of protected places and persons soon came to be regarded as regrettable, but unavoidable.

In response, a few moralists attempted to fill the void. In particular, John Ford wrote a groundbreaking article in 1944, ''The Morality of Obliteration Bombing,'' in which he emphasized that large classes of those killed in the bombing of cities could not possibly be considered combatants. Surely, Ford argued, children, the elderly, the sick, mothers not working in munitions factories, and many other groups must be considered noncombatants and, therefore, innocents* to be protected from indiscriminate attack.

While Ford's argument was sound, it remains, nonetheless, unpersuasive among those who possess the power to act upon it. For example, the first sec-

retary of the Air Force, Stuart Symington, demonstrated on a number of occasions how the same rationalizations used to override the laws of land warfare
worked equally well to parry Ford's argument. In particular, Symington could
not understand why Americans should be concerned with saving the lives of
enemy women and children when killing these people in their homes might save
the lives of American soldiers on the battlefield. Indeed, the most sympathetic
response to Ford's line of argument was the promise that, next time, when the
technology had been further refined, the bombing would be more precise,
thereby reducing its indiscriminate character and allowing innocent noncombatants to escape injury. The most recent rehearsal of this response was during the
Persian Gulf War*.

After World War II, a less overtly moral approach was taken by historians of
air power, such as Michael Sherry and Ronald Schaffer. These historians noted
with some indignation that independent air operations had yet to make a significant contribution to winning a war. For example, between 1965 and 1966,
the bombing of North Vietnam increased from 33,000 to 128,000 tons. However,
the *Pentagon Papers* estimated that, for each dollar of damage inflicted on North
Vietnam, the United States expended $6.60 in 1965 and $9.60 in 1966. This
stunning decrease in efficiency might have been acceptable if the bombing had
accomplished its primary missions of reducing the flow of materiel to the South
and weakening the will of the North to continue the war. But the authors of the
study found no evidence that this had occurred.

The proponents of air power have always indicted the historians for their lack
of faith in the future. For example, General Hoyt Vandenberg said in 1949,
''What you are quoting from, sir, is tactics and techniques of a war that is past
[World War II]. . . . We [now] have new tactics, new techniques, new speeds,
new altitudes, an entirely different type [i.e., nuclear] of explosive.'' A 1993
Nova documentary on the Persian Gulf War, entitled ''Can Bombing Win a
War,'' presented the same point of view: Not yet, but, with smart bombs, soon.
Perhaps, next time.

As the responses of the proponents indicate, their thinking is dominated not
by the moralist's concern for noncombatant immunity, but by the technological
imperative—by the belief that, because it will soon be technologically possible
to do something, we should do it. The budgetary success of President Ronald
Reagan's Star Wars initiative is the most recent example of this kind of reasoning. More important, if less frequently discussed, is the belief that only a bu-
reaucratically independent air force can properly employ the new air technology.

This doctrine was articulated most clearly by Guilio Douhet*, who distinguished between auxiliary aviation and an independent air force. In Douhet's
view, auxiliary aviation (i.e., tactical air power) is ''worthless, superfluous,
harmful'' because its only mission is to support naval or military forces, while
an independent air force (i.e., strategic air power) is invaluable because its independent offensive mission of bombing cities so as to crush the material and
moral resistance of the enemy will win wars even before ground forces can

mobilize. In the eyes of the prophets of air power, bureaucratic independence is the sine qua non for fullest realization of the technological imperative. In order to exploit the full war-winning potential of aircraft and missiles, the air force must be freed from the needs and concerns of ground forces.

Thus, the moral challenge of aerial warfare—the indiscriminate bombing of noncombatants—is overshadowed by the moral dilemma of the air force. As long as the air force continues to believe, as Douhet, General "Billy" Mitchell, and others have taught, that an independent mission is essential to maintaining its bureaucratic independence, it will continue bombing cities, despite the pleas of the ethicists that it is immoral, of the jurists that it violates the laws of land warfare, and of the historians that it is militarily ineffective. Relying on the technological imperative, apologists will continue to predict that, next time, when the technology has been further refined, independent bombardments will surely make a significant contribution to winning a war.

See CASUALTIES OF WAR; COLLATERAL DAMAGE; FORBIDDEN STRATEGIES.

BIBLIOGRAPHY

Ford, S. J., John C., "The Morality of Obliteration Bombing," *Theological Studies* (September 1944), 261–309.

Futrell, Robert Frank, *Ideas, Concepts, Doctrine: A History of Basic Thinking in the U.S. Air Force, 1907–1964*, 2 vols. (Washington, D.C.: Air University Press, 1971).

Schaffer, Ronald, *Wings of Judgment: American Bombing in World War II* (New York: Oxford University Press, 1985).

Sherry, Michael, *The Rise of American Air Power: The Creation of Armageddon* (New Haven, Conn.: Yale University Press, 1987).

Brien Hallett

AGGRESSION, ATTEMPTS TO DEFINE. Traditionally, the aggressor was the nation that first invaded the sovereign territory of another nation, and/or fired the first shot. Each nation maligned its neighbor's motives while praising its own. The emergence of the belief in the legitimacy of the concept of preemptive war ("first strike"*) either made all nations aggressors or made the issue otiose. The opening statement in Annex 4, "Commentary on the Definition of a Case of Aggression," of the special committee of the temporary mixed commission of the League of Nations, April 16–23, 1923 affirmed that "under the conditions of modern warfare, it would seem impossible to decide even in theory what constitutes an act of aggression." This did not prevent the League of Nations from issuing in a declaration concerning wars of aggression that "all wars of aggression are, and shall always be, prohibited." At a July 4, 1933, meeting in London, a convention for the definition of aggression was signed between Romania, the USSR, Czechoslovakia, Turkey, and Yugoslavia; on July 5, 1933, a similar convention was signed between the USSR and Lithuania; and on July 8, 1937, a treaty of nonaggression was signed in Teheran between Afghanistan, Iraq, Iran, and Turkey. The meaning of aggression, however, remained elusive.

For the past three decades the United Nations has endeavored to define aggression in such a fashion as to elicit approval of the member states. The General Assembly established in 1963 a special committee on principles of international law concerning friendly relations and cooperation among states. The committee first met in 1964 in Mexico City, and among the issues they considered was the duty to refrain from intervention. The committee met again in 1966 in New York, where the committee appealed to the Paris Peace Pact* of 1928, which they called a "general treaty for the renunciation of war." Most Western states resisted any effort at precision, based on their fear that to do so would infringe on the right of national defense. While the committee was unable to get agreement on a definition of aggression, it did draft a statement that wars of aggression constituted international crimes. The nations of the Eastern and Western blocs could not agree as to which body would determine that an act of aggression had taken place and who the aggressor nation was. On December 21, 1965, the UN General Assembly issued a resolution at its 1408th Plenary Meeting titled, "Declaration of the Inadmissibility of Intervention in the Domestic Affairs of States and the Protection of Their Independence and Sovereignty." The declaration reaffirmed the principle of nonintervention to the effect that armed intervention was synonymous with aggression, and that such aggressive acts included economic and political measures as well as armed ones. Since such intervention was a standard part of international relations, it was clear that it did not speak to the matter of aggression.

On December 18, 1967, the UN General Assembly established in resolution 2330 a special committee on the question of defining aggression. In spite of opposition from some nations that feared it would simply be a propaganda tool and others who saw the effort as futile, the committee was urged to develop a draft definition to be presented to the General Assembly in 1968. The committee chose, instead, to call for further study of all the definitions suggested and not to submit a definition for approval or rejection. Among the issues included were indirect aggression, economic aggression, ideological aggression, and atomic aggression.

On March 25, 1969, the U.S. representative to the General Assembly's special committee on the question of defining aggression submitted a draft definition cosponsored by Canada, Italy, Japan, Australia, and the United Kingdom. The draft proposed that only the Security Council be empowered to make the assessment that an act of aggression had taken place. A list of aggressive acts was included in the draft. Unfortunately, this meant that any permanent member of the Security Council would be able to veto any suggestion that it had been guilty of acts of aggression. In 1972, in its fifth year, the committee concluded its sessions with the assertion that while progress had been made, no definition was forthcoming. A fifteen-member special committee to define aggression met between 1952 and 1954; a nineteen-member committee met from 1954 to 1957; a twenty-three-member committee met between 1959 and 1967; and a thirty-five-member committee met between 1967 and 1974. On April 12, 1974, at the

2319th plenary session of the General Assembly, a draft definition was adopted without a vote. The definition included the statement that ''no consideration of whatever nature, whether political, economic, military or otherwise, may serve as a justification for aggression.'' It remained, however, that the Security Council determined whether an act of aggression had occurred and who the aggressor nation was.

See DECLARATION OF WAR; FIRST STRIKE/SECOND STRIKE; FIRST USE.

BIBLIOGRAPHY

Ferencz, Benjamin B., *Defining International Aggression,* Vol. 2 (New York: Oceana Publications, 1975).

UN Draft Definition of Aggression, March 25, 1969, *American Journal of International Law* 63 (1969), 565ff.

UN General Assembly, ''Declaration on the Inadmissibility of Intervention in the Domestic Affairs of States and the Protection of Their Independence and Sovereignty,'' *American Journal of International Law* 60 (1966), 662ff.

UN General Assembly Resolution 3314, Definition of Aggression, *American Journal of International Law* 69 (1975), 480ff.

Walters, F. P., *A History of the League of Nations* (New York: Oxford University Press, 1960).

AGGRESSIVE VERSUS DEFENSIVE WAR. We tend to share a general conception that aggressive wars are wrong while defensive wars are justified. Our general conception is that it is almost always wrong to initiate a war and almost always right to fight a war when attacked.

One possible attempt to justify our general conception is to appeal to the domestic analogy: Since individual citizens have a right of self-defense, the nation-state has a collective right to defend the lives of its citizens. But the individual right of self-defense holds that one may use only enough force to repel an attacker; one may only kill the attacker when it is reasonable to believe that doing so is the sole means to save one's own life or the life of another innocent. If we carry this analogy to the nation-state, it seems that a nation has a right to force attackers from its territory while killing as few people as possible, and only when it is reasonable to believe that doing so is the sole means to save the lives of its citizens. In most actual cases, surrender seems a more efficient means to the end of saving lives than defensive war. Rarely will an attacker kill as many under surrender as by attack.

Attacking the homeland of the invaders seems difficult to justify under this model. For instance, even though one may live in a city where violent crime is common and generally uncontrolled by the law and, thereby, presents a real threat to one's life, one is not justified in destroying gun stores, munitions factories, or even the areas of town where most attackers live, in order to defend oneself. Nor is one justified in intentionally killing the innocent family of a mugger, even if doing so would defend one from the mugger. This is so even after all legal remedies fail. Yet these parallels seem the proper ones to draw if our approach to war is based on the domestic analogy.

But perhaps the claim is that the nation-state's right of self-defense is absolute or at least extremely strong while those of its citizens are defeasible. How, then, does the nation-state's right of self-defense derive from the collective rights of self-defense of its citizens? Perhaps we could add some notion about the collective importance of individual rights to strengthen the notion of national self-defense. But how does this emergent property of collective rights work and where do we draw the line?

Further, if it is the collective lives of individual citizens that is at issue, in most actual cases the best way to defend these lives is to surrender. If, on the other hand, it is the collective way of life, or civil rights, or political structure that is to be defended, the domestic analogy wears thin. If a large corporation threatens one's way of life by moving into town, one is hardly justified in destroying property and killing innocent people to prevent the move. If one's civil rights are threatened or violated, even basic ones, generally one is not thought justified in killing the oppressor. For example, African Americans were generally not thought justified in killing their white oppressors under American legal apartheid, and some were morally horrified by the thought that Palestinians or black South Africans might violently revolt to remove the yoke of apartheid. We do not think that special interest groups or ethnic or religious minorities within nation-states, even unjust nation-states, are justified in killing innocent others to preserve their way of life or their civil rights. Why, then, are nation-states? Why are these collections of rights any different?

If civil rights are the issue, why, then, is a nation-state that does not honor the civil rights of its citizens justified in defending itself from attack? More to the point, if a nation-state does not honor the civil rights of its citizens, and civil rights is the issue, why is a war of intervention against such a state to restore civil rights unjustified?

If it is the government that deserves defense, again one wonders why all such structures deserve defense and why it is always wrong to attack one—even when it is an unjust government. The Hobbesian* argument that any state is better than none is an obvious false dilemma; a third possibility would be a war of intervention to create or restore a just or more just government. It is implausible that all such acts must end with no government.

But perhaps the domestic analogy itself is the problem. Perhaps we can justify our common opinion with the social contract theory. It is always wrong to attack another country because we put at risk the lives of those who consent to the government whose nation-state we attack. The difficulty here is that it only applies to nation-states whose citizens consent to the government, not to all nation-states. Would, then, a war of intervention to create a government to which the citizens would consent be justified?

While one might argue that to continue to live under a government is tacit consent, such an argument seems implausible. Suppose the citizenry is subject to massive and pervasive propaganda* through control of the mass media. In these cases, how is even tacit consent granted? Just what is tacit consent? Suppose citizens lack the means or are regularly denied access to leave or lack the means or are denied access to the nation-state to whose government they would consent? Again, theory seems to run up against reality.

Utilitarian approaches to our common conception seem equally problematic. Under act-utilitarianism, it seems implausible that all aggressive wars will violate utility while all defensive wars will maximize utility. Further, there are the problems of the justification of the projected consequences as well as the measurement of utility.

Rule-utilitarianism fares no better. As we have seen, a blanket rule prohibiting aggressive war while sanctioning defensive war does not seem to maximize utility, since in most cases surrender is plausibly more optimal than defense, while in many other cases intervention is plausibly more optimal than nonintervention. In addition, once such a blanket rule is in effect, the greatest mischief could be accomplished to the point where the utility of the rule is questionable (e.g., massive oppression of citizens, constant unactualized threats of attack against weaker nations to force them to continually mount an expensive defense).

Perhaps, then, we need to allow exceptions to the general conception to render it more plausible. But which exceptions? Michael Walzer has argued that intervention is justified in certain cases where the "violation of human rights* within a set of boundaries is so terrible that it makes talk of community or self-determination or 'arduous struggle' seem cynical and irrelevant, that is, in cases of enslavement or massacre*." And again, humanitarian intervention is justified when it is a response (with reasonable expectations of success) to acts "that shock the moral conscience of mankind." Adopting this approach seems to assume that the obscure could be clarified by the equally obscure. Still needed are an an account of why it is a very serious crime in every other case for a state to enter into war to alter or restrict the political sovereignty of another state, as well as an account of why it is justified in every other case for even the most unjust and unjustified nation to defend itself.

Another attempt is to define "aggressive war" in such a way that it is never justified and "defensive war" in such a way that is always justified. But this merely begs the question at issue and leaves us with rather strange definitions for our ordinary notions. Indeed, it would seem simpler and more honest to simply develop a theory of justifiable war that goes beyond the distinction between aggressive and defensive war.

Unless it can be established that nation-states have an independent, defeasible claim to use the deadly force of war to resist all movements onto their territory or all attempts to alter their structure, the case for defensive war as well as the case against the initiation of war are not yet adequately made.

See AGGRESSION; FIRST STRIKE/SECOND STRIKE; FIRST USE; JUST

WAR; MUTUAL ASSURED DESTRUCTION; NATIONAL LIBERATION, WARS OF; PEACE, CRIMES AGAINST; TOTAL WAR.

BIBLIOGRAPHY

De Roose, Frank, "Self-Defense and National Defense," *Journal of Applied Psychology* (October 1990), 159–68.

Holmes, Robert L., *On War and Morality* (Princeton, N.J.: Princeton University Press, 1989).

Lee, Steven, *Morality, Prudence, and Nuclear Weapons* (Cambridge: Cambridge University Press, 1993).

Murphy, Jeffrie, "The Killing of the Innocent," *Monist* 57, no. 4 (October 1973), 527–51.

Walzer, Michael, *Just and Unjust Wars* (New York: Basic Books, 1992).

Wasserstrom, Richard, "Book Review of Michael Walzer's *Just and Unjust Wars*," *Harvard Law Review* (December 1978), 536–45.

Richard Werner

AMERICAN REVOLUTION. *See* AMNESTY; CHRISTIANITY AND WAR; CONSCIENTIOUS OBJECTION; CONSCRIPTION; DODGE, DAVID LOW; PATRIOTISM; PROPAGANDA.

AMNESTY. In general usage, the term *amnesty* is applied to a large group of persons, while *parole* and *pardon* are applied to individuals. In all cases— whether amnesty, pardon, or parole—the offenses are against the government. The practice of granting amnesty is an ancient one. In China, from the founding of the empire in the third century B.C., general amnesties or "acts of grace" were frequently granted. In 40 B.C., Thrasybulus of Athens forbade additional punishment of citizens for past political acts and required in exchange an oath of promise not to commit the offenses again. Coming from a Greek word meaning forgetfulness, the act removed the offense from the legal books. The Edict of Nantes issued by Henry IV in 1598 declared by an act of amnesty an end to the religious persecution of Huguenots. After the English Civil War in 1650 and 1651 Charles II declared amnesty, Napoleon's decree in 1802 provided amnesty, after the civil wars of 1871 in France amnesties were declared, and in 1903 the British gave amnesty to the Boers of South Africa.

On July 10, 1795, President George Washington gave a "full, free, and entire pardon" to all who had participated in the insurrection in Pennsylvania against the U.S. government. In May 1800 President John Adams gave amnesty to those who had been in the 1799 insurrection in Philadelphia. And President James Madison in 1815 pardoned those involved in offenses regarding revenue trade and navigation near New Orleans.

Amnesties may be general (i.e., with some exceptions) or universal. After the Civil War, President Abraham Lincoln declared a general amnesty on December 8, 1863, which excluded certain classes of persons who could, by personal petition, request pardon. To get this amnesty an oath of allegiance was required. Lincoln was generous in granting such pardons. President Andrew Johnson issued a series of amnesty declarations beginning on May 29, 1865, until he declared a universal and unconditional amnesty December 25, 1868. In 1872 Congress issued an Amnesty Act that restored civil rights to most southerners except for about 500 Confederate leaders. Prisoners were, of course, paroled immediately at the close of the war. Only a few short imprisonments of Confederate officials occurred. General Robert E. Lee and his officers suffered no imprisonment. Of special concern was the thirteenth exception in President Johnson's May 29, 1865, amnesty that excluded those whose property was worth $20,000 or more. The president believed that this would surely catch all the slave owners, and while he was ready to pardon them, he wanted them to appear in person and ask for it. By January 8, 1867, eighty-six members of the lower house and a smaller number of the upper house of the Confederate Congress had been pardoned along with a dozen Confederate governors. President Jefferson Davis was the only leader to stay any length in prison, chiefly because he refused to ask for pardon. He was finally released in May 1867 to be tried in civil court. His bail of $100,000 was covered by Horace Greeley, Cornelius Vanderbilt, and others, but President Johnson's final unconditional amnesty in 1868 saved Davis from facing trial.

No universal amnesty was declared by a U.S. President after World War I, although as soon as that war had ended Italy, France, Belgium, Canada, and England had declared universal and unconditional amnesty and by 1919 virtually all objectors in those countries had been freed. The chief battle in the United States for amnesty was led by the Socialist Party and the National Civil Liberties Bureau, the forerunner of the American Civil Liberties Union (ACLU). By 1921 a government Joint Amnesty Committee was formed, although the federal authorities claimed that there were no political prisoners, meaning all in prison had been duly sentenced for a crime. President Woodrow Wilson refused any amnesty. President Warren Harding did grant amnesty to twenty-one persons, including Eugene Debs*. Senator William E. Borah (R-ID) sponsored a resolution to free all political prisoners, and on March 5, 1924, President Calvin Coolidge gave amnesty to those soldiers who had deserted military service. On December 25, 1933, President Franklin D. Roosevelt gave general amnesty to those convicted under the Espionage Act and for conspiracy to violate Section Five of the Selective Service Act of 1917 who had paid the penalty the law had imposed, but it did not pardon those who were fugitives or who had been sentenced by military courts (which included most of the conscientious objectors).

At the end of World War II the United States had 15,805 antiwar prisoners, and a large number of men who had fled the country. A. J. Muste* organized a group to push for universal amnesty, which included Thornton Wilder, Henry Seidel Canby, and Henry Luce. In 1946 President Harry Truman declared amnesty for soldiers who had served at least twelve months and had criminal records. He also appointed a three-man Amnesty Board that in 1947 pardoned 1,523 of the 15,805 who had been convicted under the Selective Service Act. Those pardoned did not include blacks who had refused to serve in a segregated army, Hopis whose religion forbade killing, Puerto Rican nationalists who saw no reason to fight for a country that did not recognize their statehood, over 4,000 Jehovah's Witnesses, and a number of nonreligious objectors. This left 10,000 outside the amnesty.

In 1970 Amnesty International published a list of persons to whom amnesty should be given for their actions during the Vietnam War*. The list included men who had applied unsuccessfully for conscientious objector (CO) status and had refused military duty, men who had gone absent without leave (AWOL) on grounds of objection to the war, soldiers who had refused to go or to train others to go to Vietnam, soldiers who had spoken against the war and been charged with sedition, and civilian sympathizers who had aided or urged men to evade the draft or committed such acts as pouring blood on draft files. On January 21, 1977, President Jimmy Carter pardoned most of the remaining 10,000 Vietnam war protestors.

See CONSCIENTIOUS OBJECTION; PACIFISM.

BIBLIOGRAPHY

Amnesty, Hearings Before the Subcommittee on Courts, Civil Liberties, and the Administration of Justice of the Committee on the Judiciary, House of Representatives, 93rd Congress, 2d session, March 8, 11, and 13, 1974 (Washington, D.C.: U.S. Government Printing Office, 1974).

Amnesty International Report 1989 (New York: Amnesty International, 1989).

Dorris, Jonathan Truman, *Pardon and Amnesty Under Lincoln and Johnson* (Chapel Hill: University of North Carolina Press, 1953).

McKnight, Brian E., *The Quality of Mercy: Amnesties and Traditional Chinese Justice* (Honolulu: University of Hawaii Press, 1981).

Schardt, Arlie, William A. Rusher, and Mark O. Hatfield, *Amnesty? The Unsettled Question of Vietnam* (Lawrence, Mass.: Sun River Press, 1973).

Schlissel, Lillian, ed., *Conscience in America* (New York: Dutton, 1968).

ANDERSONVILLE PRISONER OF WAR CAMP. *See GENERAL ORDERS 100;* LIEBER, FRANCIS; WIRZ, CAPTAIN HENRY.

ANGIERS SYNOD (990). The synod issued a Peace of God* document under the leadership of Guy of Anjou, Bishop of Puy, which endeavored to qualify the concept of military necessity*. The following prohibitions were listed, and in every case save one, the qualification of military necessity under the permission of a clerical order allowed the combatant to violate the prohibition: (1) No person (soldier) shall break into a church unless it is for the purpose of collecting taxes for the bishop; (2) no clergy shall bear arms, and no unarmed persons accompanying clergy shall be harmed, unless such force is needed by a bishop or archdeacon to collect taxes; (3) no person shall seize livestock, unless needed for a lawful expedition; (4) no one shall seize peasants, men or women, with the intent to make them pay ransom, unless such peasants have already forfeited their freedom or in cases where a lord is dealing with his serfs; (5) no one shall seize church lands, unless ordered by a bishop; (6) no one shall seize or rob merchants. In each case the notion of protected places or persons was urged, unless some clerical (military) necessity ruled otherwise.

See CHAPLAINS AND ETHICS IN THE ARMY; CHRISTIANITY AND WAR; COMBATANT-NONCOMBATANT DISTINCTION; FORBIDDEN STRATEGIES; PILLAGE.

BIBLIOGRAPHY

Keen, Maurice Hugh, *The Law of War in the Late Middle Ages* (London: Routledge & Kegan Paul, 1965).

Schroeder, H. J., *Disciplinary Decrees of the General Councils* (London: Herder, 1937).

Thatcher, Oliver, and Edgar H. McNeal, *A Sourcebook for Medieval History* (New York: Charles Scribner's Sons, 1907).

ANTIBALLISTIC MISSILES/STAR WARS. During World War II, the Germans used jet- and rocket-powered missiles (the V-1 and V-2) to bomb London. By 1960, both the United States and the Soviet Union had developed intercontinental ballistic missiles (ICBMs), armed with thermonuclear warheads, with a striking range of over 5,000 miles.

From the mid 1950s, each side engaged in research to develop defenses against incoming ICBMs. All types of such defenses fall into the category of ballistic missile defense (BMD). Antiballistic missiles (ABMs)—missiles designed to shoot down incoming missiles—form one important type of ballistic missile defense. Another important type is space-based missile defense: space stations or other devices designed to intercept ICBMs with laser beams, X-rays, charged particles, or other means. In the popular press, space-based missile defenses are referred to as ''Star Wars'' defenses, in homage to George Lucas's science fiction film of 1977.

The technical problems of ballistic missile defense are formidable. An incoming ICBM is small and has a velocity of several miles per second. After the boost phase, the missile emits little heat; it is a cold dark object against the cold of space. In a typical attack, many ICBMs will be incoming, and if a single one gets through, the result is catastrophe. Against a nuclear attack, any defense less than 100 percent effective is inadequate.

The main difficulty for defenses based on antiballistic missiles is that the velocity of the ABM is roughly comparable to the incoming ICBM; the ICBM must be struck head-on, and the problem is comparable to ''hitting a bullet with a bullet.'' Should the ICBM get by, the ABM cannot easily adjust or catch up.

The main difficulty for space-based missile defenses is that the defenses can be overwhelmed by decoy warheads and chaff scattered by incoming ICBMs. In free fall, a dummy warhead will look and behave like an armed warhead, and the defense will have to shoot down all the dummy warheads to find the real ones. (A plan to shoot down ICBMs in the boost phase, before the dummies are released, can be foiled by shortening the boost phase with fast-burn rockets.)

Despite these difficulties, the United States sought to develop ABMs, and actually constructed several ABM sites (now abandoned) in the early 1970s. In

1983, the Reagan administration initiated a substantial research program into space-based missile defenses. Several prototypes were built, and widely publicized tests promised early success. In 1993, it was revealed that these tests had been faked in order to deceive the Soviets about American advances in space-based weapons. Whether the Soviets were deceived is unknown, but the fraud did take in several members of the U.S. Congress, which funded Star Wars research at around $5 billion yearly for eleven years.

THE MORAL ISSUE

The threat posed by ICBMs is real, and the leadership on each side in the Cold War felt morally obliged to do something about it. The main remedy proposed was nuclear deterrence*: the United States assured the Soviet Union, "If you attack us with nuclear weapons, we will destroy you in return." The Soviet promised likewise, and the resulting stalemate was called Mutual Assured Destruction*.

Mutual Assured Destruction leaves each side defenseless, open to destruction at will by the other side. Furthermore, assured destruction involves a commitment to a nuclear counterattack, which is, at bottom, a commitment to mass murder. The hawks disliked weakness; the doves disliked mass murder. Each sought some alternative to deterrence. Ballistic missile defense seemed a morally superior method for dealing with the nuclear threat: "Isn't it better," Ronald Reagan said, introducing his Star Wars program in 1983, "to save lives than to avenge them?"

Reagan and other supporters of ballistic missile defense appealed to the intrinsic moral superiority of defense over offense. But the view that defense is always morally superior to offense is dubious: A good defense for Auschwitz would not have been a morally good thing. In any case, a complete separation of offense from defense was implausible: If the Soviet Union launched a massive attack at American ballistic missile defenses, the United States would probably launch a nuclear counterstrike back at the Soviets, in addition to attempting to knock down incoming ICBMs.

Furthermore, there were special problems springing from the development of ballistic missile defenses on one side only. If the United States developed missile defenses and the Soviets did not, the Soviet nuclear deterrent would be nullified and the United States could attack the Soviet Union at will. Even if not attacked, the Soviets, for fear of attack, could be blackmailed into accepting whatever fate the Americans chose for them. Rather than accept this prospect, the Soviet Union might choose to go to war sooner, before American defenses were constructed, rather than later, when the Soviet Union would be helpless. Hence, critics argued that ballistic missile defenses were destabilizing, and increased the chance of nuclear war. If the intentions of missile defense were morally superior to deterrence, the results might be morally worse. These moral perplexities about stability were one factor leading the superpowers to agree in 1972 not to construct large-scale ABM systems.

MISSILE DEFENSE AND NUCLEAR TERRORISM*

In the late 1980s, a new rationale was proposed for space-based missile defense. Though space-based defenses could not hold off a large-scale nuclear attack, they might be able to stop a small-scale nuclear attack: an isolated missile fired at the United States by a nuclear terrorist, a missile launched by mistake, a small-scale Soviet nuclear attack that attempted to evade deterrence by leaving most American assets untouched. Small-scale ballistic missile defenses would not be destabilizing, and would provide the American people with a measure of protection against nuclear disasters.

Arguments like these kept Star Wars funding going even after the Cold War came to an end. At the same time, critics wondered why a terrorist would seek to put a nuclear bomb on a missile, when it is easier to bring the bomb into an American harbor by boat. In the 1990s the optimism that every offense has a defense began to fade. ''No one,'' strategist Bernard Brodie remarked, ''has ever devised an effective defense against the *bullet*.''

See NUCLEAR DETERRENCE; STRATEGIC DEFENSE INITIATIVE (SDI); TERRORISM.

BIBLIOGRAPHY

For bibliography through 1990 see Douglas Lackey, ed., *Ethics and Strategic Defense* (Belmont, Calif.: Wadsworth, 1990). For the history of the Star Wars program see William J. Broad, *Teller's War* (New York: Simon & Schuster, 1992). For the 1993 revelations of fraud see Tim Weiner, ''General Details Altered 'Star Wars' Test,'' *New York Times,* August 27, 1993.

Douglas P. Lackey

AQUINAS, THOMAS (1225?–1274). Concerning war and ethics, Aquinas is important for two reasons: first, he assured that war would become a significant, if not major, topic for Christian theologians; second, and more importantly, he was responsible for secularizing the just war* criteria by grounding them, not upon sacred scripture, but upon the principle of double effect (also known as collateral effects or collateral damage*).

The scholastic theologians avoided the topic of war, believing it to be a matter for the canon lawyers. Aquinas, however, saw the need for a theological examination of the topic, and so he incorporated the work of the canonists (principally, Gratianus) into his *Summa Theologica,* devoting Question 40 (IIa IIae) to war. Ironically, however, the least important aspect of Question 40 is its content, which may be summarized as follows: Article 1 adduces three of the nine just war criteria (competent authority, just cause, and right intention), justifying each criterion with suitable quotations, principally, from St. Augustine*. Article 2 reasons that bishops and clerics should not fight because their lives are dedicated to a higher calling. Article 3 concludes that ambushes, when characterized as "concealment," are lawful. Article 4 teaches that wars may be fought on holy days, but only to repel sudden attacks.

Of greater interest is the placement of Question 40, which, following both reason and tradition, is found in the section entitled "Consequences of Charity." Like St. Augustine, Aquinas clearly saw that just war is an act of charity. The canon lawyers, especially the Spanish Jesuits, further refined and developed the just war criteria and theologians were encouraged to explore more fundamental issues. The most fruitful of these subsequent theological investigations was undoubtedly John Calvin's* development of his "Lesser (or Minor) Magistrates" doctrine (*Institutes* IV, xx, xxi), which explores the possibility of violating the competent authority criterion and igniting a just revolution. Calvin's work formed an important part of the intellectual background for the American and French Revolutions.

Beyond question, though, Aquinas's greatest contribution was to secularize the just war criteria by grounding them solidly in the principle of double effect. He did not do this directly, but rather indirectly and implicitly. In Question 40 there is no mention of the principle of double effect. Instead, one finds quotations from the traditional religious authorities. For example, Aquinas cites St. Augustine, "War and conquest are a sad necessity in the eyes of men of principle, yet it would be still more unfortunate if wrong doers should dominate just men" (*City of God,* IV, C. 15), and several Biblical citations such as, "He [the magistrate] beareth not the sword in vain for he is God's minister, an avenger to execute wrath upon him that doth evil" (*Rom* 13:4).

To find the principle of double effect, one must page through twenty-four additional questions to reach number 64, On Homicide, Articles 7 and 8, and understand that there is a parallel between justified homicide and justified war. That is, when Aquinas argues in Article 7 that it is not illicit to kill a man in self-defense because "A single act may have two effects, of which one alone is intended, whilst the other is incidental to that intention," one soon realizes that this same reasoning applies to soldiers caught up in combat. Likewise, when Aquinas reasons in Article 8 that an accidental killing is not a mortal sin because "In Aristotle's definition [*Physics* 197b18], chance is a cause that acts without a personal agent intending it," this same argument also applies to the collateral damage that is incidental to all combat.

But, if the parallel between justified homicide and justified war is exact, then it follows that appeals to sacred scripture of whatever sort are entirely irrelevant. For, as is implied in Question 64, Articles 7 and 8, the justifiability of a homicide, of a war, or, indeed, of any human action is not predicated upon the will of God, at least not for actors possessing a free will. Rather, it is predicated upon a well-reasoned, but not infallible, judgment that the intended positive consequences will outweigh the unintended negative consequences. And further, as Question 40, Article 1 implies, to make this judgment, an individual or a society must work through the seven *jus ad bellum* and the two *jus in bello* criteria, determining to its satisfaction that the unintended negative consequences of a war will not overwhelm the intended positive consequences, as so often happens.

Accordingly, perhaps unintentionally, Aquinas rejected Holy War*. After Aquinas, the proper theological response to a call for war is no longer to ask whether the one true God demands that the faithful slay the infidel; rather, it is to ask, with a high degree of skepticism, nine purely secular questions: Do those calling for the war possess a competent authority to do so? Is their cause truly just? Are their intentions truly right?

See CHRISTIANITY AND WAR; JUST WAR.

BIBLIOGRAPHY

Aquinas, Thomas, *Summa Theologica* (New York: McGraw-Hill, 1964).

Johnson, James Turner, *Just War Tradition and the Restraint of War: A Moral and Historical Inquiry* (Princeton, N.J.: Princeton University Press, 1981).

Russell, F. H., *The Just War in the Middle Ages* (New York: Cambridge University Press, 1975).

Brien Hallett

ARAB-ISRAELI WARS (1948–1982). There have been five major wars between Israelis and Arabs. While differing in immediate causes, objectives, and impact, each was rooted in the comparatively recent conflict between Jews and Arabs over Palestine. In 1917, the British government pledged to facilitate establishment of a ''Jewish national home'' in Palestine, and during Britain's Mandate over Palestine (1922–1948) immigration increased the Jewish presence from less than 10 percent of the population in 1918 to one-third by 1947. Overwhelming Arab opposition spiraled into rebellion during the late 1930s, prompting Britain to declare in 1939 that it was not part of Mandate policy that Palestine should become a Jewish state. However, in November 1947, the UN General Assembly recommended partition of Palestine into a Jewish state on 54 percent of mandated territory and an Arab state on 45 percent, with Jerusalem under UN administration. Publicly, most Zionists agreed to this compromise but the Arab countries were opposed, declaring the resolution to be a violation of self-determination. Fighting immediately broke out among the Palestinian Arabs and Jews, and when British forces evacuated in mid-May 1948, the better-equipped and more numerous Jewish forces established a clear superiority, capturing territory assigned to the proposed Arab state. Civilians on both sides were targeted, but massacres like that at the Arab village of Deir Yassin in April by Jewish irregulars precipitated a widespread exodus of Arabs from their homes and villages.

On May 15, 1948, the day after the official formation of Israel was declared, forces from Egypt, Syria, Lebanon, Jordan, and Iraq entered the fighting in support of Palestinian Arabs. Despite population differences, Israelis placed more soldiers in the field, and had the advantage of working in familiar terrain under unified control. UN-sponsored truces in the summer provided belligerents the opportunity to rearm, while the UN mediator, Count Folke Bernadotte of Sweden, recommended immediate repatriation of the Arab refugees as a condition for any just and lasting peace. His assassination in September by members of the Jewish underground was followed by renewed fighting in October, which lasted until early 1949. When the last armistice was signed in July, the Israel Defense Forces (IDF) occupied over 77 percent of mandated Palestine, including West Jerusalem and Galilee, and it was only the intervention of Arab armies that prevented all of mandated Palestine from coming under Jewish control. The remainder was occupied by Jordan (West Bank and East Jerusalem) and Egypt (Gaza Strip). Palestinian Arabs were not permitted to establish a state and over 800,000 became refugees through flight or expulsion. Chances for peace in 1949 were lost when Israel refused Arab demands for withdrawal to the partition plan boundaries and the return of refugees.

The defeat of Arab forces by a nascent Jewish state fostered revolutionary movements in the Arab world, notably in Egypt, where Gamal Abdul Nasser assumed power in 1952. His pan-Arab nationalism caused concern in Western capitals. When Egypt nationalized the Suez Canal in July 1956, leaders in Britain and France plotted his overthrow, envisioning a joint invasion with Israel, whose Prime Minister, David Ben-Gurion, believed Arab countries would make peace only by recognizing Israel's military superiority. Cross-border incursions by Arab *Fedayeen* into Israeli settlements and Israel's attacks on Arab villagers, and especially on Egyptian military outposts in Gaza in 1955, had already raised tensions between the two countries. But it was Egypt's military build-up, its blockade of the Straits of Tiran leading into the Gulf of Aqaba, and Nasser's promise of victory that prompted Israel's invasion of the Sinai peninsula on October 29, 1956. As British planes bombed Egyptian airfields, Nasser pulled his troops from the Sinai, allowing the IDF to occupy most of the peninsula by November 3. British and French forces intervened in the Canal Zone but failed to bring about Nasser's ouster. A UN-sponsored ceasefire was achieved by November 8.

Most Security Council members joined Arab countries in condemning the invasion. Fearful that the Soviets might use it as a means of gaining influence in the Arab world, the Eisenhower administration pressured Israel to remove its forces from Egyptian territory, but stipulated that the Gulf of Aqaba remain open to Israeli ships and UN troops be stationed in the Sinai and Gaza Strip to prevent *Fedayeen* incursions. After the IDF withdrew in early 1957 the border was quiet for almost a decade.

Nasser's resolve in the face of the Anglo-Franco-Israeli invasion enhanced his prestige in the Arab world. As the Soviets rebuilt Egypt's military, he intensified his rhetoric: Israel is an alien presence in the midst of Arab territory created and sustained by Western imperialism, and Palestine can be liberated only through a unified Arab front. His 1966 defense pact with Syria preceded Israeli-Syrian clashes in a demilitarized zone in the spring of 1967. Responding to reports of an Israeli military build-up in its north, Nasser reimposed a blockade of the Gulf of Aqaba, replaced UN troops in the Sinai with two divisions of Egyptian soldiers, and concluded a defense treaty with Jordan in late May, providing Israel with a *casus belli.* He underestimated Israel's military capability and did not anticipate its attack on June 5, which destroyed Egypt's air force and routed the exposed Egyptian forces in the Sinai, most of which it captured within three days. After fighting broke out in Jerusalem, Israel quickly overpowered the light Jordanian forces, occupying East Jerusalem and the West Bank by June 8. The same day an American reconnaissance ship was hit by Israeli bombs and torpedos that killed thirty-four American sailors. Israel claimed mistaken identification, but officers on board claimed that Israel's attack was a deliberate attempt to conceal its operations against Syria. After another three-day offensive, Israel captured the Golan Heights and a ceasefire with Syria went into effect on June 11. The defeat of the combined Arab forces was devastating, with over 15,000 Arab soldiers killed—perhaps many more—compared to Israel's loss of 750.

The Israeli victory was hailed in the Western world since Nasser was viewed as pro-Soviet and Israel had skillfully portrayed the Arabs as aggressors who forced its preemptive action. Its real victory was not its damage to Arab military capacity—this was quickly restored with Soviet assistance—but capture of territory later used for political and economic ends, a public relations bonanza bringing increased Western support and Jewish immigration, and defeat of a popular brand of Arab nationalism, a powerful ideological adversary. But there is little to support the charge that Nasser was preparing an invasion that justified Israel's strike. U.S. intelligence reports to Israelis in late May indicated that Egypt had no plans for attack and that Israel would prevail in any case, an assessment subsequently confirmed by Israeli chief of staff, Yitzhak Rabin.

Although Security Council Resolution 242 (November 1967) called for mutual recognition of all states in the region and Israeli withdrawal from occupied territories, Arab countries were unwilling to negotiate with Israel after the humiliating defeat. Hostilities continued in a war of attrition, particularly between Israel and Egypt during the early 1970s. Nasser's successor, Anwar Sadat, planned another war, not to destroy Israel—Western powers would not allow that—but to secure a more balanced treatment from the Americans. On October 6, 1973, Egyptian and Syrian forces surprised the Israeli army in the Sinai and Golan Heights. After initial Arab successes, the IDF halted the Syrian advance by October 9 and, resupplied by massive American arms shipments, stopped the Egyptians by October 14. Gulf Arab countries responded by placing an embargo on oil shipments to the United States. After the IDF broke through Syrian lines in the Golan and surrounded the Egyptian Third Army in the Canal Zone, a cease-fire, brokered by the United States and the USSR, went into effect on October 24.

In this war, Israel lost over 2,500 soldiers, and while combined Arab losses were greater, respect for Arab military capability was heightened. A more active American role fostered a disengagement agreement between Egypt and Israel in

1975, the Camp David Accords of 1978, normalization of relations in 1979, and return of the Sinai to Egypt by 1982.

In the summer of 1982, Israel warred against the Palestine Liberation Organization (PLO) in Lebanon. The PLO increased its political and military activity after the 1967 war, placing the problem of Palestinian refugees back on the international agenda. After the Jordanian civil war in 1970, Lebanon became the PLO's principal base of operations and the scene of deadly IDF reprisals. In March 1978, after Palestinian commandos hijacked a bus inside Israel and thirty-four Israelis died in a shootout, Israel invaded southern Lebanon in a campaign that left 1,000 Palestinians and Lebanese dead and drove more than 100,000 Lebanese and Palestinians northward.

Diplomatic gains in the late 1970s indicated the PLO's willingness to accept a two-state solution of the conflict, but compromise on territory in the West Bank and Golan Heights and negotiations with the PLO were opposed by the Israeli government of Menachem Begin. After intense fighting in the summer of 1981, both sides agreed to a cessation of cross-border hostilities, but Begin and his defense minister, Ariel Sharon, planned another invasion to destroy the PLO infrastructure in Lebanon. A June 3 assassination attempt on the Israeli ambassador to Britain by a radical Palestinian group opposed to PLO policy was followed by an Israeli air raid on Palestinian refugee camps in Beiruit, leaving over 200 dead. After the PLO shelled northern Israel in response, killing four people, Israel invaded Lebanon on June 6, devastating Palestinian population centers in the south and forcing a large exodus of Lebanese northward into Beruit. Israeli aircraft downed more than eighty Syrian airplanes and destroyed Syrian missile batteries, causing Syria to accept a ceasefire on June 11.

The IDF was soon on the outskirts of West Beruit, which it beseiged for a two-month period with artillery and air attacks that killed several thousand civilians. Entrenched PLO fighters foiled an Israeli attempt to enter West Beruit in early August, and after a continuous Israeli aerial bombardment on August 12, President Reagan prevailed upon the Israeli government to halt the slaughter. The Americans then arranged an evacuation of nearly 12,000 PLO fighters and 2,500 Syrian soldiers in late August, overseen by a multinational force. The assassination of the Lebanese president, Bashir Gemayel, on September 14 was followed by an Israeli occupation of West Beruit and the massacre of at least 2,400 Palestinians by Israel's Phalangist allies.

It is estimated that at least 85 percent of the 20,000 Lebanese and Palestinians killed in the June–August war, many by U.S.-supplied cluster and phosphorus bombs, were civilians. Those who claim that Israel was justified in destroying PLO bases in Lebanon overlook the disproportionate number of civilian casualties, the fact that the PLO had ceased its cross-border raids and had shown willingness to accept a two-state solution, and that it was Israel's bombing of refugee camps that reopened hostilities. Arguably, Israel's aggression failed not only the test of *jus in bello* but *jus ad bellum,* and despite its government's propaganda* about combatting terrorists, of all Israel's wars, this drew the most international and domestic criticism. Although the PLO's military presence in Lebanon was reduced, the IDF did not destroy the organization nor its political influence among Palestinians, and the continued occupation of southern Lebanon earned Israel enemies among Lebanon's Shiite population.

The Arab-Israeli conflict is one of the more intractable problems of 20th-century politics. While the five wars have occasionally prompted greater realism, none has solved the basic problems caused by the forceful establishment of a Jewish state in the middle of the Arab world. It is not surprising that the belligerents should resort to violence; indeed, British officers predicted in 1919 that the Zionist program could only succeed through the force of arms. Some might view this as a legitimate, if regrettable, means of securing the Zionist ideal, but others see it as the inevitable outcome of usurping Arab territory at the expense of the Palestinians. For all this, a peaceful resolution of the conflict is a distinct possibility. But deep-seated attachments to territory and an explosive mix of determination and outrage make long-range predictions tenuous.

See AGGRESSIVE VERSUS DEFENSIVE WAR; COUNTERFORCE VERSUS COUNTERVALUE; ISLAM AND WAR; JUDAISM AND WAR.

BIBLIOGRAPHY

Bailey, Sydney, *Four Arab-Israeli Wars and the Peace Process* (London: Macmillan, 1990).

Herzog, Chaim, *The Arab-Israeli Wars* (New York: Random House, 1984).

Khouri, Fred, *The Arab-Israeli Dilemma,* 3rd ed. (Syracuse, N.Y.: Syracuse University Press, 1985).

Smith, Charles D., *Palestine and the Arab-Israeli Conflict,* 2d ed. (New York: St. Martin's Press, 1992).

Tomis Kapitan

ARCTIC REGION. The term *Arctic Region* refers to "the area north of the 50°F summer isotherm." The center of the Arctic Region is the Arctic Ocean.

The Arctic Ocean is the smallest and shallowest of all oceans. It refers to the waters found within the Arctic Circle that connect to the Pacific Ocean via the Bering Strait and to the Atlantic by the Greenland and Norwegian Seas. It covers only 14 million square kilometers of the Earth's surface. Its mean depth is about 1,200 meters. It sits on top of the world above 66° 33' 03" north latitude. The Arctic Ocean is covered by an ice mass most of the year; it is ice-locked from October to June. It has been a long-held belief that this ice mass is stationary, but in reality the Arctic ice is in constant motion and breaks into ice floes of varying size, as an effect of currents, wind, tidal, and other climatic conditions. The Arctic ice mass contains about 90 percent of all the world's snow and ice. The countries that border the Arctic Ocean, the so-called Arctic Rim nations, include the United States (Alaska), Russia (or the former Soviet Union), Canada, and the five Nordic states of Denmark (Greenland), Finland, Iceland, Norway, and Sweden.

Strategic Issues. The ice-covered Arctic Ocean—and the Arctic region as a whole—is the ideal place for the deployment of nuclear-powered submarines. Two interrelated developments in the nuclear missile calculus have thrust the submarine into the forefront of military strategy known as antisubmarine warfare (ASW). One of these developments is the vulnerability of land-based missiles, such as the intercontinental ballistic missile (ICBM), in the case of a first pre-emptive strike launched by an enemy. Obviously, the second is the consequence of the first development: the advancement of arming the submarine with so-phisticated nuclear-powered missiles (the SSBNs)—for example, the Polaris, Poseidon, and Trident (United States) and the Delta and Typhoon (Soviet Un-ion). These missiles could be aimed at a target thousands of miles away—both as an early warning strategy and to satisfy the need for providing offensive or attack capability. Antisubmarine warfare was thus born as a powerful naval strategy and a formidable deterrent against an enemy's nuclear attack. It was estimated by the U.S. navy that by 1990, 40 percent of all naval aviators and aircraft would be involved in antisubmarine warfare. Antisubmarine warfare is generally considered to consist of the following activities or phases under the ocean: detecting the presence and movement of concealed enemy submarines that can remain submerged for a long period of time; positioning the detected submarine for continued surveillance; and attacking the detected submarine with the appropriate weapons from the ocean surface, from the air, and from under the ocean. The key to ASW is the use of an array of sophisticated devices for detecting submarines. The Stockholm International Peace Research Institute (SIPRI) has published a list of the detecting devices that include electromagnetic detection by optical, field, radar, infrared, and laser devices; acoustic detection below the ocean surface; high-powered sonar (''sound, navigation and ranging'') mounted on the hull of surface destroyers and submarines; a highly sensitive magnetometer, known as magnetic anomaly detector (MAD), which can be used by aircraft, helicopters, and underwater cable on the seabed to a depth of 3,000 feet, or 1,000 meters. According to the SIPRI report, antisubmarine warfare may involve a coordinated task force of ASW carriers, aircraft, destroyers and ''hunter-killer'' attack submarines vying against one single enemy submarine.

The ice-covered Arctic Ocean has been deployed by the two superpowers, the United States and Russia (or the former Soviet Union), as an ideal place for submarine warfare, which is basically a silent surveillance war game conducted below the surface of the ocean, a matter of watching ''the archer'' before he fires the ''arrow.'' In addition, the Arctic ice provides protection for the Russian Typhoon class and the U.S. Trident, for the ice packs create noise and currents that would interfere with underwater sonar and sound surveillance devices for antisubmarine activities. It has been pointed out that the periodic openings in the ice would also provide the submarines the opportunity to fire their missiles. The North Warning System, with fifty-two radar sites stretching from Alaska to Greenland, completed in 1992, would be able to detect movement of any Rus-sian missile. Oran R. Young pointed out that military technological develop-ments have made the Arctic the world's important military operation area.

Fundamentally, the military and strategic importance of the Arctic region lies in the geographic proximity of the powers, particularly the close distance between the two superpowers; western Alaska is separated by not more than seventy-five miles by the Bering Strait from eastern Siberia. The Northwest Passage, which links the Atlantic with the Pacific Ocean, is a continued, unresolved dispute between the United States and Canada, which claims sovereignty over it. Transboundary navigation in the Arctic Ocean poses jurisdictional disputes and claims, since two-thirds of the Arctic Ocean is within the sectors claimed by Russia and Canada. It has been the strategy of the North Atlantic Treaty Organization to ''lock'' the former Soviet Union by ''choking'' its access to the Bering Strait, the Norwegian Sea, the Greenland Pass, and the Greenland-Iceland-United Kingdom Gap.

Industrial Development and Environmental Pollution. A major contributing factor to the increasing strategic importance of the Arctic region has been the rapid industrial development in the region brought on by the exploitation of Arctic natural resources. First, there is an abundance of oil and natural gas in the Arctic Region. John Warren Kindt indicated that the estimated oil reserve for the region may be more than 500 billion barrels, equivalent to the world's total known oil reserve. Also the estimate indicates some 1,800 trillion cubic feet of natural gas reserve in the region. For instance, Alaska's Prudhoe Bay, combined with the Canning River Delta, contains an estimated reserve of about 25 billion gallons of oil. The Alaskan oil reserve, both onshore and offshore, constitutes about 40 to 50 percent of the discovered oil in the United States. Canada has been drilling natural gas reserves in the MacKenzie River Delta, estimated at 93 trillion cubic feet. Denmark and Norway have also undertaken drilling projects in Greenland and the Spitzbergen Archipelago. The former Soviet Union has been drilling offshore oil reserves on the disputed continental shelf extending more than 500 miles from its Arctic coast. In addition, the former USSR has been exploiting Siberian coal, estimated at about .5 million tons per year, and has also been mining nickel, platinum, and gold in the Kala Peninsula and Chukchi Sea.

Nuclear submarine activities and rapid industrial development for oil and gas have created serious environmental problems for the Arctic. The New York–based Environmental Defense Fund (EDF) produced a series of reports showing the spread of toxic and radioactive pollution from the Russian Arctic coast area into the Arctic Ocean. Air pollutants, mostly sulfur, from industrial activities in Eurasia moved into the Arctic Ocean, the center of the Arctic region. High levels of PCBs are found in the marine life in the Arctic. At the 1993 Tokyo G-7 summit of industrial nations, the EDF expressed concern over Russian nuclear dumping in the Arctic. It is now common knowledge that the former USSR had sunk its nuclear submarines in spring 1989 in Norwegian and Arctic waters. The Soviets had habitually dumped hazardous nuclear waste in the Arctic Ocean from 1965 to 1984. In addition, heavy metals (mercury and cadmium) have been found in Arctic beluga whales, and traces of arsenic, lead, and chromium were also found in the blubber and livers of marine mammals in the Arctic. In summary, Russian experts reported that there were four main pollutants in the Arctic: oil, heavy metals, persistent organic chemicals, and radioactive waste. These environmental hazards not only would have an impact on the marine life, but pose a danger for the indigenous population in the Arctic region. The contamination of organic chemicals such as DDT, PCBs, and chlordane originate from Europe, Asia, and North America and move via the atmosphere to the Arctic.

The Arctic Environment Protection Strategy. The 1982 Law of the Sea Convention made special mention of the Arctic Ocean and pollution in the region. Under Article 234, initiated by the Canadian delegation, negotiations at the Law of the Sea conferences accepted and granted the Arctic Rim countries the authority to adopt and enforce laws and regulations for the prevention and control of marine pollution by vessels in the Arctic.

Concerns about the Arctic region's environmental problems led to discussion by the Arctic Rim nations that began in 1989 and eventually culminated in the signing of the Rovaniemi Declaration and the Arctic Environmental Protection Strategy (AEPS) in June 1991 in Rovaniemi, Finland. The regional agreement contains a set of objectives that include the protection of the Arctic ecosystem by recognizing the indigenous peoples (Inuit, Indian, Aleut, Lapp, Altaic, and Paleoasian) and their traditional values and needs; the enhancement and restoration of environmental quality and the sustainable utilization of Arctic natural resources; and the elimination of pollution in the region. The agreement provided action plans that include conducting research projects to assess the potential effects of acidifying pollutants; implementing measures to curb the use of chlordane such as DDT and PCBs; developing multilateral agreements on oil pollution from vessels, offshore production, natural seeps, and land-based sources in the ice covered Arctic, as well as emergency plans for oil spills from vessels such as that of the Exxon Valdez disaster; encouraging budgetary commitment by Arctic Rim nations to monitor radioactive contamination; and expressing the desire for an international effort toward prohibiting dumping of radioactive waste and heavy metals in the Arctic Ocean. Special attention was urged to promote research efforts and the exchange of information for the conservation of Arctic flora and fauna.

The Rovaniemi strategy for the Arctic's environmental protection is a necessary first step toward more joint international cooperative efforts on regional bases. The aspiration of the Rovaniemi strategy can only become concrete reality through concerted and continued intergovernment cooperation, since sovereignty is dispersed among some eight competing nations in the Arctic region. For many of these regional arrangements there are present a number of disintegrative forces—political, ideological, and cultural differences, as well as unequal costs and benefits—which tend to prevent their growth as effective instruments for marine environmental protection and pollution control. One glaring deficiency, however, in the Rovaniemi strategy has been the absence of discussion for exploring the possibility of limiting military activities in the Arctic Region—particularly the need for making the Arctic Region nuclear free as in the case of the Antarctica Treaty, which had been signed and ratified by thirty-two nations by 1986.

See ENVIRONMENTAL ISSUES, POLLUTION, AND THE MILITARY; HAZARDOUS DUMPING; MILITARY USES OF THE OCEAN; NUCLEAR TESTING IN THE PACIFIC; WARNING ZONES.

BIBLIOGRAPHY

Caron, David D., "Toward an Arctic Environmental Regime," *Ocean Development and International Law* 24 (1993).

Freidheim, Robert L., "The Regime of the Arctic—Distributional or Integrative Bargaining?" *Ocean Development and International Law* 19 (1988).

Kindt, John Warren, *Marine Pollution and the Law of the Sea* (Buffalo, N.Y.: William S. Hein, 1986), vol. 4, chap. 24, p. 1959.

Kolodkin, Anthony, Natalia Mirovitskaya, and Alex Royiako, "The Arctic: Arena for International Security?" *Ocean Yearbook 10* (Chicago: University of Chicago Press, 1933), 286.

Larson, David L., "United States Interests in the Arctic Region," *Ocean Development and International Law* 20 (1989), 167–91.

Wang, James C. F., *Handbook on Ocean Politics and Law* (Westport: Greenwood Press, 1992).

Young, Oran R., "The Age of the Arctic," *Oceanus* 29, no. 1 (Spring 1986). Originally appeared in *Foreign Policy* 61 (Winter 1985–86), 160–79.

James C. F. Wang

ARMS RACE. *See* ANTIBALLISTIC MISSILES/STAR WARS; BIOLOGICAL/CHEMICAL WARFARE; COLD WAR; COUNTERFORCE VERSUS COUNTERVALUE; MASS DESTRUCTION, WEAPONS OF; MILITARISM; NUCLEAR DETERRENCE; NUCLEAR PROLIFERATION; RETALIATION, MASSIVE; STRATEGIC DEFENSE INITIATIVE (SDI); TOTAL WAR; WARISM.

ASSASSINATION. Arguably the most historically significant form of homicide after battlefield killing in wartime. In a single stroke, a single agent can force a change in the course of human affairs. Rabin, Sadat, King, the Gandhis, and the Kennedys are only some of the more recent victims of a practice as old as history itself. Nevertheless, our conception of assassination remains unsettled and controversial for two chief reasons. First, it possesses a shifting, chameleon-like definition. There is a consensus that it should be recognized as a special homicide category, but it is not at all clear what the boundaries of that definition should be. Must all assassinations be politically motivated, or must they merely have political targets? Is assassination characterized by a special *modus operandi* or is that irrelevant? Second, its moral status is Janus-faced. On the one hand, its pedestrian connotation as a forbidden act is especially widespread, yet there are those who argue that assassination is morally permissible, if not obligatory (as in the case of tyrannicide).

To understand the chameleon-like nature of assassination's definition, one need only examine the origin of the term. It is generally attributed to a sect of Ismaili Shiites who viewed themselves as the true protectors of the faith and the only interpreters of the essential meaning of Islam. Hasan Sabbah, the founder of this sect, did not invent assassination, but by the time of his death in 1124, says Franzius, he "developed the practice into a sacred ritual and the prime weapon of a small state waging war against a great power." Franzius is unsure whether the term is a variation on the word "hashish," which the members of Hasan's group were reputed to use, or whether it comes from Hasan's name or the word "Asas" ("foundation"), but it is sure that Hasan's practice had three major elements. First, the *motives* of the assassins were impersonal or, after Franzius, "politicoreligious." Second, the *circumstances* of the act involved the treacherous violation of a preestablished trust, gained by becoming members of the victim's household or by representing themselves as monks who had taken vows of nonviolence. Third, the *targets* of these acts were great personages who represented the interests of their communities.

A practice possessing all three of these elements would be classified as assassination in contemporary parlance, but does each of these elements carry equal definitional weight, or must a homicide possess all three before it can be called an assassination? Contemporary answers fall into three categories. First, there are those who emphasize the *motive* element. Ford, for example, asserts that " 'Assassination is the intentional killing of a specified victim or group of victims, perpetrated for reasons related to his (her, their) political prominence and undertaken with a political purpose in view.' " Schmitt suggests that international law also emphasizes the motive element when it addresses peacetime assassination. Indeed, he asserts that peacetime assassinations are generally construed by international law to be "the targeting of a particular individual" and "killings with political overtones."

By sharp contrast, prohibitions against wartime assassination set aside the motive element. "If political motivation makes a killing during wartime an assassination," Schmitt points out, "then all combat deaths would be assassinations." This is why Article 23(b) of The Hague* IV Convention emphasizes the *circumstance* element in its definition: "[It is especially forbidden] to kill or wound treacherously individuals belonging to the hostile nation or army." Schmitt argues that treacherous killing involves "a breach of confidence," such as "an attack on an individual who justifiably believes he has nothing to fear from an assailant." Specifically, treachery may be defined as "feigning protected status or financially encouraging the killing of an individual." It follows that the targeting of the enemy leadership during wartime is not in and of itself a contemplated assassination (although it may be classified as another form of forbidden homicide). Schmitt argues that all current U.S. military manuals are in accord with Article 23(b) of Geneva IV, including the Army's *The Law of Land Warfare* (FM 27-10), the Air Force's *International Law—The Conduct of Armed Conflict and Air Operations* (AFP 110-31), and the Navy's *The Com-*

mander's Handbook on the Law of Naval Operations (NWP-9, Rev. A). And they also accord with Executive Order 12,333, which forbids any employee or representative of the United States to engage in the act of assassination.

For yet a third view, the motives of the assailant and the circumstances of the act are largely, if not entirely, irrelevant. In this view, the identity of the *target* is most important. If the target is the paramount leader of his or her community, or if the target is implicitly or explicitly entrusted by the community with representing its interests to those outside the community, then the killing of that person by another is an assassination, regardless of the motive of the assailant or the circumstances of the act. Even if it should turn out that Booth gave Lincoln advance warning of his intentions, the killing of Lincoln would still be an assassination. Or if it should turn out that the killer of President Kennedy was motivated by a desire to get even over a sour business deal, history would not redefine the Kennedy assassination as a revenge murder. Schmitt identifies Thomas Aquinas* as one of those who emphasized the target element, while Ford finds evidence for it in Herodotus, Plato, and Aristotle.

The moral status of assassination is as controversial as its differing definitions. As already suggested, those who opt for the motive-driven definition are concerned with peacetime prohibition, and those who wish to prohibit wartime assassination focus on the circumstance-driven definition. On the other hand, those who seek assassination as justified (or even required) in certain cases are those who focus on the target-driven definition.

Prohibitions against assassination in peacetime are largely based on consequentialist and realist concerns, which are eloquently articulated by Morgenthau in Part 5 of *Politics Among Nations.* To engage in assassination is to usurp the political process, and to usurp the political process is to destabilize and corrupt the fundamental architecture of social organization and civilization. There is a perpetual impetus toward the act of assassination, but the law of reciprocity will not be denied: That which is done to others will also be done to oneself, and the inevitable result of the absence of restraint is international chaos, a condition in which reprisal, terror, and the sword are the defining factors. To preserve the international system, therefore, it is important to observe moral as well as legal prohibitions, and chief among these restrictions is the prohibition against assassination.

Wartime prohibitions of assassination are equally consequentialist and realist. The Hague IV Convention proscribes assassination, apparently not because treacherous killing violates some concept of retributive or distributive justice, but because its prohibition is an attempt to impose restraint upon the process of war or to make war less chaotic and horrible. If surrender is feigned to put the enemy off guard and make killing him easier, then all future legitimate attempts to surrender are jeopardized. That is, the preestablished rules governing surrender and the taking of prisoners* are negated, and this further magnifies the incivility of war. As Schmitt puts it, "it keeps war orderly and predictable, which contributes to the manageability of conflict."

Those who would justify assassination are no less consequentialist in their concerns, but they are less inclined to invoke prudence than their counterparts. In fact, they are far more likely to invoke liberty or justice as they argue for the only justifiable form of assassination, namely, regicide or tyrannicide. As Ford points out, the Greeks were as concerned with the communal implications of assassination as Morgenthau, but they also recognized that there are times when the stroke of a knife can restore the *polis* to health and harmony. *Sic semper tyrannis* was the justification used for the assassination of Julius Caesar, and Childress argues that it is also the justification used by Dietrich Bonhoeffer in defense of his plot against Hitler. In fact, Childress argues that Bonhoeffer viewed his plot as fully justified by just war* theory. Clearly, tyrannicide could be construed as satisfying the elements of just war: just cause, *ultima ratio,* proportionality* of means, hope of success, and so on. Granted, tyrannicide is an act of desperation, but it promises to end great suffering and injustice quickly, and thus it would seem to be a legitimate remedy for the horror of a Hitler or equivalent monster.

Yet, it is not clear that it satisfies the proportionality of ends requirement, and herein lies the great paradox of assassination: Regardless of how one defines it, when one practices it, or how evil the person against whom one directs it, to engage in assassination is to threaten destruction of the moral community itself, and this is a price most commentators are unwilling to pay.

See FORBIDDEN STRATEGIES; *LAW OF LAND WARFARE, THE.*

BIBLIOGRAPHY

Childress, James F., "Just-War Theories: The Bases, Interrelations, Priorities, and Function of Their Criteria," in Malham M. Wakin, ed., *War, Morality and the Military Profession* (Boulder Colo.: Westview Press, 1986), 256–776.

Ford, Franklin L., *Political Murder: From Tyrannicide to Terrorism* (Cambridge, Mass.: Harvard University Press, 1985), 2, 41–46.

Franzius, Enno, *The History of the Order of Assassins* (New York: Funk & Wagnalls, 1969), 45, 47–48, 52–67.

Morgenthau, Hans J., *Politics Among Nations: The Struggle for Power and Peace,* 5th edition (New York: Alfred A. Knopf, 1973), 225–56.

Reisman, W. Michael, and Chris T. Antoniou, *The Laws of War: A Comprehensive Collection of Primary Documents on International Laws Governing Armed Conflict* (New York: Vintage Books, 1994), 47.

Schmitt, Michael N., "State Sponsored Assassination in International and Domestic Law," *Yale Journal of International Law* 17 (1992), 609–85.

Patrick R. Tower

AUGUSTINE, ST. (354–430). In 383, Christianity was declared the official religion of the Roman Empire, and Christians who had previously been aloof from political and social responsibility were compelled to rethink their role. Augustine, and his teacher St. Ambrose (340–397), in part inspired by the writings of Cicero (106–43 B.C.), developed just war* criteria to show why Christians could consistently serve in the military as armed soldiers, at least in some wars. Although Augustine deplored the ambitions that promoted wars for sovereignty over others, he believed that there were conditions under which it was just to extend an empire. He argued that if this were not so, then those already under the control of some wicked leader could not be aided righteously to revolt. Wars were justified when declared by the duly constituted authority for a worthy cause, and killing by soldiers was just under these conditions (*The City of God*, Book 1, 21). As instances of worthy causes Augustine named preservation of the well-being of the state, punishment of neighbor nations that had refused to make amends for wrongs committed by their subjects, to restore what had been taken unjustly, and even to expand empire if one was taking land away from a tyrant (*Questions Concerning the Heptateuch*, Question 10; and *City of God*, Book 4, Para. 15). Augustine saw wars as "stern and lasting necessities" even when the results were misery for human beings. War was simply part of the human condition. Even good kings waged wars.

With regard to the way in which wars were fought, on the assumption that they were just in the first place, Augustine expected that Christians would wage both fewer and less vicious wars. His emphasis, however, was less on what the soldier did than on the attitude prompting military action. In his *Reply to Faustus the Manichaean* he insisted that what was important was not what the soldier did but his "inward disposition" (Book 22, Para. 76). Augustine believed that God praised the profession of soldiering (*see Letter 138*, Para. 15). Although he expressed interest in humanizing war, he insisted that if the war was just, there was no basis for quibbling over the means used. "When war is undertaken in obedience to God . . . it must be allowed to be a righteous war" (*Reply to Faustus*, Book 22, Para. 75). Christians may righteously slay their neighbors in obedience to the command of their king, provided that their hearts are pure (*City of God*, Book 19, Para. 7 and 12). In spite of this, Augustine affirmed that wars must be waged proportionally to the value of the end, especially as this required sparing the innocent*. It was not clear, however, how proportionality* was to be measured.

Augustine was convinced that Christianity had already contributed to the humanizing of war through refraining from unnecessary killing. He noted that when the barbarian hordes had invaded from the north the result had been slaughtering, looting, plundering, and general misery, and he anticipated that Christian influence would diminish the scope of such havoc.

See CHRISTIANITY AND WAR; JUST WAR.

BIBLIOGRAPHY

Augustine, *The City of God* (New York: Random House, 1950), Books 1, 3, and 4.
Marrou, Henri, *Saint Augustine and His Influence Through the Ages* (New York: Harper Torch Books, 1957).

AYALA, BALTHAZAR (1548–1584). A member of the positivist school of international law, Ayala formulated principles for going to war based on practice or custom as the source of law rather than expecting, as the naturalists did, that such laws could be derived from existing principles of justice in natural laws. Although he supported the general thesis that individual citizens should not begin a war on their own, he believed that if the prince were absent, and if great hazards would ensue if they awaited his return, the people could go to war immediately. This was inconsistent with his advice that citizens ought to follow authority. His list of worthy reasons for going to war included defense of the empire, protection of friends and allies, and taking vengeance for a wrong received (Chap. 2, Questions 11, 12, and 13). He agreed with Franciscus de Victoria* (1480–1546), however, that not even the pope or the Roman emperor could justify a war against infidels solely on the grounds that they were not Christians.

He considered that damage to civilians (collateral damage*) was a normal consequence of war. Such damage included despoiling the innocent of their goods, money, animals, and even burning of crops and buildings if this would weaken the enemy. Ayala did not provide for civilian questioning of the worthiness of a war declared by the prince. In a monarchy he advised soldiers to follow authority blindly (Chap. 2, Questions 20, 21, and 23).

See BELLI, PIERINO; BYNKERSCHOEK, CORNELIUS; GENTILI, ALBERICO; GROTIUS, HUGO; RAYMOND OF PENAFORTE; VATTEL, EMMERICH; VICTORIA, FRANCISCUS DE.

BIBLIOGRAPHY

Ayala, Balthazar, *Three Books on the Law of War* (Washington, D.C.: Carnegie Foundation, 1912).

B

BANALITY OF EVIL. The phrase was introduced by the philosopher Hannah Arendt to describe the character of the Nazi* war criminal Adolph Eichmann. Eichmann had been apprehended by Israeli agents and brought to Jerusalem for trial in 1961. Arendt covered the trial for the *New Yorker* magazine, and her articles appeared as the book *Eichmann in Jerusalem* in 1963.

The book touched off a world-wide campaign of vilification against Arendt by many Jewish groups, and it is important to distinguish the original concept of the banality of evil from what it was later falsely alleged to be. It was alleged that Arendt claimed that Eichmann was not responsible for his crimes and that the real responsibility for the Jewish Holocaust* lay with the Jews themselves, who had failed to resist the Nazis and often actively collaborated with them. On the contrary, Arendt had argued in her book that Eichmann was guilty of mass murder, that he should be hung, and that he deserved no mercy. She rejected Eichmann's defense of superior orders*, and noted that non-Jews who participated in killing Jews did so under no great compulsion, while the few Jews who directly assisted in killing did so because resistance meant certain death. What caused the trouble was that Arendt mercilessly exposed the incompetence of Eichmann's prosecutors (not his judges), and the prosecutors struck back by slandering Arendt. Arendt also did not endear herself to Jewish groups by issuing negative remarks about the role of the Jewish Councils (Judenrate) in organizing Jews for deportation in Eastern Europe.

BANALITY OF EICHMANN

What, then, was the original concept of the banality of evil? It was that Eichmann was "not Iago and not Macbeth, and nothing would have been further from his mind than to determine with Richard III 'to prove a villain' . . . one cannot extract any diabolical or dialectical profundity from Eichmann." Arendt's point was not that Eichmann was a shallow person and could be guilty only of shallow crimes. It was rather that Eichmann shows us that a shallow person can be guilty of terrible crimes.

Two years later, in *On Revolution*, Arendt distinguished a goodness "beyond virtue" and an evil "beyond vice." Goodness beyond virtue, like the goodness of Jesus in the Gospels or Melville's Billy Budd, is a goodness that has nothing to do with the normal virtues, like diligence and prudence; conversely, badness beyond vice has "nothing of the sordid or sensual"; nevertheless, it is more destructive than the normal ill effects of vicious character. Eichmann is not mentioned, but the Nazi in the earlier book is clearly worse than vicious.

BANALITY OF EVIL

Does the phrase "banality of evil" imply that all evil is banal? *Eichmann in Jerusalem* argued only that Eichmann was banal, leaving open the possibility that other Nazis embodied a nonbanal evil. But in a letter to the scholar Gerschom Scholem, Arendt wrote that "evil is never radical; it is only extreme; it possesses neither depth nor any demonic dimension. It can overgrow and lay waste the whole world precisely because it spreads like a fungus on the surface. It is thought-defying because thought tries to reach some depth, to go to the roots, and the moment it concerns itself with evil, it is frustrated because there is nothing. That is the banality of evil. Only the good has depth and can be radical."

This remarkable argument explains why Arendt's thesis disturbed Scholem and other Jewish thinkers who took the trouble to get Arendt right. For believing Jews, history is the unfolding of a divine plan in which the Jewish people play a special part. The Jewish Holocaust must therefore have some role in God's plan and its perpetrators are at war with God's people. By depriving the perpetrators of demonic character, Arendt divested the Holocaust of religious significance. Scholem and many others complained of the "flippant" tone of Arendt's book. What really disturbed them was Arendt's substitution of the Neoplatonic notion of evil as privation for the Judaic notion of evil as willed malevolence. For Arendt, Eichmann was no demon because in her metaphysics there could be no demons. In the absence of demons, what was left was depravity, the absence of goodness. Arendt's final indictment pointed at a void: Eichmann, she said, was "thoughtless."

BANALITY OF THE HOLOCAUST?

Arendt never applied her banality of evil hypothesis to the Holocaust itself. In the mid 1980s a different argument appeared (Lackey, *Journal of Applied Philosophy,* 1986) for the conclusion that the Holocaust itself represented no radical evil. In 1949, C. S. Lewis had argued that one cannot complain about the quantity of evil in the world because evils cannot be summed together. Two headaches at midnight do not sum together to a superheadache; each is experienced separately by a different person, and the deepest evil is simply the worst headache. Lewis's argument can be extended to deaths and murder; each murder is the ultimate loss for each victim, but many murders do not sum to a superloss or a supermurder. If we randomly select six million murders from the set of all the world's crimes, in what way do those six million murders represent less of an evil than the Jewish Holocaust? The conclusion is that the Holocaust represents no deeper or more radical evil than a single murder, repeated six million times.

Critics of this argument have replied that the intention of the Nazis was not to commit six million murders but to annihilate the Jewish people, and this genocidal* character adds a radical and unprecedented dimension to Nazi killing. But if genocide is the "radical evil" of the Holocaust, it is an evil that is by no means new in the world. It has been inflicted on many peoples, and the Bible itself recommends it to the Jews as the proper way of dealing with the Amorites, Jebusites, Perizzites, and other tribes in ancient Palestine. Genocide is tragically too common to serve as a singular event in human history. And in the case at hand, despite all Nazi power and will, it did not succeed.

The Nazis sought to annihilate the Jews in order (they thought) to build a better Europe. Likewise, the assassin* seeks to improve the world by ridding it of a certain politician. The Nazi and the assassin are both depraved, and it is difficult to distinguish the quality of evil of one from the other. The Nazis were murderers, but there are murderers elsewhere as cruel and merciless. The implication of the banality of evil hypothesis is that the hearts of murderers are everywhere alike.

See CRIMES AGAINST HUMANITY; FORBIDDEN STRATEGIES; HOLOCAUST, THE; HUMAN NATURE AND WAR; INNOCENTS; NUREMBERG TRIALS.

BIBLIOGRAPHY

Arendt, Hannah, *Eichmann in Jerusalem* (New York: Viking, 1963).
———, *On Revolution* (New York: Viking, 1965).
Feldman, Ron, ed., *The Jew As Pariah* (New York: Grove, 1977).

Douglas P. Lackey

BARUCH PLAN. In 1946 the United Nations Atomic Energy Commission (UNAEC) was established by the General Assembly to consist of the five permanent members of the Security Council plus Canada. Since the United States was the only nation with atomic arms, it seemed appropriate that it make the first proposal. In June 1946 the Baruch Plan was the result. The plan required that all nations agree to international control and ownership of nuclear development, and that there be a veto-free control body, the International Atomic Development Authority, to administer the program. The Soviet Union vetoed the plan and made a counterproposal (June 1946) that the United States unilaterally disarm its nuclear arsenal leaving the matter of control to be discussed later. The United States vetoed this proposal. In February 1947 a UN Commission for Conventional Armaments had been set up and the Soviets called for a straight one-third cut in conventional arms, but the United States was reluctant to consider conventional weapons prior to an agreement on nuclear ones. By 1948 the UNAEC reported to the General Assembly its inability to come to any resolution. In 1952 the UN Disarmament Commission was established, but it has not, to date (1995), resolved this thorny matter.

See BIOLOGICAL/CHEMICAL WARFARE; FORBIDDEN WEAPONS; INCENDIARIES; NUCLEAR DETERRENCE; NUCLEAR PROLIFERA-TION; NUCLEAR WEAPONS TESTING.

BIBLIOGRAPHY
Baldwin, Hanson W., *The Great Arms Race* (New York: Praeger, 1958).
Barnet, Richard J., *Who Wants Disarmament?* (Boston: Beacon, 1960).
Barnet, Richard J., and Richard A. Falk, *Security in Disarmament* (Princeton, N.J.: Princeton University Press, 1965).
Brennan, Donald G., ed., *Arms Control, Disarmament, and National Security* (New York: G. Braziller, 1961).
Gilpin, Robert G., *American Scientists and Nuclear Weapons Policy* (Princeton, N.J.: Princeton University Press, 1962).
Noel-Baker, Philip, *The Arms Race* (London: Stevens, 1958).

BAY OF PIGS INCIDENT. Following the Cuban revolution of 1958 that re-placed long-time strong man Fulgencio Batista, relations between Cuba and the United States deteriorated. The Cuban government, headed by Fidel Castro, nationalized U.S.-owned properties, and in response President Dwight Eisen-hower stopped trade with Cuba, which depended heavily on the United States for exports and imports, particularly for export of Cuban sugar.

In 1960 President Eisenhower set in motion an effort to send small bands of Cuban exiles into Cuba to organize an underground resistance to overthrow Cuba's government. Soon, however, Eisenhower abandoned that approach and initiated plans for a single decisive military action against the Cuban government by Cuban exiles under U.S. direction. The planned military action, Eisenhower hoped, would spark a general uprising by the Cuban people against the new government.

Central Intelligence Agency (CIA) operatives recruited Cuban exiles living in Florida. The CIA wanted to train the force in the United States, but the State Department feared that word might get out, so the CIA used remote sites in Guatemala instead.

In early 1961, the Cuban government learned of the training in Guatemala and publicly denounced the United States for planning an invasion of Cuba. *Time* magazine reported on the training in Guatemala. As Eisenhower left the office of president in January 1961, he informed incoming president John Ken-nedy of the plans. Kennedy decided to continue with them. The CIA increased the Cuban exile force to 1,450 men.

In April 1961, in preparation for a landing in Cuba, the CIA decided to neutralize Cuba's air defense by bombing Cuban aircraft on the ground at their bases. It sent Florida-based Cuban pilots to carry out the missions, and to cover up its role it directed the pilots to say, after landing back in Florida, that they were Cuban air force pilots defecting to the United States.

Both the Joint Chiefs of Staff and the State Department conferred with the CIA about final preparations for the landing. The CIA had established a base for the Cuban exiles in Nicaragua, and from there it sent them by sea toward Cuba, commanded by a U.S. Marine Corps colonel who had been released temporarily to the CIA for the operation. The landing site in Cuba was the Bay of Pigs, on Cuba's southern coast. There, U.S. Navy destroyers lay in the water offshore to provide logistical support to the Cuban exile force. U.S. pilots from the U.S.S. *Essex* flew strafing missions to soften the beach. In the actual assault on the beach, the Cuban exiles were led by their CIA instructors.

The anticipated uprising against the Cuban government did not materialize, and Cuban government units fought off the exiles. Of the exiles, over 100 were killed in action, and another 1,000 were taken prisoner by the Cuban government. The U.S. role in the affair was widely suspected. Soviet Premier Nikita Khrushchev charged that the invasion force was "prepared, equipped, and armed in the United States." In reply, President Kennedy denied U.S. involvement but voiced moral support for the Cubans, whom he depicted as having acted independently of the U.S. government.

Fifteen years later a U.S. Senate investigating committee acknowledged the U.S. role, writing that "the President authorized the CIA to secretly direct and finance the military invasion." The committee charged that by acting on their own and secretly, Eisenhower and Kennedy had evaded "the constitutional system of checks and balances" that governs military action abroad.

After the failure of the Bay of Pigs landing, the CIA continued covert actions against Cuba. In the following months the CIA planned for the assassination of Cuban President Fidel Castro, to be carried out by covert operatives. It also sought to foment internal dissension in Cuba by infiltrating Cuban exiles to organize underground cells of resistance to the Cuban government. More significantly, the CIA sent raiding parties of Cuban exiles from Florida into Cuba, where they sabotaged sugar refineries and oil depots. The CIA called this action "Operation Mongoose."

The Bay of Pigs operation had an unintended consequence the following year, when it was a key factor in bringing the United States and the Soviet Union to the brink of war over Cuba. The Bay of Pigs invasion, taken together with "Operation Mongoose," led to Cuba's gaining the Soviet government's agreement to install missiles in Cuba. The purpose was to deter a U.S. invasion, reported Soviet Premier Nikita Khrushchev in his memoirs.

In response to the missile emplacement, Kennedy established a blockade around Cuba, to stop Soviet vessels bearing more missiles. If a Soviet ship were to refuse to be searched, Kennedy said that the U.S. vessels would use force to stop it. The blockade thus risked a military confrontation with the USSR.

Kennedy said that the missile blockade was directed against "offensive threats" by Cuba and the Soviet Union. His administration charged at the United Nations that the missile emplacement showed that the Soviet Union was using Cuba as a "base for Communist aggression." Although the public remained ignorant of the fact, Kennedy was well aware of the U.S. role in the failed Bay of Pigs invasion and in "Operation Mongoose." Kennedy thus knew that Cuba had reason to be concerned about further offensive action by the United States and that Cuba and the Soviet Union might well view the missile emplacement as defensive.

Thus, the Bay of Pigs invasion, and the secrecy surrounding it, were a factor in bringing the world close to war between the two superpowers of the day. The crisis was averted when Khrushchev removed the missiles in exchange for a promise by Kennedy not to invade Cuba.

See AGGRESSION, ATTEMPTS TO DEFINE; FORBIDDEN STRATE-GIES; PEACE, CRIMES AGAINST.

BIBLIOGRAPHY

Colby, William, *Honorable Men: My Life in the CIA* (New York: Simon & Schuster, 1978).

Falk, Richard A., "American Intervention in Cuba and the Rule of Law," *Ohio State Law Journal* 22 (1961), 546.

Kennedy, John F., "The Soviet Threat to the Americas," October 22, 1962, *Department of State Bulletin* 47 (1962), 715.

Kirkpatrick, Lyman B., Jr., *The U.S. Intelligence Community* (New York: Hill & Wang, 1973).

"Mr. Khrushchev to President Kennedy," April 18, 1961, *Department of State Bulletin* 44 (1961), 662.

Powers, Thomas, *The Man Who Kept Secrets: Richard Helms and the CIA* (New York: Knopf, 1979).

"President Kennedy to Mr. Khrushchev," April 18, 1961, *Department of State Bulletin* 44 (1961), 661.

Schlesinger, Arthur M., Jr., *A Thousand Days* (Boston: Houghton Mifflin, 1965).

Talbott, Strobe, ed., *Khrushchev Remembers* (Boston: Little Brown, 1970).

U.S. Senate, *Alleged Assassination Plots Involving Foreign Leaders: An Interim Report of the Select Committee to Study Governmental Operations with Respect to Intelligence Activities,* 94th Cong., 1st sess., Report No. 94–465, November 20, 1975.

U.S. Senate, Select Committee to Study Governmental Operations with Respect to Intelligence Activities, *Final Report: Foreign and Military Intelligence,* Book 1, 94th Cong., 2d sess., April 26, 1976.

Wyden, Peter, *Bay of Pigs: The Untold Story* (New York: Simon & Schuster, 1979).

John Quigley

BAYONETS. In medieval war, armed conflict was normally face to face and swords were the weapon of choice. Bayonets were widely used during the 18th and 19th centuries simply as swords attached to a rifle. They had the advantage of conversion on rifles that were slow loading, and the American defeat at

Bunker Hill was attributed at least partially to the lack of bayonets. In the Yorktown campaign, Washington exhorted his men to place their principal reliance on the bayonet. Local militia were required to own a cutting sword, a hatchet, or a bayonet. While the U.S. Army manuals beginning with the 1914 version, *Rules of Land Warfare**, forbade "lances with barbed tips," this did not seem to affect putting serrations on bayonets. Will Irwin, an American journalist, commented in 1921 that uninstructed civilians wondered why so much stress was put on bayonet practice, and were told that it was a way of cultivating hate. The recruit was urged to imagine that the straw dummy into which he was plunging his bayonet was a German soldier. During World War I, under the sponsorship of the YMCA, a pamphlet was written on the "Christian use of the bayonet," in which the reader was assured that, were Jesus here, he would join the troops with a bayonet in his hand. A picture of Jesus dressed in an American army uniform and holding a bayonet graced the pages.

Modern weapons of war, for the most part, relieve the soldier from such face-to-face combat, the major exceptions being in guerrilla-type wars such as Vietnam. The recent armed involvements of the United States, such as Grenada, Panama, and the Persian Gulf, utilized primarily weapons fired at a distance either from planes, cannons, or offshore ships. The current U.S. Army manual, *The Law of Land Warfare* FM 27-10, makes no mention of bayonets although it does list lances with barbed tips as forbidden on the grounds that they cause "unnecessary injury."

See FORBIDDEN WEAPONS; MILITARY TRAINING.

BIBLIOGRAPHY

Abrams, Ray H., *Preachers Present Arms* (New York: Round Table, 1933), 69.

Peterson, Harold L., *Arms and Armor in Colonial America* (New York: Bramhall, 1956).

BELLI, PIERINO (1502–1575). His treatise on military matters began with the assumption that all nations had an equal right to declare and wage war. Any people or nation "living under its own laws," and any king or ruler "who is fully independent" may declare war whenever an occasion arises. He stated that the pope had a clear right to declare and wage war and he urged lesser prelates to get papal approval first. He listed as acceptable reasons for going to war: to protect altars, home fires, children, and wives; to escape injury; to get revenge; or to help an ally or friend. All wars were just* that were waged in defense of liberty and fatherland (Chap. 5, Para. 13). The importance of a declaration of war* was that it allowed a reasonable delay between the announcement and the attack; thus, a hasty or ill-conceived war might be avoided. He insisted that no attack should be made prior to the announcement that war had been declared, and that to do otherwise would be treacherous (Chap. 8, Para. 2–8).

Belli was undecided whether a citizen had the right to refuse the call to arms of his prince, although he cited favorably the dictum of St. Augustine* that citizens were obligated to obey even clearly wicked rulers. At the same time, he cited certain proconsuls to the effect that if the injustice of a prince was "clear and manifest," the citizen was not bound to obey, while if the injustice was not established, "obedience must be rendered" (Chap. 2, Para. 1 and 3). Soldiers, however, were rarely in any position to have bases for questioning the orders of their superiors*. He supported Victoria's insistence that women and children ought to be spared, but noted that the principle was little observed (Chap. 9, Para. 1–7).

See AYALA, BALTHAZAR; BYNKERSCHOEK, CORNELIUS; GENTILI, ALBERIEO GROTIUS, HUGO; RAYMOND OF PENAFORTE; VATTEL, EMMERICH DA; VICTORIA, FRANCISCUS DE.

BIBLIOGRAPHY
Belli, Pierino, *A Treatise on Military Matters and Warfare* (Oxford: Clarendon Press, 1936).

BENTHAM, JEREMY (1748–1832). The founder of utilitarianism, Bentham judged that acts are right insofar as they contribute to the greatest good for the greatest number. His *Introduction to the Principles of Morals and Legislation* (1789) did much to establish the discipline of international law, and perhaps of political science. On utilitarian grounds, war was obviously criminal on the grandest scale. In his analysis of the causes and cures of war, he listed: (1) the pretension that the subjects of one nation are superior to those of any other; (2) injuries from rivalries in commerce, and the cure, "General liberty of commerce"; (3) disputes over the right of succession, and the cure "liquidation of titles"; (4) disputes over boundaries, and the solution "amicable demarcations"; (5) attempts at monopoly of commerce, and the cure "limiting the number of troops"; and (6) injuries on account of religion, and the means of prevention, "progress of toleration."

In Essay 4 of *Principles of International Law*, he outlined a plan "for an universal and perpetual peace." He urged the reduction of troops with the aim of disarmament. He advocated that Great Britain should not maintain any military forces in the colonies and only keep enough of a navy to defend commerce against pirates. He proposed the elimination of all old colonies and the founding of no new colonies, and the establishment of free trade, and the establishment of a "common court of judicature" to resolve conflicts between nations. Such a court would not be armed with coercive powers. A congress or diet should be established to resolve international conflicts. To implement this procedure he recommended the abolition of secrecy in the foreign department as "altogether useless, and equally repugnant to the interests of liberty and peace."

See CHRISTIANITY AND WAR; HOLY WARS; INTELLIGENCE AGENCIES, U.S.; JUST WAR.

BIBLIOGRAPHY
Baumgardt, David, *Bentham and the Ethics of Today* (New York: Octagon, 1966).
Bowring, John, ed., *The Works of Jeremy Bentham* (New York: Russell & Russell, 1962).

BIKINI ATOLL, BOMBING OF. Bikini Atoll and the Marshall Islands symbolize the human costs of above-ground nuclear weapons testing* and the transition from atomic to hydrogen bombs. Inhabitants of Bikini Atoll and other Marshall Islands exposed to radioactive fallout suffered immediate injuries, such as skin burns and hematological damage, and delayed injuries, including carcinogenic effects. Continued above-ground testing raised serious ethical issues as knowledge increased of the medical hazards posed by radioactive fallout. In fact, medical data gathered from nuclear tests conducted between 1946 and 1958 motivated the public outcry that resulted in the termination of above-ground nuclear testing in 1963.

Ethical issues associated with population relocation were greatest for inhabitants of Bikini Atoll and Eniwetok Atoll. In 1946, shortly after the atomic bombings of Hiroshima and Nagasaki*, the United States selected Bikini Atoll as a nuclear test site, relocated its inhabitants to Rongerik Atoll where they nearly starved, evacuated them temporarily to a U.S. base on Kwajalein Atoll, and then resettled them on Kili Island. Even when the United States began returning Bikinians in the early 1970s, levels of Strontium 90 in their bodies reached such dangerous levels that they were again evacuated. Eniwetok Atoll, which also had its inhabitants relocated, was not decontaminated and resettled until the late 1970s.

In the 1980s, the Department of Defense authorized the Defense Nuclear Agency to prepare a series of studies on nuclear weapons tests to provide the Centers for Disease Control and Veterans Administration with data on radiation exposure of persons participating in about 200 atmospheric nuclear weapons tests conducted between 1945 and 1962. These volumes include *Operation Crossroads—1946* (Berkhouse et al., 1984) and *Operation Ivy: 1952* (Gladeck et al., 1982). "Crossroads," conducted at Bikini Atoll, was the first postwar nuclear weapons test series and included "Able," a 23 kiloton airburst on July 1, 1946, and "Baker," a 23 kiloton underwater detonation on July 25, 1946. On November 1, 1952, "Mike," the first of two nuclear detonations conducted on islands of Eniwetok Atoll in "Operation Ivy," was the first hydrogen bomb test. This 10.4 megaton blast destroyed Elugelab Island, leaving a submerged crater 6,300 feet in diameter and 160 feet deep.

One test, however, produced enormous controversy. In the "Bravo" test of "Operation Castle" at Bikini Atoll on February 28, 1954, the United States exploded a 15–22 megaton thermonuclear device. Extensive fallout, including radioactive ash, caused serious contamination over an area extending nearly 200 miles downwind. Seven hours after the detonation, fallout arrived at Rongerik Island, about 160 miles east of Bikini. After thirty minutes, the gamma detector exceeded the maximum end of its scale (100 milli-roentgens per hour). Even heavier fallout occurred on Rongelap Atoll and Ailinginae Atoll, both located closer to Bikini. Americans operating a weather station on Rongerik were evacuated, as were Rongelap and Ailinginae islanders. (Rongelap Island was so heavily contaminated the islanders were not returned until 1957.) Later, authorities learned that a Japanese fishing vessel, the *Fukuru Maru* (Lucky Lady), had been in the fallout path. Although the fallout was visible on Rongelap and the

Japanese fishing boat, the exposed individuals took no precautions to protect their bodies. Fifty-three Marshall Islanders received whole-body exposures of 70–175 roentgens, while the twenty-three crew members of Fukuru Maru received 170–590 roentgens. Public protests against atmospheric testing quickly followed and led to a moratorium on above-ground testing in 1958 and the 1963 Partial Test Ban Treaty, which permits only underground nuclear detonations up to 150 kilotons.

On December 23, 1954, Bertrand Russell delivered a dramatic radio address on the BBC, soon published as "Man's Peril from the Hydrogen Bomb" (*The Listener,* December 30, 1954). Russell regarded this essay as launching the phase of his responses to nuclear weapons that culminated in his *Common Sense and Nuclear Warfare* (1959). However, he had earlier made similar points in "The Hydrogen Bomb and World Government" (*The Listener,* July 22, 1954) and "A Prescription for the World" (*Saturday Review,* August 28, 1954). "Man's Peril" ends with Russell's famous line, "I appeal, as a human being to human beings: remember your humanity, and forget the rest. If you can do so, the way lies open to a new Paradise; if you cannot, nothing lies before you but universal death." In this address and henceforth, Russell explicitly rejects taking sides with either superpower. Shortly after this address, Russell and Albert Einstein issued a joint statement, known as the "Russell-Einstein Manifesto," which became the basis for the Pugwash Movement. Referring to the Bravo detonation, the manifesto, which repeats almost verbatim many passages from "Man's Peril," states "we now know, especially since the Bikini test, that nuclear bombs can gradually spread destruction over a very much wider area than had been supposed."

In the late 1950s, Albert Schweitzer, along with Linus Pauling and many other scientists, also began a sustained opposition to above-ground nuclear testing. Many of the scientific discussions, often associated with Pugwash, appeared in issues of the *Bulletin of the Atomic Scientists.* In *Peace or Atomic War?* (1958), Schweitzer declares, "We must not be responsible for the future birth of thousands of children with the most serious mental and physical defects simply because we did not pay enough attention to that danger."

The termination of above-ground testing by nearly all nuclear nations remains one of the few, but very encouraging, successes of ethical debate regarding nuclear weapons.

See HIROSHIMA AND NAGASAKI, BOMBING OF; NUCLEAR WEAPONS TESTING.

BIBLIOGRAPHY
Hines, Neal O., *Proving Ground: An Account of the Radiobiological Studies in the Pacific, 1946–1961* (Seattle: University of Washington Press, 1962).
Kiste, Robert C., *The Bikinians: A Study in Forced Migration* (Menlo Park, Calif.: Cummings Publishing, 1974).
Russell, Bertrand, *Common Sense and Nuclear Warfare* (London: Allen & Unwin, 1959).

————, ''Man's Peril from the Hydrogen Bomb,'' *The Listener* 52, no. 1348 (December 30, 1954), 1135–36.

Schweitzer, Albert, *Peace or Atomic War?* (New York: Henry Holt & Co., 1958).

William C. Gay

BINARY WEAPONS. *See* BIOLOGICAL/CHEMICAL WARFARE; BRUSSELS DECLARATION; COMBATANT-NONCOMBATANT DISTINCTION; FORBIDDEN WEAPONS; MASS DESTRUCTION, WEAPONS OF.

BIOLOGICAL AND CHEMICAL WEAPONS, UN RESOLUTIONS BANNING.

December 16, 1969, UN General Assembly Resolution banning Chemical and Biological Weapons. Passed, 80 yea, 3 (U.S.) nay, and 36 abstentions.

December 8, 1971, UN General Assembly Resolution commending the convention against chemical and bacteriological weapons. Passed, 110 (U.S.) yea, 0 nay, 1 (France) abstention.

November 20, 1969, UN Report on Human Rights in Armed Conflicts reaffirming a ban on ''weapons of mass destruction'' and so-called ''non-directed weapons'' such as nuclear, napalm, flamethrowers, gas, chemicals, and germ bombs. United States not a signatory.

December 4, 1967, UN General Assembly Resolution on the nonuse of nuclear weapons. Passed, 77 yea, 0 nay, 29 (U.S.) abstentions.

April 10, 1972, Conference between the United States, USSR, and Great Britain on the ''Prohibition of the Development, Production, and Stockpiling of Bacteriological and Toxin Weapons and on their Destruction.'' United States not a signatory.

1975, UN General Assembly Resolution to prohibit the development and manufacture of new types of weapons of mass destruction and of new systems of such weapons. Passed, 112 yea, 1 nay, 15 (U.S.) abstentions.

December 8, 1976, UN General Assembly Resolution urging the conclusion of a world treaty on the nonuse of force in international relations. Passed, 88 yea, 2 nay, 31 (U.S.) abstentions.

December 10, 1976, UN General Assembly requested a ban on the development of new types of lethal weapons to include ray weapons that affect blood and intercellular plasma, infrasound weapons designed to damage internal organs, and genetic weapons to alter heredity. Passed, 120 aye, 1 nay, 15 (U.S.) abstentions.

December 10, 1976, UN General Assembly Resolution to prohibit the development and manufacture of new types of weapons of mass destruction and new systems of such weapons. Passed, 120 yea, 1 nay, 15 (U.S.) abstentions.

December 10, 1976, UN General Assembly Resolution to restrict chemical weapons. Passed, without a vote.

November 29, 1972, UN General Assembly Resolution to support the previous Resolution unilaterally if necessary. Passed, 89 yea, 4 nay, 23 (U.S.) abstentions.

November 1981, UN General Assembly Resolution banning chemical weapons. Passed, 127 yea, 0 nay, 1 (U.S.) abstention.

1982, UN General Assembly Resolution banning chemical/biological weapons. U.S. was the only nation to abstain.

December 15, 1989, UN General Assembly Resolution to study a ban on chemical/biological weapons. Passed by consensus.

December 15, 1989, UN General Assembly Resolution banning Radiological Weapons. Passed 124 yea, 2 (U.S.) nay, and 26 abstentions.

November 30, 1992, UN General Assembly Resolution "Convention on the Prohibition of the Development, Production, Stockpiling and Use of Chemical Weapons and on their Destruction." Approved by consensus.

January 13, 1993, Chemical Weapons Convention in The Hague, to establish an Organization for the Prevention of Chemical Weapons. Passed, by a vote of 130 yea. The Preparatory Commission to do this met February 8–12, 1993 in The Hague and proposed that 180 days after the 65th ratification, but not earlier than January 1995, the Convention would enter into force.

BIOLOGICAL/CHEMICAL WARFARE. In the 5th century B.C., the Spartan army in a siege of an Athenian city ignited a mixture of sulphur, pitch, and wood under the city walls in the expectation that the fumes would make the enemy easier to capture. When Perseus arranged with a native of Tarentum to destroy the Romans by poison, Livy (59 B.C.–7 A.D.) said that he did not wage war justly*. Church councils in the Middle Ages issued prohibitions against the use of poisons in war. Some reasons given for these prohibitions were that poisons were invisible and thus not sporting, and that poisons indiscriminately killed noncombatants along with combatants*. The lack of any practical defense against poison may have influenced armies generally to agree to ban such weapons. While poisoning a water supply was banned, it was considered permissible to pollute water by more visible means, such as throwing a dead animal carcass in the springs. Richard Zouche (1590–1661) remarked that when the Spanish had been besieged by the French at Naples, the Spanish had poisoned the French water supply, an act that Zouche condemned. He also condemned the act of the Italians who sent infected prostitutes into French military camps. Samuel Rachel (1628–1691) claimed that civilized nations did not use poison, either in their missiles or against the enemy's water supply. Samuel Pufendorf (1632–1694) listed the use of poison as equally heinous with perfidy and assassination*. Emmerich Vattel* (1714–1767) classified treacheries by seriousness and listed the use of poison as worse than assassination, but he considered the use of poisoned weapons as less objectionable than poisoning the water supply.

On August 27, 1874, a conference at Brussels* issued a declaration listing specific weapons and strategies that should be banned. Poisons including deleterious gases were forbidden. The same prohibitions appeared at The Hague* in 1899 and 1907 in a declaration "Prohibiting the Employment of Projectiles Containing Asphyxiating or Deleterious Gases." The American representative at The Hague Conference, Naval Captain Alfred T. Mahan, cast the only dissenting vote. *General Orders 100** had affirmed in paragraph 70 that the use of poisons was "wholly excluded" from modern warfare. *The Rules of Land Warfare* (1914)* cited The Hague resolution 23 that it was "especially forbidden" to use poison or poisoned weapons. Although the 1914 manual forbade poisons, it did not forbid gases, noxious chemicals, and biologicals. Both the Axis and the Allies experimented with gas warfare during World War I. In August 1914 the French tried gas in the war, but it dispersed so quickly that they discarded its use. On October 27, 1914, the German army fired 3,000 shells filled with dianisidine chlorosulphate against British troops at Neuve-Chapelle, but the soldiers suffered no ill effects. To evade the Hague prohibition against the use of shells "whose sole function" was to disperse gas, the Germans devised a shell that contained an explosive as well as gas. By the end of the war such gas shells constituted 50 percent of the basic load of German artillery shells.

On September 24, 1915, the British launched the first successful Allied use of gas near Loos, Belgium. Even though the winds were not favorable, enough gas drifted into the German lines to show that the German gas masks were ineffective. Furthermore, the chlorine gas caused malfunctioning of the breechlocks of rifles, machine guns, and artillery, with a side effect that prevented the German officers from shouting commands loud enough to be heard through their masks. The Russians, French, British, and Americans all used gas with varying degrees of success. Over 3,000 different chemicals were investigated for possible weapon use. In 1917 the Germans first used mustard gas, which became the favored chemical. As late as 1918 almost all the gas material used by the Allies was produced by Britain. It was not until April 1918 that the first U.S.-manufactured gas projectiles reached the Allied Expeditionary Forces, a total of about 3,600 tons. In spite of the relatively ineffective methods of dispersal, 100,000 were killed on the Allied and Axis sides from gas, and an estimated 1,300,000 were gas-related casualties.

In 1925 a Geneva Protocol* prohibited poisonous gases and bacteriologicals. Although Great Britain was not a signatory at the time, it did accede in 1930, despite the distinguished British scientist, J.B.S. Haldane's pamphlet, *Callinicus,* meant to "prove" that gas warfare was more humane than any other kind of warfare with any other kind of weapon. Since the U.S. Senate did not ratify the prohibitions, the 1956 Army Manual, *The Law of Land Warfare**, affirmed that the United States was not a party to any treaty that prohibited the use of either chemical or biological weapons. Army Pamphlet 21-1 (1965), *Treaties Governing Land Warfare,* assured the soldier that the American army was not bound by any protocols limiting the use of either chemical or biological weapons. Although UN resolutions urged the prohibition of such weapons of mass destruction, the U.S. secretary of the Army argued that gases and chemicals should be listed as "conventional" weapons.

In 1976, under President Richard M. Nixon, the U.S. Army manual was revised to take account of the Senate ratification of the 1925 Geneva Protocol. However, the United States reserved the right to determine which chemicals were included in the ban and stated that the ban only prohibited "first use" but permitted use in reprisal*. Furthermore, the U.S. reservation included the proviso that in wars with noncompliant states, the United States was relieved of its agreement not to use such weapons. With regard to biological weapons, however, the new manual forbade any use, either first or in reprisal. President Franklin D. Roosevelt had stated during World War II that the United States would not use biological agents unless they were first used by the enemy. The U.S. Army, however, was not united in its stand on biologicals. The Army Surgeon General, for example, took the position that the "defensive" aspects of biological warfare could be pursued, while Brigadier General J. H. Rothschild, head of the Chemical Corps, argued successfully that his branch should be allowed to pursue both defensive and offensive aspects. The stockpiling of such weapons has been a constant problem, and their efficacy remains a matter of dispute. In 1988 the U.S. Army Toxic and Hazardous Materials Agency reported that "the retaliatory capability of the current stockpile is 10% useful, 18% of limited use, 11% of no use, and 61% not in useful form."

Although chemical or biological warfare was not a major issue at the Nuremberg* and Tokyo* war crimes trials, there was evidence that German doctors had maltreated prisoners by performing chemical and biological experiments on them. In the Medical Trial* conducted under Control Council Law No. 10* the experiments on hapless prisoners were of such a magnitude that all twenty-three of the accused were found guilty. On December 28, 1949, a military tribunal of the USSR tried twelve former Japanese servicemen and charged them with manufacturing and using bacteriological weapons. Among the specific charges was that a military expedition of the Japanese in 1940 was sent into the Chinese region of Nimpo supplied with the germs of typhus and cholera and a large quantity of plague-infected fleas, and that they had generated a plague epidemic. A similar Japanese expedition in 1941 sent to Changteh created another plague epidemic.

The current status of chemical/biological weapons is ambiguous. An estimated ten countries are known to possess biological weapons and about twenty are known to possess chemical weapons. The U.S. manual, *Military Biology and Biological Warfare Agents,* 3-216 and 355.6, denied that warfare with such agents would be radically worse than with most other kinds of weapons. The manual insisted that using microorganisms as biological warfare agents was simply a military adaptation of naturally occurring biological attacks, and claimed further that the suffering caused by most diseases is no greater than that caused by severe injuries inflicted by shell fragments or machine gun fire. This attitude has led to extensive experimentation on unwitting human subjects by the Department of Defense and the Central Intelligence Agency. See the entry herein on BIOLOGICAL AND CHEMICAL WEAPONS, UN RESOLUTIONS BANNING.

Whether any militarily useful weapon should be prohibited remains one of the most controversial problems that insistence on the priority of military necessity* creates. See the Intelligence Agencies* entry herein for reports of medical experiments on unwitting U.S. citizens by the Central Intelligence Agency (CIA) and the Department of Defense (DOD); and the entry on the Military-Industrial Complex* for the location of the seven United States production sites for chemical weapons and the nine storage sites, as well as the United States' major biological warfare sites, and the approximately 150 public and private chemical and biological weapons laboratories in more than thirty states and fifteen foreign countries. These do not include the thousands of research projects carried out in university, corporate, and military centers. The seriousness with which the United States carries out chemical and biological warfare research has been illustrated by the experiments conducted on unwitting American citizens by the DOD and the CIA.

See CASUALTIES OF WAR; FORBIDDEN WEAPONS; GENEVA PROTOCOL, JUNE 17, 1925; INCENDIARIES; INTELLIGENCE AGENCIES; MILITARY-INDUSTRIAL COMPLEX; NUCLEAR WAR; NUREMBERG PRINCIPLES.

BIBLIOGRAPHY

American Nuclear Guinea Pigs: Three Decades of Radiation Experiments on United States Citizens, Report prepared by the Subcommittee on Energy Conservation and Power of the Committee on Energy and Commerce, H.R., November 1986 (Washington, D.C.: U.S. Government Printing Office, 1986).

Government Sponsored Testing on Humans, Hearing Before the Subcommittee on Administrative Law and Governmental Relations of the Committee on the Judiciary, HR, 103rd Cong., 2d sess., February 3, 1994 (Washington, D.C.: U.S. Government Printing Office, 1994).

Heller, Major Charles E., *Leavenworth Papers: Chemical Warfare in World War I: The American Experience, 1917–1918* (Fort Leavenworth, Kan.: U.S. Army Command and General Staff College, 1984).

Human Drug Testing by the CIA, 1977, Hearings Before the Subcommittee on Health and Scientific Research of the Committee on Human Resources, U.S. Senate, 95th Cong., 1st sess., September 20 and 21, 1977 (Washington, D.C.: U.S. Government Printing Office, 1977).

International Committee of the Red Cross, *Weapons That May Cause Unnecessary Suffering or Have Indiscriminate Effects* (Geneva: International Committee of the Red Cross, 1973).

———, *Conference of Government Experts on the Use of Certain Conventional Weapons* (Geneva, International Committee of the Red Cross, 1976).

Is Military Research Hazardous to Veterans' Health? Lessons Spanning Half a Century, Staff Report prepared for the Committee on Veterans' Affairs, Senate, December 8, 1994 (Washington, D.C.: U.S. Government Printing Office, 1994).

Radiation Experiments Conducted by the University of Cincinnati Medical School with Department of Defense Funding, Hearing Before the Subcommittee on Administrative Law and Governmental Relations of the Committee on the Judiciary, H.R., 103rd Cong., 2d sess., April 11, 1994.

Rose, Steve, ed., *CBW Chemical and Biological Warfare* (London: George Harrap, 1968).

Thomas, Ann Van, and A. J. Thomas, Jr., *Legal Limits on the Use of Chemical and Biological Weapons* (Dallas, Tex.: Southern Methodist University Press, 1970).

BOMBING, OBLITERATION. *See* AERIAL WARFARE; ANTIBALLISTIC MISSILES/STAR WARS; CASUALTIES OF WAR; CHILDREN AND WAR; COUNTERFORCE VERSUS COUNTERVALUE; FIRST STRIKE/SECOND STRIKE; FORBIDDEN STRATEGIES; HIROSHIMA AND NAGASAKI; MASS DESTRUCTION, WEAPONS OF; NUCLEAR DETERRENCE; NUCLEAR WAR; PROPORTIONALITY; STRATEGIC DEFENSE INITIATIVE (SDI).

BRITTAIN, VERA (1893–1970). Along with Bertrand Russell and Aldous Huxley, Brittain supported the British Peace Pledge Union of 1935, with its founder, Dick Shepard. The pledge affirmed that the signers would not support any war. When the British call-up included women, the union established a women's section, which Brittain chaired along with Sybil Thorndyke and Ruth Fry. Her *Testament of Youth* contained her memoirs of nursing during World War I in the British forces. She established the Women's Peace Campaign in 1939. In 1943 she wrote *Massacre by Bombing,* printed by the Fellowship of Reconciliation, to protest the indiscriminate bombing of civilian centers, and her article was signed by twenty-eight religious leaders. Brittain estimated that she received letters 50-to-1 opposed to her concern and that at least 200 articles appeared condemning her. The Reverend Daniel Poling called her essay a "squawk" and accused her signators of being "mushy." The editors of the *Christian Century* chided her "naivete," and the *Saturday Evening Post* stated in an editorial that she was obviously mentally "unstable." Conservative ministers, the Reverends Carl McIntyre and H. J. Ockenga, called her "un-American and pro-Fascist." The little support that she did receive was from the Roman Catholic and Quaker press.

See ADDAMS, JANE; CHRISTIANITY AND WAR; DAY, DOROTHY; MUSTE, ABRAHAM JOHANNES.

BIBLIOGRAPHY

Brittain, Vera, *The Rebel Passion: A Short History of Some Pioneer Peace-Makers* (London: George Allen & Unwin, 1964).

Mitchell, David, *Women on the Warpath: The Story of the Women of the First World War* (London: Jonathan Cape, 1966).

Moorehead, Caroline, *Troublesome People: The Warriors of Pacifism* (Bethesda, Md.: Adler & Adler, 1987).

Morrison, Sybil, *I Renounce War: The Story of the Peace Pledge Union* (London: Sheppard Press, 1962).

BRUSSELS DECLARATION (AUGUST 27, 1874). A conference at Brussels was called by the Russian Czar, Alexander II, to consider ways to "diminish

... the calamities of international conflicts.'' Fifteen states were represented although their representatives were not authorized to conclude any binding agreements. Although its fifty-six Articles were never adopted by any of the powers concerned, an examination of the proposals made in the Brussels Declaration illustrates the ethical concerns of the participants of the Brussels Congress. The laws of war* were applicable both to armies and to any corps that had a responsible leader, wore a distinctive uniform, carried arms openly, and conformed to the laws of war. Spies* would be punished severely. Special emphasis was placed on the obligations toward prisoners of war*.

The major points made in Article 13 were the chief reason for the lack of support. These forbade:

1. The use of poison or poisoned weapons

2. Murder by treachery of individuals belonging to the hostile nation or army

3. Murder of an antagonist who, having laid down his arms, or having no longer the means of defending himself, has surrendered

4. The declaration that no quarter* will be given

5. The use of arms, projectiles, or substances that may cause unnecessary suffering, as well as the use of the projectiles prohibited by the St. Petersburg Declaration* in 1868

6. Abuse of the flag of truce, the national flag, or the military insignia or uniform of the enemy, as well as the distinctive badge of the International Red Cross*

Twenty-five years later the above six Brussels prohibitions were incorporated into the first Hague Congress. The provisions reappeared in Geneva Conventions*, and were appealed to in the Nuremberg Charter and by the judges at the Nuremberg trials* of German war criminals after World War II as primary evidence that laws of war existed, which named war crimes*.

See BIOLOGICAL/CHEMICAL WARFARE; FORBIDDEN WEAPONS; GENEVA CONVENTION, JULY 6, 1906; HAGUE, THE, CONGRESSES; QUARTER, NO, WARS OF.

BIBLIOGRAPHY
Friedman, Leon, ed., *The Law of War,* vol. 1 (New York: Random House, 1972), 194–203.
Scott, James Brown, *The Hague Peace Conferences,* vol. 1 (Baltimore, Md.: Johns Hopkins Press, 1909).

BUDDHISM AND WAR. Based on the teachings of its founder, Gautama Siddhartha (c. 563–c. 483 B.C.), the movement developed, like Christianity, into many sects which are divided into two main traditions: Hinayana (the ''little vehicle''), now called Theravada (school of the elders), to escape the invidious implications of being ''little''; and Mahayana (''great vehicle''). The Theravada school has predominated in Ceylon, Burma, Siam, and Indo-China, while the Mahayana school has predominated in China, Korea, Japan, Tibet, and Mongolia. Our knowledge of early Buddhism comes from Pali scriptures, the sayings of the Buddha, and monastic rules. The Pali canon are estimated to be about twice as long as the Bible. In spite of differences in emphasis between the two schools, both stress the Four Noble Truths and the Eightfold Path and both teach "thou shalt not kill," forgiveness of enemies, and the significance of motive. Both assert the Five Precepts to abstain from killing, lying, stealing, sexual misconduct, and intoxicants. According to Theravada Buddhism one of the ten duties of the ruler is to promote peace and to prevent war. The Buddha was believed to have condemned the infliction of pain and killing of all forms of life.

A primary emphasis in Buddhism was on self improvement. The aim was to gain a compassionate attitude toward one's self through practice of the Eightfold Path. The presumption was that the root of suffering lay in self-destructive habits, and wars were the external signs of inner disharmony. This led to the creation of meditation centers and a belief that if enough individuals arrived at personal peace a transformation would occur among the rest of humanity (the 100th monkey principle). Although the Dalai Lama received the Nobel Peace Prize in 1989 and Buddhism has had a general reputation for peace, a counter-tradition also existed.

Buddhism, Taoism, Shintoism, and Confucianism coexisted from the start and their interrelatedness complicates identifying a specific Buddhist view on war and peace issues. From ancient times in the Orient one of the traits desired for persons of greatness was martial prowess, and, like their Christian counterparts, frequent wars were fought by Buddhists, both clergy and laity. The millennial expectation of the end of human rule was common enough among Burmese Buddhists to make rebellion and wars relatively easy to justify. On the one hand, as in early Christianity, many early Buddhists believed that to kill or to be a soldier was an offense; on the other hand a militant tradition persisted. For two millennia Mahayana Buddhism had been providing scriptural justification for going to war. Kings led their troops into battle with a relic of the Buddha on their spears. Even monks and nuns were encouraged to exchange their robes for the uniform of soldiers. In A.D. 515 Fa-ch'ing led fifty thousand troops in rebellion against the Northern Weiu and announced that soldiers would become bodhisattvas (enlightened ones) as soon as they had killed one of the enemy.

The Mahaparinirvana Sutra (Mahayana) described how the Buddha had killed some heretical Brahmins in one of his former incarnations in order to protect Buddhism from slander, as well as to protect the slanderers from more cosmic punishment should they continue in their error. It was considered good to kill one sinner to save two potentially righteous, even though it was still believed that Buddha later had to suffer for the murders he had committed. Even the father of the Pure Land school, Hui-yuan, well-known for his compassion, remarked that if Mansjuri had run a sword through the Buddha, he would have appeared to do wrong, but actually would have been following the Way. As an extreme, a certain King Anala was said to have made killing into a divine act. He would cut off the hands or feet, gouge out the eyes, or boil in oil his subjects to make them follow the example of the bodhisattvas (comparable to medieval Christian torturing of heretics).

In China Mao Tse-tung was able to utilize Buddhist monasteries. Many monks eager to show that they were not reactionaries were pleased to cooperate, and religious justifications from scripture were offered for supporting the Maoist movement. When China entered the Korean War, a meeting of 2,500 Buddhist monks, nuns, and devotees met in Wuhan (January 21, 1951), condemned U.S. imperialism as more murderous than Fascism, and concluded that since Buddhism and such imperialism cannot coexist, Buddhists should sacrifice themselves for peace. Both monks and nuns joined the laity and went off to fight in Korea.

The history of Buddhism, like that of Christianity, portrays devotees on a spectrum from militarism to the pacifism of Thich Nhat Hanh, who remarked, "If we kill men, what brothers will we have left?"

See CHRISTIANITY AND WAR; HINDUISM AND WAR; JUDAISM AND WAR; MAOISM AND WAR; MENCIUS; MO TZU; TAOISM AND WAR; TZU, SUN.

BIBLIOGRAPHY

Fu, Charles Wei-hsun, *Buddhist Ethics and Modern Society* (Westport, Conn.; Greenwood Publishing, 1991).

Paige, Glenn D., and Sarah Gilliatt, eds., *Buddhism and Nonviolent Global Problem Solving* (Honolulu: Spark Matsunaga Institute for Peace, 1991).

Spiro, Melford E., *Buddhism and Society* (Berkeley: University of California Press, 1982).

Tambiah, S. J., *World Conqueror and World Renouncer* (Cambridge: Cambridge University Press, 1977).

Welch, Holmes, *Buddhism under Mao* (Cambridge, Mass.: Harvard University Press, 1972).

BULLETS, EXPANDING. Also called "dumdum" bullets, after the former British arsenal of the same name near Calcutta. The 1868 St. Petersburg Declaration* was the first international agreement in modern times to prohibit a specific weapon in war—exploding or incendiary bullets. Unfortunately, the declaration did not anticipate the use of the expanding bullet, developed by the British. This oversight was corrected by the 1899 Hague* Declaration 3, Concerning Expanding Bullets: "The contracting Parties agree to abstain from the use of bullets which expand or flatten easily in the human body, such as bullets with a hard envelope which does not entirely cover the core or is pierced with incisions." Article 23 of the 1907 Hague Convention 4 embraced these 1868 and 1899 agreements as "special Conventions"; they are seen as specific examples of the general prohibition in Article 23(e) against projectiles calculated to cause excessive suffering. These prohibitions are generally considered now to have gained the force of customary law.

With more modern weaponry available, the fact that exploding and expanding bullets are legally prohibited is not as important as the moral principles behind that prohibition. The treatment of these weapons in international law is based on two important moral principles emphasized for centuries in just war* theory. First, it is false that ''all's fair in war.'' Even against morally permissible targets, destruction, suffering, and injury are to be limited; this moral insight is reflected in article 22 of the 1907 Hague Convention. Second, in just war theory there is no *absolute* limit to the amount of morally acceptable destruction, suffering, and injury. Rather, the amount of morally permissible suffering depends on two things: how morally important it is to bring the war to a successful conclusion— a moral consideration largely ignored in the laws of war*—and how necessary the weapon or tactic causing the suffering is for bringing about this morally important conclusion—a military consideration emphasized by the laws of war. Thus, the laws of war permit napalm but not expanding bullets, even though the former can cause more suffering than the latter. The reason is that expanding bullets do not serve any meaningful military purpose but napalm does; napalm could be important for bringing a war to a morally successful conclusion. Similarly, modern high-velocity ammunition has some of the same effects as the expanding bullet, but it is not considered to be prohibited by international law, since its military advantages mean the associated suffering is not necessarily superfluous to the moral goal to be accomplished. Neither just war theory nor the laws of war gives an absolute prohibition against weapons that cause suffering or even terrible suffering; they prohibit those that cause useless or disproportionate suffering. Expanding bullets are not prohibited because they cause terrible suffering; they are prohibited because they cause meaningless suffering.

This does not mean that it is morally or legally correct in war to use any legally permitted weapon at any time. Commanders should use their best judgment about when the suffering caused by permitted weapons is ''superfluous'' and refrain from using them in those situations.

See FORBIDDEN WEAPONS; HAGUE, THE, CONGRESSES; INCENDIARIES; JUST WAR; LAWS OF WAR; MILITARY NECESSITY; PROPORTIONALITY; ST. PETERSBURG DECLARATION.

BIBLIOGRAPHY
Greenspan, Morris, *The Modern Law of Land Warfare* (Berkeley: University of California Press, 1959), especially Chap. 9, 313ff.
Roberts, Adam, and Richard Guelff, eds., *Documents on the Laws of War,* 2d ed. (Oxford: Clarendon Press, 1989).
Wenker, Kenneth H., ''Military Necessity and Morality,'' in *Military Ethics: Reflections on Principles* (Washington D.C.: National Defense University Press, 1987).

Kenneth H. Wenker

BYNKERSCHOEK, CORNELIUS (1673–1743). A Dutch jurist who practiced in The Hague as a member of the Supreme Court of Holland, Zeeland, and West Friesland, and from 1724 until his death served as its president. A consistent positivist, following in the tradition established by Richard Zouche

(1590–1661), he affirmed that international law was founded only on the common agreements of nations expressed in treaties and custom. He did not cite ancient authorities, but based his rulings solely on current custom. Indeed, there were so few customs that he considered international relations to be essentially anarchic. "In my opinion every force is lawful in war. . . . Does it matter what means we use to accomplish it?" (*Questions,* Book 1, Chap. 1, Para. 3). Despite the assumption that anything was permissible in war, he drew the line at "acts of perfidy*," such as misusing the white flag of surrender, wearing an enemy uniform, or shooting emissaries carrying the flag of truce. Not only did perfidy undermine proper military strategy, it gave to weaker nations an advantage over the stronger, who after all, deserved to win. So little custom existed to the contrary that he dismissed any requirement that wars even be declared. A declaration of war* is "not demanded by any exigency of reason, while it is a thing which may properly be done, it cannot be required as a matter of right" (*Questions,* Book 1, Chap. 2, Para. 6–9). The notion of the three-mile limit as the extent of territorial waters was based on the assertion that territorial rights extended only as far as a cannon shot could carry, which was at the time the range of coastal artillery. The three-mile limit was applied in 1793 when the United States, caught between France and Britain, defined its neutral waters as one sea-league (three miles). The Treaty of Ghent (1818) defined the range of Canadian fishing rights to extend three miles.

No custom seemed to exist with regard to neutrality. Hugo Grotius* (1583–1645), for example, allowed that belligerents could march at will through neutral territory, citing Moses taking the people of Israel through Idumea in Canaan as precedent. Bynkerschoek gave the first formulation of the inviolability of neutral territories, and while his insistence was not followed universally, he greatly influenced public opinion in Europe.

See AYALA, BALTHAZAR; BELLI, PIERINO; GENTILI, ALBERICO; GROTIUS, HUGO; RAYMOND OF PENAFORTE; SUAREZ, FRANCISCO; VATTEL, EMMERICH DE; VICTORIA, FRANCISCUS DE.

BIBLIOGRAPHY
Bynkerschoek, Cornelius, *Dominion of the Seas* (New York: Oxford University Press, 1923).
————, *Jurisdiction over Ambassadors* (New York: Oxford University Press, 1939).
————, *Questions of Public Law* (New York: Oxford University Press, 1930).

C

CALLEY, LT. WILLIAM. *See* SON MY/MY LAI; STOCKHOLM/ROTH-SKILDE WAR CRIMES TRIAL; WINTER SOLDIER INVESTIGATION.

CALVIN, JOHN (1509–1564). Listed five acceptable bases for a just war*. These were: to inflict public vengeance by a king, to preserve the tranquility of a territory, to suppress disturbers of the peace, to rescue victims from oppression, and to punish crimes. He viewed both church and state as divine institutions, and although he recognized that the New Testament seemed to forbid Christians* to kill, he claimed that killing done in the name of the magistrate was to fulfill the judgment of God. Calvin pointed to scripture and assured the faithful that although Moses slew 3,000 of his fellows, he was still considered a lover of righteousness, and Calvin believed that had Moses been lenient, he would have been guilty of an indiscretion. Monarchs entrusted with the preservation of the nation's land and its possessions should be allowed to wage all necessary wars, and though they were urged not to be too cruel, they should not be too humane, either.

Calvin assumed that if there was political sanction for war, then the church should be expected to add its blessing. He saw war as a chastisement from God for human sin, and as being for our own good, yet he did not believe that war was an ultimate part of the divine plan. Although the church had an obligation to aid in war for the political state, Calvin insisted that Christ's kingdom was to be promoted by spiritual power alone. He noted that the New Testament never condemned war. He insisted that Christians were obligated to obey even evil rulers, since they too ruled by divine authority. In theory, Calvin allowed Christians to disagree when the ruler advocated what was ''contrary to the laws of God'' (passive resistance), but he did not support revolution. Resistance to the ruler was equated with resistance to God. Calvin was no pacifist. His objection to armed revolution rested on his conviction that the rulers governed in the name of God. He criticized the pacifism* of the Anabaptists and asserted to the contrary that "to condemn the public use of the sword . . . is blasphemy against God himself."

See CHRISTIANITY AND WAR; GANDHI, MOHANDAS; HOLY WARS; LUTHER, MARTIN.

BIBLIOGRAPHY

Calvin, John, *Institutes of the Christian Religion* (Philadelphia: Presbyterian Board of Christian Education, 1936), Book 4, Chap. 20, Para. 12.

———, *Tracts and Treatises on the Doctrine and Worship of the Church,* vol. 2, "Forms of Prayer for the Church" (London: Oliver and Boyd, 1958).

Harkness, Georgia, *John Calvin: The Man and His Ethics* (Nashville, Tenn.: Abingdon, 1958).

CASUALTIES OF WAR. The accuracy of estimates about the number of deaths as a direct or indirect consequence of war is difficult to confirm. Nations tend to underemphasize their own casualties, while maximizing those of their opponents, and most war data are written by the victors. Furthermore, most nations where wars are waged have no accurate statistics of the number of their casualties, particularly their civilians. Gil Elliot concluded that no war statistics of deaths of the order of a million or more can claim an accuracy greater than plus or minus 20 percent. Neither British nor American official estimates of casualties beginning with World War I even approached the 20 percent accuracy level. Samuel Dumas estimated that the statistics were off as much as 100 percent. Civilian casualties are even more difficult to confirm. The United Nations International Children's Emergency Fund (UNICEF) estimated that in the wars since World War II, 85 percent of the casualties have been civilian. The *Bulletin of the Atomic Scientists* (April 1964) estimated that the ratio of civilians to soldiers in World War I was 5 percent; for World War II, 48 percent; for the Korean War*, 84 percent; and for Vietnam*, 90 percent. Yet most statistical lists make no distinction between civilian and military deaths, nor do they distinguish battle deaths from deaths due to disease or starvation. The most reliable information concerning civilian casualties in current conflicts comes from such agencies as the International Red Cross, Red Crescent, and Red Shield*, Amnesty International, Human Rights Watch, and the United Nations.

Quincy Wright compared the wide range of estimates of the French and British casualties in wars from 1875–1925, which for the French ranged from 2.25 million to 3.69 million, and for the British during the same period ranged from 1.1 million to 3.1 million. Wright estimated that during the Middle Ages 30–50 percent of those in battle were killed or wounded, and that in the Napoleonic period 80–90 percent of the total army losses were from disease. Dumas estimated that in the 19th century two soldiers died of disease for every one who died in battle. He suggested also that from 1793 to 1815, when Britain was at war with France, the British lost 6,663 soldiers in battle and 86,000 from disease. Wright affirmed that in World War I, disease accounted for 30 percent of the Russian casualties, 26 percent of the U.S. casualties, and 10 percent of the German casualties.

Table 1

War	Deaths	Wounded	Total
American Revolution	4,435	6,188	10,623
War of 1812	2,260	4,505	6,765
Mexican	13,200	4,152	17,352
U.S. Civil	498,000	282,000	780,000
Spanish-American	202,400	901,600	1,104,000
WWI	37,000,000	28,000,000	65,000,000
WWII	60,000,000	18,000,000	78,000,000
Korea	700,000	1,400,000	2,100,000
Vietnam	1,250,000	no record	no record
Gulf War	200,000	100,000	300,000
Yugoslavia	250,000	no record	no record
Panama Invasion	4,000	no record	no record

The Gulf and the Yugoslavia estimates are from the United Nations. The Panama estimate is from Amnesty International.

Although Wright stated that the number of battles had tended to decrease, Lewis F. Richardson concluded that there was no evidence that wars had become less frequent, although he did state that since 1820 there have been more large wars and fewer small wars. Increase in population seems unrelated to any increase in the frequency of wars, although modern weapons have resulted in a vast increase in the number killed, both military and civilian. Nor did he discover any evidence for the theory that certain states, because of their politics, were more belligerent than their neighbors. While language differences or similarities seemed unrelated to the frequency of wars, he observed that nations where Chinese was the major language had the fewest wars, while those where Spanish was the major language had the most wars. This latter claim was also suggested by Frederick Adams Woods, who noted that from 1500 to 1700, Spain waged war about 78 percent of the time, and between 1700 and 1900 about 51 percent of the time. The nearest to this record was achieved by Turkey. In 1994, during the war in former Yugoslavia, there were at least twenty-five other civil conflicts raging in the world.

Consider, for example, Table 1, which shows standard data on a few select wars, where no effort has been made to separate civilian from military casualties, or deaths in battle from those due to disease or starvation. Compare these data with the ''official'' U.S. estimates of American battle casualties where the wars were not fought on American soil (Table 2).

The incredible numbers of military casualties in the one battle of the Somme stagger the imagination. In the first day of fighting 60,000 British soldiers were said to have died, and the total British losses for the entire battle of the Somme were put at 410,000. For the French it was 190,000, and for the Germans the soldier deaths were put at 500,000. This was almost a million deaths in one

Table 2

War	Deaths	Wounded	Total
Spanish-American	2,400	1,600	4,000
WWI	100,000	200,000	300,00
WWII	408,000	670,000	1,078,000
Korea	53,000	103,000	156,000
Vietnam	57,000	153,000	210,000
Gulf	79	no record	no record
Panama Invasion	500	no record	no record

battle. At the Battle of Passchendale in the latter half of 1917 the British put their soldier losses at 300,000 men. The problem is to interpret the comparison in the case of World War I, for example, where the estimate was that 37 million died in total, while U.S. casualties were 100,000; or again the case of World War II, where total casualties were put at 60 million and U.S. casualties at 408,000. Should we then extrapolate to an immense number of civilian casualties or at least to the conclusion that when a war is fought on your land, even your military casualties will be excessive? Moscow estimated a loss of 4.5 million Soviet soldiers in the first year of World War II. The official Soviet figure for their casualties in World War II, soldier and civilian, was 20 million. A German study, on the other hand, listed Soviet casualties as 13 million. Elliot calculated that China lost 15 million in World War II. The official German estimate was that Germany lost 4 million of its soldiers. The official Polish estimate was that Poland lost 3 million. The data are particularly vague for the Pacific theater during World War II, where no accurate data exist for civilian casualties on the various islands. In the battle of Guadalcanal, for example, the official U.S. estimates were that 24,000 Japanese were killed, 15,000 died of disease, and 500 were taken prisoner. U.S. losses were put at 1,743 killed and 4,953 wounded. The Japanese estimated their losses in the U.S. invasion of Okinawa at 110,000 soldiers, 160,000 civilians, and U.S. casualties at 50,000. The official Japanese estimate for their total military casualties was 2.3 million and for their civilian deaths, 780,000. The Japanese hastened to note that data on civilian losses on the islands of the Pacific were unavailable.

If we extrapolate from the estimates of the *Bulletin of the Atomic Scientists,* a chancy affair at best, in World War I there would have been 1.85 million civilian deaths and 1.4 million civilian wounded. In World War II there would have been 28.8 million civilian deaths and 8.64 million civilian wounded. In China, information would suggest that there were 2 million soldiers and 9 million civilian casualties. Based on the sketchy data from the Gulf War* we may contrast the 79 U.S. casualties, most from friendly fire* and the British casualties reported at 23 soldiers killed, on the one hand, with the estimated 40,000 Iraqi soldiers and 160,000 Iraqi civilians who died. A Harvard study estimated that at least 75,000 Iraqi civilians died of disease or starvation the first summer of the siege* (blockade) after the war was over. The full story is not in on the "Gulf War Syndrome" concerning psychological and physical casualties among soldiers. The casualties from modern wars are immense in spite of ambiguities about precise numbers. Estimates from the Nigerian War, for example, are that there were 2 million deaths, and a similar number for the 1910–1920 Mexican Revolution. The old just war* criterion of proportionality* would seem difficult to calculate given such monumental casualties.

Wright concluded that although it was highly subjective, a related casualty of wars has been a consequent anti-intellectual movement in art, literature, and philosophy; waves of crime; delinquency in youth; racial and religious intolerance; and a decline in respect for international law. Of much less subjectivity has been a vast increase in economic and environmental loss.

See AERIAL WARFARE; CHILDREN AND WAR; COLLATERAL DAMAGE; FIRST STRIKE/SECOND STRIKE; FORBIDDEN STRATEGIES; FRAGMENTATION BOMBS; FRIENDLY FIRE; INCENDIARIES; INNOCENTS; MASS DESTRUCTION, WEAPONS OF; MILITARY NECESSITY; NUCLEAR DETERRENCE; NUCLEAR WAR; QUARTER, NO, WARS OF; REPRISALS; TOTAL WAR.

BIBLIOGRAPHY
Dumas, Samuel, and K. O. Vedel-Petersen, *Losses of Life Caused by War* (London: Humphrey Milford, 1923).
Elliot, Gil, *Twentieth Century Book of the Dead* (New York: Charles Scribner's, 1972).
Health Concerns of Persian Gulf Victims, Hearing Before the Committee on Veterans' Affairs, H.R. 103rd Cong., 2d sess., February 1, 1994.
Ienaga, Saburo, *The Pacific War: World War II and the Japanese 1931–1945* (New York: Pantheon Books, 1978).
Persian Gulf War Illnesses: Are We Treating Veterans Right? Hearing Before the Committee on Veteran's Affairs, Senate, 103rd Cong., 1st sess., November 16, 1993 (Washington, D.C.: U.S. Government Printing Office, 1994).
Richardson, Lewis F., *Statistics of Deadly Quarrels* (Chicago: Quadrangle Books, 1960).
Woods, Frederick Adams, and Alexander Baltzly, *Is War Diminishing?* (Boston: Houghton Mifflin, 1915).
Wright, Quincy, *A Study of War,* 2d ed. (Chicago: University of Chicago Press, 1965).

CAUSES OF WAR. Early just war* theorists like St. Augustine* and Thomas Aquinas* listed causes of wars and, at the same time, implied that some of these causes justified going to war. Worthy causes included righting wrongs against one's own nation or that of a friend, reclaiming a piece of territory that had been taken from one, defending financial interests, or more generally for national defense. The presumption was that these causes were self-evidently worthy and that leaders, on reflection, chose to go to war because of them. The Judeo-Christian scriptures assumed that wars came from lust, aggression, and covetousness and implied that as natural human tendencies these traits would perpetuate wars without further reflection.

The belief that the drive to war was part of human nature, and was thus a nonreflective drive to war, was paramount in ancient scripture. The New Testament book of James affirmed that wars came from human lust, covetousness, aggression, and a basic irrational nature. Modern psychologists have speculated, without unanimity, on the possible sources in human nature for what appear to be drives to war. Sigmund Freud (1856–1939) intimated that our libidinal impulses were unconscious drives to war, and in a letter to Albert Einstein he concluded that there was no likelihood of ever curbing mankind's aggressive tendencies. Yet far more evidence suggests that wars are brought about more by the cupidity or stupidity of leaders than their libidinal drives. H. J. Eysenck suggested that aggressive attitudes tended to be general and not specific toward war making, but that if a society was teeming with frustrations, war became a natural option. Gardner Murphy concluded that belligerence was not peculiar to any race or culture. There were no uniquely aggressive nations. Neither Germans nor Japanese had a special corner on aggressiveness, but he noted that it was relatively easy to make otherwise pacific peoples into warlike ones, especially if they were dissatisfied. Gordon Allport spoke of an expectancy of war that made it easy for leaders to provoke their citizens to fight. George Santayana (1863–1952) believed that we had ineradicable warlike urges. Carl G. Jung suggested that feelings of personal inadequacy prompted us to take aggressive actions toward others. William James*, recognizing that the excitement of war was an attractive alternative to the humdrum lives most persons lived, proposed a ''moral equivalent to war'' through deeds of public service. Edward Glover noted in 1931 that no country in the world had ever spent a penny investigating the psychological aspects of war motivation. Much of the research conducted since then has been of the order of showing the military how to make warriors out of former farmers and school teachers, yet a common psychological theme has been that war making is a sign of sickness rather than normality. One of the more hopeful signs was the UNESCO study to explore the tensions that affect international understanding. Good reasons existed for doubting that wars were ever fought for the reasons that were publicized and that the moral breast-beating explanations that usually preceded a nation's entry into war tended to be rationalizations. Charles E. Osgood coined the acronym GRIT, by which he meant the ''graduated and reciprocal initiatives in tension-reduction.'' His thesis was that American foreign policy, like that of most major nations, was not designed to make peace possible.

Plato (427?–347 B.C.) was probably not the first to claim that the primary cause for war was economic, and he concluded that the quest for unlimited wealth was the major cause of war and of most other social ills. Aristotle (384–322 B.C.) stated that poverty was the parent of revolution and crime. Eighteenth- and 19th-century thinkers such as Thomas Malthus (1766–1834), Pierre-Joseph Proudhon (1809–1865), Karl Marx (1818–1883), Frederick Engels (1820–1895),

François Fourier (1772–1837), Louis Blanc (1811–1882), and Jean-Jacques Rousseau* (1712–1778) saw poverty as part of the cause and economic greed as the rest of the cause. Rousseau, for example, believed that property ownership was the root cause of war and that wars would not end until private property had been abolished. Proudhon asserted that owning property was robbery and he was joined in this assessment by Saint-Simon (1760–1825), Robert Owen (1771–1858), and Fourier. William Godwin (1756–1836), a contemporary of Rousseau, identified economic ambition as the cause of war. Malthus believed that if society provided for the well-being of all, then war, "that great pest of the human race," would cease. David Ricardo (1772–1823), Richard Cobden (1804–1865), and Jean-Baptiste Say (1767–1832) all affirmed that the mission of economists should be to show that wars were an economic catastrophe. Marx and Engels saw the anarchy of economic competition and exploitation as the major contributors to the anarchy and exploitation of war. J. A. Hobson (1858–1940), though generally unsympathetic to Marx, argued that capitalism had an internal difficulty in the unequal distribution of wealth that capitalism produced. Since workers at home were not paid sufficiently to be consumers, capitalists invested abroad, where cheap labor and profitable ventures existed. This capitalist search for ever-expanding markets by imperialist nations led inevitably to war. Economic investments abroad were closely followed by national armies to protect them. Dwight D. Eisenhower named a military-industrial complex* that made war profitable, and this theme was further elaborated by Kenneth Boulding, who spoke of this complex as a MILORG, a military-financial organization that was its own consumer. Thorstein Veblen (1857–1929) thought that the nurture of the war spirit was the product of the leisure class, which was least personally involved in war, although its members stood to gain most by the waging of war.

Thomas Hobbes* (1588–1679) had observed that "All men in a state of nature have a desire and will to hurt." Indeed, he saw the natural state as the war of each against all. Hobbes asserted that people were naturally warlike, naturally selfish, naturally deceptive, and naturally greedy. In a world of such creatures, war was the natural means of resolving disputes. Such a view, aided by patriotic* nationalism and the paranoia generated by a belief in evil nations that could only be curbed by armed might, made the war option the most attractive. The persuasiveness of the Hobbesian view is evidenced in the almost universal commitment to the expansion of military power, the arms race, and a concomitant disinclination to support the kind of negotiation and cooperation implied by the United Nations organization. No single explanation can encompass why wars are entered into. National leaders, whatever their putative warlike urges, may be prompted by egoistic drives for power, fame, or honor as much as from any statesmanlike calculation as to what is in the national interest. Those who profit financially from war may need no further incentive to explain their support for the war option. Apart from those who are drafted into military service, those who volunteer are motivated by a host of alternative reasons, not the least of which may be the desire, as William James (1842–1910) suggested, to escape from humdrum lives.

See HUMAN NATURE AND WAR; INTELLIGENCE AGENCIES; IN-TERNATIONAL LAW; LAWS OF WAR; MILITARISM; MILITARY-INDUSTRIAL COMPLEX; NATIONALISM; PATRIOTISM.

BIBLIOGRAPHY
Benoit, Emile, and Kenneth Boulding, eds., *Disarmament and the Economy* (New York: Harper & Row, 1963).
Lewinsohn, Richard, *The Profits of War Through the Ages* (London: Routledge & Sons, 1936).
Murphy, Gardner, ed., *Human Nature and Enduring Peace* (Boston: Houghton Mifflin, 1954).
Nelson, Keith L., and Spencer C. Olin, Jr., *Why War: Ideology, Theory, and History* (Los Angeles: University of California Press, 1979).
Russell, Bertrand, *Why Men Fight* (New York: Century, 1916).
Swomley, John M., Jr., *The Military Establishment* (Boston: Beacon Press, 1964).

CHAPLAINCY, HISTORY OF THE U.S. ARMY. The roots of the U.S. Army chaplaincy are essentially medieval Roman Catholic in origin. The Council of Ratisbon (A.D. 742) first authorized the use of chaplains and also prohibited "the servants of God" from fighting or bearing arms. This European tradition of the military chaplaincy was transported to colonial America. When George Washington assumed the command of the Revolutionary Army at Cambridge, Massachusetts in July 1775, he found fifteen chaplains already serving with the twenty-three militia regiments besieging Boston. Eventually about 230 chaplains saw military duty during the Revolution. All of these clergymen were from Protestant denominations with the exception of one Roman Catholic chaplain of a French-Canadian regiment.

After the disbanding of the Continental Army in 1783, chaplains did not serve again until the U.S. Army was established under the Constitution. In 1791 John Hurt of Virginia, an Episcopalian, was appointed the chaplain of the Army's only brigade. From this point on, chaplains have served in the military. It should be noted, however, that the numerous state militia regiments in existence during the 19th century were all authorized to have a chaplain as part of their structure. In addition to their regular duties, chaplains functioned on Army posts both as schoolmasters and librarians. They also held religious services in civilian settlements; established Indian congregations; officiated at community functions; visited the sick, the imprisoned, and soldiers in barracks; served as post gardeners; and occasionally functioned as legal counsel.

An estimated 2,400 chaplains served in the Union forces during the course of the Civil War, and an additional 1,000 served in the Confederate Army. It was during this conflict that the chaplaincy, for the first time, began to mirror the increasingly diverse society of America. Both Catholic and Protestant clergy saw duty with the Union forces, the former particularly in the Irish regiments, and a smaller number of rabbis also served as chaplains. Most of the Union Colored regiments had white chaplains. However, in fourteen regiments, African Americans were commissioned as chaplains. These included Henry M. Turner of the 1st United States Colored Troops (USCT) regiment, and Samuel Harrison of the 54th Massachusetts Infantry regiment. During a seven-month period in 1864 the 1st Wisconsin Heavy Artillery regiment had a female chaplain, Ella Elvira Gibson Hobart of Massachusetts, although she was never officially confirmed by the War Department.

Except in wartime, the chaplaincy remained small during the 19th century. Reflecting the size of the Army, its peacetime strength never rose above thirty-four until after the Spanish American War. The first two decades of the 20th century witnessed the establishment of the modern Army chaplaincy, and for the first time in its history a coherent structured chaplaincy emerged that was far removed from the casual and careless approach to organization that had typified its existence since 1775. In 1899 chaplains gained the right to wear a new and distinctive insignia of their profession, the Latin Cross, and in 1914 insignia of rank. A coherent method of screening and selecting candidates was created along with a Board of Chaplains. In 1904 Congress allowed chaplains to reach the rank of major, and in 1905 lieutenant colonel. Previously, chaplains were considered captains in rank. During World War I (1918) a professional school for chaplains was established, which replaced the ad hoc monitoring system used in the past. With the establishment of the Office of the Chief of Chaplains (1920), the chaplaincy became an official and independent branch of the Army.

The historical pattern of regulating the size of the chaplaincy with the size of the Army was repeated in both World War I and World War II. In April 1917 there were seventy-four regular Army chaplains and seventy-two National Guard chaplains. By the end of World War I there were 2,217 chaplains. In 1937, when Chaplain (Col.) William R. Arnold became the fifth Chief of Chaplains, there were only 125 regular Army chaplains, although in that same year almost 300 Army chaplains from the Reserve and National Guard were serving in the Civilian Conservation Corps (CCC). Arnold was the first Roman Catholic Chief of Chaplains, a position he held for the next eight years through World War II. From December 1941 to August 1945, 8,896 chaplains had served in the Army. On the day of the Japanese surrender in 1945 8,141 chaplains were on duty (Roman Catholic 2,278; Protestant 5,620; and Jewish 243). During World War II the chaplaincy suffered 478 casualties, the third highest behind the Infantry and the Air Corps, attributed to the ''be there'' philosophy that played such a large part in the chaplains' ministry. Chaplains felt that their rightful place was with the soldier on the front line.

The chaplaincy in World War II was representative of the unique ethnic and religious diversity of the United States. The Army authorized the appointment of 790 black chaplains and by July 1942, 247 were on active duty, of which 100 were overseas. The total number of black chaplains in World War I was fifty-seven. Half of the 422 rabbis in that war had volunteered, 311 served and two were killed in action, two were wounded, and forty-six were decorated for bravery. A Greek Orthodox chaplain served an all-Greek battalion. One Buddhist chaplain was approved but never assigned to the 442nd Infantry Regiment composed entirely of Japanese Americans, being replaced by a Christian chaplain of Japanese descent. When the Women's Army Auxiliary Corps (WAACs) was established, women ministers challenged the all-male limitations and urged that female chaplains be assigned to large contingents of women. A survey indicated that few WAACs desired female ministers so the matter was dropped, although many women became chaplain assistants or directors of religious education.

Thirteen chaplains were killed during the Korean War* and another thirteen died in Vietnam*. In the latter conflict chaplains were awarded two Medals of Honor, twenty-six Silver Stars, 719 Bronze Stars, eighty-two Purple Hearts, 586 Army Commendation Medals, 318 Air Medals, and sixty-six Legion of Merits. The chaplaincy continues to mirror the changing religious, ethnic, racial, and gender composition of the Army. The first official woman chaplain was commissioned in 1974, 110 years after Ella Hobart was rejected by Secretary of War Edwin Stanton. From 1990 to 1994, Chaplain (MG) Matthew Zimmerman, an African American, served as Army Chief of Chaplains; in 1994 the first Muslim was commissioned chaplain; and in 1995 the first Buddhist chaplain will enter service.

See CHRISTIANITY AND WAR; CONSCIENTIOUS OBJECTION; DAY, DOROTHY; DODGE, DAVID LOW; HOLY WARS; PACIFISM; VICTORIA, FRANCISCUS DE; WOMEN IN THE MILITARY.

BIBLIOGRAPHY

Ackermann, Henry F., *He Was Always There: U.S. Army Chaplain Ministry in the Vietnam Conflict* (Washington, D.C.: Office of the Chief of Chaplains, 1989).

Gushwa, Robert L., *Best and Worst of Times: The United States Army Chaplaincy 1920–1945* (Washington, D.C.: Office of the Chief of Chaplains, 1977).

Honeywell, Roy J., *Twenty-Four Chaplains of the United States Army* (Washington, D.C.: Office of the Chief of Chaplains, 1958).

Norton, Herman A., *Struggling for Recognition: The United States Army Chaplaincy. 1791–1865* (Washington, D.C.: Office of the Chief of Chaplains, 1977).

Stover, Earl F., *Up from Handyman: The United States Army Chaplaincy, 1791–1865* (Washington, D.C.: Office of the Chief of Chaplains, 1977).

Thompson, Parker C., *From Its European Antecedents to 1791: The United States Army Chaplaincy* (Washington, D.C.: Office of the Chief of Chaplains, 1978).

Ventzke, Roger R., *Confidence in Battle, Inspiration in Peace: The United States Army Chaplaincy, 1945–1975* (Washington, D.C.: Office of the Chief of Chaplains, 1977).

William J. Hourihan

CHAPLAINS AND ETHICS IN THE ARMY. For more than 200 years, chaplains have served in the U.S. Army as volunteer pastors, preachers, counselors, and teachers to provide religious and moral support for soldiers in both war and peace. Endorsed by their religious denominations and commissioned as officers, chaplains have performed many religious support duties including advising the command and instructing soldiers in value formation, ethical decision making, and moral leadership. With service in every major conflict in American history since the Revolutionary War, the Army Chaplaincy has frequently been characterized as "the conscience of the Army."

The involvement of chaplains in the Army's moral leadership was not a result of a formal job description for chaplains, but rather was an answer to the Army's needs. As early as 1777, General George Washington asked his chaplains to help commanders oppose "vice and immorality of every kind" in the Continental Army. Most specifically, chaplains were to preach against swearing (the taking of God's name in vain) which might, in Washington's view, bring down the wrath of heaven upon his soldiers. General Henry Knox thought chaplains should give short discourses to young soldiers concerning "knowledge, spirit, and virtuous conduct." It was most important to the commanders of the Continental Army, and to later American armies as well, to instill patriotism* and morality into the soldiers who were frequently underpaid, underfed, and unappreciated.

From the end of the Revolutionary War to the end of the Vietnam War*, the Army expected chaplains to be a source of advice and counsel for officers but to direct most of their ethical energy toward the "moral improvement" of enlisted soldiers. If officers were well educated, the Army reasoned, they should have already developed their own moral leadership skills before they were commissioned. Hence, chaplains preached and taught the virtues of obedience, sobriety, and patriotism* to the soldiers in the ranks under the supervision and with the approval of their commanders.

There were, of course, a few exceptions to the notion that chaplains advised officers but instructed the soldiers in morals and ethics. Perhaps the first major example of officer education came at West Point following the War of 1812. In response to Thomas Jefferson's conviction that the Army would need a professional officer corps in any future war, Congress established the United States Military Academy in 1802. Chaplains from the Army's Northern Department conducted services at the Academy at West Point intermittently for ten years. Then, in 1814, Chaplain Adam Empie, an Episcopal minister and a close friend of President James Madison, was appointed Professor of History, Geography, and Ethics at West Point.

Chaplain Empie's duties included preaching in chapel once a week and teaching courses in history, geography, and ethics for the Corps of Cadets. For eighty years a series of eleven chaplains, successors to Chaplain Empie, taught not only history, geography, and ethics, but also international law, constitutional law, and English literature to such cadets as Jefferson Davis, Robert E. Lee, Ulysses S. Grant, and William T. Sherman. The subject matter discussed by the chaplains in their formal classes ranged from the legality of secession, blockades, and retaliation during war to personal rules of conduct. Lt. Gen. T. J. "Stonewall" Jackson noted in his later correspondence that the Chaplain's Course was one of his favorite courses at the Academy.

Another type of officer education in ethical conduct came as a result of teaching by example rather than by lecture in a classroom. During the Civil War, Chaplain Henry Turner of the 1st Regiment, United States Colored Troops, noticed at Petersburg that white officers paid little attention to the preaching of black chaplains. Worse yet, white officers sometimes ridiculed black chaplains not for their lack of preaching skills, but for their lack of education. Chaplain Turner accordingly refused to preach for officers unless they showed what he called "proper respect for the Gospel." He did, however, minister quite effectively to black soldiers, many of whom were decorated for heroism in the fighting around Richmond and Petersburg in 1864.

During the latter part of the 19th century and early 20th century, chaplains continued their ministries in moral leadership for soldiers. Chaplains not only preached and performed pastoral duties, but also served as school teachers on many Western posts. The goals of the command for soldierly conduct dovetailed with the religious orientation of chaplains in discouraging heavy drinking, consorting with prostitutes, gambling, swearing, and fighting in the ranks. Officers and noncommissioned officers (NCOs) were encouraged to treat the soldiers fairly and not be too harsh in disciplinary punishment.

With the advent of the two World Wars, which helped define the bloodiest century in world history, the Army Chaplaincy expanded not only in numbers but also in programs for the moral improvement of soldiers. More than 11,000 Army chaplains served on active duty from 1918 to 1945. Some 470 were killed or wounded in action. Approximately 1,000 chaplains were awarded Distinguished Service Medals, Silver Stars, Bronze Stars, or Purple Hearts. More importantly, these chaplains ministered to 15,000,000 soldiers deployed worldwide in the service of their country.

At the end of World War II, the Army formally adopted a Character Guidance Program for soldiers, which provided direction in dealing with a wide variety of moral issues including high venereal disease rates. Chaplains wrote many of the lesson plans and also did the primary instruction. Since these were command programs and not religious services, attendance was required. In 1954 some 783,000 soldiers attended Character Guidance lectures. A case could be made that from 1945 to 1975, Army chaplains delivered more lectures on personal moral ethics than any other comparable group of clergy in America.

The Vietnam War refocused the Army, the Chaplaincy, and the American people on the importance of professional ethics in the military. Incidents such as the Son My/My Lai* massacre* in March 1968, and the resulting Peers Inquiry convinced many leaders including General William Westmoreland that officers as well as enlisted soldiers needed more ethical training. Army chaplains responded, as they always had historically, in providing instruction in morals and ethics. In 1971 Chaplain (Colonel) Joseph Beasley was appointed to teach ethics at West Point, the first chaplain to do so in the 20th century. By 1974 chaplains were on the faculties of the U.S. Army War College, the Command and General Staff College, and twenty-four Army service schools teaching ethics to officers and warrant officers.

In the twenty years since the end of the Vietnam War, the Army Chaplaincy has continued to emphasize the necessity of moral leadership. In Army Regulation 165-1, *Chaplain Activities in the United States Army* (August 31, 1989), chaplains were designated as the "principal staff officer for the commander's moral leadership training program." Chaplains continue, as General George Washington requested 220 years ago, to discourage vice and immorality of every kind in the Army, not only in the enlisted ranks but also in the training of commissioned officers as well.

See CHRISTIANITY AND WAR; *GENERAL ORDERS 100;* SON MY/MY LAI; SUPERIOR ORDERS; WIRZ, CAPTAIN HENRY.

BIBLIOGRAPHY

Brinsfield, John, "Our Roots for Ministry," *Military Chaplains' Review* (Fall 1987), 23–39.

———, "The Chaplain as Professor at West Point," *Military Chaplains' Review* (Fall 1987), 63–76.

Matthews, Lloyd J., ed., *The Parameters of War* (New York: Pergamon-Brassey's, 1987).

Thompson, Parker C., *From Its European Antecedents to 1791: The United States Army Chaplaincy* (Washington, D.C.: Department of the Army Office of the Chief of Chaplains, 1978).

John W. Brinsfield

CHARROUX, SYNOD OF (989). Medieval Catholic church councils issued various declarations concerning proper weapons, strategies, and targets. At Charroux it was declared:

Anathema against those who injure clergymen. If anyone attacks, seizes or beats a priest, deacon, or any other clergyman, who is not bearing arms (shield, sword, coat of mail, or helmet), but is going alone peacefully or staying in the house, the sacrilegious person shall be excommunicated and cut off from the church, unless he makes satisfaction, or unless a bishop discovers that the clergyman brought it on himself.

While these offenses were considered as religious sins rather than moral vice, the limits beyond which war makers ought not to go were emphasized.

See CHAPLAINCY, HISTORY OF THE U.S. ARMY; CHAPLAINS AND ETHICS IN THE ARMY; CHRISTIANITY AND WAR; COMBATANT-NONCOMBATANT DISTINCTION; FORBIDDEN STRATEGIES; INNOCENTS; PROPORTIONALITY.

BIBLIOGRAPHY

Keen, Maurice Hugh, *The Laws of War in the Late Middle Ages* (London: Routledge & Kegan Paul, 1965).

Thatcher, Oliver, and Edgar H. McNeal, *A Sourcebook for Medieval History* (New York: Charles Scribner's Sons, 1907).

CHEMICAL AND BIOLOGICAL EXPERIMENTS ON HUMAN SUBJECTS. It was revealed at the Medical Case* war crimes trial that Nazi doctors had performed chemical and biological experiments on inmates of their extermination camps. These experiments were named specifically by the Nuremberg court as crimes against humanity. Subsequent revelations, however, have made evident that medical experiments on human subjects have not been the sole prerogative of German doctors. Under the U.S. Department of Health, Education, and Welfare, experiments had been conducted at Tuskeegee Institute on poor illiterate black men infected with syphilis. In the experiment the subjects went untreated for over twenty years without their knowledge; in Montgomery, Alabama, two mentally retarded teenaged poor black girls were sterilized without their knowledge; and thousands of women in Tennessee were injected with an experimental birth control agent, *Diproprovera*, without informed consent. Events such as these led to the enactment by Congress of the National Research Act of 1974, which established the Commission for the Protection of Human Subjects of Biological and Behavioral Research.

The initiative in America for human experimentation "in the interests of national defense" came from the decision in 1941 by Secretary of War Henry L. Stimson, to request the National Academy of Science to appoint a committee to make a complete survey of biological warfare (BW). In February 1942 the committee completed its efforts and reported that BW was feasible and that appropriate steps should be taken to establish a BW program for the United States. In August 1942, President Franklin D. Roosevelt approved the program and centered it at Fort Detrick with the formation of the War Research Service (WRS). George W. Merck of the pharmaceutical firm of that name was named its director. In November 1942 the WRS requested the Chemical Warfare Service (CWS) of the Army (redesignated the Army Chemical Corps in 1946) to assume full responsibility for a research and development (R&D) program. At its peak the CWS had 3,900 personnel (2,800 Army, 1,000 Navy, and 100 civilian), and established six research and development centers for research in Chemical and Biological Warfare (CBW): three Army centers in Edgewood Arsenal, Maryland; Fort Detrick, Maryland; and Pine Bluff Arsenal, Arkansas; two Navy centers at the Brooklyn Naval Base and the Naval Biological Laboratory in Oakland, California; and one Air Force center in the Armament Laboratory at Eglin Air Force Base, Florida. Between 1950 and 1971, 660 contracts for CBW had been entered, of which 272 were with universities.

The primary problems were finding the weapons and the subjects. Pine Bluff Arsenal was a leader in performing this task. In 1953 it began production of cluster bombs containing *Brucella suis* (the causative agent of undulant fever) and *Pasteurella tularensis*. Between 1954 and 1967 Pine Bluff Arsenal additionally produced Q fever, *Rickettsia*, Venezuelan Equine Encephalomyelitis,

Bacillus anthrax, Botulinus toxin, and *Staphylococcal enterotoxin.* Tests using one or more of these agents were performed in the public domain on unwitting subjects in the National Airport and the Greyhound Terminal in Washington, D.C.; San Francisco harbor; Panama City and Key West, Florida; Hawaii; Little Creek, Virginia; Dugway, Utah; the Kittakinny and Tuscarora tunnels; and the Pennsylvania Turnpike. BW tests were performed on unwitting U.S. soldiers at Fort McClellan, Wright Patterson AFB, Loring AFB, Camp Cooke, Eglin AFB, Edwards AFB, Quantico Marine Corps School, Little Creek AFB, Carswell AFB, and Camp Pendleton, to mention a few. Over 150 tests were performed on U.S. military bases and at an additional 100 civilian locations.

Tests were performed on volunteer conscientious objectors in Civilian Public Service Camps, although the implications of the tests were never explained. In 1954 the Army met with authorities of the Seventh Day Adventist Church to get conscientious objectors from their ranks who were serving in the military as noncombatants to volunteer. The experiment, called ''Operation Whitecoat,'' on an initial 2,500 men continued until 1973.

In addition to these Department of Defense (DOD) experiments, similar research was carried out under the auspices of the Central Intelligence Agency (CIA). In the course of its work between 1952 and 1972 the CIA enlisted the help of the Bureau of Narcotics, the National Institutes of Health, and the Internal Revenue Service. The victims were patients in mental institutions, prisons, and senior care centers. Exotic acronyms concealed the nature of the experiments. MKULTRA synthesized and tested new behavior-modifying drugs especially on terminally ill cancer patients and skid row derelicts. MKDELTA developed, tested, and stockpiled severely incapacitating drugs. MKOFTEN tested the behavioral and toxicological effects of certain drugs on humans. Stephen Weitzman, M.D., of the Department of Microbiology at the State University of New York at Stony Brook criticized these tests on the basis that they ignored the ethical problem of informed consent, that tests in the public domain were unpredictable as to consequences, and that biological warfare was not in the United States' best interests. Congress established the requirement in 1975 that the DOD report on its biological and chemical experiments, but subsequent hearings in 1990 established that the reports were almost uselessly vague and incomplete.

In 1986 the Subcommittee on Energy released a report that 695 persons had been used as guinea pigs in thirty-one experiments by the DOD. During 1945–1947, as part of the Manhattan Project, eighteen patients diagnosed as having terminal diseases who were expected to survive less than ten years were injected with plutonium to determine how it circulated in the human body. These experiments were carried out at Manhattan District Hospital, Oak Ridge, Tennessee; Strong Memorial Hospital in Rochester, New York; the University of Chicago; and the University of California. During 1946–1947 the University of Rochester injected radium salts into patients with good kidney function to determine the amount needed to cause renal injury. From 1961–1965 the Massachusetts Institute of Technology used twenty patients aged 63–83, most from the New England Age Center, and injected them with or fed them radium or thorium to test internal doses and measure passage. During the 1960s at Los Alamos Scientific Laboratory, fifty-seven normal adults were fed microscopic spheres containing radioactive radium and manganese. During 1963–1971, sixty-seven inmates at Oregon State Prison and sixty-four from Washington State Prison received X-rays to determine the ionizing effects of radiation on fertility. During 1956 the U.S. Air Force sent manned planes through the radiation clouds from the atomic tests at Bikini* and Enewetok atolls to measure doses to the crews. During the 1950s, Foster D. Snell, a consulting firm, carried out experiments for the U.S. Army by placing radioactive soil on the hands of about 118 human subjects and measuring the efficacy of cleaning agents to remove the contamination. Incongruously, the hearings before the Committee on Labor and Human Relations in 1994, hoping to stem the tide of these experiments, met in the Fernald School for mentally retarded children, where DOD experiments had been performed on unwitting subjects.

While most of these experiments were not carried out during war, the agents in charge of these biological and chemical experiments on human subjects were those in charge of waging war, and the onus of concern so eloquently raised at the Nuremberg and Tokyo Trials must properly be raised against Defense Department involvement in such medical experiments. The Nuremberg court ruled that such experimentation constituted a crime against humanity and that the practice could not be defended by the mere appeal to military necessity or national defense.

See BIOLOGICAL AND CHEMICAL WEAPONS; BIOLOGICAL/CHEMICAL WARFARE, UN RESOLUTIONS BANNING; CHILDREN'S RIGHTS IN WAR; CRIMES AGAINST HUMANITY; FORBIDDEN STRATEGIES; NUREMBERG PRINCIPLES; WAR CRIMES.

BIBLIOGRAPHY

American Nuclear Guinea Pigs: Three Decades of Radiation Experiments on U.S. Citizens, Report Prepared by the Subcommittee on Energy Conservation and Power of the Committee on Energy and Commerce, H.R. November 1986 (Washington, D.C.: U.S. Government Printing Office, 1986).

Biological Testing Involving Human Subjects by the Department of Defense, Hearings Before the Subcommittee on Health and Scientific Research of the Committee on Human Resources, Senate, 95th Cong., 1st sess., March 8 and May 23, 1977 (Washington, D.C.: U.S. Government Printing Office, 1977).

Biomedical and Behavioral Research, 1975, Joint Hearings before the Subcommittee on Health of the Committee on Labor and Public Welfare and the Subcommittee on Administrative Practice and Procedure of the Committee on the Judiciary, Senate, 94th Cong., 1st sess., September 10, 12 and November 7, 1975 (Washington, D.C.: U.S. Government Printing Office, 1975).

Chemical Warfare: DOD's Reporting of Its Chemical and Biological Research, Report to the Chairman of the Committee on Governmental Affairs, Senate (August 1990).

Government-Sponsored Testing of Humans, Hearing Before the Subcommittee on Administrative Law and Governmental Relations of the Committee on the Judiciary, H.R. 103rd Cong. 2d sess., February 3, 1994 (Washington, D.C.: U.S. Government Printing Office, 1994).

Human Drug Testing by the CIA, 1977, Hearings Before the Subcommittee on Health and Scientific Research of the Committee on Human Resources, Senate, 95th Cong., 1st sess., September 20 and 21, 1977 (Washington, D.C.: U.S. Government Printing Office, 1977).

Human Subjects Research: Radiation Experimentation, Hearing Before the Committee on Labor and Human Resources, Senate, 103rd Cong., 1st sess., January 13, 1994 (Washington, D.C.: U.S. Government Printing Office, 1994).

CHILDREN AND WAR. Wars kill and maim children through their direct violence. Children are killed in attacks on civilian populations, as in Hiroshima. In Nicaragua*, many children were maimed or killed by mines*. Some wars, such as those in Afghanistan in the 1980s and Bosnia since 1993, have been especially lethal to children. Many children have been killed and injured in the *initifada* in the territories occupied by Israel. Historically, conflicts involving set-piece battles in war zones away from major population centers killed very few children. However, as wars have changed form, moving out of the classic theaters of combat and into residential areas, civilians are more exposed.

It is not only a matter of exposure. Civilians are killed not only accidentally but also deliberately—even if the intention is denied. Children are sometimes targeted. In the massacre at El Mozote in El Salvador in 1981, for example, all the children were killed. Terrorists* often make a point of going after children.

The casualty* rate for children is increasing not only because they are more exposed, and not only because they have become deliberate targets, but also because children are used as soldiers. Child soldiers have participated in conflicts in Mozambique, Peru, Iran, and many other places. There are perhaps 200,000 child soldiers under fifteen in the world. It has been estimated that since 1985 children under the age of fifteen have made up a significant portion of regular armies or guerrilla* forces in at least twenty-five countries.

Wars also harm children indirectly, through their interference with normal patterns of food supply and health care. For example, in 1980–1986 in Angola and Mozambique, about half a million more children under age five died than would have died in the absence of warfare. In 1986 alone, 84,000 child deaths in Mozambique were attributed to the war and destabilization. The famines in Ethiopia in the mid-1980s and again in the late 1980s would not have been so devastating if it were not for the civil wars involving Tigre, Eritrea, and other provinces of Ethiopia. Civil war has also helped to create and sustain famine in the Sudan. In Iraq, many thousands of children died during and after the Persian Gulf War* because of the disruption of food, health, and sanitation systems together with the economic embargo. In 1992 it was estimated that at least a quarter of all Somali children under the age of five died as a result of the famine and civil strife.

A striking aspect of modern warfare is the apparent willingness to sacrifice the young, both one's enemies' and one's own. In some cases children have been held as hostages by their own national leaders. Apparently Saddam Hussein, in the hope of winning sympathy, assured that the brunt of economic sanctions against Iraq would hurt Iraqi children. When the Serbs laid siege* to Srebrenica in April 1993, the Moslem leaders in Bosnia did not want their women, children, and injured to be evacuated; in effect they wanted to hold their own people hostage* in order to strengthen their claim on the territory.

Wars also cause great psychological damage to children. The psychological trauma that war causes for children received a great deal of attention during World War II. The impact on children of the Hiroshima* bombing has been studied, and there have been several efforts to explore children's perceptions of the prospect of nuclear war*. While the psychological impacts of warfare on children have been investigated frequently, there have not been nearly as many studies of the direct physical impacts of warfare on children.

In surveying the impacts of war on children we should also take note of the fact that soldiers often father mixed-raced children who are likely to be abandoned. Active warfare, occupations, and the establishment of overseas bases often lead to the births of large numbers of children of foreign soldiers by local women. (When the bases in the Philippines were abandoned, a group of Filipino Amerasians filed suit in U.S. District Court in San Francisco asking the U.S. Navy for support and damages for the children left behind in the Philippines.) In some cases, as in Bosnia, hundreds of babies born to rape victims have been abandoned.

The establishment of armed forces can be harmful to children in other ways as well. For example, high expenditures on armed forces can result in inadequate provision of resources for the care of children. President Dwight Eisenhower made the much-quoted observation that "Every gun that is made, every warship launched, every rocket fired, signifies, in the final sense, a theft from those who hunger and are not fed, those who are cold and not clothed." World Bank figures show that the forty-three countries with the highest infant mortality rates (over 100 deaths per 1,000 live births) spend three times as much on defense as on health.

The harm inflicted on children as a result of armed conflict tends to be viewed as a kind of collateral damage, an unfortunate side effect that must be tolerated in the pursuit of greater objectives. Apparently the interests pursued are not the interests of the children.

See AERIAL WARFARE; COLLATERAL DAMAGE; COMBATANT-NONCOMBATANT DISTINCTION; RETALIATION, MASSIVE; SIEGE WARFARE.

BIBLIOGRAPHY
Children in Situations of Armed Conflict (New York: UNICEF E/ICEF/1986/CRP.2, 1986).

Children in Situations of Armed Conflict in Africa (Nairobi, Kenya: African Network on Prevention and Protection Against Child Abuse and Neglect, 1988).

Children of Hiroshima (London: Taylor & Francis, 1981).

Children on the Front Line: The Impact of Apartheid, Destabilization and Warfare on Children in Southern and South Africa (New York: UNICEF, 1987).

Dodge, Cole P., and Magne Raundalen, eds., *War, Violence and Children in Uganda* (Oslo: Norwegian University Press, 1987).

Garbarino, James, Kathleen Kostelny, and Nancy Dubrow, *No Place to Be a Child: Growing Up in a War Zone* (Lexington, Mass.: Lexington Books, 1991).

Harbison, Jeremy, and Joan Harbison, *A Society Under Stress: Children and Young People in Northern Ireland* (Somerset, England: Open Books, 1980).

Kent, George, *War and Children's Survival* (Honolulu: University of Hawaii Press, 1990).

Nixon, Anne Elizabeth, *The Status of Palestinian Children During the Uprising in the Occupied Territories* (Stockholm: Rädda Barnen, 1990).

Ressler, Everett, *Evacuation of Children from Conflict Areas: Considerations and Guidelines* (Geneva: UNHCR and UNICEF, 1992).

Ressler, Everett M., Neil Boothby, and Daniel J. Steinbock, *Unaccompanied Children: Care and Protection in Wars, Natural Disasters, and Refugee Movements* (New York: Oxford University Press, 1988).

Rosenblatt, Roger, *Children of War* (Garden City, N.Y.: Doubleday, 1983).

Tolley, Howard, Jr., *Children and War: Political Socialization to International Conflict* (New York: Teachers College Press, 1973).

Wilson, Francis, and Mamphela Ramphele, "Children in South Africa," in *Children on the Front Line: The Impact of Apartheid, Destabilization and Warfare on Children in Southern and South Africa* (New York: UNICEF, 1987), 39–67.

George Kent

CHILDREN'S RIGHTS IN WAR. Children generally have the same rights as adults under international humanitarian law, but there are some provisions that give special attention to children. Of the four Geneva conventions*, the Convention Relative to the Protection of Civilian Persons in Time of War is of particular importance for the protection of children. Beyond the Geneva conventions, in 1974 the UN General Assembly adopted a Declaration on the Protection of Women and Children in Emergencies and Armed Conflicts, Resolution 3318 (29) of December 14, 1974. The declaration made six points, including the proclamation that "attacks and bombings on the civilian population, inflicting incalculable suffering, especially on women and children . . . shall be prohibited," but as a nonbinding resolution, no means for enforcement were included.

The Convention on the Rights of the Child of 1989 enumerates a broad range of children's rights that should be honored in all circumstances including armed conflict. Article 38, however, focuses specifically on situations of armed conflict. It says:

1. States Parties undertake to respect and to ensure respect for rules of international humanitarian law applicable to them in armed conflicts which are relevant to the child.

2. States Parties shall take all feasible measures to ensure that persons who have not attained the age of 15 years do not take a direct part in hostilities.

3. States Parties shall refrain from recruiting any person who has not attained the age of 15 years into their armed forces. In recruiting among those persons who have attained the age of 15 years but who have not attained the age of 18 years, States Parties shall endeavour to give priority to those who are oldest.

4. In accordance with their obligations under international humanitarian law to protect the civilian population in armed conflicts, States Parties shall take all feasible measures to ensure protection and care of children who are affected by an armed conflict.

Article 39 is also relevant. It says:

States Parties shall take all appropriate measures to promote physical and psychological recovery and social re-integration of a child victim of: any form of neglect, exploitation, or abuse; torture or any other form of cruel, inhuman or degrading treatment or punishment; or armed conflicts. Such recovery and re-integration shall take place in an environment which fosters the health, self-respect and dignity of the child.

Other articles call upon governments to provide special assistance to children deprived of their families and to children who become refugees.

Article 38 reiterates established international humanitarian law, including the seventeen articles in the fourth Geneva Convention of 1949 specifically concerned with the protection of children. Paragraphs 2 and 3 echo paragraph 2 of article 77 of Protocol I to the 1949 Geneva Conventions.

Article 38 is known as the armed conflict article, but for the problem with which children need help the most—protection from recruitment—it has little to offer. While the rest of the convention is generally applicable to "every human being below the age of 18 years," article 38 makes a point of allowing children under 18 to take direct part in hostilities and to be recruited into a nation's armed forces.

Much more needs to be done to implement humanitarian law with respect to children. With regard to Article 38 of the Convention on the Rights of the Child (which by reference incorporates international humanitarian law generally), primary responsibility for implementation rests with the national governments that have become parties to that convention. The challenge to the international community is to find ways to assure that implementation. What can be done?

Information on law and practice with respect to children's involvement in warfare should be updated regularly by an agency with a mandate from the international community. What is needed is not a one-time research effort, but continuous monitoring. A solid monitoring program would produce information in a timely manner for those agencies that could take appropriate action; it would also let nations know that they are being watched, and that people care a great deal about whether they expose children to armed conflict. Studies should be made of national laws with respect to the exposure of children to armed conflict, and of efforts that may be underway to conform those laws to Article 38.

Organizations within each country concerned with the problems of children in armed conflict should be identified and supported in appropriate ways. In many cases these indigenous organizations will be best able to assess the current state of national law and practice.

The International Committee of the Red Cross (ICRC) could review national laws with regard to children in armed conflict. National Red Cross societies may have more latitude than the ICRC. The national Red Cross societies also could play an important role in monitoring national laws and practices.

Some national governments might choose to monitor compliance with particular articles of the Convention on the Rights of the Child. The United States regularly uses its network of embassies to monitor human rights* practices around the world.

The information that is obtained on children in armed conflict could be used in several ways. Examples of appropriate legal language could be circulated to assist nations in the process of strengthening their relevant laws. Nations could be assisted in developing effective means of implementation of those laws within their own borders. There should be clear accounts of the nature of the violations. Analyses should be made to identify the specific individuals in a position to correct violations, and action should be focused on influencing those individuals. Violators might be called to account through a systematic series of escalating steps, beginning with moderate inquiries addressed to appropriate government officials, building up to embarrassing publicity and threats of international sanctions. Responses appropriate to the concrete circumstances would need to be designed.

Many things could be done for children involved in armed conflict, but there always looms the question of agency: Who will do those things? Which individuals, which organizations will take the action that is required, under what motivations, with what resources? Those who want to do something may not have good physical access and legitimacy, while those with access and legitimacy may lack the resources or the desire.

Controlling local violence is normally the responsibility of local governments. If the local government cannot handle it, the next-higher level of government is obliged to step in, and if that does not work the national government is expected to intervene. In some cases it is not clear who ought to act. There may be a breakdown of civil order, where the rule of law is no longer effective. However, in many cases there is no such breakdown, and local law remains important. As in all other arenas of human rights, it is national laws and national governments that ought to be the principal instruments for implementation of the rights of the child.

The overwhelming problem is that in regard to children in conflict situations the national government may be more the source of the problem than the solution. In that case there is a special responsibility for the international community to find ways to intervene in behalf of children.

At the international level, the ICRC and the United Nations Children's Fund

(UNICEF) play major roles in dealing with the problem of children in armed conflict. Major responsibility for implementation of international humanitarian law rests with the International Committee for the Red Cross. The ICRC's major concern is the implementation of the four Geneva Conventions of 1949 and the two protocols of 1977, but as a private organization it is not constrained by the language of those agreements, and it often goes beyond their specific mandates. Because of its belief that the problems of children are always closely intertwined with those of adults, however, the ICRC does not have specific programs for children. Its work for children is always situated within the broader general context of assistance to the victims of conflict.

UNICEF, ICRC, and other organizations play major international roles in looking after the interests of children in conflict situations, but they are constrained. UNICEF focuses on children but does not focus on situations of armed conflict. ICRC focuses on conflict but not particularly on children. The Convention on the Rights of the Child also is limited. The UN Committee on the Rights of the Child, established by the convention, is confined by the language of the convention itself and is not free to initiate new programs. Also, the committee's responsibilities cover all of the many different concerns addressed in the convention, so situations of armed conflict occupy only a part of its agenda.

There is now no international agency publishing independent analyses of national policies and practices with respect to children in situations of armed conflict. There is no central agency systematically supporting and defending the many nongovernmental agencies around the world that work for children in conflict situations on a local, national, or regional basis. There is no agency identifying the gaps in coverage. There is no body to coordinate the established agencies' work in this area. ICRC, UNICEF, and several other organizations include the issue of children in armed conflict on their agendas, but there is no international organization whose primary concern is children in armed conflict.

Concerned international organizations such as UNICEF, ICRC, UNHCR, Defense for Children International, the International Save the Children Alliance, OXFAM, Amnesty International, Rädda Barnen, the International Federation of Terre des Hommes, and others could organize a Liaison Group on Children in Armed Conflict. It could meet perhaps once a year to review the existing situation and coordinate future action. The group would not intervene directly into situations of armed conflict, but would provide advice and support for appropriate organizations prepared to do so. It could help devise strategies and programs for local organizations, and it could help develop useful information.

Globally, the most effective organizational model would entail one agency taking lead responsibility for coordinating work on behalf of children in armed conflict. It would be the locus for cumulative learning and strategic planning. Its power would come not from its capacity to act directly, but from its role in coordinating and focusing the work of many different organizations, each of which has different capacities, interests, resources, and skills. If such an agency succeeded in aligning the efforts of the many organizations—national and international, governmental and nongovernmental—concerned with children in armed conflict, the possibilities for implementing article 38 would be greatly enhanced.

Second, while humanitarian intervention was provided for a time in Iraq by the United States, Britain, France, and the Netherlands, there also was a great deal of humanitarian assistance provided by the ICRC and by the UN system under an explicit agreement with the Iraqi government.

Third, the humanitarian actions of the United States, Britain, and France were mixed with their political and military actions. There is no way to sort out the extent to which one motive or the other prevailed. As a result, these countries are open to charges of using humanitarian intervention for their own political and military purposes. A more effective separation might have been maintained by using separate, independent agents for humanitarian action. To the extent that the United States, Britain, France, and the Netherlands were concerned with ameliorating human suffering, they could have funneled more resources through ICRC and UNHCR.

Fourth, if the international community is to claim that humanitarian intervention is warranted in some extreme situations, there is a need for clear guidelines for determining when that action is to be taken, what the action is to be, and how the relevant decisions are to be made.

Fifth, too much importance has been placed on the importance of humanitarian intervention in armed conflict situations. Historically, most effective humanitarian assistance in armed conflict situations has been provided with the consent of the conflicting parties. More attention should be given to the possibilities for obtaining such agreements.

See COMBATANT-NONCOMBATANT DISTINCTION; NUCLEAR DETERRENCE; RETALIATION, MASSIVE.

BIBLIOGRAPHY

Cahill, Kevin M., ed., *A Framework for Survival: Health, Human Rights, and Humanitarian Assistance in Conflicts and Disasters* (New York: Council on Foreign Relations/Basic Books, 1993).

Hiro, Dilip, *Desert Shield to Desert Storm: The Second Gulf War* (New York: Routledge, 1992).

Pease, Kelly Kate, and David P. Forsythe, "Human Rights, Humanitarian Intervention, and World Politics," *Human Rights Quarterly* 15 (1993), 290–314.

Schefer, David J., Richard N. Gardner, and Gerald B. Helman, *Post-Gulf War Challenges to the UN Collective Security System: Three Views on the Issue of Humanitarian Intervention* (Washington, D.C.: United States Institute of Peace, 1992).

Teson, Fernando R., *Humanitarian Intervention: An Inquiry into Law and Morality* (Dobbs Ferry, N.Y.: Transnational Publishers, 1988).

George Kent

CHRISTIANITY AND WAR. Scholars are divided in their answers to the question whether Jesus took any position on the waging of war, and whether there is a unique Christian position. Some claimed that Jesus could be understood best from a pacifist presumption. Among these were C. J. Cadoux, Leyton Richards, and G.M.C. MacGregor. Cadoux had remarked that the evidence was slight for the existence of any Christian soldiers in the Roman armies between 60 and A.D 165. Others like Umphrey Lee, Adolf Harnack, Paul Ramsey, and John Bennett claimed that the dominant early view opposed such pacifism*. Whatever may be the truth about any putative position Jesus may have had, the great majority of the early Church Fathers defended a pacifist stand as the authentic Christian position. These included Justin Martyr (100–165), Clement of Alexandria (160–230), Tertullian (160–220), and Origen (185–254). Yet, in spite of this testimony, Christians did serve in increasing numbers in the Roman legions. To be sure, Canon 12 of the Council of Nicaea in 325 stated that soldiers who converted to Christianity had to get out of the army, and if they later returned to the army they had to do penance for thirteen years. The Council of Chalcedon in 451, the Synod of Angiers in 453, and the Synod of Tours in 461 all affirmed that it was forbidden for Christians to serve in the military.

When the Christian religion became the official state religion in the Roman Empire in 383 these trends changed. Under the influence of St. Augustine*, just war* thinking provided religious justification for Christians to come to the armed defense of the country. From the middle of the 3rd century, military metaphors for the Christian life became common. Christians were soldiers, Christ was a general (imperator), the church was a camp, and baptism was a military oath of allegiance (sacramentum). In 314 the Council of Arles condemned conscientious objectors*, and early in the 5th century the Christian cross was inscribed on the shields of Roman soldiers, and non-Christians were excluded from the military profession. In 376 the Emperor Valens forced Christian monks into military service, not as chaplains*, but as armed soldiers, and for the next 1,000 years Christian Church Councils endeavored with diminishing success to persuade clergy to back out of the army or at least to show some moderation. Bishop Ambrose (340?–397) excommunicated the Emperor Theodosius for his massacre of 7,000 inhabitants of Thessalonica in retaliation for their sedition, which had resulted in the death of a number of army officers. After due penance the emperor was invited back into the good graces of the church. Early Christian monarchs were not well known for moderation in war. Once the Crusades became a standard of religious excellence and participation in them a sign of religious devotion, few questioned whether Christians could be soldiers. Clergy fought in battles with the laity and even nuns occasionally put on battle dress and fought against their own bishops. John of Salisbury* (?–1180) sanctified the role of soldiers as the secular complement of the clergy, and in the induction oath soldiers were assured that ''the high praises of God are in their throat and two-edged swords are in their hands.''

Two Christian traditions developed during the Reformation. After almost 500 years of military piety it was natural for writers like Martin Luther* (1509–1564) to adjust Christian conscience compatibly with war. While he commanded

Christians to turn the other cheek in church, they were still commanded to use the sword outside. In an essay, "That Soldiers Too Can Be Saved," Luther stated that slaying and robbing by soldiers are "a work of love." In wars it is God who really wields the sword and who "hangs, tortures, beheads, slays, and fights." In a similar fashion John Calvin* (1509–1564) asserted that while war was condemned for religious use, it was to be approved for state use. As long as princes declared wars for good reasons, Calvin assumed that the church would and should give its blessing.

In contrast, strains of Christian pacifism emerged. The Catholic thinker, Desiderius Erasmus (1466–1536), affirmed that those who engaged in war were wicked and that in making war they sinned against nature, God, and man. The pacifist Mennonite sect began in Zurich in 1523 under their leader, Menno Simons, a former Catholic priest. The Mennonite Articles of Faith (1632), known also as the Dort Confession, stated in Article 14 that Jesus had forbidden his followers to be soldiers. To combat such heresy a group of high English churchmen in 1575 listed among four "Anabaptistical errors" this Mennonite claim that no Christian should hold the sword. George Fox (1624–1691), founder of the Quaker movement, wrote in his *Journal* (1659) that anyone who claimed that he served in the army for Jesus was mistaken. Pacifist sentiments were not well received by the more militant Christian brethren. Anabaptists were burned at the stake by Catholics and drowned by Protestants; Brethren were banished; and Quakers were imprisoned.

Both militant and pacifist traditions existed in early America. The Puritans, in particular, and most of the New England clergy rejected pacifism as "smacking of Arminianism." Pacifists were accused of being no better than "anabaptists" who strove to lead Christians into slavery by sapping their will for self-defense. Many early Puritans were aggressive; they not only made slaves of the Indians but slaughtered them wholesale. Christians proudly carried scalps. Miles Standish occasionally rounded up Indians in their villages and set fire to the lot. The historic peace churches were relatively quiet. American Quakers were willing to hold political office and some participated as soldiers. However, on May 1, 1777, the Schwenkfelders stated that "for conscience sake" it was impossible for them to bear arms. Mennonites remained so aloof from their neighbors that they even refused to vote. Brethren would vote but only for Quakers. On the other hand, Scots Presbyterians hated the Quakers, whose pacifism they considered cowardly. So many Presbyterians joined the army that the British sometimes referred to the American army as "Presbyterian."

Militarism* predominated in the American Christian churches during World War I. Some clergy even urged their members to shoot pacifists in their congregations, and the rare minister who reminded his parishioners that Jesus had said, "Love your neighbor," ran the risk of both fine and imprisonment. Several religious journals stated that Quakers were not entitled to be called Christians. Norman Thomas, a Presbyterian minister and YMCA worker at the time, said that the conscientious objector (CO) was commonly treated worse by chaplains and YMCA workers than by non-Christian soldiers. While the full sentences were not finally carried out, seventeen of the 500 known war objectors were given the death sentence and many were given prison terms of twenty-five years.

Between World Wars I and II peace movements developed in the mainline denominations, although the major attitude remained sympathetic with support for wars when the nation called. In 1932 a survey was conducted at the University of Chicago to determine whether the liberalism or conservatism of a religious group influenced its attitude toward war. The investigator concluded that Catholics and Lutherans were the most militaristic, while Jews, Christian Scientists, Methodists, and those who simply identified themselves as Protestants were the most pacifistic. The investigator concluded that conservative religions tended to favor militarism, while liberal denominations favored pacifism.

During World War II, most Catholic and Protestant religious journals supported the U.S. war effort. Unlike in World War I, however, pacifists were not vilified, and most churches showed great toleration of dissident opinions. The historic peace churches endeavored with mixed success to hold firmly to their traditional pacifism. While Mennonites had the best record, only three out of five of their eligible young men filed as conscientious objectors. Fewer than one-eighth of the Brethren young men rejected military service. A survey revealed that over 60 percent of the Brethren churches even dropped the pacifist pledge as a requirement of membership. Most Quaker colleges accepted ROTC programs and three-fourths of all Quakers drafted did not claim to be conscientious objectors.

Christian theologians had difficulty deciding whether World War II was "just," "righteous," or "holy." Karl Barth criticized the British Church for declaring unequivocally that this was a war fought "in the name of Jesus." During the Vietnam war* a poll conducted by the *New York Times* (April 18, 1965) reported that only about one-third of the American clergy supported the escalation and continuation of the war. In 1959 Norman K. Gottwald of Andover Newton Theological School chided Reinhold Niebuhr for his claim that the use of nuclear weapons might be Christian. Paul Ramsey, who had joined Niebuhr in support of World War II, doubted that nuclear war* could ever be justified, although he supported nuclear deterrence* as a viable Christian threat. Yet, a commission of the Federal Council of Churches of Christ in America issued a report, "The Christian Conscience and Weapons of Mass Destruction" (1950), which rejected pacifism as "irresponsible" and denied that nuclear weapons were forbidden by any humanitarian concern. While the council denied the right of the first use* of atomic weapons, it permitted their use in reprisal*. Two members of the council, Robert L. Calhoun and Georgia Harkness, refused to sign and were permitted a dissenting statement. John Bennett believed that the military draft could be considered a Christian vocation.

Although religious conscientious objectors took some comfort from official Catholic or Protestant church pronouncements, Christian soldiering has normally had official church blessing. If we set aside the Jehovah's Witnesses, who were the majority of the religious objectors in World War II, there were more non-religious objectors who served time either in prison or in Civilian Public Service Camps during World War II than from all other Christian churches combined.

See AUGUSTINE, ST.; BRITTAIN, VERA; CALVIN, JOHN; DAY, DOROTHY; DODGE, DAVID LOW; LUTHER, MARTIN; MUSTE, ABRAHAM JOHANNES; PACIFISM; RAYMOND OF PENAFORTE; ROYDEN, MAUDE.

BIBLIOGRAPHY

Abrams, Ray, *Preachers Present Arms: The Role of the American Churches and Clergy in World War I and II with Some Observations on the War in Vietnam* (Scottsdale, Ariz.: Herald Press, 1969).

Bainton, Roland H., *Christian Attitudes Toward War and Peace* (Nashville, Tenn.: Abingdon, 1979).

Cadoux, C. J., *The Early Christian Attitude Toward War* (London: Headley Brothers, 1919).

Harries, Richard, *Christianity and War in A Modern Age* (Ridgefield, Conn.: Morehouse, 1988).

Lee, Umphrey, *The Historic Church and Modern Pacifism* (Nashville, Tenn.: Abingdon-Cokesbury, 1943).

MacGregor, G.M.C., *The New Testament Basis of Pacifism* (London: James Clarke and Company, 1936).

Ramsey, Paul, *War and the Christian Conscience* (Durham, N.C.: Duke University Press, 1961).

CIVIL DEFENSE. Because it is closely associated with sheltering citizens from nuclear attack, ethical assessments of civil defense often hinge on the probability and consequences of nuclear war*. If nuclear war is unthinkable, civil defense is unnecessary. If nuclear war is unsurvivable, civil defense is a waste of money and energy that should be redirected to preventing annihilation. If nuclear war is possible and some survival is probable, civil defense—whether undertaken by the individual or by government—may be prudent.

Civil defense is part of a larger national security system. Generally, defensive systems include civil defense and military defense. Whereas civil defense programs try to protect populations and industry, military defense systems aim to protect weapons and troops. (Civil and military defense parallel the distinction between counterforce and countervalue*.) While civil defense is usually passive, military defense is often active. This distinction, however, is not based on the presence or absence of motion but on how protection is sought. A passive defense does nothing to stop a strike; it tries to shield against or dodge the strike. Whereas a fallout shelter is a shield, the evacuation of a city is a dodge. If used to protect cities, antiballistic missiles* (ABMs) would function as an active civil defense. However, if used to protect missile fields, an ABM system would function as an active military defense.

Besides the United States and former USSR, several nations (e.g, China and Switzerland) have extensive civil defense programs. The U.S. Office of Civil

Defense was established in 1941 in case German bombings of London expanded to U.S. cities. Since the atomic bombings of Japan, civil defense in the United States has been handled by various agencies and has proceeded through four phases. Each phase has spawned ethical controversy. From construction of fallout shelters through research on Star Wars, many governmental planners have believed protection against nuclear attack is possible. For years the federal government's main civil defense booklet for citizens was even titled *Protection in the Nuclear Age.* Ethically, a central issue is whether the protection offered by civil defense is an end or a means. If it is an end, then civil defense serves a humanitarian function. However, if it is a means, then civil defense is an aid to overcoming nuclear deterrence*, that is, it serves a strategic role and is an instrument in a war-fighting orientation.

The first phase in U.S. civil defense followed the enactment of the Civil Defense Act of 1950 and focused on the Evacuation Route Program. Plans to evacuate major urban areas assumed a twelve-hour lead time, which was the time existing bombers took to reach American targets. Additionally, schools provided "duck and cover" training as a response to a surprise attack. The second phase was precipitated by the Cuban Missile Crisis* and led to the Fallout Shelter Program. Because ICBM technology shortened a nuclear strike to an hour or less and the development of the hydrogen bomb greatly increased the destructiveness of bombs, sheltering (actually, only for nontargeted, nonurban areas) was emphasized over evacuation. Beginning in 1979, the controversial Crisis Relocation Program initiated the third phase. This program assumed that a lead time of several days during a buildup of international tension will allow evacuation of major urban areas before any nuclear attack. During this phase, civil defense planning was combined with other disaster responses by the Federal Emergency Management Agency (FEMA). Since the dissolution of the Soviet Union, civil defense planning has entered a fourth phase characterized by general neglect with slight attention being given to the prospects for Third-World nuclear attack and nuclear terrorism.*

Debates concerning civil defense have occurred within the public sphere and within the strategic community. The public debate has been very wide-ranging. In the early years, clergy debated issues of "shelter ethics," such as whether to admit or shoot neighbors trying to enter a family shelter. Increasingly, both Jewish and Christian religious leaders, from Reinhold Niebuhr to Billy Graham, opposed the shelter program on moral grounds. Currently, at one extreme are ethical egoists, like Bruce Clayton, who, in *Life After Doomsday,* provides information on tools, weapons, and others supplies a survivalist will need. At the other extreme are members of Physicians for Social Responsibility, like Jack Geiger, who regard cooperation with federal planning for civil defense as a "profoundly immoral act." Within the strategic community, debate on nuclear policies is primarily between nuclear deterrers and fighters. For nuclear deterrers, like Paul Warnke, civil defense at best serves only a modest, yet worthwhile, humanitarian role. Our real security lies in the mutual vulnerability of populations as a deterrent to nuclear war. Nuclear fighters, like Colin Gray, see a strategic role for civil defense. Since deterrence of attack against oneself also entails self-deterrence (i.e., one may not be attacked, but equally one cannot dare initiate attack), overcoming self-deterrence requires development of adequate defensive systems, such as the Crisis Relocation Program and the Strategic Defense Initiative*.

Most ethical assessments of civil defense occurred during the 1960s and 1980s. Especially in the 1980s, assessments of governmental plans (such as Robert Scheer provides) have been highly critical of using civil defense as a means to enhance a war-fighting nuclear strategy.

See ANTIBALLISTIC MISSILES/STAR WARS; COUNTERFORCE VERSUS COUNTERVALUE; STRATEGIC DEFENSE INITIATIVE (SDI).

BIBLIOGRAPHY
Gray, Colin, "Warfighting for Deterrence," *Journal of Strategic Studies* 7 (1984), 5–29.
Leaning, Jennifer, and Langley Keyes, eds., *The Counterfeit Ark* (Cambridge, Mass.: Ballinger, 1984).
Scheer, Robert, *With Enough Shovels* (New York: Knopf, 1982).
U.S. Senate, Committee on Banking, Housing and Urban Affairs, Hearings, *Civil Defense,* 95th Cong., 2d sess. (Washington, D.C.: U.S. Government Printing Office, 1979).
Winkler, Allan M., "A 40-Year History of Civil Defense," *Bulletin of the Atomic Scientists* 40 (June/July 1984), 16–23.

                                                                                     William C. Gay

CIVIL DISOBEDIENCE. Best understood as the attempt to bring about a change in the status quo through the violation of a law (e.g., the American civil rights movement) or institutional practice (e.g., Socrates) that is believed to be immoral, unconstitutional, or irreligious by the agent. The end-in-view of the civil disobedient is to change the questionable law or practice in order to render the system more just or humane. The end-in-view of the criminal disobedient is normally selfish gain or profit rather than an improvement in justice or the betterment of society. Hence, to classify the civil disobedient as a mere criminal misses and blurs substantive differences. Generally, civil disobedience is considered a nonviolent, public action such that the participants accept punishment to establish their sincerity and distinguish themselves from the criminal disobedient. The goal is to draw public attention to an unjust law in the attempt to bring public pressure to bear and change the law.

The debate concerning the morality of civil disobedience is one of the oldest in social philosophy. Plato, in *Crito,* has Socrates debate the personified Laws of Athens concerning our obligation to obey the law. Borrowing the social contract theory from Protagoras, the Laws of Athens argue that Socrates is beholden to them for the protection bestowed upon Socrates during his life. By remaining in a state, we tacitly agree to obey the law. To violate the law, even an unjust one, is to harm the Laws and, thereby, do evil. Socrates argues that it is always wrong to do evil, even to return evil with evil, so it is always wrong to violate a law. Our relationship to the Laws is like that of a slave to a master or a child to his or her parents. The state, rather than the individual, is sovereign. Consequently, Socrates concludes, it is always wrong to violate the law.

Henry David Thoreau, in his "Resistance to Civil Government," argues the converse. Thoreau argues that a government is legitimate only if it has the consent of the governed. But to have the consent of the governed, each person must agree to obey the laws—not tacitly but actually. The state derives whatever legitimacy it has from the rights of individuals, rather than the reverse, as Plato argued. Since no actual government is based upon actual consent, no actual government is legitimate. Consequently, governments exercise their authority by power and coercion rather than reason and legitimacy. Consequently, we are not morally obliged to obey the law. In fact, Thoreau argues, we are morally obliged to violate unjust laws because the government lacks the legitimacy, if not the power, to make and enforce the law. Thoreau held that such acts of civil disobedience could be violent as, for example, were John Brown's.

Leo Tolstoy, in his *The Law of Love and the Law of Violence,* based his justification of civil disobedience on the teachings of Jesus. Tolstoy argues that the Gospels reveal that Jesus was a pacifist who taught and practiced the law of love in opposition to the law of violence. The state, on the other hand, teaches and practices the law of violence. Like Thoreau, Tolstoy argued that no actual state is legitimate but, instead, derives its power from violence. In opposition to the Russian Bolsheviks, Tolstoy argued that means and ends cannot be separated. Violent means cannot create a just state; only another unjust state will follow based upon the law of violence. In place of a violent revolution, Tolstoy argued for a return to a simple life based on self-sufficient communities dedicated to nonviolence and communal ownership. The Communists were correct, Tolstoy believed, in their criticisms of modern society and particularly in their claim that the internal contradictions of modern society would soon tear it apart. When the event occurred, Tolstoy believed, the small, self-sufficient communities would remain to create a just and peaceful world. Interestingly, many of Tolstoy's better arguments can be divorced from their Christian context and grounded instead in pacifism. Like Thoreau, Tolstoy practiced his belief that we are morally obliged to violate unjust laws in order to change them. But we must violate laws of violence in accord with the law of love, that is, nonviolently and with love. Indeed, by the 20th century, Tolstoy was considered the conscience of Russia because of his acts of conscience.

The teachings of both Thoreau and Tolstoy were influential on the thought of Mohandas K. Gandhi*. Gandhi was not only a brilliant theorist of civil disobedience but also one of its most able practitioners. The Indian expression *satyâgraha* contains the heart of Gandhi's teachings. *Satyâgraha* is the force that is born of both truth and love. Gandhi declared that nonviolent actions are worthless when they are not motivated by love for one's enemy. Likewise, civil disobedience is worthless when it is not motivated by truth. In combination, truth and love will be heard. The goal, then, of civil disobedience is to reveal unjust laws, to bring them to the attention of the world, in the belief that truth and love will motivate people generally to join in the nonviolent struggle against oppression. In addition, the oppressors will be forced to face their own injustice. It was extremely difficult for the British to maintain their superiority as a people while the supposedly inferior Indians, unarmed and peacefully, accepted the violence of the armed British, openly and for all to see. *Satyâgraha* attempts to overcome the oppressor by patience, love, conversion, and a change in consciousness effected by confronting the oppressors with their own reliance on unjustified violence even against unarmed, peaceful demonstrators. As Tolstoy predicted, the law of love proved more powerful than the law of violence, and India was liberated from the imperialism of the British. Again following Tolstoy, Gandhi's vision for India was a nation of small, self-sufficient communities based on nonviolence and communal ownership the symbol of which was to be the spinning wheel emblazoned on the national flag. Unfortunately, the assassination of Gandhi ended his vision.

Like Tolstoy, Martin Luther King Jr.'s* commitment to civil disobedience was largely based upon his nonviolent interpretation of the Gospels. Like Gandhi, King was a brilliant practitioner of nonviolent direct action as well as an excellent theorist. In his "Letter from Birmingham Jail," King argues that a "threat to justice anywhere is a threat to justice everywhere" and that "justice too long delayed is justice denied." In light of the massive violation of the civil rights of African Americans, King, following Gandhi, advocated a unique form of civil disobedience that included many symbolic actions—walks, marches, pilgrimages—as well as demonstrations and boycotts. King realized that the privileged do not give up their privilege simply for the asking. Again, the goal was to bring to public attention the atrocities suffered by African Americans, in the belief that sunlight is the best antiseptic. Again, civil disobedience revealed the contradiction contained in the oppressor's belief that they are superior to the oppressed when the nonviolent direct actions of the civil disobedients were met with unprovoked violence by the white oppressors. Again, the messianic leader of a successful movement based on nonviolent direct action was cut down by an assassin's bullet before the dream could be realized.

More recently, the writings of Vaclav Havel* and the nonviolent direct actions of South Africans in opposition to Apartheid give us yet other examples of the theory and practice of civil disobedience. The writings of Gene Sharp and Robert Holmes present a nonviolent direct action version of national defense called "civilian defense" to replace the traditional military. Following Gandhi, both ask what the success of civilian defense could be if we diverted the trillions of dollars spent on war and crime to a nonviolent society dedicated to peaceful means of conflict resolution.

Civil disobedience also raises many important ethical issues. Must civil disobedience be nonviolent or as Thoreau, and more recently, Howard Zinn argue, can it be violent? If civil disobedience must be nonviolent, do the practitioners

CLAUSEWITZ, CARL VON (1780–1831)   85

of nonviolent direct action contradict themselves by knowingly and intentionally
creating conditions that will produce violence? King argued that this is like
blaming the wealthy person who is mugged rather than the mugger since the
wealthy person knows that wealth creates the conditions for theft. But is King's
analogy strong enough to establish that blaming the civil disobedients is blaming
the victim? Must the civil disobedients be willing to accept punishment in order
to establish their sincerity and establish their difference from the criminal disobedient? Or is their willingness to face public scorn, violence, and the possible
loss of livelihood and life adequate, especially in light of the fact that imprisonment might mean the end of the movement and that guerrilla* action may be
more effective? Finally, is Thoreau correct in his claim that no actual state is
justified in issuing and enforcing the law but, instead, derives its power from
violence and coercion? If so, how is civil disobedience not legitimate in the face
of an unjust law? How could it not be morally required?

See BRITTAIN, VERA; CHRISTIANITY AND WAR; DAY, DOROTHY;
DEBS, EUGENE; GANDHI, MOHANDAS; HENNACY, AMMON; KING,
MARTIN LUTHER, JR.; MUSTE, ABRAHAM JOHANNES; PACIFISM;
ROYDEN, MAUDE; SUPERIOR ORDERS.

BIBLIOGRAPHY

Bedau, Hugo Adam, ed., *Civil Disobedience in Focus* (New York: Routledge, 1991).
Cohen, Carl, *Civil Disobedience: Conscience, Tactics, and the Law* (New York: Colum-
bia University Press, 1971).
Holmes, Robert L., *On War and Morality* (Princeton, N.J.: Princeton University Press,
1989).
Murphy, Jeffrie, ed., *Civil Disobedience and Violence* (Belmont, Calif.: Wadsworth,
1971).
Sharp, Gene, *The Politics of Nonviolent Action* (Boston: Porter Sargent, 1973).
Singer, Peter, *Democracy and Disobedience* (New York and London: Oxford, 1974).
Sterba, James P., *Contemporary Social and Political Philosophy* (Belmont, Calif.: Wads-
worth, 1995).
Zinn, Howard, *Disobedience and Democracy* (New York: Random House, 1968).

Richard Werner

CIVIL WAR, AMERICAN. *See* AMNESTY; CHRISTIANITY AND WAR;
CONSCIENTIOUS OBJECTION; *GENERAL ORDERS 100;* LIEBER, FRAN-
CIS; PACIFISM; PRISONERS OF WAR; QUARTER, NO, WARS OF; WIRZ,
CAPTAIN HENRY.

CLAUSEWITZ, CARL VON (1780–1831). There are two Clausewitz's—the
man and the book. The man led a demanding military life, although temperamentally not well suited for it. For twenty-two years, from 1793 as a thirteen-
year-old subaltern until 1815 as the thirty-five-year-old chief of staff of von
Thielmann's corps at Waterloo, Clausewitz fought the French, participating in
some of the bitterest fighting of that cataclysmic period. Temperamentally
though, Clausewitz was inclined toward literary and philosophical pursuits. In

other circumstances, he could well have become an aesthete. In Napoleonic
Europe, however, he became a prominent member of Scharnhorst and Gneisen-
au's circle of military reformers struggling to modernize the Prussian army after
its crushing defeat at Jena/Auerstadt in 1806.

After Waterloo, as peace descended upon the continent, Clausewitz's extensive military experience and literary inclination combined to produce the sprawl-
ing, frustratingly unfinished manuscript known as *Vom Kriege (On War)*.
Published posthumously by his wife in 1832, the book soon took on a life of
its own, its most fundamental insight—that war is but policy by other means—
being lost and distorted for the next 130 years.

The first and greatest distortions occurred in Germany. There, the book was
selectively quoted and deliberately falsified in the third edition to allege that
war was not an act of policy, but independent of policy. Once started, the politicians should withdraw, and the military should pursue victory as they saw fit
using maximum force. In time, the unrestrained use of force was taken to provide a rationale for total war*, which it was assumed was but a gloss for Clausewitz's absolute war. In France, after the defeat of 1870, Clausewitz was
studied intensively at the *École de Guerre,* where Marshal Foch in particular
argued that the book demonstrated the superiority of the offense over the defense, a strange interpretation for anyone who has read Book 6, especially Chapter 1, where Clausewitz says clearly "that the defense is the stronger form of
waging war." In the English-speaking world, there were no misinterpretations,
for the simple reason that Clausewitz was all but totally ignored. A translation
by Colonel Graham appeared in 1874, but it had no impact on British or American thinking.

In sum, by World War I, Clausewitz was either being ignored or misinter-
preted. It was not until the 1960s that a group of academic strategists seeking
to place their discipline on firm foundations rediscovered Clausewitz. Working
from the original 1832 edition, these academics—among them Raymond Aron
in France, Bernard Brodie and Peter Paret in America, and Michael Howard in
England—recognized the importance of Clausewitz's "Note of 10 July 1827"
for interpreting the first chapter of Book 1 and the importance of that chapter
for interpreting the rest of the unfinished manuscript.

Previous to July 10, 1827, Clausewitz had had trouble reconciling his theory
with reality. If war is violence, then, in theory, war should be absolute—a rapid,
unified, total act of violence. Yet, real wars were never like this; their violence
was always less than absolute, less than the theoretically possible. Then, three
years before his death, Clausewitz realized that "War can be of two kinds, in
the sense that either the objective is to overthrow [*niederwerfen*] the enemy—
to render him politically helpless or militarily impotent, thus forcing him to sign
whatever peace we please; or merely to occupy some of his frontier districts so
that we can annex them or use them for bargaining at the peace negotiations."
That is, the violence of war is regulated by its political purpose. When the
purpose is to secure a dictated peace, the violence will be high. When the

political objective is something less than a dictated peace, the violence will be proportionally less. In other words, war is an act of policy, not an act of violence.

Thus, to understand *On War,* one must understand, first, that it is radically unfinished; second, that Clausewitz did not come to this most fundamental insight until the very last years of his life; and finally, that, except for the first chapter, he was unable to revise the manuscript in light of this discovery. However, once the book is read with the two kinds of war in mind, not only does its exceptional merit become apparent, but it also provides solid foundations upon which academic strategists can build their discipline.

See GERMAN WAR BOOK; *LAW OF LAND WARFARE, THE; RULES OF LAND WARFARE,* 1914, 1934, 1944.

BIBLIOGRAPHY

Aron, Raymond, *Clausewitz, Philosopher of War* (Englewood Cliffs, N.J.: Prentice Hall, 1985).

Clausewitz, Carl L. von, *On War,* Michael Howard and Peter Paret, eds. and trans. (Princeton, N.J.: Princeton University Press, 1976).

Paret, Peter, *Clausewitz and the State: The Man, His Theories, and His Times* (Oxford: Oxford University Press, 1976).

Summers, Harry G., Jr., *On Strategy: A Critical Analysis of the Vietnam War* (Navato, Calif.: Presidio, 1982).

Brien Hallett

COLD WAR. Refers to the state of hostility that existed between the United States and the Soviet Union from 1946 to 1991. It was a war in the sense that each side viewed itself as engaged in a desperate struggle for fundamental moral values. It was ''cold'' in the sense that in its forty-five years no military engagements were fought between American and Soviet soldiers. Instead, the Cold War played itself out in proxy wars fought by soldiers of allied nations, in complex campaigns of propaganda* and subversion, and in the ghostly game of nuclear threat and nuclear counterthreat. The war reached its peak in the Cuban Missile Crisis* of October 1962. It ended with the dissolution of the Soviet Union in 1991.

IDEOLOGICAL ROOTS OF THE COLD WAR

Perhaps no subject has exercised contemporary historians more than the origins of the Cold War. Every event in Soviet-American relations from 1943 to 1946 has been minutely scrutinized to identify the spark that caused the conflict. Every American act has been interpreted as demonstrating American perfidy* or American good will; every Soviet act has been interpreted as demonstrating Soviet wickedness or Soviet patience.

A better starting point for analysis is the realization that conflict between the United States and the Soviet Union was inevitable or at least likely; it needed no spark. In the mid-19th century, Karl Marx* had discerned that the two dominant powers of the 20th century would be the United States and Russia, and tension between two dominant powers is the historical norm.

Furthermore, the ideological differences between the two nations were profound. Normally, differences in structure and beliefs between two nations need not imply conflict. But when the differences are so great and the nations so powerful, suspicions will arise even in the absence of hostile acts.

Before the Soviet Union engaged in a single act hostile to the United States, many Americans had already concluded that "bolshevism" (Lenin's version of socialism) was bad. Lenin's writings by implication called for the abolition of free elections, free speech, the free press, and the private ownership of the means of production. They called for political control by a single party, for preaching atheism in the public schools, and for violent overthrow of capitalist governments. Under bolshevism, one could not vote freely, criticize the government, accumulate wealth, or will property to one's children. Bolshevism seemed an assault on liberty, on property, and on God.

The actual development of the Soviet state seemed to confirm these fears. The concentration of power permitted under Lenin's system led to an absolute dictatorship under Stalin. For many Americans, Stalin's rule showed that communism was a system without basic liberties, under which a million persons could be killed on suspicion of disloyalty, and several millions more could be deliberately starved in a government-induced famine. Yet by 1949 one-third of the world's population was committed to this form of society. According to Marx and Lenin, it was only a matter of time before the rest of the world would follow.

Before the United States had engaged in a single act hostile to the Soviet Union, followers of Lenin had already concluded that Western capitalism was bad. For them, the fundamental fact of social life was that people produce more than they need to survive; they produce a surplus, and history is the story of the struggle to control the surplus. Under communism, the common surplus is to be used for the common good; under capitalism, the surplus produced by all is appropriated by the few. The basic moral fact of capitalism is exploitation, the systematic theft of fruits of labor. Each side viewed the other's system as unjust, dangerous, and expansionist. From this assessment of systems flowed the assessment of actions. Neither side was ever prepared to give the other the benefit of the doubt.

PREHISTORY OF THE COLD WAR

The first transformation of hostile feelings about bolshevism into hostile acts occurred in the wake of the Bolshevik Revolution in 1917. When the Russian revolution deteriorated into civil war in 1919, Western governments, including the United States, sent troops into Russian territory to support the White Russian counterrevolution against Lenin. When the counterrevolution failed, the United States refused to grant diplomatic recognition to the Soviet government, and the

Western governments put the Soviet Union under an economic quarantine designed to produce the collapse of the system. When Lenin took Russia out of the war with Germany in 1917, Russia was viewed by many as a traitor to the Allied cause. As for U.S. diplomatic recognition, this was delayed because of the Soviet expropriation of American assets without proper compensation.

To all this, the Soviets responded that the war between Russia and Germany was a mindless slaughter, and that Lenin's most admirable deed was to put a stop to the killing. If the Bolsheviks commanded minority support, they had as much support as any other political group, and millions were prepared to fight and die for bolshevism in the ensuing civil war. American troops had no more right to intervene in the Russian civil war than Russian troops had a right to intervene at Gettysburg. By 1922, the Soviet government was as legitimate as any in the world, yet the United States withheld recognition. The Soviets' accusations against the United States were mainly sins of omission. Through the 1920s and 1930s, the United States failed to stand up to fascism. The United States failed to support democratic forces fighting Franco in Spain. And after December 1941, the United States and England failed to bear a fair share of the fighting against Hitler. For three years, they refused to open a second front in Europe, as if they were content to let Russia and Germany bleed each other dry.

The sins charged to the Soviet Union in these years were mainly sins of commission. In league with Hitler, the Soviet Union in the fall of 1939 invaded eastern Poland, Latvia, Estonia, Lithuania, and Finland. In the wake of victory in Poland, several thousand Polish officers were shot on Stalin's orders in the wastes of Katyn forest. These were acts of aggression* and murder, pure and simple. In defense the Soviets could only cite "reasons of state."

EVENTS OF THE COLD WAR

When the war in Europe ended in May 1945, the red flag flew over the Reichstag in Berlin. The Red Army had fought across Northern Europe into Germany, and up the Danube through Hungary. It controlled the Balkans down to Greece, Hungary, Czechoslovakia, Poland, the Baltic States, and one-quarter of Germany. Stalin had the power to incorporate all these territories into the U.S.S.R. Instead he absorbed only the Baltic States, and let the others be ruled by their own nationals—provided that their governments were communist governments, following the dictates of Moscow on all significant issues. Popular revolts against this arrangement were forcibly suppressed in East Germany in 1953, in Hungary in 1956, and in Czechoslovakia in 1968.

The Soviet justification for this postwar disposition was not simply that might makes right. Russia had been invaded twice from the West in the 20th century, at appalling cost in Russian lives. The establishment of a buffer zone on the Soviet Union's western flank might forestall a third invasion, which the Soviets had reason to fear, given manifest Western hostility to the Soviet system. As for self-determination in the states of Eastern Europe, most of them had self-determined themselves into supporting Hitler. Given the degree of collaboration exhibited in West Germany between the American military and former Nazi officers, free elections implied a possible revival of fascism.

Most Americans considered these arguments nonsense. Certainly no one could accuse the Poles of supporting the Nazis. Nevertheless, nothing could be done about Eastern Europe in the short run. For the long run, the Truman administration adopted George Kennan's doctrine of containment: the United States should make preventing the further spread of communism its highest priority. George Kennan thought that the necessary actions were largely educative, or mildly subversive, such as the secret American support supplied to anticommunist parties in France and Italy in the late 1940s. But by 1950, *containment* came to include a large military buildup and support of anticommunist military operations. Such operations included support for the right wing in Greece in 1948 and Korea* in 1950, the overthrow of popular left-wing governments in Iran in 1953, in Guatemala in 1954, and in Chile in 1973, and unsuccessful attempts to overthrow the government of Cuba in 1961 and Nicaragua in the mid-1980s.

VIETNAM* AND COLD WAR VALUES

The doctrine of containment made anticommunism the highest moral value in American foreign policy. When conflicts arose between anticommunism and other fundamental values, anticommunism prevailed. The effect of this new American moral order was most visible in Vietnam. A former French colony, Vietnam was scheduled for its first free election in 1956. By Dwight Eisenhower's own admission, 75 percent of the people in Vietnam were prepared to vote for Ho Chi Minh, a hero in the war of liberation against the French. Since Ho also happened to be an orthodox Communist, the United States sabotaged the elections in 1956, installed a dictator to rule the southern half of Vietnam, and supported the south in a war against Ho and his successors that cost over a million lives, mostly Vietnamese. The Americans had disliked communism because it was undemocratic. But in Vietnam they came to dislike democracy when it pointed toward communism.

As the Cold War progressed, its values came more and more to displace traditional American values. American ideals of free speech were compromised in the 1950s by government and private campaigns persecuting persons who allegedly held (or had held) pro-Communist views. And the huge military establishment that developed from the 1950s through the 1980s created a secretive national security sector within the United States that was irreconcilable with an open society. When the Cold War ended in 1991, both the victor and the vanquished had been transformed by the struggle, each into a strangely distorted image of the other.

The economic costs of the Cold War were immense: Estimates of the American investment exceed $3 trillion. The risks to the combatants and to the human race were great, especially during the Cuban Missile Crisis, the first and only direct confrontation between two superpowers possessing large-scale nuclear weapons. Nevertheless, the Cold War never became hot. The reason, perhaps, lay in ideology: the Americans thought that the Soviet system would not work; the Soviets thought that capitalism would collapse in the dialectic of history. Both sides believed they could afford to wait. They waited forty-five years, and awoke to find the world had gone its own way without them.

See AGGRESSIVE VERSUS DEFENSIVE WAR; INTELLIGENCE AGENCIES; MILITARY JARGON; PROPAGANDA; RETALIATION, MASSIVE; WARISM.

BIBLIOGRAPHY

The bibliography for the Cold War is immense and almost invariably partisan. For a detailed anti-Soviet account see Hugh Thomas, *Armed Truce: The Beginning of the Cold War 1945–46* (New York: Athenaeum, 1987). For accounts more sympathetic to postwar Soviet problems see D. F. Fleming, *The Cold War and Its Origins 1917–60* (New York: Doubleday, 1961) and Gabriel Kolko, *The Politics of War: The World and United States Foreign Policy* (New York: Random House, 1968). Two accounts oriented more toward the political center are Walter LaFeber, *America, Russia, and the Cold War* (New York: Wiley, 1967) and Daniel Yergin, *Shattered Peace* (Boston: Houghton Mifflin, 1977). For more recent assessments see David Reynolds, ed., *The Origins of the Cold War in Europe* (New Haven, Conn.: Yale University Press, 1994).

Douglas P. Lackey

COLLATERAL DAMAGE. Ever since the introduction of modern war, but particularly since the advent of weapons of mass destruction*, collateral damage from war has been a major concern. When one considers the millions of deaths of noncombatants or the wanton destruction of entire cities and even nation-states accomplished during World War II, it is no wonder. Even the recent Gulf War* is credited with killing roughly 100,000 noncombatants* while causing tremendous damage to nonmilitary targets. Given that the war lasted only a few weeks and was considered a "clean" war, the importance of the issue of collateral damage is evident. If we ponder the amount of collateral damage that a nuclear war*, even a limited one, would produce, again the importance of the issue of collateral damage is clear. We can expect that a nuclear war will cause massive death to noncombatants (estimates range from the tens to hundreds of millions on up to the extinction of the species), as well as extensive destruction of the economy, infrastructure, and communications. The damage would occur directly to the nation attacked as well as to neighboring nations and, indirectly, through fallout and interruption of the economy, to nonneighboring nations.

Before the introduction of modern warfare, the convention emerged that noncombatants are not acceptable military targets. Particularly with the advent of weapons of mass destruction and the ability to deliver tremendous destructive power from the air, the death of noncombatants was accepted as an indirect consequence of attempts to destroy military targets. As long as the deaths of noncombatants was not the intended consequence, as long as the intended goal was the destruction of a military target, then collateral damage was considered acceptable even if it involved the deaths of enormous numbers of noncombatants. But we had entered upon a dangerously slippery slope. While the allies were horrified by the German Blitzkrieg and the Japanese attack on Pearl Harbor, by the end of the war the allied attacks on Dresden, Berlin, Tokyo, Hiroshima*, and Nagasaki made the earlier German and Japanese attacks pale by comparison. Entire cities were destroyed, which included tremendous numbers of civilian deaths. While Hitler lost the war, his manner of waging war won the day. Now we kill noncombatants in war with hardly an afterthought, as in Vietnam* and Iraq.

But perhaps there is justification for the change. If the issue is the killing of innocents*, it is not clear that noncombatants are any more innocent than combatants. Consider the citizen who, during a war, supports the war effort, works in the defense industry, donates free labor to support the war effort, and contributes children as soldiers. Consider the conscripted soldier who opposes the war, only fires her weapon into the air, and does nothing to support the war effort. Why is the former considered innocent and the latter not? Why is the issue of innocence construed along the lines of combatant and noncombatant*?

While this is a plausible point, it is not obvious that it supports the conclusion that noncombatants are fair game in war. While some noncombatants are clearly noninnocent, the political leaders for instance, some clearly are innocent. Babies and children* must be counted among the innocent by any reasonable test. Yet babies and children are always among the victims of collateral damage in modern war. On these grounds alone, one can condemn modern war as strongly presumptively immoral and question our ready acceptance of the legitimacy of collateral damage. The distinction between combatants and noncombatants may protect some who are noninnocent while sacrificing others who are innocent, but it is the *best* means to protect babies and children, those who are obviously innocent and in need of protection, from the ravages of war. The justification for the distinction between combatants and noncombatants, then, is pragmatic. It is the best means to support and protect an important moral insight—the wanton killing of babies and children is strongly presumptively immoral. Hence, the combatant-noncombatant distinction is a justified means of attaining the end of protecting innocent life during wartime.

George Mavrodes argues that the convention to accept the combatant-noncombatant distinction is contingent on our enemy's acceptance, since it is a convention-dependent obligation. If our enemy does not accept the convention and the most efficient means to execute the war is to attack noncombatants, then we should. Yet our obligation to refrain from the wanton killing of babies and children is, if anything is, convention-independent. The best means to observe and support that convention-independent insight during wartime is to observe the convention-dependent distinction between combatants and noncombatants. Consequently, even if our enemy refuses to observe the distinction and we can more efficiently wage the war by intentionally killing innocents, it would be strongly and presumptively wrong to do so.

Some argue that collateral damage is acceptable as long as it is not intended. If one's intended target is a military one, and one does not intend the death of innocents, then one is justified in the destruction of the military target even if the death to innocents is a foreseeable consequence of the destruction of the military target and even if the number of deaths is tremendous. If one's intended target is a ball-bearing factory in Moscow and one is targeting it with a one-megaton warhead in order to ensure its destruction, one is not responsible for the tens of thousands of collateral deaths one may cause. After all, we build highways not intending but foreseeing that innocent children will die in automobile accidents. How is the targeting of the ball-bearing factory any different?

One marked difference is that the bombing kills the noncombatants directly while the highway only indirectly creates the conditions where innocents may be killed. The direct cause of the deaths of innocents on the highway would not be the highway but the improper driving habits of those who cause accidents. It is the latter and not the builders of the highway who are responsible for the deaths of innocents on the highway. Indeed, if we fail to make the highway safe, thereby creating conditions that will cause unnecessary death to innocents, we are culpable. Consequently, there is an important moral difference between building highways and obliteration bombing.

Further, there is the issue of whose intention is relevant. Nation-states, armies, and collections of persons generally do not seem to be the sorts of entities capable of having a set intention unless every member of the group desires the end-in-view. Intentions are had by persons. It is difficult to believe that political leaders and generals do not desire the collateral deaths produced in modern war. Consider the arms race and particularly Mutual Assured Destruction (MAD). What made MAD mad was not the destruction of military targets but the wanton destruction of innocent human life one could expect from a nuclear war. The primary deterrent was the collateral damage, the realization that a nuclear war would cause the deaths of millions of innocents while destroying the nation-states involved. How, then, can MAD deter without the conditional intention, at least on the part of political leaders and generals, to kill innocents wantonly?

Likewise, consider Vietnam and Iraq. Part of the lesson of these wars for Third World countries, which is often cited by political and military leaders, is the terrible price a nation will pay if it engages the United States in war—even if the United States loses. But surely a large percentage of that price is the collateral death to innocents. Again, how are we to understand the rhetoric in any way other than voicing the conditional intention to cause the death of innocents? It seems that the intentional death of innocents is an obvious desire of both political and military leaders ever since the advent of modern war. We did not fire-bomb Dresden and Tokyo merely to destroy military targets. In fact, Dresden had few military targets. Similarly, we did not drop nuclear weapons on Hiroshima and Nagasaki merely to hit military targets. In fact, the target for the former was a church. Even if we dropped these bombs to avoid an invasion of Japan and save American soldiers' lives, which is extremely dubious in the light of recent evidence concerning President Truman's designs to stop the Soviet Union from occupying northern Japan, we were trading the lives of innocents for the lives of combatants. While trading lives is always lamentable, some trades are morally decent while others are not.

In recent wars the intentional destruction of innocent noncombatants, at least on the part of political and military leaders, has been a means of conducting the war. It is difficult to understand how such acts are morally justified, even if collateral.

See CASUALTIES OF WAR; CHILDREN IN WAR; CHILDREN'S RIGHTS IN WAR; COMBATANT-NONCOMBATANT DISTINCTION; FORBIDDEN WEAPONS; INNOCENTS; INTENTIONALITY.

BIBLIOGRAPHY
Holmes, Robert L., *On War and Morality* (Princeton, N.J.: Princeton University Press, 1989).
Lee, Steven, *Morality, Prudence and Nuclear Weapons* (Cambridge: Cambridge University Press, 1993).
Sterba, James, ed., *The Ethics of War and Nuclear Deterrence* (Belmont, Calif.: Wadsworth, 1985), especially articles by George Mavrodes and Jeffrie Murphy.
Turco, R. P., O. B. Toon, T. P. Packerman, J. B. Pollack, and Carl Sagan, ''Nuclear Winter: Global Consequences of Multiple Nuclear Explosions,'' *Science* (December 23, 1983), 1283–92.
U.S. Office of Technology, *The Effects of Nuclear War* (Washington, D.C.: U.S. Government Printing Office, 1979).
Walzer, Michael, *Just and Unjust Wars* (New York: Basic Books, 1992).
Wasserstrom, Richard, *War and Morality* (Belmont, Calif.: Wadsworth, 1970).

Richard Werner

COMBATANT-NONCOMBATANT DISTINCTION. An inherent part of just war* theory is that there are some restrictions on what warriors can do. One of the most basic restrictions is expressed by the principle of *discrimination,* under which only combatants can be attacked in war; or, the other way around, that noncombatants are immune from attack. On the face of it, discriminating between combatants and noncombatants should not be difficult. It ought to be easy enough to know whom to attack and not attack in war. Noncombatants include those in uniform in the medical service (doctors, nurses, corpsmen, ambulance drivers) and those who serve in a religious capacity (chaplains* and their assistants). There are a host of people who are noncombatants and not in uniform, including children*, mothers, teachers, civilian office workers, business executives, service workers such as plumbers, electricians and garbage collectors, many factory workers, and retired people. Combatants include all those in uniform who themselves are warriors, who directly support these warriors (e.g., by loading armaments on airplanes or by serving as mechanics for airplanes, tanks, armored personnel carriers), and who could be pressed into a warrior role should conditions warrant, even if fighting is not their main assignment.

If those disposed to follow just war theory refined and extended these lists of combatants and noncombatants a bit, and then followed the principle of discrimination, much of what just war theory seeks to accomplish with respect to justice in war would be accomplished. However, by itself, the combatant-noncombatant distinction does not do the whole job for us. In attacking an enemy warship, for example, one unavoidably attacks some noncombatants such as medical personnel and chaplains as well as combatants. As such, the distinction does not tell us whether to attack or not. In a similar vein, in attacking trains loaded with military personnel, one likely also attacks noncombatants who are in charge of running the train. Evidently a supplemental rule is needed to guide us. It might take the form of: If the ship, train, or facility is primarily manned by combatants, attack is permitted—even though some noncombatants will also be attacked. But even this rule does not tell us what to do with military storage depots manned mainly by civilians. Or what to do with munitions factories where practically all the employees are civilian, that is, noncombatants.

A distinction in terms of those in and out of uniform is of some help but, if applied by itself, would tell us that it is permissible to attack chaplains and ambulance drivers. It would also tell us that munitions workers are not subject to attack. Nor would the civilian secretary of the navy be subject to attack since he or she, if clever, would never don a uniform.

Useful in a somewhat different way is the distinction between those who participate in the war effort and those who do not. This distinction differs from the others in that it is a graded or degree concept. In contrast to someone who is or is not a combatant (although there is some vagueness here too), one can participate in the war effort by degrees. Fully participating would be combatants, officers who are not combatants but lead combatants, civilian heads of the military, and munitions workers. Civilians also fully participating would include those making computers, steel, clothing, and trucks for the war effort. Less directly, but still heavily involved, would be bridge maintenance crews, railroad workers (some here more involved than others), power plant workers, radio and TV personnel, and the like. In a sense, almost all of the enemy participate in the war effort simply because they give it social support through their speech and their kindnesses toward military personnel.

But for the participant-nonparticipant distinction to be useful some people in the enemy camp have to be excluded because their contribution is tangential. One wants to say that only those whose main work effort in life supports the war fall into the class of participants and thus are subject to attack. Evidently this is how various documents such as the U.S. Army's field manual FM 27-10 (*The Law of Land Warfare**), the 1949 Geneva Convention* (IV) concerned with civilians, and the 1899 Hague Convention* (Annex to the Convention) view it—although even they are not totally clear about the matter. FM 27-10, for example, says that buildings used for military purpose can be attacked. By inference one supposes that the noncombatants in them can also be attacked. But the problem is that there is no bright line to help us define "main work effort." So the participation-nonparticipation distinction also cannot do the whole job of telling us whom we can and cannot attack. The suspicion is that no distinction can. No simple linguistic distinction is going to act like a switch to inform us when the attack should be on and when off. Rather, all of these distinctions must guide the application of the principle of discrimination only in a rough and ready way. Any one, or some combination thereof, can at best be used to give us only loose, prima facie rules. So when the directive "Don't bomb that factory" is issued, it may be overridden. If it is discovered later that the factory is being used to some extent for military purposes, those in charge are going to have to make the difficult decision whether to bomb it, and the noncombatants therein, or not.

Under special circumstances, then, rules will be overridden. One class of such circumstances has to do with the nature of the war. In a "six-day" type war there might be reverse overridding. Even munitions workers should be spared in such a war, since their products are not likely to get to the front in time to make any difference. But in a serious and protracted war, it would be difficult to argue against expanding the circle of those people and places that should be targeted. While forbidding expansion to include everyone, and therefore violate the principles of discrimination and proportionality* in just war theory, the circle might now include not only munitions workers but others who are heavily and even moderately involved in working on behalf of the war effort.

A second set of special circumstances that encourages overridability is concerned with technology. Low-technology nations will justifiably override the principle of discrimination more than their high-technology enemies. A high-tech nation can bomb a munitions factory at night with precision when most of the munitions plant personnel are home asleep. In so doing, it will cause only minimal damage to the surrounding civilian areas. Surely it would be unforgivable if a nation that possessed the capacity to bomb in and around urban areas with precision weapons used free-falling (i.e., "dumb") iron bombs instead.

In contrast, it might be forgivable with a low-tech nation. If the only weapons it had were free-falling bombs, and if it were involved in a serious war, it might be excused if it caused a greater number of noncombatant casualties than its high-tech enemy. The low-tech nation, of course, would not be permitted free access to noncombatant targets. There still would be limitations on that nation's bombing policies. It could not attack hospitals, schools, and other such targets with impunity, but there would be fewer restrictions on it than on its high-tech opponent simply because we hold people and nations accountable only up to their level of ability. What ought to be done is restricted by what can be.

A third set of special circumstances that encourages overriding concerns enemy immoral behavior. If the enemy regularly violated the principles of discrimination and proportionality, reprisals* might be in order—especially if there were no other way to stop its atrocities. A fourth set concerns how the enemy is fighting. If it is fighting in guerrilla* fashion it will, inevitably, be more difficult to sort combatants from noncombatants. Finally, a fifth set pertains, once again, to enemy immoral behavior. An enemy might make life difficult for a nation fighting within the just war tradition by placing military equipment such as airplanes and antiaircraft weapons next to religious institutions, schools, hospitals, and other civilian structures. Certainly there would be times when these structures would be destroyed not unjustly as a by-product of the attempt to get at the military assets placed next to them.

So decisions as to whether to attack certain targets are not easy to make. A distinction such as that between combatants and noncombatants is of some help. But in dealing with hard cases this and similar distinctions are, unfortunately, not of much use.

See CASUALTIES OF WAR; CHILDREN AND WAR; CRIMES AGAINST HUMANITY; FORBIDDEN STRATEGIES; GENOCIDE; HOLOCAUST, THE; INNOCENTS; JUST WAR; NUCLEAR WAR; NUREMBERG TRIALS; PRISONERS OF WAR.

BIBLIOGRAPHY

Fotion, Nicholas G., *Military Ethics: Looking Toward the Future* (Stanford, Calif.: Hoover Institution Press, Stanford University, 1990).

Geneva Convention (IV): Convention Relative to the Protection of Civilian Persons in Time of War (August 12, 1949), in Leon Friedman, *The Law of War* (New York: Random House, 1972), 641–91.

Hague (II): Laws and Customs of War on Land (Annex to the Convention), in Leon Friedman, *The Law of War* (New York: Random House, 1972), 224–35.

Holmes, Robert L., *On War and Morality* (Princeton, N.J.: Princeton University Press, 1989), Chap. 6.

U.S. Department of the Army, *The Law of Land Warfare* (FM 27-10) (Washington D.C.: U.S. Government Printing Office, 1956).

Walzer, Michael, *Just and Unjust Wars: A Moral Argument with Historical Illustrations* (New York: Basic Books, 1977), Chaps. 9–11.

Nicholas G. Fotion

COMMUNISM. *See* MARXISM AND WAR.

CONCENTRATION CAMPS. The term *concentration camp* first appeared to designate British internment centers in South Africa that were used during the Boer War (1899–1902) to prevent Boer civilians from helping guerrillas*. Disregarding the principle that one should not be punished unless found guilty in a fair trial, concentration camps remove from society people who cannot be confined through the normal workings of a state's criminal code. In the 20th century, numerous governments have implemented them. For example, the USSR had its Gulag Archipelago, the United States interned its Japanese citizens at camps such as Manzanar during World War II, and installations of related kinds have appeared in the former Yugoslavia.

Although the concentration camp was not invented by Nazi Germany, no regime has used concentration camps in a more systematically devastating way. An early step in that process occurred at Dachau, a town about ten miles northwest of Munich, Germany, where one of the first concentration camps in the Third Reich was established in late March 1933. Its early inmates were political opponents of the Nazis*, mainly Communists and Social Democrats, who were kept under so-called "protective custody."

Heinrich Himmler (1900–1945) was the Nazi leader who established Dachau. As head of the SS (*Schutzstaffel*), he eventually presided over an empire within the Nazi state. It included a vast network of camps like Dachau. Although mostly political prisoners were incarcerated from 1933 until the outbreak of World War II in September 1939, Nazi Germany's concentration camps gradually engulfed many other types of people in addition to the Communists, Social Democrats, and trade unionists who had been targeted initially. Especially by 1937–1938, Jehovah's Witnesses, members of the clergy, "asocial elements" such as homosexuals* and those called "habitual criminals," as well as Gypsies and Jews were among the thousands of people in the camps. From person to person and place to place, treatment might vary to some degree, but exhausting labor, punishment, poor food, filth, disease, and execution were all among the possible and persistent threats. Release from a concentration camp might occur, but when was as uncertain as death was likely.

Although all of the Nazi camps derived from the impulses and intentions that brought Dachau into existence, not every camp in the Nazi system was simply a *Konzentrationslager*. Especially after World War II began with the German invasion of Poland on September 1, 1939, different but still related institutions started to appear. There were, for example, labor camps, transit camps, prisoner-of-war camps, and, most destructive of all, extermination or death camps.

The Nazis violated human rights* in virtually every possible way, but no group received more inhumane treatment from them than the Jews. In the early years, however, relatively small numbers of Jews were interned in concentration camps such as Dachau and Buchenwald. Not until the summer of 1938, and especially after the *Kristallnacht* pogrom in November 1938, were large numbers of them imprisoned solely because they were Jews. Even then, most of these Jewish prisoners were eventually released after paying a ransom or proving that they were about to emigrate from Germany. Jewish fate, however, would change catastrophically with the outbreak of World War II.

Nazi ideology regarded Jews as the chief obstacle to the racial and cultural purity that Hitler craved for the Third Reich. Political opponents would have to be dealt with ruthlessly to ensure Nazi domination of Germany, but in the long run Nazi aims identified the Jews as an even more virulent threat. Their polluting presence, Hitler believed, would have to be eliminated.

Hitler's military conquests, especially in Eastern Europe, brought millions of Jews under German domination. What gradually evolved was a policy of mass murder—the Final Solution of the Jewish question. From late 1941 until late 1944, it was implemented most systematically by the gas chambers that operated at six death camps in occupied Poland: Chelmno, Belzec, Sobibor, Treblinka, Majdanek, and Auschwitz-Birkenau.

Dachau and the other early concentration camps on German soil were never death factories like Treblinka and Auschwitz-Birkenau. But the violations of human rights initiated at the first camps were part of wide-ranging aims to stamp out every element of dissent, difference, and diversity that stood in the way of Nazi domination. Concentration camps such as Dachau did damage enough to human rights, but they also helped to pave the way to camps that were even worse because they were specifically designed to remove unwanted lives, especially Jewish ones, by unrelenting mass murder.

See CONTROL COUNCIL LAW NO. 10; CRIMES AGAINST HUMANITY; HOLOCAUST, THE; INNOCENTS; PRISONERS OF WAR; TORTURE.
BIBLIOGRAPHY
Hilberg, Raul, *The Destruction of the European Jews,* 3 vols., revised and definitive ed. (New York: Holmes & Meier, 1985).
Krausnick, Helmut, Hans Buchheim, Martin Brozat, and Hans-Adolf Jacobsen, *Anatomy of the SS State,* Richard Barry, Marian Jackson, and Dorothy Long, trans. (New York: Walker & Co., 1968).

John K. Roth

CONSCIENTIOUS OBJECTION. The passive resistance to demands or coercive efforts to cause a person to act contrary to his or her conscience, and especially when this resistance is the refusal to fight in a war, to enter military service, or to perform noncombatant service in the armed forces. Such resistance is conscientious when refusals are based on appeals to conscience, that is, when defended by firmly held religious or ethical beliefs about the sinfulness or immorality of fighting, entering military service, or lending support to a war effort. Historically, such beliefs have been derived from religious or ethical principles that prohibit taking life or inflicting injury to advance national interests, or in defense of a state or international law, or even to protect those under attack, including self-defense. These principles may also prohibit the use of violence in efforts to end conflicts of any kind.

Conscientious objection is related logically to pacifism*, although commentators disagree over whether or not conscientious objection or a commitment to it is essential to pacifism. Thus, while conscientious objection involves a moral judgment against war, it also requires a personal commitment to refuse to participate in warfare if called upon. Because of this emphasis on personal responsibility, some commentators believe one's willingness to object conscientiously should be regarded as a necessary condition for recognizing a person's claim to be a pacifist. But willingness to object conscientiously cannot be a necessary condition for pacifism.

Obviously, while one cannot be simultaneously a conscientious objector (CO) and an antipacifist, the reverse need not follow. One may be a pacifist and yet never have occasion to refuse military service. Moreover, one may happily live under circumstances in which the probabilities of being called to participate personally in or to support a war are extremely low, thus never facing the need to form a commitment to conscientious objection. Even under such fortuitous circumstances, however, one might be a pacifist, when the latter is understood broadly as opposition to war as a means of settling disputes. All the same, a commitment to conscientious objection is surely a sound test of an individual pacifist's responsibility for his behavior in regard to war and violence, and therefore, might be helpful in distinguishing "principled" pacifism from pacifist positions based on pragmatic or consequentialist (utilitarian) considerations.

Also like pacifism, conscientious objection may be either absolute or conditional. The Shakers and the early Quakers exemplified the absolutist position in demanding unconditional exemption from military duties. Early Quakers believed that their obligation to follow conscience not only prohibited bearing arms but extended to bans against paying a war tax or *corvée* and to performing alternative services in the army. By contrast, early Mennonites exemplified a conditional approach to conscientious objection. While refusing to render direct military service, to perform noncombatant service in the army, and (usually) refusing to hire substitutes to take their place in the ranks, they did accept as legitimate the payment of "commutation money," as taxes and *corvées,* as well as services to alleviate suffering.

A right to exemption from military service as a CO has often been recognized by law. The right granted by William of Orange in 1575 to the Dutch Mennonites to make commutation payments in exchange for service is the first piece of legislation providing for conscientious objection. In the United States, conscientious objection has been permitted since the earliest days of the republic, although its regulation was left to the states until conscription became a matter of national concern and subject to congressional legislation.

The granting of CO status by various Selective Service Acts appears to be a major concession, given the state's traditional hostility to challenges to its right to use force. In point of fact, however, by treating COs as exemptions, allowing for exceptional piety and sectarian discipline, the state can avoid confronting any implicit challenge to its authority. The state can grant freedom of conscience without conceding that the justice or morality of its policies are being challenged. COs are thus seen as not condemning the state's war making, but only seeking personal exemption.

The development of so-called "selective conscientious objection," however, has challenged the state's ability to avoid moral censure implicit in conscientious refusals. Two varieties of selective conscientious objection exist: one arises from claims for CO status from persons not affiliated with traditional peace churches, the other arises from persons who press claims for CO status based on their objections to participating in or supporting particular wars. In the United States the government generally has been antagonistic to selective conscientious objection of the latter type but more tolerant of cases of the former kind.

Whereas the Selective Draft Act of 1917 conditioned exemption on membership in a traditional peace church, subsequent legislation in 1940 (reaffirmed in 1967) weakened the requirement for evidence of religious scruples to "religious belief and training" not tied to any particular denomination, as opposed to a "merely personal moral code." The Supreme Court further broadened eligibility in *United States v. Seeger* (1965) by suggesting that any "sincere belief" could be called religious if it "fills the same place" in the life of an individual as belief in God fills in the life of an orthodox Christian or Jew. At the same time, as in *Gillette v. United States* (1971), the Supreme Court continues to uphold the view that beliefs that "fill the same place" as belief in God do not include, in the words of the Selective Service Act (as amended in 1948), demands made for "essentially political, sociological, or philosophical" reasons. Hence, exemptions continue to be denied in cases that could be construed as political protests against the government's war making, generally the concern when petitioners profess conscientious reasons against participating in a particular war, for example, the Vietnam War*, although not in all wars. The Supreme Court's strategy in such cases is to refuse to recognize sincerity of conscience, questioning whether, as in *Gillette,* "the objector's beliefs are 'truly held.' "

In fact, conscientious objection has never impeded conscription*. Although American COs increased from approximately 4,000 during World War I to 50,000 in World War II, the number of men conscripted rose from just under three to thirteen million. Yet protests against the Vietnam War suggest that full acceptance of selective conscientious objection might make impossible the prosecution of some wars. However, moral as well as pragmatic reasons exist for restricting access to CO status, although the law need not deal so harshly with petitioners judged insincere. At stake is the justice of a system of government that must distribute burdens as well as benefits, and COs are freed from burdens other citizens are obliged to bear. It is legitimate, therefore, to define the class of "the conscientious" fairly narrowly, if this can be done in a manner consistent with the pluralistic values of democracy*.

Conscientious objection has a venerable history. Among the earliest recorded instances is the trial and execution of the Roman Christian, Maximilianus, in North Africa in A.D. 295 for refusing military service. Maxmilianus's heroic self-sacrifice was predated by Socrates's conscientious disobedience, as related by Plato in the *Apology,* and by the refusal, according to the Second Book of Moses, of the Hebrew midwives to obey the Pharaoh's order to kill all newborn male Jews, although the latter are examples of conscientious resistance to demands of authority other than demands for military service. Other well-known COs or advocates of conscientious refusal include the Roman Tertullian, Desiderius Erasmus, Sir Thomas More, Menno Simons, George Fox*, Quaker John Woolman, David L. Dodge*, Adin Ballou, William Lloyd Garrison, Leo Tolstoy, who was indispensable in arranging for the emigration from Czarist Russia of persecuted Dukhobors, Bertrand Russell, A. J. Muste*, Norman Thomas, Dorothy Day*, Franz Jagerstatter, executed in 1943 for refusing Hitler his military service, James Peck, Benjamin Spock, Daniel Berrigan, and Muslim theologian and leader, Ustadh Mahmoud Taha, executed by the Sudanese government in 1985.

See AYALA, BALTHAZAR; BELLI, PIERINO; BRITTAIN, VERA; DEBS, EUGENE; GANDHI, MOHANDAS; GROTIUS, HUGO; JUST WAR; KING, MARTIN LUTHER, JR.; PACIFISM; SUPERIOR ORDERS; VICTORIA, FRANCISCUS DE.

BIBLIOGRAPHY
Brock, Peter, *Pacifism in Europe to 1914* (Princeton, N.J.: Princeton University Press, 1972).
————, *Pacifism in the United States: From the Colonial Era to the First World War* (Princeton, N.J.: Princeton University Press, 1968).
————, *Twentieth-Century Pacifism* (New York: Van Nostrand Reinhold Company, 1970).
Mayer, Peter, ed., *The Pacifist Conscience* (New York: Holt, Rinehart & Winston, 1966).
Muste, A. J., *Of Holy Disobedience* (Wallingford, Pa.: Pendle Hill, 1952).
Noone, Michael, F., Jr., ed., *Selective Conscientious Objection* (Boulder, Colo.: Westview Press, 1989).
Schlissel, Lillian, ed., *Conscience in America* (New York: E. P. Dutton, 1968).
Sibley, Mulford Q., *The Obligation to Disobey* (New York: Council on Religion and International Affairs, 1970).
Tolstoy, Leo, *The Kingdom of God and Peace Essays* (New York: Oxford University Press, 1936).
Walzer, Michael, *Obligations: Essays on Disobedience, War and Citizenship* (New York: Simon & Schuster, 1970).
Zahn, Gordon C., *In Solitary Witness* (New York: Holt Rinehart & Winston, 1964).
————, *War, Conscience and Dissent* (New York: Hawthorn Books, 1967).

Robert Paul Churchill

CONSCRIPTION. The practice of involuntary recruitment for military service is an ancient one. In the first chapter of the Old Testament book of Numbers, Aaron and Moses registered and classified 603,550 men as able and obligated to fight. It should be noted, however, that those of the tribe of Levi were exempted for religious reasons, an early precursor of the religious option of conscientious objection*. The desirability of serving in the Roman legions precluded any necessity of drafting recruits. The 16th- and 17th-century jurists, Franciscus de Victoria* (1486–1546) and Hugo Grotius* (1583–1645), reported that it was customary for princes to call their subjects to arms. At the same time they reported that citizens occasionally refused on grounds that the war in question was unjust. Although granting both options, most jurists concluded that the call of the prince took precedence over conscience. Grotius suggested that both might be accommodated by levying a heavy tax on the objector as a test of his conviction. Normally there was no lack of willing recruits, since the life of a soldier was a vast improvement over the grinding poverty of the masses.

The British had a long history of resistance to military conscription, believing that it was incompatible with liberty. It was well into World War I before the

British resorted to conscription (January 5, 1916). Its first peacetime conscription was in April 1939, and although it continued through World War II, it was abolished in 1960. In the late 17th century British "press gangs" forced Americans into sea service, since volunteers failed to supply sufficient numbers. Although the practice ceased at the end of the Napoleonic Wars, it established an early American resistance to compulsion to military service, although the early Pilgrims and colonists assumed that all able-bodied men were obligated to come to the common defense. In 1645 a regulation ordered company commanders to appoint 30 percent of their companies to be ready on a half hour's notice for armed service. The Continental Congress on July 18, 1775, recommended that all able-bodied men between the ages of sixteen and fifty be formed into companies of militia. Although militias were formed in several colonies, no conscription was ever issued. George Washington proposed a registration and classification of all men between eighteen and twenty-five, but the first Congress failed to issue such a law. There was much resistance to the draft, expressed in desertion and mutiny. Indeed, during the Revolutionary War the initial recruitment effort to get 700 men for the 1st Regiment was unsuccessful. The hope for bounty was a major incentive to many who did sign up. Congress on May 8, 1792 issued an act to provide for the national defense by establishing a uniform militia in which every able-bodied male of eighteen would be enrolled. This law stayed on the books for 111 years.

Daniel Webster spoke so eloquently in the House of Representatives against conscription that he defeated the 1814 legislation that proposed to draft all males between the ages of eighteen and forty-five. While the Confederate Congress adopted a conscription act, the Northern armies failed to do so until an enrollment act of 1863, which provided for a draft for three years. Brigadier General James Oakes wrote a report of his administration of the act, which served as a model for the new law of 1940. The act provoked riots, and between 1863 and 1874 there were sixteen major and numerous minor riots in New York alone.

The Spanish-American War was fought with volunteers. In 1903 the act of 1863 was repealed with a new act whereby every able-bodied male aged eighteen to forty-five was subject to call by the president for a period not to exceed nine months. In May 1917 a selective service act was enacted and nearly three million men were inducted. Senator William E. Borah (R-ID) spoke on September 28, 1917 against conscription because it was against the "essential principles of free institutions." On June 4, 1920, the Army General Staff prepared a plan for peacetime mobilization, and in 1926 the Joint Army and Navy Selective Service Committee was established to prepare a selective service act. The act was established September 20, 1940, and during World War II, of the 14.6 million who served in the military, ten million came from the draft. This act was terminated in 1947 and was succeeded by the Office of Selective Service Records. In 1949 the Selective Service Act was passed for a two-year period. Inductions of a small number of men continued until 1949, after which registration and classification continued. In June 1950 the law was extended until

July 1951. A new law on drafting men for the armed forces extended the selective service to July 1955. The new term of service was for twenty-four months. No one below age nineteen would be drafted unless there were no more available between ages nineteen and twenty-five. Both mental and physical requirements were lowered. In 1963 the act was extended four years and again in July 1967, when its name was changed to the Military Selective Service Act, it was extended until 1971. Resistance to the draft was particularly strong during the Vietnam War*. Inductions under the draft ended in December 1972. Currently (1994) every male when he reaches the age of eighteen must register for military service within thirty days prior to or twenty-nine days after his birthday, although none are inducted.

   See CONSCIENTIOUS OBJECTION; MILITARISM; PACIFISM.

BIBLIOGRAPHY

Anderson, Martin, *Conscription: A Select and Annotated Bibliography* (Stanford, Calif.: Stanford University Press, 1976).

Jacobs, Clyde E., and John F. Gallagher, *The Selective Service Act: A Case Study of the Governmental Process* (New York: Dodd, Mead, 1967).

Johnson, Julia Emily, *Peacetime Conscription* (New York: H. W. Wilson, 1945).

Moscos, Charles C., *A Case for Civic Service* (New York: Council for National Service, 1988).

CONTROL COUNCIL LAW NO. 10. Churchill, Roosevelt, and Stalin agreed at the Yalta Conference, February 1945, to the idea of separate zones of influence where the major Allies would conduct war crimes trials. The Americans on December 20, 1945 issued Council Control Law No. 10 to provide for the trials, in their zone of influence, of those Germans whose crimes had been committed in a specific country. The law cited as precedent the Moscow Declaration* of October 30, 1943, "Concerning Responsibility of Hitlerites for Committed Atrocities," and the London Agreement* of August 8, 1945, "Concerning Prosecution and Punishment of Major War Criminals of the European Axis." The European theater was divided into zones under the authority of one of the major Allies: the United States, Great Britain, the Soviet Union, and France. Each zone commander had power to determine the makeup of the courts in his jurisdiction. Acting under the provisions of this law the United States issued Military Government Ordinance No. 7, which provided that the trials conducted by the United States would consist of tribunals with three members and one alternate. Every member of a tribunal in an American zone would be a civilian lawyer from the United States. In addition to the twelve American cases there were eighty-four others prosecuted by Allied countries. The United Nations War Crimes Commission analyzed all eighty-four cases as well as five of those conducted by the United States. For example, the British conducted the Essen Lynching Case in 1945, the Zyklon B Case* in 1946, the Belsen Case in 1945, the trial of General von Falkenhorst in 1946, and the trial of Kesselring in 1947. The Australians conducted the Ohashi trial in 1946; the Netherlands conducted the trial of Susuki Motisuki in 1948 and the trial of Willy Zuehlke in 1948; the French conducted the trial of Bauer, Schrameck, and Falten in 1945, and the trial of Franz Holstein and others. Poland conducted the Hoess trial in 1947.

The United States conducted an initial twelve trials under Control Council Law No. 10. There were 185 persons indicted and, of these, 177 were tried. These trials are documented in *Trials of War Criminals Before the Nuernberg Military Tribunals Under Control Council Law No. 10* and the summation reported in Telford Taylor, *Final Report to the Secretary of the Army on the Nuernberg War Crimes Trials Under Control Council Law No. 10.* With one exception, the Milch Case, all trials involved more than one accused.

The cases were named as follows:

Einsatsgruppen (United States v. Otto Ohlendorf et al.). July 3, 1947–April 10, 1948. Twenty-three officers of the "mobile killing units" of the SS Elite Guard who were in charge of the murder of two million people were indicted, and of the twenty-two tried, thirteen were given the death sentence. Six of these were commuted to life imprisonment or less; one was sentenced to ten years and one was sentenced to twenty years, although all the sentences were commuted to time served.

Medical (United States v. Brandt et al.). October 25, 1946–August 20, 1947. Twenty-four were charged with performing medical experiments on concentration camp inmates and others. Of these, eight were acquitted, seven received the death sentence, and five were given life sentences, all of which were commuted to lesser sentences.

Pohl (United States v. Pohl et al.). January 13, 1947–December 3, 1947. Eighteen were charged with the administration of the concentration camps and/ or with conducting slave labor under the *Schutzstaffel* (SS).

Hostage (United States v. Wilhelm List et al.). May 10, 1947–February 19, 1948. Twelve generals assigned to Eastern Europe were charged with criminal disregard for the rules respecting the treatment of hostages* and civilians; and of these, ten were tried and eight were found guilty, with two serving life and the rest serving lesser prison sentences.

High Command (United States v. Wilhelm von Leeb et al.). November 28, 1947–October 28, 1948. Fourteen were tried, all of whom had held command positions, charged with ordering the killing and mistreatment of prisoners* and with deporting or abusing civilians. The maximum sentence was eighteen years.

RuSHA (United States v. Ulrich Greifelt et al.). July 1, 1947–March 10, 1948. Fourteen high officials in the Race and Settlement Office of the SS Elite Guard were charged with carrying out genocide*. One received a life sentence; for the rest the maximum sentence was eighteen years.

Ministries-Wilhelmstrasse (United States v. Ernst von Weizsacker et al.). November 4, 1947–April 13, 1949. The case charged nineteen defendants with playing an important part in the political and diplomatic preparation for war, violation of international treaties, economic spoliation, and participation in the extermination program. None received a sentence greater than ten years.

I. G. Farben (United States v. Carl Krauch et al.). May 3, 1947–July 30, 1947. Twenty-four leaders of the I. G. Farben Company were charged with spoliation of property in occupied countries and with participation in the slave labor program. None received a sentence greater than eight years, and ten were acquitted.

Krupp (United States v. Alfred Krupp et al.). August 16, 1947–July 31, 1948. Originally, twelve executives of Krupp industries were charged with spoliation and the use of slave labor. All had their sentences commuted to time served.

Flick—the "Business Men Case" (United States v. Friedrich Flick et al.). February 8, 1947–December 22, 1947. Six were charged with criminal conduct with relation to spoliation of property in occupied France and the Soviet Union, using slave labor, and the "Aryanization" of Jewish properties. Three were acquitted, and of the three remaining, the maximum sentence was seven years.

Milch (United States v. Erhard Milch). November 13, 1946–April 17, 1947. Milch had been tried and acquitted in the Medical Case*, but in the new case he was found guilty of exploitation of slave labor and making medical experiments on concentration camp inmates. His sentence of life imprisonment was commuted to fifteen years.

Justice (United States v. Josef Altstotter et al.). January 4, 1947–December 4, 1947. The case charged sixteen defendants with war crimes* and crimes against humanity* through the abuse of both the judicial process and the administration of justice. Four were given life sentences, although one was given a medical parole, and the sentences of the other three were commuted to twenty years; three were commuted to time served; one received seven years; and Altstotter received five years.

The trials posed special legal problems. Proportionality* was especially ambiguous. Were troops normally trained to use minimum force or were they trained in line with Clausewitz* to use maximum force as soon as possible? In the *Trial of Wilhelm List and Others,* the tribunal ruled that the Germans behaved excessively when they killed fifty to 100 Communists for every German soldier slain during the occupation. Yet the tribunal left unanswered what a proper number might have been, although the impression left was that there was an acceptable number. The same issue arose in the *Trial of Franz Holstein,* in which Germans were accused of burning three farms for every German soldier slain by the residents, and one farm for every German soldier wounded. In the *Trial of General Lanz* in Greece, the court determined that he was guilty of having issued an excessive reprisal* order to acts of sabotage of the underwater cable. Ten Greeks had been shot for each such act. Was there a proper number? In the cases of the extermination camps, however, the judges rejected any notion that there would have been a "proper" number to kill.

Care was taken to allow all evidence to be presented by the accused. For example, in the *Pohl* case the court met for 101 sessions on different days, 1,356 documents were received in evidence, and the entire record of the case covered more than 9,000 pages. In the *Flick* case the court met five days a week for six months, exclusive of recesses, and the record consisted of 10,343 pages. The transcript of the record in the *High Command* case contained 10,000 pages. Paradoxically, many of the complaints about the trials under Control Council No. 10 were summed up by August von Knierem, general counsel for I. G. Farben. Von Knierem had himself been charged at Nuremberg but was found innocent and acquitted. He summarized the dominant German position by asserting that Control Council Law No. 10 was based on ex post facto laws; that, contrary to Allied claims, this law contained new laws not found in past tradition, notably that individuals could be tried for obeying military orders; and that it was a violation of international law not to conduct the trials by courts of the land and to use Anglo-American legal procedures. The fact that no sentence could be appealed was also legally troubling.

No accurate reports exist of the exact number of such trials conducted since the end of World War II, most of which were not strictly based on the Nuremberg* precedent. As late as January 1961, West Germany averaged one trial every three weeks. By June 1973, 6,330 persons had been convicted in West Germany. On January 13, 1961, a Warsaw court sentenced an accused for crimes committed during the occupation. The Soviets convicted about 10,000, most of whom received twenty-five-year prison sentences. By 1973 the Soviet Union had sentenced to death forty-two of its own citizens. The Israelis sentenced and executed Adolf Eichmann in December 1961.

When the United States passed the Displaced Persons Act in 1948 the doors were opened for former Nazis to enter the United States. Although that law forbade ex-Nazis, no formal apparatus existed to determine who had been a Nazi, and furthermore the United States was in the throes of its anti-Communist purges. It was well known that Nazis were firm anti-Communists, and any immigrant who was an avowed anti-Communist was admitted with few questions asked. The U.S. Department of Justice established an Office for Special Investigations to endeavor to discover Nazis living in the United States who may have been involved in war crimes. Between 1946 and 1973 the Immigration and Naturalization Service (INS) received allegations against fifty-seven former Nazis living in the United States. Only nine of these were pursued to the point of filing charges. Since the United States had no jurisdiction to try anyone for former war crimes, the only step that could be taken by the INS was to deport them. Eleven of the fifty-seven had their citizenship taken away, but only one, Ferenc Vajta, was actually deported. He was invited to Bogota, Colombia, where he served as an economics professor at a small Catholic university. Although eleven Nazis living in America were denaturalized, the problem was to get a nation that would accept them. During the Reagan administration the United States extradited Karl Linnas to the Soviet Union and John Demjanjuk to Israel to stand trial for wartime offenses. At Dachau, to mention only one of the camps where trials were held, the U.S. military commission tried 1,672 accused Nazis, and convicted 1,416 of them. John Alan Appleman, a legal historian, estimated that up to January 1949, exclusive of trials in the USSR, there were 2,116 known hearings conducted by the United States, Great Britain, Australia, France, The Netherlands, Poland, Norway, Canada, China, and Greece. Of the total trials, 950 were conducted by the United States (500 in Europe and 450 in the Far East). Although war crimes were declared by the UN General Assembly, November 26, 1968, to have no statute of limitations, the vote of 58 yea, 7 nay, and 36 abstentions indicated little support. No Western states, including those in the anti-Nazi coalition, voted in support. Only three Latin American states (Chile, Cuba, and Mexico) voted affirmatively. Fear was expressed that such a statute would erode traditional human rights, and, in addition, it was unclear how heinous the offenses needed to be before any proposed statute of limitations should be waived. The United States has no statute of limitations for murder.

There has been little investigation as to what happened to all these convicted war criminals. A study by Frank M. Buscher (1989) of the *Einsatzgruppen* trial may be taken as typical. Fourteen of the twenty-one accused were given the death penalty, but only four were actually executed. John J. McCloy, the U.S. High Commissioner, commuted the remaining death sentences to life or term sentences, and by the fall of 1958 all had been released from prison. Indeed, by the late summer of 1958, the last inmate of the American prison for war criminals, at Landsberg, had been released.

See CASUALTIES OF WAR; CHILDREN AND WAR; COUNTERFORCE VERSUS COUNTERVALUE; NUREMBERG TRIALS; PRISONERS OF WAR; TOKYO TRIALS.

BIBLIOGRAPHY
Appleman, John Alan, *Military Tribunals and International Crimes* (Westport, Conn.: Greenwood Press, 1971).
Buscher, Frank M., *The U.S. War Crimes Trial Program in Germany, 1946–1955* (Westport, Conn.: Greenwood Press, 1989).
Jackson, Robert H., *The Case Against the Nazi War Criminals* (New York: Alfred Knopf, 1946).
Taylor, Telford, *Final Report to the Secretary of the Army on the Nuernberg War Crimes Trials Under Control Council Law No. 10* (Washington, D.C.: U.S. Government Printing Office, 1949).
Trials of War Criminals Before the Nuernberg Military Tribunals Under Control Council Law No. 10 (Washington, D.C.: U.S. Government Printing Office, 1949).
Tutorow, Norman E., *War Crimes, War Criminals, and War Crimes Trials* (Westport, Conn.: Greenwood Press, 1986).
Wells, Donald A., *War Crimes and Laws of War* (Lanham, Md.: University Press of America, 1984, 1991).

COUNTERFORCE VERSUS COUNTERVALUE. These terms refer to ways of using military force, primarily nuclear force, and, derivatively, and more frequently, to forms of military deterrence, especially nuclear deterrence*. In the case of counterforce or countervalue deterrence, the question is what kinds of threats of military force are involved. The two terms refer to the object of military force, that is, to the kind of target at which the weapons are fired or against which their use is threatened. In the case of counterforce, the weapons are fired on or their use is threatened against military targets, while in the case of countervalue, the weapons are fired on or their use is threatened against civilian targets. Civilian targets, which include population centers, production capabilities, and social infrastructure generally, are referred to as *countervalue* because they are what is of greatest value to the society in question. Most use of military force is counterforce, but countervalue use has been part of warfare since its inception. Armies through history have frequently burnt crops, looted, laid siege* to cities, and terrorized civilian populations in a variety of ways. But the possibilities for countervalue destruction have grown by several orders of magnitude with the advent of nuclear weapons, since these weapons are so fantastically destructive and easily deliverable against an opponent's society. This discussion will be restricted to counterforce and countervalue in the nuclear context.

Early in the nuclear age, after the invention of the hydrogen bomb, nuclear weapons were very powerful and the means of delivery, bombers and later missiles, were not very accurate. As a result, nuclear weapons were very good for blowing up cities, as the bombings of Hiroshima and Nagasaki* indicate, because only one bomb was necessary and a high level of accuracy was not required. But they were not very good for blowing up military targets, which were often resistant to all but a close hit. So, in the early phases of the Cold War*, nuclear threats—threats of nuclear retaliation—were, of necessity, primarily countervalue threats. This became embodied in the nuclear weapons policy, adopted by the United States in the mid 1950s, known as massive retaliation. Nuclear deterrence was primarily countervalue deterrence. But, as delivery systems became much more accurate through the 1960s and 1970s, a counterforce use of nuclear weapons became more feasible, and consequently there was a shift toward counterforce deterrence. The emerging policy of counterforce deterrence was known, on the U.S. side, by a variety of names, such as graduated deterrence, flexible response, selective options, and countervailing strategy.

The important historical point, however, is that counterforce deterrence never replaced countervalue deterrence, but rather was simply added to it. Even as the developing technology of weapons manufacture and delivery allowed more sophisticated counterforce threats to be made, the ultimate countervalue threat of societal destruction was always there in the background as something each side in the Cold War threatened against the other, as embodied in the notion of mutual assured destruction* (MAD). Thus, what the United States and the Soviet Union practiced through most of the Cold War was a strategy of nuclear deterrence that was mixed—neither purely counterforce nor purely countervalue. It was what could be called an impure counterforce strategy. What was practiced in the first part of the Cold War was close to being a pure countervalue deterrence strategy. A pure counterforce deterrence strategy was never practiced, and there were perhaps insurmountable obstacles to implementing such a strategy.

Thus, as we turn to a moral evaluation of the strategies, one relevant to the real world, what we should compare are countervalue strategy and impure counterforce strategy. Which of these two strategies is morally preferable? Proponents of counterforce strategy argue that their strategy is morally better because: (a) it is more effective and hence lessens the likelihood of war and aggression*; and (b) it respects the just war* principle of discrimination, while countervalue strategy does not. We must consider each of these arguments in turn.

Regarding (a), the truth of the claim that a counterforce strategy is more effective as a nuclear deterrent than a countervalue strategy turns on the prospects for limited nuclear war. A countervalue nuclear war would likely be an ''all-out'' nuclear war, the kind in which whole societies would be destroyed and in which civilization or even the human species itself could be at risk. In contrast, a counterforce nuclear war, because it would involve attacks exclusively against military targets, would, however great the amount of destruction, be a limited nuclear war, in the sense that cities would largely be spared. So, one question raised by counterforce deterrence strategy is whether a limited nuclear war is possible, that is, whether it is at all reasonable to expect that a nuclear war, begun in a limited, counterforce way, would stay limited. This is a matter of controversy. The argument that a nuclear war is not likely to remain limited is based on two characteristics of nuclear war. First, there is a ''logic of escalation'' in war, which would induce leaders to raise the stakes in a nuclear war in an effort to get the opponent to back down. Second, the environment created by a nuclear war would make escalation hard to control. Leaders, under extreme pressure, would have to make decisions in a very short period of time in the absence of reliable information about what was going on in the war, and the systems by which they command the nuclear forces are fragile and likely to be disrupted. In the face of such factors, things are likely to get out of hand and a limited nuclear war become unlimited. On the other hand, those who believe that a nuclear war would likely stay limited argue that the stakes would be so high that all parties would behave with extreme caution.

The question of limited nuclear war is tied in with the question of the credibility of the nuclear threat. If a threat is to be effective at deterring an opponent, it must be credible, that is, the opponent must believe that the threatener would be likely to carry out the threat. Proponents of counterforce strategy argue that this kind of strategy is more effective than countervalue strategy because counterforce strategy is more credible. They reason that the threat of countervalue retaliation is credible only if the aggression to be avoided is itself a countervalue attack. It is not credible that a nation would retaliate against the opponent's cities if its own cities had not already been attacked, because otherwise such retaliation would bring about such an attack. For example, would the United States have used nuclear weapons against Soviet cities in retaliation for a Soviet attack against Western Europe, given that the Soviet Union would likely then have retaliated against U.S. cities? So, countervalue threats cannot be effective at deterring lesser forms of aggression, while counterforce threats can, because counterforce retaliation would not bring about counterattacks on cities. But this argument makes sense only if a nuclear war is likely to stay limited, because otherwise the end result would be countervalue destruction. So, if the argument against the likelihood of limited nuclear war is sound, the argument for (a), that counterforce strategy is more effective than countervalue strategy, is unsound.

Now, considering (b), the argument is that counterforce strategy is morally better because it respects the important just war principle of discrimination, while countervalue strategy does not. The principle of discrimination requires that military force not be used against civilian targets, and it is widely understood to also preclude threats against civilian targets, because such threats involve the intention* to attack those targets should the threats fail to deter. On this understanding, it is clear that countervalue strategy violates the principle of discrimination. But counterforce strategy also does, for, as discussed above, counterforce strategy, as practiced, is in fact a mixed strategy, involving both countervalue and counterforce threats. Moreover, if counterforce strategy is not more effective than countervalue strategy, it does not make war less likely, so it cannot even promise to make it less likely that civilian damage will occur. So, there is little reason to hold that counterforce strategy is morally preferable to countervalue strategy.

Two questions remain. First, is countervalue strategy, then, morally preferable to counterforce strategy? Many argue that it is, because it is more effective than counterforce strategy. This argument turns on the notion of crisis stability, which is the likelihood that a strategy will lead to war in the midst of a crisis* between nuclear opponents. Countervalue strategy, it is argued, has a higher level of crisis stability than counterforce strategy, which implies that war is less likely under a countervalue strategy than under a counterforce strategy. This means that countervalue strategy is more effective at deterring war. The second question is whether either countervalue or counterforce strategy is morally justifiable. Even if countervalue strategy is morally preferable to counterforce strategy (or vice versa), this does not mean that either strategy is morally justifiable. Analogously, assault may be morally preferable to murder, but that does not mean that either is morally justifiable. The fact that both counterforce and countervalue strategies violate the principle of discrimination suggests that neither of them is morally justifiable. At this point, it is of interest to bring back into the discussion pure counterforce strategy, even though it has not been and perhaps could not be practiced. If pure counterforce strategy could be practiced, it would not violate the principle of discrimination, but it would be highly ineffective in comparison with either countervalue or impure counterforce strategy. This reveals one of the moral paradoxes of nuclear deterrence: the only form of nuclear deterrence that could be morally justifiable in terms of respect for the principle of discrimination is morally unacceptable on the ground that it would be ineffective, and hence much more likely to lead to war than other strategies would.

See AERIAL WARFARE; COLLATERAL DAMAGE; FIRST STRIKE/ SECOND STRIKE; MASS DESTRUCTION, WEAPONS OF; TOTAL WAR.

BIBLIOGRAPHY

Freedman, Lawrence, *The Evolution of Nuclear Strategy* (New York: St. Martin's, 1981).

Glaser, Charles, *Analyzing Strategic Nuclear Policy* (Princeton, N.J.: Princeton University Press, 1990).

Jervis, Robert, *The Illogic of American Nuclear Strategy* (Ithaca, N.Y.: Cornell University Press, 1984).

Lee, Steven, *Morality, Prudence, and Nuclear Weapons* (Cambridge: Cambridge University Press, 1993).

Steven Lee

CRIMES AGAINST HUMANITY. Used loosely, a crime against humanity is any indiscriminate killing, torture*, or other widespread brutality and persecution by the officers of a government against its own people or foreigners (enemy noncombatants, resident aliens, etc.). Used more precisely, the term *crimes against humanity* emerged during World War II as an important category to describe the criminal activity of Nazi Germany between 1939 and 1945. For example, in a speech in 1944, President Franklin Delano Roosevelt declared that "Hitler is committing crimes against humanity in the name of the German people," including "systematic torture and murder of civilians—men, women, and children," and "the wholesale and systematic murder of the Jews of Europe."

Earlier anticipations of the concept can be found in the second (1899) and fourth (1907) Hague Conventions*, where reference is made in the preamble to violations of "the laws of humanity." In 1915 the governments of France, Great Britain, and Russia described the massacres of Armenians in eastern Turkey as "crimes against humanity and civilization." In 1919, in the report at Versailles of the Commission on Responsibilities of the victorious powers at the end of World War I, Germany and its allies were condemned for "barbarous or illegitimate methods" in conducting warfare, which violated "the elementary laws of humanity." The U.S. representative on the commission, however, objected to such language on the ground, among others, that "the laws and principles of humanity are not certain. . . . There is no fixed and universal standard of humanity."

It was not until the Nuremberg Trials* of the major Nazi war criminals in 1945, at the end of World War II in Europe, that the concept was given a permanent and explicit place in international law and the protection of human rights*, and defined in contrast to crimes of war* and crimes against peace*. Count 4 of the Charter of the International Military Tribunal charged the twenty-two Nazi defendants with "crimes against humanity," and all but six were convicted on this charge. The Nuremberg Principles*, as announced in 1946, defined the term in Principle VI.c: "Crimes against humanity" include "Murder, extermination, enslavement, deportation, and other inhuman acts done against any civilian population, or persecution on political, racial or religious grounds, when such acts are done or such persecutions are carried out in execution of or in connection with any crime against peace or any war crime.'' (In later usage, the necessity of concurrent crimes against the peace or war crimes was deleted.) As interpreted by the International Military Tribunal at Nuremberg, however, crimes against humanity were limited to grave crimes committed on a mass scale; persecution as such counted as a crime against humanity only if it involved atrocious inhumane acts. Telford Taylor, U.S. chief of counsel for war crimes, summarized the idea in 1949 when he said that ''the concept of 'crimes against humanity' comprises atrocities which are part of a campaign of discrimination or persecution.''

Conspicuously absent from the language used to formulate and define crimes against humanity in 1945 was any reference to genocide*. Although this term did appear in the indictments against the Nazi war criminals tried at Nuremberg, it does not appear in the final judgment. In 1946 in a war crimes trial held in Poland, the prosecutor charged the defendant Nazi with genocide, understood to be a crime against humanity. The term is defined in international law by the Convention on the Prevention and Punishment of Genocide (adopted by the General Assembly of the United Nations in 1948, in force since 1961, but not ratified by the United States until 1988). According to this convention, genocide is ''any of the following acts committed with intent to destroy, in whole or in part, a national, ethnical, racial or religious group;'' the acts in question include ''killing members of the group,'' causing them ''serious bodily or mental harm,'' ''deliberately inflicting . . . conditions of life calculated to bring about . . . physical destruction in whole or in part'' of the group, ''imposing measures intended to prevent births within the group,'' or ''forcibly transferring children of the group to another group.'' Genocide thus differs from other crimes against humanity in that it involves intentional action that targets a definable group as the victims of criminal acts. So defined, the concept of genocide overlaps, and can be seen as a natural development from, the concept of crimes against humanity.

In 1961, the ex-Nazi officer Adolf Eichmann was charged both with the crime of genocide and with other crimes against humanity. Eichmann was well known for his role in ''the final solution''—the Nazi euphemism for expulsion and extermination of European Jewry—but he had escaped capture and trial until he was located by Israeli agents in Argentina and taken to Israel for trial before Israeli judges. The first four counts against Eichmann concerned crimes ''against the Jewish people'' and were thus equivalent to a charge of genocide. The next seven counts charged him with various ''crimes against humanity,'' whose victims included Poles, Slovenes, Gypsies, Czechs, as well as Jews. He was convicted on all these charges (as well as others), sentenced to death, and executed in 1962.

In 1966, the General Assembly of the United Nations declared that policies of racial discrimination and segregation practiced in Rhodesia were crimes against humanity. The system of Apartheid in South Africa and in Southwest

Africa were similarly described by the General Assembly. In 1970 statutes of limitation for trial of charges of crimes against humanity were declared void by virtue of an international convention. (However, as of 1992, no Western nation had signed or ratified this convention.) In 1989 the General Assembly of the Organization of American States declared involuntary disappearances to be crimes against humanity.

In the years since the end of World War II, attention has focused not only on conceptual and normative issues associated with crimes against humanity, but also on political and empirical issues: Have certain governments (or their officials) committed crimes against humanity? What can be done to prevent such crimes, or at least to judge and punish the offenders? Despite widespread accusation by individuals, groups, and various nongovernmental human rights organizations against governments in several nations during these years (for instance, in Afghanistan, Kampuchea, El Salvador, East Germany, East Timor, Iraq, Kurdistan, Rwanda, and Sudan), no governmental tribunals, either national, multinational, or created by the United Nations, have been created to address such questions. The sole exception is the action taken by the United Nations to create a tribunal to evaluate charges of atrocities by the Serbs committed in Bosnia in the early 1990s.

Twenty-five years earlier, charges against the United States for war crimes, crimes against humanity, and genocide in Vietnam were heard by a nongovernmental International War Crimes Tribunal convened in Stockholm*; this was followed by further hearings in 1971 before the International Commission of Inquiry into United States Crimes in Indochina, convened in Oslo. Both organizations judged the United States guilty as charged. No acknowledgement of any authority to render such judgments was granted by the U.S. government.

Thus, in the half-century since crimes against humanity were first explicitly identified and incorporated into international law, nations and their governments, whether acting in concert or through regional or international bodies, have not proved to be generally capable either of preventing or responding with appropriate punishment to those who commit such crimes.

See CHILDREN AND WAR; COMBATANT-NONCOMBATANT DISTINCTION; GENOCIDE; HAGUE, THE, CONGRESSES; LEIPZIG TRIALS; NUREMBERG TRIALS; STOCKHOLM/ROTHSKILDE WAR CRIMES TRIAL.

BIBLIOGRAPHY

Bassiouni, M. Cherif, *Crimes Against Humanity in International Criminal Law* (Dordrecht: Nijhoff, 1992).

Ferencz, Benjamin B., "Crimes Against Humanity," *Encyclopedia of Public International Law* 8 (1985), 107–9.

Goldenberg, Sydney L. "Crimes Against Humanity: 1945–1970," *Western Ontario Law Review* 10 (1971), 1–55.

Kuper, Leo, *Genocide: Its Political Use in the Twentieth Century* (New Haven, Conn.: Yale University Press, 1981).

Miller, Robert H., "The Convention on the Non-Applicability of Statutes of Limitations to War Crimes and Crimes Against Humanity," *American Journal of International Law* 65 (July 1971), 476–501.

Orentlicher, Diane F., "Settling Accounts: The Duty to Prosecute Human Rights Violations of a Prior Regime," *Yale Law Journal* 100 (June 1991), 2537–2615.

Schwelb, Egon, "Crimes Against Humanity," *British Yearbook of International Law* 23 (1946), 178–226.

Sunga, Lyal S., *Individual Responsibility in International Law for Serious Human Rights Violations* (Dordrecht: Nijhoff, 1992).

Hugo Adam Bedau

CRISIS THEORY. Episodes in which elites deem it essential to hazard urgent, perilous decisions that increase the danger of war concern students of ethics and warfare because they:

1. provide a window though which we can observe the actual values that guide decision makers when they feel compelled to decide between peace and war

2. mark the transition between peace and war. (To paraphrase Clausewitz, wars are the continuation of crises by other means.) Accordingly, both political actors and analysts prescribe crisis prevention as an overarching imperative

3. will likely remain a prominent and dangerous feature of international life. Accordingly, both political actors and analysts are concerned with what is morally permissible in crisis management

Considerable speculation exists as to what values inform decisions at critical junctures. Crises offer insight into the actual values that guide decisions about war and peace. Two issues arise:

1. Do crises bring out the best in decision makers? Do these harrowing episodes enhance or impair an official's cognitive ability and moral sensibility?

2. Although some consensus exists regarding the factual aspects of crises, evaluating these facts is controversial.

Presidents such as John F. Kennedy and Richard M. Nixon viewed crises as epiphanies that revealed a leader's qualities and destiny. Kennedy's texts narrated what he regarded as the almost superhuman courage and intelligence that various leaders mustered at critical junctures. Reflecting upon the six crises that marked his early career, Nixon observed: "Only then [in crises] does he discover all the latent strengths he never knew he had and which otherwise would have remained dormant." Others were more concerned by the inherent danger. For example, Robert Kennedy commented on the Cuban Missile Crisis: "this kind of pressure does strange things . . . even to brilliant, self-confident, mature, experienced men. For some it brings out . . . strengths they never knew they had, and for others the pressure is too overwhelming." And, summarizing the literature on Cold War crises, political analyst Ole Holsti argued that intense and protracted crises erode decision makers' cognitive acumen and moral sensibilities.

Turning to our second concern, agreement exists regarding the empirical dimensions of crises (e.g., the decisions made and the outcome), but the facts do not speak for themselves. Normative evaluation of the facts remains controversial. Examples from the Dwight D. Eisenhower and Kennedy administrations are illustrative. The evidence suggests that Eisenhower deemed war-prevention imperative. Many biographers endorsed Henry Kissinger's view that he was a "President who was passionately opposed to war in the way only an experienced military man can be." In 1954, after the French defeat in Indochina, Eisenhower resisted the pressure of allies and advisors, and decided against significant American intervention. Likewise, when the Egyptians nationalized the Suez Canal in 1957, he rejected proposals for military action lest the United States become embroiled in war with the Soviet Union. Rather than defining the situation as an acute crisis demanding immediate risk taking, he construed the challenge as a chronic problem to be resolved patiently and diplomatically in due course.

Increasing numbers of historians have lauded Eisenhower for his restraint. However, most members of the Kennedy administration criticized Eisenhower for his reluctance to project American power and resolve. Critics such as Kissinger reiterated such criticisms. It appears that Kennedy took serious risks in his attempt to influence the course of events. During his abbreviated administration, he risked nuclear war to resolve crises in Germany and Cuba. The propriety of such actions was contested, even among members of his administration. Dean Acheson attributed the successful resolution of the Cuban Missile Crisis to "plain dumb luck," while Theodore Sorensen lauded Kennedy's "carefully calibrated, intelligent" management.

Given the frequency of crises and the lethality of modern war, a variety of political actors and analysts have urged that crisis prevention is the *summum bonum* of international politics. Reflecting upon the Cuban Missile Crisis, Dean Rusk admonished that "we have to do what we can to prevent such crises . . . because they're just too damn dangerous." Analysts such as Alexander George recommended a series of organizational and communication strategies to reduce the likelihood of crises. Crisis discourse has become the *lingua franca* of international relations, and decision makers should resist the temptation to interpret unanticipated, ambiguous events as crises. This temptation is difficult to resist, since a "crisis" is a conceptual strategy for rendering the vagaries of international life intelligible and dramatically self-validating.

Some have claimed that the ideal of crisis prevention is unrealistic, since crises are inevitable. Contrary evidence suggests that the same event may be interpreted differently—one official's crisis may be another's mere problem. Colin Powell declared that he faced twelve crises during his tenure as chairman of the joint chiefs, and he was confident that a thirteenth crisis "out there" was waiting to happen. His fatalism was shared by those who presupposed that since crises were inevitable, they were not morally responsible for these episodes. For these fatalists, crises cannot be prevented, they can only be managed prudently.

In Robert McNamara's words, "There is no more diplomacy, just crisis management."

Whether a crisis is a concept or a thing, future crises are likely. Therefore, crisis management is an overarching concern. What is morally permissible in management strategy is contested. Pacifists argue that war should never be risked, while war is an option for advocates of *realpolitik*. Robert Kennedy was concerned about the propriety of risking nuclear war to resolve a crisis. Robert McNamara was once willing to hazard such risks, but recently recanted.

In sum, crises evoke moral ambivalence. They are seen as the supreme test of national leadership and character, or as decidedly dangerous episodes that must be prevented or managed with great restraint.

See ACCIDENTAL NUCLEAR WAR; CAUSES OF WAR; COLD WAR; CUBAN MISSILE CRISIS; DEMOCRACY AND THE MILITARY; LOW-INTENSITY CONFLICT; MILITARISM; WARISM.

BIBLIOGRAPHY

Ambrose, Stephen, *Nixon: The Triumph of a Politician* (New York: Simon & Schuster, 1989).

Betts, Richard, *Nuclear Blackmail* (Washington, D.C.: Brookings Institution, 1989).

George, Alexander, *Managing U.S.-Soviet Rivalry* (Boulder, Colo.: Westview Press, 1983).

Hirschbein, Ron, "What If They Cave a Crisis and Nobody Came?" in Joseph Kunkel, ed., *In the Interest of Peace* (Wolfsboro, N.H.: Longwood Press, 1991).

Holsti, Ole, "Crisis Decision Making," in *Behavior, Society and Nuclear War,* vol. 1, Philip Tetlock, Jo Husbands et al., eds. (Oxford and New York: Oxford University Press, 1989).

Kennedy, John F., *Profiles in Courage* (New York: Harper & Brothers, 1956).

———, *Why England Slept* (New York: Wilfred Funk, 1961).

Kennedy, Robert F., *Thirteen Days* (New York: W. W. Norton, 1969).

Kissinger, Henry, *Diplomacy* (New York: Simon & Schuster, 1994).

Lebow, Richard Ned, *Between Peace and War* (Baltimore, Md.: John Hopkins University Press, 1981).

Nixon, Richard, *Six Crises* (New York: Doubleday, 1962).

Ron Hirschbein

CRUSADES. *See* CHRISTIANITY AND WAR; HOLY WARS; ISLAM AND WAR.

CUBAN MISSILE CRISIS. By most accounts, this episode brought the world close to nuclear war. President John Kennedy revealed that the chances of such a war were one out of three, and Robert Kennedy stated that he and the president expected a nuclear war, but hoped for the best. Premier Nikita Khrushchev recollected that "the smell of burning was in the air." These thirteen days in October 1962 provide a window through which we can observe the values that guided American and Soviet decision makers when they weighed the possibility of nuclear war.

The salient facts are well known. Evaluating the facts, however, evokes controversy regarding:

1. the motives of the political actors
2. the consequences of the crisis
3. the appropriate extent of public involvement at critical junctures
4. justifying risking nuclear war

Most narratives highlight the following facts. On several occasions, President Kennedy vowed that Soviet offensive weapons would not be tolerated in Cuba; the Soviets agreed. On October 14, 1962, Kennedy learned that he had been deceived: U-2 reconnaissance revealed that the Soviets were readying forty-two nuclear missiles in Cuba. In response, Kennedy convened an ad hoc group of seventeen advisors and publicly demanded that Premier Khrushchev remove the missiles. In order to compel his compliance, the president escalated the confrontation by blockading the Soviet fleet, and by putting strategic forces at an unprecedented stage of alert. Plans were circulated for evacuating officials from Washington, and an ultimatum was given to the Soviet ambassador to dismantle the missiles promptly or they would be destroyed. Khrushchev unexpectedly complied, ending the crisis. According to Robert McNamara, Cuba would have been attacked if Khrushchev had not complied, and McNamara said he was "almost certain" that the confrontation would have escalated into a full-scale thermonuclear war.

Assessing the motives of Khrushchev and Kennedy remains controversial. Typically, early American accounts attributed malicious motives to the Soviets. Graham Allison, for example, suspected that they wanted a base near the United States because they were expansionist and wanted to intimidate the United States by assuring more accurate targeting. While this view is still endorsed by some, others share the perspective of Khrushchev's son and his speech writer, namely that Khrushchev responded to domestic and international pressure by demonstrating that the Soviets had achieved parity as a nuclear power, and that he wanted to prove that, like the United States, the Soviets could deploy weapons beyond its borders. This was an appropriate response to the recent installation of American missiles in Turkey and the American-sponsored invasion of Cuba at the Bay of Pigs*. The Soviets claimed that they knew of "Operation Mongoose" (plans for a future invasion culminating in the assassination of Fidel Castro in October 1962). Accordingly, the Soviets construed their missiles as defensive rather than offensive. In other words, the nuclear bases were a symbolic gesture, not a military threat. Khrushchev claimed that he complied with the ultimatum because risking nuclear war was "madness." Commentators such as John Somerville lauded Khrushchev for his prudence, while others, such as McGeorge Bundy, indicted him for his recklessness and adventurism.

Kennedy's motives were contested. Michael Mandelbaum (a member of the Council of Foreign Relations) claimed that Kennedy's resolution of the crisis was the high point of his administration and that he reinforced his bargaining reputation and taught the Soviets that their mischief would not be tolerated. Noam Chomsky, however, interpreted Kennedy's actions as "the lowest point in human history," since he knowingly risked nuclear destruction in pursuit of his personal and political agenda. Recently, James Blight (who organized conferences of American, Soviet, and Cuban actors in the crisis) argued that fear of nuclear war tempered Kennedy's actions. However, others read the texts differently and concluded that Kennedy's quest for heroism was undaunted, and that he knowingly risked annihilation. The author believes that the crisis was a rite of passage—a pretext for Kennedy to fulfill his preconceived destiny. Finally, postmodern explications of the crisis raised the possibility that the decision makers themselves may be unaware of their motives. Kennedy gave credence to this view when he revealed that he was unsure of the "essence of his decision."

In looking at the consequences of the crisis, many of the participants lamented that their successors learned the wrong lessons. Theodore Sorensen suggested that the gradual escalation strategy that informed the crisis served as a template for conducting the tragic Vietnam War, and Daniel Ellsberg suggested that it inspired subsequent American conventional and nuclear strategy. It is worth noting that President George Bush eschewed the gradual escalation strategy in orchestrating the Gulf War. In any case, Dean Rusk concluded that such crises were so dangerous that they must be prevented.

Others lauded Kennedy and argued that he personified carefully calibrated courage alloyed with keen intelligence. For example, Lloyd Bentsen alluded to the crisis and declared that Dan Quayle "was no John F. Kennedy." The crisis raised another issue: To what extent should citizens participate in crisis definition and management? Recent commentators have argued that the public was de facto excluded from life and death decisions. It appeared that the Kennedy brothers managed the crisis without fully informing their colleagues, the Congress, or the American people. Some argued that the urgency of the crisis along with the need for secrecy made such behavior a lamentable necessity.

However, critics demonstrated that the president was deceptive even when he went public. There was a marked difference between his public and private analysis of the situation. In public the president claimed that the missiles were a grave threat, while in private, he and Robert McNamara determined that the missiles did not bestow any strategic advantage upon the Soviets. However, they had to be removed because they would undermine the bargaining reputation of American leaders and encourage the Soviets to become adventuristic in other regions. The president also allowed that the missiles would undermine his party and his presidency. Analysts such as Henry Kissinger explained that such deception was necessary, because the exigencies of foreign relations cannot be guided by the morality of the academy. However, critics contended that such "impression management" prevented informed public debate of pivotal issues.

Historian Barton Bernstein indicted this disenfranchisement as "annihilation without representation."

It was Kennedy's intention to add a discussion of the basic ethical question involved: What, if any, justification gives this government or any government the moral right to bring its people and possibly all people under the shadow of nuclear destruction? However, he never had an opportunity to rewrite or complete it.

See ACCIDENTAL NUCLEAR WAR; AGGRESSION, ATTEMPTS TO DEFINE; CHILDREN AND WAR; COMBATANT-NONCOMBATANT DISTINCTION; FIRST STRIKE/SECOND STRIKE; MUTUAL ASSURED DESTRUCTION (MAD); NUCLEAR DETERRENCE; NUCLEAR WAR; PROPAGANDA; PSYCHIC NUMBING; TOTAL WAR.

BIBLIOGRAPHY

Allison, Graham, *The Essence of Decision* (Boston: Little, Brown, 1971).

Bernstein, Barton, "The Cuban Missile Crisis," in L. H. Miller and R. W. Pruessen, eds., *Reflections on the Cold War* (Philadelphia: Temple University Press, 1974).

Blight, James, and David Welch, *On the Brink* (New York: Hill & Wang, 1989).

Bundy, McGeorge, *Danger and Survival* (New York: Random House, 1988).

Chang, Laurence, and Peter Kornbluh, *The Cuban Missile Crisis, 1962* (New York: New York University Press, 1992).

Divine, Robert, *The Cuban Missile Crisis: The Continuing Debate* (Chicago: Quadrangle, 1971).

Hirschbein, Ron, "What If They Gave a Crisis and Nobody Came?" in Joseph Kunkel, ed., *In the Interest of Peace* (Wolfsboro, N.H.: Longwood Academic, 1991).

Kennedy, Robert, *Thirteen Days: A Memoir of the Cuban Missile Crisis* (New York: W. W. Norton, 1989).

Khruschev, Nikita, *Khruschev Remembers,* Strobe Talbot, trans. and ed. (Boston: Little, Brown, 1970).

Somerville, John, "War, Omnicide and Sanity: The Lesson of the Cuban Missile Crisis," in Joseph Kunkel, ed., *Issues in War and Peace* (Wolfsboro, N.H.: Longwood Academic, 1989).

Ron Hirschbein

D

DAY, DOROTHY (1897–1980). A socialist, pacifist*, converted Roman Catholic who established "Houses of Hospitality" for the destitute, first in New York City, and later across America. With Peter Maurin she founded the newspaper, the *Catholic Worker.* Her father, John Day, was a sports writer. In 1904 the family moved to San Francisco, but when the 1904 earthquake destroyed the plant of his paper, they moved to Chicago. Her parents were indifferently Presbyterian and Episcopalian. She was an avid reader and in her youth read Jack London, Upton Sinclair, Frank Harris, Peter Kropotkin, John Wesley's *Sermons,* Augustine's *Confessions,* Jonathan Edwards, and the Anglican prayer book. She attended the University of Illinois through a two-year scholarship, after which she went to New York City and became a reporter for the Socialist paper, the *New York Call.* In 1917 she left the paper to join the Anti-Conscription League and accepted a position with the Communist paper, *The Masses,* which the Post Office, in August 1917, refused to mail, and the Justice Department shut down in November 1917. She was arrested and jailed that year (the first of eleven times) for marching with the suffragists; in 1923 she was caught in a raid of the International Workers of the World (IWW) offices and jailed; and she was jailed six times in New York in protest against air raid drills until the drills were discontinued in 1961.

In 1923 she wrote an autobiographical novel, *The Eleventh Virgin,* for which she received $5,000 for the movie rights, although it was never filmed, and in 1929 worked briefly as a Hollywood script writer. In the summer of 1932 as a reporter of a Communist hunger march she commented that now as a Catholic pacifist she regretted that she could not be in the march with them. Her wide circle of friends included Leon Trotsky, Ben Hecht, and Ammon Hennacy*.

In 1935 she organized an American branch of the British *Pax* movement to study Catholic teaching on the morality of war. Her pacifist views appeared in every issue of *The Worker,* and as World War II became imminent she printed a box urging men not to register for the draft, but when her bishop told her to stop, she did so. The war devastated her movement, since many followers were not pacifist, and the *Catholic Worker* lost 100,000 subscriptions. Most Workers enlisted, although 135 of them served in Civilian Public Service Camps, an option that Day also opposed. In 1942 she stated, ''We are still pacifists . . . and we will not participate in any armed warfare or in making munitions, or by buying government bonds to prosecute the war, or in urging others to these efforts.'' During and after the war she saw no peace candidates and ceased voting.

She had difficulty with her religious superiors on many occasions. In 1949 the Catholic cemetery workers went on strike, and Cardinal Francis Joseph Spellman called the strike ''anti-American,'' ''anti-Christian,'' and ''against the Church.'' Day told the strikers that they were true Christians and that they were themselves the Church. After Pope Pius XII issued his Christmas message December 23, 1956, endorsing just war* doctrine and condemning conscientious objection*, she affirmed her doubts in the January 1957 issue of the *Catholic Worker* that the criteria for a just war could ever be met in the modern world. In 1963 she visited the Vatican along with over fifty Mothers for Peace (composed of representatives from *The Worker,* Women's International League for Peace and Freedom, the Fellowship of Reconciliation, and Pax Christi), but did not receive an audience with the pope or his acknowledgement of their attendance at the huge meeting in St. Peter's Square.

In addition to her monthly essays in her newspaper she authored a number of books including *From Union Square to Rome* (1938), an account of her religious pilgrimage; *House of Hospitality* (1939); *The Long Loneliness* (1952); *Loaves and Fishes* (1963); and *On Pilgrimage: The Sixties* (1973).

See ADDAMS, JANE; CHRISTIANITY AND WAR; DODGE, DAVID LOW; MUSTE, A.J.; PACIFISM; ROYDEN, MAUDE.

BIBLIOGRAPHY
Coles, Robert, *Dorothy Day: A Radical Devotion* (Reading, Mass.: Addison-Wesley, 1987).
Ellsberg, Robert, ed., *By Little and By Little: The Selected Writings of Dorothy Day* (New York: Alfred Knopf, 1983).
Miller, William D., *Dorothy Day: A Biography* (San Francisco: Harper & Row, 1982).

DEBS, EUGENE VICTOR (1855–1926). Born in Terre Haute, Indiana. At the age of fourteen he went to work in the Terre Haute railroad shops and at twenty he organized the Terre Haute lodge of the Brotherhood of Locomotive Firemen. In 1879 he was elected city clerk in Terre Haute on the Democratic ticket, and in 1885 he was elected to the Indiana Legislature. In 1892, after seventeen years in the Brotherhood, he went before the convention to turn in his resignation. His hope was to form a railroad union that would include all railroad workers. The convention initially refused to accept his resignation, but finally did so. In 1893, in the middle of a great depression, he launched the ill-fated American Railway Union. In its first year it had 150,000 members and won its first strike against the Great Northern Railroad. One year later, in 1894, he and his union came to the defense of the workers in the Pullman Company strike. President Grover Cleveland, however, called out federal troops and the workers were driven back to work. Debs and three other union officers were arrested and sent to jail for six months, during which time the American Railway Union was dissolved.

Debs came out of jail a Socialist, chiefly inspired in his conversion by Victor Berger, the first Socialist elected to the U.S. House of Representatives 1911–1913, reelected in 1918, but in 1919 excluded on a charge of disloyalty. Berger was sentenced to prison for twenty years on a charge of giving aid and comfort to the enemy, although the sentence was reversed in 1921 by the U.S. Supreme Court.

In 1900 Debs formed the American Socialist Party, serving as the party candidate for president of the United States five times: 1900 with 96,000 votes; 1904 with 402,400 votes; 1908 with 420,973 votes; 1912 with 901,062 votes; and finally, while in the Atlanta penitentiary in 1920, he received 919,799 votes. In 1905 he sponsored the formation of the International Workers of the World (IWW).

As a Socialist he saw imperialism, militarism*, and war as natural consequences of capitalism, and at the 1917 convention of the Socialist Party in St. Louis participated in writing the "Proclamation," which affirmed: "The working class of the United States has no quarrel with the working class of Germany or of any other country. . . . We brand the declaration of war by our government as a crime against the people of the United States and against the nations of the world."

In 1917 three Socialist leaders had been sentenced to one year in jail each for their antiwar statements. On his way to the Ohio state convention of the Socialist Party, Debs stopped in June 1918 to visit his comrades in prison. At the Canton, Ohio convention, knowing that federal agents were in the hall, he delivered his famous speech against the war. Four days later he was arrested for violating the Espionage Act. The indictment charged him with "attempting to cause insubordination, mutiny, disloyalty, and refusal of duty within the military forces of the United States, and the utterance of words intended to procure and incite resistance to the United States, and to promote the cause of the Imperial German Government."

He was sentenced on September 18, 1918, two months before the end of the war, to ten years in prison. While in the Atlanta penitentiary he wrote *Walls and Bars* as a critique of the American prison system. He quoted a contemporary with favor: "Every society has the criminals it deserves." His visitors included many famous persons, including Samuel Gompers, Lincoln Steffens, Norman Hapgood, and Clarence Darrow. President Woodrow Wilson refused to issue a pardon. Debs remarked, "It is Woodrow Wilson who needs a pardon from the American people, and if I had it in my power I would grant him the pardon that would set him free." President Warren Harding pardoned Debs in 1921. He wrote his creed while in Atlanta:

> While there is a lower class I am in it
> While there is a criminal element I am of it
> While there's a soul in prison I am not free.

By this time Debs was sixty-six and in broken health, and he was an invalid most of the time until his death on October 20, 1926. He was a man without bitterness and remarked that his prison experience included three county jails, one state penitentiary, and one federal prison, but ''I have no personal grievance to air.'' During his lifetime he delivered over 6,000 speeches and wrote approximately 3,000 articles for publication.

See CONSCIENTIOUS OBJECTION; CONSCRIPTION; MARXISM AND WAR; MILITARY-INDUSTRIAL COMPLEX; PACIFISM.

BIBLIOGRAPHY

Coleman, McAlister, *Eugene V. Debs: A Man Unafraid* (New York: Greenberg Publisher, 1930).

Debs, Eugene Victor, *Walls and Bars* (Chicago: Charles H. Kerr, 1973).

Rogers, Bruce, ed., *Debs: His Life, Writings and Speeches* (Girard, Kan.: The Appeal To Reason, 1908).

DECLARATION OF WAR. Until the end of the 17th century declarations of war had three significant purposes: (1) they were the end product of an elaborate political process by which a society decided to go to war, (2) they were a key element in the principal diplomatic activity of governments, and (3) they articulated the grand strategy with which a war was to be fought. Of these three, only the third survived into the 20th century.

Up to the 17th century the decision to go to war required elaborate public debate. The great barons debated the issue, first in councils of the elders or in a senate, and then in a council of warriors or a popular assembly. The debates were commonly clothed in or at least accompanied by religious rites. The political reality was that extensive public discussions were held, as documented in the Babylonian epic *Agga and Gilgamesh,* Judges 11, Thucydides, Livy, and elsewhere. The aim was to crystalize the issues into a document that could be voted up or down. In the case of war, this document listed the grievances that justified the resort to war and articulated the remedies that would restore peace. With the rise of absolute monarchs the decision-making process was radically narrowed from many public debates to a few private consultations.

Until the end of the 17th century communication and transport were so difficult that only the most vital issues could justify the expense and danger of foreign travel. War, however, was a vital issue, since leaders would delay going to war until they knew whether their opponent would accept or reject their demands. The emissaries who were sent carried a document listing the grievances justifying the resort to war. By the end of the century the difficulties of both communication and travel were less of a problem, in part because resident ambassadors were already conducting negotiations on the site. By this time declarations of war were no longer needed for political or diplomatic reasons.

Between 1700 and 1870 there were 107 undeclared wars and only ten declared ones. This ratio has remained. On June 5, 1967, Algeria, Iraq, Kuwait, Sudan, and Syria formally declared war against Israel, the first declared war since 1945.

Declarations could be either absolute or conditional. A conditional declaration (called an ultimatum when it contained a fixed date) asserted that war was inevitable unless certain demands are met. An absolute declaration affirmed that a state of war existed, usually because armed conflict had already broken out. In either case the declaration determined that a state of war existed. Declarations may also be reasoned or unreasoned, motivated or unmotivated, as defined in Article 1 of Convention 3 of the 18 October 1907 Hague Conference, "Relative to the Opening of Hostilities." A reasoned declaration is one that gives a full account of the causes and goals of war, such as was the case in the Declaration of Independence. An unreasoned declaration provides either no reasons or inadequate ones as was the case in the U.S. congressional declarations of 1812, 1846, 1898, 1917, and 1941.

The matter is further confused when different authorities issue conflicting declarations. For example, in 1941 the 77th Congress formally issued an unreasoned and absolute declaration against Japan. At the same time, President Franklin Roosevelt fixed his grand strategy in his speech, "A Date Which Will Live In Infamy." In the American Constitution the declaration of war is the function of Congress. In practice, however, Congress has made this decision only once in 200 years, namely, in 1988. In all other cases Americans went to war by a presidential decision. Abraham Lincoln observed in 1848 that this "places our President where kings have always stood."

See FORBIDDEN STRATEGIES; FIRST STRIKE/SECOND STRIKE; LAWS OF WAR.

BIBLIOGRAPHY
Eagleton, Clyde, "The Form and Function of the Declaration of War," *American Journal of International Law* (January 1938), 19–35.
Hamilton, Alexander (Pacificus/Americanus), and James Madison (Helvidius), *The Letters of Pacificus and Helvidius with the Letters of Americanus 1845,* a facsimile reproduction with introduction by Richard Loss (Delmar, N.Y.: Scholars' Facsimiles and Reprints, 1976).
Manicus, Peter T., *War and Democracy* (Oxford: Basil & Blackwell, 1989).

Brien Hallett

DELLUMS COMMITTEE. *See* SON MY/MY LAI; STOCKHOLM/ROTHSKILDE WAR CRIMES TRIALS: WINTER SOLDIER INVESTIGATION.

DEMOCRACY AND THE MILITARY. If any state has a right to use military force in self-defense, then a democracy certainly has that right. Possibly the citizens of a democracy have a greater right to self-defense, inasmuch as the governments of constitutional democracies are legitimate protectors of citizens' rights in a way in which oppressive totalitarian regimes are not. Correspondingly, it might be argued that, given greater opportunities to influence foreign policy, the citizens of democracies have greater responsibility for ensuring that the military force used by their government serves only legitimate objectives.

The presence of military force raises two special sets of problems for democracies. One type relates to possible ways in which democratic processes may be adversely affected by military power. Paradoxically, the other type relates to ways in which democratic processes may impede or obstruct the efficient, and sometimes legitimate, use of military force.

Every democracy needs to take precautions against subversion by its own military forces, or by the illegitimate use of military force by an unrepresentative faction. Of course, the frequency of military-led or -backed coups d'état, revolutions, and insurrections is testimony to the frequent failure of legal and institutional safeguards against the usurpation of power. Probably factors such as the civic culture of a nation, the strength of voluntary and nongovernmental institutions, and economic and general social stability contribute as much to the maintenance of democracy as do institutional arrangements for the separation of powers and checks and balances.

In the United States it has been difficult to distinguish between the legitimate uses of armed force by the chief executive to pursue the national interest and excesses of that authority in waging actual wars. Occasionally Congress has limited presidential initiatives, as in the case of the 1982 Boland Amendment, which prohibited U.S. funding of groups seeking the destruction of the Sandinista regime in Nicaragua. In general, however, there is no principled distinction between war and ways in which the military may be used by presidents without need for congressional approval.

The corrosive effects of the military on democracy may also be more subtle. These include the expansion of so-called expert control in the national security state over decision making that ought rightfully to be matters of public debate, the increased secrecy attached to defense policies, the tendency toward sophisticated weapons technology that, if it is to be used effectively, would preclude democratic control, and the abilities of the military-industrial complex* to influence government spending. Dwight D. Eisenhower pointedly warned the nation about the disproportionate influence of a military-industrial alliance during the last year of his presidency.

The history of the Cold War* between the United States and the former Soviet Union exacerbated these problems. For instance, however morally dubious its justification, a majority of American citizens accepted a nuclear deterrence* strategy based on a ''countervalue*'' namely, mutually assured destruction (MAD)*. In fact, however, as early as the tenure of Robert McNamara as secretary of defense, the national security establishment began to shift targeting from a ''countervalue'' to a ''counterforce'' policy, and then, under the Carter and Reagan administrations, to a questionable countervailing strategy and nuclear war-fighting posture. Efforts to fully implement a countervailing strategy, including deployment of the MX missile, proved unpopular when disclosed and publicly debated, as had proposals to deploy the neutron bomb and to establish antiballistic missile* (ABM) systems. Nevertheless, it should be of concern to democrats that presidential administrations, Democratic as well as Republican, have proceeded so far in changing nuclear weapons policies in virtual secrecy, if not outright deceit—given the gap between "declaratory" policies for public consumption, and actual "deployment" policies.

During the Cold War*, it was generally conceded by Congress and the public that, in the event of a surprise attack, the president might be required to respond appropriately, even if the result was full-scale nuclear war*. Under cover of the excuse that disclosures would compromise national security, the public was not made aware—beyond popular and scholarly conjecture—about the kinds of national emergency to which the president might respond, how he might respond (e.g., massive retaliation* or limited strikes), whether and how far authority to use nuclear weapons had been predelegated, or what sorts of targets had been selected. Yet, there seem to have been no compelling reasons for foreclosing public debate on these issues. It was argued that if citizens acquired such knowledge, so would enemies, thus weakening the deterrent effect. But this response confused the technical knowledge weapons experts needed to keep secret—for example, vulnerabilities such as the hardening of missile silos, "go codes" for launching weapons, the location of nuclear submarines on patrol, design configurations of control and command systems—with the wisdom required for the choice of sound options in the first place. Expert "guardians" certainly had no monopoly over the latter.

While the armed forces pose risks for the integrity of democracy, it is also claimed that the requirements of democratic process have adverse effects on sound military policy and strategy. To some extent, rational planning may be obstructed by the kind of lobbying and vote trading that traditionally occurs in congressional politics. In addition, antimilitarist populism may lead to a democracy's failure to attain military preparedness. This has often been charged against the popularity, especially in England, of the pacifist* movement between World Wars I and II, although failure to prepare for fascist aggression had complex causes, including a failure of leadership, low public morale, and worldwide economic depression.

Do democratic politics limit the kinds of wars democracies can wage successfully? One supposed lesson of the Vietnam War* is that citizens of a democracy will not tolerate long, drawn-out wars, when casualties* are high and success is more likely to result from attrition than from dramatic victories. This interpretation of U.S. failure in Vietnam seems weaker than alternative explanations, however, such as the inability of overwhelming military superiority to defeat an adversary undeterred by severe punishment (a hard lesson the Soviet Union insisted on learning for itself in Afghanistan).

It has been suggested that it is difficult for a democracy to engage in a war unless it is perceived by the populace as having a great moral purpose (such as Wilson's "war to end all wars") or is represented as a holy war* against evil.

Thus, it has been hypothesized that the Allies' demands for unconditional surrender* in World War II were perceived as necessary to justify the sacrifices required of citizens. Against this hypothesis one must consider that the demand for unconditional surrender was joined by the nondemocratic Ally, the Soviet Union, that the Allies feared the rapid rearmament of the Axis powers under terms less than unconditional (as Germany had rearmed after World War I), and that the Allies were already in a race to divide the world into Communist and free market spheres of influence.

Finally, is there any possibility that the spread of stable democratic governments around the world will make war less likely? There is some historical basis for an optimistic response to this question. Historically, a separate peace has been maintained for more than 150 years among republics sharing liberal principles and institutions. The most plausible reasons why democracies are capable of achieving peace among themselves are that they exercise greater democratic self-control and that they are capable of appreciating the rights of foreign nationals.

See CAUSES OF WAR; CHRISTIANITY AND WAR; COLLATERAL DAMAGE; NUCLEAR DETERRENCE; GRENADA, U.S. INVASION OF; GUATEMALA, U.S. INVASION OF; GULF WAR (DESERT STORM); HOLY WARS; INTELLIGENCE AGENCIES; JUST WAR; KOREAN WAR; MILITARISM; MILITARY-INDUSTRIAL COMPLEX; MILITARY TRAINING, BASIC; NATIONALISM; NICARAGUA, U.S. INTERVENTION IN; NUCLEAR PROLIFERATION; NUCLEAR TESTING IN THE PACIFIC; PATRIOTISM; PROPAGANDA; SON MY/MY LAI; WARISM.

BIBLIOGRAPHY
Ambrose, Stephen E., and James A. Barber, Jr., eds., *The Military and American Society* (New York: Free Press, 1972).
Churchill, R. Paul, "Democracy and the Threat of Nuclear Weapons," in Joseph C. Kunkel and Kenneth H. Klein, eds., *Issues in War and Peace* (Wolfboro, N.H.: Longwood Academic, 1989).
Dahl, Robert, *Controlling Nuclear Weapons: Democracy Versus Guardianship* (New Haven, Conn.: Yale University Press, 1984).
Doyle, Michael W., "Liberal Institutions and International Ethics," in Kenneth Kipnis and Diana T. Meyers, eds., *Political Realism and International Morality* (Boulder, Colo.: Westview Press, 1987).

                                                                        Robert Paul Churchill

DISARMAMENT. After writing seven volumes on disarmament and six volumes on international affairs, John Wheeler Bennett published *The Pipe Dream of Peace.* Disarmament is of recent vintage as a proposed solution to the problem of war. Early 17th-century proposals for securing peace were not based on any expectation that disarmament would occur. However, when the manufacture and sale of arms became a major international trade, it became evident that arms by themselves posed an incentive to war and an obstacle to peaceful negotiations.

The earliest efforts to diminish the likelihood of war recommended the diminution or abolition of standing armies. This was proposed by Abbe de St.-Pierre (1737–1814) in his "Sketch of A Project of Permanent Peace"; Jean-Jacques Rousseau* (1712–1778) in "An Opinion on Lasting Peace"; and Immanuel Kant* (1724–1804) in his *Perpetual Peace*. The universal peace plan of Jeremy Bentham* (1748–1832) published posthumously in 1843 urged holding down the size of the army and navy to that needed to curb piracy. He urged that Great Britain take the first step in this direction by removing all military force from its colonies. Montesquieu (1689–1755) warned that as nations increased their arms and armies, so also did their neighbors. In 1893, on the eve of a discussion of the military budget of the German Reichstag, and after twenty-five years of excessive European arms buildup, Frederick Engels (1820–1895) wrote *Can Europe Disarm?*, concluding that the answer was affirmative. As a first step he proposed that all standing armies be converted to militias; that the term of military service be reduced; and that Germany and France discuss mutually reducing their arms.

The history of efforts to disarm is short and dismal. The first successful attempt came in 1817, when the Rush-Bagot Agreement was reached between the United States and Canada to discontinue their major naval forces on the Great Lakes. No comparable success has been achieved since. Between 1845 and 1853, The *British Almanac Companion* reported that 2,117 petitions in favor of disarmament and against increased militia were presented and defeated in the House of Commons. It had early been urged that the arms industries be nationalized, in the belief that free enterprise in arms exacerbated the arms race. This move was opposed by nations that did not produce their own arms for fear that they would have more difficulty buying arms from nationalized firms. The two Hague Congresses* of 1899 and 1907, which were called for the primary purpose of achieving disarmament, instead expressed concern for nations that did not produce their own arms. The current U.S. arms consortium of government and private business illustrates that the sale of arms has been increased rather than diminished by even mild nationalization. Arms embargoes are political weapons while the sale of arms is merely business.

Philip Noel-Baker urged in 1958 that military research be abolished and that scientists be phased into peaceful tasks. The current military-industrial complex* in the United States, however, promotes the opposite, and the majority of government research funds have been for military purposes. The U.S. Arms Control and Disarmament Agency has exhibited little enthusiasm for disarmament and has concerned itself primarily with controlling who gets the arms and how much. The Baruch Plan* was a short-lived effort to control nuclear arms and no subsequent plan has accomplished even minor steps toward either nuclear or conventional arms reduction. The primary problem has been to get leaders who have little confidence in international diplomacy to give up the only weapons in which they do have confidence. The UN Disarmament Commission meeting, April 18–May 9, 1994, was unable to achieve consensus on guidelines for either arms transfers or nuclear disarmament.

See ANTIBALLISTIC MISSILES/STAR WARS; BIOLOGICAL/CHEMI-
CAL WARFARE; MILITARY-INDUSTRIAL COMPLEX; MILITARY
SPENDING; NUCLEAR DETERRENCE; NUCLEAR PROLIFERATION;
STRATEGIC DEFENSE INITIATIVE (SDI).

BIBLIOGRAPHY
Baldwin, Hanson W., *The Great Arms Race* (New York: Praeger, 1958).
Barnet, Richard J., *Who Wants Disarmament?* (Boston: Beacon Press, 1960).
Benoit, Emile, and Kenneth Boulding, eds., *Disarmament and the Economy* (New York:
    Harper & Row, 1963).
Richardson, Lewis F., *Arms and Insecurity* (Pittsburgh, Pa.: Boxwood Press, 1960).

DODGE, DAVID LOW (1774–1852). Author of the first anti-war pamphlets
published in America. His first, *The Mediator's Kingdom Not of This World,*
was published in 1809, followed by *War Inconsistent with the Religion of Jesus
Christ,* which came out in 1812. In August 1815 he was the leader in the establishment of the New York Peace Society, the first such society in the world,
with himself as the president. His *War Inconsistent* argued that the inconsistency
rested on three arguments: (1) war was inhuman, because it blunted the tender
feelings, oppressed the poor, spread terror and distress, destroyed human life,
and made widows and orphans; (2) war was unwise, because it destroyed property, curtailed liberty, injured the morals of society, and failed to accomplish
what it set out to do; and (3) war was criminal, because it infringed on conscience, was inconsistent with mercy, returned evil for evil, and was opposed
to the example of the Son of God. The pamphlet concluded with answers to his
objectors and the assurance that the kingdom of the Christian was not of this
world.
See CHRISTIANITY AND WAR; PACIFISM.

BIBLIOGRAPHY
Brock, Peter, *Pacifism in the United States: From the Colonial Era to the First World
    War* (Princeton, N.J.: Princeton University Press, 1968).
Dodge, David Low, *War Inconsistent with the Religion of Jesus Christ* (Boston: Ginn &
    Co., 1905).

DOUHET, GIULIO (1869–1930). Giulio Douhet was an obscure Italian artillery officer who became the best known and most frequently cited of the early
prophets of air power. He earned this accolade by writing about air power better
than anyone else, with a clarity unmatched by any of his contemporaries. The
appearance of the English translation of his *Command of the Air* in 1942 was
also fortuitous, assuring that this collection of eloquent articles would become
the primary text on air power during and just after World War II, when interest
was at its height. And, finally, Douhet's uncompromising vision of air power
as large, multiengine bombers devastating entire cities was precisely the message
that senior politicians and air officers in England and the United States wanted
the public to hear, echoing as it did their own views.

Yet, paradoxically, Douhet possessed the barest minimum of practical experience. In all probability, he never learned to fly, and his actual service was slight. He was assigned to the Italian army's Aviation section just before World War I, holding the post of director for a few months in 1913 and 1914, before his prickly personality and imperious ways led to his dismissal. He later served as a subsecretary of aeronautics in Mussolini's government in 1922. Kennett has suggested that it was precisely Douhet's lack of practical experience that made him such an effective prophet. Ignorant of and unconcerned about operational realities, he was free to imagine air power in its most radical and unfettered form.

See AERIAL WARFARE.

BIBLIOGRAPHY

Douhet, Giulio, *The Command of the Air* (New York: Coward-McCann, 1942).

Kennett, Lee B., *A History of Strategic Bombing* (New York: Charles Scribner's Sons, 1982).

Brien Hallett

DUMDUM BULLETS. *See* BRUSSELS DECLARATION; BULLETS, EXPANDING; FORBIDDEN WEAPONS; HAGUE, THE, CONGRESSES; PROPORTIONALITY; ST. PETERSBURG DECLARATION.

E

___

ENVIRONMENTAL ISSUES, POLLUTION, AND THE MILITARY. Military activity impacts the environment in the production of military equipment and weapons, in the deployment and testing of military systems, in the use of military force, and in the storage and reprocessing of military waste. Whether these systems and activities are conventional, chemical, biological, or nuclear, they contribute to environmental degradation. All of these activities pollute the hydrosphere, most also pollute the atmosphere, and testing and warfare additionally pollute the lithosphere and biosphere. Even if protecting national security justifies military systems, this benefit needs to be weighed morally against ecological concerns. At the moral extreme is ecological warfare. From a utilitarian perspective, if ecological damage exceeds the contribution to security of a military system, the morality of reliance on such a system is in question.

The concerns of environmental ethics include the interface of pursuing military activity and preserving ecological integrity. In addition, several international conventions provide legal grounds for curbing various types of military activity. Ethical assessments of the environmental effects of military activity have also increased because of concerns about nuclear weapons, especially the potential damage of radioactive releases resulting from the production, deployment, and use of nuclear weapons. One of the most explicit ethical statements on military activity and the environment, the 1984 Uppsala Code of Ethics for Scientists, comes from the scientific community itself. This code, in assuming that all scientific research has ecological consequences and stressing individual responsibility, proposes that research should be ''so directed that its applications and other consequences do not cause significant ecological damage.'' As a result, given the potential hazards of modern technological war, the code concludes that ''scientific efforts shall therefore not aim at applications or skills for use in war or oppression.''

In the first area of military activity, the production of military equipment and weapons directly contributes to environmental degradation. Numerous toxic chemicals are employed in producing conventional weapons. With nuclear weapons, from mining, milling, and enriching uranium through bomb fabrication, all phases of production pose environmental problems. These procedures left radioactive tailings on Indian reservations that caused cancer among children who played in them, and various other, less serious, radioactive releases have occurred in the other phases of nuclear weapons production. In addition, since the spent fuel from most commercial nuclear power reactors can be reprocessed to produce materials for nuclear weapons, an unavoidable connection exists between commercial and military uses of nuclear reactors and concerns about nuclear proliferation*.

In the second area, the deployment and testing of military systems also has environmental consequences. For example, the removal of paint from aircraft and oil from their engines both use hazardous chemicals, and all military maneuvers involving petroleum-fueled engines release pollutants into the atmosphere. Significantly, environmentally less destructive alternatives are available, such as nontoxic substances to remove paint from aircraft and for cleaning their engines. Also, reductions in the number and scale of military maneuvers directly decrease harmful atmospheric releases. Apart from actual war, the above-ground nuclear weapons testing* during the 1940s and 1950s caused serious human and environmental damage and even current underground testing includes some venting into the atmosphere.

The third area, the actual use of military force, is the most serious way in which military activity degrades the environment. Virtually all aspects of environmental damage that occur in the prior two stages are repeated on a larger scale during war. In addition, war in the twentieth century has added the new dimensions of biological/chemical warfare* and nuclear war*, including the use of nerve gas in World War I, the use of nuclear weapons against Hiroshima* and Nagasaki* in World War II, and the use of Agent Orange in the Vietnam War*.

At the extreme, the actual use of military force is ecological warfare. The Gulf War* is now often presented as the first conflict to rely on tactics of ecological warfare. Iraq intentionally polluted the Persian Gulf by releasing millions of gallons of oil into an almost completely enclosed body of water and, by intentionally setting fire to oil fields in Kuwait, released into the atmosphere enormous quantities of smoke that coated land surfaces in Kuwait with a layer of soot that was lethal for many plants and animals.

Of great concern are projections of what could occur. For example, the negative radiological consequences of nuclear weapons can be greatly increased by targeting an adversary's nuclear reactors. Most recently, nuclear winter has received considerable attention because of the prospect for grave environmental consequences. From an environmental perspective, Mark Harwell (1984) notes, "Human recovery could not proceed more rapidly than the recovery of natural systems." Using the prospect for nuclear winter as a normative criterion, Carl Sagan (*Foreign Affairs,* Winter 1983/1984) argues against exceeding "subthreshold" nuclear arsenals. Beginning in the 1980s, Kristin Shrader-Frechette, Michael Fox, William Gay, and several other philosophers have contended in various essays that even far less disastrous military activity than "subthreshold" nuclear war requires censure on environmental and moral grounds.

Some legal bases exist for prohibiting military activity that intentionally damages the environment. One of the more important agreements is the 1977 "Convention on the Prohibition of Military or Any Other Hostile Use of Environmental Modification Techniques" (the Enmod Convention). Earlier important conventions include the Geneva Protocol* of 1925, which bans the use of biological agents in war, and the Bacteriological and Toxic Weapon Convention of 1972, which bans the possession of such biological agents. Beyond current legal restraints are proposed conventions against the "Crime of Ecocide." As long as war continues, adherence to all of these conventions is crucial from an environmental perspective.

In the fourth area, even the storage and reprocessing of military waste pose environmental problems. In the United States alone, military installations cover over 25 million acres, onto which numerous toxic substances have been released, including fuels, toxic chemicals, unexploded shells and bombs, and high-level nuclear waste. Government officials have identified over 10,000 hazardous sites at nearly 2,000 military installations. Public concern has been greatest in relation to the potential for nuclear releases. Some plutonium was released at Oak Ridge National Laboratory in 1959, and a plutonium fire occurred at the plutonium-processing plant at Rocky Flats in 1969. Unfortunately, the costs for adequate cleanup are astronomical. Although environmental cleanup (the fastest-growing area in the post–Cold War defense budget) is now allocated several billion dollars a year, the Pentagon estimates total cleanup costs, excluding overseas facilities, may be close to $120 billion.

In the 1990s, government officials in the United States and former Soviet Union have admitted their nuclear weapons production facilities have had severe environmental and safety problems, including releases of highly radioactive materials into the adjacent environment. As a result, almost all of the facilities have been closed, despite claims by some military and governmental officials that national security requires restarting old facilities or constructing new ones.

Finally, beyond the four areas in which military activity directly contributes to environmental degradation, are additional indirect natural and human factors. Natural disasters have resulted in the release of toxic military materials into groundwater, rivers, oceans, and the atmosphere. For example, several nuclear-powered submarines with nuclear weapons aboard are sunk in the oceans because of on-board disasters. More frightening are the prospects of a natural disaster, such as an earthquake, at a nuclear facility. The U.S. Government Accounting Office (GAO) has warned that better earthquake protection is needed at the Savannah River Site, which is the facility that produced the nuclear materials for most of the U.S. arsenal and which remains a storage facility for much high-level radioactive waste.

On the human side of indirect factors is the fact that military activity is itself part of a larger social fabric. To understand the full extent of the environmental impact of military activities, their connection with broader economic and political activities needs to be considered. André Gorz makes this argument in relation to capitalist and socialist societies in *Ecology as Politics* (1980). Johan Galtung (1982) uses the term *eco-development* to refer to "the interfaces between environment and development." Obviously, military activity causes significant impacts, both direct and indirect, on development. Military activity draws on scarce resources, both human and natural. Only a limited supply of labor power is available for research and production in society, and many natural resources are nonrenewable. Diversion of these resources to military activity indirectly reduces what is available to pursue other human interests and to protect the ecosystem within which all of these activities must occur.

See BIOLOGICAL/CHEMICAL WARFARE; BIKINI ATOLL, BOMBING OF; HIROSHIMA AND NAGASAKI; GULF WAR (DESERT STORM); MILITARY-INDUSTRIAL COMPLEX; NUCLEAR PROLIFERATION; NUCLEAR TESTING IN THE PACIFIC; NUCLEAR WAR.
BIBLIOGRAPHY

Galtung, Johan, *Environment, Development and Military Activity: Towards Alternative Security Doctrines* (Oslo: Universitetsforlaget, 1982).
Harwell, Mark A., *Nuclear Winter: The Human and Environmental Consequences of Nuclear War* (New York: Springer-Verlag, 1984).
Westing, Arthur H., ed., *Environmental Warfare: A Technical, Legal and Policy Appraisal* (London: Taylor & Francis, 1984).

William C. Gay

ESCAPE, ATTEMPTS OF PRISONERS TO. *General Orders 100**, Article 77, stated that a prisoner may be shot or killed while attempting to escape, but he may not be capitally punished for having tried to escape unsuccessfully. It was assumed that prisoners of war* were not expected to pledge not to try to escape. If recaptured, they might be subjected to "closer confinement." Primarily in the light of recommendations of The Hague Congresses* of 1899 and 1907, the new U.S. manual of 1914, *Rules of Land Warfare**, reaffirmed in Article 68 that, although prisoners may be shot while attempting escape, they may not be shot for having tried to escape. A conspiracy to attempt group escape, however, may be punishable by death, but only after due trial (Article 70). Although prisoners recaptured after attempted escape may be given "disciplinary punishment," it was specifically stated that this excluded any sentence of death (Article 79). In *Rules of Land Warfare* (1934, 1940) the same limits applied to the punishment of prisoners who attempt unsuccessfully to escape. The Geneva Conventions of 1929* were cited as applicable (Article 50). The maximum permissible punishment for the attempt was greater surveillance, although food restrictions, provided they did not endanger the health of the prisoner, could be imposed. *The Law of Land Warfare** (1956) stated essentially the same rule and appealed to the Geneva Conventions of 1949* as setting the limits. The new army manual, Articles 168–171, affirmed that "prisoners who unsuccessfully attempt to escape shall be given disciplinary punishments only." Such punishments were limited to a fine of not more than 50 percent of advances in pay, discontinuance of privileges, fatigue duties not to exceed two hours daily, and confinement.

See GENEVA CONVENTIONS, 1906, 1929, 1949; HAGUE THE, CONGRESSES; PRISONERS OF WAR.

BIBLIOGRAPHY

Friedman, Leon, ed. "Geneva Convention on Treatment of Prisoners of War," in *The Law of War,* vol. 1 (New York: Random House, 1971).

EXECUTION, SUMMARY. *General Orders 100**, Article 82, stated that men who are not part of any regular army, and who plunder or raid "without commission," "shall be treated summarily as highway robbers and pirates." Articles 84 and 85 affirmed the same for "armed prowlers" and "war rebels." *Rules of Land Warfare** (1914) Article 40 stated that "summary executions are no longer contemplated under the laws of war." Article 340, however, remarked that a soldier who disobeys a superior order by pillaging "may be lawfully killed on the spot by such superior." The 1940 revision of *Rules of Land Warfare* (Article 13) repeated the same claim that summary executions were not permitted, and paragraphs 351 and 352 confirmed that unauthorized belligerents, though not entitled to prisoner of war* status, must nonetheless be given a trial before execution. *The Law of Land Warfare** (1956) Chapter 3, Section 2 listed those not entitled to prisoner of war status while still insisting that everyone was entitled to a trial before execution. Both The Hague* and Geneva* declarations were cited in support.

See FORBIDDEN STRATEGIES; PRISONERS OF WAR.

F

FEMINISM AND WAR. Although there is no separate, freestanding feminist tradition on war and peace, feminist positions have evolved in response to a number of historic traditions on war and peace. Most important among these are realism or *realpolitik,* just war*, and pacifism*. Feminists have both shared and departed strongly from these and other articulated positions. There is no clear-cut "feminist way" to discuss how war and peace have been understood. But feminists began to tend explicitly to these matters in 1792 with the publication of Mary Wollstonecraft's *A Vindication of the Rights of Women.* Wollstonecraft (1759–1797) took to task those civic republicans, including Jean-Jacques Rousseau*, who, in her opinion, misidentified civic virtue by linking it too tightly to the ideal of an armed citizenry prepared to defend the republic by force, if necessary. Wollstonecraft wanted women to bear a fair share of civic burdens but she hoped that war-fighting might no longer be among them.

Other feminists or proto-feminists veered in the direction of a pacifist dream, drawing upon Christian* articulations of a peaceable kingdom. Such feminists insisted that Christianity had itself feminized ethics, sharply calling into question older notions of warrior valor and bloody victories. This feminist trend finds frequent expression in the arguments of 19th-century suffragists in Western societies, especially but not limited to the United States, that if women were running politics, "male wars" would somehow be eliminated. Linking a male tradition to discord and violence, such feminists, among them American reformers from Elizabeth Cady Stanton (1815–1902) to Jane Addams* (1860–1935) to many contemporary voices, foresaw a time when the world would study war no more, in part because women would either have gained a parity of power with men or succeeded men altogether in the corridors of power.

Less utopian prospects beckoned for other feminists, those who did not and do not accept a sharp divide between men and women in these matters of war, peace, and ethics. Such feminists point to the overwhelming support of women for wars fought by their own societies and note the long tradition of mothers who gained civic standing and honor through the war-time sacrifice of their soldier sons. Thus, even as some women form separate organizations to fight for peace, other feminists seek what is now called a "right to fight," that is, for full entry into the armed services of their own societies. This latter stance is endorsed by mainstream liberal feminist organizations in the United States, for example. There are radical feminists who proceed from assumptions very much like those that guide historic *realpolitikers,* namely, the idea that war always threatens and the point is for one's own side to triumph. What such feminists have in mind, however, is not wars between states but a perpetual state of "war" between men and women.

Curiously enough, there is no robust feminist discussion of such matters as justifiable grounds for war, rules of engagement, proportionality, nuclear deterrence*, collateral damage*, and the whole panoply of stipulations, restrictions, and provisions of historic just war thinking. Perhaps this can be explained by the fact that women, historically, have been noncombatants*, although this has not, of course, put them out of harm's way in total warfare in this or other centuries. Given current demands for gender equality on all fronts, women— whether as feminists or not—will no doubt be compelled to pay greater attention to both grounds for war and methods of war fighting in the future. In the meantime, the profusion of often-conflicting feminist analyses and arguments prevails.

See ADDAMS, JANE; BRITTAIN, VERA; DAY, DOROTHY; ROYDEN, MAUDE; TAILHOOK; WOMEN IN THE MILITARY.

BIBLIOGRAPHY

Addams, Jane, *Peace and Bread in Time of War* (New York: Macmillan, 1922).

Campbell, D'Ann, *Women at War with America* (Cambridge, Mass.: Harvard University Press, 1985).

Elshtain, Jean Bethke, *Women and War* (New York: Basic Books, 1987).

Jean Bethke Elshtain

FINAL SOLUTION. The Nazi* project to exterminate the Jewish populations, euphemistically called the "final solution," was so unbelievable that the Jewish writer and editor, Marie Syrkin, commented in August 1942 when she read the first accounts, "I must confess to you that we read the document without the emotional capacity to accept its truth." The degree of disassociation by the perpetrators of what they were doing was characterized by euphemistic language: "final solution" meant mass murder, "evacuation" or "resettlement" meant taking people off to be murdered, "medical ramp duty" was the task of selecting those for the gas chambers, "research" was the name for the medical experiments on the inmates, and Nazi doctors insisted that the term *ethical* did not apply since the killings were a "purely technical matter." The ability to claim no knowledge of the extermination was epitomized by Albert Speer who, in his postwar writings, denied having any specific knowledge of the final solution. The momentum toward the final solution was so powerful that the plan was underway even before the death camps equipped with the gas chambers were built.

Historians suggest that the Nazis faced a quandary after their invasion of the Soviet Union as to what to do with the increasing numbers of Jews under their control. They had ghettoized the Jews, brought them to imminent starvation, and could then suggest that mass killing was the only effective solution. It was widely believed that they had tried the ''solutions'' of forced emigration or resettlement in Madagascar or Poland and they were led in March 1941 to decide to kill the Russian Jews and in July 1941 to authorize the killing of all Jews in German-held territories. Adolf Eichmann testified that in July or August 1941 Heinrich Himmler and Reinhard Heydrich acted on the assumption that Hitler had approved the extermination program. By January 20, 1942, at the Wannsee Conference dealing with the implementation of the extermination program, the death camps had been constructed and gassing had started. The process culminating in the final solution was promoted by what Lifton and Markusen called the ''genocidal mentality.''

It must not be forgotten that the anti-Semitic project was couched in anti-Communist terms. Hitler had ordered that ''the Bolshevist/Jewish intelligentsia'' must be eliminated as part of the process to liquidate ''all Bolshevist leaders.'' This rationale, which was used to justify murdering the Jews, was soon extended as applicable to killing millions of Poles, Russians, Ukrainians, Gypsies, and homosexuals.

The project would not have been possible had not science and scientists been recruited to this end. The subject of race had been of scientific and pseudo-scientific interest for at least a century, and as early as 1853 Count Arthur de Gobineau had written *The Inequality of Human Races;* the English scientist, Sir Francis Galton, had invented the term *eugenics* and had published *Hereditary Genius* (1869), and *Inquiries into Human Faculty* (1883); and as early as 1917 Fritz Lenz, a leading German geneticist, was insisting that without a major eugenics project the German race was ''doomed to extinction.'' Many Nazis emphasized that the project had nothing to do with old-fashioned anti-Semitism but simply with the eugenic aim for racial purity.

See BANALITY OF EVIL; BIOLOGICAL/CHEMICAL WARFARE; CONCENTRATION CAMPS; CONTROL COUNCIL LAW NO. 10; GENOCIDE; HUMANITY, CRIMES AGAINST; MEDICAL CASE; NUREMBERG TRIALS; PROPAGANDA; PSYCHIC NUMBING; ZYKLON B TRIAL.

BIBLIOGRAPHY

Levin, Nora, *The Holocaust: The Destruction of European Jewry, 1933–1945* (New York: Thomas Y. Crowell, 1968).

Lifton, Robert Jay, and Eric Markusen, *The Genocidal Mentality* (New York: Basic Books, 1988).

Porpora, Douglas V., *How Holocausts Happen: The United States in Central America* (Philadelphia: Temple University Press, 1990).

Rosenberg, Alan, and Gerald E. Myers, eds., *Echoes from the Holocaust: Philosophical Reflections on a Dark Time* (Philadelphia: Temple University Press, 1988).

FIRST STRIKE/SECOND STRIKE. These terms refer both to different ways to use strategic nuclear weapons and to the different policies of nuclear deterrence* involving threats to use strategic nuclear weapons in those ways. Strategic nuclear weapons are nuclear weapons that are aimed at targets on the opponent's homeland. (In contrast, tactical nuclear weapons are nuclear weapons meant for use on a battlefield. When the issue is the first or second use of tactical nuclear weapons, the relevant terms are first and second use*, rather than first and second strike.) During most of the Cold War*, a first strike would have been a counterforce* attack, that is, a strike designed to destroy military targets. In particular, the targets of a first strike would be strategic nuclear forces of one's opponent, because the purpose of a first strike would be damage limitation, that is, reduction or elimination of the nuclear damage one's opponent is able to inflict on one's own homeland. A U.S. or Soviet countervalue attack, that is, an attack aimed at the targets of greatest value to the opponent (its civilian assets such as its population, its productive capacity, and its social infrastructure) would have made no sense as a first strike, because it would simply have lead to the retaliatory destruction of the attacker's own society.

A second strike might be a counterforce attack as well, if the opponent's first strike had been a counterforce attack. So long as one's cities were intact, a countervalue retaliation would make no sense. Given the nuclear balance of the Cold War, one side's destruction of the other's cities would lead to the destruction of its own cities in response. But once one's cities had been destroyed, retaliation for such destruction would be expected to be a countervalue attack. This is how a second strike was originally conceived. Because early nuclear weapons could not be accurately delivered, and because a counterforce attack requires accurate delivery of the weapons, a nuclear attack early in the Cold War would have inevitably been a countervalue attack. Thus, a second strike would have been a countervalue retaliation for a countervalue attack. Indeed, the capacity to launch a second strike after receiving a massive attack from one's opponent, that is, having one's own nuclear weapons sufficiently invulnerable that enough of them would be left after the opponent's attack for a countervalue retaliation that would destroy the opponent's society, came to be known as a *second strike capacity.* A second strike capacity is known also as an *assured destruction capacity,* and at the point in the Cold War when both the United States and the Soviet Union had acquired an assured destruction capacity, the nuclear situation was referred to as one of *mutual assured destruction**, or MAD.

As the Cold War progressed, technological developments allowed for greater accuracy in the delivery of nuclear weapons, so that a counterforce use of the weapons became more feasible, and the idea of a first strike as a counterforce, damage limitation strike was born. But, once MAD came into being, it became questionable whether the notion of damage limitation made any sense. If the opponent had a second strike or assured destruction capacity, however much damage limitation one could achieve by a counterforce first strike would not be sufficient to keep one's society from being destroyed, and so in practical terms would be meaningless. The amount of first strike counterforce capacity necessary to insure that the opponent could not destroy one's society in retaliation was referred to as the capacity for a *disarming first strike*. But if the opponent has an assured destruction capacity, a disarming first strike is for that reason impossible. If a disarming first strike is impossible, then a first strike could provide no meaningful advantage, and no one would be tempted to launch one. If there is no first strike, there will be no nuclear war. Thus, the existence of a mutual second strike capacity, MAD, creates great stability in the relationship of two nuclear powers. In particular, nuclear war is unlikely to start between them even in a crisis* in their relationship, when tensions are high. So, when there is mutual second strike capacity, the nuclear balance is said to possess a high degree of *crisis stability*.

But nuclear technology kept improving, and the United States and the Soviet Union developed better and better counterforce capabilities. There are two reasons that this development went on, despite the fact that mutual second strike capacity seemed to make a first strike pointless. First, strategic thinkers began to believe that the two nations might fight a limited nuclear war, that is, a counterforce nuclear war that would not escalate to countervalue destruction. Second, some thought that if counterforce capacity became good enough, and included ballistic missile defenses (such as those envisioned in the Strategic Defense Initiative*), a disarming first strike capacity could be developed and the opponent's second strike capacity overcome. Thus, the idea of a counterforce first strike began to be taken more seriously. Even among some of those who remained convinced that a disarming first strike would not be possible, the idea of a counterforce second strike gained currency. It is important to emphasize, however, that this counterforce thinking and counterforce deployments were in the service of nuclear deterrence* policy. The belief was that the better U.S. counterforce capacity, the better the Soviet Union would be deterred.

Critics of these counterforce developments argued, on the contrary, that a second strike capacity was all that the United States needed to deter the Soviet Union, and moreover that the focus on counterforce first (or second) strikes made nuclear war more likely, because it degraded crisis stability. Specifically, their argument was that if each side thought that the other side thought that there was some advantage, some real damage limitation, possible through a first strike, which each might think if it had extensive counterforce capability, then, in a crisis, each would tend to believe that the other was about to launch a first strike, and hence believe that it ought to attack first. This would provide each side with a strong incentive to strike first in order to preempt what it believed to be the other side's imminent attack. Thus, the development of counterforce capacity, especially when this focused on the possibility of a first strike, made nuclear war more likely and was therefore to be rejected.

This represents the debate during the Cold War between advocates of first strike and second strike capabilities. (A discussion of the moral issues this debate raises can be found in other entries herein, including "Counterforce Versus Countervalue.") It would be incorrect to think that this issue died with the Cold War, for it represents lines of thought that will arise in the future whenever two opponents with extensive nuclear arsenals confront each other, and it seems certain that such a state of affairs will occur again, if not between the United States and Russia, then between another pair of nuclear adversaries.

See AGGRESSION, ATTEMPTS TO DEFINE; AGGRESSIVE VERSUS DEFENSIVE WAR; LAWS OF WAR; NUCLEAR DETERRENCE; NUCLEAR WAR.

BIBLIOGRAPHY

Freedman, Lawrence, *The Evolution of Nuclear Strategy* (New York: St. Martin's, 1981).

Glaser, Charles, *Analyzing Strategic Nuclear Policy* (Princeton, N.J.: Princeton University Press, 1990).

Jervis, Robert, *The Illogic of American Nuclear Strategy* (Ithaca, N.Y.: Cornell University Press, 1984).

Lee, Steven, *Morality, Prudence, and Nuclear Weapons* (Cambridge: Cambridge University Press, 1993).

Steven Lee

FIRST USE. A policy of initiating, or threatening to initiate, the use of nuclear weapons, that is, a policy of being the first to use, or threatening to be the first to use, nuclear weapons, should a war come. But a first use of nuclear weapons is understood as something different from a first strike* with nuclear weapons. First use is a policy concerning the use or threatened use of nuclear weapons on a battlefield, against traditional battlefield targets, such as troop concentrations. In contrast, first strike is a policy of using or threatening to use nuclear weapons first against the opponent's homeland targets, whether military or civilian, such as cities, industrial capacity, communications networks, and the nuclear missiles that could be used against one's own homeland targets. In the language adopted for this distinction, first use is a policy for *theater* nuclear use, whereas first strike is a policy for *strategic* nuclear use. The main debate over first use concerns whether the threat of first use is appropriate as part of a policy of nuclear deterrence*, and it is first use as a deterrence policy that will be the main focus of discussion here.

In practice, during the Cold War*, first use concerned the use of nuclear weapons in Europe in a war between NATO, the military alliance headed by the United States, and the Warsaw Pact, the military alliance headed by the Soviet Union. One of the early technological innovations in nuclear weaponry was the development of small-yield, more compact nuclear weapons, so-called tactical nuclear weapons, designed for use on the battlefield. NATO began to deploy these in Europe in the 1950s, and the Warsaw Pact soon followed suit. First use policy concerned the question of what kinds of threats should be made regarding the use of these weapons. This question was raised in light of the U.S. policy of *extended deterrence,* the attempt to use nuclear threats to deter a Soviet attack not only against the United States itself, but also against Western Europe. What kind of threats would work best to achieve extended deterrence, and, in particular, should threats of first use of tactical or theater nuclear weapons be included in such a deterrence policy? The fear was that the Warsaw Pact would launch a conventional (that is, nonnuclear) attack against Western Europe. Would a first use threat, a threat by NATO to initiate the use of nuclear weapons against a conventional attack, be part of a successful strategy for avoiding such an attack? This question was at the heart of the debate over first use policy and the critics' call for the adoption of a policy of no first use.

The argument of those advocating a NATO policy of first use in Europe was that such a policy was necessary to deter Warsaw Pact aggression. The reason was that the Warsaw Pact was thought to have superior conventional forces. NATO conventional forces were seen as no match for them, hence only the threat to use nuclear weapons against a conventional attack, that is, the first use threat, would be sufficient to deter such an attack. It was no solution to advocate that NATO increase its conventional force strength, because this was thought to be politically impossible. The members of NATO would simply refuse to spend the money and take the other measures that would be necessary to achieve conventional force parity with the Warsaw Pact. So, a first use policy was essential to achieving the U.S. goal of extended deterrence. While it is true that a first use policy increased the risk that a conventional war would turn into a nuclear war, this made deterrence more effective, because it made the Warsaw Pact more fearful of initiating a conventional war.

Those who criticized first use policy in Europe, advocates of no first use, argued that NATO conventional forces could be made adequate to deter a Warsaw Pact conventional attack and that a first use policy increased the risk of nuclear war. Part of the disagreement between the two camps was over the degree of superiority of Warsaw Pact conventional forces. Critics of first use policy believed that Warsaw Pact superiority was not great and that NATO conventional forces could readily be improved to the point where they would constitute an effective deterrent. Moreover, critics of first use policy argued that that policy was ineffective because the threat to use nuclear weapons first was not credible. The risk of nuclear escalation would be so great that it would be unlikely that NATO would ever actually carry out its threat. If nuclear weapons were used, they would destroy Europe, and what is the logic in destroying what one is trying to defend? In addition, the weapons deployment policy necessary to implement a first use threat made nuclear war more likely for another reason. In a Warsaw Pact conventional attack, caches of NATO tactical nuclear weapons would be at risk of being overrun very early in the conflict. This would put NATO in a ''use them or lose them'' situation. Unless the weapons were quickly fired, they would be captured by the enemy. This made it much more likely that they would be used. This last point is an illustration of what is called the "usability paradox": Making nuclear weapons more usable for the sake of deterrence makes it more likely that they will in fact be used, which would represent a failure of deterrence.

What are the moral issues raised by first use policy? It is, of course, a moral imperative to keep the risk of nuclear war, as well as the risk of aggression, as low as possible. Thus, a first use policy would be morally preferable only if it was a more effective deterrent. As the usability paradox suggests, however, the judgment of deterrence effectiveness must take account not only of the risk of aggression, but also of the risk that a conventional war would escalate to the nuclear level. The point of the paradox is that a first use policy in Europe may have lowered the risk of Warsaw Pact conventional aggression, while at the same time increasing the risk that a conventional war would become nuclear. If so, these two factors would have to be weighed against each other to arrive at an overall moral judgment. But the critics argue that there is a more direct route to the moral rejection of first use policy, which is a version of the moral argument against nuclear deterrence in general. Any use of nuclear weapons, even tactical nuclear weapons on the battlefield, is likely to lead to escalation to the use of nuclear weapons against civilian targets, a use prohibited by the just war* principle of discrimination. On this line of argument, any policy that increased the likelihood of such a use of nuclear weapons, as a first use policy would, is itself morally unacceptable.

The issue of first use policy may seem like a historical relic, tied as it is to Cold War confrontation in Europe. But these issues will be with us as long as nuclear weapons are. For example, the same problem arose in 1994 regarding a possible North Korean conventional invasion of South Korea, which is a strong military ally of the United States. Would a U.S./South Korean policy of threatening the first use of nuclear weapons against such an invasion more effectively deter it?

See FIRST STRIKE/SECOND STRIKE; NUCLEAR DETERRENCE; NUCLEAR WAR.

BIBLIOGRAPHY
Blackaby, Frank et al., eds., *No-First-Use* (London: Taylor & Francis, 1984).
Freedman, Lawrence, *The Evolution of Nuclear Strategy* (New York: St. Martin's, 1981).
Sigal, Leon, *Nuclear Forces in Europe* (Washington, D.C.: Brookings Institution, 1984).
                                                                                    Steven Lee

FORBIDDEN STRATEGIES. Ever since Cicero it has been affirmed that there are limits beyond which war making ought not to go. Among the strategies that are purportedly forbidden have been waging wars of no quarter*, treacherous ruses* such as the misuse of the flag of truce and the killing of emissaries, killing soldiers who were *hors de combat,* and deliberate attacks on noncombatants. Medieval practice, however, allowed a belligerent to announce a war of no quarter, following which everyone could be slain, including civilians. If a town refused to surrender on request, then custom gave the attacker the right to rape and plunder any city that refused and was later captured, while denying such rape and plunder of any city wise enough to surrender. Indiscriminate slaughter of noncombatants was customary.

Franciscus de Victoria* (1485–1546) asked whether in a just war* it was lawful to kill all of the guilty and replied that in the heat of battle everyone who resists may be slain. Hugo Grotius* (1583–1645) extended the right to kill after surrender, not simply soldiers who had borne arms, or leaders who had stirred the country to war, but everyone residing in the territory. Even prisoners of war* lacked protection. Johan Textor (1638–1701) accepted the thesis that every armed enemy could be slain in battle or whenever they were in a position to do harm, but denied that there was any right to slay soldiers who had surrendered. Both Christian Wolff (1679–1754) and Emmerich Vattel* (1714–1767) counseled moderation and rejected the practice of slaying soldiers who had surrendered. Exceptions were claimed in the cases of soldiers who had committed ''grave breaches'' and reprisals* were permitted against them. Just war doctrine, however, traditionally spoke of proportionality*. This was interpreted in two senses: the reprisal for a violation of a law of war* ought to be proportional to the offense, and no act of war should cause havoc disproportional to the value of the gain to be achieved. Victoria had once said that if the devastation was excessive, then the prince ought not to undertake the war at all.

Every U.S. Army manual has had a preliminary disclaimer in the spirit of the current Army manual, The Law of Land Warfare* (FM 27-10), that ''the law of war places limits on the exercise of a belligerent's power . . . and requires that belligerents refrain from employing any kind or degree of violence which is not actually necessary for military purposes and that they conduct hostilities with regard for the principles of humanity and chivalry'' (Para. 3). The same disclaimer appeared in the declarations of the congresses at St. Petersburg*, Brussels*, The Hague*, of the International Red Cross*, and of the United Nations General Assembly. General Orders 100* forbade waging a war of no quarter or of misusing the flag, and every revision of the manual to the present has eschewed wars of no quarter.

The deliberate attack of civilian centers had been forbidden by every U.S. Army manual on the assumption that such attacks served no military usefulness and hence could not be justified by any appeal to military necessity*. With the invention of more powerful and less discriminate weapons, however, belligerents have had difficulty in complying with the initial ban on deliberate war on noncombatants. The earlier assumption that defended places could be easily distinguished from undefended places now appeared impossible to apply or interpret. The problem became unsolvable with the advent of aerial warfare*. A 1940 British study of the Royal Air Force Bomber Command night operation revealed that two-thirds of all air crews were missing their targets by over five miles. Understandably, the Germans interpreted this as an indication that the British intentionally bombed civilian centers. German planes, as a result of a navigational error, bombed London, and the British understandably believed that these attacks were deliberate, and ordered reprisal* raids on Berlin. Hitler responded with reprisal raids on London.

A collateral question is whether the bombing of water supplies, dams, dikes, power stations, and sewage plants is equivalent to the bombing of hospitals and schools. Once the infrastructure has been destroyed then the war is against civilians. Similarly, siege warfare* and the blockade of essential civilian supplies is more damaging to noncombatants than to soldiers. If the bombing of hospitals is forbidden, what about the water and sewage facilities without which no hospital can effectively operate? Modern aerial bombing does not permit such distinctions, with the result that proposed bans on forbidden targets of war appear unworkable.

In 1956 the International Committee of the Red Cross, convinced that current rules did not provide adequately for civilian protection, issued ''Draft Rules for the Limitation of the Dangers Incurred by the Civilian Population in Time of War.'' While these rules were approved at the 19th International Congress of the Red Cross in New Delhi in 1957 and submitted to governments for their approval, virtually no response came from any government and no further action was taken. In 1965 the same resolution was proposed at the meetings of the Red Cross, and it was endorsed by the UN General Assembly in Resolution 2444 on December 19, 1968. Further UN resolutions were issued against indiscriminate aerial bombardment, but in the face of the inability to wage aerial warfare discriminately, all such resolutions failed to win approval of those nations with extensive air forces. The difficulty was not limited to the question of whether nuclear bombs could be used proportionally, since modern conventional bombs were recognized as ''near nuclear'' in their effects, as well as in their inevitable indiscriminateness.

Attempts were made at a series of diplomatic conferences sponsored by the International Red Cross to determine whether application of the proportionality* principle could serve as a working criterion of civilian protection. Conferences to this end were held in 1971, 1972, 1974, and 1975, but the lack of any proportionality calculus, and the suspicion that some acts ought not to have a calculation at all, resulted in no common agreement. Article 41 of FM 27-10 states that loss of life and damage to property ought not to be disproportional to ''the military advantage to be gained.'' Who makes this assessment, and by what criteria is the calculation made? Article 272 forbids ''collective punishment,'' that is, punishing ''protected'' persons for offenses they did not commit. The weapons of modern war make this prohibition meaningless. *Collateral damage* is the military term for the damage to civilians that is ''unavoidable,'' ''militarily necessary,'' and, most importantly, claimed to be ''proportional'' to the ends to be gained. Understandably, the assessments vary widely as to when the damage should be considered unacceptable.

See COLLATERAL DAMAGE; MILITARY NECESSITY; PILLAGE;

PRISONERS OF WAR; QUARTER, NO, WARS OF; REPRISALS; RUSES
OF WAR; SURRENDER, UNCONDITIONAL.
BIBLIOGRAPHY
Jomini, Baron Antoine Henri de, *The Art of War* (Novato, Calif.: Presidio Press, 1992).
Peters, Cynthia, ed., *Collateral Damage: The New World Order at Home and Abroad*
    (Boston: South End Press, 1992).

FORBIDDEN WEAPONS. During the Middle Ages, Catholic Church councils
proposed bans on certain weapons, including incendiaries*, poisons, the cross
bow, and lances with barbed tips. In part this was a carryover from knightly
rules of chivalry, which held that battle was carried out by men of honor and
face to face. No knight would use a long sword against a noble foe armed only
with a short sword. However, in the history of war most combatants were not
knights, and such efforts were ignored by armies that would not abandon a
militarily useful weapon solely on the grounds of humanity or chivalry.

The first U.S. Army manual, *General Orders 100** (1863), made no mention
of forbidden weapons, although it did refer to certain forbidden strategies*, such
as waging wars of no quarter*, pillage*, and deliberate attacks on civilians. In
1868 a declaration was issued at a conference at St. Petersburg* urging the
contracting parties to renounce the use in war of any projectile weighing less
than 400 grams that was explosive or "charged with fulminating or inflammable
substances." The declaration charged that such bullets "uselessly aggravate the
sufferings of disabled men, or render their death inevitable." The St. Petersburg
Declaration was reasserted at a conference in Brussels* on August 27, 1874,
which added further bans on the use of poisons, as well as such strategies as
no quarter, murder by treachery, and the killing or wounding of soldiers *hors
de combat.* The United States was neither a participant nor a signatory to these
efforts. The issue arose again in The Hague Congresses of 1899 and 1907*.
Both congresses proposed a ban on weapons that caused "superfluous injury"
(1899) or "unnecessary suffering" (1907). The Hague issued a "Declaration
Prohibiting the Employment of Bullets Which Expand or Flatten Easily in the
Human Body." Neither Great Britain nor the United States was a signatory
when it was first issued in 1899, although Great Britain did sign when the
declaration reappeared in 1907.

The U.S. Army manual of 1914, *Rules of Land Warfare**, dismissed this
declaration in article 175 and relegated it to a footnote. The United States offered
a substitute to the effect that "the use of bullets which inflict unnecessarily cruel
wounds—such as explosive bullets, and in general, every kind of bullet which
exceeds the limit necessary for placing a man immediately *hors de combat*
should be forbidden." The manual did not forbid dumdum bullets*, and, thus,
implied the U.S. belief that they did not cause unnecessarily cruel wounds.
Article 184 affirmed that such a prohibition did not apply to the use of "explosives contained in artillery projectiles, mines, aerial torpedoes, or hand grenades,
but it does include the use of lances with barbed heads, irregular shaped bullets,

projectiles filled with glass, etc., and the use of any substance on these bullets that would tend to unnecessarily inflame a wound.'' The United States believed that the prohibition applied to the scoring of the ends of bullets and the use of soft-nosed or exploding bullets. Article 176 forbade the use of poison but did not list what qualified as a poison. The Hague ban on gas and chemicals passed with only one dissenting vote by the U.S. representative, Naval Captain Alfred T. Mahan.

No significant change appeared in the subsequent revisions of the U.S. Army manual in 1934 and 1956, despite the effort of the International Red Cross in a 1925 protocol to ban the use of gas, noxious chemicals, and biologicals in war. Although revisions in 1976 disclaimed the use of germ warfare and the first use of chemical weapons, the manual did not forbid the use of atomic weapons, incendiaries, a host of fragmentation antipersonnel bombs, or the use of chemicals in reprisal*. Other than germ warfare, the only specifically forbidden weapons were the same lances with barbed heads, and so forth, that appeared in the 1914 manual.

As early as 1969 U Thant, secretary-general of the UN, urged the member states to ratify the relevant Declarations of The Hague, St. Petersburg, and Brussels, and the Geneva Protocol. He made special reference to the use of napalm, gases, chemicals, and nuclear weapons as weapons that caused ''unnecessary suffering.'' The UN General Assembly has continued to endorse scores of resolutions proposing bans on weapons deemed to be excessive. In 1973 the International Red Cross added new proposals to their 1949 conventions concerning ''weapons that may cause unnecessary suffering or have indiscriminate effects.'' These included proposed bans on the use of incendiaries, chemicals, germ weapons, certain small-calibre rifles, and nuclear bombs, although the nations in attendance were unable to agree whether any or all of the above should be considered forbidden. In 1975 the International Red Cross held a Conference of Government Experts on the Use of Certain Conventional Weapons. The sessions began with discussion of a British paper titled, ''Legal Criteria for the Prohibition or Restriction of Use of Categories of Conventional Weapons,'' which concentrated on the meaning of the The Hague terms ''unnecessary suffering'' and ''superfluous injury.'' No agreement was reached, either on the meaning of the expressions or on the intent of the phrase ''calculated to cause.'' A second session was held in 1976 in an effort to find some balance between the demands of military necessity* and the requirements of humanitarian concern, but no consensus was reached. Some argued that all weapons have a restricted legitimate use; others favored a total ban on the same weapons. Those in favor of the total ban argued that no commander would be able to decide in the heat of battle whether the likely use of a doubtful weapon would or would not exceed the bounds of humanitarian concern. Some were convinced that enough was known about the consequences of incendiaries for the conference to issue a protocol immediately banning their use. Others expressed doubt that incendiaries were any more injurious than many other accepted weapons.

On numerous occasions the UN General Assembly has issued prohibitions of incendiaries, fragmentation bombs, chemicals, germs, and nuclear bombs (see articles herein on UN Resolutions Banning Manufacture or Use of Nuclear Weapons; Fragmentation Bombs; Incendiaries; and Biological/Chemical Warfare), with generally overwhelming, although never unanimous, approval. The earliest U.S. manual, *General Orders 100**, had no section on forbidden weapons; the 1914 edition spoke of bans on chemicals, poisons, and weapons likely to cause "unnecessary suffering"; subsequent and current editions have paid decreasing attention to the matter. The inability to resolve the question of whether there should be forbidden weapons has paralleled a like inability to achieve agreement on whether there are or should be forbidden strategies*.

See BIOLOGICAL/CHEMICAL WARFARE; BULLETS, EXPANDING; FRAGMENTATION BOMBS; INCENDIARIES; MINES; NUCLEAR WAR.

BIBLIOGRAPHY

Gollancz, Victor, *Leaving Them to Their Fate* (London: Gollancz, 1946).

Lifton, Robert Jay, and Richard Falk, *Indefensible Weapons* (New York: HarperCollins, 1982).

Roling, Bert V. A., and Loga Sukovic, *The Law of War and Dubious Weapons* (Stockholm: Alqvist & Wiksell, 1976).

Rose, Steven, ed., *CBW: Chemical and Biological Warfare* (London: George G. Harrap, 1968).

Schwartzenberger, Georg, *The Legality of Nuclear Weapons* (London: Stevens and Sons, 1958).

Szasz, Paul, "The Conference on Excessively Injurious or Indiscriminate Weapons," *American Journal of International Law* 74 (1980).

FRAGMENTATION BOMBS. Article 23 of Hague Convention 4, Respecting the Laws and Customs of War on Land, stated that it was forbidden "to employ arms, projectiles, or material calculated to cause unnecessary suffering." The question of when suffering is unnecessary has remained unresolved for at least two reasons. In the first place, no calculus of suffering exists, and in the second place, The Hague did not specify who makes the determination. The only relevant statement in *The Law of Land Warfare** (FM 27-10), is Article 34, which interprets Hague Convention 4, Article 23 as applying only to those weapons that states refrain from using. Thus the manual states that "the prohibition certainly does not extend to the use of explosives contained in artillery projectiles, mines*, rockets, or hand grenades. Usage has, however, established the illegality of the use of lances with barbed heads, irregular-shaped bullets, and projectiles filled with glass." The mention of lances as prohibited makes it evident that the only criterion is military usefulness rather than the amount or degree of suffering caused. Thus, "necessary" is modified by what is militarily useful, such that no weapons will be considered to cause unnecessary suffering if they are militarily useful weapons. The current interpretation in the military manual is that no useful weapon will ever be forbidden. Is this all that Hague Convention 4, Article 23 meant?

Jean-Pierre Vigier, M.D., director of research at the National Center for Scientific Research and former officer-in-charge of armaments inspection for the French Army under General De Lattre de Tassigny during the Vietnam War*, emphasized the essentially indiscriminate nature of fragmentation bombs. They cannot, in any sense, be aimed, since they explode projectiles in a 360-degree radius. Such fragmentation bombs constituted 50 percent of all the bombs that fell in North Vietnam. A combined report on Antipersonnel Bombs by members of a Japanese scientific committee paid special attention to "ball bombs" (cluster or fragmentation bombs). Their report noted that such bombs did no harm to military hardware, but were designed to kill or maim as many persons as possible and that they inflicted injuries extremely hard to treat. The report compared them to dumdum* bullets in their inhumaneness, since they caused relatively little damage on entry but immense damage inside the body before exiting. Although the Pentagon claimed on May 5, 1967, that they were not using such canister bombs, the Army *Chemical Reference Handbook,* FM-38, listed them as part of the standard arsenal, and medical doctors reported that they treated civilians for wounds from such fragmentation bombs. *Aviation Week* reported in February 1967 that these bombs were normally dropped from planes at an altitude of three miles, thus vitiating any claim that they were used with any precision. In 1981 the UN General Assembly passed a resolution banning "particularly inhumane weapons," including fragmentation bombs, incendiaries*, and booby traps. Even if no clear calculus existed to show that such fragmentation bombs caused "unnecessary suffering," the fact remained that they were indiscriminate antipersonnel weapons and thus violated the rules against deliberate attacks on civilians.

See FORBIDDEN WEAPONS; GENEVA CONVENTION, 1949; HAGUE, THE, CONGRESSES; MINES.

BIBLIOGRAPHY
Aubert, Maurice, "The International Committee of the Red Cross and the Problem of Excessively Injurious or Indiscriminate Weapons," *International Review of the Red Cross* (November–December 1990), 477–97.
Human Rights Watch and Physicians for Human Rights, eds., *Landmines: A Deadly Legacy* (New York: Human Rights Watch, 1993).
Lifton, Robert Jay, and Richard Falk, *Indefensible Weapons* (New York: Basic Books, 1982).

FRIENDLY FIRE. The current Army Training and Doctrine Command (TRADOC) definition of *friendly fire* is: "the act of firing on friendly personnel or equipment, believing that you are engaging the enemy." *Fratricide* is friendly fire that results in casualties*. Equipment failures that result in casualties are excluded. Traditionally it had been assumed that about 2 percent of the casualties in war came from friendly fire. On November 12, 1758, during the French and Indian War, the troops under Colonel George Washington exchanged fire with those under Lt. Colonel George Mercer, resulting in the deaths of up to forty friendly soldiers. During World War I it was believed that the losses from friendly fire would be small enough, when compared with the enemy losses, to justify these deaths. Up to 5 percent losses were considered acceptable.

No careful study was made of fratricide deaths until World War II. The first was believed to have been made by a medical doctor, James Hopkins, who made a record of the types of wounds he treated. Since the Allied armies had some distinctive weapons, he was able to identify when Allied troops had suffered friendly fire. He concluded that 16 percent of those killed and 19 percent of those wounded were by friendly fire. The close air support bombing errors that killed a number of U.S. ground personnel including Lt. Gen. Lesley McNair during the Normandy invasion, and the event in Sicily in 1943 when of 144 C-47 transports carrying American reinforcements, twenty-three were shot down and thirty-seven damaged were both by friendly fire. A study was made of the battles at Bougainville, with the conclusion that 24 percent of the deaths were by friendly fire. In Vietnam*, due to the fact that certain weapons (M16 rifles, M79 grenade launchers, artillery, napalm, and Claymore mines), were exclusive to the U.S. armies, it was concluded that friendly casualties approached 20 percent. In the Israeli-Egyptian war more than 30 percent of the casualties were due to fratricide. During the Gulf War* the ''official'' report listed 615 U.S. battle casualties, of which 148 were fatal. Of the 148 fatalities, 35 (24%) were from friendly fire. Of the 467 nonfatal casualties, 72 (15%) were from friendly fire. Can we then calculate that if we killed 20,000 Iraqi soldiers, losing 35 of our own through friendly fire is acceptable?

This is an ethical, not a military, question, and since wars continue to be waged under conditions that make friendly casualties inevitable, it will not go away. This question is related to an equally perplexing question when we attempt to calculate how many enemy deaths are proportional*, given the supposed value of the objectives. The confusion in efforts to calculate this proportion was illustrated in the comment of Emmett Paige, Jr., an assistant secretary of defense, who urged that a ''cost-effective'' solution be found for avoiding fratricide. Presumably, if no cost-effective solution could be found we would have to live with the friendly deaths.

See CASUALTIES OF WAR; COLLATERAL DAMAGE; PROPORTION-ALITY.

BIBLIOGRAPHY
Bryan, Courtland D. B., *Friendly Fire* (New York: G. P. Putnam, 1976).
Office of Technology Assessment, *Who Goes There: Friend or Foe?* (Washington, D.C.: U.S. Government Printing Office, June, 1993).
Paige, Emmett, Jr., ''Fratricidal Friendly Fire Must End,'' Address at the Naval Postgraduate School, Monterey, August 2, 1994, in *Defense Issues* 9, no. 68.
Schraeder, Charles, *The Problem of Friendly Fire in Modern War* (Fort Leavenworth, Kan.: U.S. Army Command and General Staff College, 1982).

G

GANDHI, MOHANDAS K. (1869–1948). Born in northwest British India, through his mother he was greatly influenced by Jain teachings of *ahimsa*— nonviolence. The power of the British also impressed Gandhi. In 1888 he left to study law in London. His wife and first son remained behind.

After completing his studies, Gandhi returned and practiced law unsuccessfully. Eventually he secured a job as an attorney for a Muslim company in South Africa, where he discovered that Indians were deprived of rights enjoyed by whites. This discovery marked the beginning of Gandhi's social crusading. Between May 1893, when he first arrived, and July 1914, when he finally departed South Africa, Gandhi succeeded in uniting the entire Indian community—Muslims and Hindus alike—to negotiate and obtain various political rights in South Africa. He did this by utilizing a nonviolent method that he called *satyâgraha,* literally "holding onto truth." *Satyâgraha* entails a constructive program that develops self-reliance and a willingness to suffer for the sake of one's goals. Gandhi and many South African Indians served time in jail in pursuit of political rights.

On returning to India he was recognized for his achievements in South Africa. The Indian National Congress initially welcomed Gandhi as one who could bolster their party's strength in their bid for independence from Britain. But Gandhi was more tolerant of the British than were many in the Congress Party. He began an *ashram*—a religious community—in his home province of Gujarat. In 1917 he began a campaign against British taxes on tenant farmers in Champaran province. This campaign attracted the attention and admiration of all of India by demonstrating the power of *satyâgraha* in earning concessions from the British.

In 1919, disappointed that Britain did not reward India for her efforts in World War I by granting her Dominion status, Gandhi called for a general *hartal,* a day of prayer and fasting during which all business activity would cease. This marked the beginning of widespread civil resistance that was occasionally tarnished by violence. While Gandhi considered calling off the campaign because of the violence, a British General, R.E.H. Dyer, seeking to punish civil resisters and perhaps respond to a beating three days earlier of an English headmistress in Amritsar, ordered fifty troops to open fire on a peaceful meeting of civil resisters. Within ten minutes the soldiers killed almost four hundred men, women, and children, and wounded over a thousand. Dyer then ordered that any Indian using the street where the headmistress had been beaten was to crawl on all fours. From this point on Gandhi became more actively involved in Indian politics and in the Congress Party.

Gandhi urged Indians to spin their own clothes and avoid the purchase of cloth from abroad. He believed that India's independence lay in her becoming self-reliant by developing economic independence within the villages. He launched a national movement that looked as if it would pluck independence from the British in a matter of a year or two. However, in 1921, a number of civil resisters brutally beat and murdered some police officials in Chauri Chaura. The violence led Gandhi to call a halt to all resistance against the British. Nonetheless, Gandhi was arrested, charged with sedition, and in 1922 sentenced to six years in prison.

After almost two years in prison he was released by the British following an appendectomy. During these two years the Hindu-Muslim unity that Gandhi had cultivated had begun to break apart. The *satyâgraha* campaign had also disintegrated. Gandhi searched for means whereby he could train Indians in nonviolence and self-reliance. Early in 1930 he conceived his most famous campaign, the Great Salt March.

The making of salt was prohibited by the British, who held a monopoly on its production. Gandhi intended to march over two hundred miles in twenty-four days from Sabermati to Dandi, on the shores of the Indian Ocean, to make salt from the sea, and to thereby court arrest and imprisonment in hopes of generating a new nonviolent campaign of civil resistance. He left his *ashram* with seventy-eight women and men. When he arrived at Dandi, the marchers had increased in number to several thousand. Gandhi made salt and was arrested. A lengthy and massive nonviolent civil resistance campaign followed, which culminated in Gandhi's being invited to attend a conference in London to discuss the independence of India.

While in England Gandhi garnered much popular support for India's cause. He also delivered an overseas radio address to the United States. But in the end Britain maintained its hold on India.

In the 1930s Gandhi worked to improve the conditions of the poor, and one of his fasts on behalf of the untouchables almost cost him his life. His increasing intolerance of violence, including war, earned him and his wife a prison sentence at the outset of World War II. During this imprisonment Gandhi's wife of sixty-two years died.

When the war ended, Gandhi was released from prison. He discovered that Mohamed Ali Jinnah, a Muslim leader in the Congress Party, had used his support of the British during World War II to help convince them that when

Indian independence was granted, a separate Muslim state—Pakistan—should also be created. Gandhi opposed this division, but in the end Jinnah prevailed. Gandhi saw religious intolerance fanned by both Hindus and Muslims, and he struggled to convince Muslims and Hindus to overcome their differences and live together. There can be no doubt that Gandhi prevented much bloodshed during these years. He traveled on foot from town to town, talking face-to-face with Muslim and Hindu villagers, urging them to cooperate with each other. In the end these efforts cost him his life. Nathuram Vinayak Godse, a Hindu, was angered like many others by Gandhi's successful appeals for Hindus to make sacrifices for Muslims as a show of unity. On January 30, 1948, Godse shot Gandhi three times in the chest, killing him almost instantly.

   See CIVIL DISOBEDIENCE; CONSCIENTIOUS OBJECTION; HINDU-ISM AND WAR; ISLAM AND WAR; PACIFISM.

BIBLIOGRAPHY
Fischer, Louis, *The Life of Mahatma Gandhi* (New York: Harper & Row, 1983).
Gandhi, M. K., *Non-Violence in Peace and War* (Ahmedabad: Navajivan, 1942, 1944).
————, *Non-Violent Resistance* (New York: Schocken, 1961).

                                                                    Barry L. Gan

GENERAL ORDERS 100 (1863). On May 24, 1863, the *New York Times* noted under a heading, "Military Forces," the publication of "New Rules for the Government of the National Armies." The article not only made no mention of the significance of this manual, it failed to note most of its major contributions, especially in the areas of the treatment of prisoners of war* and of non com-batant civilians. This was the first manual ever issued by a nation for the in-struction of its armies in war.

   No consistent policy appeared to exist during the Civil War in the treatment of civilians and their possessions. It was a widespread practice to take no pris-oners (waging a war of no quarter*), and confusion existed as to whether the "customs of war" applied in this war. In July 1862, General Henry W. Halleck was put in charge of the Union Army. As a young Lieutenant during the Mex-ican War he had been consulted frequently for his opinions on matters of in-ternational law growing out of that conflict. In 1861 he had published a text on international law, and had become acquainted with Professor Francis Lieber* of Columbia University, an authority in the fields of international law, modern history, political science, and civil and common law. Professor Lieber had au-thored two texts: *Political Ethics* (1836) and *Civil Liberty and Self Government* (1853), and had also written extensively on the problems of guerrilla war*. Halleck's promotion left him no time to deal with the legal issues arising out of the war. Both President Abraham Lincoln and Secretary of War Edwin Stan-ton were concerned enough to establish a board to consider the problems. The board consisted of four Union generals: E. A. Hitchcock, G. Cadwalader, George L. Hartsuff, and J. H. Martindale, and Professor Francis Lieber. The generals deferred to Lieber, who wrote the document. They were to report to General

Halleck for suggestions and amendments. They did so February 20, 1863, and by May 20, 1863, the revised document was published.

Five thousand copies were printed and distributed to the officers of both the Union and Confederate armies. The provisions of the manual were asserted to be applicable to any war in which the United States might be involved. The basic premise was that both the Union and Confederate armies should operate within its framework, and the final section on "Insurrection–Civil War–Rebellion" stated that the laws contained therein applied equally to civil and international wars. The cover letter written by E. D. Townsend, assistant adjutant general, submitted April 24, 1863, stated that by order of President Lincoln these instructions were "published for the information of all concerned."

Many soldiers of the North had operated as if they were police and the soldiers of the South were criminals. How were civilians to be treated and how were soldiers to consider their private property? If the Southerners were like brigands, then prisoners need not be taken and their property could be confiscated as booty. Indeed, many soldiers of the Union army took the property of citizens and shipped it home for resale with the permission of their commanding officers. Some officers took pains to protect citizens in the South from marauding troops. General Irwin McDowell, for example, gave strict orders to his troops forbidding the taking of booty and the indiscriminate firing on the outposts of the enemy. Many of his troops were less than enthusiastic about not being able to pillage, and many considered his order forbidding plunder to be treasonable. In the Battle of Belmont near Columbia, Missouri, November 7, 1861, the federal troops were so involved in seizing plunder, and they became so disorganized, that they barely made it back to their boats before heavy enemy reinforcements came upon them. The Confederate army posed problems also. Confederate authorities claimed the right to send soldiers dressed as civilians inside the Union lines to lie in wait for Union forces, to destroy bridges and buildings, and to kill the unwary. The Confederate government insisted that such troops were still entitled to be treated as ordinary prisoners of war, and threatened that if the Union forces summarily executed* them as spies*, imprisoned Union troops would be shot in reprisal*.

The war had all the elements of a guerrilla war and its resulting chaos. Troops supposedly on military expeditions robbed and looted civilian homes and executed unarmed civilians. For example, on August 21, 1863, guerrilla leader William Clarke Quantrill and 450 of his men attacked Lawrence, Kansas, and after looting and burning, they proceeded to kill every unarmed male big enough to carry a gun. After four hours of shooting, approximately 150 unarmed men had been slain, leaving eighty widows and 150 orphaned children. One-fourth of the residences were burned to the ground and stores and banks were looted. The reprisal was no less indiscriminate in its treatment of civilians. In an effort to catch the offenders, Senator James Lane (D-IN) and General Thomas Ewing issued *General Orders No. 11,* which ordered the forced evacuation of most of the civilian inhabitants of four Missouri counties. Union troops went through the area and, if any possessions of Lawrence citizens were found in a house, it was burned and looted in turn. Over 20,000 homes were destroyed. Obviously some advice to troops was in order.

These instructions consisted of 157 articles. The first Section of thirty articles affirmed that laws of war* existed, and that these laws set limits to what soldiers were permitted to do. The laws forbade plunder, murder, and enslavement of the civilian population. Since military necessity* governed what was permitted, reprisals were allowed, and some collateral damage* to the innocent was inevitable. Section 2, with seventeen articles, assured protection of the private property of civilians, protection of persons, especially women and children, and protection of religion and the arts, and warned all American troops that violations would bring the most severe punishment. Section 3, with thirty-three articles, made provisions for prisoners of war and the taking of hostages*, eschewed wars of no quarter, the use of poisons, and the inflicting of additional wounds on enemies who were *hors de combat,* and, while permitting shooting of prisoners in the act of attempting to escape*, forbade the shooting of them for having unsuccessfully tried. Section 4, with five articles, provided protection for armed partisans as prisoners of war but denied the same for spies, brigands, or pirates. Section 5, with nineteen articles, specified the treatment of spies, war traitors, captured messengers, and abusers of the flag of truce. Section 6, with fourteen articles, provided for the exchange of prisoners and the proper uses of flags of truce. Section 7, with sixteen articles, explained the conditions for parole. Section 8, with thirteen articles, set the parameters for armistice or capitulation. Section 9, with one article, condemned assassination*. Section 10, with nine articles, set the punishments for insurrection, civil war, and rebellion. Article 59 of this manual served as the legal basis for the trial and execution of Captain Henry Wirz*, former commandant of the Confederate prisoner of war camp at Andersonville, Georgia, for putative crimes against prisoners.

The manual achieved almost instant international fame. The distinguished German political theorist, J. K. Bluntschli, prepared a document for the German army (*see* German War Book*), which was virtually a verbatim translation from the Lieber manual. France, Serbia, Spain, Portugal, Italy, and Great Britain used *General Orders 100* in preparing manuals for their armies. In 1874 at the Congress at Brussels, which had been convened by the emperor of Russia for the purpose of codifying the rules of war in the Brussels Declaration*, Baron Antoine Henri de Jomini, the presiding officer, said that the congress had been inspired by the Lieber code. In 1873, when the Institute of International Law* was founded, the association took the Lieber document as a possible basis for an international code of the laws of war. At the time of the outbreak of the Spanish-American War, *General Orders 100* was reissued, and used as the official manual. It provided the basis for military trials for war crimes of American soldiers (*see* Philippines War Crimes Trials*). Much of the Lieber document was formally adopted by the Congresses at the Hague in 1899 and 1907. The code remained the official army manual for the United States until its revision in 1914.

See LIEBER, FRANCIS; WIRZ, CAPTAIN HENRY.

BIBLIOGRAPHY

Davis, George B., "Doctor Francis Lieber's Instructions for the Government of Armies in the Field," *American Journal of International Law* (January 1907).

Friedel, Frank, "General Orders and Military Government," *Mississippi Valley Historical Review* 32, no.4 (March 1946).

General Orders 100: Instructions for the Government of Armies of the United States in the Field. 43rd Cong., 1st sess., H.R., Executive Document. January 24, 1874.

Hittle, Lieutenant-Colonel J. D., ed., *Jomini and His Summary of the Art of War* (Harrisburg, Pa.: Military Service Press, 1947).

Mink, Charles R., "General Orders, No. 11: The Forced Evacuation of Civilians During the Civil War," *Military Affairs* vol. 35, no. 1, part 2 (1970).

Morgan, J. H., trans., *The War Book of the German General Staff* (New York: McBride, Nast, & Co., 1915).

GENEVA CONVENTIONS, 1864, 1868. Henri Dunant, a Swiss philanthropist, was a prime mover, and the Swiss government was the convener of the first Geneva meeting in 1863, out of which emerged a Convention in 1864. The meeting established the organization known as the International Red Cross*. Dunant had personally witnessed the plight of the sick and wounded soldiers on the battlefield at Solferino (1859) during the Franco-Austrian War, and in 1862 he published *Un Souvenir de Solferino*. The Geneva Society of Public Welfare, under the presidency of Gustave Moynier, supported Dunant, and on February 9, 1863, appointed a committee composed of G. H. Dufour as president, Dunant, Moynier, Theodore Maunoir, and Louis Appia. This committee convened the international conference of 1863, which announced that those in attendance were "animated with the desire to soften, as much as depends on them, the evils of warfare, to suppress its useless hardships and improve the fate of wounded soldiers on the field of battle." Out of the sessions that began in 1863 there emerged, in 1864, a "Convention for the Amelioration of the Condition of the Wounded in Armies in the Field." At this time a red cross on a white ground was determined to be the official sign of medical personnel, and the committee urged the creation of national committees. Representatives from twelve countries were present: Switzerland, Baden, Belgium, Denmark, Spain, France, Hesse, Italy, The Netherlands, Portugal, Prussia, and Wurttemberg. The convention entered into force in early 1865. Although the United States was not present, President Chester Arthur signed a Declaration of Accession on March 1, 1882, and the Senate consented to this accession on March 16, 1882. Dunant was awarded the first Nobel Peace Prize in 1901 for his efforts.

The 1864 document contained ten articles. Article 1 established that ambulances and military hospitals should be acknowledged to be neutral and thus protected by all belligerents as long as any sick or wounded were being cared for. This neutrality would cease if the hospitals or ambulances were being held by a military force. Article 2 affirmed that all those employed in caring for the sick, including chaplains*, should have the benefits of neutrality as long as they were so employed. Article 3 stated that those mentioned in Article 2 should be allowed to remain in their duties after occupation, or allowed to return safely to their corps. Article 4 stated that all equipment in such hospitals must remain in the hospitals during retreat. Article 5 affirmed that any inhabitants of the country who assisted in caring for the sick and wounded be respected as neutrals, even when the care was in a private home. Article 6 stated that sick and wounded soldiers should be cared for. If after recovery they were deemed unfit to serve, they were to be sent home. If they were able-bodied, they should be sent home on the condition they agreed not to bear arms in that war. Article 7 confirmed the distinctive Red Cross flag. Article 8 affirmed that the convention should be regulated by the commanders-in-chief of the belligerent armies. Article 9 urged those powers present to convey the substance of the convention to those countries "which have not found it convenient to send plenipotentiaries." Article 10 affirmed that the convention would be ratified in Berne in four months (from August 27, 1864), or sooner if possible. No limits were set as to what could be done to able-bodied soldiers in the process of wounding or killing them.

On October 20, 1868, a second Red Cross Convention (Geneva) was called. It issued resolutions further elaborating the role of medical staff and outlined procedures for quartering prisoners of war. It extended the same privileges for the casualties of sea battles. Article 6, for example, provided that passengers and crew of sinking ships be rescued, and that the ships that did this rescue be considered as hospital ships until they had delivered their prisoners to a safe port. The United States was not a participant at either conference, although the president and Congress approved both the 1864 and 1868 resolutions at the same time (1874).

See RED CROSS, RED CRESCENT, RED LION AND SUN.

BIBLIOGRAPHY

Geneva Convention of 1864. Executive Document No. 177, 47th Cong., 1st sess., Senate. Washington, D.C., March 3, 1882.

Martin, Harold H., and Joseph R. Baker, eds., *Laws of Maritime Warfare Affecting Rights and Duties of Belligerents Existing as on August 1, 1914* (Washington, D.C.: U.S. Government Printing Office, 1918).

GENEVA CONVENTION, JULY 6, 1906. Issued a "Convention for the Amelioration of the Condition of the Wounded and Sick in Armies in the Field." Delegates from thirty-five nations signed an agreement regarding further details for the proper treatment of the sick and wounded who become prisoners of war. The thirty-three articles discussed the sick and wounded, personnel, materiel, convoys of evacuation, the distinctive emblem, application and execution of the convention, repression of abuses and infractions, and some general provisions to the effect that this convention would replace the conventions of 1864 and

1868*. The sense in which the convention was not binding was expressed in Article 33, to the effect that: "Each of the contracting parties shall have the right to denounce the present convention. This denunciation shall only become operative one year after notification in writing shall have been made to the Swiss Federal Council."

BIBLIOGRAPHY

Geneva Convention of 1906 for the Amelioration of the Condition of the Wounded and Sick in Armies in the Field (Washington, D.C.: Carnegie Foundation, 1916).

GENEVA CONVENTIONS, JULY 27, 1929. The 1929 Red Cross Conference was called to take account of events since World War I, involving the creation of both new weapons and strategies of warfare. Two conventions were issued.

In the first, the "Convention for the Amelioration of the Condition of the Wounded and Sick of Armies in the Field," the thirty-three articles of the 1906 convention were increased to thirty-nine. No significant alterations appeared in the first seventeen articles. Article 18 in the new convention included medical aircraft as also entitled to the same protection allowed for land ambulances. Article 34 of the 1906 convention stated that the provisions were obligatory only in wars between signatory powers. Article 25 of the new convention stated that the provisions would remain in force even if nonsignatories were involved. Article 38 retained the older provision that each contracting party had the right to denounce the convention, thus demonstrating that the convention did not have the force of international law. Forty-seven signatures were affixed by the nations represented.

The second convention issued by the 1929 conference, the "Convention Relative to the Treatment of Prisoners of War," was a new convention not found in the 1906 report. It contained forty-seven articles and an annex. The preface accepted the 1907 Hague* Convention and added new stipulations concerning the capture, evacuation, and imprisonment of prisoners of war. Article 2 affirmed that prisoners were to be treated humanely. Article 7 stated that prisoners were not to be needlessly exposed to danger while being evacuated from the war zone. Article 8 affirmed that prisoners were not to be conventionally imprisoned at all unless their safety or health required it, nor should they be housed in climates to which their bodies were unaccustomed. Article 11 required the captors to supply food for prisoners on a par with what the captor's troops had in base camp. Article 46 affirmed that "any corporal punishment, any imprisonment in quarters without daylight and, in general, any form of cruelty, is forbidden." While it allowed for prisoners to be shot while attempting to escape*, no prisoner could be shot for having tried unsuccessfully. Article 96 retained the former understanding that each contracting power had the right to denounce the convention. Forty-seven nations became signatories. An Annex consisted of a "Model Agreement Concerning Direct Repatriation and Hospitalization in a Neutral Country of Prisoners of War for Reasons of Health." It listed the diseases or wounds considered to warrant such repatriation.

The importance of these Geneva conventions can scarcely be overemphasized in view of the fact that the judges of the Nuremberg trials* appealed to them as the basis for their claim that laws existed, the violation of which constituted crimes against humanity*. However, the nations of the world have not agreed whether the Geneva conventions are mere "conventions" or whether they represent "custom," and hence have the status of international law. For example, the Israeli Supreme Court refused to review the actions of the military government in the West Bank in the light of Geneva Convention 4 because they held that the convention was wholly "conventional" rather than international law. On the other hand, the International Court of Justice* ruled in the Iranian *Hostages* case that the obligations were more than "contractual." They were obligations under general international law. In the case of the *Nicaragua* judgment the court ruled that even where a party denounces the Geneva conventions, it does not thereby relieve itself from obligations under international law or the laws of humanity. Nations have yet to reconcile what is customary international law if it is inconsistent with or absent from their own federal law. This was evidenced in the lengthy debate in the United States over whether President Ronald Reagan was legally justified in declaring that the judgment of the International Court of Justice in the *Nicaragua* case could be dismissed as mere convention.

See ESCAPE, ATTEMPTS OF PRISONERS TO; PRISONERS OF WAR; TORTURE.

BIBLIOGRAPHY

Friedman, Leon, ed., *The Law of War,* vol. 1 (New York: Random House, 1972).

GENEVA CONVENTIONS, 1949. Drafts were submitted in 1938 for a conference to be held in 1940, but due to World War II, the meetings were postponed until 1949. In the interim, new weapons and strategies had emerged, the first nuclear bombs had been dropped in war, and war crimes trials had been held. (See Control Council Law No. 10; Nuremberg Trials; and Tokyo Trials.) Since many of the offenses for which the Germans and Japanese had been charged had occurred prior to the outbreak of war, and since the mass deportations of civilians, the deliberate imprisonment of immense numbers of noncombatants, and the taking of civilian hostages* had not been anticipated, it was clear that the 1929 Geneva Conventions* were sadly inadequate. A need existed to specify rules for the protection of enemy aliens in belligerent countries, to protect sick and wounded civilians, to establish safe zones for them, and to provide for the internees of both occupied and unoccupied territories. Four conventions were issued.

The first, the "Convention for the Amelioration of the Condition of the Wounded and Sick in Armed Forces in the Field," consisted of fifty-four articles, an annex, and a long list of reservations affixed by the signatories. Article 3 posed new restrictions covering both civilian and soldier in armed conflicts, even when they were not of an international nature. Mandatory provisions for each of the high contracting parties were specified to apply to persons taking no active part in the hostilities, including soldiers *hors de combat.* The significance of these cautions was particularly pertinent in view of the observation made at the conference that in World War II, 80–90 percent of the war casualties were noncombatants. The following were forbidden:

1. Violence to life and person, in particular murder of all kinds, mutilation, cruel treatment and torture

2. The taking of hostages

3. Outrages upon personal dignity, in particular, humiliating and degrading treatment

4. The passing of sentences and the carrying out of executions without previous judgment by a regularly constituted court

The convention also provided that the wounded and sick shall be collected and cared for. What made this article so revolutionary was that it required states to treat their own nationals in accordance with the prohibitions. Sixty-one nations signed in support. The annex consisted of a "Draft Agreement Relating to Hospital Zones and Localities." Twenty-three nations listed reservations, all of them raising questions of infringement on national sovereign rights.

The second 1949 convention was entitled "Convention for the Amelioration of the Condition of Wounded, Sick and Shipwrecked Members of the Armed Forces at Sea" (see Geneva Conventions, 1864, 1868). The convention contained sixty-two articles, most importantly Article 3, which followed Article 3 of the previous convention. The same sixty-one nations signed in agreement.

The third convention, the "Convention Relative to the Treatment of Prisoners of War," contained 143 articles, including the same Article 3, but in addition provided detailed specification of the treatment of those thus interned.

The fourth 1959 convention was entitled "Convention Relative to the Protection of Civilian Persons in Time of War." The 141 articles followed the first 1959 convention in all significant details, including the inclusion of an identical Article 3. The same sixty-one nations signed in agreement. It was commonly assumed that these Geneva Conventions had the status of custom and were, hence, laws of war*. They were so construed during the Nuremberg and Tokyo trials* and those subsequent to Control Council Law No. 10*. Doubt was raised, however, following judgments issued by the International Court of Justice*, particularly in the merits phase of *Military and Paramilitary Activities in and Against Nicaragua.* On November 26, 1984, by a vote of 15 to 1, the International Court of Justice determined that it had jurisdiction to hear the case brought by Nicaragua against the United States for violating international law through their use of military intervention in Nicaragua. President Ronald Reagan, however, denied that the court had jurisdiction over U.S. actions, thus raising the question whether the Geneva Conventions are established law which nations are obligated to obey, or whether, as in the case of the United States, a nation may vitiate the law by not being a signatory.

See BIOLOGICAL/CHEMICAL WARFARE; COLLATERAL DAMAGE; CRIMES AGAINST HUMANITY; FORBIDDEN STRATEGIES; HOSTAGES; PRISONERS OF WAR; TORTURE; WAR CRIMES.

BIBLIOGRAPHY
Briggs, Herbert W., *"Nicaragua v. United States:* Jurisdiction and Admissibility," *American Journal of International Law* 79 (1985), 373.
International Committee of the Red Cross, *The Geneva Conventions of August 12, 1949* (Geneva, 1949).
Meron, Theodor, "The Geneva Conventions as Customary Law," *American Journal of International Law* 81 (1987), 351ff.

GENEVA DRAFT RULES, 1956. The overwhelming evidence of massive civilian casualties in war prompted a meeting which issued a set of twenty articles concerning "Draft Rules for the Limitation of the Dangers Incurred by the Civilian Population in Time of War." These rules were approved at the 19th international conference of the Red Cross at meetings in New Delhi in 1957, and then submitted to the various governments for their examination and hopefully their approval. Although there was virtually no reaction from the governments of the world, these rules had some influence on later attempts to increase international laws for the protection of civilian populations. The preamble stated that "all nations are deeply convinced that war should be banned as a means of settling disputes," but that in view of technical developments in new weapons and methods of warfare, the following rules should be instituted "by the requirements of humanity and the safety of the population." Article 1 asserted that operations be confined to the destruction of military resources and "leave the civilian population outside the sphere of armed attacks." In recognition that military targets and the civilian population may be in close proximity, Article 8 stated that military leaders should take account of those situations where the military advantage to be gained leaves the choice open between several objectives and select the one where the attack involves the least danger for the civilian population. Article 14, "Weapons with Uncontrollable Effects," proposed the prohibition of incendiary*, chemical, bacteriological*, radioactive or other agents; torpedoes*, and delayed-action weapons such as mines*, which were liable to affect the civilian populations in the future.

See BIOLOGICAL/CHEMICAL WARFARE; FORBIDDEN WEAPONS; FRAGMENTATION BOMBS; INCENDIARIES; MINES.

BIBLIOGRAPHY
Friedman, Leon, ed., *The Law of War,* vol. 1 (New York: Random House, 1972).

GENEVA PROTOCOL, JUNE 17, 1925. The failure of nations to comply with the recommendations of the Brussels Declaration and The Hague banning the use of gas, chemicals, and bacteriologicals in war, and the widespread use of these by both sides in World War I, prompted a renewed effort by the International Committee of the Red Cross to address the use of these "forbidden weapons.'' Forty-four nations were represented, and six did not sign in approval. Although Great Britain signed, it was with the reservation that the signature was not binding on India or any British Dominion that was a separate member of the League of Nations and did not separately sign the Protocol. Although Parliament failed to uphold the signatures, it did so in 1930. Indeed, in 1925 the distinguished British scientist, J.B.S. Haldane, had written a pamphlet, *Callinicus,* to ''prove'' that gas warfare was more humane than any other kind. While the U.S. delegates did sign, the U.S. Senate failed to ratify the document. In 1976 the U.S. Army Manual 27-10 (*The Law of Land Warfare**), was revised to show that America was then a signatory of the 1925 protocol. However, the signature was with the reservation that the United States reserved the right to determine which gases and noxious chemicals were included in the ban. Furthermore, the official American position held that the protocol banned only first use* and not the use in reprisal*. The brief protocol stated:

Whereas the use in war of asphyxiating, poisonous or other gases, and of all analogous liquids, materials or devices, has been justly condemned by the general opinion of the civilized world; and whereas the prohibition of such use has been declared in Treaties to which the majority of Powers of the world are Parties, to that end this prohibition shall be universally accepted as a part of International Law, binding alike the conscience and the practice of nations: declare that the High Contracting Parties, so far as they are not already Parties to Treaties prohibiting such use, accept this prohibition, agree to extend this prohibition to the use of bacteriological methods of warfare.

Unlike previous Geneva conventions* this protocol was declared to be in effect for each nation as it signed and would hold in wars independently of whether the participants of that war were signatories.

See BIOLOGICAL/CHEMICAL WARFARE; FORBIDDEN WEAPONS.

BIBLIOGRAPHY

Friedman, Leon, ed., *The Law of War,* vol. 1 (New York: Random House, 1972).

Noel-Baker, Philip John, *The Geneva Protocol for the Pacific Settlement of International Pursuits* (London: P. S. King and Sons, 1925).

GENEVA PROTOCOLS I AND II. Protocol I dealt with the protection of victims of international armed conflicts. The preamble to this first protocol stated that the provisions of the Geneva Convention of 1949* should be fully applied to all persons ''without any adverse distinction based on the nature or origin of the armed conflict or on causes espoused by or attributed to the Parties to the conflict.'' Such cases included armed conflicts where people are fighting against ''colonial domination and alien occupation and against racist regimes.'' In many wars in Third World countries, the participants were guerrillas* without uniform. Article 44 acknowledged that ''there are situations in armed conflicts where, owing to the nature of the hostilities, an armed combatant cannot so distinguish himself.'' But as long as he carried his arms openly, he should be considered as a combatant and entitled to the rights and privileges as such. This was not intended to permit dressing as an unarmed civilian in disguise, but as long as arms were carried openly, the requisite uniform could be dismissed in "exceptional" situations. The intent was to counter a growing tendency on the part of some countries to treat armed persons not part of a formal army as "brigands" or "terrorists" not entitled to capture or prisoner-of-war status. Representatives of the U.S. armed forces played a major role in the deliberations of the U.S. delegation.

In part 1, "Wounded, Sick and Shipwrecked," Article 8, the terms "wounded" and "sick" referred to military or civilian persons. Article 10 prohibited carrying out on persons, even with their consent: physical mutilation, medical or scientific experiments, and removal of tissue or organs for transplantation. Part 3, "Methods and Means of Warfare, Combatant and Prisoner-of-War Status," in article 36 on "New Weapons," required that, in the study, development, acquisition, or adoption of new weapons or methods of warfare, all parties were under obligation to determine whether any such methods or weapons might be prohibited by this protocol. Perfidy* and wars of no quarter* were both prohibited. Article 47 denied mercenaries the right to be considered combatants or entitled to prisoner-of-war status. Part 4, Section 1, on the "Civilian Population," required all parties to distinguish combatants from noncombatants*. Civilians should not be the object of either attack or reprisals*. Nor was it permitted to starve civilians, a point raised whenever siege warfare* is practiced. Article 75 reaffirmed that the following acts were prohibited:

violence to the life, health, or physical or mental well-being of persons: specifically, murder, torture of all kinds, corporal punishment, mutilation, outrages on dignity, the taking of hostages, collective punishments, and the threats to commit any of the foregoing acts.

The above Protocol I was to take effect six months after two parties had ratified it.

Protocol II related to the protection of victims of noninternational armed conflicts. The new protocol was to apply to all armed conflict not covered by Protocol I. It was noted at the conference that 80–90 percent of the victims of armed conflict since World War II had been the result of noninternational battles. Part 2 reaffirmed that the prohibitions of Article 75 applied to all without prejudice. This protocol took effect six months after at least two parties had ratified it. The U.S. delegates signed both protocols in approval.

In his "letter of transmittal" on January 29, 1987, President Ronald Reagan urged the U.S. Senate to ratify Protocol II and to reject Protocol I. The president listed the following as reasons to reject Protocol I:

1. It treats wars of national liberation in the same fashion as international conflicts. To judge wars of national liberation as worthy of concern introduces a "subjective distinction based on the war's alleged purpose."

2. It grants combatant status to irregular forces even if they lack a distinctive uniform.

3. As such it fails to distinguish terrorists* from legitimate soldiers.

President Reagan's letter stated that this first protocol was "fundamentally and irreconcilably flawed." He said that the Joint Chiefs of Staff (JCS) had concluded that many provisions of Protocol I were "militarily unacceptable." In 1988, Abraham D. Sofaer, a Legal Advisor in the Department of State, published "The Rationale for the United States Decision." He found the protocol flawed in the following ways:

1. The enforcement provisions do not assure compliance.

2. The protocol contains provisions unacceptable from a "military, political or humanitarian standpoint.

In its over 100-page account the JCS listed as militarily unacceptable reasons: it grants irregulars a legal status that is at times superior to that given to regular forces; it "unreasonably" restricts attacks on targets which have been traditionally legitimate; and it eliminates significant remedies (e.g., reprisal*). The JCS objected that allowing wars for "national liberation" implied that the reasons for waging wars were germane to the justice of a cause. The JCS denied that wars of "peoples . . . fighting against colonial domination and alien occupation and racist regimes" should be given a status such that those fighting for such causes would have prisoner-of-war status and, if captured, be immune from prosecution as terrorists. Both President Reagan and Mr. Sofaer objected to Article 20, which prohibited reprisals, and thus prevented attack on those persons or places that had been "traditionally legitimate." Hans-Peter Gasser, Legal Advisor to the Directorate of the International Committee of the Red Cross, wrote "An Appeal for Ratification by the United States" of Protocol I, in which he spoke both to the objections by President Reagan and by Mr. Sofaer.

See CASUALTIES OF WAR; COLLATERAL DAMAGE; FORBIDDEN STRATEGIES; FORBIDDEN WEAPONS; JUST WAR.

BIBLIOGRAPHY
"Agora: The U.S. Decision Not to Ratify Protocol I to the Geneva Conventions on the Protection of War Victims," *American Journal of International Law* 81 (1987) and 82 (1988).
Meron, Theodor, *Human Rights and Humanitarian Norms as Customary Law* (Oxford: Clarendon Press, 1989).
"Protocol Additional to the Geneva Conventions of 12 August 1949, and Relating to the Protection of Victims of International Armed Conflicts (Protocol I)," *American Journal of International Law* 72 (1978).
"Protocol Additional to the Geneva Conventions of 12 August 1949, Relating to the Protection of Victims of Non-International Armed Conflicts (Protocol II)," *American Journal of International Law* 72 (1978).

GENOCIDE. The term was coined by Raphael Lemkin in 1943 and adopted by the UN Genocide Convention in 1948 to designate the gravest of crimes against humanity*. The core of the UN definition concerns "acts committed with intent to destroy, in whole or in part, a national, ethnical, racial, or religious group, as such" (Article II). The failure of the UN since 1948 to hold accountable the leaders of even a single state guilty of genocide reflects defects in the structure of the UN and politics among sovereign states far more than disputes over the meaning of genocide.

Nevertheless, the UN definition of genocide has been extremely controversial, and some states have invoked it as a defense against claims that they have committed genocide. Two aspects of the UN definition are especially troubling. First, the definition arbitrarily excludes types of one-sided massacre that have been historically significant: both the annihilation of political groups and social classes, so-called "politicides," and the annihilation by an elite of groups that share the elite's own defining national, ethnical, racial, and religious characteristics, so-called "autogenocides." Examples of politicides include the massacre of millions of so-called *kulaks* under the rule of Stalin and the slaughter in Indonesia of supposed Communists under the Suharto regime in 1955–1956 that appears to have taken between 300,000 and 600,000 lives. The term "autogenocide" was invented to describe the slaughter between 1975 and 1979 of between 1–3 million Kampucheans by Pol Pot and the Khmer Rouge.

Exclusion of political groups and social classes from the UN definition resulted from the protest of the Soviet and Eastern bloc delegates, who argued that their inclusion would weaken the convention because the "mutability and lack of distinguishing characteristics did not lend themselves to definition" (Kuper 1981, p. 26). This is an argument without merit, however. Even when the victimized group has distinguishing national, ethnic, racial, or religious characteristics, it is not because group members possess these characteristics that they are victimized, but rather because victimizers believe that possession of one or more of these characteristics justifies the group's annihilation. Thus, it is not significant that we cannot set the boundaries of a political or social group, such as *kulaks,* "enemies of the people," or "Communists," that exists (like the Nazi myths of the Aryan race and the Jewish virus) only in the minds of the perpetrators of genocide. When a powerful group has embarked on the massacre* of members of an "outgroup" and intends the death of individuals simply by virtue of their membership in the group, the relevance of racial, religious, or ethnic characteristics lose their salience. Thus, as Chalk and Jonassohn recommend, we ought to use the perpetrator's own definition of the victim group. Chalk and Jonassohn aver that genocide is "a form of one-sided mass killing in which a state or other authority intends to destroy a group, as that group and membership in it are defined by the perpetrator" (1990, p. 23).

This succinct, serviceable definition allows us to dispense with such neologisms as politicide and autogenecide, and recognize the crucial point, made by sociologist Helen Fein, that whatever their characteristics, the victims of genocide have been defined by perpetrators as falling outside the "universe of moral obligation" (Charny 1982, p. 5), and therefore as being legitimate prey for elimination. There remains a second problem with the UN definition, specifically, its emphasis on intent as a necessary condition. It is, of course, by disclaiming the intent to destroy a group as such that genocidal governments have sought to evade condemnation under the UN convention, one recent and notable example being the disclaimers made by the Serbians concerning the massacre of Muslim Bosnians. Most commentators insist on the necessity of intentionality* and construe intent as evidence of purposive, premeditated, planned massacres organized or coordinated by government or military functionaries. These analysts insist on distinguishing between severe oppression and state terrorism*, including the use of death squads, on the one hand, and genocide on the other, even when the consequences are the same for the victim group, as with the Kurds in Iraq.

Conclusive evidence of premeditated and planned state policy is too stringent as a standard, especially since governments can lie about their intentions and obstruct efforts to uncover them. For this reason, it is necessary to impute or infer intent from consequences. Thus, genocide occurs when the foreseeable, predictable, and cumulative results of a course of action are the extermination of an outgroup and when a state either produces this outcome or acquiesces in bringing it about by consistently refusing or failing to protect victims, often in contravention of its own legal code. In his analysis of the fate of the Australian Aborigines, Barta (in Wallimann and Dobkowski, 1987) argues persuasively that genocide can result from "relations of destruction" inherent within a social system. In a genocidal society, a whole group might be subject to remorseless pressures of destruction inherent in the very nature of the bureaucratic, legal, and economic processes of the dominant culture. There is growing consensus that the Ache Indians of Paraguay were victims in the 1970s of a genocidal society, and that numerous indigenous peoples worldwide are at risk of extinction due to the relentless and cumulative effects of non-indigenous epidemics, like smallpox for the American Indians, pressures for national consolidation, personal violence and dispossession caused by invading and impoverished peasants, and the effects of commercial resource extractors, including multinational corporations.

A distinction is sometimes made between the extinctions of indigenous peoples, which are referred to as "developmental" or "colonial" genocides, and "ideological" genocides, for which the paradigm case is the Holocaust*. While developmental genocides are said to depend primarily on where the victims are—blocking alleged "forces of progress"—and what they possess, ideological genocides, as in the case of the Jews, are based on who the victims are. This distinction is extremely difficult to apply, however. The genocides of the Armenians by the Turks and of the *kulaks* under Stalin were based both on who the victims were and on where and what they possessed. In addition, when the government fails to arrest developments threatening the existence of a native people in a society dominated by relations of destruction, then who they are becomes as much a matter of their victimization as where they are and what they possess. This was the grim reality faced by the Tasmanians, for example, long after they could have been thought by European migrants to be obstructing progress. It is a fate that awaits indigenous peoples of Amazonia, such as the Koruba, Truka, and Yanomami, unless the Brazilian government makes a greater effort to protect them.

Two popular beliefs about genocide do not bear scrutiny. One is the notion that genocide is a modern crime; the second is the notion that it is uniquely a product of Western, and more particularly, European civilization. Although the concept of genocide as a crime against humanity is a 20th-century notion, circumstantial evidence indicates that genocide probably began in antiquity. In addition, there are numerous examples of genocides committed by non-Western or European peoples, including many that did not follow colonization and the rise of nationalism* associated with the modern state. But while genocide is regrettably global in incidence, it is true that the vast migrations of European peoples beginning in the 17th century, and especially the rapid expansion of an international market economy, seem unprecedented in accelerating the rate at which indigenous peoples have become victims of genocide.

The rapidity with which genocidal massacres can explode into orgies of killing, as in Rwanda in 1994, suggests to some that genocide may be linked to innately murderous or aggressive drives that occasionally break through the veneer of civilization. Psychoanalytic, sociobiological, and biological deterministic efforts to explain genocide fail to generate testable hypotheses, however. And the notion that the Holocaust had been perpetrated by psychotic killers and fanatics was exploded both by psychological studies of Nazis* at the Nuremberg war crimes trials* and by Arendt's study of Adolf Eichmann, resulting in her theory of the "banality of evil*." Close examinations of events leading up to genocide reveal a complex set of contributing factors, including the not yet fully understood role of ideology, and the functions—in social groups—of projection and scapegoating. Experimental social psychology, such as Milgram's studies of obedience to authority, plus studies of the "diffusion of responsibility" and "pluralistic ignorance," help to explain how otherwise ordinary people can become accomplices in genocide. While the search continues for a comprehensive explanation, sociologist Ervin Staub's view that genocide results from a dangerous combination of economic, ideological, and political causes and represents the endpoint of a "continuum of destruction," appears highly plausible.

See COMBATANT-NONCOMBATANT DISTINCTION; FORBIDDEN STRATEGIES; HOLOCAUST, THE; MASS DESTRUCTION, WEAPONS OF; MASSACRES; NUREMBERG PRINCIPLES; PSYCHIC NUMBING.

BIBLIOGRAPHY
Arendt, Hannah, *Eichmann in Jerusalem: A Report on the Banality of Evil* (1964), rev. and enlarged ed. (New York: Penguin, 1977).
Chalk, Frank, and Kurt Jonassohn, eds., *The History and Sociology of Genocide* (New Haven, Conn.: Yale University Press, 1990).

Charney, Israel, ed., *Toward the Understanding and Prevention of Genocide* (Boulder, Colo.: Westview Press, 1982).

du Preez, Peter, *Genocide* (London: Boyers/Bowerdean, 1994).

Kuper, Leo, *Genocide* (New York: Penguin, 1981).

Lemkin, Raphael, *Axis Rule in Occupied Europe* (Washington, D.C.: Carnegie Endowment, 1944).

Milgram, Stanley, *Obedience to Authority* (New York: Harper & Row, 1974).

Propora, Douglas, *How Holocausts Happen* (Philadelphia: Temple University Press, 1990).

Staub, Ervin, *The Roots of Evil* (New York: Cambridge University Press, 1989).

Wallimann, Isidor, and Michael N. Dobkowski, eds., *Genocide and the Modern Age* (Westport, CT.: Greenwood Press, 1987).

Robert Paul Churchill

GENTILI, ALBERICO (1552–1608). One of the first jurist writers to separate international law from its older basis in theology and ethics. After receiving his doctorate in civil law at the University in Perugia, Gentili fled in 1579 as a Protestant refugee, first to Austria and then to England. He lectured on Roman law at Oxford University, and became Regius Professor of Civil Law in 1587. He had an extensive private law practice, and in 1605 became counsel to the King of Spain. He emphasized the positivist thesis that custom was the source of law, but did not reject natural law or natural reason.

Gentili recognized that every nation assumed the right to wage war in its own perceived interest, and he doubted that an unjust war was possible even in principle, since "even a war of vengeance and an offensive war may be waged justly." He agreed with Franciscus de Victoria* (1486–1546) that wars for religion were unjustified, although he doubted that the facts gave much support to his assertion. After all, the clerics of Toledo had already decreed that heretics should be punished by war. Perhaps this was covered by his allowance that anything should be allowed if the failure to act resulted in the state suffering some harm. He assumed that justice could be on both sides of any given war, a conclusion following from the premise that nations had an undisputed right to go to war.

He was probably the first to support the right of nations to wage a war of intervention* to protect the freedom of the high seas. In Chapter 25 of Book 1 of *On the Law of War,* he discussed an "Honorable Reason for Waging War" as one being in the common interest. Wars of religion ought not to be allowed unless "a right of humanity is violated" (e.g., by human sacrifice). Such a war of intervention rested on an honorable cause. In Chapter 26 of Book 1 he defended even the right to intervene to defend subjects of another state against their own sovereign.

See AYALA, BALTHAZAR; BELLI, PIERINO; BYNKERSCHOEK, CORNELIUS; SUAREZ, FRANCISCO; VATTEL, EMMERICH DE; VICTORIA, FRANCISCUS DE.

BIBLIOGRAPHY
Brierly, J. L., *The Law of Nations: An Introduction to the International Law of Peace* (New York: Oxford University Press, 1963).
Gentili, Alberico, *On the Law of War* (Oxford: Clarendon Press, 1933).
————, *The Pleas of a Spanish Advocate* (Oxford: Oxford University Press, 1921).
Glahn, Gerhard von, *Law Among the Nations: An Introduction to Public International Law* (New York: Macmillan, 1970).

GERMAN WAR BOOK (USAGES OF WAR ON LAND). This manual was initially written by J. K. Bluntschli for the German General Staff. It was based on *General Orders 100**, and was written after the congresses at The Hague* in 1899 and 1907. In spite of derogatory remarks made by J. H. Morgan, who translated the document into English, this German Army manual was quite similar to the U.S. manual of 1914, *Rules of Land Warfare**. Both the U.S. and German manuals recognized that civilians will inevitably face hardship and havoc, that there is a problem with irregulars who may wear no visible signs that they are belligerents, that *levees en masse* should be accepted, and that military necessity* is the final arbiter of what is permissible in war. Both rejected the use of poisons*, assassination*, arms causing useless suffering, the killing or wounding of prisoners*, refusal of quarter*, and soft-nosed bullets, and decreed that prisoners were to be treated honorably. In spite of declarations of The Hague to the contrary, both manuals allowed bombing without notification even where civilians were at risk. In the matter of compelling prisoners to furnish information about their country, however, the German manual, while recognizing that "writers are unanimous" in condemnation of the practice, asserted that "the argument of war will frequently make it necessary."

See CLAUSEWITZ, CARL VON; *LAW OF LAND WARFARE, THE.*
BIBLIOGRAPHY
Morgan, J. H., trans., *The War Book of the German General Staff* (New York: McBride, Nast, & Co., 1915).

GRENADA, U.S. INVASION OF. The United States sent a 6,000-strong military force to Grenada, an island nation of 100,000 population in the eastern Caribbean, on October 25, 1983. In fighting that lasted four days, that force defeated the Grenada army, captured Grenada's leaders, and asked the Grenadan governor-general to serve as caretaker until a new government was formed.

The government overthrown by the United States had come to power only recently, in the wake of infighting within the ruling political party. That party was a thorn in the side of the Reagan administration because of its close relationship with Cuba. In a speech earlier in 1983, President Ronald Reagan had said that Cuba and the Soviet Union were militarizing Grenada as a "power projection into the region."

Reagan pointed to the ongoing construction of an airport in Grenada, being built by a Cuban construction crew, saying it was being designed for hostile military purposes. The Grenada government, backed up by the British general contractor for the airport construction, said the construction had no military aim and that the new airport would promote tourism by accommodating large jet airliners.

Reagan justified the military intervention on three grounds: (1) that the United States had been invited by Grenada's titular head of state, the governor-general, (2) that the action was taken under the auspices of a regional security organization, the Organization of Eastern Caribbean States (OECS), and (3) that U.S. citizens in Grenada were in imminent danger.

The military action was, however, criticized by the Organization of American States and the UN General Assembly, both organizations finding these justifications flawed. The UN General Assembly called the intervention a "flagrant violation of international law."

The claim of a request from the governor-general as a justification was questionable on two grounds. First, in Grenada the governor-general is merely a liaison officer with Great Britain, which ruled Grenada until 1974. He is not an official in charge of the government or the state and therefore lacks the constitutional authority to invite foreign troops.

Second, the United States said that the governor-general made his request via the OECS through Barbados Prime Minister Tom Adams, but Adams's press officer said that the governor-general did no such thing. A request letter with the governor-general's signature was later made public by the U.S. State Department, but that letter was apparently composed outside Grenada and hand-carried to the governor-general by U.S. troops.

The Reagan administration's reliance on the authority of the OECS was also problematic. Grenada was a member of the OECS, and the OECS treaty had provisions about military intervention*. The OECS did ask the United States to intervene. However, the OECS treaty allowed military intervention only in cases of "external aggression" against a member country, and Grenada had not been invaded. The OECS treaty also required a unanimous vote of all member countries before military action could be taken, and Grenada had not participated in the meeting at which the OECS asked the United States to intervene.

The reliance on a need to save U.S. citizens also drew criticism, because no harm had come to any U.S. citizen in Grenada. The U.S. citizens in Grenada were primarily students attending a U.S.-run medical college. The Reagan administration said that in the situation that existed in Grenada, the Grenadan ruling group might have taken hostages* as a way of protecting its position in power. The administration promised reporters documentary evidence of such a danger but did not provide any.

By the time of the intervention, the political infighting, which had involved violence, was at an end, and Grenada was quiet. Prior to the invasion, Grenadan officials contacted the medical college's vice-chancellor to ask if the students had any problems as result of the political difficulties, and to give assurances that the Grenadan government would help the students in any way that might be needed. There was no apparent threat of a countercoup that might lead to further political violence.

Just prior to the invasion, the State Department contacted New York-based officials of the medical school and asked them to state publicly that the students were in danger. School officials concluded that the reason for this request was to bolster the administration's claim of a danger as a pretext for military intervention. School officials declined to make the statement, finding no danger to the students.

In the week prior to the intervention, State Department officials were in contact with the Grenadan government about the possibility of evacuating the medical students. The Grenadan officials, although insisting that there was no danger to the students, cooperated by making preliminary arrangements for an evacuation of the students by ship. U.S. officials, however, did not follow up on the Grenadan offer.

Another fact that cast doubt on the rescue rationale was that the U.S. commanders, upon landing in Grenada, did not know the location of the medical students, even though the State Department had full information on that subject. The students were housed at three major campuses, one of them near the site of the first U.S. landing. U.S. commanders acknowledged that they had been informed only about that one campus, not about the other two. U.S. forces reached the other two campuses only several days after their landing.

In congressional hearings into the Grenada intervention, a former member of the National Security Council said that the students were in greater danger from the invasion itself than from the Grenada government. *Time* magazine said the administration was "disingenuous in its public explanations" about the reasons for the Grenada intervention. The *New York Times* charged the administration with "deliberate distortions and knowingly false statements of fact."

See AGGRESSION, ATTEMPTS TO DEFINE; CAUSES OF WAR; HUMANITARIAN INTERVENTION; LAWS OF WAR; NICARAGUA, U.S. INTERVENTION IN; PANAMA, U.S. INVASION OF; PROPAGANDA; WARISM.

BIBLIOGRAPHY

Bennett, Ralph Kinney, "Grenada: Anatomy of a 'Go' Decision," *Reader's Digest,* February 1984, 74.

"Grenada: Collective Action by the Caribbean Peace Force," *Department of State Bulletin* 83, 67, at p. 80 (December 1983).

Latin America Bureau, *Grenada: Whose Freedom?* (1984).

U.S. House of Representatives, *Situation in Lebanon and Grenada,* Hearing Before a Subcommittee of the House Committee on Appropriations, 98th Cong., 1st sess. (1983).

U.S. Senate, *The Situation in Grenada,* Hearing Before the Senate Committee on Foreign Relations, 98th Cong., 1st sess. (1983).

John Quigley

GRENADES. *See* FORBIDDEN WEAPONS; FRAGMENTATION BOMBS; MINES.

GROTIUS, HUGO (1583–1645). A distinguished jurist and statesman, some mark his writings to be the beginning of the science of international law (von Glahn, Fenwick), while others considered that such a judgment did a disservice to earlier writers (Brierly). Grotius's interest in international law was a practical one. He said he wrote about the laws of war* because "I saw prevailing throughout the Christian world a license in making war of which even barbarous nations should be ashamed." He was a student of law at Leiden. As an active leader of the Remonstrants, he worked for many years for a reunion of all Christian churches, but was sentenced by the States General, of which he was a member, to life imprisonment for his pains. He escaped to Paris where King Louis, of France, granted him a pension. While in France he completed and published his famous *De Jure Belli et Pacis* in 1625. In 1634 he became the Swedish ambassador to France, a post he held until 1643. He combined both the positivist commitment to custom and the naturalist belief that reason applied to natural law can arrive at international law. He believed that a commitment to international law was in the national interest. His other famous writing was a *Commentary on the Law of Prize and Booty* in naval warfare. He had been hired by the Dutch East India Company to represent them in a case where one of their ships had captured a Portuguese vessel and had sold both the vessel and its cargo as a prize of war. Grotius was asked to express an opinion on the legitimacy of the Dutch action. While most of his manuscript lay undiscovered until 1864, the twelfth chapter was published in 1609 under the title *The Freedom of the Seas.*

Grotius agreed with his predecessors on the importance of having a proper authority to declare war. He added the admonition to princes that some wars were unjust. He insisted that there should be a declaration of war*, even though he recognized that neither political nor military custom supported him. Unlike Francisco Suarez* (1548–1617), he rejected the notion of preventive war, although he did allow wars of intervention. Hersch Lauterpacht considered that Grotius's writings contained "the first authoritative" defense of the right of humanitarian intervention* of another state in defense of its citizens who had been seriously mistreated. The legitimacy of such intervention rested on the premise that only one party in a war could have justice on its side. To intervene on the side of justice was not an act of aggression, although to intervene on the side of injustice would be. Grotius allowed wars of humanitarian intervention where injuries were committed that "violate the law of nature," and in so doing admitted a prior debt to Alberico Gentili* (1552–1608), who had affirmed such intervention both on land and on the high seas.

He allowed for conscientious objection* for Christians* who might have religious scruples against killing. Indeed, he asserted that citizens could be held responsible for the crimes of their sovereign if they had consented to his illegal commands. Grotius commented on the difficulty of reconciling citizen conscience with princely demands, and in those cases where the citizen was dissatisfied with the explanations of the prince, he suggested that such citizens be given an extraordinary tax as an alternative to going to war. Such a tax would test the seriousness of the citizen's conscientious objection. As recently as the American Civil War, monetary substitutes were allowed. In the case of Christians, Grotius advocated leniency, and he stated that to refrain from military service was a mark of "a somewhat greater holiness." He denounced the idea of a professional military, preferring a civilian army mustered for the occasion. He accepted the doctrine of military necessity* and, consequently, proposed few limits to what soldiers were permitted to do.

With regard to acceptable reasons for going to war he identified three "undisputed and justifiable" reasons: defense of the country, recovery of property stolen, and punishment of offenders. In the absence of any adjudicating body, nations were, however, left on their own in justifying reasons of state. He listed as unacceptable reasons fear of what a neighbor might do, the desire for richer land owned by another, the desire to rule over others "for their own good" though against their wills, and the claim to be the self-appointed leader of the world.

Most predecessors of Grotius spoke primarily about how wars began, while Grotius added detailed discussion of how wars were to be waged legally. With respect to the means for waging war, Grotius accepted the prevailing list of "innocents*" to include women, children, merchants, and farmers. Actual practice did not accord with such suggestions, and even Grotius recognized that custom extended the right to kill the enemy even after surrender*, and not simply soldiers who had borne arms, but everyone in the enemy territory. Even prisoners of war* lacked protection. Unlike most of his predecessors, he stressed the need to consider the justice of the means. He urged moderation in warfare and stressed the importance of the status of hostages*, the needless destruction of civilian property, and respect for the religious beliefs of conquered peoples. Although he considered his remarks on these matters not to be legally binding or enforceable, he did believe that his writings offered helpful and important advice to both military leaders and political statesmen.

Grotius cited extensively the Scholastic writers, and mentioned Franciscus de Victoria* (1486–1546) in detail. Grotius distinguished between natural law and customary voluntary law, and his distinctions gave rise to three schools of thought with regard to *jus gentium*. Naturalists, like Samuel Pufendorf (1632–1694), denied that international laws were based on treaty or custom, and affirmed, as Thomas Hobbes* had, that international law was part of natural law. Positivists, like Cornelius van Bynkershoek* (1673–1743), claimed that laws derived solely from the agreements of states expressed in treaties and custom, although followers of Grotius held a third position, that both natural and positive laws had importance.

See AYALA, BALTHAZAR; BELLI, PIERINO; VATTEL, EMMERICH DE; VICTORIA, FRANCISCUS DE.

BIBLIOGRAPHY
Brierly, J. L., *The Law of Nations: An Introduction to the International Law of Peace* (New York: Oxford University Press, 1963).
Falk, Richard, Friedrich Kratochwil, and Saul Mendlovitz, eds., *International Law: A Contemporary Perspective* (Boulder, Colo.: Westview Press, 1985), 7–42.
Fenwick, Charles G., *International Law* (New York: Appleton-Century-Crofts, 1948).
Glahn, Gerhard von, *Law Among the Nations: An Introduction to Public International Law* (New York: Macmillan, 1970).
Grotius, Hugo, *The Law of War and Peace* (Oxford: Clarendon Press, 1925).

GUATEMALA, U.S. INVASION OF. In 1953, Jacobo Arbenz, president of Guatemala, nationalized land owned by the U.S.-owned United Fruit Company that was not currently cultivated. Arbenz acted because many Guatemalan peasants were hard-pressed to survive for lack of land to till. As compensation to United Fruit, two-thirds of whose land was affected by the action, Arbenz offered compensation at the value United Fruit had declared for purposes of paying Guatemalan taxes. The Eisenhower administration denounced the nationalization and said that the land was worth twenty-five times that amount.

As part of a campaign of pressure on Arbenz, the Central Intelligence Agency (CIA) planted stories in newspapers in the region condemning him as being Communist-oriented and a threat to other Central American nations. Arbenz was not himself a Communist, and no Communists served in his cabinet. Arbenz's Guatemala maintained no diplomatic relations with the Soviet Union.

To remove Arbenz from power, President Dwight Eisenhower ordered the CIA to take decisive measures to force him to resign. The CIA recruited Guatemalans living abroad into a military force, gave them weapons and aircraft, trained them at a secret location near Miami, and set up secret bases for them in Honduras and Nicaragua.* At their head the CIA put Carlos Castillo Armas, an ex-colonel in the Guatemalan army.

In January 1954 Arbenz made public letters given to him by a repentant coup plotter. The letters, containing discussion of coup plans, were between Castillo Armas and Miguel Ydígoras Fuentes, a military officer and politician who had lost the 1950 presidential election to Arbenz. Arbenz charged the United States with aiding the conspirators. The State Department ridiculed Arbenz's charge.

Next the CIA opened a clandestine radio station, to turn public opinion against Arbenz. In June 1954, Castillo Armas, with only 150 troops, entered Guatemala from Honduras. The CIA radio station reported the entry, saying the troops numbered 5,000. The station also reported a battle between Castillo Armas and government troops, although no such battle had occurred. Simultaneously with the troop entry, CIA airplanes, some of them piloted by Guatemalans and by CIA mercenaries, dropped bombs on Guatemala City.

CIA Director Allen Dulles explained his strategy in a secret cable to Eisenhower: "The use of a small number of airplanes and the massive use of radio broadcasting are designed to build up and give main support to the impression of Castillo Armas' strength as well as to spread the impression of the regime's weakness." Dulles told Eisenhower that the key to success was "deception and timing."

Arbenz brought a complaint to the UN Security Council, leveling his main charge at Honduras and Nicaragua rather than at the United States, whose role he apparently did not fully realize. The Soviet delegate, who also had no precise data on the U.S. role, nonetheless pointed the finger at the United States for the incipient coup. Henry Cabot Lodge, as the U.S. delegate, denied any U.S. involvement.

Once Castillo Armas had his small force inside Guatemala, U.S. Ambassador John Peurifoy encouraged high-ranking Guatemalan military officers to overthrow Arbenz. To gain their participation, Peurifoy promised to call off the Castillo Armas invasion if the officers acted against Arbenz. The ploy worked, and the officers successfully pressured Arbenz to resign. In a resignation address by radio, Arbenz, who by then understood the U.S. role, accused the United States of using communism as a pretext to intervene in Guatemala's internal affairs.

The military junta that replaced Arbenz countermanded his nationalization of United Fruit's land. A secret celebration was held in Washington at the White House, but Secretary of State John Foster Dulles publicly portrayed the situation as purely a Guatemalan affair. In 1936, Dulles had served as attorney for United Fruit and had drafted the concession agreements whereby United Fruit acquired the land that Arbenz nationalized.

President Eisenhower also publicly denied any U.S. role. When he received a new post-Arbenz ambassador of Guatemala to the United States, Eisenhower said that "the people of Guatemala" had "liberated themselves from the shackles of international Communist direction."

Later in 1954, the *Saturday Evening Post* reported that the CIA had sent guns and ammunition to Castillo Armas in Honduras. In his memoirs, President Eisenhower admitted authorizing the CIA to fly bombing missions over Guatemala City but did not acknowledge organizing the operation.

Information about the full U.S. role came to public attention only some years later. A detailed account was given in his memoirs by one of the main CIA participants, David Atlee Phillips. John Moors Cabot, who at the time was assistant secretary of state for American republic affairs, wrote in his memoirs that the CIA "staged" the coup. The U.S. role was analyzed in detail twenty years later by the U.S. Senate select committee on intelligence, which characterized the coup as one of "the Agency's boldest, most spectacular covert operations."

See AGGRESSION, ATTEMPTS TO DEFINE; HUMANITARIAN INTERVENTION; LAWS OF WAR; PROPAGANDA; WARISM.

BIBLIOGRAPHY

"The Ambassador in Guatemala (Peurifoy) to the Department of State," June 27, 1954, 11 P.M., *Foreign Relations of the United States 1952–1954*, vol. 4, 1189–91.

Cabot, John Moors, *First Line of Defense* (Washington, D.C.: Georgetown University School of Foreign Service, 1979).

Dulles, John Foster, "International Communism in Guatemala," June 30, 1954, *Department of State Bulletin* 31 (1954), 43.

Harkness, Richard, and Gladys Harkness, "The Mysterious Doings of CIA," *Saturday Evening Post,* October 30, 1954, 19.

"Memorandum by the Director of Central Intelligence (Dulles) to the President," June 20, 1954, *Foreign Relations of the United States 1952–1954*, vol. 4, 1174.

Phillips, David Atlee, *Night Watch* (New York: Athenaeum, 1977).

Tully, Andrew, *CIA: The Inside Story* (Greenwich, Conn.: Fawcett, 1962).

United Nations, Security Council Official Records, 9th yr., Provisional Verbatim Transcript, 675th mtg., p. 23, U.N. Doc. S/PV.675 (1954).

U.S. Senate, Select Committee to Study Governmental Operations with Respect to Intelligence Activities, *Final Report: Foreign and Military Intelligence,* Book 1, 94th Cong., 2d sess., April 26, 1976, 111.

Wise, David, and Thomas B. Ross, *The Invisible Government* (New York: Random House, 1964).

John Quigley

GUERRILLA WAR. Guerrilla or partisan warfare is an irregular type of fighting carried out by small groups acting independently. Traditionally, it has been considered illegitimate, not only because of its unconventional methods but also because partisans seldom wear distinctive uniforms to identify themselves as combatants, as required under the Hague* and Geneva* conventions. However, in the 20th century, with the rise of wars of national liberation*, from Ireland's Easter Uprising through Mao's Chinese Communist Revolution, and down to Peru's Sendero Luminoso, guerrilla wars have gained a certain respectability, if not full legitimacy.

Questions persist because, as the Spanish makes clear, a *guerrilla* is not a *guerra*; these "little" wars occupy a gray and murky terrain between brigandage and real wars: At the one extreme, assassinating* health workers, teachers, village chiefs, and the like or bombing buses, market places, and other nonmilitary targets are simply acts of terrorism*, not war. Likewise, calling extortion the "collection of revolutionary taxes" does little to conceal the essentially criminal nature of the enterprise. At the other extreme, despite their military organization and hit-and-run tactics, guerrilla forces never develop sufficient combat power to force a decision. Precisely because they are small, independent, and irregular, they can never hope to do more than harass the enemy. In order to be militarily decisive, guerrilla forces must either be reinforced by or transformed into regular forces, as military leaders from Wellington to Mao* have demonstrated.

Thus, to be both morally acceptable and militarily effective, guerrilla forces must meet two criteria: First, they must distinguish themselves from brigands by wearing distinctive uniforms and avoiding criminality and terrorism. Second, they must operate in close proximity to regular forces, forming an integral part of the regular army's operational plans by providing intelligence and disrupting enemy rear areas. Wellington's use of the Spanish partisans during the Peninsula Campaign might meet these criteria, as would most of the operations conducted by Soviet partisans during World War II. However, even in the clearest historical examples, the moral status of guerrilla operations remains uncertain. While some operations appear unobjectionable, too many others are simply acts of terrorism and gratuitous violence without militarily significant effect or result.

In particular, the second guerrilla stage of Mao Tse-tung's three-stage war of national liberation lacks moral credibility. The principal reason is that Mao's theory holds, and history confirms, that the conquest of power will not and cannot come until large main-force units (i.e., a regular armed force) become a reality in stage three. This means that all the killing and destruction of stage two, the guerrilla stage, has for its immediate purpose the creation of the third, main-force, stage, which is tantamount to saying that the guerrilla war is for the sake of the main-force war. But war for the sake of war is a morally untenable position, its value for seizing power under certain circumstances notwithstanding.

Or, coming at the problem from the other direction, assuming that the first stage—infiltrating and capturing the levers of political power at the local level—could be achieved without naked terrorism, the second, guerrilla, stage cannot meet the two criteria adduced above: At a minimum, extortion in the form of "revolutionary taxes" is required to finance the new "shadow" government and its newly organized guerrilla bands. And, once organized, the bands are devoid of any hope of military effectiveness because they will not be supported by sufficient main-force units until the final phases of stage three. This situation leads to long and bloody stalemates, as the Irish Republican Army and the Palestine Liberation Organization, among many other groups, demonstrate.

Finally, some have argued that guerrilla war can be justified as the poor man's last resort when oppressed or on psychological grounds to establish a national identity. While perhaps understandable, neither of these rationales is credible, especially after the examples of Gandhi*, Martin Luther King*, and Nelson Mandela.

See LAWS OF WAR; LOW-INTENSITY CONFLICT; VIETNAM WAR.

BIBLIOGRAPHY

Asprey, Robert B., *War in the Shadows: The Guerrilla in History,* 2 vols. (Garden City, N.Y.: Doubleday, 1975).

Geras, Norman, "Our Morals," *Discourses of Extremity: Radical Ethics and Post-Marxist Extravagances* (London: Verso, 1990).

Mao Tse-tung, *Selected Military Writings of Mao Tse-tung* (Peking: Foreign Language Press, 1963).

Brien Hallett

GULF OF SIDRA INCIDENT. Libya had claimed the Gulf of Sidra on its coast as its own since 1973. Much of the Gulf of Sidra lies beyond the twelve-mile limit recognized internationally as a country's border, so in March 1986 the United States began naval maneuvers with thirty ships in the Gulf of Sidra. Although the ostensible purpose of the maneuvers was to assert the right to freedom of the seas, most countries throughout the world saw the U.S. action as an attempt to provoke a military confrontation with the leader of Libya, Col. Muammar el-Qaddafi, whom the United States had been accusing of harboring terrorists and promoting terrorism.

According to official U.S. reports, on March 23 at 6 A.M., three ships—an air defense cruiser, a destroyer, and a guided missile cruiser—crossed the line that Qaddafi had called the "line of death." The United States said that at 7:52 A.M. on Tuesday, March 25, two missiles were fired at the ships and that five hours later four more missiles were fired. In response, the United States said that American planes attacked a radar station used to guide missile attacks; they also sank or disabled two Libyan fast attack craft. Libya claimed, on the contrary, that the United States had sunk a fishing boat, lost three fighter planes, and killed fifty-six civilians.

No reporters were on hand to witness the hostilities. During the alleged missile attacks six press pool reporters had been on board the aircraft carrier *Saratoga,* one of the other twenty-seven ships engaged in the maneuvers. When they asked they were told that nothing was happening and were flown back to Italy. Thus, all reports about events in the Gulf of Sidra came from official Libyan or U.S. sources only.

In 1981 two U.S. Navy jets shot down two Libyan jets that fired on them in the Gulf of Sidra. The United States said that they then conducted naval maneuvers in the Gulf of Sidra nineteen times, crossing the so-called "line of death" on eight occasions prior to the Gulf of Sidra incident. NATO allies supported the principle of freedom of the seas but, with the exception of Britain and West Germany, were cautious in their support of the U.S. maneuvers, which other nations labeled as "provocative" or "illegal."

Rhetoric flared between Libya and the United States in the days that followed the hostilities in the Gulf of Sidra. On April 5, 1986 a bomb exploded in a West Berlin discotheque frequented by U.S. servicemen; two U.S. soldiers and a Turkish woman were killed, and 229 others were wounded. The United States blamed Libya for the bombing, and ten days later, on April 15, the United States launched an air attack on Libya.

The attack was carried out by 14 A-6 fighter planes from two aircraft carriers—the *Coral Sea* and the *American*—operating in the Mediterranean Sea and by F-111 bombers flying from England. Bombs targeted Qaddafi's headquarters, his home, a naval diving school, military barracks, and two airports. Not all targets were hit, but some civilians and an adopted daughter of Qaddafi were killed in the attacks. One U.S. bomber was lost.

This attack marked the beginning of the end of a period of great tension between the United States and Libya. Several years later, on January 4, 1989, U.S. fighters shot down two Libyan fighter planes over the Mediterranean. The United States claimed that the fighter planes appeared to have hostile intentions. Responsibility for the bombing of the discotheque remains unclear, although most evidence gathered in the years following the incident pointed to a Palestinian who received support from Syria.

See AERIAL WARFARE; AGGRESSIVE VERSUS DEFENSIVE WAR; CAUSES OF WAR; COLLATERAL DAMAGE; COMBATANT-NONCOMBATANT DISTINCTION; FIRST STRIKE/SECOND STRIKE; INNOCENTS; JUST WAR; TERRORISM.

BIBLIOGRAPHY
Gwertzman, Bernard, "Plots on Global Scale Charged," *New York Times,* April 15, 1986, A1, col. 3.
Hersh, Seymour, "Target Qaddafi," *New York Times,* April 15, 1986, A1, col 5.
Quigley, John, *The Ruses for War* (New York: Prometheus, 1992), 223–30.
Schaap, Bill, "Disinforming the World on Libya," *Covert Action Information Bulletin,* No. 30 (Summer 1988), 71.

Barry L. Gan

GULF OF TONKIN INCIDENTS. The first incident occurred on August 2, 1964. The U.S. destroyer *Maddox* was on patrol in the Gulf of Tonkin, a large indentation in the coast of North Vietnam. The active phase of American involvement in Vietnam* was about to begin. As the *Maddox* approached the island of Hon Me, three North Vietnamese patrol boats emerged and advanced on the *Maddox*. At a distance of 10,000 yards, the *Maddox* opened fire on the boats. The North Vietnamese responded with torpedoes and bullets, one of which struck the radar tower of the *Maddox*. Returning fire again, the *Maddox* sunk two of the boats and disabled the third.

In Washington, American authorities promised that "grave consequences would inevitably result from any further unprovoked military action" against American ships "on the high seas." The North Vietnamese responded that the *Maddox* was in North Vietnamese territorial waters, four miles from Hon Me, and that the destroyer was acting in tandem with South Vietnamese commandos who had attacked Hon Me two nights before.

In Saigon, Deputy Defence Secretary Cyrus Vance announced that the bullet that struck the *Maddox* would be sent to Adlai Stevenson "for presentation to the United Nations." Subsequent research indicates that the *Maddox* was engaged in electronic surveillance of North Vietnamese radar facilities, which were deliberately triggered by conjoint South Vietnamese raids. The present whereabouts of the bullet that hit the *Maddox* is unknown.

The second incident occurred on August 4, 1964. The *Maddox* and the destroyer *Turner Joy* were on patrol in the Gulf of Tonkin, and again South Vietnamese naval commandos were engaged in nearby raids. At nine P.M. on a stormy night, the *Maddox* reported itself under attack, and commenced firing in all directions for three hours. In Washington, President Lyndon Johnson requested verification of the attack, and asked the Joint Chiefs to prepare a reprisal* air raid against North Vietnam.

Shortly before midnight (Washington time), American jets from nearby carriers struck North Vietnam, destroying twenty-five North Vietnamese patrol boats and a substantial portion of the oil supply of North Vietnam. President Johnson went on television to inform the American people that "repeated acts of violence against the armed forces of the United States must be met with positive reply. That reply is being given as I speak to you tonight."

The North Vietnamese denied ever having attacked the *Maddox* on August 4. Captain Herrick, on the *Maddox,* after interviewing his crew, could not confirm that any attack had occurred. Four years later, Robert McNamara claimed that electronic devices had intercepted a North Vietnamese attack order, but no transcripts of this intercept were ever released. In 1968, the present author interviewed John White, chief radio operator of the first American vessel to come to the assistance of the *Maddox* and *Turner Joy.* According to White, in all the radio traffic of that stormy night, no one said that they had seen or detected a single hostile boat.

On August 5, 1964, Johnson sent to Congress a resolution that authorized him to "take all necessary measures" to protect U.S. forces in the area and to "prevent further aggression," until he determined that peace and security were restored. On August 6, the resolution passed the House of Representatives (unanimously) and passed the Senate 98 to 2, with Wayne Morse (D-OR) and Ernest Gruening (D-AL) dissenting. This so-called "Gulf of Tonkin Resolution" provided the legal basis for American pursuit of the war in Vietnam, which was fought for the next eleven years without a formal declaration of war.

The U.S. Constitution reserves to the Congress the right to "declare war." Whether the Gulf of Tonkin resolution was a constitutional substitute for a declaration of war is a complex problem. On the one hand, Johnson had not himself "declared" war, usurping the Congress; the resolution did convey congressional support for military action; a precedent existed for military action without a declaration, namely, the Korean War*; and (d) formal declarations of war were the norm in the time of the framers but were increasingly uncommon in late 20th-century military affairs. But on the other hand, the resolution was nothing like a declaration of war because the enemy was not named, and the context of the resolution expressed congressional support only for the protection of the U.S. troops, not the involvement of those troops and others in a full-scale war. Later congressional unhappiness with the constitutional implications of the Gulf of Tonkin resolution led to the formal repeal of the resolution by Congress in 1970.

Regardless of judgments about the use to which the Gulf of Tonkin Resolution was put, the question remains regarding the ethics of the bombing raid of August 4. As president, Johnson was commander-in-chief of American forces and was responsible for their safety. Without congressional approval, he could authorize actions by American forces in self-defense. But actions in self-defense are legitimate only if the conditions for permissible self-defense have been met. For self-defense to be permissible, the victim must not have provoked the attack, and must not use force after the threat of danger has passed. The situation on August 4 does not seem to have met these conditions. The *Maddox* was very close to North Vietnam, working near South Vietnamese naval commandos. Captain Herrick, recognizing the provocative position of the *Maddox,* had requested putting further out to sea, but his request was denied. Most importantly, the raid on North Vietnam occurred long after the real or perceived threat to the *Maddox* had ceased.

Polls showed that 85 percent of the American people supported Johnson's decision to bomb North Vietnam. In the atmosphere of the Cold War*, Communists were necessarily bad, and bombing them was necessarily good. But critics of the war noted that the raid of 1964 probably would not have passed a Golden Rule or "role reversal" test, had it been presented to the American people in such terms. For example, suppose that Austrian commandos in 1940 had attacked the Statue of Liberty, while at the same time a German destroyer approached within four miles of the Jersey shore. American coast guard boats sailed out to investigate, and were sunk by the destroyer. Two days later, the same German destroyer sailed by in a storm, and the following night German planes flew in and destroyed the Brooklyn Navy yard and all the oil storage tanks in Perth Amboy. What percentage of Americans would accept a German argument that the bombing attack was a justifiable reprisal for an unprovoked attack on the high seas? Yet an analogous argument seems to have persuaded all but two members of the Senate on August 6, 1964.

See AGGRESSION, ATTEMPTS TO DEFINE; HUMANITARIAN INTERVENTION; PROPAGANDA.

BIBLIOGRAPHY
Goudlen, Joseph, *Truth Is the First Casualty* (Chicago: Rand McNally, 1969).
The Gulf of Tonkin: 1964 Incidents, Hearings Before the Senate Committee on Foreign Relations (Washington, D.C.: U.S. Government Printing Office, 1968).
Karnow, Stanley, *Vietnam* (New York: Viking, 1983).
Windchy, Eugene, *Tonkin Gulf* (Garden City, N.Y.: Doubleday, 1971).

Douglas P. Lackey

GULF WAR (DESERT STORM). On August 2, 1990, Iraqi forces invaded Kuwait and seized control of that nation. The Bush administration initially responded with indifference. *Time* reported that the prevailing attitude in the National Security Council was, "Too bad about Kuwait, but it's just a gas station, and who cares whether [it's] . . . Sinclair or Exxon?" Moreover, the president publicly proclaimed that he was not contemplating military action. However, on August 6, before any negotiations could begin, President Bush authorized sending 150,000 U.S. troops to the Gulf area. Bush's insistence that no negotiations occur was a rejection of the Security Council intent and the offers of the Arab League, the French, and Russia to assist in such negotiations. On November 19, 1990, the United States proposed Resolution 678 to the effect that if by January 15, 1991, Iraq had not complied, "all necessary force would be used against them." China threatened to veto such a resolution and the U.S. administration rewrote the demand to the effect that "all necessary means would be used." China abstained, and though it remained unclear whether "all necessary means" included "all necessary force," Bush persuaded enough members of the Security Council to support the U.S. campaign after January 15, 1991. The January 16, 1991, massive air attack against Iraq destroyed some military targets, killed massive numbers of civilians, and destroyed much of the infrastructure. A ground war followed, which lasted about 100 hours. American intervention produced the following results:

1. Iraqi control of Kuwait ended, and Kuwait's royal family was restored to power.

2. The Iraqi civilian and military suffered enormous casualties.*

3. American losses were minimal (148 killed in action, 25 percent by "friendly fire*").

4. The American invasion stopped at Basra, allowing Saddam Hussein to remain in power.

While the precise number is not known (see entry herein on Casualties of War), the Red Crescent, Red Cross*, Red Shield, Amnesty International, and Human Rights Watch claimed that thousands of Iraqi civilians were killed immediately and many more perished due to economic sanctions and the destruction of the infrastructure. With American encouragement, the Shiites and Kurds revolted. The Bush administration did not support the insurrection; many of these people were killed, and numerous survivors fled the country. Saddam Hussein remained in power.

Although many of the documents that reveal the decision-making process remain classified, the Department of Defense has made much information public, for example, that only 5 percent of the bombs were "smart." Nevertheless, obvious features of the conflict raise three ethical questions:

1. Is it appropriate for a U.S. president to go to war without an official declaration* from Congress?

2. Was the war justified when the territorial integrity of the United States was not threatened?

3. Was the war justified when massive civilian casualties were inevitable?

Those who take a strict constructionist view of the Constitution argue that only Congress has the power to declare war. Formalists join Edmund Burke in contending that the Constitution is a sacred compact between the past and the present. Accordingly, it is intrinsically valuable to uphold its provisions. Strict constructionists also posit a utilitarian argument that stresses the need for checks and balances and democratic influence in the exercise of war-making powers.

Specifically, it is argued that, given human frailties, dire consequences would result if the president alone were empowered to declare and conduct war. In the words of Alexander Hamilton, "The history of human conduct does not . . . make it wise in a nation to commit [war-making powers] . . . to the sole disposal of a magistrate . . . [such as] the president of the United States." He argued that to bestow such powers would make the president a king, not a constitutional ruler.

Critics argue that modern exigencies required the president to act quickly and unilaterally to protect the "national interest" and to safeguard beleaguered allies. Electronic intelligence gathering coupled with the speed and lethality of modern weapons required the commander-in-chief to act decisively in secret with minimal consultation.

In the context of this presidential powers controversy, several conclusions can be drawn about the Bush administration intervention in the Persian Gulf:

1. Although the Security Council endorsed the U.S. action, or at least did not oppose it, the position of the United Nations was that the war was U.S.-led.

2. A combination of diplomacy and economic incentives on the part of the Bush administration resulted in token participation of other nations.

3. Although the U.S. Congress did not declare war, it did endorse Bush's policies at the last moment when war seemed inevitable.

Critics charge that Bush could and should have obtained formal approval since urgent action was not required. After all, the administration took five months to prepare for the war. Those who support administration policy suggest that constitutional provisions cannot be the *summum bonum* of foreign policy in a rapidly changing world, and that certain goals are worthier than strict adherence to the Constitution. Bush justified the attack on Iraqi forces by likening Saddam's invasion of Kuwait to Hitler's aggression against his neighbors. Accordingly, Bush said that the liberation of Kuwait was as virtuous as the Allied liberation of France. Moreover, reestablishing the status quo in Kuwait was instrumental, Bush argued, in creating a "New World Order": an international regime in which sovereign boundaries would be respected. The Saddam regime, of course, did not share this perspective. The Iraqis argued that the Turks and the British had artificially separated Iraq from Kuwait, its 19th province, thus denying them a sea port. Further, the Iraqis alleged that the Kuwaitis were siphoning their oil and injuring the Iraqi economy by lowering the price of this resource.

Domestic critics stressed that Kuwait was not the only nation that had been overrun by a powerful neighbor. They wondered why America did not intervene when Israel and Syria attacked and de facto annexed Lebanon at various times, or when Turkey attacked and annexed half of Cyprus. One critic quipped, "Would Bush have intervened if Kuwait's principal export were broccoli?" Michael Walzer raised another problematic question: would America and its allies have intervened if an internal coup had overthrown the Kuwaiti royal family? (Given Kuwait's strained relations with America, Walzer suggested that such a coup might have been cause for celebration.)

Other critics argued that the conflict was about oil. They cited Secretary of State James Baker's remark: "The conflict is about oil and jobs." To be sure, no American administration would be indifferent to the vast reserves in the region; however, the United States only obtains about 4 percent of its oil from Kuwait, and it seemed likely that Saddam Hussein would continue to sell oil, since it was his only exportable resource. Those sympathetic to American policy allowed that this was the case, but they contended that Japan and the Common Market nations were dependent on Kuwaiti oil and investments, and therefore the economies of these allies would be undermined, with dire consequences for the United States.

Although sympathetic to the American cause, other critics charged that the Bush administration erred in permitting Saddam to remain in power. Henry Kissinger offered a rejoinder to this criticism, arguing that Saddam merely had to be "cut down to size" to restore the regional balance of power. Newsman Bob Woodward suggested that personal challenges presented by Margaret Thatcher and Bandar bin Sultan (the Saudi ambassador) overcame Bush's initial indifference to Iraqi aggression. Specifically, due to extensive Kuwaiti financial holdings in Great Britain, Thatcher persuaded Bush that his credibility and resolve—if not his presidency—were being challenged by Iraqi actions. And, citing lack of American resolve in Vietnam, the hostage crisis, and antipacification efforts in Lebanon, Bandar claimed that American presidents no longer had the will to project national power.

Suffice it to conclude that both champions and critics of American actions agree that Iraqi aggression did not threaten the territorial integrity of the United States. However, there has been considerable debate as to whether the primary motive of the Bush administration was the restoration of the status quo in Kuwait. Some argue that the restoration of the Kuwaiti monarchy was the harbinger of a New World Order, but both champions and critics of the Bush administration agree that this was not the only agenda.

Although the goals and accomplishments of Desert Storm are arguable, it is clear that tens of thousands of civilians were killed during the war and its aftermath. Furthermore, the very distinction between civilians and combatants was tendentious: Most of the Iraqi combatants were conscripts who were virtual hostages; if they had defected, the Saddam regime would likely have tortured or killed their families. Like most 20th-century conflicts, the Gulf War killed more civilians than combatants. Given the unprecedented magnitude of civilian destruction in recent wars, and the likelihood that future wars would be "wars without mercy," many theorists have argued that contemporary warfare is prima facie immoral.

Walzer contended that the outcome in civilian casualties did not justify the Persian Gulf War. Others, such as Charles Krauthammer, argued that the destruction of Iraqi civilians was "no cause for guilt." He argued that since American intervention was the moral equivalent of Allied opposition to Nazism*, the Americans should not undermine their troops by condemning inevitable—albeit inadvertent—civilian casualties. Krauthammer contended that the American destruction of civilians was qualitatively different from terrorist actions against the innocent and defenseless. Terrorists, according to this argument, deliberately kill civilians in pursuit of personal and political objectives. The Americans in Desert Storm, on the other hand, did not intend to commit such acts, and attempted to limit destruction to military targets. Finally, the argument continued, the lamentable civilian deaths in Iraq inadvertently occurred in pursuit of higher political objectives.

Critics of this argument charge that Krauthammer was disingenuous. They question the claimed distinction between civilian and military targets; specifically, they insist that the destruction of a putative military target such as a railway or power plant has dire, if not fatal, consequences for civilians. These critics believe that it should be obvious to American strategists that air attacks on densely populated cities would cause massive civilian casualties, and it was equally apparent that the destruction of a nation's infrastructure would result in ongoing casualties in the aftermath of the war.

See AGGRESSION, ATTEMPTS TO DEFINE; COLLATERAL DAMAGE; HUMANITARIAN INTERVENTION; INTELLIGENCE AGENCIES; MILITARY-INDUSTRIAL COMPLEX; PROPAGANDA.

BIBLIOGRAPHY

Ball, George, "The Gulf Crisis," *New York Review of Books* (December 6, 1990), 14–17.

Barnet, Richard, "The Uses of Force," *New Yorker* (April 29, 1991).

Falk, Richard, "U.N. Being Made a Tool of U.S. Foreign Policy," *Manchester Guardian* (July 27, 1991), 12.

Hirschbein, Ron, "Massing the Troops: A Critique of Persian Gulf Discourse," in Larry Bove and Laura Duhan Kaplan, eds., *In the Eye of the Storm* (Amsterdam: Rodopi, 1995).

Salinger, Pierre, and Eric Laurent, *Secret Dossier: The Hidden Agenda Behind the Gulf War* (New York: Penguin Books, 1991).

Sifry, Micah, and Christopher Cerf, eds., *The Gulf War Reader* (New York: Random House, 1991).

Walzer, Michael, *Just and Unjust Wars,* 2d ed. (New York: Basic Books, 1992).

Woodward, Bob, *The Commanders* (New York: Simon & Schuster, 1991).

Ron Hirschbein

H

HAGUE, THE, CONGRESSES. The two Congresses at The Hague were called by Tsar Nicholas II of Russia. The first in 1899 included twenty-six nations and had as its chief aims to bring about an arms reduction and to discover more peaceful ways of settling international disputes. Although no agreement was reached on arms reduction, the congress did issue three conventions and three declarations intended to outlaw certain weapons and practices of war. In his instructions to the five U.S. delegates, Secretary of State John Hay stated that they should consider as "lacking in practicability" all attempts to restrict either the use or the destructiveness of weapons. The United States did not accept the efforts to limit explosive bullets, dumdum bullets*, incendiaries*, or gas and noxious chemicals. Three conventions were issued.

CONVENTION FOR THE PACIFIC SETTLEMENT OF INTERNATIONAL DISPUTES

Issued July 29, 1899, the major recommendations were:

1. Before any appeal to arms, the signatory powers agree to have recourse to mediation using one or more friendly powers.
2. The powers may reject the advice of such mediation.
3. Where the issues do not involve either "national honor nor vital interests," the powers agree to establish a commission of inquiry to seek some system of arbitration short of war. A permanent court of arbitration with its seat in The Hague would be established. Twenty-eight articles outlined the procedure for arbitration.

With a minor reservation the U.S. Senate ratified this convention on April 7, 1900.

CONVENTION WITH RESPECT TO THE LAWS AND CUSTOMS OF WAR ON LAND

This brief convention of five articles recommended that:

The High Contracting Parties shall issue instructions to their armed land forces, which shall be in conformity with the Regulations respecting the Laws and Customs of War on Land annexed to the present Convention.

The annex, with sixty articles, proved to be a stumbling block for some member nations. The major reservations were on the following prohibitions found in article 23: (1) to employ poison or poisoned arms; and (2) to employ arms, projectiles, or material of a nature to cause superfluous injury.

CONVENTION FOR THE ADAPTATION TO MARITIME WARFARE OF THE PRINCIPLES OF THE GENEVA CONVENTION

The emphasis was on the protection of hospital ships and those carrying wounded, sick, or shipwrecked* survivors.

In addition to the three conventions, this first congress at The Hague issued three declarations:

1. Prohibiting Launching of Projectiles and Explosives from Balloons. The prohibition applied only between signatory powers.
2. Prohibiting Use of Expanding Bullets (Hague 4, 2). While twenty-four nations signed, the list did not include either the United States or Great Britain.
3. Prohibiting Use of Gases (Hague 4, 3). The same powers were signatories as was the case with expanding bullets, excluding, thus, both Great Britain and the United States.

In 1904 The Hague issued a convention regarding hospital ships, which exempted them from taxation in time of war.

In 1907 the member powers met again at The Hague. These meetings were also called by Tsar Nicholas II of Russia, and this time with special encouragement from U.S. President Theodore Roosevelt. Forty-four governments were represented, and although no agreements were reached on disarmament, by October 18, 1907, fourteen conventions had been issued, as follows:

1. Pacific Settlement of International Disputes, Hague, I (97 articles)
2. Limitation of Employment of Force for Recovery of Contract Debts, Hague, 2 (7 articles)
3. Relative to the Opening of Hostilities, Hague, 3 (8 articles)
4. Laws and Customs of War On Land, Hague, 4 (9 articles). An annex of 56 articles was attached. While article 23 of the 1899 convention had banned weapons that cause "superfluous injury," the new convention spoke of weapons that cause "unnecessary suffering." Although Article 24 of the 1899 session considered ruses of war "permissible," the new convention stated that they were "allowable." Article 25 of the old convention had forbidden attacks on unfortified cities; the new convention added the phrase "by whatever means." Article 27 of the old convention

had stated that "every care should be taken" to protect churches, hospitals, schools, and such; the new convention dropped the word "every."

5. Rights and Duties of Neutral Powers and Persons in War on Land, Hague, 5 (25 articles)

6. Status of Enemy Merchant Ships at the Outbreak of Hostilities, Hague, 6 (11 articles)

7. Conversion of Merchant Ships into War Ships, Hague 71 (12 articles)

8. Laying of Automatic Submarine Contact Mines, Hague 8 (13 articles). It was recognized that it would not be possible to outlaw submarines, although they could not comply with the naval requirement that sailors from sinking ships be rescued. It was proposed, however, that contact mines* be so constructed that they would become harmless if they came loose from their moorings, and a similar proposal for torpedoes* once they had missed their intended target

9. Bombardment by Naval Forces in Time of War, Hague, 9 (12 articles). Article 1 forbade the bombing of unfortified cities unless it was required by military exigency. Article 2 urged commanders to take steps to reduce unnecessary suffering, although the nature of such suffering was not specified

10. Adaptation to Maritime Warfare of Principles of the Geneva Convention, Hague 10 (28 articles)

11. Restrictions with Regard to Right of Capture in Naval War, Hague 11 (14 articles)

12. Establishment of an International Prize Court, Hague 12 (57 articles)

13. Rights and Duties of Neutral Powers in Naval War, Hague 13 (33 articles)

14. Prohibiting Discharge of Projectiles and Explosives from Balloons, Hague 14. This declaration proposed the ban to last for five years or until the Third Peace Conference. Since this conference was never held, the signatories entered World War I without this prohibition. Like all the preceding conventions it applied only in wars where all of the participants were signatories.

Between December 1922 and February 1923, a Hague convention on "Rules of Air Warfare" was issued with sixty-two articles; however, these rules were never adopted by the powers concerned. Some of the articles are, however, interesting as indications of what was being attempted. Article 18 stated that tracer, incendiary*, and explosive projectiles were prohibited. Article 20 stated that airmen descending by parachute* from disabled aircraft were not to be fired at in the course of their descent. Article 22 forbade bombardment for the purpose of terrorizing* the civilian population. Article 24 stated that bombing was legitimate only when directed exclusively at a military objective, and in those cases where civilians were too close to avoid hitting them, the bombardment should not be carried out.

See AERIAL WARFARE; BIOLOGICAL/CHEMICAL WARFARE; FORBIDDEN STRATEGIES; FORBIDDEN WEAPONS; GENEVA CONVENTION, 1949; INCENDIARIES; LAWS OF WAR; MINES; PARACHUTES; PROPORTIONALITY; RED CROSS; RED CRESCENT, RED LION, AND SUN.

BIBLIOGRAPHY
Scott, James Brown, *The Hague Conventions and Declarations of 1899 and 1907* (New York: Oxford University Press, 1915).
———, *The Hague Court Reports* (New York: Oxford University Press, 1916).
———, *The Hague Peace Conferences* (Baltimore, Md.: The Johns Hopkins Press, 1909).

HAITI. On August 22, 1791, a slave-led uprising in Saint-Dominique against French control began and culminated in 1804 with the creation of an independent Haiti. As part of the price for independence, France levelled a staggering double indemnity under which the Haitian economy struggled until President Louis Saloman liquidated the indemnity in 1888. Haiti was the first modern state of African origins and the only one to arise out of a slave uprising. The Haitian economy under the French was chiefly the slave trade, with the profits going to France. One consequence of the revolt was that Haiti was ostracized by other nations. Although the Netherlands and the Scandinavian countries traded, they did not recognize Haiti diplomatically, and the United States had no diplomatic relations with Haiti until 1862. The eastern two-thirds of former Saint-Dominique became the Dominican Republic.

German, French, and American business sought to profit from the new country. Between 1857 and 1900, U.S. warships intervened on behalf of U.S. business interests on nineteen occasions in both Haiti and the Dominican Republic. The 1915 U.S. intervention lasted until 1934. The American rationale was to "protect property and to preserve order," and also to forestall German and French business from getting control. The National City Bank of New York controlled Haitian funds and in 1914 impounded all Haitian revenue, and at the request of the bank the U.S.S. *Machias* landed a contingent of marines, who seized Haiti's gold reserves for "safekeeping." In 1922 the same New York bank forced a huge loan on Haiti with the intent to strangle the country's economy. By 1920 the United States controlled 60 percent of the Haitian market.

Haiti suffered from the start with either incompetent or corrupt leadership and exhibited what has been called a "kleptocracy," or a "soft state," characterized by corruption at all levels. At the time of the 1915 U.S. intervention illiteracy was probably close to 100 percent, and by 1980 was still about 90 percent. Its GNP per capita of $260 is the lowest of the nations of the world.

In 1965, a popular uprising in the Dominican Republic sought to reinstate that country's only freely elected president, Juan Bosch, elected overwhelmingly in 1962 and overthrown by a military coup in 1963. President Lyndon Johnson sent 24,000 troops to aid the coup in the fear that the uprising was Communist-dominated. In 1986, the twenty-eight-year dictatorship of the Duvalier family ended when President Jean-Claude Duvalier fled in a U.S. air force jet. A new constitution adopted in 1987 led to elections in November, but the army slaughtered peasants who dared to turn out to vote. In 1990 the nation held its first popular and fair election, in which Father Jean-Bertrand Aristide was elected

President with almost 70 percent of the vote. He opened all government buildings to anyone with a grievance, cut his own salary by 60 percent, and tried to reduce other government payrolls. He fired many Duvalier holdovers and tried to redistribute land to the poor. He tackled the military, appointing Raoul Cedras to supervise the establishment of a new police force to replace the military. In September 1991, however, a military coup led by Cedras overthrew Aristide (about 1,500 Haitians killed), and in October 1991 the U.S. State Department said that it had a thick notebook on human rights abuses under Aristide. However, the Bush administration publicly denounced the abuses of the coup, sheltered Aristide (he was flown by U.S. jet to Caracas, Venezuela), and imposed an embargo on trade with Haiti. In July 1993, General Cedras signed the Governors Island Agreement negotiated under UN auspices, but Cedras refused to implement the accord.

On June 25, 1994, President Bill Clinton issued an executive order banning private financial transactions between Haiti and the United States and through the United States between Haiti and other countries. On September 15, 1994, President Clinton ordered Secretary of Defense William Perry to call up military personnel necessary to support U.S. troops in any action undertaken. He ordered two aircraft carriers, the U.S.S. *Eisenhower* and the U.S.S. *America* into the region. On September 19, 1994 the first 3,000 U.S. soldiers landed in Haiti. On September 29, 1994, Secretary of State Warren Christopher reported this action to the UN Security Council, stating that the United States considered this action to be consistent with UN Security Council Resolutions 917 and 940. On October 15, 1994, the U.S. Air Force flew Aristide to Haiti. On January 30, 1995, UN Security Council Resolution 975 urged the replacement of the U.S.-led "multinational force" (MNF) by the United Nations Mission in Haiti (UNMIH) to be completed by March 31, 1995. The vote was 14-0-1 (China abstaining).

In sharp contrast with the U.S. incursion in Panama*, where up to 2,000 Panamanians were killed and about $1 billion in damage was done to the country, the Haiti incursion caused no financial damage and was virtually bloodless. This was due both to the caution of the State Department in its instructions to the U.S. forces and to the good negotiating offices of former President Jimmy Carter.

See CAUSES OF WAR; DEMOCRACY AND THE MILITARY; MILITARY-INDUSTRIAL COMPLEX.

BIBLIOGRAPHY

Fagg, John Edwin, *Cuba, Haiti, and the Dominican Republic* (Englewood Cliffs, N.J.: Prentice-Hall, 1965).

Foster, Charles R., and Albert Valdman, eds. *Haiti: Today and Tomorrow* (Lanham, Md.: University Press of America, 1984).

Ott, Thomas O., *The Haitian Revolution 1789–1804* (Knoxville: University of Tennessee Press, 1973).

The Situation in Haiti and U.S. Policy, Hearing Before the Subcommittees on Human Rights and International Organizations and Western Hemisphere Affairs of the Committee on Foreign Affairs, H.R., 102nd Cong., 2d sess., February 19, 1992.

HAVEL, VACLAV. Born October 5, 1936, Vaclav Havel was elected the first president of the new Czech Republic and served as president of post-Communist Czechoslovakia following the nonviolent "velvet revolution" of 1989. Accomplished as a playwright, essayist, philosopher, and politician, Havel is also a major theorist and strategist of nonviolent resistance.

A dissident for many years in Communist Czechoslovakia, Havel's opposition to what he called "post-totalitarianism" increased in 1976 with his organization of the Charter 77 movement and two years later with VONS (Committee for the Defense of the Unjustly Persecuted), both expressly formed to protect the defenseless, to advocate freedom of expression, and to pressure the government to respect the human rights identified in the 1977 Helsinki Accords ratified by the Warsaw Pact. In his "Open Letter to Dr. Gustav Husak" (1975), "Politics and Conscience" (1984), and especially *The Power of the Powerless* (1978), Havel characterizes totalitarian domination as a crisis of the spirit that is finished only when individuals end their collusion with the government and regain their integrity by "living in the truth." He outlines an "empowering ideology" that would enable the oppressed to live with integrity and suggests how nonviolent revolution, or "existential revolution," can occur through the successive stages of (1) personal transformation, (2) passive resistance to government manipulation, (3) active "independent citizen initiatives," including protests, petitions, and noncooperation, (4) the development of a (largely underground) "second culture," and finally, (3) the emergence of parallel social and political institutions, or the "parallel *polis*." Only nonviolent revolution, and self-sacrifice, if required, is consistent with the spiritual, existential transformation necessary to arrest the destructive tendencies of modern, technologized, and bureaucratized "civilization."

Imprisoned from 1978 to 1983, Havel added philosophical foundations for his nonviolent revolution in 144 unconfiscated letters to his wife, subsequently published as *Letters to Olga.* Regarded as the "conscience of his nation," Havel was also an astute strategist and tactician. The nonviolent revolution he orchestrated is to date the best demonstration of the fallacious assumptions underlying—in the terminology of Gene Sharp—the "monolith" theory of power and in favor of the "pluralist-dependency" theory of power, as well as brilliant in its use of "political karate." The latter involves identifying an authoritarian regime's weakest points and bringing incessant pressure to bear on them. Havel clearly understood the point made by the Latin poet Claudian and repeated by Montaigne that "There is no victory, except when the enemy in his own mind acknowledges himself beaten." His genius lay in finding ways of demonstrating this eternal truth to those blinded by the illusion that power is equivalent to the physical force or military violence at one's disposal.

See NONVIOLENT CIVILIAN-BASED DEFENSE; PACIFISM.

BIBLIOGRAPHY

Churchill, R. Paul, "Vaclav Havel's *The Power of the Powerless* and the Philosophy of Nonviolence," in Duane L. Cady, and Richard Werner, eds., *Just War, Nonviolence and Nuclear Deterrence* (Wakefield, N.H.: Longwood Academic, 1991).

Havel, Vaclav, *Disturbing the Peace,* Paul Wilson, trans. (New York: Alfred A. Knopf, 1990).
———, *Letters to Olga,* Paul Wilson, trans. (New York: Henry Holt, 1989).
———, *Vaclav Havel, or Living in Truth,* Jan Vladislav, ed. (London: Faber & Faber, 1990).
Sharp, Gene, *The Politics of Nonviolent Action* (Boston: Porter Sargent Publishers, 1973).
                                                                   Robert Paul Churchill

HAWAII, MILITARY LAND USE IN. Hawaii became the 50th American state in 1959. The U.S. military's interest in the land in Hawaii began nearly a century earlier when Hawaii was an independent kingdom. That interest, manifested by the 1873 arrival in Honolulu of Gen. John Schofield, was both masked and apparent. Ostensibly in Hawaii on a vacation to recuperate, Schofield, under secret orders from the secretary of war, was to assess the defensive and commercial capabilities of Hawaii and to collect information useful to the United States. His report urged the acquisition of Pearl Harbor as a defensive position for the West Coast.

American businessmen and nonnative sugar planters quickly increased their pressure on the Hawaiian government to cede Pearl Harbor to the United States; in 1887, they forced the king to sign a reciprocity treaty permitting the United States to use the harbor in exchange for allowing their sugar to enter the American market duty free.

Six years later, troops from the U.S.S. *Boston* were a key force in overthrowing the government of Queen Liliuokalani, and four days after the United States' formal annexation of Hawaii, over 1,000 American troops landed and set up camp at the foot of Diamond Head. Thus, from the earliest moments, the American military was imbricated in the formation of the sugar empire in Hawaii, the annexation of Hawaii, and American colonizing of the Pacific.

Overthrow and annexation enabled the military to come into possession and use of its current 8 percent of the state's total land mass of 6,425 square miles (the fourth-smallest state after Rhode Island, Delaware and Connecticut) with around 23 percent of that on Oahu. This is a generally accepted figure; the exact amount of land controlled by the military is contested. Readers of the *State of Hawaii Data Book* are urged to use these data cautiously, as there is no uniform method of aggregating and defining data.

The self-proclaimed provisional government set up after the overthrow took over both the lands of the government and the personal lands of the monarch (the crown lands). Merged as Public Lands, they were both leased and sold. At annexation, the remainder were ceded to the federal government. When the territory was created by the U.S. government in 1900, some ceded lands were kept by the United States for military and park purposes; the rest were transferred to the Territory of Hawaii. At the time of statehood in 1959, the federal government retained some ceded lands while transferring the rest to the state. About 24,000 acres is owned by the military in fee simple (complete and absolute ownership in land). The other 90 percent is either ceded or leased. Under the terms of the statehood act, the ceded lands are held in trust by the state and are to be used for schools and education and the "betterment of native Hawaiians." This structural use conflict between the interests of the state and the needs of native Hawaiians has fueled the energies of native Hawaiians to reclaim the ceded lands as the land base for a sovereign nation, while the military deploys the rhetoric of national security to retain and enlarge its possessions.

The most visible of such conflicts was a two-decade clash over the military's use of Kahoolawe, an uninhabited island long used for Navy and Pacific Rim nations' bombing practice. The island was finally relinquished to the state in 1994. The seventy-five military installations on Oahu alone occupy good beaches, parkland, ancient sacred areas, and the mountains; there is pressure from other parts of the community for beach access, housing, hiking trails, and conservation, all of which add more conflict over the military's use of this land for mountain training exercises using line ammunition, amphibious landings, and maintenance of the combat readiness of designated units. The secretary of war, Tojo West, Jr., resisting political pressures to turn over more rarely used areas, stated that "if the Army can't train here, then it's going to have to train somewhere else." Such remarks are a reminder by the secretary and his local supporters of the importance of military spending in the Hawaiian economy, where the military's annual estimated $3.8 billion ranks it second only to tourism's $9.4 billion.

Historically, the military has been regarded by some as the worst enemy of the land it occupies. Its most famous installation, Pearl Harbor, was nominated by the Environmental Protection Agency for inclusion on the Superfund list in 1991 for its high levels of chromium, mercury, lead, and PCBs. A number of valleys on Oahu, used during and after World War II for firing practice with live ammunition, are proving to be too dangerous for habitation and too costly to clean up. Schofield Barracks, home of the combat-ready 25th Infantry Division, has been a consistent violator of the Clean Water Act by its negligent disposal of wastewater. There is some fear that its toxic chemicals have filtered down into the nature storage system for drinking water. While the military has made some efforts to reestablish wetlands and other wildlife sanctuaries, its long occupation of land has imprinted the land with a legacy of hazardous wastes that threaten the island's aquifers, posing enormous costs in cleanup. The disproportionate number of endangered species of plants and animals in Hawaii are also at great risk of extinction from a century of contamination and training exercises.

On the island of Kauai, the military controls about 5 percent of its 353,484 acres. The most contested facility, the Pacific Missile Range Facility at Barking Sands Beach, is a testing site for "Star Wars" simulated intercontinental missiles, launched westward toward the Marshall Islands to test the ability of lasers to intercept them. The facility employs 900 civilians. Each launch releases hydrazine and freon, both linked to ozone depletion, into the upper atmosphere, which critics charge poses serious hazards to land and marine ecosystems, as well as human health. The state joined many local representatives to try to prevent the launches. The land closed off prior to the launch is ceded and there is local pressure to have the land returned to native Hawaiians.

The military's presence on Maui is negligible in terms of land mass, but its technology is not. An army installation on the upper slopes of Haleakala is a pioneer experimental station for bouncing laser beams off satellites. The effects have been cited as possibly dangerous to nesting birds in the crater and thousands of tourists below in Kihei. The largest facility on the island of Hawaii, the Big Island, is the Pohakuloa Training site (101,882 acres) for units of the 25th Infantry Division (Light), a manned combat element for the U.S. Army Pacific. Largely located on old lava flows from Mauna Kea and Mauna Loa, it is the home for the state's Endangered Species Propagation Facility at Pohakuloa State Park and the scarce or endangered nene, crow, petrel, akepa, akiapolaau, palila, iiwi, creeper, and io, as well as unnamed other species of animal and plant life, and is also used by campers at the park.

The Sikes Act mandates the preparation of natural resources management plans for military areas containing natural resources identified as of interest by the U.S. Fish and Wildlife Service. It thus commits the military to providing positive support to wildlife and improving land conservation practices. At the same time, its century of careless practices and commitment to a modern technology of great speeds, enormous power, and toxic chemicals, constitute a way of being in the world that cannot sit lightly upon any land.

See BIKINI ATOLL, BOMBING OF; BIOLOGICAL/CHEMICAL WARFARE; DEMOCRACY AND THE MILITARY; ENVIRONMENTAL ISSUES, POLLUTION, AND THE MILITARY; HAZARDOUS DUMPING IN PROTECTED MARINE AREAS; INTELLIGENCE AGENCIES, U.S.; MILITARY-INDUSTRIAL COMPLEX; PROPAGANDA; WARISM.

BIBLIOGRAPHY

Ali, Mehmed, Kathy Ferguson, and Phyllis Turnbull, ''Gender, Land, Power,'' Unpublished paper, Political Science Department, University of Hawaii, 1991.

Atlas of Hawaii (Honolulu: Department of Geography, University of Hawaii Press, 1973).

Kuykendall, Ralph S., *The Hawaiian Kingdom; 1854–1874: Twenty Critical Years,* vol. 2 (Honolulu: University of Hawaii Press, 1966).

Mardfin, Jean Kadooka, *Two Land Recording Systems,* Report No. 7 (Honolulu: Legislative Reference Bureau, 1987).

Sierra Club Legal Defense Fund, ''Update: Environmental Projects and Events'' (July 1993).

U.S. Army Support Command, Hawaii, ''USASCH Installation Environmental Impact Statement'' (Honolulu: Fort Schafter, 1979).

Kathy E. Ferguson and Phyllis Turnbull

HAZARDOUS DUMPING IN PROTECTED MARINE AREAS. During the past fifty years, as the world has become more crowded and as the developed nations have sought to test increasingly dangerous substances and dispose of their wastes, the isolated low-lying atolls of the Pacific have become inviting targets for activities and toxic products that would not be tolerated elsewhere. Severe environmental burdens have been imposed on isolated and sparsely populated atolls (which previously had pristine and unique ecosystems) such as Bikini*, Enewetok, Moruroa, Fangataufa, Johnston, and Christmas Atolls, in order to serve the security and economic needs of the developed world.

Are these activities inconsistent with the obligation of all nations to protect the marine environment, a responsibility that has been recognized repeatedly in recent treaties? Article 5 of the 1986 Convention for the Protection of the Natural Resources and Environment of the South Pacific Region requires all parties "to prevent, reduce and control pollution of the Convention Area, from any source," and Article 14 of that treaty requires parties more particularly to establish "protected areas" in order "to protect and preserve rare or fragile ecosystems and depleted, threatened or endangered flora and fauna as well as their habitat." Similarly, Article 192 of the 1982 UN Law of the Sea Convention requires parties to "protect and preserve the marine environment," and Article 194 (5) requires parties "to protect and preserve rare or fragile ecosystems." Are all low-lying atolls "rare or fragile ecosystems," almost by definition?

The creation of a coral atoll from its birth beginning as magma escaping on the sea floor to a fully developed reef is an extremely complex process of nature that occurs over millions of years. Tens of thousands of seamounts are distributed over the Pacific, but only a few have become atolls. Some are not tall enough to reach the surface. Others rise above the surface but then are eroded away by wind, rain, and wave action over time. Only when the rate of erosion is sufficiently slow to allow coral to grow at a rate that keeps pace with the erosion does an atoll emerge.

Each coral reef constitutes a unique ecosystem. The organisms of a reef contribute to its growth in three ways. The whole skeletons of the coral organisms and other marine creatures form a framework for further development. Broken skeletons are responsible for the forming of lime, sand, and mud that fill openings in the framework. Finally, other organisms such as blue-green and red algae act to cement materials into the framework.

Coral reefs thrive in localities where the mean annual temperature of the surface water ranges from 73 to 77 degrees Fahrenheit (23 to 25 degrees Centigrade). Significant reef activity or growth is rarely found in areas where the water temperature is below 65°F. Coral grows best where the variations in water temperatures throughout the year are slight, and considerable sunshine shines through the waters to encourage the growth of the reef corals.

Winds, ocean currents, tides, and the salinity of the water also have important roles to play in the creation of the shape of an individual coral atoll. All low-lying atolls are susceptible to dramatic changes when major weather systems pass through the atoll and are subject to constant erosion through the actions of wind and sea. They are not appropriate sites for hazardous activities because they are at the mercy of complex and not easily understood ocean weather systems that periodically bring hurricanes (or typhoons) and tsunamis (tidal waves) that carry waves across the atoll, affecting all facilities and creating the possibility of dispersing the land-based materials into the ocean environment. In 1972, in 1984, and again in 1994, all the hundreds of civilian and military personnel on Johnston Atoll were evacuated because of the severe winds and waves that battered and threatened the islands. Similarly, unexpected storms smashed into Moruroa in 1980–1981, requiring all the residents and employees to seek refuge on raised platforms while the winds and rains washed across the atoll.

Because of their relative isolation, unique flora and fauna almost invariably build up around these atolls. The United States has (almost ironically) recognized this phenomenon in the case of Johnston Atoll, and designated Johnston as a wildlife preserve as early as 1926. Nonetheless, the United States has permitted Johnston to be used for military missions that have imposed serious hazards on the surrounding environment. These activities have led the U.S. Fish and Wildlife Service to identify Johnston as an area requiring immediate cleanup.

All low-lying atolls should be designated as protected marine areas. The marine and bird life of the Pacific atolls are unique, and the introduction of hazardous activities to these atolls has invariably been harmful to these living resources. If these areas are designated as protected zones, then an effective surveillance system should be established to monitor environmental quality in these areas and a regional program should be established to regulate and restrict dumping, incineration, and other activities involving hazardous materials in these areas.

The regime of "specially protected areas" is not necessarily a regime intended to keep the designated locations as inviolate and pristine as areas like wilderness regions. Rather, this regime provides a planning mechanism whereby competing resources uses can be weighed against the values recognized in designating the areas as a protected zone. In particular, of course, no hazardous activities and no dumping that would detrimentally affect it should be permitted in the protected area.

A variety of environmental burdens have been imposed upon or proposed for Pacific island atolls. Nuclear explosions—the most serious environmental insult humans have yet created—have taken place in, over, or under the atoll lagoons of Bikini, Enewetok, Moruroa, Fangataufa, Johnston, and Christmas Atolls, and these atolls have all been contaminated. A major superport was proposed for Palau which, if built, would have permanently altered the pristine reef environment that exists there. Nerve gas is now stored on Johnston and a chemical incineration plant has been built there to burn these and other wastes now stored elsewhere. Agent Orange has also been stored on Johnston and an area of this atoll remains contaminated with dioxin. The Marshall Islands, and possibly other atoll communities, are considering allowing their uninhabited atolls to be used to store nuclear and other hazardous wastes. Such high-risk activities are clearly inappropriate for these unique and fragile ecosystems.

Substantial progress has been made in recent years in articulating the standards that should govern the protection of the marine environment. The 1982 Law of the Sea Convention and the regional seas conventions lay down sound principles designed to control pollution and preserve the living resources of the sea. These treaties establish the concept of specially protected zones, but leave to the present generation the job of developing criteria to designate such areas.

Because all low-lying atolls are so intimately connected with and affected by the surrounding marine environment, it is not logical to treat the land areas of these atolls separately from the marine region. The limited land areas of these atolls are the ultimate coastal zone, because they have no vertical component. They should be seen as an inherent part of the marine environment, and all the principles that govern the marine environment should also govern these low-lying atolls. This proposition is clearly supported by the text of recent conventions, particularly the 1986 Convention for the Protection of the National Resources and Environment of the South Pacific Region.

The logic of the South Pacific Environmental Convention also supports the proposition that all low-lying atolls should be designated as specially protected areas pursuant to Article 14. By their very nature, atolls have small or no populations and thus will always be underrepresented in human terms when development decisions are made. They thus need the *specially protected* designation to ensure that the special environmental concerns of these fragile ecosystems are weighed against the interests that seek to use them for some purpose. This approach would not interfere with rational resource development, but would promote careful planning and limit dumping and hazardous activities on or near these atolls to protect their unique and important environments.

See BIKINI ATOLL, BOMBING OF; NUCLEAR WEAPONS TESTING.

BIBLIOGRAPHY
"Convention for the Protection of the Natural Resources and Environment of the South Pacific Region," Article 5, done at Noumea, New Caledonia, November 25, 1986, reprinted in *ILM* 26 (1987), 38.
"United Nations Law of the Sea Convention," Article 192, held at Montego Bay, Jamaica, December 10, 1982, reprinted in *ILM* 21 (1982), 1261.
Van Dyke, Jon M., "Protected Marine Areas and Low Lying Atolls," *Ocean and Shoreline Management* 16 (1991), 87–160.
Van Dyke, Jon M., Ted N. Pettit, Jennifer Cook Clark, and Allen L. Clark, "The Legal Status of Johnston Atoll and Its Exclusive Economic Zone," *University of Hawaii Law Review* 10 (1988), 183–204.

Jon M. Van Dyke

HENNACY, AMMON (1893–1970). A pacifist, anarchist, socialist, and activist who was committed variously to Protestantism, Mormonism, and Roman Catholicism. He was born in the midst of the 1893 depression, July 24, 1893, in Negley, Ohio, and baptized at the age of twelve in the local creek by the Baptist minister. In 1906 the family moved twenty miles away to a place with no Baptist church, so he attended the Presbyterian church. After hearing evangelist Billy

Sunday, he was so revolted that he got up in church and announced that he was now an atheist. By the fall of 1910, inspired by reading Tom Paine's *The Appeal to Reason,* he became a socialist. After reading Upton Sinclair's *The Jungle,* about the Chicago Stockyards, he became a vegetarian.

His first year at college was at Hiram in Ohio, and a chance meeting with Zona Gale led him to transfer in his second year to the University of Wisconsin in Madison. During that year he met Emma Goldman and Bob LaFollette, and took a course from Horace Kallen. His third year of college was at Ohio State, where he was head of the Socialist Club and a delegate to the state convention of the Socialist Party in 1916. He wrote an antidraft leaflet for the party urging young men to resist the draft and to refuse to register. On April 5, 1917, he was arrested for speaking at a rally against the war on the charge of disturbing the peace. He was sentenced to two years in the Atlanta federal penitentiary, and after this term was to serve an additional nine months for refusing to reg- ister. Most of the two years in Atlanta were spent in solitary confinement, where his only reading material was a Bible. He came out an anarchist Socialist.

In 1920 he received a scholarship to attend Rand, a Socialist school in New York City. While there he worked with Roger Baldwin in the American Civil Liberties Union. For four years he and his wife hitchhiked around the country speaking on socialism, pacifism*, and anarchism; from 1940 to 1942 he was a social worker in Milwaukee, and, inspired by Dorothy Day*, sold *The Catholic Worker* and worked with her at her House of Hospitality in New York City. In the summer of 1961 he opened his Joe Hill House in Salt Lake City, inspired by Day's House of Hospitality. In 1943 he began a life-long protest against paying taxes, and on August 7, 1950, in Phoenix, he began a five-day fast protesting both the Korean War* and taxes. On November 17, 1952, he was baptized a Roman Catholic at the Peter Maurin Farm in Hutchison, Minnesota.

In 1955 he was jailed for selling *The Catholic Worker* in New York City (the first time he was jailed since 1917, thirty-five years before). Subsequently he was arrested many times for picketing in protest against air raid drills, the Omaha Missile Base, Kohler Plumbing, the Spanish embassy, the death penalty, the Las Vegas Atomic Energy Commission, the payment of taxes, and the chem- ical warfare site at Dugway, Utah.

See BIOLOGICAL/CHEMICAL WARFARE; CHRISTIANITY AND WAR; CONSCIENTIOUS OBJECTION; DAY, DOROTHY; DEBS, EUGENE; JUST WAR; PACIFISM.

BIBLIOGRAPHY
Hennacy, Ammon, *The Book of Ammon* (Self-Printed, 1965).
Troester, Rosalie Riegle, ed., *Voices from The Catholic Worker* (Philadelphia: Temple University Press, 1993).

HINDUISM AND WAR. There are several streams of thought in the Indian Hindu tradition regarding war and ethics, one being Kautilya's Machiavellian- ism*, in which a political realist philosophy is advocated. Kautilya's advice was acted on by Chandragupta, first king of the Mauryan empire around 300 B.C. Kautilya's critics claim that his account is a description of that period or those times and how best to deal with the prevailing circumstances and not a prescription for other times and situations. There were Indian monarchs ruling along Machiavellian lines but there were many more who ruled on the basis of political idealism. Early treatises such as the *Laws of Manu* insist that the ruler be moral and promote Dharma, defined as morality, righteousness, or justice.

One finds in Hinduism the notion of just war*, such as the supposed war in the *Bhagavad Gita* between the Kauravas and Pandavas, descendants of the same lineage. The central character, Arjuna, a Pandava and Kshatriya, becomes despondent as he looks out on the battlefield and sees his kinsmen in the opposing army drawn up to fight. Should he go ahead and fight and kill, or renounce his warrior role and leave the battlefield? Filled with doubt, Arjuna turns to the Lord Krishna who, after a long dialogue, persuades Arjuna to fight.

The Gita is as important to the Hindu as the Bible is to the Christian. The virtues it enjoins are supported by other Hindu scriptures. Krishna's position on war has been questioned, however. Was there ever such an actual battle or war? Is the Gita based on fact or is it a legend propounded to inculcate some moral principle or religious belief? If there was such a war, did it meet just war* criteria? Were the Kauravas, as supposed, really the evil-doer and the Pandavas the innocent* wronged? Had all other means of resolving the dispute been exhausted? Was the Gita written as an apologia for caste? Was its author a Brahmin who insisted that God created the caste system with the Brahmin as the highest rank and that the duties of each caste, being ordained by God, should never be forsaken lest the whole social order should disintegrate? Furthermore, there is no guarantee that an action is virtuous just because it is done out of duty rather than reward, or because it is done out of love, devotion, and faith in God, and in the belief that one is carrying out God's will. To consider only the purity of the motive is insufficient. The results or consequences, the taking of human lives, must be taken into account as well.

The Gita may be interpreted in two ways, literally or allegorically. Its critics usually interpret it allegorically. Gandhi*, for example, viewed the Gita not as an account of an actual battle by soldiers faithfully doing their martial duty, but a legendary account of the conflict going on eternally within every individual between his higher and lower selves. The orthodox literalist, however, believes the battle actually took place and thus sees the Gita as a divine summons to caste obligation and justifiable killing. Warfare is the exception rather than the rule in India's history. Swami Ranganathananda writes that Indian people have been uniformly nonaggressive and have not engaged in aggressive warfare outside India. K. Shridharan points out that a foreign observer cannot help but be impressed by India's long religious tradition of nonviolence and the revulsion of Indians toward bloodshed and killing. He notes that legends glorifying the effectiveness of nonviolence abound in Indian folklore. Ranganathananda claims that India's people are not aggressive because they are disciplined in the tenets of Hinduism and its sister religions, Buddhism and Jainism. Buddha taught the virtues of compassion, love, forgiveness, nonhatred, and nonviolence. Jainism is known especially for its emphasis on noninjury, portrayed even today by the Jain monk sweeping the path he walks lest he tread on an insect which might wander underfoot.

Jainism and Hinduism share metaphysical and epistemological presuppositions that have ethical implications. Both view truth as relative and reality as nondialectical. Thus, it would be invalid to proclaim one view of truth as the absolute truth, or to divide reality, including people, into absolute and exclusive categories of good and evil or right and wrong, or to universalize and absolutize one particular religion. Such a metaphysical and epistemological position leads to the attitude of tolerance and acceptance that has long characterized Jainism and mainstream Hinduism.

Complementing tolerance is *Ahimsa,* usually translated as nonviolence. Its devotees admit the existence of evil but refuse to requite evil with evil, insisting that only moral means must be used to attain good ends. Practicing Ahimsa inevitably entails suffering but, rather than impose suffering on another, suffering is taken upon oneself. The devotee believes in the transforming power of sacrificial love, in the innate goodness in every person, that truth will triumph in the end, and that there is a force greater than the physical at work in the world. Practicing Ahimsa requires much courage and self-discipline, unlimited love and compassion, and the detesting of the evil deed but not the doer. Ahimsa thus incorporates many elements of the Hindu-Indian ethical tradition. It has found expression in nonviolent tactics long practiced in India such as the *Hartel* (suspension of work or business as a form of political protest), *Duragraha* (persistence in action), *Hijrat* (voluntary emigration to avoid an oppressor), *Dharna* (sitting on the doorstep of a wrongdoer in order to call public attention), fasting, and the boycott. Its 20th-century adherents point to Gandhi as proof that Ahimsa works. Through it he and his followers accomplished what has been done rarely in history, the freeing of one people from another's rule without resorting to war.

The impact of Hindu ethics in recent times is reflected in Bhave's Bhoodan Movement, initiated in 1958, under which many acres of land were given voluntarily to poor peasants by large landholders, Nehru's tenure (1947–1964) as India's first head of state, during which India avoided border wars with China and Pakistan, and the prominence of philosophical and religious leaders like Tagore, Ramakrishna, and Radhakrishnan, who shared a broad, universalistic outlook in contrast to the extremist Hindu Mahashaba, who opposed Gandhi's anti-untouchability campaigns and non-violence and took as their motto "Hinduize all politics and militarize Hinduism."

That the Hindu extremists and Gandhi both utilized phrases and precepts found in the same Hindu writings points up the paradox found in Hinduism as well as the literature of other religions. If you view Kautilya's *Arthasastrya* as prescriptive, a manual of action for all times and places, you can then rationalize

Machiavellian rule as valid universally. If you see it as a product of a particular time and circumstances, it cannot validly be universalized. If you interpret the Gita literally, you can rationalize a just war; if interpreted allegorically, you cannot. If the Kshatriya caste is your model, you will emphasize power, resolve, fearlessness, competitiveness, obedience, and duty as virtues. If the genuine Brahmin is your ideal, you will emphasize as virtuous compassion, love, contentment, nonattachment, generosity, forgiveness, forbearance, tolerance, freedom from hatred and pride, self-control, and truthfulness. Which side of the paradox is dominant in Hinduism and Hindu India? The great majority of Indians would agree with Shridharani's statement that "the tradition of nonviolence is deeply rooted and continuous in our country," and would assert the latter.

BIBLIOGRAPHY

Bondurant, Joan, *Conquest of Violence* (Princeton, N.J.: Princeton University Press, 1988).

Shridharani, K., *War Without Violence* (New York: Garland Publishing, 1972).

Donald H. Bishop

HIROSHIMA AND NAGASAKI, BOMBING OF. In August 1945 the Truman administration devastated Hiroshima and Nagasaki with atomic bombs. A uranium weapon killed tens of thousands of people in Hiroshima on August 6, and a plutonium weapon had the same impact on Nagasaki on August 9. At the time, this action elicited little controversy among America and its allies. On the contrary, it was a cause for celebration, and the attack was widely interpreted as a demonstration of American technological superiority and as retribution for Japanese aggression and atrocities, and most importantly, it was believed that the bombing precipitated Japanese surrender. The event became something of a cultural icon in the American remembered past. In 1994 the Postal Service announced plans to issue a stamp to commemorate the fiftieth anniversary of the nuclear destruction of the Japanese cities. The stamp features an atomic mushroom cloud with the following gloss: "Atomic bombs hasten the war's end, August 1945." In 1995 the stamp design was altered to a general World War II theme. In addition, the Smithsonian Museum planned to exhibit the *Enola Gay* (the B-29 named after the pilot's mother) that bombed Hiroshima. Acceding to harsh criticism, the Smithsonian changed the exhibit to show less sympathy for the Japanese victims and more sympathy for the American rationale for using the weapon.

Officials and mainstream historians defended the destruction of Hiroshima and Nagasaki as a lamentable necessity for ending the war with a minimal loss of American and Japanese lives. McGeorge Bundy (an aide to Secretary of War Henry Stimson and national security advisor to President John Kennedy) offered an account of the decision to drop the bomb that was representative of the widely accepted, mainstream narrative. He began by attempting to contextualize the decision to use atomic weapons. He argued that a precedent existed for destroying cities to demoralize enemies, and that the U.S. desire to end the war quickly and decisively determined the Truman administration's decision. According to Bundy, the overriding objective was "to win the war as fast as possible, and . . . the use of the atomic bomb against cities was a legitimate instrument to this end." Specifically, he acknowledged that, in hindsight, other options might have ended the war, but given the tenor of the times and historical exigencies, the use of atomic weaponry was understandable, if not unavoidable. In his view, these weapons did not win the war, but they ended it quickly and effectively.

Bundy's analysis of the moral problems posed by this decision is of considerable interest to students of ethics and warfare. He argued that it was necessary to destroy two Japanese cities in order to show American resolve and to demonstrate the awesome power of the weapons. Revisionist historians, however, offer a contesting interpretation. He also rejected what he regarded as the most salient objection to the use of atomic weapons, summed up in Michael Walzer's contention that the use of atomic weapons was prima facie immoral because the rights of noncombatants were not respected. Bundy argued that, had Walzer's perspective been adopted, no modern war could be fought, because the search for victory invariably involves the killing of civilians. The just war* criterion of proportionality* is implicit in Bundy's analysis, as is the assumption that a lesser evil is justified if it prevents a greater evil. In any case, according to Bundy, most decision makers and combatants simply did not perceive the destruction of Japanese cities as immoral. As he explained, "The change in strategy and tactics required by . . . [Walzer's] argument is one that no political leader could have imposed."

Revisionist historians offer a contesting narrative that rejects Bundy's historical analysis and normative presuppositions. This narrative can be reconstructed from a variety of sources. Unknown to the American public, many prominent officials argued against the use of atomic weapons for strategic and humanitarian reasons. These historians conclude that bureaucratic imperatives and hegemonic aspirations account for the American decision. For example, General Eisenhower expressed his dismay when he learned of the decision:

I voiced to him [Secretary Stimson] my grave misgivings, first on . . . the belief that Japan was already defeated and that dropping the bomb was completely unnecessary, and secondly because I thought that our country should avoid shocking world opinion by the use of a weapon . . . [that was,] I thought, no longer mandatory as a measure to save American lives. . . . Japan was, at that very moment, seeking some way to surrender with a minimum loss of "face."

And Admiral Leahy expressed similar views.

According to the revisionists, the bomb was dropped for bureaucratic and hegemonic reasons. It appears, for example, that bureaucratic imperatives guided General Groves (the director of the Manhattan Project). His declassified diary reveals that he was fearful that unless Congress got something for its money (a usable nuclear weapon), he would spend the rest of his life testifying on Capitol Hill. Evidently, other participants in the project had also staked their careers and reputation on nuclear weaponry. Some have argued that the zeal that informed the Manhattan Project was typical of an ecclesiastical bureaucracy—a new religion that sought national salvation in the magic of the atom.

Revisionists also suggest that the decision was based on anticipated hegemonic competition with the Soviet Union in the postwar period. For example, Joseph Rotblatt, a Manhattan Project physicist, revealed that as early as 1943 General Groves told him that the real purpose behind building the bomb was intimidating the Soviets after the war. According to the revisionists, the destruction of the Japanese cities was intended to send a message to the Soviets rather than to the Japanese. It was widely believed that the American nuclear monopoly would usher in an "American Century," an epoch of uncontested American economic, political, and military supremacy.

In any case, it is clear, in retrospect, that options other than using the bombs on civilian targets were not seriously entertained. Most mainstream and revisionist historians share Bundy's lamentation: "Whether broader and more extended deliberation would have yielded a less destructive result we shall never know. Yet one must regret that no such effort was made."

See AGGRESSION, ATTEMPTS TO DEFINE; BANALITY OF EVIL; CASUALTIES OF WAR; CHILDREN AND WAR; COLLATERAL DAMAGE; COMBATANT-NONCOMBATANT DISTINCTION; COUNTERFORCE VERSUS COUNTERVALUE; CRIMES AGAINST HUMANITY; FORBIDDEN STRATEGIES; FORBIDDEN WEAPONS; GENEVA CONVENTION, 1949; HOLOCAUST, THE; INCENDIARIES; INNOCENTS; INTENTIONALITY AND DOUBLE EFFECT; MASS DESTRUCTION, WEAPONS OF; MILITARY NECESSITY; NUCLEAR WAR; PROPORTIONALITY; SHIMODA CASE.

BIBLIOGRAPHY

Alperovitz, Gar, *Atomic Diplomacy* (New York: Simon and Schuster, 1965).

Bernstein, Barton, "The Atomic Bomb and American Foreign Policy, 1941–1945," *Peace and Change* (Spring 1974), 1–16.

———, "The Perils and Politics of Surrender: Ending the War with Japan and Avoiding the Third Atomic Bomb," *Pacific Historical Review* (February 1977), 1–28.

———, "A Postwar Myth: 500,000 U.S. Lives Saved," *Bulletin of the Atomic Scientists* (March 1984), 38–40.

Eisenhower, Dwight, *Mandate for Change* (New York: Doubleday, 1963).

Herken, Gregg, *The Winning Weapon* (New York: Alfred Knopf, 1980).

Hirschbein, Ron, *Newest Weapons/Oldest Strategy: The Dialectics of American Nuclear Strategy* (New York: Peter Lang, 1991).

Leahy, William, *I Was There* (New York: McGraw-Hill, 1950).

Ron Hirschbein

HOBBES, THOMAS (1588–1679). English political philosopher, best known for his view that without an absolute sovereign government, humanity degenerates into perpetual warfare. This view may be understood as Hobbes's response to the English civil war (1642–1660) between monarchists and parliamentarians. Hobbes advocated a return to monarchy, alleging that the civil war was caused by individuals who ignored the civil order in search of personal power. Today, the word *Hobbesian* refers to theories that only the unbridled exercise of political power can create national or international stability.

In his masterpiece *Leviathan* (1651), Hobbes describes human nature in the absence of government. Human thoughts are produced by the motion of objects acting on the body. Since each body is different and there is no system of education, each person thinks different thoughts and communication is impossible. Further, each isolated person is equal to every other in that each person has the ability to kill every other. Therefore, when two people desire the same thing they compete rather than cooperate. Competition leads to diffidence, the need to protect oneself from attack through preemptive strike. As a reputation for strength is the best protection against attack, people come to attack others simply for the sake of glory. In the absence of government, these behaviors are neither good nor bad; they are simply survival techniques. In this state of war, there is no industry, farming, geography, arts, or sciences, and life is ''solitary, poor, nasty, brutish, and short.''

Hobbes admits that this state of nature is a fiction, which he creates to use in his argument. Even so, he says, certain aspects of the state of nature are present in our political societies. States attack one another for competition, diffidence, and glory; citizens lock their doors and carry weapons because they fear attack from fellow citizens; and, in civil war, the power of government degenerates to where it cannot keep order.

The way out of the state of war, Hobbes argues, is through the use of reason. People recognize that the best route to self-preservation is through peace. They agree to lay down their arms as well as their right to fulfill all their desires on the condition that others do the same. In other words, they contract with one another to live together peacefully. But the contract has no binding force without a sovereign who has the power to enforce it with the sword. Therefore, in making the contract, people agree with one another to follow the sovereign, who is not bound by the contract to lay down arms and give up rights. The sovereign has absolute power to make, enforce, and adjudicate laws; appoint all ministers; make war and peace; censor speech and writing; make the rules of propriety; and create social and economic classes. Though this looks like a miserable condition for citizens, Hobbes says it is better than civil war.

See CLAUSEWITZ, CARL VON; DEMOCRACY AND THE MILITARY; GENEVA CONVENTION, 1949; HAGUE, THE, CONGRESSES; INTELLIGENCE AGENCIES, U.S.; JOHN OF SALISBURY; MACHIAVELLI, NICOLO; PATRIOTISM.

BIBLIOGRAPHY
Hobbes, Thomas, *Leviathan,* C. B. Macpherson, ed. (Baltimore, Md.: Penguin Books, 1971).

Kraynak, Robert P., *History and Modernity in the Thought of Thomas Hobbes* (Ithaca, N.Y.: Cornell University Press, 1990).

Laura Duhan Kaplan

HOLOCAUST, THE. Referring to their regime as the Third Reich, Adolf Hitler and the Nazi Party ruled Germany from 1933 to 1945. The Holocaust happened during those years. It was Nazi* Germany's planned total destruction of the European Jews and the actual murder of nearly six million of them. The genocidal* campaign carried out by Nazi Germany and its collaborators—it was the most systematic, bureaucratic, and unrelenting the world has seen—also destroyed millions of non-Jewish civilians. They included Roma and Sinti (Gypsies), Slavs, Jehovah's Witnesses, Freemasons, homosexuals*, the mentally retarded, the physically handicapped, and the insane. The Nazis believed that the threat of these groups to the Third Reich approached, though it could never equal, the one posed by Jews.

Although Europe's Jews resisted the onslaught as best they could, by the end of World War II two-thirds of the European Jews—and about one-third of the Jews worldwide—were dead. The vast majority of the Jewish victims came from Eastern Europe. More than half of them were from Poland. There, the German annihilation effort was 90 percent successful. At Auschwitz alone—located in Poland, it was the largest of the Nazi killing centers—more than one million Jews were gassed.

To see how the Holocaust happened, note that Adolf Hitler (1889–1945) became chancellor of Germany on January 30, 1933. He soon consolidated his power through tyranny and terror. Within six months, Hitler's decrees were as good as law, basic civil rights had been suspended, thousands of the Third Reich's political opponents had been imprisoned, and the Nazis stood as the only legal political power in Germany.

Emphasizing the superiority of the German people, Nazi ideology was anti-Semitic and racist to the core. The Nazis affirmed that German racial purity must be maintained. Building on precedents long-established by Christianity's animosity toward Jews, the Nazis went further and vilified Jews as the most dangerous threat to the goal of racial purity. Here it is important to underscore that Jews are not a race but a people unified by memory and history, culture, tradition, and religious observances that are widely shared. Any person can become Jewish through religious conversion. Nevertheless, Nazi ideology defined Jewish identity in biological and racial terms.

German law established detailed conditions to define full- and part-Jews. To cite three examples, if one had three Jewish grandparents, that condition was sufficient to make one fully Jewish. If one had only two Jewish grandparents and neither practiced Judaism nor had a Jewish spouse, then one was a *Mischlinge* (mongrel) first-class. A person with only a single Jewish grandparent would be a *Mischlinge* second-class. The identity of one's grandparents was determined, paradoxically, not by blood but by their membership in the Jewish re-

ligious community. Once these Nazi classifications were in effect, the identity
they conferred was irreversible.

Defining Jewish identity was crucial for identifying the population targeted
by the Nazis' anti-Semitic policies. Those policies focused first on segregating
Jews, making their lives intolerable, and forcing them to leave Germany. Between 1933 and the outbreak of World War II in September 1939, hundreds of
decrees, such as the Nuremberg Laws of September 1935, deprived the Third
Reich's Jews of basic civil rights. When Jews tried to emigrate from German
territory, however, they found few havens. In general, doors around the world,
including those in the United States, opened reluctantly, if at all, for Jewish
refugees from Hitler's Germany.

World War II began with Germany's invasion of Poland on September 1,
1939. With the notable exception of its failure to subdue England by air power,
the German war machine had things its own way until it experienced defeats at
El Alamein and Stalingrad in 1942. By the end of that year, four million Jews
had already been murdered.

As Hitler's forces advanced on all fronts, huge numbers of Jews came under
Nazi domination. These newly captured Jews far exceeded the relatively small
Jewish population—about 600,000 and less than 1 percent of the total German
population—when Hitler first came to power. For more than a year after the
war began, Nazi planning still aimed to enforce massive Jewish resettlement,
but there were no satisfactory ways to fulfill that intention. Other tactics had to
be found. The Holocaust did not result from a detailed master plan that timed
and controlled every move in advance. When one step reached an impasse,
however, the next was always more drastic, because the Nazis did not deviate
from their basic commitment: Somehow the Jews had to be eliminated.

In the spring of 1941, as plans were laid for the invasion of the Soviet Union,
Hitler decided that special mobile killing units—*Einsatzgruppen*—would follow
the German army, round up Jews, and kill them. In the fateful months that
followed, a second prong of attack in Nazi Germany's war against the Jews
became operational, as well. Instead of moving killers toward their victims, it
would bring victims to their killers.

Utilizing a former Austrian military barracks near the Polish town of Oświę-
cim, the Germans made their Auschwitz concentration camp operational in June
1940, when 728 Polish prisoners were transferred there. By the summer of 1941,
the original camp (Auschwitz I) had been supplemented by a much larger camp
at nearby Birkenau (Auschwitz II). Within the next year—along with five other
sites in occupied Poland (Chelmno, Belzec, Sobibor, Treblinka, and Majdanek)—Auschwitz-Birkenau became a full-fledged killing center. Auschwitz
"improved" killing by employing fast-working hydrogen cyanide gas, which
suppliers offered in the form of a deodorized pesticide known as Zyklon B*.
Efficiency at Auschwitz-Birkenau was further improved in 1943 when new cre-
matoria became available for corpse disposal. Optimum "production" in this
death factory meant that thousands of Jews could be killed per day. When SS

(*Schutzstaffel*) leader Heinrich Himmler (1900–1945) ordered an end to the systematic killing at Auschwitz in late 1944, his reasoning was not based entirely on the fact that Soviet troops were nearby. For all practical purposes, he could argue, the "Final Solution*" had eliminated Europe's "Jewish problem."

With Hitler's suicide on April 30, 1945, and the subsequent surrender of Germany on May 7, a chapter ended, but the history and legacy of the Holocaust continue. Everyone who lives after Auschwitz is affected by this event. The Holocaust is forgotten at humanity's peril. Remembering it provides warnings that perhaps can make a shield for the future.

See BANALITY OF EVIL; CHILDREN AND WAR; COMBATANT-NONCOMBATANT DISTINCTION; FINAL SOLUTION; FORBIDDEN STRATEGIES; HUMAN RIGHTS; MASSACRES; NAZISM; ZYKLON B WAR CRIMES TRIAL.

BIBLIOGRAPHY
Berenbaum, Michael, *The World Must Know: The Story of the Holocaust as Told in the United States Holocaust Memorial Museum* (Boston: Little, Brown, 1993).
Hilberg, Raul, *The Destruction of the European Jews,* 3 vols., rev. and def. ed. (New York: Holmes & Meier, 1985).
Rubenstein, Richard L., and John K. Roth, *Approaches to Auschwitz: The Holocaust and Its Legacy* (Atlanta, Ga.: John Knox Press, 1987).

John K. Roth

HOLY WARS. A holy war may be understood as a war in which some or all of the following conditions apply: (1) the objectives of the war are identified as religious; (2) religious leaders claim that the killing in war is licit, obligatory, or glorious; (3) religious authorities proclaim "heavenly" or extra-mundane rewards for supreme sacrifice or participation; (4) it is waged against a group with a different religion, and often a different nationality and ethnicity; (5) it is generally waged by societies that deploy specially trained personnel, combatants distinct from a priestly class or religious officials; and (6) war is recognized as generally a secular and worldly affair, and a holy war as a sanctified exception, and therefore, perfectly consistent with prohibitions against wars among coreligionists or citizens of the same nation.

Conditions (5) and (6) are important in distinguishing holy wars from wars fought by societies with tribal religions in which there is no distinction between the secular and the sacred. When religion encompasses all of the community's life, war is an activity in which the gods of the people are also involved in combat, and war is surrounded with prayer, ritual, sacrifice, and purification. Religious observance related to war among the ancient Greeks and Romans was tribal in this sense, as well as among the Etruscans, Celts, early Germans, early Scandinavians, Native-American peoples, and the Yoruba of West Africa, among others.

The transition from tribal religion warfare to holy war can be traced in the history of Judaism*. The historical books of the Bible are full of battles, and the Ark of the Lord represents the very presence of God in the campaign (1 Sam. 4.1–11). But by the 5th century C.E., rabbinical interpreters were distinguishing between two kinds of war, *milchemet reshut,* optional war, and *milchemet chovah,* obligatory war, also called *milchemet mitzvah,* religious war. This second category included the war against the seven tribes of Canaan (Deut. 20.16–18), war against the Amalekites, who had been guilty of unprovoked aggression (Deut. 25.17–19), but not the massacre of the house of Ahab and the Baal-worshipers (2 Kings 9–10) or the wars of David to expand his kingdom. The main justification for holy and obligatory war was defense against attack from without, and a majority of rabbis rejected preventive war as falling in this category.

Among Christians, the conversion of the Emperor Constantine confused the mission of the Peace Church with the fortunes of the state. According to Eusebius, writing under Constantine, the providence of God was equally at work in both, and there were therefore two levels of Christian vocation. The clergy were to be totally dedicated to God and to live in accordance with the strictures of the New Testament; the laity were to exercise the normal obligations of citizenship. Hence, Ambrose, bishop of Milan, could pray for the victory of the Roman armies against the invading Germanic peoples; the Church and empire were interdependent and the defense of the empire was a holy war. Likewise, Augustine* interpreted the pacifist teachings of the New Testament as injunctions for the inward, spiritual life, and insisted on absolute pacifism* in personal relations, while simultaneously expanding Cicero's doctrine of the just war* by arguing for the military defense of the innocent* from aggression*. Just war was, for Augustine, the instrument of divine judgment on wickedness.

Although the doctrines of just war and holy war are not distinguished in early Christian theology, they diverged greatly during the years of the Crusades (1095–1272). Pope Urban II initiated the First Crusade in 1095, supposedly to rescue the Holy Sepulcher from the Seljuk Turks. But the pope was probably motivated as much by interest in discouraging internecine strife within Christendom by concentrating military energy on an external enemy. Proclaiming the crusade a righteous war against the infidel, Urban promised those who participated blessings in heaven as well as the temporal rewards of booty. The motives for subsequent crusades became increasingly complex, and only some can be regarded as holy wars: Pope Eugenius III called for the Second Crusade, and the Fourth Crusade, which resulted in the sacking of Christian Constantinople, had been supported by Pope Innocent III, who was also responsible for initiating in 1208 the Albigensian Crusades against the Cathar heresy.

The crusades were waged in ways that disregarded the limitations imposed by doctrines of the just war, as elaborated, for example, by Gratian in 1140 (although Huguccio argued that just war could be initiated against heretics and infidels). Subsequently, Aquinas* in the 13th century reaffirmed Augustine's notion of a just war as one in response to the wrongdoing of an enemy, and intellectuals, at least, ceased to confuse just war with holy war.

Among Protestants after the Reformation, John Calvin* was militantly theocratic, seeing the state as a positive instrument in support of true belief. Likewise, Oliver Cromwell is claimed to have believed that he had a divine commission for the "holy wars" he waged, and some Puritan settlers in New England in the 17th century were inclined to interpret their wars with natives, such as their massacre* of the Pequot, as holy wars. But in subsequent centuries, Christian views about the holiness of fighting became increasingly irrelevant in the face of nationalistic* and patriotic* forces, as well as the interests of commercial enterprise and imperialism.

In contrast to Judaism and Christianity, the concept of holy war in Shintoism and Islam* retained prescriptive influence well into the 20th century. By imperial decrees of 1868 and 1870, Shinto became the established state religion of Japan. Although Buddhists, Confucians, and Christians were not forced to recant, all worshipers were obligated to participate in state Shinto practices. In effect, state Shinto was a form of religious nationalism. The Emperor, the Son of Heaven, was believed to be descended from Amaterasu, the sun-goddess, and was himself regarded as divine. Thus, the fusion of religion and national policy made all of Japan's wars holy wars. The watchword of imperial policy at the outbreak of World War II was "The Whole World Under One Roof," and the instrument of this religious and imperialistic policy was the imperial army. Combatants were sometimes led to believe that their fighting was divinely guided, as exemplified, for example, by the Kamikaze ("Divine Wind") suicide missions. With Japan's defeat in World War II, state Shinto shrines were disestablished, Emperor Hirohito renounced the divinity of imperial rule, and Shintoism dissolved into a number of loosely connected sects.

In Arabia, Prophet Muhammad established the religion of Islam* in 622 C.E. among the community of believers, or *umma,* at Medina. Muhammad banned intertribal raiding within the *umma* of Islam, but waged war both to overcome threats and to spread the faith, capturing Mecca in 630. With the expansion of Islam after the death of the Prophet, the central concept of *jihad,* or striving in the service of God, came more and more to be identified with a holy war undertaken for the faith. Many Muslims no longer interpret the obligation of *jihad* as military struggle, but Muslim fundamentalists still do and some *imams,* or religious leaders, believe that a soldier who lays down his life for the cause of Allah achieves instant immortality.

See AUGUSTINE, ST.; CALVIN, JOHN; CHRISTIANITY AND WAR; ISLAM AND WAR; JUDAISM AND WAR; JUST WAR; NATIONAL LIBERATION; PATRIOTISM; PEACE OF GOD; PROPAGANDA; SHINING PATH; VICTORIA, FRANCISCUS DE.

BIBLIOGRAPHY

Bainton, Ronald H., *Christian Attitudes Toward War and Peace* (Nashville: Abingdon Press, 1960).

Ferguson, John, *War and Peace in the World's Religions* (New York: Oxford University Press, 1978).

Robert Paul Churchill

HOMOSEXUALITY. Homosexuality in the military was not a significant public issue until presidential candidate Bill Clinton told a group of gay fundraisers in Los Angeles in the course of the campaign that, once in office, he would lift the ban on gays serving in the military. He reaffirmed his pledge soon after taking office in 1993. Encouraged by the new president's words, a number of gay and lesbian officers publicly announced that they were gay, and gay rights organizations such as the Campaign for Military Justice conducted protest marches urging a change in policy.

Gays in the military soon became one of the most controversial issues of Clinton's first year in office. Opposition surfaced immediately in the military, in Congress, and in the press. In January 1993, President Bill Clinton ordered Secretary of Defense Les Aspin to conduct a review of the policy banning homosexuality and to bring forward recommendations for its revision by mid-July. In the meantime, the president ordered a halt on military discharges based on sexual orientation but supported continued prosecution for sexual misconduct such as sodomy under the *Uniform Code of Military Justice**.

Homosexuality in the military was first formally regulated in 1943, with a ban on people "who engage in homosexual conduct or who, by their statements, demonstrate a propensity to engage in homosexual conduct." During World War II, homosexuality was generally tolerated, as it was attributed to soldiers responding to wartime pressures and conditions. Exclusion of homosexuals was first widely enforced in the early 1950s during the McCarthy era. In the 1970s, as the U.S. gay rights movement went public, the military reacted by asking recruits about their sexual orientation.

Critics of the policy banning gays charged a double standard in its enforcement. While heterosexuals charged with engaging in a one-time homosexual sex act were regularly exonerated, homosexuals were discharged from the military merely for being identified as such. A General Accounting Office study of the U.S. Army found that, from 1988 to 1992, there were, on average, 380 discharges annually for homosexuality; less than 10 percent of these resulted in court martials for homosexual misconduct. While these data were differently interpreted as indicating either a major or minor problem, it was clear that the number of court martials was high enough to force gays to hide their identity. Yet, the number of prosecutions for homosexuality was far lower than those for sexual misconduct by heterosexuals.

The debate over whether or not to lift the ban excluding homosexuals from the military has been based on many different arguments and has been waged in many different arenas. A common military objection has been that allowing homosexuals to serve would undermine unit cohesion, morale, and discipline, and would generally weaken combat effectiveness. The proponents for lifting the ban countered that many gays had served and were serving in the military with distinction and with no apparent effect on military effectiveness. They argued that there was no evidence to suggest that homosexuals inhibited military performance.

Commentators in the press and Congress addressed the issue of potential sexual harassment, claiming that acceptance of homosexuals would mean promotion of a gay lifestyle, unwelcome sexual advances made by soldiers toward other soldiers, a rise in sexual promiscuity and attendant sexually transmitted diseases including AIDS, and the general feminization of the military. Proponents countered that an end to discrimination based wholly on identity would not necessitate any changes in standards of conduct.

Gay rights advocates and others also made constitutional arguments, stating that the ban violated the principle of equal protection of the laws and the individual right to privacy. Opponents claimed that military service was not a right, but a privilege. Other grounds put forward for lifting the ban were the costs of prosecuting cases, the acceptance of gays in the armed forces of many other Western countries, and the double standard of discharging homosexuals for their sexual orientation, when heterosexuals were merely sanctioned for unacceptable behavior.

The issue of homosexuals in the military divided every major U.S. political institution. Congressional opposition for lifting the ban revolved around conservative members of Congress who threatened to enshrine it in legislation. Two openly gay representatives, Barney Frank (D-MA) and Gerry Studds (D-MA), led the gay rights forces, with the support of some Vietnam War* veterans. Senator Samuel Nunn (D-GA), chair of the Senate Armed Services Committee, a key player who commanded wide respect and could influence many votes with his position, indicated his early opposition to lifting the ban.

The Clinton administration was divided between those who sought to lift the ban, even if it meant a major defeat in Congress, and those who sought a workable compromise, even if it meant that the president had to renege on his promise to gays. The Joint Chiefs of Staff opposed lifting the ban but were ordered by the Pentagon to try to find ways to modify the policy in a way that would be acceptable to them. The Department of Justice was concerned that any new policy be defensible in court.

After six months of internal debate, the Clinton administration presented in July 1993 a compromise policy that sought to distinguish between homosexual orientation and conduct. Referred to in the press as ''don't ask, don't tell,'' the policy removes the military's right to ask about or investigate sexual orientation but maintains the ban and penalties for open declarations of homosexuality and all homosexual behavior. Senator Samuel Nunn held hearings on the compromise policy and confirmed that the military leadership was agreeable to the compromise and willing to enforce it, with the result that he ostensibly ceased his opposition. The compromise won majority support as well in public opinion polls. Press reports of reaction in the military emphasized a sense of relief that the issue had been dealt with, but concern that the vagueness of the new policy would make it problematic to enforce.

Gays in the military who had declared their homosexuality in anticipation of a policy change expressed their sense of betrayal. Gay rights groups immediately proceeded to challenge the new policy in court. In 1993, a gay officer's lawsuit making its way through the federal courts succeeded in district court in winning a ruling that the ban was unconstitutional. The Clinton administration sought and won a ruling from the Supreme Court that the district court judgment only applied to the specific case at hand, leaving the administration free to go forward with the compromise. It also appealed the district court case.

At the same time, congressional support for the compromise wavered. While advocates of lifting the ban lost a congressional vote, Senator Nunn and others passed legislative amendments to permit the armed services to ask recruits about their sexual orientation. Unlike gender issues in the military, homosexuality promised to be an issue that would not soon recede from the scene.

See MILITARY AS A PROFESSION.

BIBLIOGRAPHY

Shilts, Randy, *Conduct Unbecoming: Lesbians and Gays in the U.S. Military: Vietnam to the Persian Gulf* (New York: St. Martin's Press, 1993).

Ellen Boneparth

HORS DE COMBAT. *See* CRIMES AGAINST HUMANITY; GENEVA CONVENTIONS, 1864, 1906, 1929, 1949; HAGUE, THE, CONGRESSES; NUREMBERG TRIALS; NO QUARTER, WARS OF; PRISONERS OF WAR; RED CROSS, RED CRESCENT, RED LION AND SUN.

HOSTAGES. The practice of taking hostages was widespread in ancient and medieval times, either to raise money through ransom or to pressure the enemy to surrender*. A medieval city that surrendered on request was assured that rape and pillage would not take place, while any city that resisted the request exposed its entire citizenry to annihilation. Debate continued over whether children, women, and old men should be taken as hostages, but, since knights commonly lived by rapine and pillage, civilians were generally fair game.

*General Orders 100** (1863) noted (para. 54) that the practice was rare at that time. If a person was a hostage, however, he was to be treated as a prisoner of war*. *Rules of Land Warfare** (1914) listed as reasons for taking hostages: (1) to insure proper treatment of the wounded and sick left behind; (2) to protect the lives of prisoners of war; (3) to protect lines of communication in a footnote it was noted that in the war of 1870 with France, the Germans had placed a resident of Alsace on all trains so that harm to the train would entail harm to one of their own; and (4) to ensure compliance with requisitions or contributions. The 1934 U.S. Army manual, *Rules of Land Warfare**, contained the identical information. The current U.S. Army manual, *The Law of Land Warfare**, paragraphs 11, 273, and 497, affirms that the taking of hostages is forbidden, and it cites support for this prohibition from the Geneva Convention of 1949*, "Relative to the Protection of Civilian Persons," Articles 33 and 34.

Since in modern wars most casualties* are civilians, the use of civilians as pawns has continued. The various theories of nuclear deterrence* endorsed forms of hostage taking inasmuch as they involved the threat to kill the civilian populations of the Soviet Union in either a first or second strike* to deter a Soviet nuclear attack. The U.S. doctrine of massive retaliation* estimated that, should such retaliation be done, up to 350 million casualties (primarily civilian) would result. In his discussion of mutual assured destruction (MAD)*, Herman Kahn was asked how many American deaths would be acceptable under that policy, and his reply was 200 million (again primarily civilian). The practices of siege* and embargo are also forms of hostage taking, since the primary sufferers are civilians. The practices of aerial warfare* during World War II as in Dresden, Hamburg, Tokyo, and Hiroshima* and Nagasaki*, and in Vietnam* and the Gulf War*, also involved holding civilians hostage.

The taking of hostages as a way to put pressure on an enemy has been utilized also by terrorists*, in much the same fashion as was practiced in the medieval period, in order to get the release of imprisoned members or to gain ransom. Military efforts to gain the release of hostages, in the absence of a formal declaration of war*, have proved difficult. The issue of hostage taking arose at war crimes trials after World War II. In the trial, *United States v. Wilhelm List et al.,* called the *Hostage Case,* twelve generals assigned to southeastern Europe were charged with criminal disregard of the laws of war in their treatment of hostages and other civilians. In a broad sense, modern war strategies where the primary targets and casualties are civilians inevitably utilize them as hostages.

See AERIAL WARFARE; COMBATANT-NONCOMBATANT DISTINCTION; FORBIDDEN STRATEGIES; INNOCENTS; SIEGE WARFARE.

BIBLIOGRAPHY

Contamine, Philippe, *War in the Middle Ages* (Oxford: Basil Blackwell, 1985).

Eichelman, Burr, David Soskis, and William Reid, eds., *Terrorism: Interdisciplinary Perspectives* (Washington, D.C.: American Psychiatric Association, 1979).

Keen, Maurice Hugh, *The Laws of War in the Late Middle Ages* (London: Routledge & Kegan Paul, 1965).

HUMANITARIAN INTERVENTION. Assistance provided to people within a nation by outsiders without the consent of the national government. Humanitarian intervention pierces the veil of sovereignty, the basis for the integrity of nation-states in the international system. The idea of inviolable national sovereignty has served the international system well since the Treaty of Westphalia of 1648, but times have changed. There have been massive violations of human rights* by national governments, especially in this century. Also in this century, there is new international law with regard to human rights, and there are new international mechanisms for implementing and monitoring that law, especially in the United Nations* system. There is increasing acknowledgment that the doctrine of noninterference in the internal affairs of nations should be revised. The practice of nations has already moved ahead of international law in this area, as illustrated by the delivery of international humanitarian assistance without the consent of the national governments in Iraq*, Bosnia*, and Somalia.

Some writers equate humanitarian intervention with any sort of humanitarian assistance in armed conflict, but it is more useful to take intervention to mean the delivery of assistance without consent. Some use the term humanitarian intervention to refer to the use of coercive military action to free civilians from oppressive situations, situations in which there are serious violations of human rights. In such cases, the action may be wholly military in character. Here, however, the focus is on the provision of humanitarian assistance involving such things as the delivery of food and medicine or providing temporary housing.

Some define humanitarian intervention as armed intervention for humanitarian purposes, but this does not recognize the possibilities of unarmed coercive measures such as sanctions or noncoercive assistance such as airdrops of food.

Further confusion may arise from the fact that military units are often used in noncoercive ways to deliver disaster relief. Military resources were used for the Berlin airlift in the late 1940s, but they were not used as instruments of coercion. Military resources may be used even where there is no conflict. The U.S. armed forces, for example, were used to help provide relief following floods in Bangladesh and in the aftermath of the Mount Pinatubo eruption in the Philippines.

In some cases, nongovernmental organizations have provided humanitarian assistance without consent, more by stealth than by coercion. *Médecins sans Frontières* (Doctors Without Borders), for example, specializes in delivering medical care to civilians in conflict situations, even when those in power do not agree to their providing such services. Thus, the actions of nongovernmental organizations sometimes can be viewed as a form of humanitarian intervention, even though they are not undertaken under the aegis of any official national or international body.

The situation in Iraq in 1991 is worth elaborating because it has elements of both humanitarian intervention and consent-based assistance and shows how the two can become entangled and confused. On April 5, 1991, the UN Security Council passed Resolution 688, condemning Iraq's repression of the Kurds and calling for humanitarian assistance. On the same day, President George Bush ordered the U.S. military to begin airdropping emergency humanitarian supplies to Kurdish refugees camping along the Iraq-Turkey border. On April 7, U.S. military aircraft began airdropping relief supplies for Kurdish refugees. On April 16, President Bush announced that American, British, and French troops would construct secure camps in northern Iraq for the Kurds. The humanitarian assistance provided to civilians in Iraq in April 1991 is often cited as a breakthrough representing the first time in which humanitarian intervention was internationally sanctioned. For example, Mario Bettati, a French professor of international law, said that Resolution 688 "broke new ground in international law, for the first time approving the right to interfere on humanitarian grounds in the hitherto sacrosanct internal affairs of member states." Similarly, David Scheffer, an international lawyer with the Carnegie Endowment for International Peace, said the resolution "established an unprecedented set of rights and obligations for aid agencies and the host government. In the past, UN aid agencies worked within sovereign borders only with the consent of the host government. Resolution 688 marked a significant change in that operating procedure wherever the local government is resistant to any intervention.''

The case is really not so clear. Several points need to be to made to correct or qualify these positions. There have been many previous cases of humanitarian intervention, under various definitions of that term. For example, in 1979–1980, while the people of Cambodia were suffering under Khmer Rouge terror and Vietnam's invasion, the United States encouraged and paid for the provision of food and medicine across the border by nongovernmental organizations and the United Nations without the permission of the de facto authorities. In 1983–1984 the U.S. government provided extensive assistance to Afghans who remained in parts of Afghanistan not under Soviet control. Both the Afghan government and the Soviet Union complained about this intervention. Several other cases are enumerated in the literature on humanitarian intervention.

If this was not the first time humanitarian intervention had taken place, it might be argued that this was the first time that such action had international approval. Or it might seem to have been the first time international approval was given for humanitarian intervention specifically by UN forces. As a reading of the resolution itself shows, there was no clear approval of that sort. The language does not plainly authorize either unilateral or multilateral intervention for humanitarian purposes. The resolution asks that ''Iraq allow immediate access by international humanitarian organizations to all of those in need of assistance.'' It does not say that assistance will be provided whether or not Iraq allows it.

The language of the resolution was ambiguous. On April 16, 1991, the United States, Britain, and France announced that under their interpretation of it, they were entitled to send troops to northern Iraq and establish secure encampments to provide supplies for Kurdish refugees. They then proceeded with ''Operation Provide Comfort'' to establish safe havens for Kurds in northern Iraq.

There was and is a great deal of opposition to humanitarian intervention of the sort suggested (though not actually articulated) in Resolution 688. In his history, *Desert Shield to Desert Storm,* Dilip Hiro points out that ''Of all the resolutions on the Gulf crisis and its aftermath, resolution 688 emerged as the one which met the most opposition, with five of the 15 members voting against or abstaining.'' More generally, ''Many Third World countries saw resolution 688 as the beginning of a process by which the Western powers, using the forum of the UN Security Council, meant to diminish their political independence and sovereignty.'' It may be significant that most of the commentators who hail Resolution 688 as a breakthrough in international law are from countries that are likely to do the intervening, not from countries that might be the purported beneficiaries of humanitarian intervention.

In *Pandaemonium,* Senator Daniel Moynihan (D-NY) observes that the Security Council actually justified the intervention on the basis of the questionable argument that ''the massive flow of Kurdish refugees over Iraq's borders and into Turkey and Iran had created a 'threat to the peace' and, therefore, justified further action by the Council under Chapter VII of the Charter.'' International lawyer Richard Gardner also points out that the U.S. government relied for legal authority on the authorization to use force to restore international peace and security and that the Security Council ''at no time asserted a collective right to intervene for exclusively human rights purposes.'' The resolution justified intervention partly on the basis of the threat to international peace and security, and not on humanitarian grounds alone.

Resolution 688 was passed, and the action was taken after the truce in the Persian Gulf War*. The armed conflict to which this humanitarian assistance related was not the Persian Gulf War but the Iraqi government's attempts to suppress the Shia insurgency in the south and the Kurdish insurgency in the north. Neighboring Turkey and Iran were troubled by the heavy influx of refugees, but they did not threaten military action. What was the threat to international peace and security?

On April 18, Iraq's foreign minister signed a memorandum of understanding on the role of UN humanitarian centers (UNHUCs). In Hiro's account:

Baghdad welcomed UN efforts to promote the voluntary return home of Iraqi displaced persons and to take humanitarian measures to avert new waves of refugees, and allowed the UN to set up UNHUCs, staffed by UN civilians, all over the country in agreement with Baghdad, to provide food aid, medical care, agricultural rehabilitation and shelter. It promised to make cash contributions in local currency to help cover the UN's in-country costs. The arrangement was ''without prejudice to the sovereignty, and territorial integrity, political independence, security and non-interference in the internal affairs of Iraq.''

Thus, after April 18, Operation Provide Comfort, designed to set up safe havens for Kurdish refugees inside Iraq, was undertaken with the agreement of the Iraqi government. The agreement expired in 1992.

Humanitarian assistance was provided in the period following the Gulf War cease-fire by the International Committee for the Red Cross* (ICRC) in the south as well as the north. In September 1991, in accordance with Iraq's agreement with the United Nations, the UN High Commissioner for Refugees (UNHCR) took over the assistance programs that had been handled by the ICRC, except in the Penjwin region, where the ICRC continued to provide assistance for some 10,000 Kurdish families.

The major problematic issue in Iraq was not whether assistance would be provided, but how the different agencies would coordinate their services. The resolution did not describe any general guidelines or principles for deciding when the international community would undertake humanitarian intervention. Why Iraq? Why not other places as well?

The U.S.-British-French-Netherlands intervention to establish camps and the subsequent Memorandum of Agreement regarding humanitarian assistance were designed to help Kurds in the north. No comparable assistance was provided to the Shia in the south or to the general Iraqi population. This is especially significant in view of the suffering inflicted on the Iraqi population as a consequence of the economic sanctions following the Persian Gulf war. The lack of guidelines for the delivery of assistance opened the possibility that humanitarian intervention would be undertaken selectively to serve political purposes.

Several conclusions can be drawn from this analysis of the Iraq case. First, resolution 688 did not plainly authorize humanitarian intervention.

Second, while humanitarian intervention was provided for a time in Iraq by the United States, Britain, France, and the Netherlands, there also was a great deal of humanitarian assistance provided by the ICRC and by the UN system under an explicit agreement with the Iraqi government.

Third, the humanitarian actions of the United States, Britain, and France were mixed with their political and military actions. There is no way to sort out the extent to which one motive or the other prevailed. As a result, these countries are open to charges of using humanitarian intervention for their own political and military purposes. A more effective separation might have been maintained by using separate, independent agents for humanitarian action. To the extent that the United States, Britain, France, and the Netherlands were concerned with ameliorating human suffering, they could have funneled more resources through ICRC and UNHCR.

Fourth, if the international community is to claim that humanitarian intervention is warranted in some extreme situations, there is a need for clear guidelines for determining when that action is to be taken, what the action is to be, and how the relevant decisions are to be made.

Fifth, too much importance has been placed on the importance of humanitarian intervention in armed conflict situations. Historically, most effective humanitarian assistance in armed conflict situations has been provided with the consent of the conflicting parties. More attention should be given to the possibilities for obtaining such agreements.

See NATIONALISM; PROPAGANDA; PROPORTIONALITY.

BIBLIOGRAPHY

Cahill, Kevin M., ed., *A Framework for Survival: Health, Human Rights, and Humanitarian Assistance in Conflicts and Disasters* (New York: Council on Foreign Relations/Basic Books, 1993), 202–20.

Hiro, Dilip, *Desert Shield to Desert Storm: The Second Gulf War* (New York: Routledge, 1992).

Pease, Kelly Kate, and David P. Forsythe, ''Human Rights, Humanitarian Intervention, and World Politics,'' *Human Rights Quarterly* 15 (1993), 290–314.

Schefer, David J., Richard N. Gardner, and Gerald B. Helman, *Post-Gulf War Challenges to the UN Collective Security System: Three Views on the Issue of Humanitarian Intervention* (Washington, D.C.: United States Institute of Peace, 1992).

Tesón, Fernando R., *Humanitarian Intervention: An Inquiry into Law and Morality* (Dobbs Ferry, N.Y.: Transnational Publishers, 1988).

George Kent

HUMAN NATURE AND WAR. Since the beginning of civilization, it is likely that people have wondered if war and social violence are inevitable results of human nature, or whether they are social inventions that could be replaced by the invention of peace and nonviolence. After all, war seems to be as old as civilization itself. The earliest known cities were surrounded by walls that evidently were erected to defend against armed attack.

In modern times, the theory that war is determined by human nature has been popularized by writers such as Thomas Hobbes* (1588–1679) in the 16th century, by Social Darwinists such as Herbert Spencer (1820–1903) in the 19th century, and more recently by Konrad Lorenz (1966) and Edmund O. Wilson (1975). The Social Darwinists made use of the evolutionary theory of Charles Darwin (1809–1882), while Lorenz and Wilson used information from recent scientific studies of animal behavior.

A great deal of publicity has been given to these recent claims that war is inherent in human nature. The most prestigious publishing houses, journals, and book reviews have given wide coverage to each new supporter of this point of view. Although the question is not new, it would seem to have taken on a new urgency in the past few years.

Why at this moment of history has the question become so important? We may speculate that in the past, when there seemed no chance to abolish the institution of war, the question was confined to philosophical speculation. Now, however, the abolition of war is on the agenda of history. The advent of nuclear weapons has transformed international war to the point that even the winner could be totally destroyed. With the end of the Cold War*, the United Nations* has begun to realize the potential for which it was created, "to save succeeding generations from the scourge of war."

Given its new relevancy, the question of the nature of war needs to be addressed in realistic fashion, using the sharpest analytic methods of the natural and social sciences. It was for this reason that twenty eminent scientists were convened in Seville, Spain, for the UN International Year of Peace in 1986. They came together, in conjunction with a meeting of the International Society for Research on Aggression, to answer the question: "Do modern biology and social sciences know of any biological factors that are an insurmountable or serious obstacle to the goal of world peace?" They brought to Seville the results of studies about animal behavior, psychology, brain research, genetics, and other related issues.

Among the studies brought to Seville, two played an especially important role in their formulation of the question: "The Behaviors and the Genetics of Aggression," by the celebrated behavioral geneticist, Benson Ginsburg, and "The Biological Basis of Warfare," by the founder of animal behavior studies in the United States, John Paul Scott.

The twenty scientists concluded that "biology does not condemn humanity to war" and that "the same species who invented war is capable of inventing peace.'' They based their conclusions on five propositions, abbreviated in the following presentation:

1. It is scientifically incorrect to say that we have inherited a tendency to make war from our animal ancestors. Although fighting occurs widely throughout animal species, only a few cases of destructive intraspecies fighting between organized groups have ever been reported among naturally living species, and none of these involve the use of tools designed to be weapons. The fact that war has changed so radically over time indicates that it is a product of culture.

2. It is scientifically incorrect to say that war or any other violent behavior is genetically programmed into our human nature. While genes are involved at all levels of nervous system function, they provide a developmental potential that can be actualized only in conjunction with the ecological and social environment. While individuals vary in their predispositions to be affected by their experience, it is the interaction between their genetic endowment and conditions of nurturance that determines their personalities.

3. It is scientifically incorrect to say that in the course of human evolution there has been a selection for aggressive behavior more than for other kinds of behavior. In all well-studied species, status within the group is achieved by the ability to cooperate and to fulfill social functions relevant to the structure of that group.

4. It is scientifically incorrect to say that humans have a ''violent brain.'' While we do have the neural apparatus to act violently, it is not automatically activated by internal or external stimuli. How we act is shaped by how we have been conditioned and socialized.

5. It is scientifically incorrect to say that war is caused by ''instinct'' or any single motivation. The emergence of modern warfare has been a journey from the primacy of emotional and motivational factors, sometimes called ''instincts,'' to the primacy of cognitive factors. Modern war involves institutional use of personal characteristics such as obedience, suggestibility and idealism, social skills such as language, and rational considerations such as cost-calculation, planning, and information processing.

The text of the Seville Statement has been reprinted over a hundred times in more than thirty languages, some of which are listed below in the bibliography. UNESCO, which adopted the Seville Statement in 1989, has produced a brochure that includes the text, commentary, and a bibliography that includes supporting scientific documentation.

The Seville Statement on Violence has been endorsed by numerous scientific organizations, including the American Anthropological Association, American Psychological Association, and American Sociological Association.

Of course, other issues have arisen that were not dealt with in the Seville Statement on Violence. For example, in another publication it has been pointed out that ''biology does not make men more aggressive than women.'' Also, a controversy has arisen recently about whether there is a biological factor that makes people tend to distrust or be aggressive toward others who are of different racial or ethnic groups. The latter is expected to be addressed soon by a group of experts similar to those who gathered in Seville.

Some criticism of the Seville Statement exists, as pointed out in the pages of the *Seville Statement Newsletter,* which has been published three times a year since 1986 and is distributed now by the International Peace Research Association. Most prominent have been complaints from specialists who feel that the statement implies that they should discontinue their search for biological factors in war. Therefore, one should point out, when using the statement, that research should be continued because conclusions in science are never final and must be constantly revised in the light of new data. In the words of the statement itself, one must recognize "that science is a human cultural product which cannot be definitive or all encompassing."

The Seville Statement notes that the tasks of constructing peace are not only institutional and collective, but "also rest upon the consciousness of individual participants for whom pessimism and optimism are crucial factors. Just as 'wars begin in the minds of men,' peace also begins in our minds." This has been studied scientifically. It was found that those young people who believed that war is intrinsic to human nature were less likely, when asked in a subsequent questionnaire, to have taken part in any activity for peace. Apparently, they believed that since war was inevitable, such activity was of no use.

Belief that war is intrinsic to human nature is widespread. It was found in a cross-cultural study of 5,000 university students from eighteen nations published in 1972 that about half of them believed that "war is a result of the inherent nature of men." Other studies have confirmed these results.

Given the widespread belief in the biological inevitability of warfare and the effect of this attitude on people's behavior, it is clear that the debate on this question needs to be expanded to include as many people as possible. The Seville Statement on Violence can play a useful role in this debate, although new materials, including those based on new research, need to be developed as well.

See BANALITY OF EVIL; FEMINISM AND WAR; MILITARY TRAINING, BASIC; PSYCHIC NUMBING; WOMEN IN THE MILITARY.

BIBLIOGRAPHY

Adams, David, "Biology Does Not Make Men More Aggressive Than Women," in *Of Mice and Women,* K. Bjorkqvist and P. Niemela, eds. (London: Academic Press, 1992), 17–25.

————, *The Seville Statement on Violence: Preparing the Ground for the Constructing of Peace* (Paris: UNESCO, 1991).

Adams, David, and Sarah Bosch, "The Myth That War Is Intrinsic to Human Nature Discourages Action for Peace by Young People," in *Essays in Violence,* Martin Ramirez, Robert Hinde, and Jo Groebel, eds. (Seville: University of Seville, 1987), 121–37.

Barnett, S. A., "Models and Morals: Biological Images of Man," in *Multidisciplinary Approaches to Aggression Research,* Paul F. Brain and David Benton, eds. (Elsevier: North Holland Biomedical Press, 1981), 515–29.

Eckhardt, William, "Crosscultural Theories of War and Aggression," *International Journal of Group Tensions* 2, no. 3 (1972), 36–51.

Ginsburg, Benson E., and Bonnie F. Carter, "The Behaviors and the Genetics of Aggression," in *Essays in Violence,* Martin Ramirez, Robert Hinde, and Jo Groebel, eds. (Seville: University of Seville Press, 1987), 121–37.

Leeds, Anthony, and Valentine Dusek, "Sociobiology: A Paradigm's Unnatural Selection Through Science, Philosophy, and Ideology," *Philosophical Forum* 13 (1981), 1–35.

Lorenz, Konrad, *On Aggression* (New York: Harcourt, Brace & World, 1966).

Scott, John Paul, "The Biological Basis of Warfare," in *Essays in Violence,* Martin Ramirez, Robert Hinde, and Jo Groebel, eds. (Seville: University of Seville Press, 1987), 121–37.

"The Seville Statement on Violence," *Unesco Courier* 46 (February 1993), 40 (published in 32 languages).

Wilson, Edmund O., *Sociobiology: The New Synthesis* (Cambridge, Mass.: Harvard University Press, 1975).

David Adams

HUMAN RIGHTS. Human rights are whatever entitlements all persons have: rights they have because they are human beings. Thus, the idea of human rights is the idea of rights that persons have regardless of their nationality, race, religion, sex, color, aptitude, merit, or any other characteristic that distinguishes some humans from others. Accordingly, human rights may be contrasted with special rights that only some have by virtue of their personal circumstances, such as the rights people have with respect to each other arising from some agreement between them; and also with legal rights that can be created and can cease, such as the rights one has by virtue of winning an elective office for a term of years.

Human rights, like legal rights, may take any or all of four different forms: (1) *privileges,* as when a person's right to do something arises from the lack of any duty not to do that thing; (2) *powers,* as when someone, exercising the right to do something, changes the moral situation of another person (e.g., by appointing someone to be one's agent); (3) *immunities,* as when someone's right to do something is not vulnerable to the power of anyone else; and (4) *claims,* that is, someone's right to do something is that person's claim against someone else with regard to that thing. (This fourfold analysis of rights is from W. N. Hohfeld.) Typical human rights—such as the grand political rights of life, liberty, and property—are in fact a cluster of Hohfeldian rights. Thus, the right to life includes the privilege to stay alive (e.g., to act in self-defense), various powers (e.g., to buy, trade, or otherwise acquire food), immunities (e.g., not to be forced to risk one's life for others), and—above all—claims (e.g., others have the duty not to commit murder).

Today's human rights have their historical origins principally in the various doctrines of natural rights advocated by leading European philosophers of the 17th and 18th centuries. Thomas Hobbes* thought there was but one natural and inalienable right, namely, each person's right of self-preservation. John Locke argued that all persons had many natural and inalienable rights, among them the rights of life, liberty, and property. Other leading thinkers in this period (notably Hugo Grotius*, Jean-Jacques Rousseau*, and Immanuel Kant*) developed alternative lists and conceptions.

Of more influence than any of these philosophical accounts was the French Declaration of the Rights of Man and of the Citizen, proclaimed in 1789 shortly before the French Revolution and defended by Thomas Paine in his widely read *The Rights of Man* (1791). Article 1 proclaimed "Men are born and remain free and equal in respect of rights," and Article 2 declared that "the natural and imprescriptible rights of man" consist of "liberty, property and resistance to oppression." The remaining fifteen articles spelled out various other rights, including due process of law (Articles 7, 8, and 9), freedom of religious worship (Article 10), and freedom of speech (Article 11), all familiar to the British from their Bill of Rights (1689) and to the Americans from their Bill of Rights incorporated in the federal constitution (1791). The French Declaration, however, also included hortatory language ("The law ought to prohibit only actions hurtful to society"), thereby blurring the distinction between genuine human rights and other good things.

Today, the standard list of human rights is that provided by the General Assembly of the United Nations in its "Universal Declaration of Human Rights," adopted and proclaimed on December 10, 1948. This declaration states that the "equal and inalienable rights of all members of the human family" included in this list are to be understood as "a common standard of achievement for all peoples and all nations." This language unfortunately suggests that the so-called "rights" about to be listed are not really rights at all, but instead are only goals to aim at. Be that as it may, the listed rights include the familiar rights of "life, liberty, and security of person" (Article 3), equal protection and recognition before the law (Articles 4, 6, and 7), due process of law (Articles 5, and 8–12), freedom of conscience and speech (Articles 18–19), freedom of assembly (Article 20), self-government (Article 21), as well as rights not widely acknowledged prior to this declaration: the right to seek asylum (Article 14), the right to a nationality (Article 15), and especially various socioeconomic or "welfare" rights, such as the right to work (Article 23), the right to leisure (Article 24), the right to an adequate standard of living (Article 25), and the right to education (Article 26).

Exactly what duties of nations, peoples, and especially governments arise from these rights is less clear. Which rights, if any, should be given priority over others if a conflict of rights arises (e.g., a conflict between raising the standard of living, on the one hand, and free speech and assembly on the other) is also unclear. Real progress with these issues as well as general enforcement of human rights has depended on the agreements of national governments to incorporate these rights into various conventions and covenants having the force of treaties, such as the Convention Relating to the Status of Refugees (1951) and the International Covenant on Economic, Social, and Cultural Rights (1966).

Natural and human rights have usually been claimed by their advocates and defenders to be inalienable—that is, such as cannot be given away, sold, or traded, even if the right-holder were to consent to such alienation. Theorists have been equally firm that such rights can, however, be forfeited, as they must be if punishment for crimes is not to be in violation of the offender's rights.

Philosophers have differed over the source or originating principles of human rights. Theorists such as Locke derive natural rights from divine law for mankind and the duties such laws entail. Utilitarians such as J. S. Mill treat human rights as essential elements in a universal moral code by virtue of the incomparable utility for all mankind that such rights identify and protect. Other theorists have defended such rights either as conceptually embedded in notions of "justice as fairness" (John Rawls) or products of even more basic facts about human beings, our capacity to recognize and see ourselves as subject to moral laws, with each of us having "inherently individual interests" to protect and pursue (Judith Jarvis Thomson).

Are human rights absolute? Probably not; rights are weighty matters deserving respect, but it is too much to claim that no circumstances can arise in which a human right ought to be overridden by other considerations. Also, since human rights are many, not just one, it is extremely difficult to decide—in a nonarbitrary way—which right(s) is (or are) the one(s) that is (or are) absolute and which are not.

Do human needs give rise to human rights? Certainly not, or at least not without considerable complex qualifications. A starving person may justifiably steal from those with a surfeit of food, but not because starvation creates or gives one a right to the food belonging to others. Persons in dire need of organ transplants have no right to demand the needed organs from others. Yet if we had no needs, and especially no permanent needs (for food, shelter, security), we would have no use for rights.

Doctrines and theories of human rights have not gone without their critics. Jeremy Bentham regarded statements of natural rights as purely rhetorical expressions ("nonsense on stilts") and as a misleading way of asserting that something ought to be made the legal right for all persons. For Karl Marx the natural rights of his day were no more than bulwarks of bourgeois society tacitly determined by the requirements of public order in a capitalist society. Others have complained that all known doctrines of human rights are devices of Western cultural imperialism (not very persuasive, given the evidence of moral principles akin to if not identical with human rights in every culture). And others have objected at the "rights explosion" of the late 20th century, in which individuals and groups affirm their desires as though they had a right to the satisfaction of those desires, whatever the cost and consequences. The practices of free enterprise economics frequently exemplify this. What these and other objections principally show is the need to formulate the list of human rights from within the framework of a sound moral theory, something in which both the French Assembly of 1789 and the UN General Assembly of 1948 were lacking.

See COMBATANT-NONCOMBATANT DISTINCTION; GENEVA CON-

VENTION, 1949; MASS DESTRUCTION, WEAPONS OF; MUTUAL AS-
SURED DESTRUCTION (MAD).

BIBLIOGRAPHY

Brownlie, Ian, ed., *Basic Documents on Human Rights* (Oxford: Clarendon Press, 1971).

Donnelly, Jack, *Universal Human Rights in Theory and Practice* (Ithaca, N.Y.: Cornell University Press, 1989).

Nickel, James, *Making Sense of Human Rights* (Berkeley, Calif.: University of California Press, 1987).

Thomson, Judith Jarvis, *The Realm of Rights* (Cambridge, Mass.: Harvard University Press, 1990).

Werhane, Patricia H., A. R. Gini, and David T. Ozar, eds., *Philosophical Issues in Human Rights: Theories and Applications* (New York: Random House, 1986).

Winston, Morton E., ed., *The Philosophy of Human Rights* (Belmont, Calif.: Wadsworth, 1989).

Hugo Adam Bedau

I

IMMUNITY. *See* AERIAL WARFARE; CHILDREN AND WAR; CHILDREN'S RIGHTS IN WAR; CHRISTIANITY AND WAR; COMBATANT-NONCOMBATANT DISTINCTION; CRIMES AGAINST HUMANITY; GENEVA CONVENTIONS 1864, 1906, 1929, 1949; MASS DESTRUCTION, WEAPONS OF; PRISONERS OF WAR; QUARTER, NO, WARS OF.

INCENDIARIES. Prohibitions against the use of fire were among the earliest efforts to identify forbidden weapons* and strategies, such as bans against flaming arrows and torching cities. The Second Lateran Council in 1139 declared that incendiaries should be forbidden, and such weapons were the most frequently deplored during the medieval period. Attempts were made by both the Axis and the Allies in World War I to use gasoline in flamethrowers, but their efforts were both risky to the user and ineffective against the enemy. Treaties at Saint-Germaine-en-Laye in 1919 and Trianon in 1920 prohibited the manufacture and use of flamethrowers, and the United States negotiated several treaties with the Central Powers to ban incendiaries and chemicals. But in Article 29 of both the 1934 and 1940 editions of *Rules of Land Warfare** soldiers were informed that the United States was not bound by any treaty to refrain from the use of incendiaries.

At the beginning of World War II the U.S. Army Chemical Warfare Service enlisted the assistance of both private companies and university faculty in developing a useful agent. Harvard Professor Louis Fieser, a noted organic chemist, invented napalm. It was used extensively in World War II, Korea*, Vietnam*, and in the Gulf War*. It has been praised by the military as ''the best all around weapon.'' The question of the use of incendiaries was to have been considered at the 19th International Conference of the Red Cross* (ICRC) in New Delhi in 1957, but incendiaries in general and napalm in particular were not even mentioned. The discussion concentrated on nuclear weapons*. It was obvious that since nuclear weapons are incendiaries, a ban on incendiaries would be a ban on nuclear weapons as well. In 1969 U Thant, the secretary general of the United Nations, encouraged the ICRC to study the effects of incendiaries and napalm in particular. The ICRC and the UN issued declarations* listing incendiaries as forbidden weapons*, and a special study was published in 1972, *The United Nations Study on Incendiary Weapons and All Aspects of Their Use.* This resulted in a UN resolution in 1972 proposing a ban on napalm and other incendiaries. While it passed by a vote of 99 yea, O nay, there were 15 abstentions, including the United States. The current Army manual, *The Law of Land Warfare**, states in Article 36 that the use of weapons that employ fire, such as flamethrowers, napalm, and other incendiaries, does not violate international law. The *U.S. Army Field Manual 3-8, Chemical Reference Handbook* has over thirty pages of descriptions of chemicals and incendiaries in the official arsenal. The British manual concurs, but warns that incendiaries are not to be used so as to cause "unnecessary suffering." Since incendiaries are basically antipersonnel weapons, it is unclear how they are to be used without causing "unnecessary suffering."

See BIOLOGICAL/CHEMICAL WEAPONS; FORBIDDEN WEAPONS; GENEVA CONVENTIONS, 1906, 1929, 1949.

BIBLIOGRAPHY

Cookson, John, and Judith Nottingham, *A Survey of Chemical and Biological Warfare* (London: Sheed & Ward, 1969).

Rose, Stephen, ed., *Chemical and Biological Warfare* (London: George Harrap, 1968).

United Nations Document No. A-8803, *The United Nations Study on Incendiary Weapons and All Aspects of Their Possible Use* (October 9, 1972).

INCENDIARIES, UN RESOLUTIONS BANNING.

November 29, 1972, UN General Assembly Resolution to ban Napalm and Other Incendiary Devices. Passed, 87 yea, 0 nay, and 27 (U.S.) abstentions.

December 9, 1974, UN General Assembly Resolution banning napalm and other incendiaries. Passed, 108 yea, 0 nay, and 13 (U.S.) abstentions.

December 10, 1976, UN General Assembly Resolution to study banning special conventional weapons deemed to cause excessive injury. Passed without a vote.

December 19, 1977, UN General Assembly Resolution against incendiaries. Passed, 115 yea, 0 nay, and 21 (U.S.) abstentions.

December 14, 1978, UN General Assembly Resolution urging the prohibition of new types of weapons of mass destruction. Passed, 118 yea, 0 nay, and 24 (U.S.) abstentions.

December 14, 1978, UN General Assembly Resolution to prohibit new types of weapons of mass destruction. Passed, 103 yea, 18 (U.S.) nay, and 18 abstentions.

November 21, 1980, UN General Assembly Resolution on prohibition of the "Development of New Types of Weapons of Mass Destruction." Passed, 117 yea, 0 nay, with 26 (U.S.) abstentions.

December 12, 1980, UN General Assembly approval of Protocol I of the Treaty of Tlateloco. Passed, 138 yea, 0 nay, 5 (U.S.) abstentions.

1981, UN General Assembly Resolution banning "particularly inhumane weapons," to include booby traps, mines, fragmentation bombs, and incendiaries. The United States was not a signatory.

BIBLIOGRAPHY

Dispatch (Washington, D.C.: U.S. Department of State, fortnightly publication).

United Nations Resolutions (Dobbs Ferry, N.Y.: Oceana Publications, 1985).

United States Participation in the UN, Report by the President to the Congress (Washington, D.C.: U.S. Government Printing Office, yearly).

INNOCENTS. Almost everyone would agree that, except for very rare instances, there are always some innocent victims of war, that is, civilians who are in no way responsible for war and pose no harm to others. The controversy surrounding innocents, therefore, concerns both the moral significance that should be attached to the distinction between "innocents" and "noninnocents," and the question whether, in "total wars*," the distinction can be meaningfully made.

The principle of discrimination in the *jus in bello* section of the doctrine of just war* prohibits attacks on the innocent. Often the innocent have been construed as civilians or noncombatants*, so that *jus in bello* is held to permit or excuse attacks (if they are proportionate*) on combatants, while prohibiting attacks on noncombatants. Some commentators have called attention to two difficulties with this distinction. First, it does not coincide with guilt or evil intention: Why should a young conscript who voted against the war be a legitimate target for attack, when civilians behind the battle lines who favor military aggression are not? The latter, not the former, have guilty or evil intentions. Secondly, some wars, such as guerrilla* wars, may be conducted in ways that defy efforts to distinguish clearly between combatants and noncombatants. Much of the war effort may be conducted by persons engaged most of the time in civilian pursuits and who melt back into the general population after completing a military mission. Given these realities, it is objected that the distinction between the so-called innocent and the noninnocent is of little, if any, moral significance.

This is not, of course, to advocate indiscriminate attacks on infants and children*, hospitalized invalids, or the inmates of asylums; indeed, many who advance these objections characterize themselves as pacifists* and advance them as reasons for rejecting the concept of *jus in bello*. Others, who believe that wars can be justified on grounds additional to just war considerations, regard these objections as reasons for giving priority to "military necessity*," that is, doing whatever is most efficient in winning the war, over the principle of discrimination.

It may be argued, however, that the innocent should be understood in terms of the original Latin meaning of innocence as *in* (not) *nocens* (harming or hurting). Thus, the distinction between innocents and noninnocents is not intended to be based on evil intention alone, as is also the case for domestic crimes. Nor need this distinction be restricted to the distinction between officially commissioned, identifiable combatants and non-combatants*. It is morally imperative, even if difficult, to distinguish between those who may do injury to us and those we have an obligation to defend, on the one hand, and those who do not pose this threat of injury. Discrimination permits or excuses the incapacitation of those who threaten imminent injury, including the civilian who is on a military mission, but not those who do not expose us to injury, including the prisoner of war and the peasant who is no longer engaged in guerrilla* warfare.

A second type of objection claims that total war makes it impossible to be discriminate in the conduct of war. It may be argued either that everyone, or almost everyone, on the enemy's side is contributing to the war effort, or that it is necessary to use modern weaponry, such as aerial bombardment or use of nuclear devices, that are indiscriminate in their effects. In this way, wars are ended more quickly, and fewer lives, including civilian lives, are lost. Respondents regard the first claim as false. Civilians who produce food or clothing for the use of combatants would produce food or clothing for civilian consumption if their country were not at war. Such contributions to the war effort are quite unlike working in a munitions plant, which is a legitimate target, and do not excuse the targeting of these civilians, any more than feeding prisoners of war* turns one's own soldiers into traitors. In response to the second claim, studies show that obliteration bombing is ineffective, and perhaps counterproductive, and therefore does not save lives by ending wars more quickly. Japan did surrender quickly after A-bombs fell, but it is not clear that alternatives, such as an offshore display or the bombing of an unpopulated site, would not have produced equal results. In any case, only the requirement of unconditional surrender*, a morally dubious objective in itself, made it plausible to argue that an invasion might have been more costly in civilian lives than dropping the atomic bombs. Finally, how could it be moral to use weapons almost certain to take the lives of persons not endangering us, for purely speculative benefits?

See CASUALTIES OF WAR; CHILDREN AND WAR; CHILDREN'S RIGHTS IN WAR; COLLATERAL DAMAGE; CONCENTRATION CAMPS; CRIMES AGAINST HUMANITY; FORBIDDEN STRATEGIES; GENEVA CONVENTIONS, 1906, 1929, 1949; GENOCIDE; HIROSHIMA AND NAGASAKI, BOMBING OF; HOLOCAUST, THE; HUMAN RIGHTS; MASSACRES; MUTUAL ASSURED DESTRUCTION (MAD); NUCLEAR WAR; PROPORTIONALITY; REPRISALS; RETALIATION, MASSIVE; SIEGE WARFARE; TERRORISM.

BIBLIOGRAPHY
Lackey, Douglas P., *Ethics of War and Peace* (Englewood Cliffs, N.J.: Prentice-Hall, 1989).
Walzer, Michael, *Just and Unjust Wars* (New York: Basic Books, 1977).
Wasserstrom, Richard, ed., *War and Morality* (Belmont, Calif.: Wadsworth, 1970).

Robert Paul Churchill

INTELLIGENCE AGENCIES, U.S. The oldest of the current agencies, the Federal Bureau of Investigation (FBI), was first proposed in 1907 by Attorney

General Charles Joseph Bonaparte. Although both the House of Representatives and Senate rejected his request, three days after Congress had adjourned, on May 30, 1908, Bonaparte quietly established a secret police force in the Department of Justice. The congressional fear expressed at the time was that such an agency would not limit itself to crime, but would become a self-appointed custodian of ideology and thus threaten First and Fourth Amendment rights. J. Edgar Hoover was appointed director in 1924, and by 1935 the agency used its power fully as a watchdog of political orthodoxy. The FBI has shared its files with the Army since 1962.

The Office of Strategic Services (OSS) was created by President Franklin D. Roosevelt in 1941 to collect data on the enemy and to conduct clandestine operations behind enemy lines. At this time several branches of government had their own intelligence offices: State, Treasury, Justice, Army, and Navy. In November 1944, OSS director William J. Donovan recommended to the White House the creation of an independent intelligence agency. President Harry S. Truman disagreed so strongly that in October 1945 he relieved Donovan of his post, abolished the OSS, and divided intelligence matters between the State and War departments.

By January 1946, however, President Truman was persuaded to establish the Central Intelligence Group (CIG) under a director, and a National Intelligence Authority (NIA). This NIA consisted of the secretaries of War, State, Navy, and a representative of the president, Admiral William Daniel Leahy. Truman said at this time that he feared that this new agency might become a ''Gestapo,'' and he severely limited its duties. In 1947, after considerable congressional debate, the National Security Council (NSC) and the Central Intelligence Agency (CIA) were established. At House hearings on Truman's bill to establish these two groups, on April 25, 1947, Republican Congressman Clarence J. Brown (R-OH) asked James V. Forrestal, secretary of the Navy, ''Does this agency . . . allow the President to have a Gestapo of his own?'' At the same hearings, Representative Henderson L. Lanham (D-GA) asked Vannevar Bush, director of the U.S. Office of Scientific Development and Research, whether there was danger of the CIA ''becoming a Gestapo.'' The new NSC included the president as chair, the secretaries of Defense, Army, Navy, Air Force, State, and the chair of a new committee, the National Security Resources Board (NSRB). An act of 1949 removed from the membership the secretaries of Army, Navy, Air Force, and the NSRB, but added the vice-president. Thus denied membership, the military continued their own spy agencies independent of this federal agency. President Truman attended only ten of the first fifty-seven formal meetings held up to the time of the Korean War*, denying, by his absence, any significant presidential oversight.

The military had intelligence branches before World War II. Although they operated briefly in the National Security Council, today they function as somewhat independent, although cooperative, agencies. Their domestic intelligence programs are carried out by the U.S. Army Intelligence Command

(USAINTC), the Continental Army Command (CONARC), the Office of the Director of Civil Disturbance Planning and Operation (DCDPO), and the Army Counterintelligence Analysis Branch (CIAB). USAINTC, for example, had 304 stateside offices, staffed by thousands of agents.

In July 1948 President Truman issued a memorandum stating that the NSC and the CIA did not determine policy nor supervise operations, but no one was assigned the task of enforcing this. The NSC was supposed to establish policy for the CIA through two committees: the NSC Intelligence Committee, created in 1971, and the "40 Committee," which had existed in some form since 1948. The Rockefeller Committee, established by President Gerald R. Ford on January 4, 1975, to investigate charges that the CIA was violating civilian rights, reported on June 6, 1975 that the CIA had never submitted any of its domestic activities to the "40 Committee" for its approval. The CIA has four directorates: (1) intelligence, to evaluate, correlate, and disseminate foreign intelligence; (2) operations, to conduct clandestine activities; (3) science and technology, to do research and development; and (4) administration, to handle housekeeping chores. These directorates were compartmentalized, operated on a need-to-know basis, and commonly did not share information with each other. In 1956, Senator Michael Mansfield (D-MT) introduced a bill to establish a joint congressional watchdog committee to oversee these agencies. However, his resolution, and every similar effort since, was killed in committee. An emasculated House Armed Services and Appropriations Committee gave perfunctory surveillance. They met once a year for two hours. One member, Congressman Walter Norblad (R-OR), stated, "we accomplished nothing." Present policy is that the NSC and the CIA report, if at all, only to the president. Congress must request information in order to get any. The spy agencies have no obligation otherwise to provide information.

On January 20, 1975, Senate Democrats caucused and voted to set up a bi-partisan committee to investigate the FBI and CIA. On January 21 Senator John Pastore (D-RI) introduced Senate Resolution 21 to form an eleven-member committee, chaired by Senator Frank Church (D-ID). The committee revealed the Huston Plan, a particularly egregious violation of Fourth Amendment rights. Tom Huston, a young attorney on the White House staff, participated in a group called the Ad Hoc Interagency Committee on Intelligence. Watergate was one of this committee's projects. The committee had been formed by President Richard M. Nixon and included White House aides H. R. Haldeman and John Erlichman. The Church committee also discovered that the CIA had employed religious missionaries as spies, had impersonated clergy, and had established agencies pretending to be churches. Since the CIA had the right to censor all such reports, the committee findings were never formally accepted.

The House created several committees to investigate the FBI and CIA. The first was created on February 19, 1975, by H.R. 138, chaired by Rep. Lucien Nedzi (D-MI), and abolished on July 17, 1975. A second committee was formed on July 17, 1975, by H.R. 591 and chaired by Rep. Otis Pike (D-NY). In spite of much investigation containing serious allegations, the Pike committee report was never officially printed. On July 17, 1977, H.R. 658 created another committee to conduct oversight, chaired by Rep. Edward Boland (D-MA). The committee met for eight years until 1985, but its reports were never formally acted upon.

Two presidential commissions made similar efforts. The first commission was established by President Lyndon Johnson in February 1967 to investigate charges that the CIA had financed the National Student Association and covertly infiltrated civilian groups. The committee consisted of its chair, Nicholas Katzenbach, under-secretary of State; John W. Gardiner, Secretary of Health, Education, and Welfare; and Richard Helms, Director of the CIA. By the end of February the commission submitted an initial report, and by March 30, 1975, less than two months after its formation, a final report was given to the president. The report recommended that the CIA cease giving support to any U.S. educational or private voluntary organizations and that a public/private government-sponsored group should be formed to provide the CIA with funds for overseas activities. In spite of reservations by Gardiner, the other members of the committee determined that no obstacles would be put in the way of the CIA, which continued financial support of U.S. college faculty and student groups.

President Gerald Ford created a second commission on CIA activities within the United States on January 4, 1975, by Executive Order 11828. The commission set out to: (1) determine if the CIA was violating its mandate not to operate in the United States, (2) see if sufficient safeguards existed to limit such activities, and (3) make recommendations to the president. Vice-President Nelson A. Rockefeller was named the chairman. The initial findings were that the CIA had spied on American citizens, kept illegal dossiers on those who disagreed publicly with various government policies, intercepted and opened private mail for over twenty years, infiltrated student protest groups, assisted in illegal wire taps, and improperly assisted other government agencies. The final recommendations of the commission, however, after CIA censorship, were too modest to change the situation.

A report of Senate hearings in the fall of 1975, a document over 1,200 pages long, revealed that the CIA and the Department of Defense (DOD) had used American citizens as human subjects in chemical and biological warfare experiments*. Of particular importance were hearings in 1977 before the Subcommittee on Health and Scientific Research of the Committee on Human Resources, chaired by Senator Edward M. Kennedy (D-MA), revealing experiments on unwitting American citizens dating back to 1952 using such lethal agents as tularemia, undulant fever, syphilis, botulinus, Q Fever, and Venezuelan Equine Encephalomyelitis. Both the CIA and the DOD carried out experiments on unwitting citizens in local jails, prisoners, patients in mental hospitals, terminally ill cancer patients, prostitutes, soldiers in army bases, and the general population in public places.

These findings raised crucial questions about the role of such spy activities in a democratic society, of who is empowered rightfully to determine when the Constitution may be violated in the name of national security, and whether limits exist beyond which a society can not legally go to preserve its perceived best interests.

See FORBIDDEN STRATEGIES; MILITARY AS A PROFESSION; MILITARY EDUCATION; MILITARY TRAINING, BASIC; SPIES.

BIBLIOGRAPHY

Biological Testing Involving Human Subjects by the Department of Defense, Hearings Before the Subcommittee on Health and Scientific Research of the Committee on Human Resources, Senate, March 8 and May 23, 1977 (Washington, D.C.: U.S. Government Printing Office, 1977).

Biomedical and Behavioral Research, Human-Use Experimentation Programs of the Department of Defense and Central Intelligence Agency, Joint Hearings Before the Subcommittee on Health of the Committee on Labor and Public Welfare and the Subcommittee on Administration Practice and Procedure of the Committee on the Judiciary, Senate, September 10, 12, November 7, 1975 (Washington, D.C.: U.S. Government Printing Office, 1975).

History of the Office of the Secretary of Defense: The Formative Years 1947–1950 (Washington, D.C.: U.S. Government Printing Office, 1984).

Human Drug Testing by the CIA, 1977, Hearings Before the Subcommittee on Health and Scientific Research of the Committee on Human Resources, Senate, September 20–21, 1977 (Washington, D.C.: U.S. Government Printing Office, 1977).

Human Subjects Research: Radiation Experimentation, Hearing of the Committee on Labor and Human Resources, Senate, 103rd Cong. 1st sess. (Washington, D.C.: U.S. Government Printing Office, 1994).

Intelligence Activities–Mail Openings, Hearings Before the Select Committee to Study Governmental Operations with Respect to Intelligence Activities of the United States Senate, October 21, 22, and 24, 1975 (Washington, D.C.: U.S. Government Printing Office, 1975).

Military Surveillance of Civilian Politics: A Report of the Subcommittee on Constitutional Rights, Committee of the Judiciary, U.S. Senate, October 28, November 12, December 15, 1981 (Washington, D.C.: U.S. Government Printing Office, 1981).

U.S. Intelligence Agencies and Activities Risks and Control of Foreign Intelligence, Hearings Before the Select Committee on Intelligence, H.R., November 4, 6, December 2, 3, 9, 10, 11, 12, and 17, 1975 (Washington, D.C.: U.S. Government Printing Office, 1975).

INTENTIONALITY AND DOUBLE EFFECT. A single act can have many effects, some good, some bad. Suppose that one is contemplating an act that has, one foresees, good consequences for some people but bad consequences for others. Is it morally permissible to perform this act? Within the framework of a strict ethic that contains the principle, "Do no harm," the act is prohibited. But suppose that we locate the moral center of the act not in the external performance, but in the intentions with which the act is performed. The relevant moral rule becomes, "Do no intentional harm." Now, suppose that with this act one intends the good effects and regrets the bad effects. By the rule, "Do no intentional harm," the act is permissible.

If we add considerations of intentionality, we may change the moral rating of an act. The testing procedures for changing moral ratings of acts through the consideration of intentionality constitute the "doctrine of double effect," an established principle of Catholic moral theology. In many cases, an act that is normally prohibited becomes permissible when the doctrine of double effect is applied.

This loosening of moral strictures has special consequences for the ethics of war. Many acts of war that are prohibited by normal moral standards become permissible under the doctrine of double effect. For example, suppose that the act in question is the bombing of a bridge near which civilians are known to live. Normally, one cannot use violence that foreseeably kills civilians. But in this case, one might desire only to blow up a bridge and might regret killing the civilians. Under double effect, the bombing is permissible.

Consider a given act that has good and bad consequences. The doctrine of double effect, as developed in the 17th century, will condone the act if and only if:

1. The act is not inherently immoral, that is, immoral on the basis of what kind of act it is, apart from its consequences. For example, if the act is an act of blasphemy, or an act of deception, then it is not sanctioned regardless of effects or intentions.

2. The foreseeable good effects of the act outweigh the bad effects. This weighing procedure will be difficult in many cases but easy in many others. For example, if the act involves killing one innocent person to save five, then requirement 2 is satisfied. If the act involves killing five innocent people to save one, then this requirement is not satisfied.

3. The bad effects must be side effects, not the means by which the good effects are produced. To do so would violate St. Paul's dictum (Rom. 3:8) that Christians never do evil that good may come. If one intends the end, one intends the means. To avoid intending the bad effects, they must not be the means to the good effects. Requirement 3 rules out an application of double effect suggested by Aquinas*. In arguing that it is permissible to kill in order to save one's own life, Aquinas had argued that one intends to save one life and one regrets taking life, hence self-defense is permissible. But since killing the aggressor is the means by which saving one's life is obtained, killing in self-defense is not sanctioned by requirement 3. (It may be permissible to kill in self-defense for some other reason.)

4. The good effects must be intended, and the bad effects not intended. The sense of "intended" here differs significantly from "intended" in common law. In law, "intended" is roughly interchangeable with "foreseen." In the doctrine of double effect, "intended" is roughly interchangeable with "desired." In some versions of the doctrine of double effect, the distinction between "intended" and "unintended" effects is subjectively drawn: one intends the effects about which one had positive feelings; one does not intend the effects about which one has negative feelings. In other versions, the distinction between intended effects and unintended effects is drawn by the "counterfactual test": If one would perform the act even if one thought that the bad effects were not forthcoming, then the good effects are intended and the bad effects

not intended. For example, if one would still bomb the bridge if civilians were not present, then the deaths of the civilians are unintended evils.

The doctrine of double effect provides a method by which those who believe in strict duties can on occasion behave like utilitarians. Furthermore, the doctrine provides a useful technique for restraining even the "good side" in war: in World War II, the tactical bombing of military objectives by the Allies was permissible by double effect; the terror bombing of Dresden was not.

Nevertheless, every element of the doctrine has come in for criticism. Pacifists* have complained that the distinction between inherently immoral acts and acts immoral through their effects (Requirement 1) is arbitrarily drawn: for pacifists, taking life is inherently immoral. Those who argue that the weighing and measuring characteristic of utilitarian ethics is an intellectual sham are equally critical of the weighing and measuring implied in Requirement 2. Students of causal relations have suggested that the distinction between "means" and "side-effects" central to Requirement 3 is spurious. If causes are defined as necessary and sufficient conditions, then if the act is the cause of the good and bad effects, the bad effects will be necessary and sufficient conditions, that is, causes, of the good effects.

The severest criticisms have been directed at Requirement 4. To declare that a bad effect is "unintended" because one feels regret about it puts moral judgments at the whim of feelings; to say it is unintended because of the counterfactual test is to indulge in an unverifiable guess about what a person would do if conditions were different. (Can one be sure that one would bomb the bridge if civilians were not present? Perhaps the enemy uses human shields, and the absence of civilians proves that the bridge is unimportant.) Furthermore, every event has multiple descriptions, and I may regret an event described one way but not regret it described another way. One might honestly say, "I never intended to kill him, only to blow him to bits. His dying is a regrettable side effect of blowing him up." In a war, one might claim that the intention of every act is victory, and all the killing is a regrettable side effect. By such maneuvers, every act becomes permissible.

See AERIAL WARFARE; BANALITY OF EVIL; CASUALTIES OF WAR; CHILDREN AND WAR; COLLATERAL DAMAGE; FORBIDDEN STRATEGIES; FORBIDDEN WEAPONS; HIROSHIMA AND NAGASAKI; HOLOCAUST, THE; INNOCENTS; JUST WAR; MASS DESTRUCTION, WEAPONS OF; MASSACRES; NUCLEAR DETERRENCE; NUCLEAR WAR; PROPORTIONALITY; REPRISALS; SIEGE.

BIBLIOGRAPHY

For a history of the Doctrine of Double Effect see Joseph Mangan, "A Historical Analysis of the Principle of Double Effect," *Theological Studies* (1949). A modern defense of double effect is given in Charles Fried, *Right and Wrong* (Cambridge, Mass.: Harvard University Press, 1978). Problems with the doctrine are explored in P. Foot, "The Problem of Abortion and the Doctrine of Double Effect," *Oxford Review* (1967), and in Jonathan Bennett, ''Morality and Consequences,'' *Tanner Lectures on Human Values,* vol. II, S. McMurrin, ed. (Cambridge: Cambridge University Press, 1981).

Douglas P. Lackey

INTERNATIONAL COURT OF JUSTICE (WORLD COURT). Much of the history of international adjudication is embedded in treaties. On November 19, 1784, U.S. Secretary of State John Jay signed a treaty with Great Britain that established three boards of arbitration to resolve a series of disputes. In each case the boards resolved the issues and, where relevant, fixed responsibility and assessed damages. The Treaty of Washington in 1871 established four arbitrations dealing with British conduct during the American Civil War. The most famous was the Alabama Claim, named after a British-built ship that the Confederates had used from British ports to raid Union ships. The hearings were in Geneva, Switzerland before a board of five members consisting of three neutrals and a representative from the United States and the United Kingdom. The tribunal awarded $15.5 million to the United States for the failure of the UK to remain neutral. President Benjamin Harrison praised a Pan-American treaty issued at a conference in 1889–1890 as a worthy alternative to war. Unfortunately, no nation in attendance, including the United States, ever ratified the treaty. President William J. McKinley praised the Olney-Pauncefote Treaty between England and the United States as a forward step, but the U.S. Senate refused to ratify the treaty.

Based on the principles of The Hague* Congresses on the Pacific Settlement of Disputes (1899), a permanent court of arbitration was established. However, it was not ratified by the U.S. Senate, and lacked power to do more than hear cases. President Calvin Coolidge called it a ''convenient instrument to which we can go, but to which we could not be brought.'' The last U.S. effort to support this court was on January 29, 1935, when it failed again to pass the Senate. Between 1900 and 1914 this court worked on more than 120 general arbitration treaties.

The League of Nations General Assembly on December 16, 1920, adopted the Statute of the Permanent Court of International Justice. By September 1921 a majority of the states had ratified the court, which lasted until April 16, 1946, at which time the League of Nations was formally dissolved. The court functioned alongside of the Court of Arbitration and during its life handled sixty-six cases, of which thirty-eight were contentious and twenty-eight were advisory.

The United Nations established the International Court of Justice (ICJ) in 1946 under Article 7 of the UN Charter, and under Article 92 this new court was established as the official judicial organ of the UN. Neither the Court of Arbitration (The Hague) nor the Permanent Court of Justice (League of Nations) had any official status with its founding body. The new court consisted of fifteen members, no two of whom could be from the same state. Efforts were made to be representative geographically in relation to different legal systems. There were no lower or upper age limits. Candidates were nominated through ''national groups," which could name four persons for any vacancy. When President Jimmy Carter tried to get Arthur Goldberg on the court he was overruled by the "national group," which preferred Richard R. Baxter of the Harvard Law School. Nominees were then elected by simple majority by the General Assembly and the Security Council to serve a nine-year term, and remained in office until whatever case they were working on had been decided. In the event that a party refused to comply with the court's decision, recourse could be sought in the Security Council. Any of the five permanent states could, however, veto such an appeal. The United States never accepted the compulsory adjudication clause of the court. A number of U.S. congressional actions indicate a general mood of indifference to international law, such as the Nancy Kassebaum (R-KA) Amendment (1993), the Gramm-Rudman-Hollings law (1985), and section 151 of the Foreign Relations Authorization Act (1987), the Sundquist Amendment, which under the concern of deficit reduction sequestered funds for foreign aid. In its first forty years the court issued 115 decisions in contentious cases and/or advisory proceedings. This court has generally been underused. Indeed, during the first four decades there were seventeen years in which the court rendered no advisory opinions. Only seven states have appeared more than once before the court: Great Britain (8), France (4), the United States (3), and Belgium, West Germany, India, and Norway (2).

Fewer than one-third of the member states accept the compulsory jurisdiction of the court (45 out of 160), and some of these have reservations. Among those states supporting the compulsory jurisdiction of the court are: Barbados, Botswana, Colombia, Costa Rica, the Dominican Republic, Gambia, Haiti, Honduras, India, Kenya, Liberia, Malawi, Mauritius, Nigeria, Pakistan, Panama, Somalia, Swaziland, Togo, Uganda, and Uruguay. Among Western nations accepting compulsory arbitration are: Australia, Austria, Great Britain, Belgium, Canada, Finland, Malta, the Netherlands, Portugal, Sweden, Switzerland. Among those accepting limited jurisdiction of the sort provided by the U.S. Connally Reservation are Mexico, the Philippines, and Sudan. In spite of U.S. reticence to submit to adjudication by the court, many treaties bind this country by clauses requiring or at least allowing submission to the World Court. By the end of the 1980s the United States was obligated through treaties to submit cases to the court with thirty-one nations under bilateral agreements and with more than 160 nations under multilateral treaties and conventions. ·

Nicaragua brought a case (1985) before the court charging the United States with violations of both treaties and UN Charter obligations. The court found the United States culpable and subject to a fine that could have run as high as $400 million. At that time the U.S. State Department terminated the American agreement to accept the jurisdiction of the court effective April 7, 1986, thus nullifying the court's judgment. The United States was not alone in such action. In 1972 the Soviet Union refused to comply with the judgment of the court that member states must pay their assessed share of UN peacekeeping operations; Iran refused to obey the court in the *Hostages* case; Albania did not appear in the early stages of the *Corfu Channel* case and refused to obey the court when the judgment went against it. In 1973 France refused to appear before the court to respond to the claims of Australia and New Zealand that nuclear testing in the South Pacific was unlawful, and while the case was pending, France, like the United States later, revoked its acceptance of court jurisdiction. Iceland refused to abide by the decision of the court in the *Fisheries Jurisdiction* cases and Turkey (1978) refused to appear in the *Aegean Sea Continental Shelf* case. Despite this record, most countries, like the United States, insist that they support the World Court even though they deny its compulsory jurisdiction. In June 1994 a coalition of citizen organizations including the International Peace Bureau, the International Physicians for the Prevention of Nuclear War, and the International Association of Lawyers Against Nuclear Arms made a formal presentation to support a ban on nuclear weapons. It was the first time the ICJ had admitted a citizen presentation, although citizen groups have no legal standing to be able to argue a case in the court.

   See INTERNATIONAL LAW; LAWS OF WAR; NATIONALISM.

BIBLIOGRAPHY
Damrosch, Lori Fisler, *The International Court of Justice at the Crossroads* (Dobbs
       Ferry, N.Y.: Transnational Publishers, 1987).
Franck, Thomas M., *Judging the World Court* (New York: Priority Press, 1986).
Gamble, John King, *The International Court of Justice* (Lexington, Mass.: D.C. Heath,
       1976).
Rosenne, Shabtai, *The World Court* (New York: Oceana Publications, 1963).
Weston, Burns H., Richard A. Falk, and Anthony A. D'Amato, "Statute of the Inter-
       national Court of Justice," in *Basic Documents in International Law and World
       Order* (St. Paul, Minn.: West Publishing Company, 1980), 23–29.

INTERNATIONAL LAW. From the 16th to the 18th centuries, a group of jurists attempted to formulate international laws. Their primary locus of concern was war. These writers included Franciscus de Victoria* (1480–1546), Pierino Belli* (1502–1575), Balthazar Ayala* (1548–1584), Francisco Suarez* (1548–1617), Alberico Gentili* (1552–1608), Hugo Grotius* (1583–1645), Emmerich da Vattel* (1714–1767), and Cornelius Bynkerschoek* (1673–1743). Two options were explored in the search for the bases of international law: (1) some, like Victoria and Belli, attempted to show that such international laws could be derived using Aristotelian natural law theory as modified by Roman Catholic thinkers, and illustrated by quotations from Judeo-Christian scriptures and early Christian Church Fathers; (2) others, like Ayala, Gentili, Vattel, and Bynkerschoek, were positivists, who attempted to ground international law in custom. Grotius combined the two positions. With the demise of natural law theory, efforts to establish international laws depended on whether customs existed among nations of sufficient universality and persistence that violators of such customs could be accused of having broken a law.

   In 1874, Francis Lieber* urged Rolyn-Jacquemyns to establish an Institute of

International Law. The annual report in 1878 recommended that Gustave Moy-nier research the military codes of nations to see if there was enough uniformity to conclude that some international laws of war existed. Moynier drafted a sample code in 1880, which the Institute accepted. Textbooks in international law appeared, giving some credence to the thesis that international laws existed, and the major arguments rested on the view that such laws were embodied in treaties and customary practice.

The Nuremberg Trial* judges faced the formidable task of specifying such laws in order to justify the legal bases for the war crimes trials. The judges argued that the Geneva* conventions had established laws the breaking of which constituted crimes against humanity; that the declarations of The Hague* established laws the breaking of which constituted war crimes; and that the Paris Peace Pact* had established a law the breaking of which constituted a crime against the peace. Lewis Oppenheim defined laws of war as "generally binding customs and international treaties." But how international did a custom or treaty need to be? The 1864 Geneva conventions were initially approved by the delegates of only the twelve attending nations, while only twenty-six national delegates attended the sessions at The Hague. At what point did enough nations ratify these declarations and conventions for the conclusion to be drawn that these established international law? The question became moot when UN resolutions with over 150 nations in approval were still considered merely advisory, and provisions in both the Hague and Geneva conventions permitted nations to repudiate them if they proved inconvenient. In addition, many of the major nations (including the United States and the Soviet Union) did not recognize the jurisdiction of the World Court.

The debate over whether nations had a right of reprisal was typical of the ambiguity. Evelyn Speyer Colbert observed that the claim for such a right "reflected the absence of law enforcing machinery," and Oppenheim noted that reprisals were commonly used as a "convenient cloak for violations of international law." Did international laws exist that set limits to acceptable weapons? The U.S. Army manual, *The Law of Land Warfare**, states that no international laws exist prohibiting weapons such as incendiaries, noxious chemicals, gases, or nuclear bombs. The only possible exception, for the United States, were biological weapons, which were determined in 1976 to be the "only clearly forbidden weapon in international law" (this conclusion was reached in spite of the long UN list of weapons of "mass destruction" whose use was asserted to be "contrary to the rules of international law"). George Manner examined supposed international laws with regard to war and concluded that unless the offense was a domestic one, no claim for the existence of an international law could be substantiated, and that, in addition, it was axiomatic that individuals were not subjects of international law.

Although Sir Hersch Lauterpacht, the new editor of Oppenheim's *International Law,* referred to the judgments of the Nuremberg Tribunal as being "evidence of international law," he also noted that the Allies would have added to this stature if they had agreed to have their own nationals tried. He noted further that there was no guarantee that international law as a whole would survive the current onslaught of lawlessness. Such a suspicion was reinforced by the results of the effort of the UN Commission on International Law to formulate principles derivable from Nuremberg, but the UN General Assembly refused to ratify any such proposal. Indeed, uneasiness over the legal bases for the Nuremberg trials was expressed by legal writers such as F. B. Schick, Marion Lozier, Alwyn W. Freeman, Erwin Knoll, Judith Nies McFadden, Howard Taubenfeld, and Hans Erhard; while Thomas Dodd and Quincy Wright insisted that the trials were models of international procedure, and in Wright's case sufficiently well established to condemn the U.S. war in Vietnam as a violation of international law. Articles in the international law journals commonly refer to international laws, especially as they may apply to war, as in grave need of revision.

See LAWS OF WAR.

BIBLIOGRAPHY

Colbert, Evelyn Speyer, *Retaliation in International Law* (London: King's Crown Press, 1948).

Falk, Richard A., *The Status of Law in International Society* (Princeton, N.J.: Princeton University Press, 1976).

Midgly, E.B.F., *The Natural Law Tradition and the Theory of International Law* (London: Paul Elek, 1975).

Stockholm International Peace Institute, *The Law of War and Dubious Weapons* (Stockholm: Almqvist & Wiksell, 1971).

INTERVENTION. *See* AGGRESSION, ATTEMPTS TO DEFINE; AGGRESSIVE VERSUS DEFENSIVE WAR; FIRST STRIKE/SECOND STRIKE; HUMANITARIAN INTERVENTION; PARIS PEACE PACT; REPRISALS; RETALIATION.

IRAN-IRAQ WAR (1980–1988). From September 1980 until August 1988, the northern edge of the Persian Gulf was the scene of war between Iraq and Iran. By the time fighting stalemated and a peace accord was signed in August 1990, billions of dollars had been spent, hundreds of thousands of lives had been lost, and neither country had been able to achieve any of the goals that had initiated and sustained the conflict. Despite this, the leadership in both countries consolidated their hold on power.

Three divisions underlay the animosities that led to the war: (1) the rivalry between Arabs and Persians (Iran is the Persian homeland while Iraq is mostly Arab); (2) the Sunni-Shiite schism (Iran is predominantly Shiite, and though over half of Iraq's population is Shiite, its Sunni minority has been politically dominant); and (3) the antagonism between the Arab nationalism of the Baath party, which has ruled Iraq since 1968 and the pan-Islamism of Iran's Shiite clergy, which gained power in 1979. Of the three, the last provides a more immediate backdrop for understanding the war.

When an independent Iraq was carved out of formerly Ottoman territory after World War I, it inherited a border dispute between the Ottomans and the Iranians centering on the Shatt al-Arab (also called the Arvand River), the 110-mile waterway that carries the waters of the Tigris and Euphrates into the Persian Gulf. The Shatt is Iraq's only outlet to the gulf, on which is located its major port and second-largest city, Basra. The Iranian cities of Khorramshahr and Abadan are located downstream. In 1937, the two countries negotiated a treaty fixing the common border as the Shatt's east bank, placing the river inside Iraq but granting navigation rights to Iran. The Shah of Iran abrogated the treaty in 1969, and in the early 1970s, together with the United States and Israel, supported an insurgency by the minority Kurds against the Baghdad government. Border clashes also occurred during this period. Hostilities abated after the 1975 treaty, in which Iraq consented to the *thalaweg*—the median line through the main navigable channel in the Shatt—as the common boundary, while Iran agreed to end assistance to the Kurds.

This rapprochement between the Shah and the Baathists was opposed by Ayatollah Khomeini, the Shiite clergyman living in Iraq in exile from his native Iran since 1964. When Khomeini's call for the ouster of the Shah began to have its dramatic effect in 1978, the Iraqi leader Saddam Hussein expelled him from Iraq. After Khomeini eventually returned to Tehran to preside over Iran's revolutionary movement, tensions between the two countries mounted. The Iraqi call for the return of territory specified in the 1975 treaty was ignored by Iran, and Khomeini's emphasis on export of the Islamic revolution led him to condemn the Baathist's Arab nationalism, creating apprehension in Baghdad and Arab Gulf countries. After an attempt on the lives of some Baathist leaders in April 1980, Iraq expelled several thousand individuals of Iranian origin and executed a prominent Shiite clergyman. Khomeini urged Iraqi Shiites to revolt. On September 17, arguing that Iran had not complied with the terms of the 1975 agreement and was refusing to negotiate outstanding border disputes, Iraq renounced the unpopular treaty and claimed sovereignty over the Shatt.

Border skirmishes in September 1980 constituted the main *casus belli*. Noting that the hostage dispute with the United States cut Iran off from U.S. military supplies, and resentful that Iraq had been pressured to sign the 1975 treaty, Saddam Hussein found circumstances propitious for an invasion. Observers are divided about his aims. The Iraqis stated that resort to force was necessary to halt Iranian provocations and to settle outstanding border disputes, but some suggest that the Iraqis were aiming at a takeover of Arabstan, a portion of the oil-rich province of Khuzestan bordering Iraq in the southeast. Others speculate that Saddam's objective was to intimidate, if not to overthrow, the Khomeini regime.

As to the latter, the September 22 invasion had the opposite effect. Although the Iraqi forces took Khorramshahr and within two weeks controlled 5,400 square miles of Khuzestan, their advance was soon halted. The Iranian clerics used the war to consolidate power by diverting the attention of the military and generating popular support for a unified response to the invasion. Refusing calls for a cease-fire in October, they used the hostages* to bargain for American arms from supporters of Ronald Reagan's candidacy for U.S. president. The latter, with the Israeli government as an intermediary, arranged for the sale of arms to Iran in exchange for release of the hostages after the 1980 elections.

By April 1982, the Iranians had pushed the Iraqi forces back to the border, retaken Khorramshahr, and cut Iraqi access to its oil export facilities in the Persian Gulf, demanding $150 billion in reparations and a dismantling of the Baathist government as the price for peace. In response to Iraqi bombardment of their oil terminal on Kharg island in July 1982, the Iranians invaded Iraq but were eventually repelled by Iraqi resistance. Iranian forces retreated and pre-pared for a renewed offensive during the next rainy season, a strategy that they repeated for five years, but that gave the Iraqis an opportunity to prepare de-fenses. Thousands of young men were recruited to serve in its Revolutionary Guard movement, which favored large-scale invasions of Iraqi territory. Iraq responded to massive human wave attacks with heavy artillery and poison gas— which Iran used as well—exacting severe casualties. Despite this, the Iranians gained a foothold in Iraqi territory, notably in the Faw peninsula within sight of Kuwait, during the 1986 campaign, where they remained until successful Iraqi counteroffensives in spring 1988.

Damage to Iraq's economy and fear of Iranian incursions into Arab territory led the Gulf Arab countries to subsidize Iraq's war effort. The flow of arms generated a massive buildup of Iraq's military; by 1985, Iraq had mobilized 450,000 soldiers, established air superiority, and began firing short-range mis-siles into Iranian cities. Iran responded with missile attacks on Baghdad, and by 1988, Iraq was sending long-range missiles into the Iranian capital, Tehran. Both sides stepped up attacks on shipping in the gulf which led, in turn, to the Amer-ican reflagging of Kuwaiti tankers in 1987. Security Council Resolution 598 (July 1987) called for an immediate ceasefire, which Iraq accepted but Iran rejected. It was not until the failed Iranian offensives of 1987, the successful Iraqi counterattacks in early 1988 costing Iran 40 percent of its major military equipment, and the increased involvement of the superpowers, that the Iranian leaders finally agreed to a truce in July 1988.

Casualty* figures are uncertain. Minimal estimates are that 140,000 Iraqis were killed, mainly soldiers, while the Iranians lost 300,000, including 80,000 civilians. Some observers place Iranian losses at nearly a million. It is estimated that battlefield casualties were the greatest since World War II. The economies of both countries were ravaged; Iranian oil output was reduced to a tenth of what it had been at its height, and Iraq's war debt was estimated at $100 billion, most of it to the Arab Gulf countries.

The political impact of the war extended far beyond the gulf. Iran's need for weapons in 1980 prolonged the hostage crisis, which contributed significantly to Jimmy Carter's defeat in the 1980 presidential elections. With attention shifted to another Middle Eastern conflict, Israel bombed Iraq's nuclear reactor at Osirak in February 1981 and invaded Lebanon in 1982. A dispute over re-payment of its war debt led Iraq to invade Kuwait in August 1990 which, in turn, brought about a stiff response from the United States and its allies. The resulting war in early 1991 further devastated Iraq's economy and led to a U.S. military presence in the gulf likely to extend well into the next century.

It is doubtful that Iraq's initial invasion of Iran is justifiable under interna-tional law* or just war* ethics. Its border dispute with Iran should have been referred to arbitration or the Security Council. But the Iranian leadership was at fault for prolonging the war, refusing the Iraqi offer of cease-fire and a return to the status quo in the spring of 1981, and using young Iranians in human wave assaults upon well-entrenched Iraqi artillery—up to 70,000 died in the 1987 Karbala V offensive. The employment of chemical weapons* by both sides was perhaps a violation of *jus in bello*. As with most wars, there were parties on the outside, notably those in the United States, Europe, and Israel, who profited, politically and economically, and whose policies and deceptions as-sured that neither side would emerge victorious.

See BIOLOGICAL/CHEMICAL WARFARE; GULF WAR (DESERT STORM).

BIBLIOGRAPHY

Ismael, T., *Iraq and Iran: Roots of Conflict* (Syracuse, N.Y.: Syracuse University Press, 1982).

Joyner, C., ed., *The Persian Gulf War* (Westport, Conn.: Greenwood, 1990).

Khadduri, M., *The Gulf War* (Oxford: Oxford University Press, 1988).

Pelletier, F., *The Iran-Iraq War* (New York: Praeger, 1992).

Rajaee, F., ed., *The Iran-Iraq War: The Politics of Aggression* (Gainesville: Florida University Press, 1993).

Tomis Kapitan

IRAQ COMMISSION OF INQUIRY. The commission was formed to deter-mine if war crimes* had been committed by the United States in the Gulf War*, and was led by former U.S. Attorney General Ramsey Clark. It held its first hearing in New York on May 11, 1991. Subsequent commissions were held in fifteen countries, and public hearings took place in twenty-eight U.S. cities. At the first hearing a nineteen-point indictment was issued. Included in the list were the following charges: the United States prevented negotiations and bribed the members of the Security Council to vote in favor of immediate armed retaliation; the initial bombing was on civilian centers destroying the infrastructure, and the siege* that followed held the civilian populations hostage*; the so-called "smart" bombs missed their targets 25 percent of the time, and "dumb" bombs missed 75 percent of the time, thus denying the U.S. claim that the war spared civilians; the U.S. earth-movers buried alive over 8,000 Iraqi soldiers; the "Highway of Death" occurred eight days after Iraq had surrendered and two days after President George Bush had declared the cease-fire; many, if not most, of the oil well fires were started by U.S. bombing; antipersonnel fragmentation

bombs* and napalm were used (banned by both UN* and Geneva Declarations*); and the casualty* ratio of about 4,000 Iraqi for every one American
indicated that, contrary to the U.S. claim that Iraq was a formidable foe, it was,
as one U.S. pilot called it "a turkey shoot."

Like the Stockholm-Rothskilde trials* (led by Bertrand Russell and Jean-Paul
Sartre) for putative U.S. crimes in Vietnam*, the Shimoda trial* in Tokyo of
the United States for the bombing of Hiroshima and Nagasaki*, the North Vietnamese Commission to "Investigate the U.S. Imperialist War Crimes in Vietnam," and the Tokyo Tribunal organized by the Japanese philosopher,
Yoshishige Kosai, the Iraq Commission was without legal status, although the
questions they raised were of profound ethical significance.

See CASUALTIES OF WAR; COLLATERAL DAMAGE; CRIMES
AGAINST HUMANITY; FORBIDDEN STRATEGIES; FORBIDDEN WEAP-
ONS; GULF WAR (DESERT STORM); PROPAGANDA; WAR CRIMES.

BIBLIOGRAPHY
Clark, Ramsey, et al., *War Crimes: A Report on United States War Crimes Against Iraq*
(Washington, D.C.: Maisonneuve Press, 1992).
Dispatch (U.S. Department of State fortnightly reports, which contain all UN Security
Council resolutions on the Gulf War, 1991–1993).
Duffett, John, ed., *Against the Crime of Silence: Proceedings of the International War
Crimes Tribunal* (New York: Simon & Schuster, 1968).
Falk, A. Richard, "The Shimoda Case: A Legal Appraisal of the Atomic Attacks Upon
Hiroshima and Nagasaki," *American Journal of International Law* (October
1965).

ISLAM AND WAR. In both the main traditions of Islam, *Sunni* and *Shia,*
pacifism* has not been accepted as an integral doctrine. The Prophet Muhammad
had no compunction about the legitimacy of force when he believed the situation
demanded it, and those dubious about "fighting in the way of Allah" were
regarded as letting their scruples weaken their nerve or allowing their love of
domestic peace to become a *fitnah,* or temptation, to them.

The close historical connection between Islam and militarism* can be traced
to the role of Muhammad as both religious and secular leader of the *umma,* the
"brotherhood," or community, of Islam. While banning intertribal warfare
within the *umma,* Muhammad supported war in defense of the *umma* as well as
raids on infidel tribes in Arabia, including the capture of Mecca in 630 C.E.
Subsequent to Muhammad's death in 632, Islam continued to be spread by
military conquest and the central concept of *jihad,* or "striving in the way of
Allah," was interpreted to include war against unbelievers and enemies of the
faith. Since the Qur'an enjoined the obligation of *jihad,* or striving to strengthen
the faith, on all believers (61,11) this was in turn interpreted as an obligation
on the faithful to offer their wealth and lives in holy war*. Muslims who died
on the battlefield were said to be guaranteed entry into paradise and exemption
from trial on the Day of Judgment (Qur'an 3, 163). In addition, the interpretation

of *jihad* as holy war was also seen as consistent with the central vision of the Qur'an of a single, worldwide Islamic state (21, 23).

The world was divided between *dar-al-Islam,* the realm of Islam, and *dar-al-harb,* the realm of war. Non-Muslims were offered the choice of free accession to the *umma* or military subjugation, and under the Umayyad caliphs of Damascus, the armies of Islam swept across North Africa, took Sicily and Spain, and were stopped from further advance into Europe only by their defeat at Poitiers in 732. Turning eastward, Muslim armies under Muhammad ibn Qasim penetrated into India. Yet, despite the interpretation of *jihad* as holy war, Islamic conquerors did not coerce those of other convictions into the faith, even though Islam is understood by Muslims as offering a total vision of life. This tolerance of Muslim caliphs and *imams,* or religious leaders, for other confessions exposes the conflation of the sacred and secular aspects of Islam. As long as non-Muslim, ''People of a Book''—mostly Jews, Christians, Buddhists and Hindus*—accepted the political control of Islam, they were allowed to retain their beliefs. Hence, Muslim rule in Spain and India represented tolerance, not persecution.

Unlike Christianity* and Judaism*, no distinction developed in Islam between a holy war and a just war. The doctrine of the *jihad* had become a definition of just war. Nevertheless, Muslim jurists such as Ibn Khaldun (1332–1406 C.E.) submitted the *jihad* to close analysis. In general, four kinds of holy war were recognized: defensive war, or the *ribat; jihad* against the People of a Book; *jihad* against polytheists; and *jihad* against Muslim apostates, dissenters, and bandits. For the most part, defeated polytheists, apostates, dissenters, and bandits were treated very harshly.

The jurists also laid down certain rules of war, some of which parallel those of the doctrine of just war. It was agreed that only the caliph or *imam* had legitimate authority to declare *jihad,* that war must be waged with good intention, that there should always be an invitation to accede to Islam before attack, and that noncombatants* should be spared unless they were indirectly helping the enemy cause. There was considerable controversy regarding other rules concerning the despoiling of crops and slaughter of animals, the poisoning of wells, the division of spoils, and suspension of warfare in the sacred months.

By the 20th century, many Muslims had taken the view that there had been a suspension of *jihad* as holy war. The spread of this view coincided with the rise of nationalism*, the deemphasis of the Qur'anic vision of a universal, theocratic state, and the division of Islam into separate states with national interests sometimes in conflict. Many Muslims interpret *jihad* as the striving of the individual for personal self-mastery and purification, a view consistently maintained by a tradition of spirituality within Islam, known as *Erfan* or Sufism and begun by Hasan of Basra (?–728). The Sufi interpretation is often supported by al-Jilani's (?–1166) reading of the Prophet's words, ''We have returned from the lesser *jihad* to the greater *jihad,*'' as meaning that self-mastery is more important than the conquest of external enemies. The quasi-pacifistic Ahmadiyya

movement (claiming about 10 million followers) interprets *jihad* further as en-
joining assistance for the weak and oppressed.

In the late 20th century, however, there has been a resurgence of Islamic
militants and Muslim fundamentalists who have reinvoked the militant interpretation of *jihad* by advocating holy war against secular governments "corrupted"
by Western influences. In this group one must include the Ayatollah Khomeini
and Islamic resurgents in the overthrow of the shah's regime in Iran, the assassination of Anwar Sadat by members of the radical *al-Jihad* group that had
infiltrated the Egyptian army, and the exploits of extremist Shiites in Lebanon,
including the terrorism of *Hizb Allah* (The Party of God). Militant interpretations
of *jihad* remain potent sources for ideologies of warfare in Islam. Their effects
may continue to be blunted by divisions within Islam itself (such as those provoked by Iraq), the prospects for peace between Israel and the Palestinians, and
resistance to neofundamentalist efforts for "re-Islamization" by Muslims
strongly influenced by beliefs in democracy, limited government, and human
rights*.

See ARAB-ISRAELI WARS; ISLAM AND WAR; JUDAISM AND WAR;
SABRA AND SHATILLA MASSACRE.

BIBLIOGRAPHY
Behishti, Muhammad Hosayni (Ayatullah) and Hujjatul-Islam Javad Bahonar, *The Phi-
    losophy of Islam* (Salt Lake City: Islamic Publications, n.d.).
Boulares, Habib, *Islam: The Fear and the Hope* (London: Zod Books, 1990).
Lewis, Bernard, *The Political Language of Islam* (Chicago: University of Chicago Press,
    1988).

Robert Paul Churchill

J

JAMES, ST., DECLARATION (JANUARY 1943). In anticipation that there should be war crimes trials after World War II and to avoid the difficulties faced by the Leipzig Trials*, some of the nations occupied during World War II joined in proposing that those guilty of war crimes should be punished through some channel of justice. Many international legal authorities raised doubts whether such a declaration rested on established legal traditions and whether conducting such trials would entail making rules after the fact. Current international law tradition assumed that criminal acts of war would first have to constitute crimes within the community where the alleged crimes had been committed, and it was further noted that by tradition individuals were not subject to international rules of war. Only states could be prosecuted; thus, capital punishment would be inappropriate. Resolution of these issues was required before the subsequent trials could be legally defended.

See CRIMES AGAINST HUMANITY; LAWS OF WAR; MOSCOW DECLARATION; NUREMBERG TRIALS; PEACE, CRIMES AGAINST; TOKYO TRIALS; WAR CRIMES.

BIBLIOGRAPHY

Appleman, John Alan, *Military Tribunals and International Crimes* (Westport, Conn.: Greenwood, 1971).

Manner, George, "The Legal Nature and Punishment of Criminal Acts of Violence Contrary to the Laws of War," *American Journal of International Law* 37 (July 1943).

JAMES, WILLIAM (1842–1910). The first distinguished American psychologist, he is also one of the most important philosophers the United States has produced. His lasting reputation rests primarily on three of his books: *The Principles of Psychology* (1890), *The Varieties of Religious Experience* (1902), and *Pragmatism: A New Name for Some Old Ways of Thinking* (1907). James is also well-known for an important essay, "The Moral Equivalent of War" (1910). These writings reflect what James called meliorism, a fundamental dimension of his moral philosophy.

Meliorism emphasizes three ideas. First, change and open-endedness characterize all existence. In particular, human experience is forever new and never duplicates itself exactly. The world that persons feel and know is not fixed and finished. It is the moving, growing result of interaction between human beings and their environments.

Second, freedom pervades human existence. Entailing ambiguity and risk, freedom means that human beings are incomplete and forced to struggle for identity and meaningful ways of living. Although no guarantees for success exist, freedom also involves opportunity. Human decisions affect the world and what humanity's place within it will be. Specifically, human beings can move the world toward ideal ends.

Third, the human heart beats with hope. No starry-eyed optimist, James knew that evil haunts existence and that life smells of death. Still, James had no use for pessimism. In a world of freedom, hope springs eternal. Hope means that the past and present are not good enough and that the future can be better.

James applied his meliorism in "The Moral Equivalent of War." That essay denies that human nature and history are structured deterministically. War has plagued human life, but James argued that war is not inevitable and that it can be eliminated. Pacifism* was one of James's ideals, but he recognized realistically that two major obstacles stand in its way. First, horrible as it is, war magnifies powerful goals. To defend one's country against threats or to extend its influence through maintenance of military superiority or overt conquest are causes that seem compelling to many people. Second, a militaristically oriented lifestyle and even war itself can provide demanding tests that require and produce courage, discipline, communal spirit, and endurance—virtues a nation must possess to assure its health.

While acknowledging how formidable those two perspectives could be, James disagreed with the naive and romanticized views of war on which they were based. Instead, he defended "the moral equivalent of war" by arguing that there are ample opportunities for the best ideals of a militaristic lifestyle to be cultivated by declaring war on human suffering, poverty, disease, and injustice. Anticipating the formation of agencies such as the Peace Corps, James believed that victory in these humanitarian battles, which requires the highest virtues of the militaristic lifestyle, not only would be the best defense of everything that human beings rightly hold dear but also could lead to the abolition of war itself.

See CAUSES OF WAR; HUMAN NATURE AND WAR; MILITARISM; MILITARY TRAINING, BASIC; PATRIOTISM.

BIBLIOGRAPHY

McDermott, John J., ed., *The Writings of William James* (Chicago: University of Chicago Press, 1977).

Myers, Gerald E., *William James: His Life and Thought* (New Haven, Conn.: Yale University Press, 1986).

John K. Roth

JIHAD. *See* CHRISTIANITY AND WAR; HOLY WAR; ISLAM AND WAR.

JOHN OF SALISBURY (1115–1180). Studied under Abelard (1136–1138), was secretary to Archbishop Theobald at Canterbury (1150–1164), was a supporter of Thomas Beckett and was present at his murder (1170), and became Bishop of Chartres (1176–1180). He was the author of a biography of Beckett and Anselm; *Metalogicus* (1159); and *Policraticus* (1159). The last dealt with matters of diplomacy and contained remarks on the relationship between the soldier and the Christian faith. He dedicated *Policraticus* to Beckett, in whose service he had worked for ten years prior to the latter's murder.

John supported the two-sword theory, one papal and the other secular, and he classed military service as on a par with religious obligation. Obedience to the king in war was equated with obedience to God, a relationship that has continued to the present and is reflected in part in the role of the military chaplain*. Like the religious chaplain, the duly ordained soldier's task was "to defend the Church, to assail infidelity, to venerate the priesthood, to protect the poor from injuries, to pacify the province, to pour out their blood for their brothers, and, if need be, to lay down their lives." Unlike their spiritual brothers, however, the soldier was to give his service independently of the worthiness of the cause. For this reason John emphasized obedience to superior orders* as a legal protection for the soldier who might be asked to do in war what would be a punishable offense in peacetime. Soldiers' actions were morally neutral. "It makes no difference whether a soldier serves one of the faithful or an infidel, so long as he serves without impairing or violating his own faith."

Were there no limits to what soldiers should do while carrying out the orders of their superiors? John dealt with the question in a chapter titled, "That Soldiers Are to Be Punished with Severity if in Contempt of Military Laws They Abuse Their Privileges." What might these contemptible acts be and what were the punishments prescribed? He included a prohibition against theft and rapine. Soldiers guilty of such deeds would be more severely punished than laymen, in view of the fact that soldiers were professionals. Other proscribed acts included luxurious living, intemperance, disobedience, and lack of discipline. The punishments ranged from loss of pay, reduction in rank, banishment to Sicily, or barley rations for up to seven years. Cowardice was commonly punished by opening a vein and withdrawing an excessive amount of blood. But what if the superior commanded a soldier to commit theft or rapine? John's answer was clear. "In the military there must be no questioning of the commander's orders. . . . If you bid me plunge my sword in my brother's heart or my father's throat, or into the womb of my wife big with child, I will do in full your bidding, though with an unwilling hand."

See CHRISTIANITY AND WAR; MILITARY AS A PROFESSION; MILITARY TRAINING, BASIC.

BIBLIOGRAPHY
Dickenson, John, trans., *The Statesman's Book of John of Salisbury* (New York: Russell
& Russell, 1963).
Keen, Maurice Hugh, *The Laws of War in the Late Middle Ages* (London: Kegan Paul,
1965).

JUDAISM AND WAR. Three attitudes toward war are that it is never, it is
always, and it is sometimes justifiable. They are epitomized by the absolute
pacifist*, a Clausewitz* or Machiavelli*, and the Medieval just war* doctrine.
Two types of just war are the secular, fought for humanistic values such as
freedom, justice, and equality, and the religious, fought for sacred ends in the
name of God. In actual situations the two types often overlap. Soldiers in World
War I fighting to make the world safe for democracy believed God was on their
side.

Pentateuchal Judaism, Islamic *Jihad,* and the Medieval Crusades exemplify
the holy war* type. Participants in "holy wars" believe that God is on their
side only, and that they have a divine mission, are carrying out God's will, have
a righteous cause, and God will ensure their success. They distinguish sharply
between good and evil, and see themselves as the former and the enemy as the
latter to be defeated and eliminated by whatever means necessary.

Pentateuchal Judaism illustrates the holy war model in several ways. The
Israelites who left Egypt and invaded Canaan believed that God revealed himself
and his will to Moses, selected the Jews as his chosen people, and gave them
the land of Canaan as exclusively theirs. Moreover, God not only led but actually
joined the Israelites in their violent, bloody conquest and devastation of Canaan.
Thus, the Canaanite conquest was a justifiable holy one, being sanctioned and
even participated in by God in order to secure the promised land for his chosen
people. The holy war syndrome surfaced recently in the Palestine-Israeli conflict
in the form of the Gush Emunim, a radical settlers' movement whose leaders
reiterated, vivified, and applied the tenets of Pentateuchal Judaism to the contemporary situation, substituting the Palestinian Arabs for the Canaanites of old
and insisting they be dealt with in the same harsh way.

Two groups opposed Gush Emunim fundamentalism: secular Jews sharing
the original image of a democratic, heterogeneous Israel, and moderate religious
Jews adhering to the broader Judaism of the later prophets. Both would have a
peaceful, pluralistically religious society. The Oz Vesham and Netivot Shalom
are two religious groups advocating compromise and peace with the Palestinians
and an end to the Intifada. Many secular Jews joined the broad-based peace
movement begun in the 1970s, whose followers supported Palestinians' desire
for independence, detested the atrocities of the Israeli occupation army and insisted on an end to military rule, rejected the good Jew/bad Arab stereotype,
lamented the increasing militarizing of Israeli society, and believed that the end
of a greater Israel encompassing Gaza, the West Bank and even the Sinai was

neither necessary nor historically and scripturally justifiable and that the means of achieving contravened the dictates of justice and morality.

Very much a minority in Jewish history is the absolute pacifist position that war is never justifiable. Some American Jewish conscientious objectors* were imprisoned in WW I for refusing military service and World War II saw a small number, as well. Prior to 1948 in Palestine, Nathan Chofshi and Joseph Abileah were two of a small pacifist group. Abileah opposed the formation of a Jewish state, supported the Bret Shalom and Kedma Mizracha groups promoting Arab-Jewish rapprochement, believed only moral means should be used to achieve moral ends, and refused both combatant and noncombatant* service in the Israeli army. Since Israeli law makes no provision for exemption from military service on conscientious grounds, refusal to serve is only occasional, such as the four Israeli youths whose open letter in July 1971 to defense minister Dayan refusing army service on grounds of conscience led to their imprisonment.

Between the two world wars a major peace movement, quite pacifist in nature, came into being worldwide and especially in the West, joined by mainline Protestant groups and the historic peace churches. Rabbis like Stephen Wise stood alongside Protestant and Catholic clergy denouncing war. British and American Jews joined the religious Fellowship of Reconciliation and the secular War Resisters' League International. The movement died out with the advent of World War II. Its Jewish adherents like Rabbi Wise modified or reversed their earlier stance, and Reform and Conservative branches of Judaism supported the war against Germany.

The holy and just war traditions dominate Judaic history. The first began with the Canaanite conquest and continued with the wars of the Judges and Kings, the Maccabbean wars against the Seleucids and later revolts by zealous Jews against Rome in 66 C.E. Two Medieval proponents were the 13th-century Nachmanides, whose apologist writings appealed to the Gush Emunim and the earlier poet philosopher Judah Halevi whose views, accepted by the Gush Emunim, were portrayed by a contemporary Hebrew University professor as racist, ethnocentric, anti-Christian and anti-Muslim. In contrast, Maimonides* (1135–1204), like Spinozoa (1632–1677), advocated a humanistic, rationalistic outlook. The Torah is not to be understood literally when it conflicts with reason. God is not a personal deity leading his followers in battle. Look positively at Muslims, as they are monotheists too. Restrain anger, avoid revenge, and follow Aristotle's golden mean.

The just war view appealed especially to sectarian Jews of the Diaspora in the modern era and those who had given up an orthodox but retained a nominal Judaism. They had been culturally assimilated, assumed civic obligations, and were influenced by the Enlightenment ideals of freedom, equality, and justice. Their acceptance of the view may explain in part Jews fighting for Prussia in the 1813 Napoleonic war and the American revolution and the forming of a British Jewish legion in World War I and a British brigade group in World War II. It may also explain the selective pacifism of 2,500 veterans of the Lebanon

1982 war who concluded it was unjust and whose refusal to serve there again led to a number being jailed.

Events since the 1940s have led some Jewish leaders to question the just war thesis and the use of force to resolve disputes. Rabbis criticized the Vietnam War. Einstein was horrified by the bombing of Hiroshima. David Lilienthal opposed the development of the hydrogen bomb. Reform Judaism, the Orthodox Jewish Congregations, and the Synagogue Council of America opposed Reagan's nuclear policies and the growing American nuclear arsenal. Jewish intellectuals like Alfred Lilienthal criticized the wars Israel fought since its 1948 formation as well as the latest Israeli-Palestinian confrontation. On the other hand, many Jews supported the Vietnam War and the development of nuclear weapons and their deterrence use, with Norman Podhoritz, *Commentary* editor, being one example. And Israel's actions have likewise received broad Jewish support inside and outside Israel, whether it be for the wars it fought (claimed to be defensive), or the development of nuclear weapons (supposedly for defensive use only). In summary, unqualified pacifism has been virtually nonexistent in Judaic history. The vast majority of Jews have supported what they believed to be either a holy or just war or a combination of both.

See ARAB-ISRAELI WARS; HOLY WARS; NATIONALISM; SABRA AND SHATILLA MASSACRE.

BIBLIOGRAPHY

Lilienthal, Alfred, *The Zionist Connection* (New York: Dodd, Mead, 1978).

Rosenwasser, Penny, *Voices from a Promised Land* (Willimantic, Conn.: Curbstone Press, 1992).

Shindler, Colin, *Ploughshares into Swords* (London: Y. B. Tauris, 1991).

Donald H. Bishop

JUSTICE, CAN BOTH SIDES HAVE? According to just war* theory, it is unproblematic that there may be wars in which one side acts justly and the other unjustly, and wars in which both sides act unjustly. What is problematic is whether there can be wars in which both sides act justly.

At stake in this issue is the just war theory's coherence. For to say that one side acts justly in war implies that the other acts unjustly, which would mean that if both are acting justly, then both are also acting unjustly. In that case, the war would be just and unjust at the same time, a conclusion that no one but an ethical relativist is likely to embrace.

But the question whether both sides can have justice can be understood in either of two ways: (1) Can both sides have a just cause? (2) Can both sides be acting justly, all things considered? Question 1 asks only whether, of the various conditions for justice in the recourse to war (*jus ad bellum*), both sides can satisfy the specific requirement of just cause. Question 2 asks whether all of the conditions justifying the resort to war (just cause, legitimate authority, right intention, etc.) can be met simultaneously on both sides.

Only question 2 raises directly the issue of the moral coherence of war. For even if both sides had a just cause, it would not follow that either side (much less both) satisfied all of the other just war conditions (both might, for example, still be acting unjustly by virtue of having evil intentions, in which case the war would be unjust all around).

But since both sides having a just cause is a necessary condition of their both acting justly in the sense of question 2, let us begin by asking whether question 1 can be answered affirmatively.

If one takes at face value most formulations of just cause, there is no obvious reason why both sides could not have a just cause. In representative formulations, Augustine* understands just cause as the necessity to avenge the violation of a right; the American Catholic Bishops more recently understand it as the need ''to protect innocent life, to preserve conditions necessary for decent human existence, and to secure basic human rights*'' (which implies there may be a just cause in going to the aid of others even if one's own nation has not been wronged).

Although they may assume it, these and similar formulations do not preclude the possibility that a nation that has been wronged by another (giving the first a just cause against the second), has itself also wronged the other (giving the second a just cause against the first).

But there is a paradox here. If to have a just cause against B, A must either have been wronged (or about to be wronged) by B, or have correctly judged that B is wronging (or has wronged, or is about to wrong) others—and vice-versa for B—then the very circumstances that give each a just cause would also put each in the wrong.

The two wrongs, of course, might not be commensurate, or sufficiently grave to give rise to a just cause (the Catholic Bishops' inclusion of ''comparative justice'' among the conditions of *jus ad bellum* suggests there may be varying degrees of justice on both sides). But if they are commensurate and sufficiently grave, just war theory does not expressly preclude the possibility that both sides have a just cause.

If each side should have a just cause, can each, as question 2 asks, also be acting justly on balance? In other words, can both meet all of the conditions of justice in war? It seems not.

Although both sides can easily satisfy the conditions of legitimate authority and right intention, they cannot both meet the conditions of probability of success, proportionality, and last resort.

For A to have a probability of success in war against B, it would have to be the case that B does not have a probability of success in war against A. And for more good than evil to be achieved by A's prevailing against B, it would have to not be the case that more good than evil would be achieved by B's prevailing against A. Can the condition of last resort ever be satisfied? A would have to have exhausted all peaceful alternatives to war, meaning it would have to have tried, and failed, to persuade B to settle their differences peacefully. But in that case, B would not have exhausted all peaceful alternatives, since it will, by hypothesis, have refused to accede to the peaceful solutions proposed by A. And if B has not exhausted all peaceful alternatives, then if it goes to war, it will not do so as a last resort. If, by hypothesis, *B* were also acting justly, then, of course, all of the foregoing considerations would apply on its side as well. In that case, *A* could not invoke probability of success, proportionality, and last resort, in which case it would not be acting justly, all things considered.

So although the answer to question 1 is yes, both sides conceivably could have a just cause (however unlikely that might be in practice), the answer to question 2 is no, all of the conditions of justice cannot be met on both sides at the same time. For that would be to say that each side is acting both justly and unjustly, on balance and in the same respect at the same time. And that would be to make wars in which both sides are acting justly extensionally equivalent to wars in which both sides are acting unjustly.

It is sometimes supposed that Augustine thought that both sides could have justice in war. But he does not say this. Indeed, he says in another connection (the treatise *On Lying*) that to say that the same thing is both just and unjust is absurd. In the 16th century, Victoria* and Gentili* maintained that in the strictest sense, war cannot be just on both sides. But they allow that there can be some sense of justice—what might be called a subjective sense, reflecting what each side believes, understandably or excusably, to be just—on both sides. By the 17th century, the issue seems to have been widely discussed, though not in great depth, and often with considerable unclarity. Suarez refers to the opinion that both sides can act justly in some circumstances, but he disputes that contention. Grotius* distinguishes different meanings of "just," saying that with regard to the thing itself, war cannot be just on both sides, because a moral quality cannot be given to opposites as to doing and restraining. Yet he also says that no one acts unjustly without knowing that he does an unjust thing, and so sometimes each side may justly "plead his case." While this stops short of saying that both sides can act justly, it implies a subjective sense of justice, reflecting conviction of one's justice, which may characterize both sides.

Stratmann is probably correct that until the end of the 16th century certain moral guilt was considered necessary to give one just cause to fight (where it was most likely assumed, though unstated, that such guilt on one side precluded it on the other). The relaxing of this condition gave rise to the possibility that there could be some measure of justice on both sides, as represented by the recognition of "comparative justice" as a condition of *jus ad bellum.*

There is little sustained discussion of this issue among late 20th-century writers, though Michael Walzer, in *Just and Unjust Wars,* expresses uncertainty about the coherence of what he calls the "moral reality" of war, an issue particularly relevant to his account of supreme emergencies. The point is that even in the course of waging a just war, one may have to do things that are morally prohibited. While Walzer stops short of saying this makes the war both just and unjust, and does not, in any event, say that war can be just on both sides, this provides a springboard from which arguments to those conclusions might be launched.

See AGGRESSION, ATTEMPTS TO DEFINE; JUST WAR; PATRIOTISM.

BIBLIOGRAPHY

Gentili, Alberico, *De Jure Belli: Libri Tres,* in *The Classics of International Law,* James
    Brown Scott, ed. (Oxford: Clarendon Press, 1933), 31–32.

Grotius, Hugo, *De Jure Belli ac Pacis Libri Tres,* in *The Classics of International Law,*
    James Brown Scott, ed. (Oxford: Clarendon Press, 1925), 565–66.

Holmes, Robert L., *On War and Morality* (Princeton, N.J.: Princeton University Press,
    1989), 150–52.

Pastoral Letter on War and Peace of the National Conference of Catholic Bishops, *The
    Challenge of Peace: God's Promise and Our Response* (Washington, D.C.: U.S.
    Catholic Conference, 1983).

Stratman, Franziscus, *The Church and War: A Catholic Study* (New York: P. J. Kennedy
    and Sons, 1928), 61–77.

Tucker, Robert W., *The Just War: A Study in Contemporary American Doctrine* (Balti-
    more, Md.: Johns Hopkins University Press, 1960), 98–101, 166–67.

Walzer, Michael, *Just and Unjust Wars: A Moral Argument with Historical Illustrations*
    (New York: Basic Books, 1977), 13–22, 304–27.

Robert L. Holmes

JUST WAR. The concept of just war has been a part of Western culture from its beginnings. Written accounts of war invariably include efforts to explain, defend, condone, or otherwise justify making war. Groups seem virtually incapable of mass armed violence in the absence of reasons for seeing their cause to be in the right. Throughout history, nations and leaders assert their righteousness as participants in war while questioning that of their enemies.

The long tradition of expecting and providing moral justifications for war and acts of war has continued, despite the absence of clearly universal value standards by which such judgments are made. In fact there is no consensus about value standards to this day. There is wide disagreement on who should make the judgments and on the standards by which they should be made. All that exists is a just war tradition, not a single precise and explicit doctrine of an international body, government, treaty, church, or moral theory. The tradition consists of generally accepted yet variously interpreted guidelines about morality and war that have been evolving for centuries. It involves broadly cultural values as well as narrowly religious, military, and professional elements; sources include ancient literature and philosophy, medieval theology, modern history, contemporary military codes of conduct, and the like.

The very earliest attitude about war seems to have been what is now called "war realism." It is the view that war happens outside of morality, that war is just a fact, a natural and normal activity, and that when war happens the best thing to do is win first and worry about being moral after the war is over. The old adage, "all's fair in love and war," is an effort both to exempt war from usual moral standards and to justify doing so on moral grounds.

Perhaps out of self-interest or perhaps out of moral recognition of the suffering of victims of war, moral restraint in undertaking and conducting war emerged early in history. Ancient texts such as Homer's epic *Iliad* reveal codes of conduct concerning rules of war. Cicero makes reference to the Amphictyonic Council whereby twelve Greek tribes united on an equal basis for the purpose of caring for Delphi, the religious center of the ancient world, and for observing rules of battle. This is the earliest known European organization dedicated to eliminating cruelty in war. In his *Republic*, Plato offers perhaps the earliest systematic theoretical account of war in which grounds for moral restraint in war are presented.

The fiercely independent city-states of the ancient Greeks were consolidated in the conquest of Alexander the Great, but the widest military domination of the Mediterranean world and Europe came as the Roman Empire swallowed the Greek world. From the end of the 2nd century until the fall of Imperial Rome at the close of the 5th century, the empire was constantly at war. While the early Christian church embraced pacifism* to the point of nonresistance despite Roman persecution of Christians, church and state united in embracing a notion of just war after Emperor Constantine's conversion in 313.

The teachings of St. Augustine* on war, developed near the beginning of the 5th century, became standards for the church for generations to come. They were built from the ancient codes of Cicero and Plato but with Christian additions. Killing and Christian love could go together for Augustine because salvation, not the life of the body, was of supreme importance. Attitudes, not actions, were the locus of right and wrong. Since the goal was to avoid hate, even destruction of the body may benefit the sinner. With just intent, war could vindicate justice. Fought without atrocities, war could create peace. Just as Augustine consolidated and built upon values from earlier generations, so his guidelines have been refined, extrapolated, and expanded into the broad cultural standards of just war operative today.

As it has evolved to the present, the western just war tradition is made up of two distinct but related themes: (1) the *jus ad bellum*, or moral justification for going to war, and (2) the *jus in bello*, or moral guidelines for conduct in war. Each involves several conditions to be satisfied. For a war to be considered just under this tradition, both the conditions which justify resorting to war and the conditions which justify conduct in war must be met.

The *jus ad bellum*, or justification for going to war, involves six distinct conditions: (1) the cause must be just, (2) a right authority must make the decision to go to war, (3) groups going to war must do so with a right intention, (4) war must be undertaken only as a last resort, (5) the goal of the war must be a likely emergent peace, and (6) the war must be proportionate, that is, the total evil of a just war cannot outweigh the good achieved by the war. Each of these conditions must be met independently prior to a decision that it is just to go to war.

Just Cause. The just war tradition maintains that aggression* is impermissible and that a war is justly undertaken in response to aggression. A use or threat of force by one state against the political sovereignty or territorial integrity of another constitutes aggression. Self-defense is the obvious rationale for going to war. But the principle of just cause has been extended to cover defense of another state against aggression, intervention to protect potential victims of massacre*, assisting secessionists, and even preemptive strikes against potential aggressors.

Right Authority. Historically, right authority meant legitimate decisionmakers of government. This has included, in varying contexts, heads of state, rulers, monarchs, presidents, generals, prime ministers, legislative bodies, and so on. Over the past few hundred years the principle of right authority has shifted from resting with single individuals to resting with the collective will of those people directly affected by the potential gains and burdens of the war in question. Revolutionary wars are justified by appeals to defense against exploitation and aggression, and by claims to rights of self-rule, as well as rights to security and freedom.

Right Intention. The only right intention for a just war is the will to right the wrong of aggression and to bring about peace. Intending revenge, domination, harm, cruelty, or personal or national self-interest are always wrong.

Last Resort. For war to be justly undertaken, all avenues for righting the wrong of aggression must have been exhausted first. The just war tradition presumes the moral abhorrence of war and insists that war must be avoided if possible.

Emergent Peace. The just war tradition requires that war be undertaken only if it is likely to generate conditions of lasting peace. Such conditions would have to set right the problems that provoked the aggression that broke the peace.

Proportionality.* Finally, war is taken up justly only where the total good to come from the war is likely to outweigh the total evil of making war. If the price of the projected war is too great in total dislocation, suffering, and death, including all human, economic, and cultural costs, in comparison to the good likely to come of it, again, considering all the likely gains, then the war is disproportionate.

Deciding when it is just to go to war, given these six factors, is a complex and difficult task. It is not a simple matter of measuring a proposed war against a formula. Many factors must be considered, and there is room for disagreement and difference in interpretation along the way. If agreement can be reached by the appropriate decision makers that conditions are met to justify going to war, then attention must turn to the conditions guiding conduct in war. That is, even if a war satisfies the conditions for justly going to war, still it is not a just war unless moral guidelines for conduct in the war are satisfied as well.

The *jus in bello*, or moral guidelines for conduct in war, consist of three parts: (1) discrimination, or the immunity of innocents, as governed by (2) double effect, or the intended results as distinct from those unintended, and (3) proportionality again, this time regarding specific acts within war rather than the overall proportionality of the war.

Discrimination. The principle of discrimination means that in just war, noncombatants should be immune from attack. It is always wrong to kill innocents, and participants in just war must discriminate between legitimate and illegitimate targets of acts of war. The notion of noncombatant immunity seems to have its origins not in moral sensitivity but in a code of chivalry from the Middle Ages. Knights were professional soldiers and there was no glory in taking arms against nonknights. Peasants, serfs, craftspeople, and merchants were sources of wealth to the knightly class. It was considered cowardly to attack a knight indirectly through attack on his servants, workers, and noncombatant subjects rather than engaging the knight directly.

Today it seems obvious that children, the elderly, and the infirm all are inappropriate targets of military action. Noncombatant immunity is not as easy as it may seem, however. Defense plant workers are usually considered legitimate targets, since they work for the war effort. The residential dwellings of ordinary people and their families have traditionally enjoyed immunity, but modern warfare has reached into neighborhoods of traditionally immune noncombatants on the grounds that they support the war.

Double Effect. The principle of double effect was developed by Christians in the Middle Ages to come to grips with the inevitable "spillage" of war. The basic thrust of the notion is that while the injury or death of innocents is always wrong, either may be excused if it was not the intended result of a given act of war. The point is that acts of war may have more than one effect: the intended effect is the injury or death of the legitimate military target; the second effect is the unintended injury or death to the innocent person whom it is always wrong to target (hence the term, *double effect*). As long as acts of war do not target and thus intend the injury and death of innocents, they may be excused as unintended or collateral* losses.

The principle of double effect is complex and provokes paradoxical difficulties. The use of nuclear weapons on Hiroshima and Nagasaki*, for example, may be said not to involve intending the injury or death of noncombatants, and thus the principle of double effect would justify hundreds of thousands of injuries and deaths. Yet such casualties were foreseen. It is difficult to grasp the distinction between unintended yet foreseen casualties.

Proportionality. Finally, the conduct of a just war is guided by the principle of proportionality. As in the justification of going to war above, the issue is one of weighing the evil of war against the good results to be gained by war. But rather than consider the total good and evil in the balance of going to war, here the consideration is with a given act, a particular campaign, a specific event contemplated as a part of the overall war. According to this guideline, each act must meet the proportionality test: Is it likely that the evil of doing a given act will be offset by the likely good to be gained from the act? If not, the act is disproportional and thus prohibited.

The elements justifying both the resort to war and the conduct in war fit together. A war is just only if all of both sets of conditions are met. If any condition goes unmet, the war is not justified morally. This means that even if all six of the *jus ad bellum* conditions are met, but the war cannot be fought under the guidelines of the *jus in bello* conditions, then the war is not just and thus should not be undertaken. The same can be said for wars that can be justly fought but fail to meet standards to justify going to war.

The just war tradition is a complex, subtle, living set of standards that has evolved over more than two thousand years and continues to evolve as wars present themselves for moral consideration. It is not a straightforward doctrine with clear and measurable conditions that can be tested empirically. The tradition itself gets various interpretations by different individuals for a variety of situations and purposes. Those using the tradition to justify or to deny justification for any particular war must interpret the complex set of interrelated principles, and in doing so they inevitably weigh various aspects of the tradition differently. While the tradition has provided a broad and general guide to considerations of morality and war, it cannot answer all questions definitively. People are left bearing the burden of having to make moral judgments of war. The just war tradition can help, but the final responsibility is ours.

See AUGUSTINE, ST.; CHRISTIANITY AND WAR; FORBIDDEN STRATEGIES; FORBIDDEN WEAPONS; JUSTICE, CAN BOTH SIDES HAVE?; MASSACRES; NATIONAL LIBERATION, WARS OF; NUCLEAR WAR; PROPORTIONALITY; TOTAL WAR.

BIBLIOGRAPHY

Bainton, Roland H., *Christian Attitudes Toward War and Peace* (Nashville, Tenn.: Abingdon Press, 1960).

Cady, Duane L., *From Warism to Pacifism: A Moral Continuum* (Philadelphia: Temple University Press, 1989).

Holmes, Robert L., *On War and Morality* (Princeton, N.J.: Princeton University Press, 1989).

Johnson, James Turner, *Can Modern War Be Just?* (New Haven, Conn.: Yale University Press, 1984).

Ramsey, Paul, *The Just War: Force and Political Responsibility* (New York: Charles Scribner's Sons, 1968).

————, *War and the Christian Conscience: How Shall Modern War Be Conducted Justly?* (Durham, N.C.: Duke University Press, 1961).

Teichman, Jenny, *Pacifism and the Just War* (Oxford: Basil Blackwell, 1986).

Walzer, Michael, *Just and Unjust Wars* (New York: Basic Books, 1977).

Duane L. Cady

K

KANT, IMMANUEL (1724–1804). German philosopher influential in the development of written codes for the conduct of warfare. The argument behind the concept of a war crime may have gotten its clearest philosophic analysis from Kant. In addition, his views of the role of war in human history, and of the problem of eliminating war, have been and still are matters of intense interest.

Perpetual Peace, published in 1795, held that since the object of war is to win a favorable peace, "some confidence in the character of the enemy must remain even in the midst of war, as otherwise no peace could be concluded and the hostilities would degenerate into a war of extermination." To maintain this level of confidence between belligerents, what he called "dishonorable stratagems" must not be used. Among such acts to be forbidden, he listed employment of assassins*, of poison, breach of capitulation, and incitement to treason. Each of these acts is forbidden under the Hague* and Geneva* Conventions. Kant's viewpoint on these matters is followed in the U.S. Army's manual, *The Law of Land Warfare** (FM 27-10), in which the purposes of the restrictions on warfare are explained in Kantian terms as facilitating the restoration of peace and safeguarding certain fundamental human rights*. (The manual also adds the purpose of protection from unnecessary suffering, something not mentioned by Kant.)

Kant insisted that a war of extermination can bring the destruction of both parties, and result in peace only "in the vast burial ground of the human race." Therefore, such a war and the means leading to it "must be absolutely forbidden." Obviously, atomic and nuclear* weapons would come under this heading.

Kant held that these dishonorable stratagems and "infernal arts, vile in themselves" would be continued in use after a war, and would undermine the peace. As an example of something of this sort that would continue after war, he mentions the use of spies*. A spy will lie and therefore undermine trust in his side. Early in *Perpetual Peace,* Kant stressed the need to avoid "bad faith" with the enemy. This point is also stressed in the U.S. Army manual at paragraph 49: ''Absolute good faith with the enemy must be observed as a rule of conduct,'' and again, in paragraph 453, ''in all non-hostile relations the most scrupulous good faith shall be observed by both parties, and no advantage not intended to be given by the adversary shall be taken.'' Against Kant's view, however, this manual and the history of warfare accept spying as a legitimate activity.

On the matter of eliminating warfare, Kant is quite clear. Nations cannot be allowed to remain in the present ''state of nature,'' relying on themselves for their protection. A world government, a League of Nations, must be created. Such a world government would have as its purpose only the prevention of war between states, not the administration of civil law in every state in the world. He gives a number of steps that can lead to such a world legal system, and to ''world citizenship.'' Among them: aggression* by one state against another; the use of mercenaries, and war on credit should all be forbidden; voluntary self-defense military exercises are acceptable but national standing armies should in time be abolished.

Kant held that the natural state of man is one of war. Peace must be established. While war has brought benefits, and he applauds those, it ought to and can be eliminated. He proposed that nations give up their savage freedom, adjust themselves to the constraints of public law, ''and thus establish a continuously growing state . . . which will ultimately include all the nations of the world.''

While Kant is well known for his strong opposition to exploiting individuals, to using them for purposes other than their own, and for formulating this as an absolute moral principle, the categorical imperative, his view of war may surprise readers. His philosophy of history regards conflict as a necessary means of progress. While asserting that war is the greatest source of the evils of our civilized world, he insists that ''In the present state of human culture, war is an indispensable means to the still further development of human culture.'' Wars will eventually force nations to ''step from the lawless condition of savages into a league of nations.''

Also surprising but understandable is his comment comparing the statesman and the general: ''Even in a fully civilized society there remains this superior esteem for the warrior . . . because his mind cannot be subdued by danger. . . . Even war has something sublime about it if it is carried on in an orderly way and with respect for the sanctity of the citizens' rights.''

Despite Kant's respect for the display of courage, his strong message is that we must work for ''the goal of world citizenship,'' and for a world government that ends the sovereignty and war powers of individual nations.

See CAUSES OF WAR; HUMAN NATURE AND WAR; PROPAGANDA.

BIBLIOGRAPHY

Axinn, Sidney, *The Logic of Hope: Extensions of Kant's View of Religion* (Atlanta, Ga.: Editions Rodopi, 1994).

Kant, Immanuel, "Conjectural Beginning of Human History," Emil L. Fackenheim, trans., in *On History,* Lewis White Beck, ed. (Indianapolis, Ind.: Bobbs-Merrill, 1963), 66–67, 121.

———, *Critique of Judgment* (Indianapolis, Ind.: Hackett Publishing Company, 1987), 121–22, 262–63.

———, *Perpetual Peace,* in *On History,* Lewis White Beck, ed. (Indianapolis, Ind.: Bobbs-Merrill, 1957), 85–90, 343–47.

U.S. Department of the Army, *The Law of Land Warfare* (FM 27-10), July 1956 (Washington, D.C.: U.S. Government Printing Office, 1988).

Sidney Axinn

KELLOGG-BRIAND PEACE PACT. *See* AGGRESSION, ATTEMPTS TO DEFINE; PARIS PEACE PACT; PEACE, CRIMES AGAINST.

KING, MARTIN LUTHER, JR. (1929–1968). Born in Atlanta, Georgia, his father was a Baptist minister. Many events in King's childhood influenced his indignation toward the segregation practiced in the U.S. South during that time. He recalled two such events: once when two of his white childhood friends were forbidden to play with him, and once when his father stormed out of a shoe store, angry at being forced to move to the rear of the store in order to make a purchase.

At fifteen, King began college at Morehouse College in Atlanta. At nineteen, upon completion of his studies, he continued his studies at Crozier Theological Seminary in Pennsylvania. During this time he experienced a crisis of faith. He was studying to be a minister but did not see how the teachings of Christianity could help to alleviate the plight of blacks in the South. He was both impressed and troubled by Nietzsche's critique of Christianity. When he came across the teachings of Gandhi, he believed he had found a thinker and person of action able to apply Christ's teachings at a political level. King admired Gandhi's ability to take the notion of turning the other cheek and of self-suffering, and to transform it into political action, into civil disobedience as Thoreau spoke of it. He also saw in Gandhi a man who genuinely practiced self-suffering for the sake of his own redemption and the redemption of others. These ideas all fitted closely with King's own sense of Christianity.

When he finished at Crozier in 1951 he went on for a doctoral degree at Boston University, where he met Coretta Scott, whom he eventually married. Upon completion of his studies in Boston, King moved with his wife to take a job as a minister in Montgomery, Alabama. Within a short period of time he became involved in the event that catapulted him to national recognition as a leader of civil rights for blacks in the United States—the Montgomery bus boycott.

As in many cities throughout the South, blacks were required to sit in the rear of buses, leaving the front seats for whites. The arrest of Rosa Parks, who one day decided not to give up her seat to a white man, sparked a boycott by blacks of the City of Montgomery's bus company. King emerged during the year-long boycott as the leader of blacks in Montgomery, the chief strategist for the boycott, and the chief negotiator with the city. The struggle was prolonged. At the end of one year, with the city on the verge of declaring illegal the car pools organized by the black community, the U.S. Supreme Court declared the bus segregation laws unconstitutional. The black community under King's leadership was able to negotiate an acceptable settlement with the city of Montgomery.

During the bus boycott, King and others helped to establish the Southern Christian Leadership Conference, a group dedicated to working to promote the dignity of black people throughout the United States. As leader of this group King worked during the 1950s to secure voting rights for blacks. In the 1960s he was involved in two major civil rights struggles.

The first of these was the effort to desegregate Birmingham, Alabama. Efforts to integrate lunch counters, bus stations, and retail stores in Birmingham eventually landed King in jail. There he wrote his most famous essay, ''Letter from Birmingham Jail,'' in which he defended his own actions and the principle of nonviolent civil disobedience on Catholic, Protestant, Jewish, and secular grounds. Eventually, business people in Birmingham were willing to make concessions to the demands of the black community. Following this successful campaign King gave the most famous speech of his career at a march for jobs and freedom held in Washington, D.C. during the summer of 1963. This was the ''I Have a Dream'' speech, which helped to inspire passage of the Civil Rights Act of 1964. In 1964 King earned the Nobel Peace Prize.

The second major civil rights struggle in which King was involved in the 1960s was the struggle to secure voting rights for blacks in Alabama. King's efforts to conduct a march on Selma were met with resistance by both police and private citizens. Eventually, through federal intervention, King gained the protection of the National Guard and completed the march. These events inspired passage of the Voting Rights Act of 1965.

Between 1965 and 1968 King turned his attention to what Gandhi had called the worst violence of all—poverty. King saw connections between the normal workings of the U.S. economy and poverty and between the war in Vietnam* and poverty. He became an outspoken critic of the war in Vietnam. He criticized black leaders who supported violence as a means for gaining rights.

When a protest march that he had led in Memphis turned violent, King, after leaving the city, decided to return there to help soothe tempers and restore calm to the city. The day after his arrival, after giving a speech that foreshadowed his death, King was shot to death as he stood on a balcony outside his motel room.

See CHRISTIANITY AND WAR; CIVIL DISOBEDIENCE; CONSCIENTIOUS OBJECTION; PACIFISM.

BIBLIOGRAPHY
Ansbro, John, *Martin Luther King, Jr.: The Making of a Mind* (New York: Orbis Books, 1982).
King, Martin Luther, Jr., *Stride Toward Freedom: The Montgomery Story* (New York: Harper & Row, 1958).
Peck, Ira, *The Life and Words of Martin Luther King, Jr.* (New York: Scholastic, 1968).
Barry L. Gan

KOREAN WAR. The war in Korea, 1950–1953, between its northern and southern administrations, saw the United States actively participate on the side of the south. Major hostilities broke out in June 1950. The Truman administration, saying that the north had invaded the south, convinced the UN Security Council to approve military action on behalf of the south, under U.S. command. The Truman administration's portrayal of the onset of the hostilities was, however, contested by Korea's northern administration, which said that the south initiated the hostilities.

Harry Truman further said that the north was encouraged to start the war by the Soviet Union, which did provide some material support to the north. After several months of fighting, Chinese soldiers entered the war on the side of the north. Truman portrayed the war as an effort by international communism to take territory.

The question of which side started the war has remained a matter of controversy. The fighting began along the 38th parallel, which divided the two sectors, at the parallel's western end, an area known as the Ongjin peninsula. For an invasion by the north, this would be an inappropriate choice, because it would lead the northern forces, after a few miles, to a dead end at the sea. For an attack by the south, however, the Ongjin peninsula would be a logical starting point, because it affords easy access to Pyongyang, the northern capital.

Although the southern administration, like Truman, said that it had been invaded by the north, it acknowledged a piece of evidence heavily relied upon by the north, namely, that one of the first actions of the fighting was the capture by the south of the northern city of Haeju, located five miles north of the 38th parallel. U.S. military intelligence confirmed that Haeju had been captured by the south, identifying the southern force as its 17th regiment.

The northern administration said that this occurred on June 23, two days before hostilities began all along the 38th parallel. The southern administration said that it took Haeju only on June 25. However, a southern admiral, Young Woon Lee, recounted some years later, having led the attack on Haeju, which is just one mile inland, that it was on June 23. The admiral also said that on June 23 the south's chief of staff ordered commanders to "go into action at 5 [A.M.], June 25" for a general invasion of the north. In order to divert attention from the south's planned invasion, said the admiral, the southern army started partial attacks beginning at 10 P.M. on June 23, including the attack on Haeju. The U.S. ambassador reported on June 26 that the northern army was withdrawing northward, all along the 38th parallel, a fact that suggests that the south attacked first.

Within a few days, however, the northern army took the offensive and rapidly moved south, capturing the south's capital city of Seoul. The north's rapid advance has been cited to prove that the north was the aggressor. The June 25 hostilities were not the first along the 38th parallel. Intermittent fighting had occurred throughout the previous year. Mid-1949 had seen major hostilities, mostly precipitated by the south.

When the United States approached the UN Security Council, a number of delegates showed hesitancy over the issue of who started the fighting. The delegates of the UK, France, India, Egypt, Norway, and Yugoslavia were concerned that the Security Council possessed too little information on the issue. In council session, Yugoslavia abstained on the resolution that condemned the north for aggression, stating that reports from the scene were too contradictory for a firm conclusion as to responsibility. It asked that the council hear a representative of the north before condemning it for aggression, but the council refused. The UK voted for the resolution but made the curious accompanying statement that the council should not take "action which might go beyond the bounds of the evidence" on the issue of who started the fighting.

In early 1950, the north was pressing its demand for reunification with the south. On May 30, southern president Syngman Rhee was marginalized politically when elections resulted in a parliament with a large anti-Rhee majority. This situation made it difficult for Rhee to maintain his position that the two Koreas should remain separate. Given this political situation, both U.S. and British intelligence estimated in early 1950 that the north had such good prospects of defeating Rhee politically that it was unlikely it would invade the south. In the spring of 1950, Rhee said he was planning to invade the north, and he moved troops to the 38th parallel.

On June 18, John Foster Dulles, a consultant to the State Department, told the national assembly of the south that if the north attacked, the United States would assist the south. This statement gave Rhee, failing politically, a motive to provoke the north to hostilities.

Truman attributed the north's alleged invasion to the "international Communist conspiracy." At the United Nations, the U.S. representative asked, "Can there be any doubt that the armed attack upon the Republic of Korea is part of a Soviet Communist plan of world domination?" adding, "The Communist masters of the North Korean puppets revealed by the attack their willingness to resort to armed force . . . to achieve imperialistic aims of world domination."

There is little evidence, however, that, even if the north was the aggressor, the Korean hostilities were part of a Soviet plan. In 1948 the Soviet Union had voluntarily withdrawn its postwar occupation force from north Korea, and after that it had supplied only outdated military equipment on a commercial basis and left only a handful of military advisors. As the fighting began, the Central Intelligence Agency (CIA) in Washington informed the National Security Council, in a secret briefing, that it had no evidence that the Soviet Union would support the north. The U.S. ambassador in Moscow, in a top secret cable to Secretary of State Dean Acheson, opined that the Soviet Union was "not disposed to enlarge the conflict into a general Asian or world conflagration."

In late June 1950, the Soviet Union was boycotting UN Security Council sessions because of the council's refusal to seat the mainland Chinese government as the representative of China. If the Soviet Union had plotted a north Korean attack on the south, it would not likely have absented itself, because the Security Council was sure to be a forum for discussion of the Korea fighting. The Soviet Union enjoyed a power of veto under council procedures, and its absence let the council condemn the north and set up a UN command to fight for the south.

A possible motive for President Truman's eagerness to send troops to Korea can be found in a policy paper written in April 1950 by his National Security Council and titled "United States Objectives and Programs for National Security." The United States had demilitarized rapidly after World War II. The paper, subtitled N.S.C. 68, argued that the United States must remilitarize rapidly to confront communism, less in Asia than in Europe. A war in Korea gave Truman access to congressional funding for a general remilitarization.

One major aspect of the Korean War was China's participation. In late 1950, poorly equipped Chinese fighters, called "volunteers" by China's government, entered Korea from China. This followed a push into north Korea, nearly to China's border, by U.S. troops. Since Truman was depicting the hostilities as a campaign by world communism, the Chinese government feared that he might send troops into China. Truman had recently declared that he would defend Taiwan if the mainland Chinese government tried to oust the Taiwan government headed by Chiang Kai-shek. This declaration suggested that the United States planned involvement in China's affairs. Gen. Douglas MacArthur, Truman's commander in Korea, fed China's fears by refusing to state that he had no intention of invading China.

China was also concerned about electrical generating stations in north Korea, just south of the Chinese border, that supplied much-needed power to China. A takeover of these stations by the U.S. forces would deprive southern China of electricity. MacArthur refused to issue an assurance to China about its electrical supply in the event that U.S. troops occupied the power stations.

The first troops that China sent into Korea occupied the area of the power stations, and a CIA analysis concluded that China's aim was the limited one of protecting its border and securing the power stations. After Chinese forces entered Korea, MacArthur attacked them, and President Truman threatened to use the atomic bomb against China.

There is little evidence to support Truman's portrayal of the Korean War as an advance by world communism. Even as to the genesis of the hostilities in June 1950, the historical record remains unclear. The war ended with no clear winners. Ceasefire talks began in July 1951 and continued with sporadic fighting until an armistice was signed July 27, 1953. U.S. troops have remained in South Korea and U.S. military and economic aid have continued.

See AGGRESSION, ATTEMPTS TO DEFINE; AGGRESSIVE VERSUS DEFENSIVE WAR; CAUSES OF WAR; TERMINATION OF WAR.

BIBLIOGRAPHY
"The Ambassador in Korea (Muccio) to the Secretary of State," June 26, 1950, *Foreign Relations of the United States 1950,* vol. 7, 165.

"The Ambassador in the Soviet Union (Kirk) to the Secretary of State," July 6, 1950, 9:00 P.M., *Foreign Relations of the United States 1950,* vol. 7, 315.

Committee for a New Direction for U.S. Korea Policy, *Conference for a New Direction in U.S. Korea Policy* (1977).

Cumings, Bruce, *The Origins of the Korean War: Vol. 1, Liberation and the Emergence of Separate Regimes, 1945–1947* (Princeton, N.J.: Princeton University Press, 1981).

———, *The Origins of the Korean War: Vol. 2, The Roaring of the Cataract 1945– 1950* (Princeton, N.J.: Princeton University Press, 1990).

Hastings, Max, *The Korean War* (New York: Simon & Schuster, 1987).

Kolko, Joyce, and Gabriel Kolko, *The Limits of Power: The World and United States Foreign Policy, 1945–1954* (New York: Harper & Row, 1972).

"Memorandum by the Director of the Central Intelligence Agency (Smith) to the President," November 1, 1950, *Foreign Relations of the United States 1950,* vol. 7, 1025–26.

"Memorandum of Conversations by Mr. Charles P. Noyes, Adviser on Security Council Affairs, United States Mission at the United Nations," June 25, 1950, *Foreign Relations of the United States 1950,* vol. 7, 144.

"Memorandum of National Security Council Consultants' Meeting," June 29, 1950, *Foreign Relations of the United States 1950,* vol. 1, 327.

"A Report to the President Pursuant to the President's Directive of January 31, 1950," April 7, 1950, *Foreign Relations of the United States 1950,* vol. 1, 234.

Ross, John C., U.S. Deputy Representative in the Security Council, "The Threat of Communist Imperialism," August 23, 1950, *Department of State Bulletin* 23, (1950), 380.

Stone, I. F., *The Hidden History of the Korean War* (New York: Monthly Review Press, 1952).

Truman, Harry S., "The Korean Situation: Its Significance to the People of the United States," July 19, 1950, *Department of State Bulletin* 23 (1950), 163.

United Nations Security Council Official Records, 5th yr., Provisional Verbatim Transcript, 473rd mtg., UN Doc. S/PV.473 (1950).

John Quigley

L

LAW OF LAND WARFARE, THE (1956, 1976). In May 1953, an Anglo-American conference in Cambridge, England considered revisions of the army manuals of the two countries. Major Richard Reeves Baxter, later a Harvard professor, was a U.S. representative, who ultimately wrote the new version that appeared in 1956. Reference was made to the Nuremberg* and Tokyo* trials, and a section on war crimes*, crimes against humanity*, and crimes against the peace* was included. No mention was made, however, of any of the declarations of the newly formed United Nations*. Ambiguity remained in the relation of military necessity* to the principles of humanity and chivalry. In spite of vast increases in chemical warfare weapons, article 38 stated that the Geneva Protocol of 1925* was not binding on the United States. This was qualified by a revision in 1976 to the effect that while biological weapons* were forbidden both in first use* and in reprisal*, chemical weapons were to be allowed in reprisal, although banned in first use. Although article 34 affirmed that it was forbidden to "employ arms, projectiles, or material calculated to cause unnecessary suffering," article 35 approved of the use of atomic weapons*; article 36 approved incendiaries* such as napalm and flame throwers; and article 38, even after its 1976 revision, accepted gas and chemicals as not causing unnecessary suffering. In spite of the massive development of aerial weapons, including the planes to carry them, the sections on bombardments, assaults, and sieges* remained in much the same form as in 1934. (This issue is discussed elsewhere in this volume under the headings Aerial Warfare; Biological/Chemical Warfare; and the Combatant-noncombatant Distinction.) The manual's sections on prisoners of war* were expanded to include the Geneva Conventions of 1949*. Work on a new revision is currently underway under the direction of Colonel W. Hays Parks.

See BULLETS, EXPANDING; FORBIDDEN STRATEGIES; FORBIDDEN WEAPONS; FRAGMENTATION BOMBS; INCENDIARIES; MASS DE-STRUCTION, WEAPONS OF; NUCLEAR WAR; PROPORTIONALITY;

RETALIATION, MASSIVE; SIEGE WARFARE; TERMINATION OF WAR.

BIBLIOGRAPHY

U.S. Department of the Army, *The Law of Land Warfare,* FM 27-10 (Washington, D.C.: U.S. Government Printing Office, 1956).

U.S. Department of the Army, *The Law of Land Warfare,* Change No. 1 (Washington, D.C.: U.S. Government Printing Office, July 15, 1976).

Wells, Donald A., *The Laws of Land Warfare: A Guide to the U.S. Army Manuals* (Westport, Conn.: Greenwood Press, 1992).

LAWS OF WAR. The assumption that there should be laws or rules of war is as ancient as Cicero, Aristotle, and Augustine*. Medieval church councils made reference to the existence of such laws. A brief review of the U.S. Army manuals since the first, in 1863, *General Orders 100*, evidences the nature of this belief and the grounds for it. *General Orders 100* stated that "the law of war imposes many limitations and restrictions on principles of justice, faith, and honor" (Article 30). *Rules of Land Warfare** (1914) affirmed (Article 1) that "the conduct of war is regulated by certain well-established and recognized rules that are usually designated as 'the laws of war,' which comprise the rules both written and unwritten, for the carrying on of war, both on land and on sea." The same phrase appeared in the 1934 version, and a similar formulation appears in the current *The Law of Land Warfare* (1976, revised)*.

On the matter of written sources, *Rules of Land Warfare* (1914 and 1934) stated that "during the past 50 years many of these rules have been reduced to writing by means of conventions or treaties entered into by the principal civilized nation of the world after full discussion at The Hague*, Geneva*, Brussels*, and St. Petersburg*." The list of some of these conventions (Article 3) includes some that the United States did not ratify, such as St. Petersburg, Brussels, and The Hague declarations forbidding projectiles that had for their "only object the diffusion of asphyxiating or deleterious gases," and the ban on dumdum bullets*. It was not clear whether the failure of a nation to ratify a declaration meant that it was not a law for that nation while remaining a law for those nations that did ratify. Indeed, the current U.S. Army manual, *The Law of Land Warfare,* continues the ambiguity by advising that "military commanders will be instructed which, if any, of the written rules herein quoted are not legally binding as between the United States and each of the States immediately concerned" (Article 7a).

The unwritten sources for the common law of war were affirmed by the 16th–18th-century jurists and by Professor Francis Lieber* to be customs and usages. Where nations, as a matter of practice, have tended to follow certain practices, we may refer to these as the "usages" of war. Where the usages have become virtually universally the case, we may refer to these as customs of war. From the 1914 Army manual to the present, such customs have been asserted to have been created within the limiting controls of military necessity*, the "principle of humanity," and the "principle of chivalry." Military necessity presumes that whatever is necessary to win a war cannot be denied by custom. The principle of humanity prohibits whatever is not "militarily necessary," and the principle of chivalry "denounces dishonorable means, expedients, or conduct." The section in the current manual on the "Force of the Law of War" states that all such lawmaking treaties were "binding only between the States that have ratified or acceded to, and have not thereafter denounced . . . and only to the extent permitted by the reservations." Laws of war, under this interpretation, appear to be misnamed, since they do not limit war but are themselves limited by military necessity.

See AERIAL WARFARE; BIOLOGICAL/CHEMICAL WARFARE; COMBATANT-NONCOMBATANT DISTINCTION; CRIMES AGAINST HUMANITY; FORBIDDEN STRATEGIES; FORBIDDEN WEAPONS; FRAGMENTATION BOMBS; INCENDIARIES; WAR CRIMES.

BIBLIOGRAPHY

Draper, Colonel G.I.A., "The Ethical and Juridical Status of Restraints in War," *Military Law Review* 55 (Winter 1972).

Keen, Maurice Hugh, *The Law of War in the Late Middle Ages* (London: Routledge & Kegan Paul, 1965).

Kunz, Josef L., "The Laws of War," *American Journal of International Law* 50 (April 1956).

Wells, Donald. A., *The Laws of Land Warfare: A Guide to the U.S. Army Manuals* (Westport, Conn.: Greenwood Press, 1992).

———, *War Crimes and Laws of War* (Lanham, Md.: University Press of America, 1991).

LEIPZIG TRIALS. At the end of World War I, the Allies appointed a "Commission on the Responsibility of the Authors of the War and on Enforcement Penalties." Articles 228–230 of the Versailles Treaty (1919) required Germany to turn over to the Allies suspected war criminals for trials by Allied tribunals. Reports were submitted by the delegates from Great Britain, France, Belgium, Greece, Serbia, Poland, Rumania, and Armenia to the commission, which in turn reported to the Paris Peace Conference on February 6, 1920. The Allies formally demanded the extradition of 896 Germans accused of violating the laws of war*. The commission report included the recommendation that acts that provoked the war and accompanied its inception, and violations of the laws and customs of war and of humanity, should be tried as crimes. Offenders, regardless of rank, would be liable for prosecution. A high tribunal was proposed, to consist of three members from each of the five major Allied powers, and one each from the rest of the Allied nations. Six questions were raised and answered by this commission:

1. Did Germany and Austria premeditate going to war? The commission reported that the Central Powers, together with their allies, Turkey and Bulgaria, deliberately com-

mitted acts in order to make war unavoidable, and that Germany, in agreement with Austria-Hungary, deliberately defeated all peace proposals. The commission determined that there had been premeditation.

2. Was the neutrality of Belgium and Luxembourg violated? The commission concluded that the neutrality of Luxembourg had been guaranteed by Article 2 of the Treaty of London, May 11, 1867, and had been violated by the penetration of German troops August 2, 1914.

3. Were there violations of the laws and customs of war? The commission ruled that the Axis powers had committed the following violations of the laws and customs of war: systematic terrorism*, murders, massacres*, killing hostages*, torture* of civilians, deliberate starvation of civilians, rape, abduction of women and girls for enforced prostitution, deportation of civilians, internment of civilians under inhumane conditions, compulsory enlistment of soldiers in occupied countries, the deliberate bombing of undefended places, collective penalties, deliberate bombing of hospitals, churches, schools, and historical monuments, the use of deleterious and poisonous gases, explosive and expanding bullets*, demand for no quarter*, ill treatment of prisoners of war*, and the misuse of flags of truce.

4. Who was to be held personally responsible? The commission concluded that no reason existed why rank or high position should relieve any from responsibility. Even though heads of state were immune in national courts, there was no reason why this should be the case in international courts.

5. What should be the proper procedure for an appropriate tribunal? The commission ruled that two classes of culpable acts should be prosecuted: the acts that provoked the war and violations of the laws of war and humanity. The offenses included crimes of omission as well as commission.

6. How should the tribunal be set up? The commission ruled that the courts should be in the country of the accused, and that all, regardless of rank, would be subject to trial; however, the consent of the offending state was required before its citizens could be tried.

The United States submitted a ''Memorandum of Reservations'' to the commission, explaining why it would not participate in the trial process. The reservations included the claim that the only courts legally entitled to prosecute the accused were military courts from the country of the accused; the United States did not approve of an international tribunal of the victors; and although the American delegates accepted that violations of the laws of war could be considered war crimes, they opposed the idea that there was a class of crimes against humanity*. They argued that the legitimate deeds of war were inhumane under any conventional interpretation, and that, thus, inhumaneness alone could not be an offense. The United States rejected ''negative responsibility,'' whereby a person could be tried for failing to stop some event, and that heads of state could be tried. While granting that from a moral point of view such heads of state were guilty, the United States insisted that no laws existed to support the effort to find them so legally. The U.S. report emphasized military necessity* as the primary defense for acts of war, and since the methods of destruction inherent in war are admitted to be cruel and contrary to normal decency, it followed that slaying and maiming by themselves were not sufficient cause for condemning acts of war. Furthermore, even wantonly cruel acts are excusable if the soldier who committed them did not know that the acts were cruel, or if he was following the orders of his superior*.

On February 3, 1920, a list of 896 alleged war criminals was submitted to Baron von Lersner, the German legate. He refused to accept the list. The list was then sent directly to the German government on February 7, 1920, but the Cabinet refused to turn over the offenders to German courts. The Allies finally agreed to accept an offer from the Supreme Court of the Reich of Leipzig to try a select number of the cases. Forty-five names were proposed, although only twelve were ever brought to trial: six were nominated by Britain, five by France, and one by Belgium. Chancellor Hermann Muller approved of a secret fund to pay the court expenses of the German defendants, and announced that his government had compiled a 381-page list of Allied war criminals that he might publish. Considerable German sentiment existed to condemn Allied war crimes, and during the fall of 1920 a retired army officer, Major Otto von Stulpnagel, wrote a book, *The Truth About German War Crimes,* which achieved national fame. The government of Germany never published a list of Allied war criminals. Seven of the German accused were found guilty and given sentences ranging from six months to four years. The rest were acquitted.

The Allied commission was so infuriated by these light sentences that they withdrew in protest and recommended on January 14, 1922, that no more cases be submitted. They proposed to try the cases themselves. Hundreds of Germans were tried and the issue of war crimes was emphasized as a diplomatic weapon to force the Germans to pay reparations. These trials ceased after the Locarno Treaty of 1925 improved relations with Germany. The French, however, continued a policy against those Germans who had been convicted of denying them entry into France as late as 1929. Three military concepts made the trials difficult to conduct: military necessity*, the right of reprisal*, and the obligations of soldiers to obey their superiors. No nation was expected to refrain from a militarily needed act of war on the mere grounds that it was an inhumane act. Winning a war was the soldier's business, and only cruel acts that had no military significance could serve as the basis for a charge. The right of reprisal against an enemy who had committed some violation of the laws of war was well established. Indeed, it was presumed that the reprisal act could be of the same kind as the first act that posed the offense. Thus, even the needless bombing of innocent civilians could be justified if it was in reprisal against an enemy who had done this first. Obedience to superior orders* was fundamental to military discipline, and the suggestion that soldiers should assess the orders that were given seemed alien. Unlike civilian life, where reservation or abstention were constitutional rights, the army insisted that it could not operate without unquestioning obedience down through the ranks.

The Allies, in particular the British, made an effort to punish Turkish war criminals, but made little effort to do the same for those in Austria, Hungary, or Bulgaria. Bulgaria did conduct a few trials, especially of the ministers of state who had led Bulgaria into the war. Authorities in Turkey court-martialed a few soldiers and the British imprisoned over 100 Turkish soldiers accused of crimes in Malta. While they were imprisoned for over two years, they were never brought to trial. By the time the nationalist revolution had put Mustapha Kemal Pasha in power, his government compelled the Allies to stop the trials. The Allies had urged Yugoslavia, Rumania, and Greece to prosecute Bulgarians for war crimes. The three Balkan countries urged the formation of a tribunal to be composed of seven judges (one each from Britain, France, Italy, and Belgium, and three from their own countries), but the Allies rejected the idea of any such international court. Later the Allies proposed that the Bulgarian courts try their own offenders, but the results were meager.

See BIOLOGICAL/CHEMICAL WARFARE; CASUALTIES OF WAR; LAWS OF WAR; *RULES OF LAND WARFARE;* SUPERIOR ORDERS; WAR CRIMES.

BIBLIOGRAPHY

Friedman, Leon, ed., *The Law of War* (New York: Random House, 1972).

Willis, James F., *Prologue to Nuremberg: The Politics and Diplomacy of Punishing War Criminals of the First World War* (Westport, Conn.: Greenwood Press, 1982).

LIBYA. *See* GULF OF SIDRA.

LIEBER, FRANCIS (1800–1872). The primary author of the first U.S. Army manual, *General Orders 100*: Instructions for the Armies of the United States in the Field* (1863). Born and educated in Berlin, Germany, he joined the Prussian army in 1815 as a volunteer, fought in battles at Ligny and Waterloo, and was severely injured in an assault on Namur. He served as a volunteer in the cause of Greek independence. He came to the United States in 1827. He was the initiator and editor of the thirteen-volume *Encyclopedia Americana* (1829–1833). From 1835 to 1856 he was a professor of history and political economy at the University of South Carolina, Columbia, and during his tenure there he published three major works: *Manual of Political Ethics* (1838–1839), *Legal and Political Hermeneutics* (1839), and *On Civil Liberty and Self Government* (1853).

In 1858 he was appointed Professor of History and Political Economy at Columbia College, New York City. As the acknowledged authority on the rules for guerrilla warfare*, insurrection, and rebellion, he was requested by General Henry W. Halleck to write, for use in the Civil War, a volume titled, *Guerilla Parties, Considered with Reference to the Law and Usages of War* (1863), and most significantly to be the primary author of a first U.S. Army manual for the guidance of soldiers in the armies of both the South and the North.

In 1865 he was selected as the superintendent of a bureau in Washington, D.C. to oversee the preservation of the records of the Confederate government.

In 1870 the governments of the United States and Mexico used him as an arbitrator in several important cases between the two countries. He died before finishing the tasks.

See *GENERAL ORDERS 100;* WIRZ, CAPTAIN HENRY.

BIBLIOGRAPHY

Davis, George B., "Doctor Francis Lieber's Instructions for the Government of Armies in the Field," *American Journal of International Law* (January 1907).

Freidel, Frank, "General Orders and Military Government," *Mississippi Valley Historical Review* 32, no. 4 (March 1946).

Lieber, Francis, *On Civil Liberty and Self-Government* (Philadelphia: J. B. Lippincott, 1877).

Root, Elihu, "Francis Lieber," *American Journal of International Law* 7 (1913).

LIMITATIONS, STATUTE OF. As trials under Control Council Law No. 10* wound to a close, the question arose as to whether a statute of limitations existed for alleged war criminals. If such a law did exist, then by 1952 any as yet untried criminals would be safe from prosecution. There is no statute of limitations for murder in the United States. On November 26, 1968, the United Nations General Assembly approved a resolution that ruled that crimes against humanity* and war crimes* had no time limit for their prosecution. The resolution, however, had little support from the member nations, with a vote of 58 yea, 7 nay, and 36 abstentions. No Western states, including members of the anti-Nazi coalition, signed, and only three Latin American states voted affirmatively (Chile, Cuba, and Mexico). Objectors feared that such a resolution would undermine traditional human rights*, and in addition it was unclear how serious offenses needed to be before the statute deserved to be waived. Nations could not be compelled to extradite accused persons, although, as in the case of the Eichmann trial, Nazi hunters continued to carry out prosecutions. The current efforts of the UN Security Council to conduct war crimes trials, while not affected by any statute of limitations, suggest that Nuremberg* may be believed to have set a precedent.

See CONTROL COUNCIL LAW NO. 10; CRIMES AGAINST HUMANITY; NUREMBERG TRIALS; TOKYO TRIALS; WAR CRIMES.

BIBLIOGRAPHY

Borchard, Edwin, "Editorial Comment: The Effect of War on Law," *American Journal of International Law* 40 (July 1946).

Bosch, William J., *Judgment on Nuremberg: American Attitudes Toward the Major War-Crimes Trials* (Chapel Hill: University of North Carolina Press, 1970).

Hankey, Lord, *U.N.O. and War Crimes* (London: John Murray, 1951).

McNair, Lord, and A. D. Watts, *The Legal Effects of War* (Cambridge: Cambridge University Press, 1968).

Schick, F. B., "The Nuremberg Trial and the International Law of the Future," *American Journal of International Law* 41 (October 1947).

Taylor, Telford, *Nuremberg and Vietnam: An American Tragedy* (New York: Time Books, 1970).

Wright, Quincy, "The Nueremberg Trial," *Journal of Criminal Law and Criminology* 37 (March 1947).

LONDON AGREEMENT ON WAR CRIMINALS (1945). In World War II, the Allied governments issued a number of declarations of their intent to prosecute and punish war criminals. On October 7, 1942, the Allies announced that a UN War Crimes Commission would be established. This was done on October 20, 1943. The Moscow Declaration* of October 30, 1943, attended by the United Kingdom, the United States, and the USSR, stated that the German war criminals would be judged and punished in the countries where their crimes had been committed, while "major criminals" whose offenses crossed national borders would be punished by a joint decision (the Nuremberg trials*). This decision was drafted at a London conference conducted by France, the USSR, the United Kingdom, and the United States, June 26–August 8, 1945. An additional international tribunal for the Far East was established by a special proclamation by Gen. Douglas MacArthur in 1948.

The London agreement contained seven articles, which provided for an international military tribunal that would follow the jurisdiction and functions set out in the charter annexed to the agreement. The tribunal would prosecute those accused of crimes that had "no particular geographical location." Governments of the United Nations were urged to adhere to the agreement. Article 7 stated that the duration of the agreement would be for one year. The tribunal would consist of four members (each with an alternate), with the presence of all four required to constitute a quorum. Conviction required a majority vote, and in the event of a tie, the president of the tribunal would cast the deciding vote. Annexed to the agreement was a charter that contained the constitution that determined how the tribunal would operate. Articles 1–4 established the membership of the tribunal. Article 6 identified the three offenses as crimes against the peace*, war crimes*, and crimes against humanity*. Articles 7–12 established that both individuals and organizations may be established as criminal. Articles 14–24 outlined the judicial procedures. Articles 26–29 affirmed that the judgments of the tribunal would be final and not subject to review. The four major Allied nations became signatories August 8, 1945, and by December 22, 1945, nineteen other governments had acceded to the proceedings.

See CONTROL COUNCIL LAW NO. 10; NUREMBERG TRIALS; SHIMODA CASE; STOCKHOLM/ROTHSKILDE WAR CRIMES TRIAL; TOKYO TRIALS.

BIBLIOGRAPHY
Friedman, Leon, ed., *The Law of War,* vol. 2 (New York: Random House, 1972), 883–93.

LOW-INTENSITY CONFLICT. The expression was created during the Reagan administration to separate small-scale wars like Grenada*, Nicaragua*, Afghanistan, Cambodia, and Panama*, the air strikes on Libya, and the occupation of Beirut, Angola, El Salvador, and the Philippines, from a "mid-intensity" conflict like Korea* or the Gulf War*, and a "high-intensity" conflict like World War II. A commitment was made to develop special military forces to engage in these small wars, sometimes called "frontier wars," and during the Bay of Pigs incident* called "subliminal warfare." *U.S. Army Operational Concept for Low Intensity Conflict,* published by the Army Command and General Staff College, defined low-intensity conflict as "a limited politico-military struggle to achieve political, social, economic, or psychological objectives," a definition accepted by the Joint Chiefs of Staff in 1986.

On January 18, 1962, President John F. Kennedy authorized the formation of a new Cabinet-level body for "Counter-Insurgency." This body first consisted of Attorney General Robert Kennedy; Maxwell Taylor, Chairman of the Joint Chiefs of Staff; John A. McCone, the director of the Central Intelligence Agency (CIA); the heads of the U.S. Information Agency (USIA) and the Agency for International Development (AID); and Averill Harriman for the Department of State. An International Police Academy was formed and met in an old streetcar barn in Georgetown, at which senior police officers from client states received training in counterinsurgency. At its peak in 1969, the program had a budget of $37 million and maintained training and advisory missions in about forty countries. The academy was phased out by Congress in 1974 amid charges that it was involved in terrorism and the repression of political dissent.

In 1985 a two-volume, thousand-page *Final Report* was published on the concepts, strategies, and guidelines of low-intensity war fighting doctrine in the Third World. In January 1986, Caspar Weinberger, secretary of defense, hosted the Pentagon's first Low-Intensity Warfare Conference at the National Defense University at Fort Leslie J. McNair in Washington, D.C. The same month an Army/Air Force Center for Low-Intensity Conflict was established "to improve the Army/Air Force posture for engaging in low-intensity conflict." Lieutenant Colonel Oliver North was director of the National Security Council's Counterterrorism and Low-Intensity Warfare Group. This led to the formation of Special Operations Forces (SOF) like the Army's Green Berets; the Navy's SEALs; the 160th Army Aviation Task Force, Night Stalkers; and the CIA Delta Force.

Robert S. McNamara, secretary of defense under Presidents John F. Kennedy and Lyndon Johnson, saw such limited war as a promising way to deter Communist aggression without "the necessity of arousing the public ire." Since such forces were usually sent clandestinely without congressional input, such actions undermined the democratic checks and balances process and involved a reckless disregard of customary international law. Low-intensity conflicts had the advantage from the perspective of the Pentagon that they would not have to be defined as wars, no draft would be required, fewer soldiers would be involved, and hopefully there would be fewer American casualties. On the negative side, however, by evading congressional oversight, being secret from the press and the public, advocating assassination*, violating Geneva* and UN Charter concerns, and almost by definition being aligned with right wing dictatorships, plans for such low-intensity conflict undermined the American democratic processes.

See GRENADA, U.S. INVASION OF; NICARAGUA, U.S. INTERVEN-

TION IN; PANAMA, U.S. INVASION OF (OPERATION JUST CAUSE);
RUSES OF WAR; TERRORISM.

BIBLIOGRAPHY
Barnet, Frank, ed., *Special Operations in U.S. Strategy* (Washington, D.C.: National
    Defense University Press, 1984).
Cable, Larry E., *Conflict of Myths: The Development of American Counterinsurgency
    Doctrine and the Vietnam War* (New York: New York University Press, 1986).
Johnson, W. P., and E. N. Russell, *Strategic Studies Project: U.S. Army Strategy for
    Low-Intensity Conflict* (Washington, D.C.: Industrial College of the Armed
    Forces, 1985).
Klare, Michael T., and Peter Kornbluh, *Low Intensity Warfare* (New York: Pantheon,
    1988).

LUTHER, MARTIN (1483–1546). In an essay, "That Soldiers, Too, Can Be
Saved," Luther insisted that God had no more difficulty saving soldiers than
saving priests. He remarked that "although slaying and robbing do not seem to
be the work of love . . . yet in truth even this is a work of love," and he affirmed
that "the hand that wields the sword is not really man's but God's." It is God
who really "hangs, tortures, beheads, slays, and fights." Luther had a long
scholastic tradition behind him in favor of viewing war as universal, rational,
and in accord with the spiritual life. However, he opposed religious crusades
and doubted that priests and bishops should bear the sword. Christian laymen,
however, lived in both worlds and they must wield the sword whenever their
earthly prince commanded.

Luther's views have been open to a wide variety of interpretations. Some
have maintained that Luther paved the way for the secular control of religion,
which reached a culmination in the fascist state (he recommended burning Jewish synagogues, and either making slaves of Jews or banishing them). Others
asserted that he established the way for the democratic separation of church and
state. Still others held that he was a medievalist at heart and that his position
reflected no change from the prevailing Roman Catholic one of his day. A
review of Luther's writings would seem to indicate that he held successively
different views. In 1520, when he issued his *Address to the Christian Nobility,*
he seemed confident that an appeal to them would protect the Lutheran Church
against Roman Catholicism. At this period he favored integration of church and
state as being in the interests of religion. In 1523, when he published his book,
Concerning Secular Authority, he seemed disillusioned with integration and favored a separation of the church from the state. This disillusionment came after
the judgment was issued against him at the Diet of Worms in 1521. While he
was suspicious of entrusting matters of religion to any emperor, he did state that
religious persons ought to be obedient to their secular rulers. He later proposed
that under special circumstances rebellion against the emperor might be warranted, even to the point of war. He did not, however, support the peasants in
their rebellion. A fourth position reasserted the sanctified status of the secular

ruler, and appealed in support of this to the fourth Mosaic commandment in support of the idea that secular powers were divine and holy. He agreed with Plato, Aristotle, and Cicero that the state is responsible, not only for enforcing laws, but for making the citizens moral, improving their character, and curbing their passions, and thus, he presumed secular government to be an earthly Kingdom of God.

See CHRISTIANITY AND WAR; PACIFISM; SUPERIOR ORDERS.

BIBLIOGRAPHY

Koenigsberger, H. G., ed., *Luther: A Profile* (New York: Hill & Wang, 1973).

Luther, Martin, *Works* (Philadelphia: A. J. Holman, 1915–1932).

Oberman, Heiko A., *Luther: Man Between God and the Devil* (New Haven, Conn.: Yale University Press, 1982).

M

MACHIAVELLI, NICCOLO (1469–1527). Machiavelli's writings were consistently lacking in ethical or moral concerns, yet his reflections gave important insight into the realpolitik presumptions of most political discussion. Starting with the premise that men were bad and would not observe good faith, it followed that princes who would succeed had best learn the art of deceit and the art of war. He concluded that "all armed prophets have conquered and unarmed ones failed." War was the only art that was necessary for one who would command, and a strong army was the only adequate defense. Since the army was the life's blood of a healthy and strong nation, the wise leader should be lenient in punishing its generals for their excesses. Since the safety of a country depended on its army, and since the defense of the country was always good, "no matter whether effected by honorable or ignominious means . . . no considerations of justice or injustice, humanity or cruelty, nor glory or of shame, should be allowed to prevail."

See DEMOCRACY AND THE MILITARY; HOBBES, THOMAS; MILITARY AS A PROFESSION; MILITARY TRAINING.

BIBLIOGRAPHY

Butterfield, Herbert, *The Statecraft of Machiavelli* (New York: Macmillan, 1956).

Fleischer, Martin, ed., *Machiavelli and the Nature of Political Thought* (New York: Atheneum, 1972).

Gilbert, Allan H., *Machiavelli's Prince and Its Forerunners* (New York: Barnes & Noble, 1938).

MAIMONIDES, MOSES (1135–1204). A Jewish philosopher who studied under Arabic scholars, in 1148 he emigrated from his birthplace, Cordoba, Spain, to Cairo, where he was the physician to Saladin, the sultan of Egypt, and served as the rabbi of Cairo. In his *Guide for the Perplexed* he discussed, as one of the three evils of man, evils that people do to each other. He remarked, surprisingly, that this kind of evil was not widespread in any country in the whole world. He remarked, "It is of rare occurrence that man plans to kill his neighbor or to rob him of his property."

His comments on war raised no ethical questions and he supported the right of the king to wage both "primary" and "optional" wars. Primary wars were those waged for a religious cause. In the case of such a war the king need not seek any sanction from the court. "He may at any time go forth of his own accord and compel the people to go with him." Optional wars were those waged to extend the boundaries of Israel and "to enhance his [the king's] greatness and prestige." In such a war, however, the king must have the sanction of the court of seventy-one.

See JUDAISM AND WAR.

BIBLIOGRAPHY

Maimonides, Moses, *Guide for the Perplexed* (New York: Dover, 1956).

MANUALS, U.S. ARMY. *See GENERAL ORDERS 100; RULES OF LAND WARFARE; THE LAW OF LAND WARFARE.*

MAOISM AND WAR. Early Chinese culture was molded by three major schools of thought, Confucianism, Taoism* and Buddhism. Two minor schools, Moism and Legalism, existed also. Mo Tzu (c. 400 B.C.), "the first pacifist statesman in history," advocated universal, equalitarian love: Love all people equally, others' parents as much as your own, others' children as much as your own, people in other states as much as those in yours. Mo-tzu argued that partiality was the chief cause of wars and human suffering; a universality of outlook and action was the only sure remedy. Obviously such a view led to the condemnation of interstate rivalry and wars of aggression. Moism flourished for two centuries and then languished because of circumstantial and ideological reasons. The Legalists, the Machiavellians* of ancient China, became predominant in the warring states period, when heads of states vied to form an empire. The last and most prominent was the Chin dynasty (221–206 B.C.), which ruled by military force, absolute power, intrigue, harsh laws, and punishment and reward. This led to the alienation of the people, a revolt, and Chin's and the Legalists' eclipse.

Mao Tse-tung (1893–1976) was born into a peasant family in Hunan province. His father was a Confucianist, his mother a devout Buddhist from whom Mao inherited the Buddhist ethic of caring and compassion. At the village school he learned the Confucian classics by heart. From 1913 to 1918 Mao attended two Changsha normal colleges, where he read and admired the writings of Liang Chi-chao and the idealist-universalist Kang Yu Wei, and took part in revolutionary political activities. When he was young he came under the influence of the patriotic and pragmatic school of Wang Fu-chih and took the side of poor peasants in his district when they revolted during a famine.

In 1920 Mao organized and became secretary of the first Communist group in Hunan province and attended the first Congress of the Chinese Communist Party in 1921 as the Hunan representative. He was elected to the Central Committee at the third Congress in 1924, and became the party chairman in 1925.

In 1930 his wife Yang Kai-hui was executed by the nationalist Kuomintang. Following the Nationalists' defeat and retreat to Taiwan in 1945 he proclaimed the establishment of the People's Republic of China.

Mao was neither a Moist nor Legalist. His attitude toward war is seen in his statement that "there are only two kinds of war in history, just* and unjust," that "we support just wars and oppose unjust wars," and that "all counter-revolutionary wars are unjust, all revolutionary wars are just." This means that Mao and his countrymen who fought in the Opium Wars, the Taiping and Boxer Rebellions, and the anti-Japanese and other wars were fighting just wars, since they were wars of revolt against nations who had forced, or were attempting to force, themselves upon China or wars seeking freedom from a foreign yoke, just as was the American revolt against British control. On the other hand, those seeking to retain their control by putting down any revolt through war or force were fighting an unjust war. From Mao's remarks above we can see that two of the just war criteria developed in the West are met: right intention and self-defense. The intent was the freeing of China from foreign rule, and obviously China was fighting defensive wars, since it was being invaded rather than invading.

A third just war criterion is proportionality*. To be just, a war must be fought with as small a loss of life and destruction of property as possible. The more excessive a war becomes, the less just it is. How is Mao to be appraised in regard to this? On the one hand we find statements in the *Christian Century* (October 1959) that the first decade of the revolution in China had cost 15 or 20 million lives and in a 1970 issue of the *New York Times* that Mao "had slaughtered, exiled and imprisoned more than the total number of people killed and mutilated by Stalin and Hitler combined."

Hensman suggests that such statements are the exaggerations of the McCarthy era, made by a hostile press of a hostile nation when negative, stereotyped views of China dominated the West and America especially. Such statements could not be based on evidence, since Americans were not allowed in China from 1949 to 1978, and other sources put the figures much lower. It should also be noted that there was much violence and killing by Japan and Western powers in pre-Maoist China, and that Chiang and his armies killed large numbers of Chinese. Hensman admits that there undeniably was violence and killing, but concludes that "the violence does not appear to have been out of proportion, given the magnitude of the revolution and the external threats to the new regime." [Robert McNamara, for example, calculated openly that "a single nuclear attack on China would dispose of 50 million Chinese."]

In regard to proportionality and the loss of lives in a war, Mao himself wrote that "Of all things in the world, people are the most precious"; "A revolution is not a dinner party but is an uprising, an act of violence whereby one class overthrows another"; and "As far as our own desire is concerned, we do not want to fight, even for a single day. But if circumstances force us to fight, we can fight to the finish." From the above and many similar statements found in

Mao's writings we may conclude, now that we are beyond McCarthyism, the China lobby, and the China-bashing period, the Cold War*, and Vietnam*, that Mao, if a warrior, was a reluctant one. He did not relish or glorify war. It was to be fought only if necessary and as a last resort, with as little loss of life and destruction as possible. Violence was to be viewed as a temporary expedient, a necessary means to good ends and turned to only under unusual circumstances. It was the final means of dealing with those who, benefiting from the status quo, would do anything to defend it.

A realist in regard to means, Mao was an idealist in terms of ends. Not only from Marx but even more from the idealist and universalist Kang Yu-wei, Mao conceived of utopia, the "realm of the Great Harmony," as the ultimate goal to be reached. Mao was one of a number of Chinese in the 19th and 20th centuries involved in a "self-strengthening movement." Their goal was a unified, prosperous China, free from foreign domination and taking its rightful place in the world. Mao empathized with Third World countries undergoing revolutions like China's and thus deserving of China's support. He shared the aspirations of the Chinese people and the ethical tradition he inherited from his Confucianist father, Buddhist mother, and the Chinese peasants of caring, compassion, benevolence, mutuality, helpfulness, unselfishness, honesty, persistence, simplicity, and hard work. Although his revolutionary zeal made him intransigent to most criticism, he continued and exemplified the Chinese political tradition of the centralization of power, the morality of the ruler, and government's function of serving the people.

See BUDDHISM AND WAR; CAUSES OF WAR; MARXISM AND WAR; TAOISM AND WAR.

BIBLIOGRAPHY

Hensman, C. R., *Yellow Peril; Red Hope* (London: SCM Press, 1968).

Rejai, M., *Mao Tse-tung on Revolution and War* (Garden City, N.Y.: Doubleday, 1969).

Donald H. Bishop

MARTENS CLAUSE (1899). Although the laws of war had been formally elaborated in international agreements such as those at St. Petersburg*, Brussels*, Geneva*, and The Hague*, it was never intended that the existing list would exhaust or displace customary law. The Martens Clause, which first appeared in the preamble to the 1899 Hague Convention II, was intended to emphasize that much of the law with respect to war still rested on customary practices. This clause emphasized that laws of war were not limited to what had been documented in treaties:

Until a more complete code of the laws of war is issued, the high contracting Parties think it right to declare that in cases not included in the Regulations adopted by them, populations and belligerents remain under the protection and empire of the principles of international law, as they result from the usages established between civilized nations, from the laws of humanity, and the requirements of the public conscience.

Fedorovich Martens (Frederic Frommhold Martens), 1845–1909, was a professor of law at the Imperial Alexander Lyceum and a member of the Russian delegation to The Hague Conference of 1899.

See HAGUE, THE, CONGRESSES; *LAW OF LAND WARFARE, THE;* LAWS OF WAR.

BIBLIOGRAPHY

Scott, James Brown, ed., *The Hague Conventions and Declarations of 1899 and 1907* (New York: Oxford University Press, 1915).

MARXISM AND WAR. Disciples of Karl Marx (1818–1883), like those of Jesus, represent no univocal position on issues of war and peace. During World War I, many Marxists went to war in their respective countries while others served time in prisons as conscientious objectors*. American socialists were similarly divided in World War II. The American Socialist Party, traditionally pacifist*, opposed going to war, while the American Communist Party sold war bonds and urged its members to enlist. Where did Marx and the earlier disciples stand on the matter of war and ethics?

At almost every congress of the two Internationals between 1864 and 1914, the question was raised: "What should be the attitude of the working man toward war?" Marx felt keenly enough about the question to propose at the London planning session in 1864 that an antiwar plank be included in the platform of the First International. In a speech of July 23, 1870, Marx reaffirmed his basic thesis that wars under capitalism would always promote a "playing upon national prejudices, and squandering in piratical wars the people's blood and treasure." In *The Civil War in France* he had announced, "Let our voices unite in one cry of reprobation against war." But was this sentiment more than a bit of doctrinal rhetoric? The record is not unequivocal.

Item 8 on the agenda of the Lausanne Congress of the First International, September 2–8, 1867, raised the question again of the place of the working man. Since the members at that congress had been invited to send delegates to a further peace congress in Geneva on September 9, the delegates took the occasion to make two points: (1) war is a bourgeois tool for the exploitation of the proletariat, and (2) it makes sense, however, before capitalism has been abolished, to work for the end of war through the abolition of standing armies, the maintenance of peace, and the freeing of the workers from the power of capital. Marx was not present at this congress when these two items were voted on. His reaction was one of incredulity that any socialist could imagine that war could be diminished without first abolishing capitalism. He referred to this Geneva group as "these peace windbags." At the congress at Brussels, September 6–15, 1868, the first item of concern was again, "what should be the attitude of the workers in the event of war between the European powers?" The delegates made two points: (1) since the cause of war is the capitalist economic system, communists should call a general strike against going to war; and (2) such a strike could end war, even though the economic system remained capitalist. Marx was equally displeased with this vote, which he called a piece of "Belgian stupidity." Marx believed that the proletariat were not sufficiently well organized to succeed in a general strike. The patriots of their respective countries would martyr them and nothing would have been accomplished.

When war did break out in 1870 Marx wrote a manifesto, signed by all the members of the General Council, asserting that Germany was fighting a war of self-defense, while France was fighting a war of aggression*. German socialists generally supported their country until the French were defeated. But when Germany attempted to annex Alsace, after the French defeat, many German socialists resisted their government. Friedrich Engels (1820–1895) felt so strongly that Germany was in the wrong that he offered his services to the French army. French socialists reacted similarly, except in reverse order. In the case of the war in 1870, both Marx and Engels conceded that the capitalist countries, Germany and France, could wage legitimate wars of self-defense. That they could also wage dynastic wars was equally conceded. Thus, German and French proletarians killed each other.

Not all German socialists held this view. Wilhelm Liebknecht (1826–1900), for example, voted against German war credits to show his antagonism to Prussianism. Auguste Bebel (1840–1930), on the other hand, fearing that such a vote would be interpreted as a vote for Bonapartism, persuaded Liebknecht to join him and refrain from voting altogether. Karl Kautsky (1854–1938) and Otto Bauer (1881–1938) rejected the war as a clear case of bourgeois oppression of the proletariat, while Lasallean socialists followed the recommendations of Marx and Engels and voted for war credits.

At the Brussels Congress of the Second International in 1891, the question of the workingman and war arose again. The general sentiment of the congress was to support verbal protest only. Although the Dutch delegation moved that all socialists declare a general strike, of the sixteen nations present only the Dutch, French, and British delegations supported the motion. No congress down to 1914 at the outbreak of the war had majority support for any action save verbal denunciation. Feelings of national allegiance outweighed their opposition to bourgeois war.

At the Stuttgart Congress in 1907, Gustave Hervé (1871–1944), a French socialist, recommended more positive action. He rejected the distinction between aggressive and defensive war as irrelevant from the standpoint of the proletariat. Although he insisted that international war should always be countered by proletarian revolution, the congress did not support him. Both Hervé and Pierre Proudhon (1809–1865) maintained that "the proletariat have no fatherland," but again the congress failed to support this view. By the time of the Brussels Congress of 1914, the majority of Marxists were indistinguishable from the conventional bourgeoisie on the issue of war. Rosa Luxemburg (1870–1919), Karl Liebknecht, and Auguste Bebel were exceptions in their open opposition to all war. Luxemburg, in particular, saw the failure of socialists to prevent World War I as a failure of the spirit of humanistic Marxism.

After World War I, Nikolai Lenin (1870–1924) saw the war as having paved the way for a proletarian nation. He insisted that "the slogan of peace is stupid and wrong. . . . It signifies philistine moaning." In a speech in 1917 Lenin affirmed, "We are not pacifists. We are opposed to imperialist wars for the division of spoils among capitalists, but we have always declared it to be absurd for the revolutionary proletariat to renounce revolutionary wars that may prove necessary in the interests of socialism." When Leon Trotsky (1877–1940) stated in 1919 that now that there was a socialist nation, wars were class affairs where proletarians fought bourgeoisie, Rosa Luxemburg replied that this was mistaken Marxism. But most Marxists were indistinguishable from bourgeois nationalists.

Many Marxists were convinced that the proletarian revolutionary war was like a Christian crusade. Lenin explained that when war was waged by the proletariat to conquer the bourgeoisie, "such a war is legitimate and just." Marxists, like Christians in the 4th century, now had a nation, and all the implications of nationalism led them to the similar conclusion that just wars* could be fought.

See CHRISTIANITY AND WAR; DEBS, EUGENE; MUSTE, ABRAHAM JOHANNES; NATIONAL LIBERATION, WARS OF.

BIBLIOGRAPHY

Engels, Frederick, *The Role of Force in History* (New York: International Publishers, 1968).

Korovin, Eugene A., "The Second World War and International Law," *American Journal of International Law* 40 (October 1946).

Marx, Karl, *The Civil War in France* (New York: International Publishers, 1940), 23ff.

Somerville, John, *The Philosophy of Marxism* (New York: Random House, 1967).

Stekloff, G. M., *History of the First International* (New York: International Publishers, 1928).

Trainin, I. P., "Questions of Guerrilla Warfare in the Law of War," *American Journal of International Law* 40 (July 1946).

MASSACRE. The term *massacre* refers to those situations in which one side enjoys an overwhelming advantage and as a consequence kills an excessive number of the enemy, perhaps even the total enemy force. Wars of no quarter* were historically forbidden primarily because they resulted in a massacre. The term is a denigrating one denoting an a priori unjust situation. Unlike just war* theory, there is no counterpart for massacre. The term "just massacre" is seen as an oxymoron. Part of the negative attitude toward massacres and the consequent rejection of wars of no quarter derives from a perceived unfair advantage one side has over the other, and the further judgment that annihilation is rarely required by military necessity. Where one side enjoys an overwhelming advantage in sheer numbers and/or sophisticated technology, and where no prior concern with proportionality is present, the temptation to massacre exists. Just war theorists will debate whether a given battle amounts to a massacre and their problem will be to determine if there exists some ideal number of enemy to be slain. In the absence of any adjudicating body, such debates tend to be subjective. In normal disputes, one accuses the opponent of massacres while reserving a less pejorative term for the slaughter caused by one's own side. It would seem obvious that killing soldiers after they have surrendered would be a case of massacre. The Nazi slaughter of the Jews, commonly referred to as the Holocaust*, seems a clear case of massacre, not simply because of the overwhelming Nazi advantage in killing unarmed prisoners*, but because such killing served no military purpose. Killing unarmed men, women, and children has been called massacre ever since the biblical story of the "massacre of the innocents."

Massacre is not a neutral, analytic concept in discourses on war and peace. On the contrary, the term is often used as a tendentious, rhetorical device. It is part of the ideological lexicon designed to bestow virtue on one's cherished group while demonizing an adversary. Due to its virtue, our side wins decisive victories, and we slay only the deserving, while due to their treachery, the enemy side commits heinous massacres, both because they slay the innocent* and because they do so in such numbers. Understandably, the Iraqi press might portray the United States' land war against them (called a Turkey Shoot by some U.S. airmen) as an obvious case of massacre. The Iraqis crushed Kuwaiti resistance and conquered that nation in a matter of hours, but did they commit a massacre? Due to its overwhelming strategic superiority, the United States defeated the Iraqi military in a matter of hours. Was this a massacre? Not surprisingly, neither the Iraqi nor the American press refers to the actions of its respective government as a "massacre"; honorific terms such as "liberation" are invoked.

However, the term *massacre* can be used in a more neutral, analytic sense to reveal the dramatic change that has occurred in 20th-century violent conflicts. John Dewey was perhaps prescient when he observed in 1927 that "war" no longer adequately described modern conflicts: "The dynamic conflicts of the seventeenth century are called by the same name . . . 'war.' The sameness of the word too easily conceals from us the difference and significance [of twentieth-century violent conflict]."

Reflecting upon World War I, Dewey suggested that the word *war* did not adequately convey the horror and tragedy of defenseless civilians perishing at the hands of powerful armies. Most wars that occurred after Dewey's observation resulted in the death of more civilians than combatants. Indeed, various contemporary analysts conclude that conflicts since the end of World War II have killed more children than combatants. For example, consider the civilian casualty* ratio of some typical modern conflicts. The civilian deaths in Guatemala were 72 percent; in the Sudan, 99 percent; in Lebanon, 63 percent; in Afghanistan, 62 percent. Are all these results properly called massacres? Similar data exist for the wars in Vietnam*, Panama, Grenada*, Iraq, and Somalia, where civilian casualties vastly outnumbered soldiers.

Perhaps it is difficult to have a concern with massacres where the enemy is "demonized." During World Wars I and II, entire populations were so demonized that massive casualties as at Dresden, Hiroshima, and Nagasaki* were not seen as massacres. More recently, however, American policy is more selective in its portrayal, and commonly only the leaders are depicted as demons. For example, President George Bush had several occasions to state that "our quarrel is with Saddam Hussein, not the Iraqi people." Yet despite this salutary change in discourse, large numbers of Iraqi civilians were killed. A study by members of the Harvard medical faculty in the spring of 1991 estimated that by the end of that summer an additional 75,000 Iraqi children would have died from starvation or disease due to the damage to the infrastructure caused by the U.S. air war. Many authors suspect that "wars without mercy" (massacres) may well characterize conflicts for the foreseeable future.

See CASUALTIES OF WAR; COLLATERAL DAMAGE; GULF WAR (DESERT STORM); MASS DESTRUCTION, WEAPONS OF; NUCLEAR WAR; RETALIATION, MASSIVE; TOTAL WAR.

BIBLIOGRAPHY

Addington, Larry H., *The Patterns of War Since the Eighteenth Century* (Bloomington: Indiana University Press, 1984).

Dewey, John, *The Public and Its Problems* (Chicago: Swallow Press, 1927), 127.

Eliott, Gil, *Twentieth Century Book of the Dead* (New York: Scribner's, 1972).

Harkavy, Robert E., and Stephanie G. Neuman, eds., *The Lessons of Recent Wars in the Third World,* vols. 1 and 2 (Lexington, Mass.: Heath, 1985, 1987).

Schloming, Gordon, *Power and Principle in International Affairs* (New York: Harcourt Brace, 1991), 16–17.

Ron Hirschbein

MASS DESTRUCTION, WEAPONS OF. There are four basic types of weapons of mass destruction: ballistic missiles, nuclear weapons,* chemical weapons, and biological* weapons. Ballistic missiles are divided into intercontinental ballistic missiles (ICBMs), which travel over 3,400 miles, and short-range guided ballistic missiles (GBMs), which travel shorter distances. Ballistic missiles of both types are weapons of mass destruction when they are used to deliver nuclear, chemical, or biological warheads.

An ICBM is essentially a rocket that lifts outside the earth's atmosphere and is armed with one or more warheads that it then delivers to a target. Multiple independently targeted reentry vehicles (MIRVs) allow ICBMs to carry several warheads, each of which can be targeted separately.

The United States employs 950 Minuteman and fifty MX missiles for strategic purposes. Of these, all of the MX missiles and 550 Minutemen missiles are MIRVed. The MIRVed Minutemen carry three warheads, while the MXs carry ten. The MX is a large, extremely accurate missile capable of destroying enemy missile silos. Because of their extreme accuracy, weapons like the MX gave the United States a viable first-strike* weapon by the late 1980s. The Soviet Union had an ICBM force of roughly 1,400 at its peak. The Soviets employed far more of their nuclear warheads on ICBMs than the United States, which maintained rough equality among ICBMs, nuclear submarines, and strategic bombers—the strategic triad. Soviet warheads are generally larger and their ICBMs have a larger "throw weight" (the mass of payload that they can carry) than their U.S. counterparts. The Soviet emphasis on size, often used by the United States to justify American buildups, was largely intended to compensate for inferior technology, particularly with respect to warhead accuracy and miniaturization.

Solid-fueled missiles are preferable to liquid-fueled ones because the latter are more dangerous, deteriorate more quickly, and require more preparation time to launch. The United States did away with liquid-fueled ICBMs by the mid-1960s. With the sole exception of the SS-13, which appeared in 1969, the Soviets did not deploy solid-fueled ICBMs until the late 1980s. Even at that time, most of their ICBMs remained liquid-fueled. Currently, both the SS-24s and SS-25s are solid-fueled. They are also both mobile. Approximately 60 percent of the Soviet ICBMs are the older SS-17s, SS-18s, and SS-19s. These missiles, deployed between 1978 and 1985, are MIRVed with an average of seven warheads. The huge SS-18s, with a throw weight eight times as great as the Minuteman IIIs, have ten warheads each.

The U.S. SLBM force, carried on thirty-three submarines, including twenty Trident subs, can deliver more than 5,000 nuclear warheads—enough warheads to destroy the former Soviet Union roughly ten times. Nuclear submarines are the least vulnerable leg of the strategic triad because they can hide undetected beneath the oceans. With the introduction of the Trident II (D-5) in 1990, the United States had a first-strike capability on submarines—and may have earlier with the Trident Is (C-4s). The Trident II, with a range of 7,000 miles, has the accuracy of the MX and carries eight warheads.

Soviet SLBMs lagged years behind the United States. By the 1980s the Soviets added the Typhoon submarine. It carries twenty SS-N-20 missiles with ten warheads each. By the early 1990s, the Soviets had 930 missiles on sixty-two submarines, which could deliver 3,600 warheads—but they lacked the accuracy of the Tridents and their first-strike capability.

Besides the ICBMs, there are guided ballistic missiles. Twenty-five countries have acquired or are attempting to acquire GBMs. Most are developing countries, many in the most volatile regions of the world. In the Middle East, nine countries have missile programs.

Israel's Shavit space launch vehicle could be used as an ICBM capable of delivering a half-ton payload at intercontinental ranges. Israel's Jericho 2 can deliver at least two tons on any Arab country. India's Agni missile is roughly comparable to the Jericho 2. Saudi Arabia purchased its missiles from China. The DF-3 has a range of 3,500 kilometers and a one-ton payload. It is the largest missile deployed outside of the five nuclear powers. The Soviet Scud-B missile is capable of delivering a one-ton payload at a range of 300 miles. It was modified by Iraq to carry a much smaller payload at ranges of 600 kilometers, which allowed their use against Israel during the Gulf War*. A more extensive modification, the al-Abbas, may be capable of delivering a half-ton warhead at similar ranges. The current U.S. sea-launched cruise missile has a payload of less than 500 kilograms at a range of 1,300 kilometers.

GBMs with ranges greater than a few hundred kilometers are extremely inefficient for the delivery of conventional warheads. A missile armed with a Hiroshima-sized nuclear weapon is roughly 10,000 times more deadly than the same missile armed with high explosives. While the development of nuclear weapons* is expensive, easy to detect, and relatively easy to stop with export controls, the same is not true of chemical and biological warheads. Hence, it is reasonable to assume that the future will yield many more nations with GBMs capable of delivering chemical and biological warheads and, quite possibly, nuclear warheads.

The Hiroshima* bomb had an explosive force of twelve kilotons, or twelve thousand tons of TNT. H-bombs with an explosive force greater than a megaton, or a million tons of TNT, are common today. Most U.S. strategic nuclear weapons range in size from forty kilotons to 1.2 megatons—from more than three times the power of the Hiroshima bomb to 100 times its power. The average size is about 250,000 kilotons, or more than twenty thousand times the Hiroshima bomb. Soviet weapons tend to be somewhat larger, averaging about 600,000 kilotons, or more than fifty thousand times the Hiroshima bomb.

By the 1980s, both superpowers had enough deliverable nuclear weapons to destroy each other over twenty-five times. Their combined firepower could destroy the earth roughly ten times. These numbers represent ''the overkill ratio'': the number of times one nation can destroy the vast majority of the others' population and industrial base.

Nuclear weapons cause destruction by their initial or direct radiation, the electromagnetic pulse, thermal radiation, the blast wave, and radioactive fallout. They are the most destructive weapons known today. The immediate deaths, medical consequences, lethal fallout, and destruction to industry, agriculture, communication, and medical facilities would make even a small, limited nuclear war horrific. Similarly, the global effects are numbing. Global fallout, damage to world economy and communications, damage to the ozone layer, and the possibility of a nuclear winter could all contribute to massive global death. Some scientific experts estimate that a nuclear exchange involving as few as one hundred megatons (less than 1 percent of the combined total of the superpowers) would plunge us into a nuclear winter resembling the conditions present during the ice age. Even without the effects of nuclear winter, some experts conclude that a nuclear war would end civilization as we know it. Other experts contend that the consequences of a nuclear war, while involving the deaths of tens to hundreds of millions as well as massive destruction to industry and infrastructure, would leave the world with the opportunity to rebuild to present standards.

It is claimed that one dozen to two dozen countries stockpile or are actively seeking chemical weapons, but only the United States, the Soviet Union, and Iraq admit to stockpiling these weapons. Egypt, India, Iran, Israel, North and

South Korea, Libya, Pakistan, Syria, and Taiwan are strongly suspected of stockpiling or producing chemical weapons.

A variety of chemical agents have been developed that kill and incapacitate. Choking agents attack the respiratory system, causing irritation and inflammation of bronchial tubes and lungs. Blood agents act by preventing the utilization of oxygen in the blood. Both can be lethal. Both can be defeated by gas masks. Blister agents injure and kill by absorption through the skin as well as by inhalation. As liquids, their effects cannot be defeated by gas masks and their use is easier to control than a gas.

Nerve agents are far more deadly. When inhaled, nerve agents are lethal in concentrations over ten times smaller than other chemical weapon agents. They are also absorbed through the skin. Production costs are low. If a chemical warhead on a missile with a one-ton throw weight is used against an unprepared city with a population density of 35 per hectare (e.g., Tel Aviv or Riyadh), 200 to 3,000 would be killed and a somewhat larger number seriously injured, depending on weather conditions. This is 40–700 times as many deaths, and 20–300 times as many injuries, as would result from a conventional warhead.

No nation is known to possess biological weapons today, but the United States, the United Kingdom, and Japan developed such weapons in the past, and Iraq and Syria are suspected of stockpiling such weapons today. Biological agents can be divided into two categories: toxins (toxic chemicals produced by living organisms) and pathogens (living organisms that produce disease). Toxins do not seem to have real advantages over nerve agents for missile attacks.

Pathogens have significant advantages over nerve agents in their ability to kill large numbers of civilians. In particular, *bacillus anthracis,* the bacteria that causes anthrax, is ideal for delivery by missiles because it forms spores that survive explosions as well as exposure to sun, air, and rain. It is not infectious but is spread by spores. Anthrax is deadly in concentrations 1,000 times smaller than nerve agents. Left untreated, anthrax kills nearly all who contact it within a few days. Anthrax produces lethal concentrations over an area 100 times larger than does the most potent chemical agent (sarin). Thus, even when used against a prepared population, anthrax warheads could rival small nuclear weapons in their ability to kill people. Unlike chemical agents, however, anthrax spores can survive for decades in the soil. Like nuclear weapons, they make the taking and holding of territory complicated. Used against a well-protected population, nuclear weapons are 100–1,000 times more deadly than chemical weapons and about ten times as deadly as an anthrax warhead.

See ANTIBALLISTIC MISSILES; BIOLOGICAL/CHEMICAL WARFARE; INCENDIARIES; MINES; NUCLEAR WAR; PROPORTIONALITY; RETALIATION, MASSIVE; TOTAL WAR.

BIBLIOGRAPHY

Fetter, Steve, "Ballistic Missiles and Weapons of Mass Destruction," *International Security* 16, no. 1 (Summer 1991), 5–42.

Gervasi, Tom, *The Myth of Soviet Military Supremacy* (New York: Harper & Row, 1986).

Perkins Jr., Ray, *The ABC's of the Soviet-American Nuclear Arms Race* (Pacific Grove, Calif.: Brooks/Cole Publishing, 1991).

Schell, Jonathan, *The Fate of the Earth* (New York: Knopf, 1982).

Turco, R. P., O. B. Toon, T. P. Packerman, J. B. Pollack, and Carl Sagan, "Nuclear Winter: Global Consequences of Multiple Nuclear Explosions," *Science* 23 (December 1983), 1283–92.

U.S. Office of Technology Assessment, *The Effects of Nuclear War* (Washington, D.C.: U.S. Government Printing Office, 1979).

Richard Werner

MEDICAL CASE. Officially designated *United States v. Karl Brandt et al.*, was the first trial under Control Council Law No. 10*. The trial opened December 9, 1946, and closed July 19, 1947. The bench was composed of three U.S. judges: Walter B. Beals of the Supreme Court of Washington, Harold L. Sebring, Judge of the Supreme Court of Florida; and Johnson T. Crawford, Judge of the District Court of Oklahoma. Victor C. Swearingen, former Assistant Attorney General of Michigan, was the alternate member. The indictment named twenty-three defendants. They included Karl Brandt, Reich Commissioner for Health and Sanitation, with supervisory authority over all military and civilian medical services; Lt. General Siegfried Handloser, chief of the medical services of the entire Wehrmacht; Lt. General Oscar Schroeder, chief of the medical services of the Luftwaffe; Karl Gebhardt, chief surgeon of the SS and president of the German Red Cross; and a number of distinguished medical doctors.

The principal count of the indictment charged the defendants with "criminal responsibility for cruel and frequently murderous medical experiments performed without the victims' consent." Experiments were carried out at Dachau for the Luftwaffe to investigate the limits of human endurance at high altitudes and to determine treatment for flyers who had been severely frozen. At Dachau, Buchenwald, and other concentration camps, inmates were deliberately infected with malaria, epidemic jaundice, typhus, and other diseases to test vaccines. Brandt and three other defendants were charged with a so-called "euthanasia" program, which involved the killing of the aged, insane and incurably ill, deformed children, and others by various means, such as gas and lethal injections. The relatives of the victims were told that they had died of natural causes.

The primary argument of the defense was that they were acting under superior orders*, and that some of the subjects were to have been executed in any case. The judgment of the tribunal of August 19, 1947, stated that "judged by any standard of proof the record clearly shows the commission of war crimes* and crimes against humanity*. . . . These experiments were not the isolated and casual acts of individual doctors and researchers working solely on their own responsibility." They were part of an official policy at the highest governmental levels. Fifteen were convicted of criminal responsibility: seven were sentenced to death by hanging, five to life imprisonment, three to long terms, and one to ten years. Seven were acquitted because their guilt could not be established beyond a reasonable doubt. Erhard Milch was one of these, but he was later tried in *United States v. Milch* for his involvement in the slave labor program. The sentences were confirmed by the military governor, and after the U.S. Supreme Court (by a 5-to-3 vote) refused to review the cases, the executions were carried out at Landsberg prison, where America's prisoners were confined.

This case was not an isolated one. The issue of medical experimentation arose in the Dachau, Mauthausen, Flossenberg, Buchenwald, and Nordhausen concentration camp cases. Numerous instances of medical experiments on prisoners surfaced following World War II. Hundreds of Japanese doctors and nurses were charged with performing surgical experiments on the Chinese in Shanxi Province, central China, between February 1942 and August 1945. Japanese Army Unit 731 was charged with killing at least 3,000 Chinese, Russians, Koreans, and Mongolians in experiments involving the injection of disease germs such as anthrax, typhus, and dysentery, and with human vivisection and shrapnel-induced gangrene. On December 28, 1949, a USSR Military Tribunal charged twelve former Japanese servicemen with manufacturing and using biological* weapons. Among the specific charges was that a 1940 Japanese military expedition in the Chinese region of Nimpo spread the germs of typhus and cholera, and plague-infected fleas resulting in a plague epidemic. Similarly, in 1941, in Changteh, a similar experiment was conducted. A U.S. Army commission at Yokohama in the *Kyushu University* case established that eight American fliers had been killed in experimental operations at the University clinic. Evidence showed that some of the victims were alive when the experiments began. Although one offender committed suicide before he could be tried, twenty-two others were found guilty and four, including a lieutenant general, were sentenced to be hung.

See BIOLOGICAL/CHEMICAL WARFARE; CONTROL COUNCIL LAW NO. 10.

BIBLIOGRAPHY

Materials on the Trial of Former Servicemen of the Japanese Army Charged with Manufacturing and Employing Bacteriological Weapons (Moscow: Foreign Language House, 1950).

Tutorow, Norman E., *War Crimes, War Criminals, and War Crimes Trials* (Westport, Conn.: Greenwood Press, 1986).

Whiteman, Marjorie M., ed., *Digest of International Law* (Washington, D.C.: U.S. Government Printing Office, 1968), vol. 11.

MEDICAL PERSONNEL. *See* COMBATANT-NONCOMBATANT DISTINCTION; GENEVA CONVENTIONS, 1864, 1868, 1906, 1929, 1949; PRISONERS OF WAR; RED CROSS, RED CRESCENT, RED LION AND SUN.

MENCIUS. Perhaps the most famous and faithful follower of Confucius, flourished well over a century after his "master's" death (372–289 B.C.). Like Confucius, he preached the doctrine of humanheartedness (*jen*). In giving consideration to others, this doctrine focuses on human nature* rather than on social status or ethnic origin. People should be given consideration as human beings first and foremost, and only secondarily as teachers, administrators, citizens of a particular state in China, or whatever. As such, there was an inherent notion of equality built into the concept of *jen.*

However, neither Mencius nor Confucius believed in equality of social status. Both recognized that some sort of hierarchy is needed in order to permit the society to function efficiently. Parents, rulers, teachers, and older brothers, among others, must be given their due by those beneath them. Yet the duty of superiors is never to act selfishly, but to show concern for those beneath them. Mencius also followed Confucius in emphasizing the role of ritual (*li*) in human lives. For both thinkers, our tendency to act morally (i.e., to act in accord with the principle of humanheartedness) needs to be disciplined. Good habits are what make us act well, not moments of inspiration. *Li* disciplines us by giving us the good habits we need. When we are trained to show respect for our parents on a daily basis, and when we similarly practice etiquette day after day, we gradually acquire the habits to act well. *Li,* then, is part of a person's education, a process that emphasizes the human being's role in society.

Mencius also shared with Confucius a belief in the importance of the ''gentleman,'' the *chun tzu* (sometimes translated as the superior man). Such a person has of course been educated properly and thus has good habits and is committed to the doctrine of humanheartedness. This commitment expresses itself in such practices as, if one is a teacher, allowing all qualified students the opportunity to enter one's classes regardless of their social status. It also expresses itself in the *chun tzu*'s dealings with the emperor and his other superiors. The *chun tzu* does not practice blind obedience, because humanheartedness overrides obedience. If the ruler acts immorally he must be made aware of the nature of his actions. The *chun tzu* is expected to correct the superior, politely but firmly. Mencius himself regularly acted in the capacity of a *chun tzu* in criticizing rulers and other powerful officials. In one passage of his writings (actually probably student notes) it is recorded how he asked King Hui of Liang whether there is a difference between killing with a stick or a sword. The king replied there is not. Then the king was asked if there is a difference between killing a man with a sword or a style of government. Again, of course, the king replied, this time reluctantly, in the negative. Mencius then pointed out to the king that his governmental policies are starving the people—even while the king and those living in the palace have an abundance of food (Book 1, Chapter 4, 132–33). Needless to say, Mencius was not always popular with those whom he criticized.

This line of thinking with the king begins to show how Mencius justified civil rebellion. In an audience with another king he presented the following argument. It is wrong to overthrow kings. However, if a king acts badly with respect to his people, and therefore has lost his mandate of Heaven, he is not really a king—because he is not acting in a kingly way. As such, if his ministers overthrow him, they are not really overthrowing a king but a mere fellow who happens to be sitting on the throne (II, 9, 167). And, of course, there is nothing wrong with overthrowing such a fellow.

Mencius's views in these matters have a utilitarian flavor. The good king cannot be overthrown justly; but beyond that he would not be, in actual fact, overthrown. He would no more be attacked by his subjects, Mencius believes, than a good parent would be attacked by his children. However, the utility of being a good king extends beyond what happens within the kingdom. By providing an environment in which to make his people happy (i.e., by providing them with the opportunity to have a family, build a home, grow food, make clothing, and by helping them become educated), they become willing to fight for the kingdom. Happy people make good soldiers. Enemies will think twice before attacking a kingdom composed of happy people. Besides, the kingdom that deals justly with its people and neighboring states is less likely to be attacked for another reason. If such a kingdom is to grow, the best way to do so is by example, not by invasion. Neighboring territories will want to join the just state rather than fight it. Mencius would conquer others by having the state exercise virtue rather than its cavalry.

For those occasions when the just state must deal with an unjust state, Mencius, for all his dislike of war, was not a pacifist. *Jen* dictates that we love others. If those others are oppressed by their ruler, they will require help. It is the duty of the just state to help those who are oppressed. In this he is in agreement with Mo Tzu, a thinker from the generation before him, with whom he otherwise has little in common.

So we have in Mencius an example of the early beginnings of just war* theory. He focuses his attention mainly on issues pertaining to justice of the war. But it is clear, if not by actual statement then by direct implication of his theory of *jen,* that there are good and bad ways to fight a war, as well.

See JUST WAR; MAOISM AND WAR; MO TZU (MO TI).

BIBLIOGRAPHY
Creel, Herrlee G., *Chinese Thought: From Confucius to Mao Tse-tung* (Chicago: University of Chicago Press, 1953), chap. 5.
Legge, James, *The Chinese Classics: The Works of Mencius* (Oxford: Oxford University Press, 1935).

Nicholas G. Fotion

MILITARISM. Academic and ideological debate on militarism, primarily between liberals and Marxists, began in the 19th century. Since World War II, debate has focused on differences in the militarism of developing versus developed nations. From primitive militarism to totalitarian militarism, a basic definition includes belief in and practice of constant preparation for war and subordination of civil control and interests to the military and their sympathizers. However militarism is defined, it is broader than its expressions in imperialism and total war*, but narrower than problems of civil military relations and warism*. While warism and pacifism* are opposites, militarism and civilianism, contrary to Vagts, are not opposites, since militarism can occur under civilian rule and even in democratic states. Ethical concern about militarism often focuses on peacetime expressions, since just war* theory and other moral principles generally suffice for assessing actual wars.

Analyzing studies of primitive militarism, William Eckhardt (like Rousseau*) notes its correlation with the rise of private property and resulting tendencies toward social injustice and war. He concludes that overcoming militarism requires subordinating property rights to human rights and pursuing a more altruistic and democratic civilization. Modern militarism is closely connected with the transition from agrarian to industrial society. Besides Rousseau, early critics of war preparations and standing armies include Diderot and Voltaire. In the 19th century, Pierre-Joseph Proudhon began the use of the term *militarism* and Herbert Spencer, in *Principles of Sociology* (1897), distinguished industrial and militant societies.

While Friedrich Engels's "The Tactics of Social Democracy" (1895) addresses ties among military, industry, and government, Lenin's *Imperialism, the Highest Stage of Capitalism* (1916) is the classic Marxist text that argues capitalism is by nature imperialistic (hence, militaristic). Karl Liebknecht's *Militarism and Anti-Militarism* (1917 and 1969) stresses the connections of militarism to class society and class struggle. Prior to World War I, European Marxists emphatically opposed imperialism and militarism. After the war began, Lenin, Liebknecht, and Rosa Luxemburg maintained this position, but most socialist parties, succumbing to nationalism, supported the war efforts of their nations.

The origin of the liberal position—also an influence on Lenin's position—is J. A. Hobson's *Imperialism* (1902 and 1938). Unlike Marxists, liberals do not view militarism as resulting from class struggle and are generally vague about the prospect that the ruling class can use both civilian and military authority to support their interests. Alfred Vagts's *A History of Militarism* (1937 and 1959) is probably the most cited liberal exposition of militarism. However, his key distinction between a proper "military way" and an improper "militaristic way" can mask ways in which societies that practice the "military way" can still be militarist in a manner that exceeds merely being warist.

Marxists* are correct that 19th- and early 20th-century capitalism exhibits a close connection between imperialism and militarism. Critics correctly note that socialist economies have practiced their own versions of militarism, such as Soviet militarism. While Marxists who deny that socialism can be militaristic are incorrect, equally incorrect are those who argue that Western parliamentary democracies cannot be militaristic. Absence of civilian subordination to the military does not imply absence of militarism; civilian leaders can be militarist in their thinking and policies. In this regard, C. Wright Mills was suspicious of the view that postwar industrial societies are antimilitaristic. Furthermore, since few liberals or Marxists are pacifists, a fine line exists between what one side views as legitimate militarily and the other regards as excessively militaristic.

World War II spawned extreme cases, which some writers refer to as fascist or totalitarian militarism. Militarism in Germany, Italy, and Japan was coupled with autocratic and oligarchic political structures. These expansionist governments intentionally used military force to build empires. Georges Sorel contributed to the philosophy of violence that supported Italian Fascism. In Germany, Georg Thomas argued for a war-preparedness economy (*Wehrwirtschaft*) in times of peace as well as war, and Ernst Jünger proposed that the entire society be organized along military patterns and become involved when war ensues. In his classic *A Study of War* (1942 and 1964), Quincy Wright uses the term *totalitarianization of war* to characterize such 20th-century warfare in which all phases of national life are organized for total war.

Since World War II, the forms of militarism in developing countries and in the industrial north have sharply diverged. In developing countries, authoritarianism in the military is increasingly coupled with military rule in government. By contrast, the superpowers and several other nations never demobilized and shifted to what Seymour Melman terms *permanent war economies.* Some writers contend the resulting arms race deterred military expansionism or at least largely checked 19th- and early 20th-century forms of militarism. Nuclear weapons also restrained militarism, with shifts toward limited war strategies.

Currently, within the industrial north, attention is focused on the military-industrial complex*. Many writers view the military-industrial complex as distinct from militarism or as different from earlier forms. Scholars who contend that the military-industrial complex is militaristic often regard it and limited war theories as modifications of permanent war economies and total war strategies. Global trends are toward increasing military over civil spending, as noted annually in Ruth Leger Sivard's *World Military and Social Expenditures.*

Militarism, in whatever form or degree, raises serious ethical issues. For the military and government, militarism encourages centralization and discourages democracy. Militarism also encourages technological progress at the expense of social equality. Finally, militarism poses problems in relation to the relative importance of civilian versus military authority, human versus property rights, and altruistic versus egoistic values.

See DEMOCRACY AND THE MILITARY; MARXISM AND WAR; MILITARY AS A PROFESSION; MILITARY EDUCATION; MILITARY TRAINING, BASIC.

BIBLIOGRAPHY

Berghahn, Volker, *Militarism: The History of an International Debate 1861–1979* (New York: St. Martin's Press, 1982).

Eide, Asbjørn and Marek Thee, eds., *Problems of Contemporary Militarism* (New York: St. Martin's Press, 1980).

Melman, Seymour, *The Permanent War Economy* (New York: Simon & Schuster, 1976).

Vagts, Alfred, *A History of Militarism: Civilian and Military* (New York: W. W. Norton, 1937; Meridian Books, Inc., revised, 1959).

William C. Gay

MILITARY AS A PROFESSION. The military profession in the broad sense comprises all who serve in the armed forces as a vocation. In the strict sense, it encompasses only the career officer corps. It is they who set the standards of performance and ethics for enlisted personnel, who are craftsmen acting under the professionals' direction, and for reserve officers, who are quasi-amateurs taking their lead from the professionals.

The function of the officer corps is to manage the state's monopoly of force to promote the ''national interest,'' noble or ignoble, as defined by the commander-in-chief. Its mission is to win wars of any magnitude in which the commander involves the nation, from minor skirmishes all the way up to total war* involving weapons of mass destruction*. The corps is a profession similar to medicine, law, and engineering in the sense that practitioners are endowed with exclusive authority by society to discharge its function and carry out its mission. Furthermore, society provides the training, in some cases lifelong, to employ the skills, manage the personnel, and operate the machines necessary to do so.

The officer corps, like other professions, enjoys great autonomy. It selects its members, controls their education*, and monitors their behavior through a rigidly hierarchical organization. It inculcates in its members a distinctive culture and segregates them from contact with society so that they will identify with the group and look askance at outsiders. As a consequence, military officers tend to think in terms of a distinctive political philosophy—political realism—and adhere to a distinctive ethic—the professional military ethic.

The military mind thinks of political matters in Hobbesian* terms: humans are basically self-interested and would be engaged in an endless war of all against all if they were not restrained by force concentrated in the political sovereign. Nations exist in a state of nature in relation to each other, so every other nation is a potential enemy. Hence, the nation must maintain maximum military strength and use it as needed to defend its place in the world. Pacifism* and disarmament are foolish, if not treasonable. The slow arts of diplomacy are a reflection of weakness and indecision.

The military ethic demands the basic virtues of discipline, obedience, loyalty, honor, courage, and integrity. In many contexts these require sacrifice of personal desire, safety, and comfort. Examples of self-sacrifice make it possible for officers to take pride in their work despite its purpose of homicide and destruction. Such examples also allow the public to admire successful officers and glorify the military profession.

Nevertheless, there are distinctive vices to which military officers are prone. Some of these the military ethic combats, without complete success. Others it actually encourages. The vices include blind obedience to immoral orders; excessive loyalty to comrades, the corps, or the country at the expense of the welfare of humanity; a concern for honors rather than being honorable; rashness that jeopardizes those who depend on one; and careerism or sacrifice of integrity in order to advance in rank.

The existence of a professional officer corps encourages war in a number of ways. The corps, through a vigorous program of public relations, communicates its political philosophy to the public, defining for the public the meaning of security and national honor and the importance of war and military strength. It not incidentally promotes a key role for itself in society and lays claim to a large portion of society's wealth to provide it with the tools of its trade. By keeping the nation militarily strong, it feeds delusions of national grandeur and power. The availability of an effective corps, disposed as it is to follow orders and believing as it does in the efficacy of force, makes it easy for the state security apparatus to resort to violence in times of crisis*.

See DEMOCRACY AND THE MILITARY; MILITARISM; MILITARY EDUCATION; MILITARY-INDUSTRIAL COMPLEX; MILITARY TRAINING, BASIC; WARISM.

BIBLIOGRAPHY

Hartle, Anthony E., *Moral Issues in Military Decision Making* (Lawrence: University of Kansas Press, 1989).

Huntington, Samuel P., *The Soldier and the State* (Cambridge, Mass.: Harvard University Press, 1957).

McGrath, James H., and Gustaf E. Anderson, III, "Recent Work on the American Professional Military Ethic: An Introduction and Survey," *American Philosophical Quarterly* 30, no. 3 (July 1993), 187–208.

John Kultgen

MILITARY EDUCATION. The preparation of women and men in the art and science of war. Military education occurs at various levels in the United States: Junior reserve officer training (JROTC) in high schools; college-level education at military service academies and in reserve officer training (ROTC) units at civilian universities; postgraduate commissioning via officer candidate school (OCS) (a ninety-day course for college graduates); and midcareer education for selected officers at various "war colleges" (supported either by one branch of the military service or jointly by all three branches at the National War College, Washington, D.C.). The war college level focuses predominately on command and staff issues. In order to be commissioned as an officer in the U.S. military, a person must have earned a baccalaureate degree. Since 1973, military service has been voluntary in the United States. Registration for conscription is maintained, but the population is not subject to compulsory military education via the draft, although enlisted personnel are provided with boot camp training.

In 1974, President Gerald Ford signed a law that mandated the inclusion of women in the student bodies of service academies. Since that time there has been increasing emphasis on educating women for positions in combat. This emphasis has occasioned an effort to relax the laws excluding women from combat, accompanied by a backlash against increased participation by women in combat. The military in general and military schools in particular have wrestled with the meaning of gender equity in the preparation and deployment of women.

Contemporary military education has two major focuses: the science and technology required to understand and operate mechanized and computerized weapons systems (e.g., nuclear submarines and intercontinental ballistic missiles); and the moral reasoning and ethical behavior necessary to function in our interdependent world amidst the rigors of combat as representatives of a constitutional democracy. Because of the first focus, military service academies have become engineering colleges. The second focus has been more slowly recognized, since the service academies tend to emphasize training rather than education.

The standards of morality for military officers are similar to those for civilians (truth telling, promise keeping, honesty) but also involve what some regard as virtues especially needed by military personnel (obedience, loyalty, courage, and integrity). Because of both the large, spread-out dimensions of modern military campaigns and the stresses of combat, officers and enlisted personnel must obey orders even if they do not understand the purpose to be served by obeying. The military officer is "trained" to fit into a hierarchical, bureaucratic, and highly competitive organization. The primary way to succeed within this organization (i.e., to be promoted) is to satisfy one's superiors to the highest degree possible.

It is also important for an officer to obey the laws of the land in the conduct of warfare. Included in these are various treaties and conventions that have been ratified by the United States. Specifically, the Hague* and Geneva* conventions discuss the parameters within which war can be waged, touching on issues including the treatment of prisoners, regard for innocents (noncombatants) caught in battle zones, and forbidden weapons. Further, military officers are expected to understand and act in accordance with the Constitution of the United States. In their oath of office they swear to uphold and defend that Constitution. The Iran-Contra scandal of the late 1980s resulted in increased emphasis on educating students in service academies in the letter and spirit of the Constitution. In particular, given the acknowledged lying to Congress by members of the armed services in this scandal, there is great stress placed on the notion of the separation of powers and of the civilian control of the military. Given the structure of government in the United States, it is important not to have the military take over the government using its massive resources in a coup d'état.

Military education combines the two areas of knowing and doing. Officers and enlisted persons are expected both to possess technical and ethical knowledge and to act on that knowledge in appropriate ways. The military deals with major life and death issues in the lives of its own people and the lives of enemies. It is important that military officers at all levels be able to reflect on the overall nature of their profession as well as on the morality of specific activities they are asked to undertake.

Officers are not dealing merely with machines (weapons systems). The bureaucracy is not merely a huge machine deploying people as interchangeable parts. The Kantian imperative to treat people not merely as means but as ends in themselves needs to be a central part of the ethical education of the military.

See DEMOCRACY AND THE MILITARY; FEMINISM AND WAR; HO-

MOSEXUALITY; *LAW OF LAND WARFARE;* LAWS OF WAR; MILITA-RISM; MILITARY AS A PROFESSION; MILITARY TRAINING, BASIC; SUPERIOR ORDERS; *UNIFORM CODE OF MILITARY JUSTICE;* WOMEN IN THE MILITARY.

BIBLIOGRAPHY
Hartle, Anthony E., *Moral Issues in Military Decision Making* (Lawrence: University of Kansas Press, 1989).
Huntington, Samuel P., *The Soldier and the State* (Cambridge, Mass.: Harvard University Press, 1957).
McGrath, James H., and Gustaf E. Anderson III, "Recent Work on the Professional Military Ethic: An Introduction and Survey," *American Philosophical Quarterly* 30, no. 3 (July 1993), 187–208.
Pratt, George K., *Soldier to Civilian* (New York: Whittlesly House, 1944).

David E. Johnson

MILITARY-INDUSTRIAL COMPLEX. On April 27, 1946, General Dwight D. Eisenhower, Chief of Staff of the U.S. Army, issued a policy statement formulating the idea of a close relationship between civilian industry, scientists, universities, and other government agencies with the military. He indicated: (1) all civilian resources should be redirected to support the plans of the military in times of peace; (2) universities and industries should be encouraged financially to direct their energies toward military ends; and (3) officers of the armed services should become aware of the advantages the military can derive from this arrangement. Most citizens were aware that in wartime the regimentation of resources and national effort was required, however, the suggestion that this might be in order in peacetime marked a radical reformulation.

Fifteen years later, on January 17, 1961, then President Eisenhower warned in his farewell address of the implications of this policy. He remarked:

This conjunction of an immense Military Establishment and a large arms industry is new in American experience. . . . In the councils of government we must guard against the acquisition of unwarranted influence . . . by the military-industrial complex. . . . We must never let the weight of this combination endanger our liberties or our democratic processes.

A new terminology was adopted to conceal these changes. The former war department was called the "defense department," warriors were called "peace keepers," and those formerly known as the "merchants of death" were called "defense contractors." This complex altered American society in a number of ways.

What Seymour Melman called "pentagon capitalism" was created. One result was that a primary function of government and business became the manufacture and sale of weapons of war. In part, this was made easy by the policy of industry to hire retired military officers to serve as paid members of their boards and to serve as lobbyists for their wares. Malcolm Moos, Eisenhower's speech writer, said that this was what the president had in mind when he gave the warning. Senator Paul Douglas (D-IL) conducted an inquiry into the employment of retired officers of the rank of Colonel/Navy Captain or higher in the 100 largest defense contractors, which led to an effort by the Hebert Subcommittee (1959) of the Armed Service Committee to forbid such hiring. The motion was defeated by one vote. Ten years later, Senator William Proxmire (D-WI) found that while in 1959 the 100 largest defense contractors hired 768 retired officers of the rank of Colonel/Navy Captain or higher, in 1969 there were 2,072. The ten companies with the most retired military accounted for more than half the total defense contracts.

The United States also became the number one weapons dealer in the world. In 1990, the U.S. share of the global arms market rose to 40 percent, while the Soviet share decreased to 29 percent. In the decade from 1980 to 1989 the United States supplied $128 billion in weapons to 125 of the world's 169 countries. This included many nations with chronic human rights abuses, such as Iran, Iraq, Saudi Arabia, Egypt, South Korea, and Thailand.

In addition to weapons, the United States became the primary exporter of troops, with 395 major military bases in thirty-five countries, plus hundreds of smaller bases. Nearly one-third, $90 billion, of all military spending went to these bases. The Soviets, until the breakup of their country, had European bases in East Germany, Czechoslovakia, Poland, and Hungary, and access facilities in Bulgaria and Mongolia. In the rest of the world the Soviets had bases in Cuba, Syria, Libya, Ethiopia, Angola, South Yemen, the Seychelles, and Guinea.

The United States also became the major producer of nuclear arms. For more than forty years, America spent about $1.5 billion a week making nuclear bombs and producing them with such secrecy that the process was virtually exempt from congressional oversight, making a total of about $1 trillion. The United States has four nuclear weapons research development and testing facilities: Livermore, California; and Los Alamos and Albuquerque, New Mexico; and Las Vegas, Nevada; six nuclear materials production sites: Fernald, Ohio; Hanford, Washington; Idaho Falls, Idaho; Paducah, Kentucky; Piketon, Ohio; and Savannah River near Aiken, South Carolina; and six nuclear weapons production sites: Kansas City, Missouri; Dayton, Ohio; Amarillo, Texas; Clearwater, Florida; Denver, Colorado; and Oak Ridge, Tennessee. The international sale of nuclear components is big business. The 1993 meetings of the Nuclear Suppliers Group included twenty-seven nations, with an open invitation to Argentina to attend as an observer. Two nations, China and North Korea, threatened to withdraw their membership.

None of this was without risk. In 1991 the U.S. government identified 21,000 polluted sites on military bases and nuclear weapons plants. The world's navies had accidents leaving over fifty nuclear warheads and nine nuclear reactors lying on the bottom of the ocean. U.S. accidents with nuclear weapons from 1951 to 1981 included two fires aboard nuclear armed planes, eight nonnuclear explosions aboard planes carrying nuclear weapons, four instances of nuclear contamination aboard nuclear planes, seven bombs or warheads lost and not recovered from planes and one from a submarine, twelve accidents aboard nuclear-powered submarines, four aboard nuclear ships, and four on nuclear missiles. The Department of Defense (DOD) revealed that between 1975 and 1987 there were 173 accidents involving trucks carrying radioactive materials.

Further, United States became the major producer of chemical weapons. In 1969, under President Richard Nixon, the United States ceased building chemical weapons. Nixon stated that such weapons were "morally repugnant to the conscience of mankind." In 1975 Congress stated that chemical weapons production would not be resumed without a presidential certification that it was "essential to the national interest." Neither President Gerald Ford nor Jimmy Carter gave such certification, but under pressure from President Ronald Reagan, Congress approved in 1987 the production of binary chemical warfare weapons. Twice (in 1983 and 1986) Vice-President George Bush broke tie votes in the Senate in favor of making chemical weapons. In 1993, the United States had seven production sites for chemical weapons and nine storage sites. Production sites are located in Van Nuys, California; Rocky Mountain Arsenal, Denver, Colorado; Pine Bluff Arsenal, Arkansas; Shreveport, Louisiana; Muscle Shoals, Alabama; Newport, Indiana; and Aberdeen, Maryland. Storage sites are located in Johnson Atoll; Umatilla, Oregon; Toele, Utah; Pueblo, Colorado; Pine Bluff, Arkansas; Anniston, Alabama; and Aberdeen, Maryland. The United States is not alone in chemical weapons manufacture. An estimated twenty countries are suspected of either possessing or seeking to possess chemical weapons. The British, for example, have twenty-three known chemical weapons experimental centers in universities.

The United States has also had a major role in biological weapons* research and production. Major biological warfare facilities exist at Dugway Proving Ground near Salt Lake City, Utah; Salk Institute in Swiftwater, Pennsylvania; and Fort Detrick, in Frederick, Maryland. In addition, the United States has approximately 150 public and private chemical and biological weapons laboratories in more than thirty states and fifteen foreign countries. This does not include the biological and chemical weapons research carried out in thousands of university, corporate, and military centers. Senate and House hearings revealed that chemical and biological experiments on U.S. citizens were conducted under the auspices of the DOD and the Central Intelligence Agency (CIA). These included 156 experiments in the public domain and 141 on military bases, all on unwitting subjects.

A significant influence of the military/industrial complex has been noted in colleges and universities. This development is influenced by the fact that 75 percent of government research funds during the 1960s to 1980s were administered by the DOD and the CIA. University faculty taught courses in mind control, spying, and the overthrow of foreign governments. Project "Camelot," for example, sponsored by the DOD and the CIA, paid social scientists to determine how the CIA could overthrow the duly elected government of Chile.

Most such research was so classified that not even the university administration knew what was being researched. Since the intellectual life of institutions of higher learning traditionally has rested on shared research duly criticized by a jury of one's peers, secret research undermined the academic enterprise. The total effect on American society of this complex arrangement has been immeasurable, and serious ethical questions have emerged for a democratic society. Questions remain as to who is empowered to determine both domestic and foreign policy, and especially as to whether such military and business domination is really in the national interest.

See BIOLOGICAL/CHEMICAL WARFARE; DEMOCRACY AND THE MILITARY; HAZARDOUS DUMPING IN PROTECTED MARINE AREAS; MILITARISM; NUCLEAR PROLIFERATION; STRATEGIC DEFENSE INITIATIVE (SDI); WARISM.

BIBLIOGRAPHY

Biological Testing of Human Subjects by the Department of Defense, 1977 Hearings Before the Subcommittee on Health and Scientific Research of the Committee on Human Resources, Senate, March 8 and May 23, 1977 (Washington, D.C.: U.S. Government Printing Office, 1977).

Cookson, John, and Judith Nottingham, *A Survey of Chemical and Biological Warfare* (London: Sheed and Ward, 1969).

Defense Monitor 18, no. 3 (1989); 18, no. 4 (1989); 18, no. 6 (1989); 18, no. 7 (1989); 20, no. 4 (1991).

Employment of Chemical and Biological Agents, Army Field Manual No. 3-10, Naval Warfare Information No. 36-2, Air Force Manual No. 355-4, and Marine Corps Manual No. 11-3 (Washington, D.C.: U.S. Government Printing Office, March 31, 1966).

Human Drug Testing by the CIA, 1977, Hearings Before the Subcommittee on Health and Scientific Research of the Committee on Human Resources, U.S. Senate, 95th Cong., 1st sess. September 20 and 21, 1977 (Washington, D.C.: U.S. Government Printing Office, 1977).

Rose, Steven, ed., *CBW: Chemical and Biological Warfare, London Conference on CBW* (London: George Harrap & Company, 1968).

MILITARY JARGON. In 1947 under President Harry Truman the War Department became the National Military Establishment (retitled in 1949 as the Department of Defense), and the Secretary of War became the Secretary of Defense. Soldiers no longer waged wars, they waged defense, and the defense budget was defended as a social welfare program. Thus entered the linguistic transformation of neologisms that concealed what was going on from both our potential enemies and from ourselves. The deception ranged over the entire operations and hardware of what had previously been understood to encompass war.

Nowhere was the designed ambiguity greater than in the areas of atomic weapons and production. When the 1975 Sunshine Act required that all meetings of the Nuclear Regulatory Commission be open to the public, the commission held "nonmeeting gatherings." The risks involved in nuclear production were hidden by euphemisms. A nuclear breakdown, resulting in radioactive contamination, was called an "immediate high consequence." Nuclear mismanagement was called "multiple management breakdown." An explosion in a nuclear power plant was called an "energetic disassembly," and a fire was an event of "rapid oxidation." Radioactive, contaminated waste was simply "spent fuel," and deaths or injuries from nuclear accidents were called "health effects." Plans for massive evacuation in the event of a nuclear attack were described as a "fallout sojourn in the countryside."

New weapons were given comforting names. It was suggested that the MX missile be called the "peacemaker," and Robert McFarlane, national security advisor, conjectured that "widowmaker" would not be acceptable. After President Ronald Reagan mistakenly called it the "peacekeeper," that name became established. The bomb that killed an estimated 130,000 people in Hiroshima was named "Little Boy"; the one dropped over Nagasaki was "Fat Man," and it killed at least 70,000 instantly. War planes were given names comparable to those for new cars: Harrier, Dagger, Lynx, Puma, and Hawkeye. Deadly missiles were called Sea Darts, Rapiers, Blowpipes, or Sidewinders. The twenty-four nuclear-armed missiles on a Trident submarine are called the "Christmas Tree Farm," and other nuclear weapons, now called "devices," are given the names of cheeses, trees, or golf strokes. The concentration of 100 missiles is called ambiguously a "dense pack," and the highly volatile and deadly fuel air incendiary bears the name "Daisy Cutter." Terry Egan at the Department of Energy stated that the names must be easy to pronounce and must not connote or imply that they are weapons to be used to kill. The smoke used in smoke bombs is a "universal obscurant."

A missile that goes out of control is described as having "impacted the ground prematurely," or "terminated five minutes earlier than planned." The failure of a missile to hit the target is described as an event where "we acquired the target," and a badly constructed missile is one whose "product integrity is marginal." When the ordinary 13-cent steel nut, called by the Pentagon "a hexiform rotatable surface compression unit," and costing $2,034, failed to work, the Pentagon reported that the piece had "suffered dramatically degraded useful operational life."

Killing the enemy is called "servicing the target," the indiscriminate spraying of an area by machine gun fire is called "reconnaissance by fire," refugees are "ambient noncombatant personnel," and enemy troops who survive are "interdictional nonsuccumbers." The practice of bombing civilians is portrayed as "eroding the will of the population." When U.S. ships are positioned off a foreign territory they are said to be in a "target rich environment." The use of Agent Orange in Vietnam* to poison vegetation was called "resources control." A retreat is a "tactical redeployment" or a "backloading of augmentation personnel." The invasion of Grenada* was called a "pre-dawn vertical insertion," and its object was claimed to be a "rescue mission." Indeed, although the U.S.

Army awarded over 8,500 medals, the report stated that the task was done by the ''Caribbean Peace Keeping Forces.'' A sub-holocaust attack is named a ''surgically clean counter-force strike.'' All these strategies conceal the ethical issues of war.

The use of grossly misleading expressions was particularly egregious by the Nazis when they discussed the Holocaust*. At the Wannsee Conference of January 20, 1942, the German leaders proposed the language for discussion of the Holocaust. The genocidal* war against the Jews was called ''the final solution''; the problem of how to exterminate the Jews was the ''Jewish question''; the acts of killing the Jews were ''special treatment'' or ''cleansing''; the act of removing them from the ghettos was called ''thinning out''; the mobile gas chambers were ''auxiliary equipment''; the compliance sought from the Jews was called ''cadaver obedient.'' When the Nazis shifted from shooting Jews to gassing them, this new practice was called ''humanizing,'' meaning that it was psychologically easier on the killers.

See MILITARY-INDUSTRIAL COMPLEX; PATRIOTISM; PROPAGANDA; WARISM.

BIBLIOGRAPHY
Caldicott, Helen, *Missile Envy* (New York: Bantam Books, 1986).
Lutz, William, *Doublespeak* (New York: Harper & Row, 1989).

MILITARY LAND USE. *See* ARCTIC REGION; BIKINI ATOLL, BOMBING OF; BIOLOGICAL/CHEMICAL WARFARE; ENVIRONMENTAL ISSUES, POLLUTION, AND THE MILITARY; HAWAII, MILITARY LAND USE IN; HAZARDOUS DUMPING IN PROTECTED MARINE AREAS; NUCLEAR WEAPONS TESTING; OKINAWA, MILITARY OCCUPATION OF; ZONES OF PEACE.

MILITARY NECESSITY. This ancient military concept has posed the primary problem in all efforts to set humanitarian limits to what should be allowed in war. *General Orders 100** mentioned military necessity as referring to those acts ''which are indispensable for securing the ends of war'' (Article 14). It allows all destruction of ''those armed enemies and any others whose death is unavoidable,'' although it does not allow ''infliction of suffering for the sake of suffering, or for revenge, nor of maiming or wounding except in fight'' (Article 16). Furthermore, military necessity does not allow the use of poison, wanton devastation, or acts of perfidy. It was unclear whether these acts were not allowed because they were never militarily required, or that they were not allowed even where it would be militarily useful to do them. Military legalists generally claimed that laws of war had been written taking account of military necessity, which appeared to mean that whatever was militarily necessary would never be declared illegal. The problem for the soldier was to know when such acts were unavoidable, when he might be causing suffering for the sake of suffering, or when revenge was playing a part.

Rules of Land Warfare (1914)* added the principles of humanity and chivalry as conditioning military necessity. Humanity prohibited acts of violence that were not militarily necessary, and chivalry demanded ''a certain amount of fairness.'' But it was not clear whether humanity or chivalry might forbid acts that were deemed militarily necessary. The same ambiguity persisted in the 1934 manual revision, and in the current manual, *The Law of Land Warfare* (1956)*. The current formulation still leaves unclear whether military necessity is inviolate or whether appeal to it can ever be overruled. The judges at Nuremberg stated that military necessity cannot be used as a defense for acts forbidden by the conventional and customary laws of war*. However, it was not suggested that a militarily useful strategy would ever be abandoned on the sole grounds of humanitarian concern. The extermination camps were forbidden because they lacked any military justification, and hence were not required for German victory.

The unanswered question is whether the function of laws of war is to protect all militarily necessary acts or to serve as a judge of those militarily necessary acts that should be forbidden. Debate at the war crimes trials* after World War II revolved around whether militarily necessary acts of war should ever be forbidden by laws of war. The judges at Nuremberg* affirmed in the *Hostage Case (United States v. List et al.)* that no appeal to military necessity could justify wanton devastation of a district or the infliction of suffering serving no military function. The judges did state that the appeal to military necessity might be overruled by other customary or conventional rules, but such instances appeared to need to be settled case by case. The judges at the *Krupp* trial agreed with those at the *Hostage* trial. But did the judges establish that war crimes*, crimes against humanity*, and crimes against the peace* were criminal even where it might be militarily expedient to act otherwise, or was the conclusion that these crimes were always militarily unnecessary?

Confusion still exists in distinguishing between military necessity and self-preservation. One of the aspects of the question raised at the trials was whether a nation involved in an illegal war was entitled to appeal to military necessity, and the judges ruled that military necessity was a proper appeal only in legitimate wars. Not all international jurists have maintained that every state has a fundamental right of self-preservation independently of laws of war. In most wars there will be a victor and a vanquished. To allow the losing side to violate all laws of war to avoid being conquered would open the door to the abandonment of all semblance of war limits. There is a widespread suspicion that there really are no laws of war. After all, The Hague Conventions* were prefaced by the formula, ''if military circumstances permit,'' and the Conventions of Geneva* provided that nations could renounce them.

See CRIMES AGAINST HUMANITY; FORBIDDEN STRATEGIES; FORBIDDEN WEAPONS; HOSTAGES; NUREMBERG TRIALS; SIEGE WARFARE; WAR CRIMES.

BIBLIOGRAPHY

Brierly, J. L., *The Law of Nations* (Oxford: University Press, 1963).

Draper, Colonel G.I.A., ''The Ethical and Juridical Status of Restraints in War,'' *Military Law Review* 55 (Winter 1972).

Falk, Richard A., *The Status of Law in International Society* (Princeton, N.J.: Princeton University Press, 1970).

Kunz, Josef L., ''The Chaotic Status of the Laws of War and the Urgent Necessity for Their Revision,'' *American Journal of International Law* 45 (January 1951).

MILITARY POLLUTION. *See* ARCTIC REGION; BIKINI ATOLL, BOMBING OF; BIOLOGICAL/CHEMICAL WARFARE; ENVIRONMENTAL ISSUES, POLLUTION, AND THE MILITARY; FORBIDDEN WEAPONS; GENEVA PROTOCOL, JUNE 17, 1925; HAWAII, MILITARY LAND USE IN; HAZARDOUS DUMPING IN PROTECTED MARINE AREAS; INTELLIGENCE AGENCIES, U.S.; MASS DESTRUCTION, WEAPONS OF; MILITARY-INDUSTRIAL COMPLEX; NUCLEAR ACCIDENTS; NUCLEAR PROLIFERATION; NUCLEAR TESTING; WARNING ZONES AND MILITARY EXCLUSION ON THE HIGH SEAS.

MILITARY TRAINING, BASIC. From the point of view of the military, the function of basic training has been to create soldiers who would perform well under battle conditions. S.L.A. Marshall stated, ''What we need to seek in training are any and all means by which we can increase the ratio of effective fire.'' What his studies revealed, however, was that even among the most seasoned troops, only about 25 percent of the soldiers would fire their weapons even when they were severely attacked. The average was closer to 15 percent. These results were more true for riflemen than for machine gunners or those firing in small groups. Marshall concluded that in ''civilized'' nations the average and healthy individual had such a strong resistance to killing that he would not of his own volition take a life if there was any way to avoid it. What information exists indicates that this was less of a problem in the navy and air force. If average individuals do have a resistance to killing, then the very remoteness of the targets in navy and air force engagement meant that the psychological problems were less likely to arise. Air crews dropped their missiles from a vast distance and were spared cries of anguish, the sight of mutilated bodies, and even the sound of their bombs. The problems of basic training for troops under fire is peculiarly different for the army. No effort is made here to question whether the training is adequate to the task, although Marshall's concerns are timely and important. The intent is to raise ethical questions about what is required to make civilians into soldiers and what problems arise in converting them back into civilians.

The conversion of civilians into foot soldiers, generally referred to as ''basic training,'' has traditionally consisted of two kinds of instruction. On the one hand, the recruit learned skills in marching, marksmanship, military courtesy and customs, and field fortification. None of these had any meaningful civilian use. On the other hand, the recruit was conditioned to obey without question the orders of his superiors*, whatever they might be. Such training was inimical to constructive life in a democratic society. The relationships among the staff were caste structured and, thus, alien to democratic egalitarianism. The relations between officers and enlisted persons were rigidly stratified, with immense power over those at lower ranks and servile powerlessness toward those of higher ranks. Military justice was also caste ridden. Noncommissioned persons would probably be reduced in rank to the bottom for infractions, while officers were commonly merely transferred to another place. Colonel Thomas R. Phillips commented in 1943 that Army regulations on discipline were patterned from those of 1821, which were copied unchanged from the regulations of the noble and peasant army of Royal France of 1788. Nowhere were the contradictions between the profession* of soldiering and the obligations of citizenship in a democratic society more obvious than in both military rank and training.

The social structure of the military is medieval, with hierarchical control and rigid separation by rank, with clearly specified privileges for the elite, while privilege for the lower ranks rests on the whim of the upper ranks. Overall, there is an almost total lack of the kind of moral accountability we expect in civilian life. Otherwise efficient workers in civilian life are trained to lose personal initiative and are taught to wait for orders from above before daring to act. Procedures are simple and learned easily, but further information trickles down slowly, if at all, from ranks above. Liddell Hart once commented that a lifetime in the military curbing original thought often results, on retirement, in there being nothing to express. Soldiers are so impersonalized that they are known by a number. The perfectly trained soldier is one whose civilian initiative has been reduced to zero. Recruits are trained to depend on the military, and normal civilian attitudes of responsibility toward property, society, and social institutions are largely ignored.

The general attitude of the leadership toward those in basic training has been exemplified in the ways in which recruits were used as guinea pigs in chemical, biological, and radiological experiments, and in the unwillingness after wars to compensate recruits for illnesses that they suffered as a consequence of their service. Congressional hearings in 1977 revealed that between 1944 and 1977 over 140 biological and chemical experiments were performed on unwitting soldiers at military bases by the Central Intelligence Agency (CIA) and the Department of Defense (DOD). Just as the experiments with Agent Orange and nuclear exposure to tests were denied by the military to have caused any negative results on soldiers after World War II and Vietnam*, so also following the Spanish American War the government denied that the returning soldiers had typhoid and refused to treat them. From the very beginning of experiments with atomic bombs, soldiers were exposed deliberately to radiation to aid in scientific experiments.

Writers such as Willard Waller in his book, *The Veteran Comes Back*, George

K. Pratt in his *Soldier to Civilian,* and Eliot A. Cohen in *Citizens and Soldiers: The Dilemmas of Military Service,* conclude that the army machine destroys individual will, alienates the individual from normal society, substitutes the Army for society, plays havoc with family relationships, virtually abolishes ordinary democratic freedoms, stresses instant obedience without reflection, forces persons into jobs they did not want, and trains men to kill, a task with no useful civilian function. The overall training was found inconsistent with the democratic ends of the preservation of life, liberty, and the pursuit of happiness. Many concluded that the Victorian notion that the "Army makes a man out of you," was false as far as living in a democratic society. As far as training was concerned, a colonel once remarked, "Show me a private with fifteen years experience, and I'll show you a private with one year of experience repeated fifteen times."

Military training requires the soldier to suppress aggression toward military superiors, whom they may detest, and bestow it on persons whom they have never met and toward whom they probably have no feelings at all. Recent studies (Dixon) suggest that the military organization may attract a minority of persons who are already a menace to society and furthers those very attitudes that will prove destructive to society on their return. The medieval caste system, the emphasis on a macho image, and the generally unregulated power of the upper ranks over the lower, have been attractive to both sadists and masochists. Reports of widespread maltreatment of recruits exist. Congressional hearings reported, for example, that at the camps at Parris Island, South Carolina and at San Diego, recruits were beaten to death, shot, marched to death in excessive heat, thrown down stairs, forced into acts of self-flagellation, or drowned. On one occasion at Parris Island a drill sergeant took raw recruits on a forced night march that resulted in the drowning of six soldiers in Ribbon Creek. Recruits were hazed, forced to run up and down ladders, forced to ingest more food or drink than their systems could handle, made to eat paper or other foreign objects, made to march with ballast, required to attack one another violently, and made to stand in unnatural positions for unduly long periods. At Fort Jackson, South Carolina, on June 29, 1978, sixty recruits arrived and began training. Ten hours later two were dead of heat stroke. One had been required to run around the parade ground carrying a sand bag and a log, the other was compelled to beat his chest against a tree. A General Accounting Office report (GAO/NSIAD-94-82) for fiscal years 1989 through 1992 reported that at least 700 uniformed personnel lost their lives in training accidents, and noted that the armed services do not identify all training-related deaths.

When soldiers are mustered out, the problems of conversion to civilian society once again subject the soldiers to new and serious readjustments. Dixon Wecter's *When Johnny Comes Marching Home* was paradigmatic. Vietnam veterans were neither the first nor the last to return angry, to discover that their military skills were useless at home, that the cruelty, horror, fear, and guilt generated by their war experiences ill-prepared them for civilian life, and that society was commonly less than appreciative of what they had been commanded to do or endure. Soldiers who had been sheltered in the womb of military paternalism found themselves adrift, unsupported, and unappreciated by both the citizens and the government. Psychologist Elizabeth Rosenberg commented, ''It would be surprising if the inevitable release of aggressive impulses in active warfare failed to produce more or less pathological reactions of anxiety or guilt.'' The problems faced by returning soldiers due to official diffidence and neglect go back to the American Revolution and continued through the Civil War, Spanish American War, and World War I. The only U.S. war in which returning soldiers received respect or appreciation was World War II, and this was no model, given the medical experiments conducted on recruits. U.S. soldiers returning from the over forty wars that they have fought since World War II (from Korea* through the Gulf War*) have faced both an angry citizenry and an indifferent administration. One cannot overemphasize the significance of the widespread ''post-traumatic stress disorder,'' referred to by psychologists as an old problem, not created in Vietnam, because it highlights the fact that no matter what the process of military training is, many cannot be conditioned to kill or to tolerate the slaughter of war.

Obviously, beyond basic training, soldiers may learn mechanical, electrical, engineering, or computer skills. These, however, are not dependent upon basic training and are already handled in civilian society. It may well be that so-called basic training prepares recruits for the rigors of war and that without it men and women would be unable to do their soldierly duties, but in a volume on war and ethics it is timely to note the price such training exacts, and the degree to which such training is inconsistent with the duties of responsible citizenship in a democratic society. Pericles proclaimed the virtues of military training in urging citizens to go to war ''whether the ostensible cause be great or small.'' But Aristotle observed that ancient tyrants were demagogues precisely because they were trained military men. Adam Smith (1723–1790) saw military training as inimical to republican liberties. Even a Social Darwinian like Herbert Spencer (1820–1903) recognized that the military spirit ''perpetually tramples on justice.'' Liebknecht concluded that the proper spirit for military training consisted of a ''crazy jingoism, narrow mindedness, and arrogance . . . lack of understanding or even hatred of every kind of progress.''

See DEMOCRACY AND THE MILITARY; INTELLIGENCE AGENCIES, U.S.; MILITARISM; MILITARY AS A PROFESSION; MILITARY EDUCATION; PSYCHIC NUMBING; SUPERIOR ORDERS; UNIFORM CODE OF MILITARY JUSTICE; WARISM.

BIBLIOGRAPHY

American Journal of Sociology 51, no. 5 (March 1946).

Deaths and Abuses of U.S. Army Trainees, Hearings Before the Investigations Subcommittee of the Committee on Armed Services, H.R., 96th Cong., 1st sess., June 6, 7 and July 11, 1979 (Washington, D.C.: U.S. Government Printing Office, 1979).

Dixon, Norman, *On the Psychology of Military Incompetence* (London: Jonathan Cape, 1976).

Lifton, Robert Jay, *Home from the War: Vietnam Veterans: Neither Victims nor Executioners* (New York: Simon & Schuster, 1973).

Marine Corps Recruit Training and Recruiting Programs, Hearings Before the Subcommittee on Military Personnel of the Committee of the Armed Services, H.R., 94th Cong., 2d sess., May 24, 25, 26, June 2, 3, 9, 23, 29, and August 9, 1976 (Washington, D.C.: U.S. Government Printing Office, 1979).

Marshall, S.L.A., *Men Under Fire* (New York: William Morrow, 1968).

Military Training Deaths, Report to the Honorable Dave Durenberger, U.S. Senate, GAO/NSIAD-94-82 (May 1994).

Pratt, George K., *Soldier to Civilian* (New York: Whittlesey House, 1944).

Severo, Richard, and Lewis Milford, *The Wages of War* (New York: Simon & Schuster, 1989).

Sonnenberg, Stephen M., Arthur S. Blank, and John A. Talbott, *The Trauma of War: Stress and Recovery in Viet Nam Veterans* (Washington, D.C.: American Psychiatric Press, 1985).

Uhl, Michael, and Tod Ensign, *GI Guinea Pigs: How the Pentagon Exposed Our Troops to Dangers More Deadly Than War: Agent Orange and Atomic Radiation* (New York: Wideview Press, 1980).

Waller, Willard, *The Veteran Comes Back* (New York: Dryden Press, 1944).

Wecter, Dixon, *When Johnny Comes Marching Home* (Cambridge, Mass.: The Riverside Press, 1944).

MILITARY USES OF THE OCEAN. A maritime nation, large or small, must use its sea power for these related purposes: to obtain access to the seas; to control the seas for unimpeded navigation, which in turn is essential for commerce or the acquisition of resources; and finally, to provide national security both in terms of self-defense and the ability to project military force overseas in times of war and peace. For major seapowers such as the United States and the former Soviet Union, naval presence and mobility in the world's oceans are indicative of global influence and dominance. Two recent developments have had some impact on the traditional uses of military power on the seas. First is the creeping jurisdiction of national claims over the ocean space that resulted in the establishment by the 1982 Law of the Sea Convention of new ocean regimes that tend to reduce naval mobility. The second is the rapid developments in modern naval strategy and weaponry that have made military uses of the oceans no longer limited to surface activities. Military activities in the oceans are now increasingly and inextricably linked to strategic nuclear warfare and the antisubmarine activities of underwater detection, identification and surveillance of nuclear-powered submarines capable of firing ballistic missiles with nuclear warheads—submarine-launched ballistic missiles (SLBMs).

Peacetime antisubmarine warfare conducted underneath the ocean surface, as well as the traditional military uses of warships on the ocean water, first of all raise the question of the legality of these military uses in the context of the new law of the seas convention. Then there is the need by the world community to find ways by which the use and testing of explosive nuclear devices on and under the oceans may be regulated, if not prohibited, by international or regional consensus. This consideration is necessitated by the overall need for maintaining the existing power balance and guaranteeing international stability and state security. Accordingly, it is useful to discuss briefly the legal principles established by the 1982 Law of the Sea (LOS) Convention for the peacetime military uses of the ocean.

First, the coastal state has complete sovereignty over its internal waters and territorial sea. Therefore, no other state's vessels, including warships, can enter into the internal waters, the airspace above, or the seabed underneath, without the explicit permission of the coastal state, except for the purpose of transient passage. In peacetime it is not permissible for another state to deploy underwater antisubmarine surveillance devices, such as sonobuoys. Such activities constitute a violation of international law, and the coastal state can remove such emplacements from its internal waters. However, David Larson estimated that Soviet submarines had committed a total of 122 underwater penetrations or incursions between 1969 and 1982 in Swedish and Norwegian internal waters. Article 19(2) of the 1982 LOS Convention specifies the types of activities engaged in by a foreign state in internal waters or the territorial sea that are "prejudicial to the peace, good order or security" of a coastal state. These are: the use of force against the sovereignty, territorial integrity, or political independence of the coastal state; any exercise or practice with weapons of any kind; any act of propaganda; and the launching, landing, or taking on board of any aircraft or any military devices. Articles 17–45 of the 1982 LOS Convention provide coastal states with the right to control and regulate their territorial seas and transit through their straits with respect to innocent passage. The March and April 1986 U.S. military actions involving air strikes against Libya and the show of force and missile exchange around the Gulf of Sidra* were incidents of aberration that pose questions of legality in the military uses of the ocean.

On the high seas there is a considerable uncertainty about the right of states to engage in military activities in the area beyond the limits of national jurisdiction. While the high seas are open for use by all nations with guarantees of the basic freedoms of navigation, overflight, fishing, cable laying, and scientific research, Articles 88 and 89 of the 1982 LOS Convention stipulate that "the high seas shall be reserved for peaceful purposes." Also, "no state may validly purport to subject any part of the high seas to its sovereignty." The language of Article 88 is rather ambiguous, for it does not clearly distinguish between nonmilitary uses and nonaggressive uses of the high seas. If nonmilitary purposes are the only kind permitted, then navigation by warships on the high seas surely must be prohibited; but, if nonaggressive purposes are allowed, then any nation's navy may use the high seas for any military purpose if such activities are not considered aggressive. Zedalis takes the position that warships must use the high seas as guaranteed by the established freedom of navigation principle, so long as such military activities are "reasonable in nature" and do not prevent other nations and their warships from transiting, and so long as a nation does not claim exclusive jurisdiction over others on the high sea area. David L. Larson feels that the provisions of the 1982 LOS Convention do not by themselves restrict the use of naval weapons on the high seas. Thus, in Larson's view, with the exception of specific prohibitions by other treaty arrangements, all naval weaponry, including strategic nuclear ballistic missile submarines and strategic nuclear attack submarines, is permitted.

Under Article 73 of the LOS Convention, the coastal state has the right to enact enforcement laws and regulations in the exclusive economic zone for economic exploitation, navigation, and security. Thus the deployment of limited range antisubmarine devices in the zone is permitted. Article 2(1) of the 1959 Convention on the Continental Shelf and Article 77 and 79 of the 1982 LOS Convention grant sovereign rights to the coastal states for the purpose of exploring and exploiting the natural resources on the continental shelf.

The interpretation of these provisions, as well as state practice, seem to indicate that military uses on the continental shelf are specifically prohibited. Thus, in the exercise of the sovereign rights of the coastal states, military uses can be permitted as long as they do not interfere with (1) the exercise of navigational freedoms of other states, including laying submarine cables and pipelines, and (2) the coastal state's right to explore and exploit resources on the continental shelf. However, the continental shelf is the prime area for emplacing antisubmarine detection and surveillance devices. The legality of emplacing such electronic and acoustic devices on the continental shelf is a matter of debate. David Larson argues that it may be permissible to emplace the antisubmarine detecting devices beyond two hundred nautical miles with or without the coastal state's approval. But another state's emplacement on the continental shelf of antisubmarine electronic devices that would interfere with a coastal state's exploration and exploitation of the continental shelf resources is questionable at best. In the context of superpower competition, military and strategic considerations often outweigh the question of legal permissibility. Such has been the case of the employment of the sound surveillance system (SOSUS) off the Kuriles and Aleutians in the Pacific, and off the North Cape between Iceland, Greenland, and the United Kingdom. The U.S. Navy's SOSUS system, which cost about $16 billion during the Cold War, is now facing drastic budget cuts. For the 1995 fiscal year, the Clinton administration has requested only $60 million, as compared to $165 million in 1994 and $335 million in 1991. While the SOSUS system once maintained a network of more than 1,000 undersea microphones linked by more than 30,000 miles of cables to the Navy's monitoring stations, the Navy dismantled most of these undersea listening devices in the early 1990s. The remaining undersea listening devices are being used for monitoring the migrations of whales, detecting earthquakes, measuring ocean temperature, and for other undersea scientific research.

In the case of the high seas, it is generally accepted as permissible to emplace strategic ballistic nuclear submarines and other naval weaponry on the deep seabed—if there are no specific prohibitions by treaty arrangements. However, Article 141 of the 1982 LOS Convention does call for the international area reserved for deep sea exploration and exploitation be used exclusively for peaceful purposes. If the term "peaceful purposes" means the absence of aggressive use in the deep seabed area, then military activities are permitted. But, if the term refers to all military activities, then such uses are in violation of Article 141. Aside from the continuous debate among scholars as to whether the deep seabed area is *res communis* or *res nullius,* there is really no clear or specific prohibition of the emplacement of detecting surveillance devices on the seabed as long as there is no exclusive use. In the future, the deep seabed will become a prime area for antisubmarine activities, for, as pointed out by David Larson, the ocean regime is a legal vacuum and the use of naval weaponry is "unrestricted and unrestrained."

The issue of military uses of the ocean was neglected at the UN Law of the Sea Conferences. As potential conflicts develop between the claims of the coastal states and the need for the sea to be accessible to the world's navies, there are many issues concerning the military uses of the ocean that need clarification. Will the high seas and the deep seabed continue to be used for peaceful purposes in the future against the trend of naval weaponry becoming more sophisticated and more destructive?

There is a deadly game of hunting-and-be-hunted under the ocean waters being engaged in by the superpowers and their submarines, which can slip through the waters of each other's coasts. It is now technologically possible for a Russian skipper to hear his pursuer under water before he is detected by the U.S. Navy's listening devices. The balance of power under the ocean waters is changing as new technology develops. The key question to be posed now is, can the evolving new law of the sea and future arms controls restrict the future military uses of the oceans? It may be reasonable to ask that the issue of military uses in the ocean should be a key item for negotiation at the next (the fourth) law of the sea conference. The neglected issue of military use of the oceans should be the priority item for discussion since the Law of the Sea Convention came into force on November 16, 1994.

See BIKINI ATOLL, BOMBING OF; ENVIRONMENTAL ISSUES; HAZARDOUS DUMPING IN PROTECTED MARINE AREAS; NUCLEAR TESTING IN THE PACIFIC; POLLUTION IN THE MILITARY.

BIBLIOGRAPHY

Booth, Kenneth, "The Military Implications of the Changing Law of the Sea," in *Law of the Sea: Neglected Issues,* John King Gamble, Jr., ed. (Honolulu: Law of the Sea Institute, University of Hawaii, 1979), 328–421.

Larson, David L., "Naval Weaponry and the Law of the Sea," *Ocean Development and International Law* 18, no. 2 (1987), 125–90.

Laursen, Finn, "Security Aspects of Danish and Norwegian Law of the Sea Policies," *Ocean Development and International Law* 18, no. 2 (1987), 199–233.

Modelski, George, and William R. Thompson, *Seapower in Global Politics, 1494–1993* (Seattle: University of Washington Press, 1988).

Richardson, Elliot L., "Power, Mobility and the Law of the Sea," *Foreign Affairs* 58, no. 4 (Spring 1980), 902–19.

Wang, James C. F., *Handbook on Ocean Politics and Law* (Westport, Conn.: Greenwood Press, 1992).

Zedalis, Rex J., "Military Uses of the Ocean Space and the Developing International Law of the Sea: An Analysis in the Context of Peacetime ASW," *San Diego Law Review* 16, no. 13 (April 1979), 591–96.

James C. F. Wang

MINES. Hague Convention 8, Article 1, para. 1. of October 18, 1907, listed three kinds of mines: (1) observation mines anchored and connected by wires so they can be exploded by electricity; (2) anchored automatic contact mines attached to heavy weights and exploded by contact; and (3) unanchored automatic contact mines also exploded by contact. The convention was concerned especially with unanchored automatic mines. It stated that "it is forbidden to lay unanchored automatic contact mines unless they be so constructed as to become harmless one hour at most after those who laid them have lost control over them." Furthermore it was forbidden to lay such mines off the coasts and ports of the enemy for the sole object of intercepting commercial ships. In practice, all such mines were claimed not to have this sole object, and hence the ban was without effect. Anchored mines were to become harmless as soon as they had broken loose. Neutral nations were permitted to lay mines off their own coasts, however, all mines by whomever laid were to be removed at the close of the war. The Hague* had urged that "every precaution must be taken" to protect the innocent, but in the absence of either an adjudicating authority or a precise rule as to the meaning of "every precaution," this rule was largely functionless.

Rules of Land Warfare (1914)* Articles 432–443 discussed the matter of mines and urged nations to construct mines that would satisfy the conditions. Article 440, however, cited Hague 8, Article 6, which modified the prior admonitions, since it stated that nations whose technology did not allow them to manufacture safe mines should "undertake to convert the material of their mines as soon as possible," but left the time frame unspecified. Thus, there was nothing to prevent a belligerent nation from violating the entire Hague intent. The mines in question were antisubmarine mines. The same reference to Hague Convention 8 was discussed in *Rules of Land Warfare* (1934)*, but again only mines laid in water were referred to.

In *The Law of Land Warfare* (1956)*, all reference to mines, whether on sea or land, was deleted. Article 34 merely mentions that explosive mines are not forbidden. No mention in the current or previous manuals was made of antipersonnel land mines. The 1977 Geneva Protocol II* urged limits to the use of these antipersonnel mines, which were indiscriminate, and unlike most weapons of war, remained on the scene for years afterward, and in agricultural Third World countries prohibited normal work and living. Over 100 million uncleared antipersonnel mines are estimated to remain in the field in over sixty countries, and the costs of removing them are expected to exceed the cost of supplying them in the first place. While the United States was a signatory to Protocol II, neither President Ronald Reagan nor George Bush presented the protocol for congressional ratification. Although President Bill Clinton has expressed support for ratification, this has not been done to date (1995).

Almost 100 companies and government agencies in forty-eight countries have manufactured more than 340 different kinds of antipersonnel land mines. The United States heads the list in varieties produced (37), followed by Italy (36), the former USSR (31), Sweden (21), Vietnam (18), Germany (18), Austria (16), the former Yugoslavia (15), France (14), China (12), and the United Kingdom (9). The location of these unexploded mines, in order of number, are: Africa, the Middle East, East Asia, South Asia, Europe, and Latin America. The United States provided its troops with over 275,000 antipersonnel mines for use in the Gulf War*. The export of such mines is a flourishing business, and American-made mines were used in Angola, Cambodia, Iraq, Mozambique, Nicaragua, and Somalia. Discussion at Geneva* suggested that the use of mines constituted perfidy, and should, hence, be considered a violation of the laws of war*. On October 23, 1992, the U.S. Congress approved the Landmine Moratorium Act, which imposed a one-year ban on the sale, export, or transfer abroad of land mines (the Leahy-Evans Amendment). This moratorium was extended in 1993 for three years, and in 1993 the UN General Assembly unanimously approved a resolution calling for moratoriums on landmines, although the reservations and qualifications introduced by UN member nations leave most of the issue ambiguous.

See COMBATANT-NONCOMBATANT DISTINCTION; FORBIDDEN WEAPONS; FRAGMENTATION BOMBS.

BIBLIOGRAPHY

Hidden Death: Land Mines and Civilian Casualties in Iraqi Kurdistan (New York: Human Rights Watch/Middle East, 1992).

Landmines: A Deadly Legacy, The arms project of Human Rights Watch and Physicians for Human Rights (New York: Human Rights Watch, 1993).

U.S. Department of State, *Hidden Killers: The Global Problem with Uncleared Landmines* (Washington, D.C.: U.S. Department of State Political-Military Affairs Bureau, Office of International Security Operations, July 1993).

MORAL EQUIVALENT OF WAR. *See* CIVIL DEFENSE; HUMAN NATURE AND WAR; JAMES, WILLIAM; NONVIOLENT CIVILIAN-BASED DEFENSE.

MOSCOW DECLARATION. On October 30, 1943, the three Allies, Great Britain, USSR, and the United States, issued a declaration in anticipation of war crimes trials to be conducted after the war. The declaration made two principal points: (1) those Germans whose war crimes had been committed in a particular country would be tried by the people of that country and at the place where the offenses had been committed; and (2) those Germans whose crimes had no specific locale would be tried on the basis of a joint decision to be published later by the Allies. In July 1944 the UN War Crimes Commission was established, and by August 8, 1945, the Allies had established an International Military Tribunal for the prosecution of those Nazis whose crimes had no specific locale. The charter of the tribunal established three kinds of offenses: crimes against the peace*, war crimes*, and crimes against humanity*. Subsequent to the proceedings in Nuremberg*, Allied Control Council Law No. 10* provided that uniform legal trials would be conducted of those Germans whose crimes had been in a particular place.

See CONTROL COUNCIL LAW NO. 10; LONDON AGREEMENT ON WAR CRIMINALS; NUREMBERG PRINCIPLES; NUREMBERG TRIALS; WAR CRIMES.

BIBLIOGRAPHY

International Law, 27-161-2, vol. 2 (Washington, D.C.: Headquarters, Department of the Army, October 1962), chap. 8, I, b.

Trials of War Criminals Before the Nuerenberg Tribunals Under Control Council Law No. 10, vol. I (Washington, D.C.: U.S. Government Printing Office, 1949), viii.

MO TZU (MO TI). Lived during the "hundred philosophers" period, being born soon after the death of Confucius (551–479 B.C.) and dying a generation before the birth of Mencius (371–289?), Confucius's most famous follower. The dates usually ascribed to him are 470–391 B.C. He seems to have come from humble origins but, nonetheless, was well educated—possibly in Confucianism. Not surprisingly, he shared with Confucius the thought that rulers must serve all the people in a society and not just some special class within it. But he went beyond Confucius and his followers in preaching his doctrine of universal love. For Mo Tzu, and unlike Confucius, we are not supposed to privilege our own family. We are supposed to be as kind to other people's fathers as we would be to our own. Further, his universal love doctrine demands that a ruler not privilege his own people, either. All people must be treated as equals, as they are treated, he says, by God. Following a form of utilitarian theory, he said that the right thing to do is to maximize the welfare of all people. This meant that, given the limited resources available to societies in those days, Mo Tzu would not countenance the extravagant lifestyle of the ruling classes—something the followers of Confucius apparently did. He condemned the elaborate funerals of the day. These funerals, according to the Confucionists, were a way of showing respect for ancestors. Mo Tzu wondered, as he saw much money spent on them and on other aristocratic indulgences such as musical extravaganzas, clothes, jewelry and houses, whether more good could be done by giving people simple clothes, basic good food, and simple but warm and safe housing. He wanted a society for the people even if he did not want (perhaps because the people were not ready for it) a society of the people.

Mo Tzu's attitude toward war is consistent with these thoughts. He saw wars of aggression as terribly costly activities—especially to the people. In the short run these wars might benefit the ruler or some special class within the society, but as they traveled away from home to conquer other states, soldiers and their leaders would not be doing their normal work of farming, fishing, laboring, and administering. The society would suffer during their long absence. Further, the society would suffer because there would be casualties and much loss of supplies and equipment. Not only that, the conquered people would suffer. Aggressive wars*, Mo Tzu thought, seem to bring the least, rather than the greatest, good to the greatest number. This was especially true as the occupation of the enemy territory continued and what was originally a traditional war between two armies turned into a guerrilla war*. He also said that aggressive wars represent thievery. He could not understand how people could condemn horse thieves and murderers, but then turn around and praise those rulers who are horse thieves and murderers on a grand scale. He argued that a red patch is red whether it is small or large. So a large act of thievery, as is represented by aggressive war, is thievery, just as is a small act of thievery committed by a pickpocket. If we wish to be consistent we should condemn the former just as we do the latter.

No doubt, then, Mo Tzu was no lover of war. But he was no pacifist* either. In fact he condoned going to war, even starting one, under certain conditions. If a neighboring state's ruler systematically abused his citizens by overtaxing them in order to pay for a war of aggression, build new castles, or simply pay for a fancy lifestyle, Mo Tzu would say that the ruler had lost his mandate of Heaven. That ruler would deserve to be deposed, especially under the aegis of the principle of universal love, which says that we are supposed to care for our neighbors as much as for our family. Mo Tzu distinguished these so-called punitive wars from wars of aggression. The former are permitted; the latter are not.

Mo Tzu went beyond merely teaching what seems in retrospect to be an early version of just war* theory. He was a man of action as well as words. He had a following of perhaps several hundred students. His students did not just study Moist doctrines, they also participated in military activities. Whenever Mo Tzu heard that some state was planning aggression upon another, his well-trained student troops would make themselves ready to help defend the potential victim state. While they were waiting for the aggressor, Mo Tzu, it is said, was typically engaged in negotiations to bring about a peaceful settlement of the dispute. On one occasion he is said to have dissuaded the ruler of Chu from attacking the state of Sung. Apparently a strategist by the name of Kung Shu Pan had created "cloud ladders" to be used for storming fortifications. This encouraged the ruler of Chu to plan an invasion. Mo Tzu presented himself before that ruler and showed him how he would deploy his forces and the forces of Sung to repel each and every attack planned by Kung Shu Pan. The king was impressed by Mo Tzu's presentation. Kung Shu Pan, however, said he had one last secret plan. Mo Tzu surmised that this involved killing Mo Tzu. His response was that he anticipated Kung Shu Pan's last move and, as a result, had already placed his men in position to defend Sung no matter what happened to him. It was at this point that the king of Chu decided to keep his troops at home.

In Mo Tzu we have one of the earliest of just war theorists. Like most theorists in this tradition, and certainly like many thinkers in China before and after him, he was fully aware of the horrors of war. It was his concern, as both a just war* thinker and warrior, to do something about placing restraints on that horror.

BIBLIOGRAPHY

Creel, Herrlee G., *Chinese Thought: From Confucius to Mao Tse-tung* (Chicago: University of Chicago Press, 1953).

Mo Tzu, *Basic Writings,* Burton Watson, trans. (New York: Columbia University Press, 1963).

Nicholas G. Fotion

MUSTE, ABRAHAM JOHANNES (1885–1967). As a pacifist* clergyman he helped found a Boston chapter of the Fellowship of Reconciliation and opposed the U.S. entry into World War I. Born in Zierkzee in the Dutch province of Zeeland, his family emigrated to America in January 1891, and settled in Grand Rapids, Michigan. The family joined the Fourth Dutch Reformed Church, which taught predestination, original sin, and salvation by grace. He graduated from Hope College and then went on to New Brunswick Theological Seminary, during which time he took courses at Columbia University. In 1912 he joined the Socialist movement and voted that fall for the Socialist, Eugene Debs*, for president.

In 1915 he was called to Newtonville, Massachusetts Congregational Church as their minister, a post from which he resigned in March 1918 on request because of his opposition to the war, and he joined the Society of Friends in Rhode Island. He came under the influence of Rufus Jones, Sherwood Eddy, Roger Baldwin, Jane Addams*, Garrison Villard, W.E.B. DuBois, and Norman Thomas. In 1919, prompted by concern for the textile workers' strike in Lawrence, Massachusetts, he accepted the post as head of the Boston Defense Committee, and by the end of the year was executive secretary of the Amalgamated Textile Workers Union, a position he resigned in 1921 to become director of Brookwood Labor College in Katonah, New York.

He was actively involved in the Scottsboro Case and was secretary of the Tom Mooney Pardon Conference. In 1933 his followers, dubbed ''Musteites,'' established the American Workers Party, to include Socialists and Communists, but to maintain a third way between socialism and communism. In October 1936 Muste broke with the Marxist contingent and renewed his work with the Fellowship of Reconciliation (FOR), and accepted a post as minister of the Presbyterian Labor Temple in New York City. At the outbreak of World War II he resigned from the Temple to become the executive secretary of the FOR, effective April 1, 1940. Although he initially supported the National Service Board for Religious Objectors (NSBRO) in their support for alternative service for war objectors, he later advocated that the FOR break its ties with the NSBRO because it did not adequately defend nonreligious objectors and those who refused even alternative service. He strongly supported the pamphlet by Vera Brittain*, *Massacre by Bombing,* which opposed the Allied practice of obliteration bombing.

After the war, Muste promoted a Tax Refusal Committee, and in March 1960 the Internal Revenue Service took him to court for failing to pay taxes since 1948. Since he lived solely on gifts he had no income that could be taxed. He was a lecturer at Union Theological Seminary, active in the Congress of Racial Equality (CORE), the War Resisters League, the Committee for Nonviolent Action, and the World Peace Brigade. He opposed the war in Vietnam* and served on numerous antiwar committees, supported draft card burnings, and spoke whenever he was asked. In January 1967 (then aged 83) he and Pastor Niemoller (75), Anglican Bishop Ambrose Reeves (67), and American Rabbi Abraham Feinberg (67) were guests by invitation in Hanoi, North Vietnam. He wrote back with a message to Washington, "For God's sake stop lying. . . . Let us stop this bombing practice." One month later he died of an aneurism. A long-time friend commented, "He allocated eighty-two years to living but only one day for dying." *Time* magazine called him "The Number One U.S. Pacifist"; J. Edgar Hoover branded him a "long time Communist fronter"; and Martin Luther King, Jr.* said that without Muste the "American Negro might never have caught the meaning of nonviolence."

See CHRISTIANITY AND WAR; CONSCIENTIOUS OBJECTION; PACIFISM.

BIBLIOGRAPHY
Muste, A. J., *Nonviolence in an Aggressive World* (New York, 1940).
————, *Not By Might* (1947) (New York: Garland Library, reprint, 1971).
Robinson, Jo Ann Ooiman, *Abraham Went Out: A Biography of A. J. Muste* (Philadelphia: Temple University Press, 1981).

MUTUAL ASSURED DESTRUCTION (MAD). A doctrine of the nuclear age, before which only the loser in a war could fear total or near-total destruction. But historically, when the Soviet Union and other nations followed the United States into the nuclear age, the possibility arose that even the purported winner in a war could lose everything.

More specifically, the original, or what might be called the classic, MAD doctrine is composed of three claims: (1) No matter how successful an aggressor* nation's initial nuclear attacks are, the victim nation could still mount attacks that would be successful enough to destroy the aggressor. Of course, this claim presupposes that the nations involved have numerous nuclear weapons and the means of delivering them to various targets—a presupposition long since satisfied by several nations. (2) There is no effective defense against nuclear attacks, especially those delivered by missiles. Part of the force of this claim is that even a very effective defense against nuclear attacks, up to 95 percent effective, would not be good enough, since the destructive power of the remaining 5 percent would be great enough to destroy any nation. (3) All those nations possessing a significant number of nuclear weapons believe the first two MAD claims. This third claim is essential to MAD, for even if the first two claims were true, but were not believed by someone whose hand was on a nuclear trigger, that person might (irrationally) launch an attack on one or more of the other nuclear powers. MAD would thus fail to deter, and the mutual destruction predicted in the first claim would become a reality.

It should be clear that MAD is not just a descriptive doctrine that reports how things are. Rather, it is primarily a prescriptive doctrine addressed to all nuclear powers. In what will henceforth be called the narrow version of MAD, the first claim can be viewed as a threat aimed at potential aggressor nations: "If you initiate a major nuclear attack and, in so doing, defeat another nation, you in turn will be defeated by the defeated nation." In this same narrow version the second claim reads "Don't build defensive weapon systems," and is aimed at both potential aggressors and victims. The third claim is aimed at believers, and urges them to "Convince nonbelievers of the correctness of the other two claims."

Although MAD as a general doctrine is controversial, the narrow version is the least controversial of three versions. If MAD "works," it does so paradigmatically in an all-out nuclear war* between two or more major nuclear-armed nations. In contrast to this narrow version, the somewhat narrow version argues that the MAD doctrine applies even in wars where the involved nations initially use nuclear weapons sparingly. The talk here is of a nuclear threshold. Once nations cross that threshold, the argument is, they cannot easily avoid escalation. One nation might use a small nuclear weapon to thwart a dangerous conventional enemy attack employing tanks, planes, and artillery backed with hordes of infantry. If it did, the likelihood is that its enemy would retaliate* by using a somewhat larger nuclear weapon. Or perhaps the retaliation would take the form of using two small shots. Whatever the enemy did, the first user* would likely retaliate in turn. The end result would be open-ended escalation and a collapse of the somewhat narrow into the narrow version. Both versions lead to mutual destruction. They come to the same thing.

The extended version of MAD is the most controversial of the three. It argues that MAD doctrine applies to any major wars fought directly between two nuclear powers. For this version, war, not just nuclear war, is the threshold that should not be crossed. This is because it is assumed that a major conventional war fought between nuclear powers will inevitably lead to situations where one side or the other will be tempted to use nuclear weapons. The nation succumbing to this temptation might be on the verge of victory, needing an extra punch to help bring it about. Or it might resort to nuclear weapons as it finds its back to the wall. Or still another possibility is that those in charge of the war see using small nuclear weapons as just a small escalation, given that the conventional war they are fighting is already so destructive. Other possible scenarios can be imagined. All these possibilities are so real, according to extended MAD, that the fear of escalation to nuclear war prevents these nations from confronting each other militarily in any kind of war. In this extended version, MAD expresses the thought that holding nuclear weapons in place not only prevents nuclear war but all major wars between nations possessing these weapons. The sheer fear of what might happen is enough to freeze these nations into a state of peace, albeit an uneasy one.

Opposition to MAD comes from two sides. On the one, there are those who suppose that war is still a viable option even while the participants have a variety of nuclear weapons in hand. On the other, there are those who argue from some pacifist* position and also certain versions of the just war* position.

The most benign criticism from the warrior side questions the extended version of MAD, but not the other two. It argues that fear of crossing the nuclear threshold is so great that a major conventional war between two nuclear powers will not likely escalate to the nuclear level. It would be nice, these critics say, if all nations were convinced that MAD applied to all wars. If they were convinced, they would have no reason to buy large numbers of bombers, fighter planes, tanks, helicopters, artillery, aircraft carriers, and submarines. Unfortunately, extended-version MAD is believed by so few of them that the United States, Russia, Great Britain, France, Germany, China, and almost all other nations continue to build their conventional military arsenals. They do so not just to fight potential enemy nations devoid of nuclear weaponry, but to directly face potential nuclear enemies as well.

A more radical warrior criticism suggests that a flexible response is possible on the nuclear level. Here, the challenge is not only to the extended version but also to the other versions of MAD. According to this view, scenarios can be conceived where a nation could use nuclear weapons and win without losing. It might work something like this: Aggressor nation A launches an attack on victim nation V's missile silos, airfields, and submarine pens. That is, it launches a series of counterforce strikes. It successfully destroys both a large portion of V's nuclear retaliatory potential and a good portion of its economy. However, it avoids directly attacking civilian, that is, countervalue, targets. By doing so it places itself in the position of holding those targets hostage* to attack. Before V can retaliate, it is told that if it does not, A will not attack V's cities. V is supposedly paralyzed—unable to retaliate. But it is still in the throes of a crushing defeat. In this scenario A has won, but yet has avoided defeat.

Criticism of MAD by pacifists and certain just war theorists takes at least two forms. One is straightforwardly consequentialist. It argues that the warrior flexibility argument is not convincing. V would not hesitate to retaliate, indeed is trigger-ready to do so, so there would be no negotiating window for A to try to gain some advantage. The result would be that the immorality of A's attack in killing millions of innocent* people would be matched by the immorality of V's counterattack. More generally, the consequentialist argument says that we are inevitably forced into a MAD position if nations continue to hold a large number of nuclear weapons in a ready-to-use mode. But beyond that, the argument is that MAD itself won't work. It will fail because sooner or later accidents will happen or some crazy leader will turn the switch.

Nonconsequentialist arguments focus on the inherent immorality of MAD. According to these arguments, the use of nuclear weapons is clearly immoral. There is no meaningful way to draw the distinction between counterforce and countervalue* targets. Too many military targets are too close to too many civilian centers for something as devastating as nuclear weapons to destroy the former without massively destroying the latter. But, the argument continues, MAD itself is immoral even before war begins, because it openly threatens devastation to countervalue targets as well as to counterforce ones. Further, it is not as if governmental officials who practice MAD are only pretending they will strike back if attacked. They mean to use these weapons if provoked. But meaningful threats to do something immoral are themselves immoral. So MAD itself is immoral and therefore ought to be abandoned.

MAD defenders reply to the warrior flexible-response argument by agreeing with the pacifists. For them there is no window for achieving victory and avoiding defeat. In turn, they reply to the pacfists in most general terms by admitting that MAD may not sound palatable to many people. After all, it is a doctrine based on mutual terror. Yet it is the best doctrine available. In their eyes it certainly makes sense to significantly diminish nuclear stockpiles and thereby diminish the nuclear threat. But it is unrealistic to talk about eliminating all nuclear weapons. They ask how the world would verify that all nations have eliminated all their weapons, and they reply that there is no way. The monster is out there and the only realistic response to its presence is to keep it under control. MAD is the only meaningful doctrine for doing that.

Defenders of extended MAD have another argument to use against pacifists: Pacifists want peace, of course, as does almost everyone else. But they want peace on their own terms via total disarmament. But their view of how peace must be achieved blinds them from seeing that extended MAD has already given them what they want. They already have peace, even if it has been given to them through terror, not love. The paradox they have placed themselves in is that by ridding the world of MAD, pacifists are also ridding themselves of the peace they want and already have.

Some have suggested that MAD is not so much wrong or immoral as it is dead, now that the Cold War* is dead. Clearly this suggestion is wrong. MAD has proliferated just as nuclear weapons have. MAD originally was an exclusive relationship between the United States and the Soviet Union. Soon the Soviet Union found itself having MAD relationships with Great Britain, France, and China as well. But as other countries have joined the nuclear club, they too are forming relationships. India and Pakistan have had a MAD relationship for some time. North Korea has formed MAD relationships recently with both the United States and China. Very likely, MAD relationships will continue to proliferate.

MAD proliferation suggests an interesting if terrifying change on the world scene. If MAD fails, it may do so, not as many feared, as a result of a massive nuclear exchange between the two major nuclear powers; it may fail regionally, on a small scale, as it were. We have only to wait to see what happens.

Proliferation may be triggering another change, this one in the MAD doctrine itself. The classic version argues against building significant defense systems to stop nuclear attacks. Defenses of the near future certainly will still not be good enough to stop nuclear attacks significantly above the 95 percent level. So full-bodied defenses still make no sense. But defense systems may become good enough to stop small attacks by maverick nations or ones caused by accident. With proliferation of nuclear weapons it may be, therefore, that MAD will be modified to permit robust, if not maximal, defense systems. If MAD is modified in this way in the near future, the trick will be to build defenses that are good enough, but not too good.

See ACCIDENTAL NUCLEAR WAR; ANTIBALLISTIC MISSILES/STAR WARS; MASS DESTRUCTION, WEAPONS OF; NUCLEAR WAR; RETALIATION, MASSIVE; TOTAL WAR.

BIBLIOGRAPHY
Brodie, Bernard, *Escalation and the Nuclear Option* (Princeton, N.J.: Princeton University Press, 1966).
———, *War and Politics* (New York: Macmillan, 1973).
Hardin, Russell, John J. Mearsheimer, Gerald Dworkin, and Robert E. Goodin, eds., "Symposium on Ethics and Nuclear Deterrence," *Ethics* 95, no. 3 (April 1985), 409–728 (twenty articles by various authors).
Jervis, Robert, "What Deters? The Ability to Inflict Assured Destruction," In *American Defense Policy*, 5th ed., John F. Reichart and Steven R. Sturm, eds. (Baltimore, Md. and London: Johns Hopkins University Press, 1982), 161–70.
Nitze, Paul, "Deterring our Deterrent," *Foreign Policy* 25 (Winter 1976–77), 195–210.

Nicholas G. Fotion

N

NAPALM. *See* FORBIDDEN WEAPONS; INCENDIARIES; INCENDIARIES, UN RESOLUTIONS BANNING.

NATIONALISM. It was generally understood by jurists, by the end of the 18th century, that the ends of sovereign nationalism were inconsistent with the hope for laws of war*. Every effort to establish international laws of war was conditioned by overriding national presumptions. These included: (1) war was a basic right of sovereign nations, such that no international rule could ban war on principle where the hegemony of a nation was involved. No nation could be required to surrender; (2) national armies were guaranteed the right to win and no rule that might hinder military success could be proposed; (3) even where nations might agree to be guided by some rules, as in the case of declarations of The Hague*, Geneva*, or the UN* General Assembly, such agreements could be withdrawn in the interests of national security; (4) national commitments precluded that any delegate to any international congress could commit the nation to a rule overriding the nation's sovereignty. Nationalism presumed international anarchy, and thus international war was preferable to being subject to any larger authority. As such, nationalism remains as a persistent cause of war*.

See CAUSES OF WAR; DEMOCRACY AND THE MILITARY; PATRIOTISM.

BIBLIOGRAPHY

Brierly, J. L., *The Law of Nations: An Introduction to the International Law of Peace* (New York: Oxford University Press, 1963).

Colbert, Evelyn Speyer, *Retaliation in International Law* (London: King's Crown Press, 1948).

Kalshoven, Frits, *The Law of Warfare: A Summary of Its Recent History* (Leyden: A. A. Sitjhoff, 1973).

Noel-Baker, Philip John, *The Geneva Protocol for the Pacific Settlement of International Disputes* (London: P. S. King and Sons, 1925).

Pictet, Jean, *The Principles of International Humanitarian Law* (Geneva: International Committee of the Red Cross, 1966).

NATIONAL LIBERATION, WARS OF. The emergence since World War II of wars of "liberation" has exacerbated the problem of whether all warriors should be bound by the same rules. In wars of national liberation, the oppressed are commonly far weaker than their oppressors, so that if the oppressed must comply with the normal rules of large armies, especially those regarding uniforms, no war of liberation could ever be won. Actually, in most of the current wars, ideology has played a major role, and thus the temptation has been great, even for conventional armies, to claim that the virtue of their cause justifies some loosening of the rules. If one side is the bearer of virtue and the other side is the evil oppressor, surely the evil side is not entitled to the deference normally claimed for the enemy. Eugene A. Korovin, Professor of International Law at the University of Moscow Juridical Institute, believed that struggling national resistance groups ought not to be required to abide by the strict rules of war*. The temptation is great, however, for all beleaguered warriors to draw the same conclusion, and to do whatever is required either to avoid defeat or to assure victory. The question has been raised for UN troops as well: Are they to be bound by the same rules of warfare as national armies? The prevailing view of the Geneva conventions* is that wherever there is armed conflict, the rules of war should apply, at least as far as giving all belligerents the right of being prisoners of war* and not the victims of a war of no quarter*. The problem remains, however, that in wars of national liberation it is difficult to distinguish the combatants from the noncombatants*, and this is especially important when the oppressed behave like regular armies in making war on civilians.

Every warrior tends to claim that his war is an exception. In wars of religion, the true believers doubt that conventional rules of chivalry should apply in wars against the heathen. Crusaders rarely worried about the strategies they used against unbelievers, and many religious leaders doubted that faith needed to be kept in wars with Muslims. Even Franciscus de Victoria* (1486–1546), who had rejected wars over religion, allowed that in wars against unbelievers, the enemy could be slain even after surrender, while in wars against Christians a more humane rule should be followed. The temptation in wars over ideology has been to assume that the enemy has given up any right to humane treatment.

See COMBATANT-NONCOMBATANT DISTINCTION; FORBIDDEN STRATEGIES; LAWS OF WAR; PRISONERS OF WAR; RUSES OF WAR; SHINING PATH (SENDERO LUMINOSO).

BIBLIOGRAPHY
Korovin, Eugene A., "The Second World War and International Law," *American Journal of International Law* 40 (October 1946).
Trainin, I. P., "Questions of Guerrilla Warfare and the Law of War," *American Journal of International Law* 40 (July 1946).

NAZISM. The word is a contraction of the term *Nationalsozialismus* (National Socialism). It identifies a type of fascism essentially linked to Adolf Hitler (1889–1945). A 20th-century German political movement, Nazism advocated a racist form of nationalism that emphasized anti-Semitism, single-party dictator-ship, a state-controlled economy, and territorial expansion through war.

During World War I (1914–1918), Hitler spent four years on the Western Front, where he served with distinction and was wounded. In October 1918, shortly before the war ended, he was temporarily blinded in a gas attack. By the time he recovered, Germany had surrendered. Along with many other Germans, Hitler was stunned by the surrender. The intensity of his belief that Germany had been "stabbed in the back," betrayed from within by Jews, was matched only by his disdain for the conditions imposed on Germany by the Treaty of Versailles.

Assigned to an army intelligence unit after the war, Hitler's tasks included the investigation of a small right-wing group known as the *Deutsche Arbeiter-partei* (DAP) or German Workers' Party. Finding its ideas coinciding with his own, Hitler joined this party, and by 1921 he had become its leader. Hitler changed the party's name to the National Socialist German Workers' Party (*Nationalsozialistische Deutsche Arbeiterpartei*)—NSDAP or Nazis, for short. Two years later, he led his Nazi followers in an attempt to overthrow Germany's postwar Weimar Republic. Staged in Munich on November 8, 1923, this coup was unsuccessful.

Following a trial for treason, Hitler spent little more than a year in prison. While in jail, he began writing one of the most influential books of the twentieth century, *Mein Kampf* (My Struggle), which was published in 1925. By 1933, *Mein Kampf* had sold more than one million copies. Its royalties made Hitler a wealthy man.

Mein Kampf argued that nature's basic law is one of eternal struggle, in which conflict is the means to greatness. Drawing on Social Darwinism and racial theory that could be traced back to the 19th century, Hitler maintained that some human races are culture-creating and others are culture-destroying. They are locked in a struggle for survival of the fittest. At the top of the culture-creating races is the Nordic-Aryan-Germanic "master race," which deserves to dominate inferior races. In Hitler's view, however, the racially superior German people were especially threatened by racial pollution. Thus, Poles, Russians, Ukrainians, and other Slavic peoples, as well as "defective" and "asocial" Germans (for example, the mentally and physically disabled, homosexuals, and criminals) would become Hitler's targets. Heading this list, however, was the racial enemy Hitler regarded as the most unrelenting of all: the Jews.

Mein Kampf testifies that wherever Hitler saw a threat to the racial and national survival he prized, wherever he sensed an obstacle to the geographical expansion he craved, he ultimately found the Jews. According to Hitler, Jews plundered, subverted, and infected the very people who deserved to dominate the world. To defend themselves, the German people had to defeat the challenge of these "culture destroyers" once and for all. Under his leadership, Hitler believed, the Nazis could and would provide the power to do so.

In the years before the Great Depression, the Nazi party remained a fringe political group, but the devastating economic situation gave Hitler and his Nazi followers the chance they needed. Capitalizing on Hitler's power as a spell-binding speaker, the Nazis' following increased as Hitler promised a better life for the German people.

Hitler's political fortunes did not rise without difficulty—the Nazis never won a majority in any freely contested national election—but on January 30, 1933, Hitler got the power he wanted. Germany's president, Paul von Hindenburg, was persuaded to invoke emergency dictatorial power granted him under the Weimar constitution to prevent an overthrow of democratic order. Ironically, when Hindenburg used his authority to appoint Hitler chancellor (prime minister of Germany), he ensured the very result his action was supposed to prevent.

Once Hitler became chancellor, the Nazis took power and "coordinated" German society to fit Hitler's view of what all Germans should think and do. Democracy was dead in Germany. Within six months, Hitler's decrees were as good as law, basic civil rights had been suspended, books had been burned, the Nazis stood as the only legal political party in Germany, and thousands of the Third Reich's suspected political opponents had been sent to concentration camps* as Nazism's tactics of terror and tyranny became ever more obvious.

As Hitler and his political party developed their relentless Nazi propaganda*, Nazism emphasized the survival and destiny of the German *Volksgemeinschaft*. This racially, ethnically, and culturally homogeneous community, devoid of dissent and obedient to the *Führer* who embodied and expressed its will, depended on obtaining sufficient land (*Lebensraum*) to sustain the vitality and purity of the German people's destiny. Thus, while Hitler spoke of peaceful international relations, he rearmed Germany and prepared for war. In 1938, Nazi Germany annexed Austria and the German-speaking Sudetenland of Czechoslovakia. Hitler then ordered German troops to invade Poland on September 1, 1939. World War II, which took the lives of between fifty and fifty-five million people, was under way.

With the notable exception of its failure to subdue England by air power, the German war machine had things its own way until it experienced defeats at El Alamein and Stalingrad in 1942. Meanwhile, as Hitler's forces advanced on all fronts, huge numbers of Jews came under Nazi domination. Somehow, Nazism decreed, the Jews had to be eliminated.

The huge system of concentration camps, ghettos, murder squadrons, and killing centers that became essential elements of Nazism took more than twelve million defenseless human lives. Between five and six million of them were Jewish, including about 1.5 million children* under fifteen. The Nazi intent was to rid Europe, if not the world, of Jews. Hitler went far in meeting that goal. By the time he committed suicide on April 30, 1945, and Nazi Germany surrendered in ruins on May 7, two-thirds of the European Jews—and about one-third of the Jews worldwide—were dead.

Nazism assaulted Western liberalism and democracy by denying human* and civil rights and by committing ruthless aggression in international relations. Unfortunately, its legacy includes various neo-Nazi groups whose racist propaganda preaches hate and incites violence. By no means are those groups confined to Germany. They are ignored at humanity's peril.

See CONTROL COUNCIL LAW NO. 10; CRIMES AGAINST HUMANITY; HOLOCAUST, THE; NUREMBERG TRIALS.

BIBLIOGRAPHY
Hitler, Adolf, *Mein Kampf,* Ralph Manheim, trans. (Boston: Houghton Mifflin, 1971).
Jäckel, Eberhard, *Hitler's Weltanschauung: A Blueprint for Power,* Herbert Arnold, trans. (Middletown, Conn.: Wesleyan University Press, 1972).
Lifton, Robert J., *The Nazi Doctors: Medical Killing and the Psychology of Genocide* (New York: Basic Books, 1986).
Sax, Benjamin, and Dieter Kuntz, *Inside Hitler's Germany: A Documentary History of Life in the Third Reich* (Lexington, Mass.: D. C. Heath, 1992).

John K. Roth

NICARAGUA, U.S. INTERVENTION IN. During the Ronald Reagan and George Bush administrations, the United States became involved in a political and military conflict affecting Nicaragua. In the 1970s, a movement formed in Nicaragua to oppose long-time strongman Anastasio Somoza Debayle. The movement called itself Sandinista, after Augusto Sandino, a Nicaraguan general who waged a guerrilla* campaign against the U.S. Marines after they occupied Nicaragua in the 1920s. At that time, the United States organized a National Guard for Nicaragua, headed by Anastasio Somoza García. Through that position Somoza came to control the government, and he ruled in an authoritarian fashion. Power remained in the Somoza family, and by the 1970s the leader was Somoza's son, Anastasio Somoza Debayle.

In 1979, the Sandinista party overthrew Somoza, and remnants of Somoza's National Guard regrouped in neighboring Honduras. From there they launched military raids back into Nicaragua. The Central Intelligence Agency (CIA) assisted these forces, which came to be called ''contras,'' by paying soldier salaries, planning combat missions, and training recruits at bases in Florida, Texas, and California. Under the cover of military exercises, U.S. Army engineers built command posts for the contras in Honduras. The CIA organized a second contra force in Costa Rica.

In Miami, the CIA organized a committee of exiled Nicaraguan businessmen as the political leadership of the contras. The CIA produced a pamphlet for contra soldiers, explaining how to operate in Nicaragua. The pamphlet suggested assassinating* local officials of the Nicaraguan government, to show the populace that the government could not rule effectively. These efforts were undertaken by the U.S. government without public knowledge. In 1982, reporters discovered the U.S. role, and a congressional committee asked CIA Director William Casey to explain. Casey acknowledged the CIA assistance but denied that the aim was to overthrow the Nicaraguan government. He said that the purpose was to stop arms shipments from Nicaragua to insurgents in El Salvador, where a civil war was in progress.

Other administration officials, however, admitted that the goal was to overthrow Nicaragua's government. In response to this information, Congress forbade the CIA and the Defense Department to provide military support "for the purpose of overthrowing the Government of Nicaragua."

During 1983–1984, aircraft bombed Nicaraguan economic installations, and speedboats raided the Nicaragua coast, blowing up oil depots. Undersea explosive mines* appeared in the waters off Nicaragua's major port. Ten ships, flying the flags of Liberia, Panama, the Netherlands, and the USSR, were hit by the mines. Nicaragua's government announced that the mines killed two crew members and injured fourteen, and it temporarily closed its ports.

The contras announced that they had done the mining. However, contra publicity director Edgar Chamorro, who subsequently abandoned the contra cause, later said that the contras were not involved. He said that a CIA official gave him a Spanish-language press release, written by the CIA, proclaiming contra responsibility for the mining, and Chamorro read the release over a CIA-funded contra radio station in Honduras.

The Soviet government accused the United States of responsibility for these attacks, but the Reagan administration denied involvement. Soon, however, a classified CIA report became public that detailed dates and places of CIA speedboat raids and of a CIA role behind the mining. The raids, it turned out, had been carried out by Latin American mercenaries. CIA trainers launched the mercenaries into small boats from "mother ships" to plant the mines.

The U.S. Senate, upon learning that the Reagan administration had concealed its role, resolved that no funds be used "for the purpose of planning, executing or supporting the mining of the ports or territorial waters of Nicaragua." Congress strengthened its prior language on U.S. aid to the contras with a law that forbade not only the CIA and Defense Department, but "any other agency or entity of the United States involved in intelligence activities" to support "directly or indirectly, military or paramilitary operations in Nicaragua."

To evade the Congressional prohibition, the administration created a nominally private organization to finance and train the contras. The administration solicited funds from private individuals and from several foreign governments, including those of Saudi Arabia and Brunei. It got Israel to contribute weapons. It sold arms clandestinely to Iran and gave the proceeds to the contras. It collected privately contributed equipment in the United States, and a CIA-owned airline, Southern Air Transport, ferried the equipment to the contras.

As an additional means of generating funds for the contras, Southern Air Transport pilots brought contra cocaine and marijuana into the United States on return trips from Central America. Drug Enforcement Administration agents confirmed the contents, and the pilots claimed they had administration protection for the drug-running. The Medellín cartel of Colombia rented cargo space from the contras on some of these flights to the United States. The administration also cut off trade with Nicaragua and imposed economic sanctions on it. Eventually, in a major political reversal, Congress, at the urging of the Reagan administration, decided to fund the contras.

Nicaragua sued the United States in the International Court of Justice* (ICJ), arguing that it was the victim of aggression* by the United States. The United States took the position that the court did not have jurisdiction over the case, but the court decided that it did and in 1986 found against the United States, calling its attacks on Nicaragua acts of aggression. Hard-pressed economically, the Nicaraguan government survived until 1990, when national elections resulted in bringing to power a coalition of parties opposed to the Sandinistas.

See AGGRESSION, ATTEMPTS TO DEFINE; INTELLIGENCE AGENCIES, U.S.; PROPAGANDA.

BIBLIOGRAPHY

Brinkley, Joel, "Contra Arms Crews Said to Smuggle Drugs," *New York Times,* January 20, 1987, A1, col. 4.

Cockburn, Leslie, *Out of Control* (New York: Atlantic Monthly Press, 1987).

"Guns, Drugs and the CIA," Transcript, Frontline Special, WGBH, Public Broadcasting System (1988).

President's Special Review Board, *Report of the Special Review Board,* February 26, 1987 (Tower Commission Report).

Rogers, David, and David Ignatius, "How CIA-Aided Raids in Nicaragua in '84 Led Congress to End Funds," *Wall Street Journal,* March 6, 1985, 1, col. 1.

Senate Select Committee on Intelligence, *Report on Preliminary Inquiry,* January 29, 1987.

Walker, Thomas, ed., *Reagan Versus the Sandinistas: The Undeclared War on Nicaragua* (Boulder, Colo.: Westview Press, 1987).

John Quigley

NONVIOLENT CIVILIAN-BASED DEFENSE. A subcategory of nonviolent action, with the specific purpose of defending a social or political group. Other related terms are defensive defense, nonoffensive defense, nonprovocative defense, social defense, and alternative defense. As a result, perhaps, of both the increasing dangers of high technology weapons and increased civilian efforts to develop and preserve security, research into these less violent methods of defense expanded during the 1980s. Serious research on the effectiveness of different methods of nonviolent action has been a major effort of Gene Sharp for over twenty years, and work on the conditions under which nonviolent action succeeds constitutes the majority of the work at the Program on Nonviolent Sanctions in Conflict and Defense, which he founded at Harvard. Sharp's work has focused on the pragmatic utility of nonviolent action as the functional equivalent of war, and especially on the use of civilian-based defense. His book, which addresses the question of the use of nonviolent sanctions in making Europe unconquerable, was favorably reviewed by George Kennan in the *New York Review of Books.* Kennan's review, which is reprinted in Sharp's book, notes that Sharp implies no less than a change in political philosophy when he writes that "all political power is rooted in and continually dependent upon the cooperation and obedience of the subjects and institutions of the society.'' An edited work (Conser et al.) demonstrates that nonviolent action was also critical to the U.S. independence movement.

Much of the other work on alternative, defensive, or nonoffensive defense is centered in Northern Europe, especially in the UK, West Germany, and the Nordic countries. The *Non-Offensive Defense Newsletter* is published in Copenhagen. Some of the work of the Alternative Defense Commission in Bradford, England examines a range of both military and nonmilitary defensive defense options open to a nonnuclear Britain, and looks at the option of dealignment from superpower blocs. Johan Galtung offers movement toward defensive defense, along with nonalignment, inner strength, and outer usefulness, as four roads within the concept of alternative security systems. Dietrich Fischer, drawing on his earlier work on the Swiss concept of defense, contributes to an understanding of the role of defensive defense as one of the methods of preventing war in the nuclear age, and a book by Jan Oberg, Wilhelm Nolte, and Fischer explores some of the possible relationships of military and nonmilitary methods of defensive defense.

Alex P. Schmid is one of the few researchers who examines the conditions under which social defense can be practicable. He sets out ten conditions (not all of which he sees as necessary) for a viable social defense and applies these to Soviet military intervention and especially to four East European case studies: the Lithuanian resistance against Soviet reoccupation, the East German uprising of June 17, 1953, the Hungarian uprising of 1956, and the Czechoslovakian resistance of 1968. His conditions for success include:

• knowledge of nonviolent resistance and willingness to use it
• independence
• adequate internal communication
• a democratic tradition and politically conscious population
• perceived political legitimacy greater than that of the attacker
• a high level of social cohesion
• dependence of the attacker on the defending unit or its ally
• opportunities for individual interactions
• legitimate status with public opinion, foreign governments, or the attacker
• some rationality in the adversary

Schmid notes, in conclusion, that he did not achieve "a formalized hierarchical set of noncontradictory, theory-based conditions," and that a broader framework for analysis is needed. He notes the inherent differences between centralism and decentralism in different theories of social defense, suggesting, by implication, that it is crucial to deal with this question.

Work on trans-armament—moving from military solutions to the use of nonviolent sanctions—is proceeding apace, with more limited work on simply moving from more offensive to more defensive weapons systems. There is an increasing interest in both movements in a great number of countries among researchers, publics, and governments. A number of research groups have formed in the United States, including the Alternative Defense Working Group of the Institute for Defense and Disarmament Studies in Boston, which focuses primarily on the military end of the spectrum. The Dibb Report to the Australian government and submissions to the Corner Committee in New Zealand both reflect increased interest in more defensive methods of national defense.

At the time of the end of the Cold War*, the use of nonviolent action in the Eastern European states, especially the Baltic states, was significant both in bringing about the independence of states from the Soviet empire and in defending regimes from coups. Researchers on nonviolent civilian-based defense became consultants to many of these governments as they emerged, and Sharp's work in particular was translated into many languages. Certain of the Baltic states even wrote elements of nonviolent civilian-based defense into their constitutions. Both policy-oriented and more basic research continue in the United States and especially in the Scandinavian countries and elsewhere in northern Europe.

See MILITARISM; PACIFISM; PEACE RESEARCH AND PEACE STUDIES

BIBLIOGRAPHY

Alternative Defence Commission, *Defence Without the Bomb* (London: Taylor and Francis Ltd., 1983).

Alternative Defence Commission, *The Politics of Alternative Defence: A Role for a Non-Nuclear Britain* (London: Paladin, 1987).

Conser, Walter H., Ronald M. McCarthy, David J. Toscano, and Gene Sharp, eds., *Resistance, Politics, and the American Struggle for Independence* (Boulder, Colo.: Lynne Rienner, 1987).

Fischer, Dietrich, *Preventing War in a Nuclear Age* (Totowa, N.J.: Rowman & Allenheld, 1984).

Galtung, Johan, *There Are Alternatives! Four Roads to Peace and Security* (Nottingham: Spokesman, 1984).

Oberg, Jan, Wilhelm Nolte, and Dietrich Fischer, *Frieden gewinnen* (Fribourg: Dreisam Verlag, 1987).

Schmid, Alex P., *Social Defence and Soviet Military Power: An Inquiry into the Relevance of an Alternative Defence Concept* (Leiden: Center for the Study of Social Conflict, 1985).

Sharp, Gene, *Making Europe Unconquerable: The Potential of Civilian-Based Deterrence and Defense* (Cambridge, Mass.: Ballinger, 1985).

Carolyn M. Stephenson

NUCLEAR ACCIDENTS. The U.S. Nuclear Regulatory Commission (NRC) issued *Reactor Safety Study: An Assessment of Accident Risks in U.S. Nuclear Power Plants* (1975) and estimated that there would be at least one major core-damaging accident every twenty years. In operation, U.S. nuclear power plants averaged two emergency shut-downs a day. At one time in 1986 all nine Tennessee Valley Nuclear Plants were shut down for repairs. The issue was real enough that Sandia National Laboratory issued estimates of the human casualties and financial consequences of nuclear power reactor accidents for nine major plants. Possible human casualties were estimated at 500,000, and the financial costs at over $1 trillion. In spite of these concerns, in 1992 the NRC decided that sixty-three of the 109 licensed nuclear power plants did not need to meet the minimum requirements of its own General Design Criteria.

Less well publicized are military nuclear accidents. While these are not solely due to human incompetence, the *Bulletin of the Atomic Scientists* (November 1980) reported that in a three-year period, 1975–1977, military personnel with access to U.S. nuclear weapons programs were removed in the following numbers and for the following reasons: 4,809 for drug abuse; 3,746 for mental, physical, and behavioral traits that prejudiced reliable performance; 2,552 for behavior contemptuous of the law; 2,268 for negligence or delinquency on duty; 1,083 court martialed for civil offenses; and 609 for alcohol abuse, for a total of 15,067. These data are particularly troubling since four officers acting together in a Minuteman squadron of fifty intercontinental missiles could launch the missiles without authorization or impediment. Independently of these data are accidents involving the transportation of nuclear weapons due to a combination of human or mechanical failures. Such accidents have been given names: a "Broken Arrow" is a serious nuclear accident; a "Bent Spear" is a less serious nuclear accident; a "Nucflash" is a "Broken Arrow" that risks starting a nuclear war; a "Dull Sword" is less serious than a "Bent Spear" and a "Faded Giant" is an accident involving a nuclear reactor.

Faded Giants included the following accidents: On December 12, 1952, at the nuclear power plant at Chalk River, Ontario, Canada, by human error, three or four valves that should not have been opened were opened. When the supervisor came to the basement he closed the valves, then went upstairs to call the operator. He told the operator to push buttons 4 and 1. The operator had to put down the phone to do this, so when the supervisor realized he should have said buttons 4 and 3, the operator could not hear him. All that could be done was to dump the heavy water and shut down the plant. In 1957 at Windscale in Cumbria, England, at a gas-cooled graphite modified reactor designed to produce plutonium for the military, the entire system was shut down by a human error. This was called "the worst nuclear accident in the Western world." On October 5, 1966, the Enrico Fermi Atomic power plant was shut down and reported in *We Almost Lost Detroit.* In 1970 an explosion occurred at the Gorki submarine yards, after which the Volga River and Black Sea estuary were radioactively contaminated. On March 28, 1979, the catastrophe at Three Mile Island was caused by six human errors, four improper safety functions, and one equipment failure. April 26, 1986, the radioactive release at Chernobyl was estimated at 1,000 times greater than at Three Mile Island.

Between 1950 and 1981, Broken Arrows included four fires aboard nuclear airplanes, one fire aboard a nuclear submarine, and one in a nuclear weapons storage plant; eight instances of nuclear contamination from airplanes; nine instances of losing a nuclear bomb from an aircraft and two from nuclear-armed submarines. Bent Spears included twenty-four accidents on nuclear submarines and fourteen accidents on nuclear-carrying surface ships. Dull Swords included ten nonnuclear explosions on nuclear-armed aircraft. In 1981 a truck carrying nuclear bombs in West Germany caught fire.

There have been numerous Nucflashes over the years. In 1956 an unarmed B-57 crashed into a nuclear weapons stockpile in East Anglia, Great Britain, and in 1957 a B-57 accidently dropped a 1 megaton bomb near Mars Bluff, South Carolina. In 1960 a nuclear weapon fell from an American plane flying over Laos. In 1962 a B-52 broke up in mid-air, releasing two nuclear bombs. One was twenty-four megatons and was found hanging by its parachute in a tree with five of its six safety switches tripped. In 1968 a B-52 crashed and burned at Thule Air Base, Greenland, destroying all four of its nuclear bombs by fire; in 1970 a Soviet nuclear-armed submarine collided with an Italian cruise liner and another exploded and sank off the coast of Great Britain; in 1980 twice in June and once in November a short circuit in a computer chip announced that Soviet nuclear missiles had been fired. In 1980 a mechanic dropped a wrench, rupturing the fuel tanks of a Titan missile near Damascus, Arkansas, and the explosion tossed the nine-megaton warhead 200 yards. In 1981 a Soviet submarine apparently on a spying mission and armed with nuclear-tipped torpedoes was grounded near a top secret Swedish naval facility near Karlskrona. In 1984 a Soviet nuclear-armed submarine collided with the U.S. aircraft carrier *Kitty Hawk* in the Sea of Japan, and in 1984 an errant submarine-launched cruise missile overflew Norwegian air space and later crashed in Finland. Between 1946 and 1975 the American Strategic Air Command with its nuclear warheads was put on alert thirty-three times, indicating a perilous combination of Pentagon paranoia and instrumental unreliability. Between 1977 and 1984 the U.S. early warning system generated 20,784 false indications of missile attacks requiring a Missile Display Conference, and 1,035 were serious enough to require a Missile Attack Conference at North American Air Defense Command (NORAD). These numbers are no longer released to the public.

Nuclear accidents constitute a kind of collateral damage*, and as in other instances of collateral damage, some calculation is required to determine whether the risks outweigh the possible gains. These nuclear accidents constitute potential collateral damage to the entire human race in their biological, geological, and social environments. Given that approximately one-fourth of the world's population live under military rule, and that military leaders tend to accept collateral damage as an acceptable risk, insufficient concern is likely to be the rule.

See COMBATANT-NONCOMBATANT DISTINCTION; COUNTER-FORCE VERSUS COUNTERVALUE; ENVIRONMENTAL ISSUES, POLLUTION, AND THE MILITARY; HAZARDOUS DUMPING IN PRO-

TECTED MARINE AREAS; NUCLEAR WAR; NUCLEAR WEAPONS TESTING; PROPORTIONALITY.

BIBLIOGRAPHY

Cantelon, Philip L., and Robert C. Williams, *Crisis Contained: The Department of Energy at Three Mile Island* (Carbondale: University of Southern Illinois Press, 1982).

Curtis, Richard, and Elizabeth Hogan, *Perils of the Peaceful Atom: The Myth of Safe Nuclear Power Plants* (New York: Doubleday, 1969)

Flavin, Christopher, *Reassessing Nuclear Power: The Fallout from Chernobyl* (New York: Worldwatch Institute, 1987).

Fuller, John G., *We Almost Lost Detroit* (New York: Thomas Crowell, 1975).

Harris, John B., and Eric Markusen, eds., *Nuclear Weapons and the Threat of Nuclear War* (New York: Harcourt Brace, 1986).

Kidron, Michael, and Dan Smith, *The War Atlas* (London: Pan Books, 1983).

Novick, Sheldon, *The Careless Atom* (Boston: Houghton Mifflin, 1969).

Pollard, Robert D., *The Nugget File* (Cambridge, Mass.: Union of Concerned Scientists, 1979).

Reactor Safety Study: An Assessment of Accident Risks, U.S. Nuclear Regulatory Commission Report (Washington, D.C.: U.S. Government Printing Office, 1975).

Report to Congress on Abnormal Occurrences, U.S. Nuclear Regulatory Commission (October 1984–September 1993).

Union of Concerned Scientists, *Safety Second: The NRC and America's Nuclear Power Plants* (Bloomington: Indiana University Press, 1987).

NUCLEAR DETERRENCE. This is the practice of preventing undesirable acts by opponents by threatening to attack them with nuclear weapons. Since nuclear deterrence requires the possession of nuclear weapons, it has so far been practiced only by nuclear nation-states. Nothing in the definition, however, prevents the use of nuclear deterrence by terrorist groups or sub-state organizations that come to possess nuclear weapons.

Nuclear deterrence is one species of deterrence, a widely utilized method of social control. All forms of deterrence require an agent, an opponent, and an undesired act A. To practice deterrence, the agent must communicate with his opponent in such a way that the opponent comes to believe that if he performs A, some sanction, S, will follow. A deterrent policy is successful if the opponent does not perform A, but would have performed A, save for fear of suffering S. Thus, nuclear deterrence shares with all forms of deterrence the following features: (1) it is irreducibly psychological, since it relies on the creation of beliefs and fears; (2) it is coercive, since it requires the issuing of threats of harm; and (3) its success is unverifiable, since even if the opponent does not do A, it cannot be shown that he would have done A, save for fear of the sanction. (Perhaps he never planned to do A at all.)

There are several varieties of nuclear deterrence, depending on the specification of the act to be deterred. Suppose that the agent practicing deterrence is the United States. If the United States is committed to using nuclear weapons only in response to perceived aggression against itself, we have what is often called "finite" deterrence. If the United States is committed to using nuclear weapons in response to perceived aggression against one of its allies, we have "extended" deterrence. If the United States is prepared to use nuclear weapons only in response to a nuclear attack, we have "minimal" deterrence. If the United States is prepared to use nuclear weapons in response to a nonnuclear attack, we have "nonminimal" deterrence. Since nonminimal deterrence permits the use of nuclear weapons before the opponent has used them, it is often identified as a "first strike"* posture. Since minimal deterrence permits the use of nuclear weapons only after the opponent has used them, it is often identified as a "second strike" posture.

There are also several types of nuclear deterrence, depending on how the agent plans to use its nuclear weapons in carrying out deterrence. Again using the United States as an example, if the United States responds with a nuclear attack on its opponent's cities and economic assets, we have what is called "countervalue"* deterrence. If the United States responds with a nuclear attack on the opponent's military forces, we have what is called "counterforce"* deterrence. The distinction between countervalue deterrence and counterforce deterrence can be combined with the distinction between minimal and nonminimal deterrence to produce four different subtypes. Add further distinctions, and the permutations multiply. Much of the discussion of deterrence among professional strategists in nuclear states has been devoted to guessing which type of nuclear deterrence is best suited to securing national objectives.

Throughout the Cold War*, the United States was prepared to use nuclear weapons in response to a nonnuclear attack by the Soviet Union against Western Europe. In 1980, President Jimmy Carter announced that the United States was prepared to use "any means," that is, nuclear means, in response to a Soviet intrusion into the Persian Gulf, presumably a nonnuclear intrusion. From 1946 to 1962, the United States was committed to using nuclear weapons primarily against Soviet cities. From 1962 on, the United States was prepared to launch nuclear attacks against Soviet cities, or Soviet military installations, or both. Accordingly, through 1962 the United States was practicing extended, nonminimal countervalue nuclear deterrence. After 1962 it was practicing extended, nonminimal, mixed counterforce/countervalue nuclear deterrence—at least in theory. Whether these fine-grained choices of one form of nuclear deterrence over another can be implemented by adjustments of military directives and changes in weaponry is a matter of debate.

HISTORY OF NUCLEAR THREATS

There are numerous instances of nuclear gunboat diplomacy since 1945. In most cases, the goals were trivial and the threat largely symbolic. Nevertheless, there are five incidents in which the goal was significant and the threat was real. In each case, success is claimed for American nuclear deterrence. Supporters of deterrence argue that threats of nuclear attack (1) induced Japanese surrender in August 1945, (2) prevented a Soviet invasion of Western Europe between 1945 and 1991, (3) forced North Korea* to accept a settlement at Panmunjon in 1955, (4) pressured Khrushchev to withdraw nuclear missiles from Cuba in 1962, and (5) prevented Soviet intervention on the side of Egypt during the Yom Kippur war in 1973. These widely accepted historical claims are attacked by critics who argue that (1) the Emperor of Japan was resolved to peace before the atomic bombings occurred, (2) the Soviet Union never planned to invade Western Europe, (3) the North Koreans were defeated on the battlefield before nuclear threats were made—if they were made, (4) Khrushchev in 1962 sought only a balance in intermediate range missiles, a balance he secured by an implicit promise to remove American missiles from Turkey, and (5) the Soviets were not prepared to fight the United States on behalf of Egypt, even if the United States had not possessed nuclear weapons. Furthermore, any claim for success must also take into account the costs of maintaining the posture of deterrence, including the economic costs of manufacturing nuclear weapons* and delivery systems, the ecological cost of the weapons plants, the political cost of a system that requires extensive secrecy in the midst of a democratic state, and the risk that the system will malfunction and cause an accidental nuclear war.

HISTORY OF NUCLEAR STRATEGY

The revulsion caused by the destruction of Hiroshima and Nagasaki* produced three proposals to forestall further atomic attacks on cities. Most atomic scientists favored the internationalization of nuclear weapons material, but this idea foundered on East-West suspicions in 1946. Most military planners favored the development of smaller nuclear weapons for battlefield use; this idea foundered on technical problems in the late 1940s. The third idea, sponsored by Bernard Brodie and the new breed of civilian nuclear strategists, was to restrict the uses of nuclear weapons to deterrence only.

At first sight, nuclear weapons seem ideally suited for deterrence: If the opponent performs the undesired act, the result is his own destruction. But from the beginning, the deterrence only proposal was beset by a paradox. If nuclear weapons are too terrible for use, then they are too terrible for threats, since one will not have the heart to carry out the threat. The weapons prove to be self-deterring.

The remedy was either to make nuclear weapons smaller, less terrible, and more likely to be used, or to make them bigger and more terrible, to compensate for self-deterrence. Robert Oppenheimer favored the first approach, Edward Teller the second, and both sorts of weapons were produced by the early 1950s. In 1954 the American secretary of state assured the Soviets that undesirable Soviet acts would be met by "massive retaliation" with these new weapons. But by the late 1950s, American attempts at deterrence were confounded by the development of Soviet nuclear weapons and Soviet ICBMs: now American use of nuclear weapons against the Soviets would provoke a Soviet nuclear response against the United States. As Jacob Viner had discerned even in 1946, there is no joy in destroying your opponent if the likely result is your own destruction a few hours later.

What deterrence needed in order to be credible was laid out by William Kaufmann in "The Requirements of Deterrence" in 1956. The problem was how to meet the requirements. Two suggestions dominated the late 1950s. The first, associated with Thomas Schelling, was to make the response to the undesired act automatic, therefore eliminating the possibility that the sanction would not be applied. This, Bertrand Russell noticed in 1959, turned nuclear deterrence into a variety of Highway Chicken. The second, associated with Herman Kahn, was to develop American weapons and civil defenses, so that in a nuclear exchange the Soviet Union would be destroyed and the United States would survive. What Kahn considered survival, however, most Americans considered a nightmare. In the end, neither strategy prevailed. By the middle 1960s, the United States settled simply for "assured destruction," that is, the ability to destroy the Soviet Union should the Soviet Union launch a nuclear first strike against the United States. Assured destruction, practiced by both sides by the late 1960s, became Mutual Assured Destruction*, or MAD, solemnified by the SALT I and ABM Treaties of 1972.

Through the 1970s, both doves and hawks expressed discontent with MAD. Doves pointed out that assured destruction required the maintenance of a complex nuclear war–making system, which sooner or later would malfunction, with catastrophic results. Hawks pointed out that assured destruction provided no safety against a small Soviet nuclear attack, since the United States could not respond for fear of losing whatever assets had survived the small Soviet first strike.

With the election of Carter in 1976, the doves temporarily prevailed, but when Cyrus Vance's "deep cuts" proposals failed in 1977 and the Soviet Union invaded Afghanistan in 1979, official opinion swung back toward the nuclear war–winning proposals of Herman Kahn. Precise new weapons systems, introduced in the late Carter years, promised incapacitation of Soviet missiles by an American first strike, and provided "countervailing" strikes against any type of Soviet first strike, large or small. By 1979, strategist Colin Gray could proclaim that "victory is possible." Kahn's proposals for civil defense were revived in a new form by Ronald Reagan in his "Star Wars" proposals of 1983, and Reagan's secretary of defense announced that in any nuclear war, the United States would "prevail."

In the end, the United States did prevail, not because of nuclear deterrence, but because of the internal economic collapse of the Soviet Union. In the wake of the Cold War, little interest exists in nuclear threats and nuclear deterrence. The costs to the nations that practiced nuclear deterrence were great, and the conjectural gains were counterbalanced by real risks. Ironically or justifiably, the post–Cold War economic world is dominated by nations like Germany and Japan, that never played the deterrence game.

ETHICS AND NUCLEAR DETERRENCE

Nuclear deterrence involves a commitment to use nuclear weapons in certain circumstances. For many persons, any use of nuclear weapons is immoral, because nuclear explosions in war necessarily kill civilians and poison the earth. Thus, deterrence involves a conditional intention to do an immoral deed. If it is immoral to intend to do an immoral deed, nuclear deterrence is immoral.

This argument, first circulated by several Catholic British philosophers in 1961, provoked many responses. Paul Ramsey suggested that the sole answer was to restrict nuclear weapons in such a way that their use was moral. Others argued that the conditional intention in deterrence was not the real intention of deterrence, which was, at bottom, to prevent nuclear war. Philosopher Gregory Kavka, in 1978, argued that the argument was invalid because the principle that it is immoral to intend an immoral deed is false, and that in strategic situations it may be morally required to make oneself impure through commitments to violence. David Gauthier argued in 1984 that since deterrence is moral—it kills no one and prevents nuclear first strikes—it must be moral to carry out what deterrence requires, even if that be a nuclear second strike. Jefferson McMahan wondered how one could verify what the intentions of the American government, or any government, actually are.

If the intentions of deterrence are inscrutable, the risks of deterrence are not. Deterrence requires nuclear weapons and delivery systems, and these systems create the possibility of accidental nuclear war. If one multiplies the size of this catastrophe by even a small chance that it will occur in any given year, the result is a large negative "expected value," and we have a utilitarian criticism of deterrence. This argument, circulated in the early 1980s, was assisted by the computer analyses showing that the explosion of American nuclear weapons as intended in existing war plans would generate enough dust to kill most life on earth.

The disaster that a nuclear war would be was acknowledged on all sides. The challenge to the utilitarian critique of deterrence was to supply an alternative policy that had a smaller risk of nuclear war than deterrence. Many felt that although deterrence had risks, the alternatives were even riskier. As it turned out, the utilitarian critique impressed the Soviets more than the Americans. In the late 1980s Gorbachev abandoned deterrence, not because of its intentions, but because of its costs.

See ACCIDENTAL NUCLEAR WAR; COLD WAR; MASS DESTRUCTION, WEAPONS OF; NUCLEAR ACCIDENTS; RETALIATION, MASSIVE.

BIBLIOGRAPHY

Anscombe, G.E.M., "War and Murder," in *Nuclear Weapons: A Catholic Response,* W. Stein, ed. (London: Merlin, 1961).

Ford, John C., "The Morality of Obliteration Bombing," *Theological Studies* (1944).

Kavka, Gregory, "Some Paradoxes of Deterrence," *Journal of Philosophy* (June 1978).

Lackey, Douglas, "Missiles and Morals: A Utilitarian Critique of Nuclear Deterrence," *Philosophy and Public Affairs* (Summer 1982).

———, *Moral Principles and Nuclear Strategy* (Totowa, N.J.: Rowman & Allanheld, 1984).

Lee, Steven, *Morality, Prudence, and Nuclear Weapons* (New York: Cambridge University Press, 1994).

Ramsey, Paul, *War and the Christian Conscience* (Durham, N.C.: Duke University Press, 1961).

Douglas P. Lackey

NUCLEAR PROLIFERATION. Since the start of the nuclear era, people have worried about the potential spread, or "proliferation," of nuclear weapons. In 1962, President John F. Kennedy warned of the possibility that by the 1970s the United States could "face a world in which fifteen or twenty or twenty-five nations may have these weapons." However, only China (1964) joined the United States (1945), the USSR (1949), the UK (1952), and France (1960) as formal members of the "nuclear club," the only nations with openly declared or acknowledged nuclear arsenals. With the breakup of the USSR in 1991, eight nations are now known to possess nuclear weapons, as the former Soviet republics of Russia, Ukraine, Kazakhstan, and Belarus inherited the USSR's arsenal.

An additional number of countries are widely believed to have approached or perhaps even crossed the nuclear weapons threshold. India, Israel, and Pakistan are suspected either to already possess some undeclared nuclear weapons capabilities or to be able to produce a limited number of nuclear weapons within weeks or months of a decision to do so. By one unofficial estimate, India has the components with which to assemble forty to sixty nuclear weapons on short notice, Pakistan could likely make five to ten weapons. In 1974, India became only the sixth country to test a nuclear explosive. Based upon information made public in 1986 by Mordechai Vanunu, a former technician at Israel's Dimona nuclear complex, many experts believe that Israel may already have produced as many as 100–300 nuclear weapons. Following the 1991 Persian Gulf War*, UN inspection teams confiscated documents confirming the existence of an aggressive nuclear weapons program in Iraq. Algeria, Iran, Libya, and North Korea are also widely suspected of seeking nuclear weapons capabilities. In 1993, South Africa made public that it secretly produced, but has since dismantled, six nuclear weapons. Argentina, Brazil, South Korea, and Taiwan also are believed to have had at one time, but to have since apparently shut down, programs to develop nuclear weapons. The C.I.S. nuclear weapons on the chart are those

U.S. Nuclear Weapons

U.S. Nuclear Warheads on...	January 1993 (START II signed)	November 1994	2003 Under START II	2003 Under Nuclear Posture Review
Inter-Continental Ballistic Missiles	2,450 warheads; 1,000 ICBMs	2,240 warheads; 730 ICBMs	500 warheads; 500 ICBMs	450-500 warheads; 450-500 ICBMs
Submarine-Launched Ballistic Missiles	3,840 warheads; 480 C-4 and D-5 SLBMs; 24 Poseidon and Trident subs	2,688 warheads; 336 C-4 and D-5 SLBMs; 14 Trident subs	1,750 warheads; 432 or less C-4 and D-5 SLBMs; 18 Trident subs	1,750 warheads; 336 or less D-5 SLBMs; 14 Trident subs
Bombers	3,776 warheads; 236 B-52 and B-1 bombers	3,452 warheads; 192 B-52, B-1, and B-2 bombers	est. 1,250 warheads; 94 B-52 bombers	1,250 warheads; 66 B-52 and up to 20 B-2 bombers
Total Deployed Strategic Weapons:	10,066 warheads; 1,718 missiles and bombers	8,380 warheads; 1,258 missiles and bombers	3,500 warheads; 1,026 missiles and bombers	3,500 warheads; 872 missiles and bombers
Est. Total Active Tactical Weapons	Est. 1,350 warheads; 1,000 in Europe and 350 SLCMs in U.S.	950 warheads; 600 in Europe and 350 nuclear SLCMs in U.S.	950 warheads; 600 bombs in Europe and 350 SLCMs in U.S.	830 warheads; 480 USAF bombs deployed in Europe; 350 SLCMS in U.S.
Est. War Reserve Weapons	Est. 7,500 warheads	Est. 6,000 warheads	Est. 4,000 warheads	Est. 4,000 warheads
Est. TOTAL warheads:	Roughly 19,000 warheads	Roughly 15,000 warheads	Roughly 8,500 warheads	Roughly 8,300 warheads

342

C.I.S. Nuclear Weapons

C.I.S. Nuclear Warheads on...	January 1993 (START II signed)	November 1994	Projected 2003 Under START II	2003 Post Clinton-Yeltsin Sept. 94 Summit
Inter-Continental Ballistic Missiles	6,115 warheads; 1,015 ICBMs	5,905 warheads; 1,067 ICBMs *	800 warheads; 800 ICBMs	no change
Submarine-Launched Ballistic Missiles	2,696 warheads; 832 SLBMs; 55 subs	2,384 warheads; 520 SLBMs; 31 subs #	1,696 warheads; 408 SLBMs; 24 subs	no change
Bombers	1,426 warheads; 140 bombers	1,374 warheads; 109 bombers !	1,000 warheads; 75 bombers	no change
Total Deployed Strategic Weapons:	10,237 warheads; 1,987 missiles and bombers	9,663 warheads; 1,696 missiles and bombers +	3,496 warheads; 1,283 missiles and bombers	no change
Est. Total Active Tactical Weapons	Est. 4,000 warheads	Est. 3,300 warheads #	Est. 2,750 warheads	no change
Est. War Reserve Weapons	Est. 15,000 warheads	Est. 15,000 warheads #	Est. 5,000 warheads	no change
Est. TOTAL warheads:	Roughly 29,000 warheads	Roughly 25,000 warheads	Roughly 11,000 warheads	no change

Sources: DOD, DOE, CDI, ACA, NRDC, and SIPRI.
Notes: * ICBM Warheads: 3,811 Russia, 1,120 Ukraine, 920 Kazakhstan, 54 Belarus
      ! Bomber Warheads: 810 Russia, 564 Ukraine
      + Total Strategic Warheads: 7,005 Russia, 1,684 Ukraine, 920 Kazakstan, 54 Belarus
      # All Submarines, tactical nuclear weapons, and war reserve weapons are based in Russia.

343

of the former Soviet Union, referred to as the Commonwealth of Independent States.

That more nations have not acquired "the bomb" can be credited in large part to an assortment of institutions, policies, and agreements that have been forged by the world's nations to counter nuclear proliferation. These have included supply-side strategies that seek to prevent sensitive nuclear weapons knowledge, equipment, and materials from falling into "the wrong hands," and demand-side strategies that focus on making nuclear weapons unattractive and on easing the underlying tensions that fuel the demand for nuclear weapons. Measures to prevent the spread of nuclear weapons to additional countries have included: the 1968 Nuclear Nonproliferation Treaty; the designation of nuclear-weapon-free zones (Antarctica, Latin America, outer space, the ocean seabed, and the South Pacific); controls on the export of nuclear materials and technology; inspection of nuclear materials by the International Atomic Energy Agency; negotiations to reduce regional tensions; agreements by the United States and the USSR to reduce their existing nuclear weapon stockpiles; and negotiations to end all nuclear test explosions.

The main international barrier to nuclear proliferation remains the Nuclear Nonproliferation Treaty, or NPT, now signed by more than 160 countries (the most notable nonsignatories are India, Israel, and Pakistan). The NPT established an international norm against the acquisition of nuclear weapons by additional countries. It is a bargain between nuclear-weapon "haves" and "have-nots." In signing the NPT, non-nuclear-weapon nations pledge to forswear nuclear weapon aspirations in return for the right to the safeguarded peaceful exploitation of nuclear energy. For their part, nuclear-weapon nations are committed under Article VI of the NPT "to pursue negotiations in good faith on effective measures relating to cessation of the nuclear arms race and an early end to nuclear disarmament*."

At the request of a majority of the NPT signatories, the treaty will be reviewed every five years. The NPT also mandates that a decision be made twenty-five years after it entered into force, by majority vote, as to "whether the Treaty shall continue in force indefinitely, or shall be extended for an additional fixed period or periods." As the NPT took effect in 1970, this extension conference was set to take place in 1995. At the close of the first part of this conference (April 6, 1995) the thirty-eight members issued a pledge not to use nuclear weapons against non-nuclear-weapon states. The conference was unable, however, to re-establish the Ad Hoc Committees on security assurances, prevention of the arms race in outer space, expansion of membership, definitions of a nuclear explosion, verification, and implementation. The testing issue was still challenged by a Chinese nuclear test in August (its second for the year) and the threat of France to resume nuclear testing in the South Pacific. An extension for only a fixed period would likely spell doom for the treaty. At each of the four NPT review conferences to date, the slow progress in implementing Article VI of the NPT has received the most attention by delegates. The failure to negotiate a comprehensive ban on nuclear weapons tests* has proven to be the single most contentious issue. Both Article VI and the preamble to the NPT call for such negotiations.

Also standing in the path of nations that may be seeking to "go nuclear" are the considerable technical challenges associated with nuclear weapons development and production. The primary obstacle is acquiring the fissile material needed to fuel the chain reaction necessary to generate a nuclear explosion, the minimum requirement for which is generally regarded to be about twenty-five kilograms of highly enriched uranium or eight kilograms of weapons-grade plutonium. Some nuclear scientists believe that as little as 1 to 3 kilograms of plutonium may be sufficient to build a crude nuclear bomb. Weapons-grade uranium is produced by enriching the concentration of uranium-235 in natural uranium by 90 percent or more. Plutonium is chemically separated, or "reprocessed," from used, or "spent," nuclear fuel; that is, fuel that has been discharged from a nuclear reactor because it can no longer efficiently sustain a nuclear chain reaction. Some advanced nuclear weapons nations also use tritium to increase the energy release, or yield, of nuclear explosives.

Verifying that sensitive nuclear materials and technologies are not diverted from civilian to military uses is the responsibility of the International Atomic Energy Agency (IAEA). Established in 1957, this UN-affiliated agency performs two seemingly contradictory roles, one promotional, the other regulatory. On the one hand, the IAEA promotes nuclear energy generation and facilitates the transfer of nuclear materials and technology for peaceful purposes. On the other hand, it serves as the primary verification mechanism and policing arm of the NPT. Within 18 months after signing the NPT, non-nuclear-weapon nations with peaceful nuclear programs are required to sign on to an IAEA program of routine audits and on-site inspections, collectively referred to as safeguards. The IAEA has a huge mandate, but only a small staff and annual budget. Its 200 inspectors regularly visit over 900 nuclear facilities in more than fifty countries. Some have proposed dividing the IAEA into two separate agencies to alleviate this burden and also to eliminate any possible conflict of interests in its dual missions.

In September 1991, Director General of the IAEA Hans Blix made the following recommendations for strengthening the agency:

The case of Iraq demonstrates the challenges that may need to be met and the ability of the Agency to meet them. . . . I conclude that the lesson to be learnt from the present case is that a high degree of assurance can be obtained that the Agency can uncover clandestine nuclear activities if three major conditions are fulfilled: first, that access is provided to information obtained, *inter alia* through national technical means, regarding sites that may require inspection; second, that access to any such sites, even at short notice, is an unequivocal right of the Agency; and third, that access to the Security Council is available for backing and support that may be necessary to perform the inspection.

In an address to the UN on September 27, 1993, President Bill Clinton identified an "increased threat" of nuclear proliferation as being among the foremost national security threats facing the United States. He remarked:

One of our most urgent priorities must be attacking the proliferation of weapons of mass destruction. . . . I have made nonproliferation one of our nation's highest priorities. We intend to weave it more deeply into the fabric of all our relationships with the world's nations and institutions.

President Clinton also proposed that nations end all production of fissile material for weapons:

We will pursue new steps to control the materials for nuclear weapons. Growing global stockpiles of plutonium and highly enriched uranium are raising the danger of nuclear terrorism for all nations. We will press for an international agreement that would ban production of these materials for weapons forever.

As part of a new "counterproliferation initiative," the Pentagon has stepped up its focus on high-tech weaponry such as warheads capable of destroying underground command bunkers and interceptors that can knock down approaching enemy missiles. The major new weapon system that the military hopes to develop under this program, the Theater High Altitude Area Defense System (THAAD), is a multibillion-dollar, mobile antimissile interceptor for use against short- and medium-range ballistic missiles.

The breakup of the USSR has bred concern that "loose nukes" might find their way into the hands of terrorists or "rogue" nations. There is also concern that all fissile material and nuclear technology in the former USSR may not be fully accounted for and safeguarded. In addition, there is concern about a possible "brain drain"; that is, that former Russian nuclear weapons scientists and engineers, their status and incomes reduced, might sell their services to the highest bidder.

Ultimately, nations interested in acquiring nuclear weapons must be persuaded that their national interests are better served by not possessing nuclear weapons than by acquiring them. The burden falls on the members of the "nuclear club" to take steps that will minimize the perceived military and political value of nuclear weapons in international affairs.

See ACCIDENTAL NUCLEAR WAR; ANTIBALLISTIC MISSILES/STAR WARS; CAUSES OF WAR; COLD WAR; DISARMAMENT; HIROSHIMA AND NAGASAKI; MASS DESTRUCTION, WEAPONS OF; MILITARY-INDUSTRIAL COMPLEX; NUCLEAR WAR; NUCLEAR WEAPONS TESTING; NUCLEAR WEAPONS TESTING, UN RESOLUTIONS BANNING; NUCLEAR WEAPONS, UN RESOLUTIONS BANNING MANUFACTURE AND USE OF; STRATEGIC DEFENSE INITIATIVE (SDI); TOTAL WAR.

BIBLIOGRAPHY
Center for Defense Information, *The Defense Monitor* 21, no. 3 (1992).
Gray, Peter, *Briefing Book on the Nonproliferation of Nuclear Weapons* (Washington, D.C.: Council for a Livable World Education Fund, 1993).
Spector, Leonard S., with Jacqueline R. Smith, *Nuclear Ambitions,* Carnegie Endowment for International Peace (Boulder, Colo.: Westview Press, 1990).
Martin L. Calhoun

NUCLEAR TESTING IN THE PACIFIC.

AMERICAN NUCLEAR TESTS

Testing in the Marshall Islands was first conducted between 1946 and 1954. After the 1945 nuclear explosions in Hiroshima and Nagasaki*, U.S. policy-makers became curious about the meaning and magnitude of this new force that had been unleashed. The military community was interested in seeing just what the new weapon could do, and scientists were interested in its biological effects. The U.S. government planned a series of tests to address these questions called Operation Crossroads, a name symbolic of the position at which the world found itself.

After reviewing sites in the Atlantic and the Caribbean, the U.S. planners selected a section of the Marshall Islands as most appropriate. These atolls were inhabited by only small numbers of people and were not near any large population areas. The people inhabiting Bikini* and Enewetok Atolls were moved to facilitate this testing. In July 1946, the United States began its tests with one bomb burst about 520 feet above a fleet of naval vessels anchored in the Bikini lagoon, and a second test detonating an atomic device 90 feet below a ship, about halfway to the bottom of the lagoon. This second detonation produced a mile-high column of radioactive seawater.

The second round began in 1948 at Enewetok Atoll. Called Operation Sandstone, it was a series of three detonations on 200-foot towers. In April 1951, the tests on Enewetok resumed with Operation Green House, consisting of four blasts. Then on November 1, 1952, came the first hydrogen bomb test on Enewetok's Elujelab Island (test ''Mike''). After the test, only a crater 200 feet deep and a mile in diameter remained where the island once stood.

The first serious fallout accident occurred on March 1, 1954, after test Bravo in the Castle series on Bikini Atoll. The yield was about seventeen megatons, and the winds in the upper atmosphere caused the radioactive cloud to drift over and deposit fallout on several inhabited atolls to the east: Rongelap, Ailinginae, and Utirik, with 64, 18, and 157 islanders, respectively, and Rongerik, with 28 Americans. Rongelap received snow-like fallout ash about five hours after the detonation; Rongerik received a mist of fallout about two hours later; and Utirik was exposed about twenty-two hours after the blast. A Japanese fishing vessel, the *Lucky Dragon,* located 100 miles away, experienced the fallout within two hours of the explosion.

Although the U.S. government has repeatedly stated that the fallout was an accident, increasing evidence has revealed that the dangers were foreseen. The Rongelap people were given no official warning prior to the Bravo test. The radioactive dust soon formed a layer on the island two inches deep. It turned the drinking water brackish yellow and contaminated the food. By nightfall, the islanders began to show the effects of acute radiation exposure, such as itching and burning of the skin, eyes, and mouth; severe vomiting; and diarrhea.

About two days after the blast, the Rongelap islanders and the exposed persons on the other atolls were evacuated to Majuro by the U.S. Navy, but by then their exposure was already quite high. Within about two weeks after the bomb test, the majority of the Rongelap people had skin burns on their necks, arms, and feet and lost some of their body and scalp hair. Cesium-137 and strontium-90 body burdens became quite high among Rongelap islanders because they had eaten irradiated foods.

The Utirik people, whose original estimated exposure in 1954 of fourteen rads was less than one-twelfth of the exposure received by the Rongelap people, also developed a significant rate of thyroid cancer. By 1976, ten out of 157 (6%) of the people at Utirik who were exposed in 1954 had developed thyroid tumors.

The twenty-three crewmen aboard the Japanese fishing vessel, *Lucky Dragon,* saw the flash of light on March 1, 1954, and the mushroom cloud that formed on the test site of Bikini Atoll, but they did not immediately connect this experience with the heavy, gritty ash falling on them about ninety minutes later. Unfamiliar with fallout, some crewmen even tasted it to determine what it was. They washed themselves and their clothing to try removing the ash that began burning their skin, but were unable to do a very thorough cleansing of the ship under the circumstances. So they sailed back to Japan, some 2,000 miles away, in a contaminated environment.

Upon arrival in Japan almost two weeks later, they were nearly all suffering from radiation sickness similar to that experienced by the Rongelap people— itching and burning of the skin, nausea, and vomiting. After six months, the radio operator on the *Lucky Dragon,* who had been exposed to an estimated dose of 510–590 rads, died. Scientists estimated the other twenty-two fishermen had been exposed to radioactive materials ranging from a low of 190–220 to a high of 660–690 rads.

The twenty-eight American servicemen stationed at Rongerik also suffered from skin burns on their necks, arms, and feet and lost body and scalp hair beginning about two weeks after their exposure. Since their initial examination in 1954, however, the military men who were on Rongerik have apparently received no regular medical follow-up from the U.S. government, despite their exposure to a radiation dose at least five times that of the Utirik people.

The Bikini and Enewetok people have moved from island to island looking for a satisfactory permanent location. The Bikinians returned to their home in 1971 but had to evacuate again in 1978 because of the radioactivity. The Enewetok people returned to their atoll in April 1980 even though the northern half of the atoll is still so radioactive that it remains uninhabitable and will be off-limits permanently to the returning population. In October 1982, the residents of Enewetok filed a lawsuit in the U.S. Court of Claims for $500,000,000 in damages, accusing the United States of neglect and broken promises. In 1983, the United States established a fund of at least $183,700,000 to compensate Marshall Islanders for injuries and damages related to the nuclear testing.

ATMOSPHERIC NUCLEAR TESTS IN FRENCH POLYNESIA: 1966-1974

In the mid-1960s, France relocated its nuclear weapons testing program to Moruroa Atoll in the Tuamotu Archipelago, in French Polynesia. Between 1966 and 1974, forty-one atmospheric tests were announced. Testing effects have been recorded as far away as Mexico, where fish were found to have increased levels of radioactivity, and in Fiji, where the rain was found to be contaminated.

New Zealand and Australia first attempted to end the French atmospheric testing program through diplomatic channels and then finally in frustration brought suit in the International Court of Justice in 1973. The Fiji government also sought to join as an intervenor in the proceedings. Without deciding the merits of the case, the Court granted a temporary order restraining France from conducting further tests until the case had been heard. Australia and New Zealand contended that the French atmospheric tests violated international law. New Zealand in particular claimed that the ''maturing of national and international attitudes towards nuclear weapons . . . is evidenced by a series of treaties and resolutions.'' It went on to argue that not only was New Zealand's territorial sovereignty violated by the tests, but that they could cause damaging effects as well, including among other things, ''apprehension, anxiety and concern.'' In 1974, the newly elected French President Giscard d'Estaing announced that beginning in 1975, all tests would be conducted underground. The International Court then accepted France's contention that the case should be considered to be moot because no further dispute existed. It can reasonably be assumed that these suits and the court's interim order influenced France's decision to end its atmospheric program.

Subsequently, France moved its tests underground and continued them until a moratorium was announced in the early 1990s. The French underground testing raised fears of radioactive contamination. Because the atolls of French Polynesia are made of coral and are relatively porous, some observers have predicted that radioactive material will leak into the ocean. In addition, occasional mishaps undermined confidence in the commitment of the facility to high standards of safety.

CONCLUSION

The long and unfortunate history of the Pacific's role in the Atomic Age has shaped present Pacific attitudes toward continued and proposed nuclear activities within the region. Ironically, this region, having no nuclear activities of its own—with basically rural economies and little advanced technology of any sort—has had more direct experience than nearly any other area of the world with the physical, political, and social impacts of nuclear energy. With this in mind, it is not difficult to understand the current antinuclear mood and the impatience expressed by many islanders with the risk analyses coming into use in the developed countries for decisions involving technology risk. To the islander, the quantitative risks are nearly irrelevant.

See BIKINI ATOLL, BOMBING OF; CHEMICAL AND BIOLOGICAL EXPERIMENTS ON HUMAN SUBJECTS; ENVIRONMENTAL ISSUES, POLLUTION, AND THE MILITARY; NUCLEAR WEAPONS TESTING.

BIBLIOGRAPHY

Conard, R., *A Twenty-Year Review of Medical Findings in a Marshallese Population Accidentally Exposed to Radioactive Fallout* (Upton, N.Y.: Brookhaven National Laboratory, 1977).

————, *Summary of Thyroid Findings in Marshallese Twenty-Two Years After Exposure to Radioactive Fallout* (Upton, N.Y.: Brookhaven National Laboratory, 1977).

Hines, N. O., *Proving Ground: An Account of the Radiological Studies in the Pacific 1946–1961* (Seattle: University of Washington Press, 1962).

Johnston, Giff, *Bulletin of the Atomic Scientists* 36, no. 24 (1980).

Kiste, R., *The Bikinians: A Study in Forced Migration* (Menlo Park, Calif.: Cummings, 1974).

Micronesian Support Committee, *Marshall Islands: A Chronology 1944–1981* (Honolulu: University of Hawaii Press, 1981).

Nuclear Test Cases (*Australia v. France, New Zealand v. France*), 1973 ICJ 253, 12 *ILM* 749 (1973).

Van Dyke, Jon M., ''Protected Marine Areas and Low-Lying Atolls,'' *Ocean and Shoreline Management* 16 (1991), 87–160.

Van Dyke, John M., Kirk R. Smith, and Suliana Siwatibau, *Nuclear Activities and the Pacific Islanders* (Honolulu: East-West Center, 1984).

Jon M. Van Dyke

NUCLEAR TREATIES. More than 50,000 nuclear weapons exist in the world, containing an explosive power equal to 300,000 Hiroshima* bombs. Several treaties concern the accumulation and spread of nuclear weapons. However, they scarcely affect the massive arsenals of the United States and the former Soviet Union. Furthermore, no treaty to date cuts the nuclear arsenals of the United Kingdom, France, and China. More importantly, no treaties currently on the horizon change the grim future—a future in which the Earth and its inhabitants will continue to be threatened by the awesome power of the mushroom cloud.

The United States has agreed to several treaties that limit where nuclear weapons can be deployed. The 1959 Antarctic Treaty prohibits the signatories from establishing military bases, carrying out military maneuvers, or testing weapons in Antarctica. The 1967 Outer Space Treaty prohibits the deployment of weapons of mass destruction in outer space. The 1967 Latin American Nuclear Free Zone Treaty commits the United States, the Soviets, and others to respect the denuclearized status of the Latin American zone where receipt, storage, installation, deployment, and possession of nuclear weapons are prohibited. The 1971 Seabed Treaty prohibits the deployment of nuclear weapons on the ocean floor.

The Nuclear Non-Proliferation Treaty (NPT) is a multilateral treaty that has been signed by more than 160 countries. The treaty was first signed in 1968 and went into effect in 1970. The NPT prohibits nations from developing, acquiring, or maintaining nuclear weapons, with one exception. Those nations that already had nuclear weapons are permitted to keep them, at least for the time being.

In exchange for the right to keep their nuclear weapons, the United States, the Soviet Union, Britain, France, and China agreed to share the peaceful benefits of nuclear power with nations that did not have nuclear weapons. Perhaps most importantly, the nuclear weapons states agreed to pursue a complete ban on nuclear testing* and "the elimination from national arsenals of nuclear weapons and the means of their delivery."

The NPT has not solved all proliferation* problems. Several countries that have nuclear weapons programs and may already possess nuclear weapons have not signed the NPT, including Israel, India, and Pakistan. Furthermore, the signing of the Non-Proliferation Treaty does not guarantee that a signatory nation will not seek nuclear weapons. Both North Korea and Iraq signed the NPT, but still sought nuclear weapons. The NPT, however, does give participating nations some modicum of enforcement authority.

The Anti-Ballistic Missile (ABM)* Treaty of 1972 is a bilateral treaty between the Soviet Union (and now its successor states) and the United States. This important treaty limits the deployment of missile defenses that could intercept incoming long-range ballistic missiles traveling at high speed. The ABM Treaty does not allow for the deployment of a national missile defense system, whether it be in space or at various locations on the ground.

The ABM treaty had two main purposes: to keep the arms race out of the heavens and to stop a missile defense race before it began. A race for more and increasingly effective missile defenses would only add fuel to the already inflamed race for offensive nuclear weapons.

Only one treaty to date addresses nonstrategic nuclear weapons—the Intermediate-Range Nuclear Forces (INF) Treaty. This treaty was signed in December 1987 and went into force in June 1988. The INF treaty successfully eliminated all U.S. and Soviet land-based nuclear missiles with a range of 300–3,400 miles.

The Strategic Arms Reduction Treaties (START I and II) of 1992 and 1993 are the first treaties to eliminate a certain number of long-range or strategic nuclear weapons. The START I and II treaties, when ratified and fully implemented, will cut the nuclear arsenals of the United States and former Soviet Union by two-thirds by the year 2003. This will leave the United States and Russia with 3,500 and 3,000 strategic or long-range nuclear weapons, respectively. British, French, and Chinese nuclear forces are unaffected by the START treaties.

While the START treaties will reduce the overkill of U.S. and Russian nuclear arsenals, they do not relieve the threat of a nuclear holocaust. The destructive power of the remaining weapons is very real. Secretary of State Warren Christopher pointed out in congressional testimony that there was ''no question that even the remaining one-third of our strategic forces are extremely powerful and have a capacity to destroy civilization as we know it several times over.''

If the START treaties and various initiatives concerning battlefield nuclear weapons are implemented as scheduled, by the year 2003 the United States alone will still have upwards of 5,000 deliverable nuclear warheads—3,500 long-range and roughly 1,500 short-range. This would be equal to the explosive power of 70,000 Hiroshima bombs.

The Partial Test Ban Treaty (1963), the Threshold Test Ban Treaty (signed in 1974 and entered into force in 1990) and the Peaceful Nuclear Explosions Treaty (signed in 1976 and entered into force in 1990) limit the location, explosive power, type, and purpose of nuclear explosions. Despite efforts since 1950 to ban all nuclear test explosions, the international community has yet to agree to a Comprehensive Test Ban (CTB) treaty. Such a treaty would be the sign that the nuclear powers are ready to move toward the reversal of the nuclear arms race.

Under the leadership of President Bill Clinton, the United States is observing a nuclear testing moratorium. The United States last tested in September 1992. Only China and France have tested nuclear weapons since. A complete ban on testing is being negotiated at the United Nations Conference on Disarmament (CD) in Geneva.

The CD is also negotiating a ban on the production of nuclear materials for military purposes. This ban on the building blocks of nuclear weapons was proposed by President Clinton. It would not, however, have any impact on the more than 420 electrical generating nuclear power plants that operate in twenty-nine countries, nor would it affect the fifty-four countries to date that have nuclear research reactors. Every nation that has a nuclear reactor potentially has the raw materials—uranium and plutonium—to make nuclear weapons.

Numerous multilateral and bilateral talks have been conducted concerning stopping the spread of nuclear weapons and halting and reversing the nuclear arms race. Much, however, remains to be done. The world will not be safe from the threat of nuclear weapons until nations work together to eliminate forever nuclear weapons from national arsenals, as stated in the NPT treaty, or, better yet, from the planet entirely. No negotiations aimed at eventually eliminating the nuclear threat are planned.

See ACCIDENTAL NUCLEAR WAR; ANTIBALLISTIC MISSILES/STAR WARS; COLD WAR; NUCLEAR DETERRENCE; MASS DESTRUCTION, WEAPONS OF; NUCLEAR PROLIFERATION; STRATEGIC DEFENSE INITIATIVE (SDI); NUCLEAR WEAPONS TESTING, UN RESOLUTIONS BANNING; NUCLEAR WEAPONS, UN RESOLUTIONS BANNING MANUFACTURE OR USE.

BIBLIOGRAPHY

"Arms Control and Disarmament Agreements: Texts and Histories of the Negotiations," U.S. Arms Control and Disarmament Agency (1990).

Bunn, George, Roland Timerbaev, and James Leonard, *Nuclear Disarmament: How Much Have the Five Nuclear Powers Promised in the Non-Proliferation Treaty?* (Lawyers Alliance for World Security, Committee for National Security, and the Washington Council on Non-Proliferation, June 1994).

"Nuclear Weapons After the Cold War: Too Many, Too Costly, Too Dangerous," *Defense Monitor* 22, no. 1, Center for Defense Information (1993).

Kathryn R. Schultz

NUCLEAR WAR. Throughout the nuclear age, philosophers have reflected on the nature, use, and consequences of nuclear weapons. These reflections have progressed through four phases. The first phase stretches from Hiroshima* to Bikini* and focuses on atomic weapons from their initial use in 1945 to the testing of the hydrogen bomb in 1952. During the 1950s and 1960s, the second phase concerns above-ground nuclear testing*, as well as postwar tension between the United States and the Soviet Union. The third phase focuses on increasing shifts during the 1970s and 1980s toward counterforce* weapons and war-fighting strategies. The fourth phase responds to the dissolution of the Soviet Union in 1991 and problems of nuclear proliferation* and nuclear deterrence* theory in the post-Cold War* world.

Nuclear weapons undercut the traditional distinction between military combatants and civilian noncombatants*. In fact, if deterrence fails, noncombatants will be the primary victims, and just war* principles of proportionality* and discrimination will be violated. Moreover, because of radioactive fallout, the use of nuclear weapons entails ecological warfare, the results of which cannot be contained within the territorial boundaries of the fighting nations.

Nuclear war is a contingent event; it is neither necessary nor impossible. Instead of resignation to or denial of nuclear war, we should learn about the possibilities. This knowledge is based on three sources: (1) studies of actual nuclear weapons detonations; (2) projections on limited and full-scale nuclear war, which normally extrapolate casualties* and damage to military and industrial bases; and (3) computer simulations and speculative models on possible catastrophic consequences. Our empirical knowledge alone, however, suggests that even limited nuclear war will have consequences significantly more severe than the worst of most conventional wars.

During the first phase of philosophical response, the theme of social responsibility was raised by several famous philosophers. On August 8, 1945 (two days after the bombing of Hiroshima), Albert Camus was the first to voice ethical concern with an essay in *Combat,* and Bertrand Russell began his prolonged responses with an essay in *Forward* on August 18. Also in 1945, Jean-Paul Sartre responded with "La Fin de la Guerre" (*Temps Modernes*), and John Dewey wrote his seminal essay "Dualism and the Split Atom" (*New Leader*). Pierre Teilhard de Chardin also made several contributions. Briefly, some philosophers, including Russell, considered whether the Soviet Union should be prevented, militarily if necessary, from developing nuclear weapons. Also, even before the Soviet Union tested its first atomic bomb in 1949, philosophers addressed whether world government was now needed and feasible. In addition to writings by Russell and A. C. Ewing, *Ethics* published essays in 1946 and 1947 on this topic. Finally, even at this time, John Somerville and several other philosophers raised the prospect that nuclear war could bring about the end of the human species.

Especially significant is T. V. Smith's *Atomic Power and Moral Faith* (1946), which is the first book by a philosopher to address nuclear weapons. Smith stresses the economic, military, and social implications of atomic energy, provides a critique of religious and political sectarianism in the atomic age, and pioneers the call for improving U.S.-Soviet relations. Also notable is Daniel S. Robinson's *The Principles of Conduct* (1948), which develops his view that, within applied philosophy, concern about the atomic age should be preeminent for political ethics.

During the second phase, debate on the extinction thesis received increased attention. The reality of the Cold War replaced the hope for international control of atomic weapons, the hydrogen bomb was developed, the Chinese Revolution succeeded, and the Korean War* began. Against this backdrop, in 1958 Russell and Sidney Hook carried on a heated exchange, with Russell arguing that nuclear war would destroy all humanity and Hook arguing that Soviet communism would destroy all freedom. Continuing to be the philosopher who spoke most extensively about the nuclear war, Russell made a dramatic broadcast for the BBC, initiated the Pugwash movement, contributed to the Campaign for Nuclear Disarmament, and published his classic *Common Sense and Nuclear Warfare* (1959).

One practical result of the criticism by ethicists and scientists of above-ground nuclear testing* was the Partial Test Ban Treaty. Along with the "Russell-Einstein Manifesto," one of the compelling pleas to protect the innocent came from Albert Schweitzer in *Peace or Atomic War?* (1958). Nevertheless, the position of Hook also had influential representatives, including Karl Jaspers, who published *Die Atombombe und die Zukunft des Menschen* (1958). Like Hook, he advocated risking destruction of humanity in nuclear war over the alternative of losing our "humanity" under totalitarianism. Less known in this phase are some of the metaphysical assessments of the nuclear age. Martin Heidegger, for example, discussed the metaphysics of nuclear weapons in several writings, and several philosophers subsequently drew on his argument that metaphysical reflection on the nuclear age helps us diagnose our plight as would-be controllers (and, potentially, destroyers) of the Earth.

The third phase was swept up with renewed public concern over the nuclear threat during the 1970s and 1980s. The American Academy of Sciences warned of the dangers of ozone depletion from nuclear detonations, the Physicians for Social Responsibility declared the unmanageability of medical problems after nuclear war, Johnathan Schell used the term "second death" in his famous *The Fate of the Earth* (1982) to refer to the meaning of annihilating humanity in nuclear war, and Carl Sagan warned of the prospect of nuclear winter. With these Apocalyptic forecasts, the extremes in arguing about nuclear war were reached. John Somerville summed up these concerns in his term "omnicide"— the irreversible extinction of all sentient life. Beyond revisiting the extinction thesis, philosophers in the 1970s and especially the 1980s produced a deluge of writings seeking to "counter counterforce*"—arguing against nuclear war-fighting policies and first-strike* weapons. Key journal issues were published by *Philosophy and Social Criticism* (1984, Gay, ed.) and *Ethics* (1985, Hardin et al., eds.), and several important anthologies were published, including *Nuclear Weapons and the Future of Humanity* (1984, Cohen and Lee, eds.) and *Nuclear War* (1985, Fox and Groarke, eds.). Substantial contributions were made by Douglas Lackey, especially in his *Moral Principles and Nuclear Weapons* (1984) and Gregory Kavka, especially in his *Moral Paradoxes of Nuclear Deterrence* (1987).

During the 1980s, two professional associations of philosophers formed in response to the threat of nuclear war. Concerned Philosophers for Peace (founded in 1981) and IPPNO, the International Philosophers for the Prevention of Nuclear Omnicide (founded in 1983), hold annual conferences and conduct programs at divisional meetings of the American Philosophical Association. In addition to their respective newsletters, Concerned Philosophers for Peace has published several books that address various philosophical topics concerning nuclear weapons. These volumes include *Issues of War and Peace* (1989, Kunkel and Klein, eds.), *In the Interest of Peace* (1990, Klein and Kunkel, eds.), and *Just War, Nonviolence and Nuclear Deterrence* (1991, Cady and Werner, eds.).

In the fourth phase, philosophers are responding to the dissolution of the Soviet Union and the proliferation of nuclear weapons. Steven Lee argues in *Morality, Prudence, and Nuclear Weapons* (1993) that, even with the dissolution of the Soviet Union, the threat of nuclear war continues and a strong case can still be made for the immorality and imprudence of nuclear deterrence*. Lee supports delegitimization of nuclear weapons and, to achieve this goal, contends that war itself needs to be delegitimized. In an effort to address such broader concerns, William Gay and T. A. Alekseeva edited *On the Eve of the 21st Century* (1994), a collaborative volume by Russian philosophers at the Institute of Philosophy in Moscow and American philosophers in Concerned Philosophers for Peace. In this volume, Russians and Americans criticize the persistence of *Realpolitik* as inspired by Hobbes* and the morality of nuclear deterrence. They also argue for nonviolent* approaches to national security and reassess the future of socialism and role of Russia in the post-Cold War world.

Beginning with *From the Eye of the Storm* (1994, Bove and Duhan Kaplan, eds.), Concerned Philosophers for Peace launched a book series with Rodopi Press on the "Philosophy of Peace." This series reflects the changed ways in which philosophers are responding to the nuclear threat and the prospects for global peace in the post-Cold War world. Increasingly, topics of regional conflicts, along with concerns about nuclear proliferation, are receiving attention by this group and by individual philosophers. The final verdict on how philosophers and the world community will respond ethically and politically to the prospects for increased nuclear proliferation and the attendant threat of nuclear war remains to be seen.

See COLD WAR; COMBATANT-NONCOMBATANT DISTINCTION; COUNTERFORCE VERSUS COUNTERVALUE; ENVIRONMENTAL ISSUES, POLLUTION, AND THE MILITARY; HOBBES, THOMAS; JUST WAR; MARXISM AND WAR; MUTUAL ASSURED DESTRUCTION (MAD); NUCLEAR DETERRENCE; NUCLEAR PROLIFERATION.

BIBLIOGRAPHY

Gay, William, and Michael Pearson, *The Nuclear Arms Race* (Chicago: American Library Association, 1987).

Kavka, Gregory, *Moral Paradoxes of Nuclear Deterrence* (Cambridge: Cambridge University Press, 1987).

Lackey, Douglas, *Moral Principles and Nuclear Weapons* (Totowa, N.J.: Rowman & Allenheld, 1984).

Lee, Steven, *Morality, Prudence, and Nuclear Weapons* (Cambridge: Cambridge University Press, 1993).

William C. Gay

NUCLEAR WEAPONS, UN RESOLUTIONS BANNING MANUFACTURE OR USE OF.

November 24, 1961, UN Resolution classifying nuclear weapons as causing "unnecessary suffering." United States not a signatory.

November 28, 1966, UN General Assembly Resolution to plan for a Ban the Bomb Conference. Passed, 80 yea, 0 nay, and 23 (U.S.) abstentions.

November 29, 1972, UN General Assembly Resolution to hold a world disarmament conference. Passed, 105 yea, 0 nay, 1 (U.S.) abstention.

December 11, 1979, UN General Assembly Resolution against stationing nuclear weapons in non-nuclear weapons countries. Passed, 99 yea, 18 (U.S.) nay, and 19 abstentions.

In 1979, The UN General Assembly approved 39 resolutions on arms and disarmament issues. Of these, the United States supported 29, abstained on 7, and voted nay on 3.

November 1981, UN General Assembly Resolution banning weapons of mass destruction. Passed, 116 yea, 0 nay, and 27 (U.S.) abstentions.

November 25, 1981, UN General Assembly Yugoslavian Resolution on the cessation of the nuclear arms race. Passed, 136 yea, 0 nay, and 9 (U.S.) abstentions.

December 15, 1989, UN General Assembly Resolution for a Nuclear Freeze. Passed, 136 yea, 13 (U.S.) nay, and 5 abstentions.

December 17, 1989, UN General Assembly Resolution Prohibiting the Use of Nuclear Weapons. Passed, 134 yea, 17 (U.S.) nay, and 4 abstentions.

1990, UN General Assembly Resolution on Preventing Nuclear War. Passed, 132 yea, 12 (U.S.) nay, and 9 abstentions.

1990, UN General Assembly Resolution to Freeze the production of nuclear weapons. Passed, 125 yea, 17 (U.S.) nay, and 10 abstentions.

1991, UN General Assembly proposal for comprehensive disarmament. Passed, 123 yea, 6 (U.S.) nay, and 32 abstentions.

1991, UN General Assembly Resolution to prohibit the use of nuclear weapons. Passed, 122 yea, 16 (U.S.) nay, and 22 abstentions.

1991, UN General Assembly Resolution on the ''Prohibition of the production of fissionable materials for weapons purposes.'' Passed, 152 yea, 2 (U.S.) nay, and 3 abstentions.

NUCLEAR WEAPONS TESTING. On July 16, 1945, the United States conducted the world's first explosive test of a nuclear weapon at Alamogordo, New Mexico. Since then, six nations—the United States, the former USSR, the UK, France, China, and India—have acknowledged detonating nuclear explosives, primarily for test purposes. The former USSR first exploded a nuclear device in 1949, the UK in 1952, France in 1960, China in 1964, and India in 1974. In total, there have been 2,037 nuclear explosions worldwide (including the bombs dropped on Hiroshima and Nagasaki*), an average of one every nine days. Not all of these explosions were announced before they occurred. On December 7, 1943, U.S. Energy Secretary Hazel O'Leary divulged that there were 204 ''secret,'' or unannounced, U.S. nuclear explosive tests between 1963 and 1990. The United States now acknowledges conducting 1,054 nuclear tests (including twenty-four joint tests with the UK), the former USSR 715, the UK 45 (including twenty-four joint tests with the United States), France 204, China 40, and India 1.

Nuclear weapons have been exploded atop towers, on barges, while suspended from balloons, after being dropped from aircraft, after being lifted by rockets, in the atmosphere, underground, and underwater. About 25 percent of all nuclear tests occurred in the atmosphere. The United States conducted 215 atmospheric tests, the former USSR 207, the UK 21, France 45, and China 23. These 511 atmospheric tests contained a combined explosive power of about 438 megatons, or 29,000 times the force of the bomb dropped on Hiroshima. More than half of this megatonnage was unleashed in a sixteen-month period from September

1961 to December 1962. The largest nuclear blast ever, measuring 58 megatons, was conducted by the former USSR in 1961.

U.S. nuclear explosions have taken place in Alaska, Colorado, Mississippi, New Mexico, and Nevada, and also outside U.S. borders in Japan, in the Pacific Ocean, and over the South Atlantic. Since 1974, all U.S. nuclear tests have been conducted at the Nevada test site, sixty-five miles northwest of Las Vegas. The former USSR utilized two principal test sites. One was Semipalatinsk, in the republic of Kazakhstan; the other was Novaya Zemlya, an island 500 miles north of the Arctic Circle. The UK initially tested nuclear weapons in Australia and on South Pacific islands. Since 1962, all British tests have been conducted jointly with the United States at the Nevada test site. France initially tested nuclear weapons in the Sahara Desert, but since 1966 it has used the South Pacific atolls of Mururoa and Fangataufa. All Chinese nuclear tests have taken place at Lop Nur, in the province of Sinkiang. India's lone nuclear test occurred beneath the Rajasthan Desert.

Nuclear tests have been used to develop nuclear weapons, enhance their safety, check their reliability, determine how nuclear explosions affect military equipment and personnel, study the physics of nuclear explosions, and train weapons designers. About 85 percent of all nuclear explosions have been for purposes of developing, testing, and refining new nuclear weapons. Such weapons-design tests have made it possible to produce 200-kiloton cruise missile warheads that weigh only 270 pounds. By comparison, early 20-kiloton atomic bombs weighed five tons. A second type of nuclear test, weapons-effects tests, are conducted for purposes of assessing the survivability of military equipment and electronic components in a nuclear environment. A third type of nuclear test, weapons-reliability tests, entail detonating a nuclear warhead to ensure that others of its type will work as intended. Nuclear weapons have also been tested to ensure that they are safe. Weapons-design and weapons-reliability tests are conducted in vertical shafts, 600–3,600 feet deep, and cost about $30 million each. Weapons-effects tests are conducted in horizontal tunnels, 1,000–8,000 feet long, and cost about $50–$60 million each.

In the past, governments gave nuclear weapons testing priority over public health, safety, and environmental considerations. As a result, many tens of thousands of people were exposed to radioactive fallout, in some cases deliberately. A 1991 study by International Physicians for the Prevention of Nuclear War predicted that the radiation from atmospheric testing absorbed by humans through the year 2000 will cause 430,000 cancer deaths. It estimated that as many as 2.4 million people will die from cancer as a result of the legacy of atmospheric testing. Nuclear tests conducted underground have also released radioactive debris into the atmosphere through the phenomenon of "venting." In a 1970 underground test at the Nevada test site, code-named "Baneberry," the ground above the explosion collapsed and a large radioactive cloud containing some three million curies of radioactivity drifted as far away as Canada.

In the 1950s, the United States and the former USSR conducted hundreds of tests of hydrogen bombs. The radioactive fallout from these tests spurred public protest around the world and led to the signing of the Limited Test Ban Treaty in 1963, which banned nuclear explosions in the atmosphere, in outer space, and underwater. After 1962, the United States, the former USSR, and the UK conducted nuclear tests underground only. France last tested in the atmosphere in 1974, China in 1980. Two additional treaties place limits on nuclear testing. The 1974 Threshold Test Ban Treaty banned underground nuclear weapons tests having an explosive force of more than 150 kilotons, the equivalent of 150,000 tons of TNT. The 1976 Peaceful Nuclear Explosions Treaty extended this 150-kiloton limit to nuclear explosions conducted for peaceful purposes.

A complete ban on nuclear testing was the goal of every U.S. president from Dwight D. Eisenhower to Jimmy Carter. Formal negotiations to secure a comprehensive test ban first took place in 1958. The 1963 Limited Test Ban Treaty obliges signatories to seek ''to achieve the discontinuance of all test-explosions of nuclear weapons for all time.'' The preamble to the 1968 Nuclear Non-Proliferation Treaty (NPT), in addition, restates the commitment of the world's nations to ban nuclear tests.

Temporary nuclear testing moratoriums are currently being observed by the United States, Russia, and the UK. Only China and France continue to test. The United States has not tested a nuclear weapon since September 1992, Russia since October 1990, and the UK since November 1991.

Despite its expressed commitment to achieving a test ban that, according to President Bill Clinton, ''can strengthen our efforts worldwide to halt the spread of nuclear technology in weapons,'' the Clinton administration is considering ordering a series of extremely small nuclear explosions known as ''hydronuclear tests.'' These tests are being justified by the military as necessary to ensure the reliability and safety of nuclear warheads that are expected to remain in the U.S. arsenal during a comprehensive test ban. Critics counter that current U.S. nuclear warheads already have been certified as safe and reliable and that hydronuclear tests would violate the spirit of a Comprehensive Test Ban Treaty and undermine U.S. efforts to halt the spread of nuclear weapons to additional countries.

A complete ban on nuclear testing would curtail the design and development of new nuclear weapons. It would slow the technological push to create new and potentially more deadly weapons. An end to all nuclear testing would also lend needed credibility to ongoing efforts to prevent the spread of nuclear weapons to additional countries. An NPT extension conference was held in 1995 to determine the future of the treaty that remains the main international barrier to nuclear proliferation*. In August 1995 President Clinton announced that he would press for a permanent ban on nuclear testing, with the proviso that if U.S. security was in jeopardy and if Congress concurred, he might support a renewal of underground testing. Unfortunately for the NPT deliberations, China tested a nuclear bomb in August, the same month as President Clinton's announcement (China's second test in 1995), and France announced its intention of further nuclear tests in the South Pacific. A majority of the signatories to the

NPT have demanded that a Comprehensive Test Ban Treaty be concluded before the NPT is extended. Another benefit of banning nuclear tests is that by doing so we would be sparing the environment from further damage.

See ACCIDENTAL NUCLEAR WAR; ANTIBALLISTIC MISSILES/STAR WARS; BIKINI ATOLL, BOMBING OF; BIOLOGICAL-CHEMICAL WAR-FARE; CHILDREN AND WAR; COUNTERFORCE VERSUS COUNTER-VALUE; ENVIRONMENTAL ISSUES, POLLUTION, AND THE MILITARY; HAZARDOUS DUMPING IN PROTECTED MARINE AREAS; HIROSHIMA AND NAGASAKI; MASS DESTRUCTION, WEAPONS OF; MILITARY-INDUSTRIAL COMPLEX; NUCLEAR ACCIDENTS; NU-CLEAR PROLIFERATION; NUCLEAR TESTING IN THE PACIFIC; NUCLEAR WEAPONS TESTING, UN RESOLUTIONS BANNING; STRA-TEGIC DEFENSE INITIATIVE (SDI); ZONES OF PEACE (ZOP).

BIBLIOGRAPHY
Center for Defense Information, *Defense Monitor* 11, no. 8 (1982); 13, no. 5 (1984); 14, no. 5 (1985); 14, no. 8 (1985); 18, no. 1 (1989); 18, no. 8 (1989); 20, no. 3 (1991); 22, no. 5 (1993).
Goldblat, Josef, and David Cox, eds., *Nuclear Weapon Tests: Prohibition or Limitation?* Stockholm International Peace Research Institute (New York: Oxford University Press, 1988).
International Physicians for the Prevention of Nuclear War and the Institute for Energy and Environmental Research, *Radioactive Heaven and Earth: The Health and Environmental Effects of Nuclear Weapons Testing In, On, and Above the Earth* (New York: Apex Press, 1991).

Martin L. Calhoun

NUCLEAR WEAPONS TESTING, UN RESOLUTIONS BANNING.

1963, Treaty between USSR and the United States banning testing in the atmosphere, under the sea, and outer space, but not underground.

December 9, 1971, UN General Assembly Resolution to suspend nuclear and thermonuclear tests. Passed, 74 yea, 2 nay, and 36 (U.S.) abstentions.

November 29, 1972, UN General Assembly Resolution on the suspension of nuclear and thermonuclear tests in the atmosphere as well as in all environments. Passed, 105 (U.S.) yea.

December 9, 1974, UN General Assembly Resolution for the cessation of nuclear and thermonuclear tests. Passed, 95 yea, 3 nay, and 30 (U.S.) absten-tions.

November 29, 1972, UN General Assembly Resolution urging that all nations cease testing independently of any agreement on a verification scheme. Passed, 80 yea, 4 nay, and 29 (U.S.) abstentions.

December 10, 1976, UN General Assembly Resolution urging the cessation of nuclear and thermonuclear tests and the conclusion of a comprehensive test ban. Passed, 105 yea, 2 nay, and 27 (U.S.) abstentions.

December 11, 1975, UN General Assembly Resolution on the urgent need for cessation of nuclear and thermonuclear tests and to work for a comprehensive test ban. Passed, 106 yea, 2 nay, and 24 (U.S.) abstentions.

December 11, 1975, UN General Assembly Resolution on a treaty on the complete and general prohibition of nuclear-weapons tests. Passed, 94 yea, 2 nay, and 34 (U.S.) abstentions.

December 11, 1975, UN General Assembly Resolution to establish a nuclear-weapon-free zone in the South Pacific. Passed, 110 yea, 0 nay, and 20 (U.S.) abstentions.

December 15, 1975, UN General Assembly Resolutions urging general and complete disarmament: Resolution 3484A banning tests, passed, 97 yea, 5 nay, and 24 (U.S.) abstentions; Resolution 3484B to strengthen the role of the UN in disarmament, passed, 108 yea, 2 nay, and 14 (U.S.) abstentions; Resolution 3484C regretting the slow response of the USSR and the USA toward disarmament, passed, 102 yea, 10 (U.S.) nay, and 12 abstentions. Resolution 3484D requesting that the secretary general take steps to strengthen the disarmament division of the UN, passed, 115 yea, 0 nay, and 13 (U.S.) abstentions.

December 10, 1976, UN General Assembly Resolution to establish a nuclear-weapon-free zone in South Africa. Passed, 91 yea, 2 nay, and 43 (U.S.) abstentions.

December 14, 1976, UN General Assembly Resolution to conclude a treaty of the complete and general prohibition of nuclear-weapon tests. Passed, 95 yea, 2 nay, and 36 (U.S.) abstentions.

December 14, 1976, UN General Assembly Resolution to cease all nuclear tests. Passed, 95 yea, 2 nay, and 36 (U.S.) abstentions.

December 14, 1978, UN General Assembly Resolution to ban further nuclear testing. Passed, 130 yea, 2 nay, and 8 (U.S.) abstentions.

December 11, 1979, UN General Assembly Resolution condemning any attempt on the part of Israel to manufacture, acquire, store, or test nuclear weapons. Passed, 97 yea, 10 (U.S.) nay, and 38 abstentions.

December 12, 1980, UN General Assembly Resolution for a Comprehensive Test Ban. Passed, 129 yea, 0 nay, and 35 (U.S.) abstentions.

November 23, 1981, UN General Assembly Australian Resolution on a Comprehensive Test Ban. Passed, 140 yea, 0 nay, and 5 (U.S.) abstentions.

1990, UN General Assembly Resolution for a Nuclear Test Ban. Passed, 140 yea, 2 (U.S.) nay, and 6 abstentions.

In January 1991 and again in August 1991, President Reagan reaffirmed his position that underground nuclear testing was necessary to maintain the credibility of the U.S. deterrent.

1992, UN General Assembly Resolution by Mexico for a Comprehensive Test Ban passed, 124 yea, 2 (U.S.) nay, and 19 abstentions. A Soviet Resolution on the same issue passed, 115 yea, 4 (U.S.) nay, and 26 abstentions; and an Australian Resolution also on a Comprehensive Test Ban passed, 111 yea, 1 (U.S.) nay, and 35 abstentions.

In 1992, the U.S. Congress directed that a test ban be negotiated by 1996 and established an interim moratorium on nuclear testing. Shortly before that moratorium was to expire, President Clinton, on July 2, 1993, extended the ''Moratorium on U.S. Nuclear Testing'' until September 1994. He reported that his administration had determined that the nuclear weapons in our arsenal were safe and reliable and that further testing was counterproductive after September 1994.

NUREMBERG PRINCIPLES. Frequent appeals have been made to what are called the Nuremberg Principles. The current formulation of them was done at the request of the UN General Assembly by the International Law Commission during June and July 1950. These were deduced from the Nuremberg Charter and the process by which the Nuremberg Trials* were conducted. The seven principles are as follows:

1. Any person who commits an act that constitutes a crime under international law is responsible therefor and liable to punishment

2. The fact that domestic law does not impose a penalty for an act that constitutes a crime under international law does not relieve the person who committed the act from responsibility under international law

3. The fact that a person who committed an act that constitutes a crime under international law acted as a head of state or responsible government official does not relieve him from responsibility under international law

4. The fact that a person acted pursuant to an order of his government or of a superior* does not relieve him from responsibility under international law, provided a moral choice was in fact possible to him

5. Any person charged with a crime under international law has the right to a fair trial on the facts and law

6. The crimes hereinafter set out are punishable as crimes under international law:

   a. Crimes Against Peace*:
      (i) Planning, preparation, initiation or waging of a war of aggression* or a war in violation of international treaties, agreements or assurances
      (ii) Participation in a common plan or conspiracy for the accomplishment of any of the acts mentioned under (i)
   b. War Crimes*: These are violations of the laws or customs of war, which include, but are not limited to, murder, ill-treatment or deportation to slave-labor or for any other purpose of civilian population of or in occupied territory, murder or ill-treatment of prisoners of war or persons on the seas, killing of hostages*, plunder of public or private property, wanton destruction of cities, towns, or villages, or devastation not justified by military necessity*
   c. Crimes against humanity*: These consist of murder, extermination, enslavement, deportation, and other inhuman acts done against any civilian population, or persecutions on political, racial, or religious grounds, when such acts are done or such persecutions are carried out in execution of or done in connection with any crimes against the peace or any war crime

7. Complicity in the commission of a crime against peace, a war crime, or a crime against humanity as set forth in Principle 6 is a crime under international law.

See CONTROL COUNCIL LAW NO. 10; LONDON AGREEMENT ON WAR CRIMINALS; MOSCOW DECLARATION; NUREMBERG TRIALS; TOKYO TRIALS.
BIBLIOGRAPHY
Bailey, Sydney D., "Comments of the ILC on the Seven Nuremberg Principles," *Prohibitions and Restraints in War* (New York: Oxford University Press, 1972), 163–70.
Department of the Army Pamphlet 27-161-2, *International Law,* vol. 2 (Washington, D.C.: Department of the Army, October 1962), 303–4.
Heydecker, Joe, and Johannes Leeb, *The Nuremberg Trials* (London: Heineman, 1962).
Jackson, Robert H., *The Case Against the Nazi War Criminals* (New York: Knopf, 1946).

NUREMBERG TRIALS. In January 1942, some of the occupied nations joined in issuing the St. James Declaration, which proposed that those guilty of war crimes should be punished through some channel. Legal tradition at this time did not support such a plan. In the first place, only nations could be found guilty, and individual soldiers were protected under military rules when they were following superior orders*. Furthermore, no nation could legally prosecute the citizens of another nation and no act could be considered a crime unless it was a crime in the country in question. Although The Hague* conventions had named war crimes, they never specified punishment. In addition, no universal agreement existed to support the thesis that The Hague established laws of war*. This St. James Declaration was not supported by American traditions. The framers of the Nuremberg Charter were aware that their efforts would be conditioned by certain overriding national and military commitments, which included the established tradition that war making was a national right and that no rule should be invented that would ban war making whenever the hegemony of a state was at stake. Armies had the right of reprisal* and to appeal to military necessity* whenever a rule might hinder military success. The matter of reprisal came up at the trials, and the courts had two options: they could deny that the victims of extermination had committed any prior crime for which they were being punished, or argue that the reprisals of the Germans were disproportionate to the supposed offense. Both options were explored.

In October 1943, the major Allies issued the Moscow Declaration*, which made two principal points: (1) those Germans guilty of war crimes would be tried by the people and in the area where the crimes had been committed, and (2) those Germans whose crimes had no specific locale would be tried pursuant to a joint decision to be published later by the Allies. A UN War Crimes Commission was established in July 1943 to gather evidence of war crimes. The primary focus of the commission was on the treatment of prisoners of war*, atrocities against civilians, inhumane treatment in concentration camps, the execution of hostages*, and the killing of noncombatants*. In November and December 1943 the Soviets began to try and prosecute some Germans and their Russian accomplices as war criminals, and trials took place in Kiev and Kharkov. American and British news correspondents were invited to attend both the trials and the hangings that resulted. In the summer of 1944, the staff of General Dwight D. Eisenhower at the Supreme Headquarters of the Allied Expeditionary Forces (SHAEF) prepared a *Handbook for Military Government in Germany*. This handbook proposed the automatic arrest and detention of about 250,000 high-ranking Nazis, and the mandatory arrest of all members of the Gestapo, the *Sicherheitsdienst* (SD), the higher members of the *Sturmabteilung* (SA), the *Schutzstaffel* (SS), and the regular army. Secretary of the Treasury Hans Morgenthau promoted his own plan, which proposed that the "major" criminals would be captured, identified, and summarily executed* by a UN firing squad. Lesser criminals would be given a trial.

The Allies faced a number of questions. Could leaders of states be tried? At the end of World War I the British had said yes, and the Americans had said no. Now the positions were reversed. Viscount Simon feared that even to have a trial would be a propaganda weapon in favor of the Axis, so he proposed the offending Germans be considered as outlaws who could be shot on sight without trial. The Soviet Union agreed with the United States, and together they persuaded Great Britain to participate. On August 8, 1945, an agreement was reached by the United States, Great Britain and Northern Ireland, France, and the USSR to hold two kinds of trials. The first trial type would be of the top leaders whose crimes had no specific locale and who could not plead superior orders. The second type of trial would prosecute those accused of crimes in a specific country, and the United States issued Control Council Law No. 10, which initiated a group of ten such trials. For the first trial at Nuremberg, the court would consist of four members and a vote of three was required for conviction.

A charter was prepared that listed the offenses. These were: (1) crimes against peace*, (2) war crimes*, and (3) crimes against humanity*. With regard to crimes against peace, the tribunal charged that aggressive war* was a crime. There was, however, no agreed-on definition of what such a war would be. Most nations accepted the strategy of first strike*, and this eliminated the standard definition of who was the aggressor. Nations had long ago abandoned the requirement even to make a declaration of war*, thus, even the Japanese attack on Pearl Harbor did not violate any clear law. The German lawyers pointed out that no international rules defining aggression existed. The prosecution, for its part, argued that the Paris Pact of 1928* (Kellogg-Briand Peace Pact) outlawed war as a national policy and that it was binding on the sixty-eight nations that had signed it. But the pact never mentioned aggressive war, nor did it specify any punishments for violations. The tribunal added criteria to the offense that made it generally inapplicable to most purported offenders. Before one could be found guilty, he or she had to have actual knowledge that an aggressive war was intended and that if launched it would be aggressive. In addition, the person with such knowledge must have been in a position to shape or influence the national policy. Although every defendant at the Tokyo trials* was found guilty of this crime, only eight of the twenty-four at Nuremberg were. The idea that conspiracy was a crime found little support from books on international law. What was not in question was that the Nazis were being charged with planning and initiating wars against Poland, the United Kingdom, France, Denmark, Norway, Belgium, The Netherlands, Luxembourg, Yugoslavia, Greece, the USSR, and the United States.

Part of the claim that laws forbidding breaking the peace existed was the charge of the tribunal that Germany had a ''common plan or conspiracy'' to wage aggressive war. This plan was to commit war crimes, crimes against humanity, and crimes against the peace. The Nazi Party was named as the central agency that carried out this plan. The Nazis were accused of violating the Treaty of Versailles, which had set restrictions on German rearmament, of attempting to retake territories lost after World War I, and of acquiring further territory for *lebensraum*. Nazis were charged with promulgating the doctrines of the Aryan master race, the ''leadership principle'' that put all power in the hands of the fuhrer, and that war was a noble activity. The Nazi party was charged, further, with having destroyed free trade unions, promoted beliefs incompatible with Christian teaching, persecuted pacifists, directed the economy to war making, planned to invade many neighboring countries, and collaborated with Japan and Italy for aggressive war.

The charge of war crimes was based by the tribunal on certain declarations of The Hague*. Unfortunately, these declarations were never considered binding on nonsignatories, and even signatories were relieved of compliance in wars with nonsignatories. Until 1944, even the U.S. Army manual, *The Law of Land Warfare*, stated that soldiers obeying superior orders* could not be found guilty of any war crimes. Although this was changed in the manual in 1944, there was no evidence that such a change established an international law that pleading superior orders* was not a sufficient excuse.

The tribunal defined war crimes as acts of murder and ill-treatment of civilian populations of or in occupied territories and on the high seas and included shooting, hanging, gassing, starvation, overcrowding in camps, systematic undernourishing, the assigning of tasks beyond the physical ability of the workers, inadequate medical care, kicking, beating, applying hot irons, the performance of medical experiments on living human subjects, arrests and sentencing without trial, and deliberate attempts to annihilate groups by virtue of their racial, national, or religious background. The charge included deportation for slave labor of civilians, murder and ill-treatment of prisoners of war*, killing of hostages*, pillage* of private and public treasures, looting or destruction of works of art, wanton destruction of towns not justified by military necessity, exacting heavy collective penalties, the conscription of civilian labor, and the Germanization of occupied territories. The judges concluded that the extermination camps were excessive, and that they served no viable military purpose. However, the courts did not consider whether some conventional weapons, such as flamethrowers, napalm, chemical and biological agents*, and nuclear explosives* were indiscriminately destructive.

Crimes against humanity were affirmed by the tribunal to have been established by certain declarations of Geneva International Red Cross* conventions. The list of offenses was similar to that for war crimes but emphasized the civilian deaths in extermination camps. The British did not accept the notion of crimes against humanity. Their position was that war was, in principle, inhumane, thus the crime against humanity was either an indictment of all war or irrelevant. The word genocide* was not named at this time as either a national or an international crime, and when the UN attempted in 1948 to get nations to endorse a resolution naming it as such, the U.S. Senate did not ratify it until our own laws made it a crime almost forty years later. In spite of any ambiguity on this score, the Nuremberg court charged every accused whom they hung with this crime.

The tribunal determined that it had the power to try heads of state, to declare that certain German organizations were criminal, and to find that membership in those organizations was tantamount to being criminal. By April 26, 1946, the tribunal had received 81,433 applications to be heard, most of these coming from prisoner of war camps. The defense counsel visited eighty prisoner of war camps gathering data, and by August 1946 the tribunal had 313,213 affidavits of persons to be interviewed. They saw that this would be an endless enterprise and abandoned this in favor of one trial of twenty-four national leaders. Of these, eleven were sentenced to hanging, three to life imprisonment, two to twenty-year prison terms, one to fifteen years, and one to ten years. One was pardoned, two were found not guilty, one was not tried, and two committed suicide before the end of their trials.

The preponderance of the debate at Nuremberg as well as at the Tokyo* and later trials was whether the civilian or soldier deaths were militarily necessary. If it could be shown that the acts were militarily necessary and that the deaths served a military purpose, even Allied jurists recognized that such acts would not be criminal. Given that the Allied air forces' policy of carpet and blitz bombing of German and Japanese cities had the inevitable result that a majority of the casualties* were civilians, the air forces of both Germany and Japan were immune to charges of crimes. Given that Allied submarines sank enemy ships, both civilian and military, without rescuing the survivors, no German or Japanese submarine commanders were charged with war crimes. This left only one clear area where German offenses seemed unmatched by Allied practice, and this was in the treatment of prisoners of war, both civilian and military.

Legal criticisms of the trial process surfaced from the start and continued after the trials were over. Telford Taylor, who wrote the final report for the secretary of the army on the post-Nuremberg trials, was aware that there were serious problems. Were offenses against one's own people war crimes or crimes against humanity? Were they offenses in international law? Taylor saw the main contribution of this first trial to lie in its charter, but he remarked that the charter would set no precedent unless most nations supported the principles. Taylor noted that since war consisted of acts considered criminal if committed in times of peace, custom had established that soldiers had a "blanket of immunity" from any charges as long as they were obeying orders. The task of the court was to show that this immunity had limits. Although scholars such as Quincy Wright thought that the procedure was a model for an international criminal tribunal, others, such as Hans Erhard, asserted that the Allies had invented the offenses after the fact. George Finch admitted that although it was accepted international law that a belligerent has the authority to try and punish individuals for crimes when they can catch them, that this is simply "victor's justice." Many believed that the trials violated military law that protected soldiers when they were obeying superior orders. Some legalists, including some in the United States, challenged the legitimacy of the court's dismissal of military necessity when the German lawyers appealed to it.

Of some interest was the claim of "McCarthyites" in America that the trials were a Jewish plot against noble German Aryans, and that it was a Communist plot against good free enterprising capitalists. Representative John E. Rankin (D-MS) and Senator William Langer (R-ND) said that the trials were an American disgrace and a Jewish/Communist plot. Would these trials continue indefinitely or did a statute of limitations apply here? If such a limitation did exist, then by 1952 any as yet untried criminals would be safe from prosecution. On November 26, 1968, the UN General Assembly approved a convention ruling that crimes against humanity and war crimes had no time limit, but the convention had little support. Fifty-eight voted in favor, seven voted against, but thirty-six abstained. No Western nation including members of the anti-Nazi coalition signed, and only three Latin American states approved (Chile, Cuba, and Mexico). The objectors and abstainers feared that such a convention would erode fundamental human rights. In addition, it was unclear how serious the offenses needed to be before the statute of limitations should be waived. Nations could not be compelled to extradite any accused, although, as in the Eichmann case, Nazi-hunters might continue as best they could to conduct their searches. Thus, the era of these trials came officially to a close. Did they establish a precedent? The distinguished international jurist, Lewis Oppenheim, referred to the judgments of the Nuremberg tribunal as being "evidence of international law." Yet, when the UN Commission on the Codification of International Law proposed to formulate principles derivable from the Nuremberg precedent, the General Assembly refused to ratify them.

See AGGRESSIVE VERSUS DEFENSIVE WAR; CHILDREN AND WAR; COLLATERAL DAMAGE; COMBATANT-NONCOMBATANT DISTINCTION; CONCENTRATION CAMPS; EXECUTION, SUMMARY; FORBIDDEN STRATEGIES; FORBIDDEN WEAPONS; GENEVA CONVENTION, 1929; GENOCIDE; HAGUE, THE, CONGRESSES; HIROSHIMA AND NAGASAKI; HOLOCAUST, THE; HOSTAGES; INNOCENTS; MILI-

TARY NECESSITY; PARIS PEACE PACT; PEACE, CRIMES AGAINST; PROPORTIONALITY; REPRISALS; SUPERIOR ORDERS; TOTAL WAR.

BIBLIOGRAPHY

Davidson, Eugene, *The Trial of the Germans* (New York: Macmillan, 1966).

Jackson, Robert H., *The Case Against the Nazi War Criminals* (New York: Alfred Knopf, 1946).

————, *Report to the International Conference on Military Trials* (New York: AMS Press, 1971).

Taylor, Telford, *Nuremberg and Vietnam: An American Tragedy* (New York: Time Books, 1970).

Trials of the Major War Criminals Before the International Military Tribunal, 42 vols. (New York: AMS Press, 1971).

O

OKINAWA, MILITARY OCCUPATION OF. Okinawa is the principal island of the Ryukyu Islands and the administrative center for Okinawa prefecture of Japan. It is sixty-five miles long, averages seven miles in width, with an area of 454 square miles. Its population is 1.1 million. Okinawa was the scene of the final and bloodiest battle of World War II. After an invasion by U.S. forces, the 84-day-long battle lasted from April 1 to June 23. Okinawans call it ''The War'' and the ''Typhoon of Steel.'' Twelve thousand Americans were killed, 35,000 were wounded, and 90,000 Japanese soldiers died. Caught in the crossfire, 150,000 Okinawan civilians (one-third of the population) died from wounds, exposure, starvation, and disease. Every family was affected. The southern third of the island and smaller offshore islands such as Iejima were completely devastated, along with cultural treasures. As a prefecture of Japan, Okinawa was made an ''island of sacrifice'' by the Japanese government so as to prevent or delay the expected invasion of Japan's main islands.

Before its forcible annexation by Japan in 1879, Okinawa had a 450-year history as an independent kingdom and a 300-year peace heritage. As a prefecture of Japan for sixty-six years (in effect, military occupation), Okinawans were treated as second-class citizens. The governor came from the main islands. Teaching of Okinawan history and language were prohibited.

Japan's surrender on August 15, 1945, marked the beginning of what has become fifty-years of U.S. occupation, administration, and military control. The post-World War II occupation and military presence in Okinawa and the other islands may be divided into three periods. The vast majority of Okinawans, however, regard this as fifty years of foreign occupation.

The Nimitz Proclamation in 1945 initiated U.S. military rule, with first a naval then an Army government. Initially, Okinawans' impression of individual American soldiers was on the whole favorable, but the situation deteriorated due to official U.S. policy or lack of policy. Many Okinawan civilians were gathered into refugee camps. Food, shelter, and medical care were provided. Okinawans said, however, that while they were helpless in detention camps and other temporary shelters, much or all of their farm land and other property was confiscated by the U.S. military. This was done under the "Rules of Land Warfare." Eighty to 90 percent of some towns was taken—usually the best agricultural land. What could not be seized in that way was taken under the U.S. Law of Eminent Domain, with no appeal possible. A "red line" was arbitrarily drawn on military maps, designating areas to be taken in the future as needed for U.S. military purposes. Land was commandeered for air bases, artillery and missile practice ranges, equipment storage, military headquarters, dependent housing, golf courses, and rest centers. Toward the end of this period, construction of permanent military structures and facilities was begun, sometimes expanding Japanese installations but often building in entirely new areas on the small island.

Permanent reconstruction of Okinawa's public buildings, as with all reconstruction on Okinawa, lagged behind that of mainland Japan by several years. While Okinawan civilians continued to exist in poverty or substandard conditions, military families enjoyed comparatively spacious houses surrounded by broad lawns, occupying the space of five or six Okinawan homes. During those years, with notable exceptions, Okinawa was regarded as a place of exile for less competent military personnel, served as a military dump, and was called by those assigned there "The Rock." However, those persons who continued to suffer most were displaced Okinawan people.

The basic decision to conquer and keep Okinawa was made by the United States during World War II in 1942, even while repeatedly stating that the war was not being fought for territorial aggrandizement. An immediate factor in the final decision to retain Okinawa and the other islands was the outbreak of the Korean War*.

Positive aspects of U.S. policy during the period included some reconstruction of highways, bridges, and public buildings; some rebuilding of schools, hospitals, and welfare facilities; training of nurses; founding of the University of the Ryukyus; scholarships for Okinawan youth to American universities; and voluntary gifts by members of U.S. military chapels to rebuild churches destroyed or damaged by war. Negative aspects, as viewed by Okinawans, included loss of their land; exclusion of Okinawan landowners from U.S. bases even for cultivating their fields and visiting their ancestral family tombs (related to Okinawan religion); trials in U.S. military courts for crimes committed by U.S. soldiers against Okinawans; crimes by U.S. personnel often not admitted by the U.S. occupation forces; and inadequate or no compensation for personal injuries, deaths, and property damage.

The commander of the U.S. Ryukyu Forces (later to be appointed by U.S. Presidential Order) was an Army general with supreme local authority; his power extended even to cancelling decisions made by Okinawan officials and later by popular elections. Next in command was a second Army general appointed as civil administrator of the Ryukyu Islands (USCAR). Before the first period of seven years ended, the attitude of Okinawans toward the United States was rapidly changing for the worse.

Whereas the San Francisco Peace Treaty of 1951 (ratified in 1952) officially ended the U.S. occupation of mainland Japan, Okinawa and all the Ryukyu Islands were politically severed from Japan and placed under U.S. administration. Okinawans, however, viewed this as continued occupation. Furthermore, U.S. bases were used as a forward staging area for the conduct of the Korean War, creating hostile feelings toward Okinawa in the minds of Asian neighbors.

In 1952, the Gunto governments of each major island group (*gunto*) were replaced by a tripartite central government of the Ryukyu Islands (GRI), with its chief executive an Okinawan appointed by the U.S. High Commissioner, the Ryukyu legislature with members elected by popular vote, and a judiciary composed of higher, district, and summary courts. Laws gave first place to U.S. presidential orders, then to proclamations and orders promulgated by the high commissioner within the limits of the presidential order, and last to laws enacted by the Ryukyu legislature that did not conflict with American laws. The high commissioner continued to rule Okinawa with absolute authority. The first U.S. civilian was appointed as civil administrator in the late 1950s; but the high commissioner retained final authority. Popular election of the Okinawan chief executive was not permitted until 1968, only four years before reversion to Japan. In 1960, the U.S.-Japan Security Treaty became effective, by which the two governments promised mutual military assistance, but reinforced feelings of Okinawans of being left as political orphans, with their island even more subject to use by the occupying power. In 1955, a U.S. congressional committee visited Okinawa, held hearings, and made recommendations, most of which ignored the basic requests of Okinawans.

Poison gas and nuclear weapons* were introduced and stored on Okinawa. During 1954 and 1955, three forcible seizures of land at gunpoint occurred in Oroku village, Iejima, and Isahama village, accompanied by the wounding and mistreatment of Okinawans, the bulldozing and burning of homes and barns, and the random shooting of livestock. During the Vietnam War*, Okinawa was again used by the United States as a major staging and supply area, despite Okinawan protests. This U.S. policy, combined with inadequate compensation, repeated cases of deaths, injuries, and property damage, gave impetus to a growing sentiment favoring reversion to Japan and removal of U.S. bases. The often-reiterated U.S. policy, however, was that although Japan had "residual sovereignty" over the Ryukyu Islands, the United States would retain control "for the foreseeable future." Thus, Okinawa became the only U.S. colony in the world created by World War II. Many consider this to be an outgrowth of racist attitudes of certain American leaders and citizens.

On May 15, 1972, reversion to Japan became effective. Okinawa again became a prefecture of Japan, with elected representatives in the Japanese Diet. Although Okinawans had asked to be placed on the same level as other prefectures, the United States and Japan agreed secretly to the retention by the United States of all its military bases. In addition, Japan Self Defense Forces (JSDF) were brought in over Okinawan objections. Before reversion, entire U.S. Marine bases in mainland Japan had been moved to Okinawa. The U.S. military command of Okinawa was later transferred from the Army to the Marines.

As of 1994, there are on Okinawa: 45 U.S. bases of all four branches of military service, 32,000 military personnel, and 20,000 dependents and civilian employees; this comprises 75 percent of all U.S. bases and 61 percent of all U.S. military personnel on Japanese soil. Okinawa has only 0.6 percent of all Japan's land area. Okinawans consider land as life, not as a commodity to be bought and sold. Nevertheless, they are excluded from their ancestral lands and prevented from using it for agriculture and industry. Contrary to Japan's post–World War II "Peace Constitution" and three nonnuclear principles, it is an open secret that U.S. nuclear weapons are stored on Okinawa, and port calls are made by U.S. nuclear submarines. U.S. bases include one of the largest bomber bases in East Asia, jet fighter and other air bases, several Marine bases, artillery and missile practice ranges, jungle and urban guerrilla* warfare training areas, communications facilities, golf courses, and beaches. This U.S. military presence has continued to result in numerous deaths, injuries, and property damage, as well as in murders, rapes, destruction of the environment*, and severe noise pollution. There is continuing exploitation of women for prostitution and gross violation of their human rights. In spite of Okinawan objections, U.S. personnel participate regularly in joint military maneuvers named "Operation Team Spirit" (OTS) and "Peace Keeping Operation" (PKO). With the closing of U.S. bases in the Philippines, there has been a net increase in the number of U.S. military personnel on Okinawa, despite repeated official requests by the governor of Okinawa that bases be reduced or eliminated. Military bases hinder Okinawan community and economic development.

The American response to Okinawan criticism has been to claim: (1) the United States has the right to keep and use Okinawa due to military victory in 1945; (2) the United States is protecting Okinawans and "defending the Free World"; (3) Okinawans should be grateful for what the United States has done for them economically and socially, and for their defense. Less openly stated is the U.S. and Japanese position that Okinawa and other southern islands are necessary for defending the 1,000 miles of sea lanes to the Middle East that supply oil to both nations. Okinawa was a main staging area during the Gulf War and for the U.S. military support of South Korea against North Korea.

Okinawan newspaper polls taken between 1982 and 1994 indicated that 80–90 percent of Okinawans oppose the presence of U.S. military bases. Most maintain that, in addition to other adverse effects, the U.S. military presence on their island invites attack and total destruction by present and future enemies of the United States. Rather than be known as the military "Keystone of the Pacific," they wish their island to be the "Bridge of Peace."

The Annex to the Hague Convention* No. IV (1907) states: "The foregoing prohibition (regarding confiscation of private property) extends not only to outright taking in violation of the law of war but also to any acts which, through the use of threats, intimidation, or pressure by actual exploitation of the power of the occupant, permanently or temporarily deprive the owner of the use of his property without his consent or without authority under international law." U.S. Ambassador to Japan Edwin O. Reischauer stated that there was no moral justification for Okinawans to be assigned "indefinitely to the status of colonial people." After fifty years of U.S. occupation and military presence, we are presented with an anomaly of history and political ethics. The peaceable people of Okinawa prefecture in Japan, who opposed Japan's wars of conquest most strongly and suffered most from the effects of World War II, are those who still are forced to bear the greatest suffering and the violation of their basic human rights.

See ENVIRONMENTAL ISSUES, POLLUTION, AND THE MILITARY; HAWAII, MILITARY LAND USE IN; MILITARY USES OF THE OCEAN; WARNING ZONES.

BIBLIOGRAPHY

Feifer, George, *Tennozan* (New York: Ticknor & Fields, 1992).

Keys to Okinawan Culture (Okinawa Prefectural Government, Naha, Okinawa, 1992), 11–28.

Okinawa Voice (Ginowan, Okinawa: Okinawa Christian Heiwa Center, December–April 1994).

Ota, Masahide, ed., *A Comprehensive Study of U.S. Military Government on Okinawa, An Interim Report* (Ginowan, Okinawa: University of the Ryukyus, 1987).

Price, Melvin, "Report of a Special Sub-Committee of the Armed Services Committee, House of Representatives," No. 86 (Washington, D.C.: U.S. Government Printing Office, 1956).

Reischauer, Edwin O., *The United States and Japan* (Cambridge, Mass.: Harvard University Press, 1961).

U.S. Military Bases on Okinawa: A Message from the Land of Courtesy (Ginowan, Okinawa: Military Base Affairs Office, Okinawa Prefectural Government, 1994).

C. Harold Rickard

OXFORD MANUAL. The document was issued by the Institute of International Law, a nongovernmental body established in 1873 and composed of legal scholars from a number of nations. The inspiration for the institute came from the work of Francis Lieber* and the organizational efforts of the Belgian publicist, Rolin-Jaequemyns. Its aim was to promote the development of international law by assisting in its codification. The manual adopted at Oxford, England, September 9, 1880, was drafted by Gustave Moynier, and unanimously adopted by the institute. The aim was to provide the world with a manual for nations in their relations with each other during war, with the hope that sovereigns would "make these laws known among all people."

The document contained eighty-six articles. Under "General Principles," the manual stated the requirements for a legitimate army to include wearing a distinctive uniform, having a responsible chief, and the open carrying of arms. Article 4 recognized that belligerents do not have "unlimited liberty as to the means of injuring the enemy." Article 8 listed as forbidden: the use of poison, keeping assassins*, feigning surrender, attacking under the presumption of being a noncombatant force, and improper use of military insignia. Article 9 forbade methods calculated to cause superfluous suffering, notably projectiles weighing less than 400 grams that were charged with explosives or incendiary* substances, killing enemy who have surrendered or are *hors de combat,* and waging a war of no quarter*. Articles 10–18 provided for the care of the sick or wounded. Articles 21–22 identified who were entitled to prisoner of war* status. Articles 32–34 forbade pillage* and attacks on undefended places. Articles 35–40 provided for the protection of medical personnel and hospitals. Articles 61–78 named provisions for prisoners of war. Article 84 affirmed that "offenders against the laws of war are liable to the punishments specified in penal law." Although article 85 stated that "reprisals* are formally prohibited in case the injury complained of has been repaired," Article 86 affirmed that in "grave cases" where reprisals seem necessary, "their nature and scope shall never exceed the measure" of the initial offense.

See GENERAL ORDERS 100; GENEVA CONVENTIONS, 1864, 1868; HAGUE, THE, CONGRESSES; *LAW OF LAND WARFARE;* LAWS OF WAR; *RULES OF LAND WARFARE;* ST. PETERSBURG DECLARATION.

BIBLIOGRAPHY

Institute of International Law, *The Laws of War on Land* (Oxford: Institute of International Law, September 9, 1880).

P

PACIFISM. Moral opposition to war and other forms of violence. The concept embraces a wide range of positions from an absolute prohibition of all use of force against persons to a selective and pragmatic rejection of particular forms of force under varying circumstances. Pacifists differ on their moral grounds for rejecting war and other forms of violence and on the grounds for their commitments to varieties of nonviolence.

Etymologically, the term *pacifism* comes from the Latin *pax,* or *pacis,* "peace," originally "compact," plus *facere,* "to make." Literally, pacifism means "peacemaking." Often pacifism is incorrectly identified as *passivism,* which derives from the Latin *passivus,* "suffering," and means being inert or inactive, or suffering acceptance. Pacifists may be passivists but often are activists, choosing nonviolent means to resolve conflict and to work toward personal and social goals.

Pacifism consists of two parts: opposition to war and violence, and commitment to cooperative social and national conduct based on agreement. Beyond the mere absence of war, peace is a condition of group order arising from within by cooperation among participants, rather than order imposed from outside the group by domination from others. The antiviolence and especially the antiwar aspect of pacifism is much more frequently reflected in philosophic literature than the positive peace aspect.

Absolute pacifism, the purest, most extreme form of pacifism, is the position that it is wrong always, everywhere, for everyone to use force against living things. This view has few if any adherents, although it has aspirants. Since the extreme use of violence between persons is war, much of the pacifist literature discusses pacifism as it relates to war.

Moral opposition to war is discussed across the history of Western philosophy. While early considerations of the morality of war can be found in ancient Greek texts (e.g., in Plato's *Republic*), pacifism as the moral opposition to war, as distinct from the moral opposition to particular wars, seems to emerge in Western culture among 1st-century Christians. While Imperial Rome was virtually always at war, the most devoted followers of early Christianity* carried pacifism to the extreme of nonresistance to evil despite their own persecution by Romans. Controversy over Christianity and pacifism persist to this day. Jesus himself is quoted both for and against pacifist views. Whatever his convictions on the subject, the idea of the moral superiority of peace and cooperative order over war and forced order emerged among Jesus's followers.

With Constantine's declaration of tolerance to Christianity (in 313) and his own conversion to Christianity, the church moved away from pacifist values. After the union of empire and church, soldiers could be Christians and vice-versa. In the early 5th century, Augustine* combined the classical code of war with Christian doctrine to develop a just war* position. Jesus's expression, "resist not evil," was taken to apply not to actions, but attitudes. If one could avoid hate, then killing and love were compatible because salvation, not the life of the body, was central. Injury and death could even benefit a sinner if justice were vindicated and peace restored. War could be just if massacre*, looting, and atrocities could be avoided.

Pacifism was largely dormant from the time of Constantine until 16th-century reforming sects such as the Mennonites and Anabaptists. More philosophical treatments come from Erasmus, also in the 16th century, and Kant* in the late 18th. Adin Ballou articulated pragmatic pacifism in the mid-19th century and William James explored pacifist philosophy in the early 20th.

The volume of pacifist literature has grown exponentially this century, in part on the heels of the work of notable pacifists such as Leo Tolstoy, Jane Addams*, Albert Schweitzer, Mohandas Gandhi*, Dorothy Day*, and Martin Luther King, Jr.* Their actions as well as their thoughts have inspired serious philosophical consideration of alternatives to war and violence. Other reasons for the rapid increase in theoretical considerations of pacifism include the massive scale on which war has been undertaken throughout the 20th century and the technological refinements of the means of war together with the proliferation of weapons that have made large-scale killing possible for most nations.

Arguments for pacifism tend to focus on the evils of war, including human suffering—especially that of innocents*—and on the moral degradation of participants as well as the uncontrollability of warfare. There is no one pacifist position. A spectrum of pacifist positions can be understood as varying degrees of moral opposition to war and moral commitment to cooperative social order.

Less extreme than the absolutist pacifism discussed above, collectivist pacifism is a position that opposes war yet allows some force, perhaps even lethal force, under restricted circumstances. There is no contradiction in maintaining a moral opposition to war while at the same time claiming the right to defend oneself by force against an unprovoked attacker. One's position on small-scale, interpersonal violence need not follow directly from one's moral objections to war. Collectivist pacifism helps clarify why large, messy wars are easier for pacifists to condemn (and harder for just warists to defend) than small, neat ones. Meanwhile, just warists often select scale-reducing analogies (military "policing" actions, "surgical" bombing, and so on) to ease their burden of justification.

A fallibility pacifist—sometimes called an epistemological pacifist—concedes the moral justifiability of war in principle yet denies it in fact. The reasoning is that even if war were justifi*able,* in order for it to be justifi*ed* a great deal that must be known in fact is not known. The fallibility pacifist takes war as it occurs to be too subtle and complex to feel confident in the knowledge of relevant factors required to warrant injury and death on a mass scale.

Technological pacifists also may grant the justifiability of war in principle yet deny it in fact. But for such thinkers the problem is not so much the lack of knowledge as the uncontrollability of the "spillage" of war. Modern war has gotten to the point (this point may vary for different technological pacifists) that the moral rules guiding restraint in war of the just war tradition cannot be met due to the nature of the means of war. Perhaps when volunteers met in remote battlefields with spears, war was justifiable; but modern war alters war to a point where the "front" cannot be identified. Weapons can reach behind allied and enemy lines to strike deep into civilian centers without discrimination or precise control over effects.

Nuclear pacifism is a contemporary variety of technological pacifism. According to the nuclear pacifist, nuclear weapons* have made war unlike anything in its history. The weapons are of such magnitude of destructive power with such uncontrollable effects that the nuclear pacifist finds their use unthinkable.

Ecological pacifism focuses on the impact of war, but rather than restricting concern to nuclear weapons, the impact of the full arsenal of conventional as well as nuclear weapons is considered, especially as it affects ecosystems. Ecological pacifists object not only to the fighting of wars but to the research, development, testing, and deployment of weapons, since all aspects of contemporary war capability risk disastrous consequences for sustainable ecosystems.

Perhaps the weakest form of pacifism is pragmatic pacifism, where the moral opposition to war is selective rather than categorical. Some pragmatic pacifists will reject virtually all wars on moral grounds based on the historical record of war not accomplishing what it had been expected to accomplish. Despite the promises of justifications of war, wars have rarely made things better. They have contributed mightily to death, dislocation, suffering, and destruction. Based on empirical consideration, war seems a bad risk.

Other pragmatic pacifists will oppose a given war on moral grounds only because it seems unlikely to yield the desired objectives. Some in Martin Luther King, Jr.'s civil rights action in Birmingham in 1963 thought violence perfectly justifiable but unlikely to succeed at delivering the objectives, so they supported King. The same could be said for many of Nelson Mandela's supporters during the struggle for racial equality in South Africa. A sort of pacifism is followed, but it is of a selective and pragmatic sort.

Peace is not just the absence of war—negative peace—but the presence of cooperative order—positive peace. So beyond moral opposition to war, pacifism involves commitments to cooperative social order that arise from within societies by agreement rather than order imposed on societies by domination from the outside. Again, pacifists take a variety of positions.

Perhaps the first choice of a means to peace is discussion leading to consensus. Where consensus cannot be achieved, those committed to peaceful resolution of conflict may need to go beyond discussion to negotiation and even arbitration. The next level of nonviolent* action includes political protest, demonstration, letter-writing campaigns, petitioning, lobbying, picketing, wearing symbols, marches, teach-ins, and so on. All are directed to persuasion of authorities.

Further approaching physical confrontation are methods of noncooperation. Social and economic boycotts, strikes, slow-downs, tax protests, walk-outs, reporting "sick," economic embargoes, and the like are included. Beyond such noncooperation is nonviolent intervention. Fasting, development of underground newspapers and electronic media, forming shadow governments, as well as various acts of civil disobedience* are all short of the step to violent intervention, the step pacifists refuse to take. Pacifists may fall anywhere along the range of commitments to cooperative and internal order making.

Pacifism is a varied set of positions opposing war and other forms of violence and embracing a positive notion of peace as cooperative internal order. Its history is long, its heroes are many, and its variety is far from the popular stereotype of the unrealistic and naive extremist. The body of pacifist literature is rich and engaging beyond the sketch provided here.

See BRITTAIN, VERA; CONSCIENTIOUS OBJECTION; DAY, DOROTHY; DODGE, DAVID LOW; GANDHI, MOHANDAS; HENNACY, AMMON; KING, MARTIN LUTHER, JR.; MUSTE, ABRAHAM JOHANNES; QUAKERS; ROYDEN, MAUDE.

BIBLIOGRAPHY
Brock, Peter, *Pacifism in Europe to 1914* (Princeton, N.J.: Princeton University Press, 1972).
———, *Twentieth Century Pacifism* (New York: Van Nostrand Reinhold, 1970).
Cady, Duane L., *From Warism to Pacifism: A Moral Continuum* (Philadelphia: Temple University Press, 1989).
Gandhi, Mohandas K., *Nonviolent Resistance,* Bharatan Kumarappa, ed. (New York: Schocken Books, 1951).
Holmes, Robert L., *On War and Morality* (Princeton, N.J.: Princeton University Press, 1989).
King, Martin Luther, Jr., *A Testament of Hope: The Essential Writings of Martin Luther King, Jr.,* James M. Washington, ed. (New York: Harper & Row, 1986).
Ruddick, Sara, *Maternal Thinking: Toward A Feminist Peace Politics* (Boston: Beacon, 1989).
Sharp, Gene, *Power and Struggle,* Part 1 of *The Power of Nonviolent Action* (Boston: Porter Sargent, 1973).
Wells, Donald A., *The War Myth* (Indianapolis: Bobbs-Merrill, 1967).

Duane L. Cady

PANAMA, U.S. INVASION OF (OPERATION JUST CAUSE). On December 20, 1989, President George Bush sent 12,500 U.S. troops to augment the 12,000 already in Panama. The justifications for the incursion varied and included: to restore democracy in the area, to protect U.S. interests in the Panama Canal, to remove from power General Manuel Noriega who had become a recalcitrant opponent of U.S. interests, to protect American citizens in the area, and to stop the drug trade. Noriega had been an employee of the Central Intelligence Agency (CIA) under Director George Bush, during which time he had been of assistance in the U.S. war in El Salvador by helping the CIA set up a second Contra army in Costa Rica and allowing the Contras to train in Panama. Noriega had also cooperated with the U.S. Drug Enforcement Administration (DEA) in their efforts to stop the cocaine traffic through Panama. At the same time Noriega was profiting tidily from the drug trade. On occasions when his drug connection was raised by Congress, CIA Director William Casey intervened to remind the protesters of Noriega's help in fighting the Contras and the matter would be dropped.

Whatever the motives prompting the Bush administration action, the U.S. invasion was criticized by several sources. The UN Security Council voted a majority condemnation of the invasion, but the United States used its veto to defeat the judgment. The UN General Assembly "strongly deplored" the intervention and demanded the immediate removal of American forces by a Resolution which passed 75–20 (with an immense number of abstentions) on the grounds that the action was a violation of the UN Charter which guaranteed national sovereignty from armed invasion. The Organization of American States (OAS) called the American action a "violation of the rights of the Panamanian people to self-determination without outside interference." In addition, the Bush administration had sent $10 million to aid the election of Guillermo Endara, Noriega's opposition, a clear violation of both U.S. and OAS election policy which forbade foreign contributions in domestic elections. The United States had put economic pressure on Panama by withholding funds, freezing assets in U.S. banks, and an economic embargo. Such actions were in violation of the OAS Charter, which ruled that such economic pressures were acts of war.

Just war theory* had insisted that if a war was not justified in the first place, it made no sense to argue that the war had been waged justly. No serious effort was made by the Bush administration to defend the war based on *jus in bello* or *jus ad bellum* arguments. However, the matters of proportionality* and protection of civilians should have been raised. The U.S. forces included highly armed helicopters, tanks, and even the Stealth bomber, and entailed the bombing of civilian centers. Aerial warfare is notoriously indiscriminate and when coupled with concentration on civilian centers like El Chorillo, it was inevitable that collateral civilian damage would be excessive. No adequate estimates exist of the casualties or the extent of collateral damage*, although in monetary terms the Panamanian loss was estimated at $1 billion. The U.S. military estimated

Panamanian casualties at 314 soldiers and 202 civilians; the Noriega government estimated 8,000 Panamanian casualties; a Red Cross official estimated 2,000; the Panamanian Catholic Church estimated 655 deaths; former U.S. Attorney General, Ramsey Clark, estimated 3,000–4,000; America's Watch estimated the ratio of civilian to military deaths as six civilians for every soldier and joined with Physicians for Human Rights in accepting the estimate of 300 Panamanian deaths and at least 3,000 wounded. In hearings before the House of Representatives attempting to discover the extent of casualties, the official U.S. diffidence was illustrated by the comment of Brigadier General James R. Harding, "there is no historic precedent for U.S. military forces having to account for non-U.S. casualties inflicted during armed combat." Such a position violates the oldest Geneva conventions which have considered it obligatory for the contestants to account for both their own and their opponents' casualties. Indeed, if a war is unjust in the first place, one death would be too many. U.S. forces buried Panamanians in mass graves, some even on U.S. military bases, hence inaccessible to UN, Red Cross, or Human Rights Watch scrutiny. The resulting devastation by bombing and burning of civilian homes left thousands homeless, a condition not corrected as late as 1995, six years after the event.

   See AGGRESSION, ATTEMPTS TO DEFINE; CHILDREN AND WAR; CHILDREN'S RIGHTS IN WAR; COUNTERFORCE VERSUS COUNTER-VALUE; DECLARATION OF WAR; DEMOCRACY AND THE MILITARY; FIRST STRIKE/SECOND STRIKE; FORBIDDEN STRATEGIES; FORBIDDEN WEAPONS; GENEVA CONVENTION, 1949; GRENADA, U.S. INVASION OF; GUATEMALA, U.S. INVASION OF; INNOCENTS; INTELLIGENCE AGENCIES, U.S.; LAWS OF WAR; PROPAGANDA; RUSES OF WAR; SIEGE WARFARE; TOTAL WAR.

BIBLIOGRAPHY
The Laws of War and the Conduct of the Panama Invasion (New York: Americas Watch, May 1990).
Post-Invasion Panama: Status of Democracy and the Civilian Casualties Controversy, Hearings before the Subcommittee on Western Hemisphere Affairs of the Committee on Foreign Affairs, H.R., 102nd Cong., 1st sess., July 17 and 30, 1991 (Washington, D.C.: U.S. Government Printing Office, 1991).
Quigley, Jon, *The Ruses for War* (New York: Prometheus Books, 1992).
U.S. Military Intervention in Panama, Bulletin No. 169 (Geneva: International Committee of the Red Cross, 1990).

PARACHUTES, PERSONS DESCENDING BY. Paragraph 30 of *The Law of Land Warfare** (1956) states that "the law of war does not prohibit firing upon paratroops or other persons who are or appear to be bound upon hostile missions while such persons are descending by parachute. Persons other than those mentioned in the preceding sentence who are descending by parachute from disabled aircraft may not be fired upon." In modern aerial warfare*, where the sky may be filled with descending parachutists, some from disabled planes and others not, it is unlikely that troops on the ground would be in a position to make this distinction. The aim of the rule is to provide for aerial warfare a distinction similar to that for sailors in the sea from sinking ships. However, parachutists who land on the ground are ready and able for battle, unlike sailors from sinking ships, and are equally dangerous no matter the condition of the plane from which they descend. Efforts to protect military personnel who were *hors de combat* grew out of medieval notions of chivalry as well as the hope that one's own soldiers would receive like treatment. Modern weapons and strategies, however, are so indiscriminate that it is impossible to single out for protection soldiers who are *hors de combat.*

See PRISONERS OF WAR; SHIPWRECKED SAILORS.

PARIS PEACE PACT (KELLOGG-BRIAND PEACE PACT) (1928). The representatives of fifteen participating nations issued this treaty in Paris, the implications of which have been a subject of international dispute. The text of this brief pact is as follows:

Persuaded that the time has come when a frank renunciation of war as an instrument of national policy should be made to the end that the peaceful and friendly relations now existing between their peoples may be perpetuated; convinced that all changes in their relations with one another should be sought only by pacific means and be the result of a peaceful and orderly process, and that any signatory Power which shall hereafter seek to promote its national interests by resort to war should be denied the benefits furnished by this Treaty; hopeful that, encouraged by their example, all the other nations of the world will join in this humane endeavor and by adhering to the present Treaty as soon as it comes into force bring their peoples within the scope of its beneficent provisions, thus uniting the civilized nations of the world in a common renunciation of war as an instrument of their national policy.

The distinguished international jurist, Lewis Oppenheim, considered that the pact constituted an official renunciation of war as a national policy, even if it did not outlaw war as a means of national defense. Oppenheim observed a contradiction in the notion that war had been outlawed and the continued belief that proper laws of war* existed. The judges at the Nuremberg trials* appealed to this pact as evidence that going to war constituted a crime against the peace*, and that the pact was binding on the sixty-three nations that had signed it. The French, however, held a widely expressed reservation that if any country violated this pledge, then all countries were automatically released from their pledge, and that the pact was only a renunciation of starting war, while still permitting war in defense.

Although the Paris pact did not distinguish between aggressive* or defensive wars, the Nuremberg tribunal referred to the pact as having outlawed aggressive war. The ambiguity seemed important enough that some jurists, including Franz B. Schick, concluded that if crimes against the peace were basic to the legitimacy of the trials, and if the Paris pact did not provide a basis for such crimes, then all the subsequent charges against the Axis participants would collapse. Conventional customs of war would have protected the Germans from most of the remaining charges. Disagreement as to the implications of the pact existed among the counsels of the Military Tribunal of the Far East, and even the president of that tribunal expressed doubt whether there was any precedent for the claim that aggressive war was a crime and whether the Paris pact was ever intended to establish it. The current U.S. Army Pamphlet 27-1, *Treaties Governing Land Warfare,* makes no mention of the pact in its list of treaties to which the United States is bound.

See AGGRESSION, ATTEMPTS TO DEFINE; FIRST STRIKE/SECOND STRIKE; JUST WAR; LAWS OF WAR; MUTUAL ASSURED DESTRUCTION (MAD).

BIBLIOGRAPHY

Renunciation of War Treaty, Paris, August 27, 1928 (Washington, D.C.: U.S. Government Printing Office, 1928).

Schick, Franz B., "Crimes Against the Peace," *Journal of Criminal Law and Criminology* 38, no. 5 (January–February 1948).

Wright, Quincy, *The Role of International Law in the Elimination of War* (Manchester: Manchester University Press, 1961).

PATRIOTISM. The basic meaning is love of one's own country. Not surprisingly, patriotic attitudes are encouraged in all countries, since the sentiment of attachment helps motivate people to perform their civic duties.

Though somewhat neglected by philosophers, patriotism is a contentious ideal. Strong advocates of patriotism have invoked the slogan "My country, right or wrong" to promote the idea that patriotism requires unquestioning support of one's country, especially in wartime. Antiwar thinkers often denounce patriotism as an immoral attitude that artificially divides human beings and promotes hostility, war, and militarism*. Both sides frequently share the assumption that patriotism requires exclusive, unconstrained, and unquestioning loyalty.

According to this conception, patriotism combines:

• belief in the superiority of one's country

• exclusive concern for one's country

• automatic support of one's country's military policies

While these attitudes are common during wartime, there seems to be a widespread recognition that they are undesirable. The ordinary terms for these attitudes all have negative connotations. "Chauvinism" is an unjustified feeling of national superiority, while "xenophobia" is unwarranted fear toward people of other countries. "Jingoism" is excessive enthusiasm for war.

A crucial question is whether patriotism is necessarily chauvinistic, xenophobic, and jingoistic. If it is, there would seem to be an inherent conflict between patriotism and morality.

While patriotism often takes this extreme form, a more moderate form does seem possible. It includes:

• special affection for one's country—but without belief in its superiority

• special concern for one's country—but of a sort that is not exclusive and so permits a concern for people of other countries

• conditional support of one's country's policies—an attitude that permits evaluation and criticism of national policies, including decisions involving war

This moderate form of patriotism appears to escape the criticisms often made of extreme patriotism.

Any form of patriotism must also include a willingness to act for one's country, even if this involves personal sacrifice. Perhaps for this reason, military service is often seen as the paradigm of patriotic action.

There are two problems with identifying patriotism and military service. First, fighting in war, like any action, can arise from many different motives. People may fight for money, for adventure, because they have been conscripted, or because they fear the punishment or scorn that refusal to fight might bring. Fighting for these reasons is not a patriotic act because it is not motivated by concern for one's country.

The second problem with the military service paradigm of patriotism is that it defines patriotic action too narrowly and thus excludes the possibility of a pacifist* being a patriot. While the focus on fighting for one's country correctly brings out the idea that genuine patriots must be willing to act on their country's behalf, it mistakenly suggests that military service is the only type of patriotic action. Yet, pacifists and others can have special affection and concern for their country and can show their concern for it through different forms of public service.

Where willingness to act and sacrifice are lacking, then one has a false form of patriotism. Hypocritical patriots express patriotism for personal ends. Superficial patriots are infatuated with their country—after perhaps a military victory—but their affection does not commit them to action. Ritual patriots may love the trappings of patriotism—parades, holidays, and flags—but lack genuine commitment to the country's well-being.

All genuine patriots possess four features:

1. special affection for their country

2. a sense of personal identification with their country

3. special concern for their country's well-being

4. willingness to sacrifice to promote their country's good

This definition is both neutral and comprehensive. It is broad enough to include both extreme and moderate forms of patriotism and does not prejudge whether patriotism is morally good or bad.

The definition excludes false patriotism, as well as extreme universalist or globalist perspectives. Globalists often reject patriotism because they believe we have equally strong moral duties toward all people. Patriots, even those who respect the rights of people outside their own country, see themselves as having special duties toward their own country that they do not have toward others. While moderate forms of patriotism incorporate aspects of universalism, they retain the element of particular loyalty that extreme universalists reject.

See CAUSES OF WAR; DEMOCRACY AND THE MILITARY; MILITA-RISM; MILITARY EDUCATION; NATIONALISM; PROPAGANDA.

BIBLIOGRAPHY

Dietz, Mary, "Patriotism," in *Political Innovation and Conceptual Change,* T. Ball et al., eds. (Cambridge: Cambridge University Press, 1989).

Gomberg, Paul, "Patriotism Is Like Racism," *Ethics* 101 (1990).

MacIntyre, Alasdair, "Is Patriotism a Virtue?" *The Lindley Lecture* (Lawrence: University of Kansas Press, 1984).

Nathanson, Stephen, *Patriotism, Morality, and Peace* (Lanham, Md.: Rowman & Littlefield, 1993).

Oldenquist, Andrew, "Loyalties," *Journal of Philosophy* 79 (1982).

Tolstoy, Leo, "Patriotism," and "Patriotism, or Peace?" in *Tolstoy's Writings on Civil Disobedience and Non-Violence* (New York: New American Library, 1968).

                                                                                        Stephen Nathanson

PEACE, CRIMES AGAINST. The Nuremberg* tribunal named the Paris Peace pact* of 1928 as the basis for its charge that waging aggressive war or waging it as an "instrument of international policy" constituted a crime. Twelve of the twenty-four tried at Nuremberg were found guilty of crimes against the peace, while all twenty-five of those tried at Tokyo were found so guilty. Serious legal reservations were expressed as to whether the Paris pact provided a sufficient foundation for such a charge. The distinguished British jurist, Lewis Oppenheim, observed that if the pact had outlawed war, then there would be no reason to have laws of war at all. The French held a widely expressed reservation that if any country violated the pledge, then all countries were automatically released from their pledge. This made the pact, at most, a renunciation of "first strike*," while reserving the "second strike" option. No nation imagined that the pact denied the national right of self-defense. Telford Taylor once noted that rules of war that "interfered significantly with military success" were unenforceable. The interpretation that the pact outlawed war surely "interfered significantly." Indeed, the U.S. Army Pamphlet 27-1, *Treaties Governing Land Warfare,* made no mention of the pact in its list of treaties to which the United States felt bound; nor was aggressive war a topic of concern.

Since charging a nation with a crime presumed that aggressive war could be distinguished from defensive war, the general failure to establish such a distinction seriously undermined the initial charge. It proved difficult to determine whether any of the accused knew that his country was planning a war of aggression*, and, even if he did, that he was in a position to alter national policy. The tribunal ruled that both knowledge and power to change policy were required before guilt could be established. Traditionally, such a crime presupposed that whoever fired the first shot or whoever invaded the land of another was the guilty party. The wide acceptance, however, of the right of preemptive war*, and the legitimacy of first-strike undermined any traditional argument as to who was the aggressor. Even those who defended nuclear deterrence* were open to the charge that such a policy was tantamount to planning the commission of a crime against the peace.

See AGGRESSION, ATTEMPTS TO DEFINE; NUREMBERG TRIALS; PARIS PEACE PACT; TOKYO TRIALS; VIETNAM WAR.

BIBLIOGRAPHY
Department of the Army Pamphlet, 27-161-2, *International Law,* Vol. 2 (Washington, D.C.: U.S. Government Printing Office, 1962).
Department of the Army Pamphlet, 27-1, *Treaties Governing Land Warfare* (Washington, D.C.: U.S. Government Printing Office, 1956).
Schick, Franz B., "Crimes Against the Peace," *Journal of Criminal Law and Criminology* 38, no. 5 (January–February 1948).

PEACE OF GOD. A document by this name was issued in 989 following a council in Charroux, France. The point of this document was to govern the conduct of warfare by banning violence against certain groups of people including the clergy, women, and pilgrims. The primary focus was on the safety of unarmed people. This document also forbade assaults on certain nonhuman entities including churches, cemeteries, and fruit trees. The Peace of God was followed in 1027 by the Truce of God, which outlawed all violent conflict at certain significant times of the church year, rather than designating protected groups of people. The concepts promulgated in the Peace of God found their way into later attempts to codify the rules of warfare, most notably those of Grotius*.

See CHARROUX, SYNOD OF; CHRISTIANITY AND WAR; COMBAT-ANT-NONCOMBATANT DISTINCTION; FORBIDDEN STRATEGIES; GROTIUS, HUGO; HOLY WARS; INNOCENTS; JUST WAR; LAWS OF WAR; MASSACRES; TERRORISM; TOTAL WAR.

BIBLIOGRAPHY
Christopher, Paul, *The Ethics of War and Peace* (Englewood Cliffs, N.J.: Prentice-Hall, 1994).
Head, Thomas, and Richard Landes, *The Peace of God* (Ithaca, N.Y.: Cornell University Press, 1992).
Nussbaum, Martha, *The Therapy of Desire* (Princeton, N.J.: Princeton University Press, 1994).
Russell, Frederick H., *The Just War in the Middle Ages* (New York: Cambridge University Press, 1975).
Yoder, Paul, *The Politics of Jesus* (Grand Rapids, Mich.: Wm. B. Eerdmans Publishing, 1972).

David E. Johnson

PEACE RESEARCH AND PEACE STUDIES. Both are generally regarded as covering research and teaching on the causes of war* and the conditions of peace. In the United States, the term *peace studies* usually includes both research and education. In British systems, *peace studies* generally refers to research and teaching at the tertiary or university level, while the term *peace education* is reserved for the elementary and secondary levels. In both types of systems, peace education is derived from the field of peace research and is solidly based within it. Although disagreement exists over the exact content of the field, it remains clear that peace studies focuses around the causes of the increase and decrease of massive violence, the conditions associated with those changes, and the processes by which those changes happen. Peace researchers investigate war, peace, and conflict. Peace studies incorporates the interaction of research and education.

General agreement exists on a number of elements relating to the study of peace: (1) the field is interdisciplinary at its best, or at least multidisciplinary; (2) it is international and/or more often transnational; (3) it is policy-oriented— meaning directed to the real-life political environment of both policymakers and peace movements; (4) it is value-explicit. Generally peace studies includes commitment to some experiential component of learning, such as an internship. Finally, agreement exists that peace research is located largely within the social sciences. Peace studies, on the other hand, seems to have a broader disciplinary base, and includes all the social sciences (including history), philosophy, physics, biology, religion, art, language and linguistics, and other fields as well.

Probably the most serious division in the field of peace research occurs over the definition of peace. As is the case in political science for power and politics, there is no agreement over what is the central object of study. The major question has been whether peace is to be defined simply as the absence of war (''negative peace'') or whether the concept encompasses both the absence of war and the presence of social justice (''positive peace''). Those who argue that peace should be narrowly defined hold that broadening the concept reduces its clarity. To some degree this division can be identified geographically. In northern Europe and much of the Third World, the concept of positive peace is more widely accepted, while in the United States a larger number of peace researchers limit themselves to work on negative peace. The two individual peace researchers most often associated with the two poles of this debate, Johan Galtung, who is credited with the invention of the term *positive peace* in the mid-1960s, and Kenneth Boulding, among whose ''twelve friendly quarrels'' with Galtung include this one, fit the geographical expectations.

THE ORIGINS OF PEACE RESEARCH AND PEACE EDUCATION

Although the issues of war and peace can be traced back to Thucydides and later to the works of Thomas Hobbes* and John Locke, the origins of peace research as a separate field of inquiry are probably better traced only within the 20th century. There have been three primary waves of peace studies worldwide since its beginnings between the world wars.

The First Wave. Quincy Wright and Lewis Richardson, independently in the United States and the United Kingdom in the 1930s, were among the first to do quantitative analyses of war, to some degree out of the belief that the outbreak of war was based largely in the ignorance of foreign policy makers of what might be the consequences of their decisions. Both concluded that improving the knowledge base was a necessary part of dealing with the problem of war, and that evaluation and application of that knowledge would also be important. Wright's analysis of the causes of war found that each of six great wars over the course of more than twelve centuries showed a combination of idealistic, psychological, political, and juridical causes. Richardson looked at the attributes of states, among other factors, and found that homogeneity in culture, language, and religion did not preclude war breaking out among them.

Although Richardson and Wright were clearly the forefathers of the field, peace studies could not be said to have begun in earnest as an academic field until the late 1940s or early 1950s. Two research institutes were founded in this period at the close of World War II. In France, the Institute Français de Polémologie was founded in 1945. Bert Roling was a central figure in polymologie (war research), thinking its study was essential to the development of international law, and he introduced it to the Netherlands. In the United States in the same year, Theodore Lentz founded the "oldest continuously operating peace research center in the world," to encourage the mobilization of social scientists for a science of peace, which would bring about a scientific revolution involving both changes in fact and value.

A letter published in April 1951 by Arthur Gladstone and Herbert Kelman in the *American Psychologist,* arguing that pacifist challenges to the assumptions underlying conventional foreign policy deserved the systematic attention of psychologists, led to the 1952 formation of the Research Exchange on the Prevention of War and its *Bulletin.* It split the functions of the Research Exchange and exchanged the *Bulletin* for the more formal *Journal of Conflict Resolution: A Quarterly for Research Related to War and Peace,* which began publication in 1957 at the University of Michigan. The Center for Research on Conflict Resolution was organized, as was the Correlates of War Project, headed by J. David Singer, to look at some of the state and systemic factors thought to be associated with the frequency, severity, magnitude, and intensity of war.

In 1959 two institutes in very different traditions were founded. The Peace Research Institute Dundas (Canada) was founded by Hannah and Alan Newcombe, largely in the negative peace tradition. The Peace Research Institute Oslo (Norway) began as part of the Institute of Social Research and became independent in 1966. The radical critique of peace research was predominant here in the late 1960s, and Johan Galtung's concept of "positive peace" was to be a central focus both of the institute and of the *Journal of Peace Research,* which began publication at the institute in 1964. International organizations of peace researchers also began at this time. The Peace Research Society (International), which now prefers the term *peace science,* was set up at a meeting in Sweden in 1963 by Walter Izard of the United States. The Polemological Institute at the University of Groningen in the Netherlands, of which Bert Roling became the first director in 1961, was the first site of the International Peace Research Association (IPRA), founded in 1964 as a result of a Quaker International Conference and Seminar in Clarens, Switzerland in August 1963. It is regarded as the major international professional organization in the field of peace research.

The Second Wave. What might be regarded as the second wave of peace studies began in the late 1960s/early 1970s, and may be regarded as the democratization of peace research. The reaction to Vietnam* led to a radical critique of peace research in Northern Europe, and in the United States to the development of peace education. If the first wave of peace studies was primarily peace research with a touch of education, primarily at the graduate level, then the second could be regarded as primarily a new focus on peace education, both at the graduate, especially at the undergraduate and university levels. It was occasioned by the realization of peace researchers that their research had a relevance for the undergraduate classroom and even more so for the troubled campuses of the era of Vietnam protests around the world. While Manchester College in Indiana had established the first undergraduate peace studies program in the United States as early as 1948, stressing the interdisciplinary and cross-cultural emphasis that was to characterize later efforts as well, it was not until the early 1970s that a wave of peace studies programs was to be created. As with the Manchester program, many of these began in small, religious-based liberal arts colleges.

The Third Wave. In this phase, the impetus came from public peace movements concerned with the nuclear arms race rather than from the peace research/ education community. Antinuclear concerns led first to the development of antinuclear organizations within professions, to such organizations as Physicians for Social Responsibility, International Physicians for the Prevention of Nuclear War, Artists for Social Responsibility, and the like, as well as to local referendums on nuclear-free zones and to the more familiar development of arms control and disarmament movements. Out of all of these came a concern with educating the public, and eventually with educating students at all levels, focusing not only on college-level education, but on the education of teachers and the direct education of elementary and secondary students in peace studies.

A second component of this third wave was a tremendous increase in the emphasis on conflict resolution and particularly the use of third parties or mediation. This ranged from training in neighborhood centers in divorce mediation through the development of new types of mediation appropriate for use in public budgetary and environmental disputes through the development of university-level training and research programs and the development of national and international organizations in the field. In the United States a number of national groups emerged: the National Institute on Dispute Resolution (NIDR), the Society of Professionals in Dispute Resolution (SPIDR), and the National Conference on Peacemaking and Conflict Resolution, which held its first conference in 1982 to try to link conflict resolution with other parts of the field and to link professional conflict-resolvers with researchers and educators. Local and international mediation centers and firms were founded, joining older efforts in the labor and commercial field such as the American Arbitration Association, and universities began programs of research and education, beginning largely at the graduate or postgraduate level. The Program on Negotiation, a consortium of Boston groups based at the Harvard Law School, was joined by programs at the Universities of Hawaii, Michigan, Minnesota, George Mason, Wisconsin, Colorado, Syracuse, and others. While many of these focus largely on individual or domestic conflict, some programs, including Hawaii, Syracuse, and Colorado, make explicit linkages between conflict resolution and peace studies as more broadly defined.

A new field of research and teaching was introduced into peace studies in the 1980s, that of alternative international security systems, and the largely neglected conditions of peace began to join the well-researched causes of war as a major focus of the field. This field encompassed not only conflict resolution, but also nonviolent action and other methods for the maintenance and development of peace and security. What appears to have been the first conference on the subject, the COPRED 1979 meeting, produced a book reviewing various approaches. UNESCO's first Disarmament Education Conference, held in 1980, included references to the need for developing alternatives as a part of disarmament education. The work of Gene Sharp on nonviolent struggle and civilian-based defense*, begun over a decade before, and the Program on Nonviolent Sanctions in Conflict and Defense at Harvard, came into public view and greater acceptance.

Finally, governments began a new phase of institutionalization of peace research and education. The states of California, Ohio, and Hawaii, and the government of New Zealand, among many others, began to develop peace education in the public school and university systems. National institutes were formed: the University for Peace, loosely associated with the United Nations, was formed in Costa Rica, as well as the Austrian Peace Research Institute (1983), the Canadian Institute for Peace and International Security (1984), the Australian Peace Research Centre (1984), the U.S. Institute of Peace (1984), and the Scientific Research Council on Peace and Development in the USSR (1979), followed by similar councils in Bulgaria (1981) and Hungary (1982) and a Peace Research unit in the Academy of Sciences in Czechoslovakia (1982). In at least some of these countries where peace studies was being institutionalized, the debate over whether peace studies should be policy-relevant and work toward the improvement of state practice related to war, peace, and justice issues, or whether peace studies should remain independent and critical of the state, was rekindled by the sudden growth of resources in the field. Nor was this the only debate; the tremendous growth of peace action, peace research, and especially peace education at all levels, and the joining together of those who had long worked in the field with a large number of new individuals and organizations, was the occasion for both the reawakening of the debates discussed above and the awakening of new debates.

PEACE RESEARCH AND PEACE EDUCATION AFTER THE COLD WAR

Although there were predictions of the end of conflict, the end of history, and the end of the need for peace research as the Cold War ended in the late 1980s, it took only a very few years for it to be apparent that conflict and violence had not abated but simply taken different forms, and that research and education on the causes of war and the conditions of peace were still needed. Attention that had been focused on international conflict, and especially East-West ideological conflict backed up by nuclear deterrence*, began to focus on other conflicts that had been going on all this time in other parts of the world, and on new conflicts in regions where violence had been low. As demands for human rights expanded from individual civil and political, economic, and social, to group rights, and as ethnic and national identities became the focus of conflict and often violence, peace research turned to look both at these conflicts and at the means for their control and resolution. Economic and environmental conflict also became the focus of peace research. While work on low-intensity conflict* during the 1980s was limited, attention to subnational conflict and violence became a major focus, together with work on conflict resolution, early warning systems, and UN* preventive diplomacy, peacekeeping, peacemaking and peacebuilding and enforcement. Debate continued over world government and enforcement power, over unilateral or multilateral control of economic and military power, and over violent versus nonviolent means of carrying on and resolving conflict. Peace studies would still need to fight the battles over whether research, education, or activism were to be priorities, but there was by this time no question that such a field as peace research existed.

See CAUSES OF WAR; DEMOCRACY AND THE MILITARY; MILITARY AS A PROFESSION; MILITARY EDUCATION; MILITARY TRAINING, BASIC; PROPAGANDA.

BIBLIOGRAPHY

Boulding, Kenneth, ''Twelve Friendly Quarrels with Johan Galtung,'' *Journal of Peace Research* 14 (1977), 75–86.

Burton, John, *Resolving Deep Rooted Conflict: A Handbook* (Lanham, Md.: University Press of America, 1987).

Dedring, Juergen, *Recent Advances in Peace and Conflict Research* (Beverly Hills, Calif.: Sage, 1976).

Fisher, Roger, and William Ury, *Getting to Yes: Negotiating Agreement Without Giving In* (New York: Penguin, 1981).

Galtung, Johan, *Essays in Peace Research,* Vol. 1 (Copenhagen: Christian Ejlers, 1975).

Kelman, Herbert C., ''Reflections on the History and Status of Peace Research,'' *Conflict Management and Peace Science* 5, no. 2 (Spring 1981), 95–110.

Louis Kriesberg, *Social Conflicts,* 2d ed. (Englewood Cliffs, N.J.: Prentice-Hall, 1982).

Pruitt, Dean G., and Jeffery Z. Rubin, *Social Conflict: Escalation, Stalemate, and Settlement* (New York: Random House, 1986).
Richardson, Lewis F., *Statistics of Deadly Quarrels* (Pittsburgh, Pa.: Boxwood, 1960).
Sharp, Gene, *Making Europe Unconquerable* (Cambridge, Mass.: Ballinger, 1985).
Singer, J. David. ''Accounting for International War: The State of the Discipline,'' *Journal of Peace Research* 18, no. 1 (1981).
Stephenson, Carolyn M., ed., *Alternative Methods for International Security* (Washington, D.C.: University Press of America, 1982).
Wright, Quincy, *A Study of War,* 2 vols., rev. ed. (Chicago: University of Chicago Press, 1965).

Carolyn M. Stephenson

PEERS COMMISSION. *See* CRIMES AGAINST HUMANITY; GENEVA CONVENTION, 1949; SON MY/MY LAI; STOCKHOLM/ROTHSKILDE WAR CRIMES TRIALS; WINTER SOLDIER INVESTIGATION.

PERFIDY. *See* FORBIDDEN STRATEGIES; GENEVA CONVENTIONS, 1929, 1949; RED CROSS, RED CRESCENT, RED LION AND SUN; RUSES OF WAR.

PHILIPPINES WAR CRIMES TRIALS. *General Orders 100** was used by American military tribunals to try several officers of the U.S. Army for violating the laws of war in the Spanish-American War (1899–1902). By American estimates, more than 200,000 Filipino people were killed and another 900,000 died of starvation as a result of the conflict. Brigadier-General Jacob H. Smith, U.S. Army, was tried April 24–May 3, 1902 for having given orders to Major L.W.T. Waller of the U.S. Marine Corps to take no prisoners on the island of Samar, Philippine Islands. When Major Waller had asked whether he was to kill every person capable of bearing arms, he said that the General had replied affirmatively. When the Major had asked whether there was a lower age limit, the General had stated that ten years was the lower limit. Article 60 of *General Orders 100* had affirmed that it was against the usage of modern war to give no quarter*, and article 68 had stated that ''unnecessary or revengeful destruction of life is not lawful.'' The official charge against General Smith was ''conduct to the prejudice of good order and military discipline.'' Although the court martial found General Smith guilty as charged and recommended that he be retired, the final sentence was commuted to an admonishment.

Major Edward Glenn of the Fifth U.S. Infantry was tried May 23–29, 1902 for using torture* to get information from one of the leaders of the insurrection, Tobeniano Ealdama. The form used was the ''water cure,'' in which large quantities of water were forced into the stomach through the mouth. Torture of prisoners to exact information had been forbidden by Article 16. Furthermore, *General Orders 100,* Articles 56, 71, and 75, had forbidden maltreatment of prisoners*. Major Glenn appealed to military necessity*, a matter discussed in

Articles 15 and 16. The latter articles stated that military necessity did not "admit of cruelty to exact information," and the tribunal rejected the plea. His sentence, however, was suspension from command for a month and the forfeiture of $50 in pay.

Lieutenant Preston Brown of the Second U.S. Infantry was tried in June 1901 for shooting a prisoner for having tried to escape*. *General Orders 100,* Article 77 had ruled that while prisoners could be shot during an escape attempt, they should not be punished capitally for having tried unsuccessfully. This rule has continued to the present revised 1976 Army manual, *The Law of Land Warfare*, Article 168. The court found him guilty as charged and sentenced him to dismissal from the service and five years imprisonment at hard labor. The sentence was reduced by President Theodore Roosevelt to forfeiture of half pay for nine months and a reduction in line-ranking as a lieutenant.

In 1902, reports came to the Judge Advocate General's Office that Captain Cornelius M. Brownell had applied the "water cure" to a Catholic priest, Father Augustine de la Pena, under which the priest had died. While the facts were certified as true, the judge ruled that since Brownell was no longer in the military, he could not be tried. Furthermore, an act of June 6, 1900, had ruled that extradition of a person who had committed a crime held only if the crime was in a foreign country. Since the Philippine Islands were not considered a foreign country, extradition was not possible. After these trials, a civilian commission headed by Charles Francis Adams confirmed the judgments of these military tribunals.

See FORBIDDEN STRATEGIES; *GENERAL ORDERS 100;* TORTURE.
BIBLIOGRAPHY
Friedman, Leon, ed., *The Law of War,* vol. 1 (New York: Random House, 1972).

PILLAGE. Since ancient times, one of the fringe benefits of soldiering was the opportunity allowed for taking property as booty. During the American Civil War many private marauding groups were formed precisely for this purpose. Indeed, one of the reasons for the creation of the first U.S. military manual, *General Orders 100* (1863)*, was to point out that such a practice was forbidden by the laws of war*. Articles 34, 35, and 36 affirmed that it was forbidden to pillage or plunder national treasures. Articles 37 and 38 guaranteed protection for the private property of the residents from such plunder or pillage.

Rules of Land Warfare (1914)* cited Hague Resolutions (HR) 28 and 47 to the effect that "the pillage of a town or place, even when taken by assault, is prohibited." Indeed, a footnote to Article 339 stated that such acts may be punishable by death if committed by a soldier in active service. *The Law of Land Warfare* (1956)* reaffirmed the same prohibitions, citing in addition to HR 28 and 47, the Geneva Convention Relative to the Protection of Civilian Persons* (1949), Article 33. Article 99.6 of the *Uniform Code of Military Justice* (UCMJ)* condemned soldiers who "quit their place of duty" to commit pillage, implying that pillage while not on duty might be considered differently. Pillage by all sides in wars has been widespread, and pillage and plunder by the Germans during World War II were the bases for some of the sentences during the war crimes trials.

See CONTROL COUNCIL LAW NO. 10; *GENERAL ORDERS 100;* NUREMBERG TRIALS.

BIBLIOGRAPHY

Colby, Elbridge, "The Military Value of the Laws of War," *Georgetown Law Journal* 15 (1926–27).

Keen, Maurice Hugh, *The Laws of War in the Late Middle Ages* (London: Routledge & Kegan Paul, 1965).

Thatcher, Oliver, and Edgar H. McNeal, *A Sourcebook for Medieval History* (New York: Charles Scribner's, 1907).

POISONS. *See* BIOLOGICAL/CHEMICAL WARFARE; BRUSSELS DECLARATION; CHEMICAL AND BIOLOGICAL EXPERIMENTS ON HUMAN SUBJECTS; CRIMES AGAINST HUMANITY; FORBIDDEN WEAPONS; GENEVA PROTOCOLS I AND II; HAGUE, THE, CONGRESSES; HAZARDOUS DUMPING IN PROTECTED MARINE AREAS; NUCLEAR WEAPONS TESTING.

PREEMPTIVE STRIKE. *See* AGGRESSION, ATTEMPTS TO DEFINE; AGGRESSIVE VERSUS DEFENSIVE WAR; FIRST STRIKE/SECOND STRIKE.

PRISONERS OF WAR. Traditionally, wars of no quarter* were forbidden. However, practice did not accord with this ban, and thus historically, little attention was paid to what to do with soldiers who had surrendered or become *hors de combat* before the final conflict had been resolved. Rules existed under which by the display of certain flags or pennons a town could be asked to surrender. A town that refused to do so exposed its citizens to total annihilation. Towns that surrendered on request might be spared this result. As late as Franciscus de Victoria* (1486–1546) and Hugo Grotius* (1583–1645), it was the custom to kill solders even after surrender. While the entire peoples of a vanquished nation were, in some sense, prisoners, little consideration was given to the fate of prisoners before the end of a war.

The first U.S. Army manual, *General Orders 100**, provided explanations to the questions of both who is entitled to be a prisoner of war and how prisoners of war should be treated. Article 49 of this first manual listed those entitled to prisoner of war status as including: all soldiers, all citizens involved in an uprising *en masse,* all those attached to an army, disabled soldiers, those who have thrown away their arms and asked for quarter, citizens who accompany the army, such as sutlers, reporters, all members of the royal family, and diplomatic agents. Chaplains* and medical staff could be prisoners if they stayed with the wounded troops. The manual affirmed that prisoners were to be adequately housed, clothed, fed, and medically treated. Although prisoners could be shot while attempting escape*, they should not be capitally punished for being unsuccessful. Spies*, brigands, or bandits were not entitled to prisoner of war status. Marauding troops like those of Quantrell, and even conventional troops commonly took no prisoners or at best simply left the wounded and sick where they lay.

In 1864, the first Geneva Conference* provided extended details for the care of prisoners on land, and a similar conference in 1868 did the same for shipwrecked sailors*. Ships needed to be protected as they carried the shipwrecked to the nearest land prison. These suggestions, together with a similar Geneva Conference in 1906, were added to the revised army manual of 1914, *Rules of Land Warfare**, where Articles 45–47 endorsed the further requirements of the Geneva sessions. The 1934 manual contained additional instructions for the care of prisoners citing the Geneva Conventions of 1929, which insisted that prisoners captured after an attempt to escape should not be given excessive punishment such as execution or deprivation of food or liberties guaranteed by the convention. The 1956 U.S. Army manual, *The Law of Land Warfare**, quoted from the 1949 Geneva Conference.

Data from the war crimes trials after World War II established that prisoners were grossly mistreated by both Germany and Japan, and at the same time, that both France and the United States maltreated German prisoners. Current Geneva conventions speak to the matter of who is entitled to be a prisoner; how prisoners are to be fed, clothed, housed and medically treated; how they may be required to be employed and the pay for such employ; that their confinement must not be like a prison; how they may be exchanged or paroled; and that they may not be exposed to ill-treatment, torture, murder, starvation, disease or reprisal, or subjected to medical experiments. A primary incentive quite apart from humanitarian considerations was that maltreatment of enemy prisoners exposed one's own soldiers who were imprisoned to like treatment.

On no other matter has there been such agreement among warring belligerents as on the treatment of prisoners of war. Indeed, if there is any belief that rules exist with regard to war, it is in this area. The first U.S. war crimes trial of Captain Henry Wirz* was over the maltreatment of prisoners of war, and no offense loomed larger in the trials after World War II than the treatment or maltreatment of this group. Trials by the United States of some of its own soldiers in the Philippines War Crimes Trials* were for maltreatment of prisoners of war. Most of those charged in the Leipzig trials* were for offenses against prisoners. Most of the Nuremberg*, Tokyo*, and Control Council Law No. 10* trials dealt with crimes against prisoners. Data from the Korean War indicate that American prisoners suffered in violation of the Geneva rules. Evidence from the Vietnam War* reveals that Americans were responsible for the torture of North Vietnamese soldiers.

See BIOLOGICAL/CHEMICAL WARFARE; CONCENTRATION CAMPS;

ESCAPE, ATTEMPTS OF PRISONERS TO; FORBIDDEN STRATEGIES;
HOLOCAUST, THE; HOSTAGES; REPRISALS.

BIBLIOGRAPHY
American Prisoners of War in Southeast Asia, Hearings Before the Subcommittee on
    National Security Policy and Scientific Developments of the Committee on For-
    eign Affairs, H.R., 92nd Cong., 2d sess., part 3, February 3, March 16, 1972
    (Washington, D.C.: U.S. Government Printing Office, 1972).
Bacque, James, *Other Losses: An Investigation into the Mass Deaths of German Pris-
    oners at the Hands of the French and Americans After World War II* (Toronto:
    Stoddart, 1989).
Friedman, Leon, ed., *The Law of War,* vol. 1 (New York: Random House, 1972), 504–
    5.
Sargant, William, *Battle for the Mind* (Westport, Conn.: Greenwood, 1957).

PROPAGANDA. In common use, propaganda involves deliberate deception,
either by omission of truth or the commission of falsehood, in the interests of
some cause. Currently the term is a pejorative, but this was not always the case.
In 1622, Pope Gregory XV organized a College of Propaganda to supervise the
spreading of important doctrine in the foreign mission field. The church believed
that the doctrines were true and their enthusiasm in spreading them was not
only bolstered by this conviction, but involved no intent or effort at dissimu-
lation. Thorstein Veblen (1857–1929) observed that "once a warlike enterprise
has been entered upon so far as to commit a nation to hostilities, it will have
the cordial support of popular sentiment even if it is patently an aggressive war."
Toward the end of World War I Karl Liebknecht (1871–1919) described this
willingness as "the obedience of the corpse." The self-hypnosis of this acceptance of the crassest propaganda has been called "puppy patriotism" by the
New York League of Women Voters and a "prodigious mass of humbug" by
G. B. Shaw, and was typified by the candid claim of Carl Clausewitz* that
"even when the likelihood of success is against us, we must not think of our
undertaking as unreasonable or impossible."

National war slogans exhibit the quality of deception. The announced reasons
and the real ones for going to war are rarely the same. The American Revolution
was hailed by the slogan, "no taxation without representation," but this concealed the fact that the colonists did not want to pay taxes at all and would
probably have objected even if they had representation. Part of the stimulus for
that war was the desire for land speculation, which the British controlled and
in which many colonists wanted a share. Parenthetically, so little enthusiasm
existed for the cause of independence that about 25,000 colonists joined the
British forces, and George Washington had great difficulty in getting anyone to
volunteer for the army. A similar deception was involved in the U.S. war with
Mexico. Mexico had passed a law in 1827 for the gradual abolition of slavery,
while Texas was a slave state and its constitution as late as 1837 legalized
slavery. At the time of that war Mexico included California, New Mexico, Ar-

izona, Utah, Nevada, and part of Colorado, so that the motive to gain new territory played a significant role for the United States. The Massachusetts legislature resolved in April 1847 that the Mexican war had been unconstitutionally commenced for the dismemberment of Mexico. Even General Ulysses S. Grant in his memoirs had said that it was "one of the most unjust ever waged by a stronger against a weaker nation." The official propaganda, however, claimed much loftier aims.

In February 1918, Lord Northcliffe (Alfred C. W. Harmsworth), who was in charge of British propaganda against Germany, called an Inter-Allied Propaganda Conference in London to consolidate the propaganda policies of the Allies. His aim was to wage a war of ideas against Germany, and among other ends, to claim that Germany had sole blame for the war. President Woodrow Wilson spoke of this as a "war to end all wars," and his Fourteen Points were announced as the reasons for U.S. involvement. By an executive order in April 1917, a U.S. Committee on Public Information was established, chaired by George Creel, former editor of the *Rocky Mountain News,* and it was to include the secretaries of War, Navy, and State. The committee, however, held only one meeting, after which Mr. Creel ran the program alone. At the same time that he promoted Wilson's Fourteen Points, he stirred up anti-German sentiment. As symptomatic of some results were the renaming of "hamburger" to "Salisbury Steak," and "sauerkraut" to "Liberty Cabbage." It was Creel who announced that the war was not only to "rewin the tomb of Christ, but to bring back to earth the rule of right, goodwill to men, and gentleness which He taught." It was a war to "make the world safe for democracy." In like manner, German philosopher Rudolf Euken said that the German cause possessed the "soul of humanitarianism," and Adolf Harnack, the distinguished German biblical scholar, accused England of having broken down the ramparts of European civilization. Paul Sabatier, the distinguished French religious biographer, asserted that his country was fighting for "the salvation of all mankind." Self-deception has been easy, and the usual casualties of war include good sense and a respect for facts. Such military propaganda is basically chauvinism. Many Americans still believe that Pearl Harbor justified the U.S. entry into World War II, that the Gulf of Tonkin incident* justified the U.S. bombing of North Vietnam*, or that the UN Security Council Resolution 678 justified the U.S.-led Gulf War* against Iraq in January 1991.

The first political post held by Adolf Hitler in the German Workers Party was that of chief of propaganda. When he became leader of the Third Reich he appointed Joseph Goebbels as minister of propaganda. In 1942, playwright Robert E. Sherwood was given the job of organizing the U.S. Foreign Information Service of the Office of Coordinator of Information. On July 13, 1942, President Franklin D. Roosevelt established the Office of War Information (OWI) to conduct psychological warfare, since called "sykewar" (psychological war). Initially the rhetoric of Roosevelt's Four Freedoms and the remarks of Churchill about self-determination, equal trading rights, and general security provided the bases for what World War II was all about. Roosevelt, however, preferred to keep the war aims in vague generalities like "winning the war," so that long before the war was over most Americans did not know what the outcome was supposed to be. Out of this OWI came the Office of International Information and the International Broadcasting Division, notable functions of which were The Voice of America, the International Press and Publications Division, the International Motion Pictures Division, and the Advisory Commission on Educational Exchange. President Harry S. Truman abolished the OWI on August 31, 1945, and it was ultimately replaced by the Central Intelligence Agency (CIA).

Branches of government became proficient in distortion. In the Navy, for example, the practice of "gundecking" became common. It involved the falsification of records. It was common to redefine battle efficiency so that if the target was missed the report simply changed the target so that every salvo was a success. Those who fired did not want to be accused of inaccuracy, so if a spotter said he did not see any hit, the report stated that the spotter had been looking in the wrong direction. One way to justify the immense number of rounds sent was to "recreate" the target as located where all the shells had landed. Troops "rectified their lines"; they never "retreated." Enemy soldiers became subhuman "gooks," "slants," or "Huns." The practice of shooting everyone in sight was concealed by the expression "free fire zone." Congressional hearings on the roles of the CIA in deception, not only abroad but also in the halls of Congress, revealed how widespread deliberate falsification was. It was common for nations to demonize their opponents in order to justify violations of the laws of war.

Linguistic changes implemented the confusion. The former War Department became the Defense Department, warriors were peacekeepers, and military projects were given misleading titles like "Project Restore Hope," for an armed intervention, "Project Comfort" for a bombing mission, and "Project Just Cause" for an illegal invasion of another nation. Project "Desert Storm" sounded a lot better than "the bombing of civilian centers" like Baghdad. "Project Camelot" concealed a secret project of the CIA to undermine the duly elected government of Chile. President Ronald Reagan's plan in 1982, called "Project Democracy," was a covert plan to influence the governments of foreign countries. A regrettable consequence of all this was a general lack of confidence of the citizenry in either their news media or their government leaders.

See MILITARY JARGON; MILITARY TRAINING, BASIC.

BIBLIOGRAPHY

Dovring, Karin, *Road of Propaganda: The Semantics of Biased Communication* (New York: Philosophical Library, 1959).

Lavine, Harold, and James Wechsler, *War Propaganda and the United States* (New Haven, Conn.: Yale University Press, 1940).

Winkler, Allan M., *The Politics of Propaganda: The Office of War Information 1942–1945* (New Haven, Conn.: Yale University Press, 1978).

PROPORTIONALITY. One of the criteria used by just war* theorists to determine two different issues: (1) whether one is justified in fighting a given war at all (*jus ad bellum*) and (2) whether one is justified in conducting a war in a particular way (*jus in bello*). Just war theory lies on a continuum between pacifism* at one end and holy war* on the other end. Several positions of pacifism exist along the continuum. In this entry, *pacifism* refers to antiwar pacifism.

The characteristics distinguishing pacifism, just war, and holy war can be stated as follows. Antiwar pacifism argues that human beings have a duty to refrain from killing. Holy war theory argues that human beings have a duty to engage in warfare in God's cause, a "righteous" war. Just war theory claims that there may be occasions in which participation in warfare can be justified, but the burden of proof is on those who would justify warfare. All three positions share the view that warfare can be morally evaluated. A contrary view that, while conflict within a nation can be morally assessed and regulated, conflict between nations cannot, is often called realism. These distinctions provide a context within which to understand the criterion of proportionality.

In addition to proportionality, *jus ad bellum* rules include: competent authority, right intention, just cause, last resort, and just peace. The rule of proportionality is variously stated. Lackey affirms that "the rule of proportionality states that a war cannot be just unless the evil that can reasonably be expected to ensue from the war is less than the evil that can reasonably be expected to ensue if the war is not fought." A difficulty in applying this rule is in trying to measure the two evils that can reasonably be expected to occur. A second problem lies with the apparent incommensurability of the goods and evils in our lives. Can we say that the loss of a certain number of lives is a greater evil than the loss of certain rights or freedoms? If all our values cannot be ranked on the same scale, it is hard to know how to interpret more and less evil.

Further, this rule seems to imply that a war is just only if there will be more death, suffering, and so forth if the war is not fought than if the war is fought. On this view the rule would censure most wars and just war theory would be difficult to distinguish from antiwar pacifism.

The rule of proportionality in the *jus in bello* part of the just war doctrine holds that the harm committed in fighting the war must be proportionate to the value of the objective. If the *jus ad bellum* rule governs political decisions, then it should govern military strategy. For example, based on the *jus in bello* proportionality requirement, the American Roman Catholic Bishops issued a pastoral letter in 1983 stating that the use of nuclear weapons violated the rule of proportionality. In other words, military personnel conducting warfare by means of nuclear weapons would be engaged in an unjust form of warfare. The confrontation generated by this letter raises a general question of the relation between the proportionality rule and military technology. Has technological advance rendered this rule obsolete? Or, would the application of this rule inhibit the use of technology? Can we continue to utilize rules that were generated in the middle ages when warfare was so different?

The rule of proportionality serves to place some limits on the violence of warfare. Historically, this rule was developed by a religious institution to show how far believers should go during warfare. In the 20th century, does this rule govern the decisions of political and military leaders in secular states?

What if following this rule jeopardizes the chances of winning the battle or the war? Those who want to conduct warfare in a just manner may disagree about strategy with those who want to win the war at any cost. In the 20th century, no effective sanctions exist that can be levied on those who violate this rule. Can this rule be justified? Historically it was justified by appeal to the will of God as interpreted by the church. Can a secular justification be provided for this rule? We might try to argue that the rule has utility for each side in an armed conflict. Our side will hold to it because we want the other side to hold to the same rule. Is it possible to apply this rule with any degree of certainty? Determining proportionality involves making educated guesses rather than operating on knowledge. The rule is, therefore, susceptible to problems generally confronting moral decision making that appeal to the possible consequences of those decisions.

See CASUALTIES OF WAR; CHILDREN AND WAR; COLLATERAL DAMAGE; FORBIDDEN STRATEGIES; FORBIDDEN WEAPONS; HOLOCAUST, THE; INNOCENTS; JUST WAR; MASSACRES; MASS DESTRUCTION, WEAPONS OF; NUCLEAR WAR; PACIFISM; SIEGE WARFARE; TORTURE; TOTAL WAR.

BIBLIOGRAPHY

Cady, Duane, *From Warism to Pacifism: A Moral Continuum* (Philadelphia: Temple University Press, 1989).

The Challenge of Peace: God's Promise and Our Response (Washington, D.C.: United States Catholic Conference, 1983).

Lackey, Douglas P., *The Ethics of War and Peace* (Englewood Cliffs, N.J.: Prentice Hall, 1989).

David E. Johnson

PROTECTED PLACES. *See* AERIAL WARFARE; BIKINI ATOLL, BOMBING OF; CHILDREN AND WAR; COLLATERAL DAMAGE; COMBATANT-NONCOMBATANT DISTINCTION; COUNTERFORCE VERSUS COUNTERVALUE; FORBIDDEN STRATEGIES; FORBIDDEN WEAPONS; GENEVA CONVENTION, 1949; HAZARDOUS DUMPING IN PROTECTED MARINE AREAS; *LAW OF LAND WARFARE, THE;* MILITARY USES OF THE OCEANS; NUCLEAR ACCIDENTS; NUCLEAR DETERRENCE; NUCLEAR WEAPONS TESTING; OKINAWA, MILITARY OCCUPATION OF; RETALIATION; SIEGE WARFARE; STRATEGIC DEFENSE INITIATIVE (SDI); TOTAL WAR; ZONES OF PEACE (ZOP).

PSYCHIC NUMBING. The concept was introduced in 1967 by psychiatrist Robert Jay Lifton in *Death in Life,* his pioneering study of survivors of the atomic bomb dropped on Hiroshima* in August 1945. During in-depth interviews with seventy-five survivors, Lifton found that virtually all of them reported losing their capacity to feel the intolerably painful emotions aroused by witnessing death and destruction on a massive scale. According to Lifton, "They simply ceased to feel. They had a clear sense of what was happening around them, but their emotional reactions were unconsciously turned off" (1967, p. 31). Later in the book, Lifton argued that psychic numbing was a prominent symptom in survivors of the Nazi concentration camps* (500–539). In a later work, Lifton succinctly defined psychic numbing as "the loss of feeling in order to escape the impact of unacceptable images. This numbing, psychologically necessary at the time, can later give rise to despair, depression, and withdrawal" (1987, 62).

The importance of psychic numbing among survivors of massive trauma was recognized by the American Psychiatric Association (APA) when it introduced posttraumatic stress disorder into its Diagnostic and Statistical Manual and included psychic numbing among the defining symptoms. According to the APA, "Diminished responsiveness to the outside world, referred to as 'psychic numbing' or 'emotional anesthesia,' usually begins soon after the traumatic event." The APA added that "the ability to feel emotions of any type, especially those associated with intimacy, tenderness, and sexuality, is markedly decreased" (American Psychiatric Association 1987, 248).

Not only are the victims of violence susceptible to psychic numbing, but so are those who inflict it on others. Indeed, Lifton has asserted that "it is probably impossible to kill another human being without numbing oneself toward that victim" (Lifton 1986, 442). Thus, in *Home from the War,* his study of American veterans of the Vietnam War*, Lifton argued that the "business-like demeanor" of the men who slaughtered defenseless Vietnamese civilians in the infamous My Lai massacre* reflected "an advanced state of psychic numbing" (Lifton 1973, 51). Weapons technology that allows killing to be done from a distance promotes numbing, Lifton found. Thus, bomber pilots who killed from high altitudes "need not experience the searing inner conflicts" that could afflict ground troops (Lifton 1973, 346). Likewise, in his study of German physicians who contributed to the Holocaust*, including selecting Jews at Auschwitz for the gas chambers, Lifton found extensive evidence of psychic numbing as a facilitator of mass killing. Interviews with twenty-eight former Nazi doctors revealed that their previous medical training had placed a high value on "coldness" and "hardness"; that their professional peers in the camp encouraged them to regard the Jewish victims as subhuman and therefore undeserving of any empathic feelings; and that the euphemistic language in which the entire killing enterprise was couched had the effect of numbing the killers to the suffering of their victims (Lifton 1986, 442–47). *The Genocidal Mentality: Nazi Holocaust and Nuclear Threat* (Lifton and Markusen 1990) examined ways in which numbing and related psychological processes facilitated the involvement of otherwise humane men and women in the preparations for nuclear holocaust.

These included a preoccupation with the technical tasks at hand, utilizing a euphemistic vocabulary, and regarding the potential human targets of the weapons as anonymous enemies rather than vulnerable men, women, and children.

Psychic numbing is not limited to victims and inflicters of violence and trauma. Lifton has also identified the "numbing of enhancement" and the "numbing of everyday life." The former involves the reduction of feeling "in · some spheres of the mind in order to make possible more accomplished behavior or more intense feeling in other spheres" (Lifton 1982, 106). As an example, he pointed to surgeons who must shut out worries about failure of an operation in order to concentrate on doing the best possible job. The latter refers to peoples' needs to shut out distracting, disturbing images and stimuli in order to function in their jobs and personal lives. If one were to become too empathically pained by all the bad news reported in the press and television, for example, one's ability to perform responsibilities and care for one's family could be impaired. Lifton argues that threats to individual and collective survival posed by nuclear weapons*, global environmental* crises, overpopulation, and the pervasiveness of violence have created an "age of numbing." There is a real danger that the widespread tendency to become numbed to such threats will prevent people from confronting and striving to reduce them.

See BANALITY OF EVIL; BIOLOGICAL/CHEMICAL WARFARE; CASUALTIES OF WAR; CHEMICAL AND BIOLOGICAL EXPERIMENTS ON HUMAN SUBJECTS; CHILDREN AND WAR; CRIMES AGAINST HUMANITY; FINAL SOLUTION; FORBIDDEN STRATEGIES; GENEVA CONVENTION, 1949; GENEVA PROTOCOLS, 1977; GENOCIDE; HOLOCAUST, THE; HUMAN NATURE AND WAR; HUMAN RIGHTS; INNOCENTS; JUST WAR; MASSACRES; MILITARISM; MILITARY TRAINING, BASIC; NUCLEAR WAR; NUREMBERG PRINCIPLES; NUREMBERG TRIALS; TERRORISM; TORTURE; WAR CRIMES.

BIBLIOGRAPHY
American Psychiatric Association, *Diagnostic and Statistical Manual of Mental Disorders: DSM-III-R* (Washington, D.C.: American Psychiatric Association, 1987).
Lifton, Robert Jay, *Death in Life: Survivors of Hiroshima* (New York: Random House, 1967).
———, *The Future of Immortality and Other Essays for a Nuclear Age* (New York: Basic Books, 1987).
———, *Home from the War: Vietnam Veterans—Neither Victims nor Executioners* (New York: Simon & Schuster, 1973).
———, *The Life of the Self* (New York: Touchstone Books, 1976).
———, *The Nazi Doctors: Medical Killing and the Psychology of Genocide* (New York: Basic Books, 1986).
Lifton, Robert Jay, and Richard Falk, *Indefensible Weapons: The Psychological and Political Case Against Nuclearism* (New York: Basic Books, 1982).
Lifton, Robert Jay, and Eric Markusen, *The Genocidal Mentality: Nazi Holocaust and Nuclear Threat* (New York: Basic Books, 1990).

Eric Markusen

Q

QUAKERS. Quakers' fundamental belief is that there is "that of God in every one." Quakers resist formalization of their theology or social doctrines, and have considered themselves to be seekers after truth, believing that in "waiting upon the Lord" they will find unity both with the divine and with each other.

The movement arose as small bands of seekers in Cromwellian England in the mid-1600s sought to restore primitive Christianity*, and the depth of the power of religious experience in it. The name *Quaker* arose because they trembled with emotion at their meetings. The term was first used by Justice Gervase Bennett of Derby in 1650 in reproach (Jones 1958, p. 35). Quakers originally called themselves "Children of the Light," but by 1652 had begun to call themselves the Society of Friends, after Jesus's words "I have called you friends."

George Fox (1624–1691), considered the founder of the Society, as it came to be called after 1665, was born in Fenny Drayton, England, in July 1624. Early in life he found a conflict between the simple religion of the Bible and both the theology and the way of life of the strict Calvinist church in which he grew up. Leaving home, he traveled widely, seeing visions and growing strong in his beliefs, which included a mystical experience of light, and a distrust of "steeplehouses" and hireling priests, and of art and music. He and other Quakers were severely persecuted and were imprisoned. In spite of this, the Society grew until, by the time of Fox's death in 1691, there were between 50,000 and 60,000 Friends in England.

Among those who became convinced of the Quaker religion were Robert Barclay, whose 1676 publication of his *Apology for the True Christian Divinity, as the same is held forth and preached by the people called, in scorn, Quakers* made Fox's thought readily available to Quakers. William Penn's (1644–1718) 1667 "convincement" led him to found Philadelphia in 1682 as a "city of brotherly love," on land granted to Penn by Charles II as Pennsylvania. Penn's "holy experiment in government" was based on the Quaker principles of peace and equality between all human beings.

Friends are generally organized into what are called Monthly Meetings. Each Meeting holds a worship meeting each first day of the week, and a meeting for business monthly. Among early Friends, meetings for worship involved waiting in silence for the spirit, and this remains the practice for the "unprogrammed" meetings that exist largely in England and on the East Coast of the United States. The practice of using pastors grew up among certain American Quakers after various splits in the sect in the late 1800s, and continues in that part of Quakerism that holds "programmed" meetings. By 1672 a Yearly Meeting of all Quakers was set up in England. This Meeting recognized Quaker "testimonies" against war, oaths, and superfluities as already existent. Current monthly meetings are usually organized into quarterly meetings and then into yearly meetings and sometimes broader groupings representing differences in practice, in beliefs, and in the acceptability of evangelism. Unprogrammed, or silent meetings, are generally governed by committees of ministry and oversight that attend to the spiritual welfare and pastoral care of the membership. In meetings for business, Friends wait upon the spirit, as they do in worship, and decisions are made by consensus, not by majority rule. A clerk, the leader of the meeting, is one who has learned to read the "sense of the meeting" and formulate it into a minute that will be acceptable to all and allow unity.

In the mid-1990s there are approximately 300,000 Quakers worldwide, of which roughly one-third are in Kenya, one-third in the United States, and one-third throughout the rest of the world. Only roughly 18,000 remain in England. Most Friends worldwide are united in the Friends World Committee for Consultation (FWCC), which was created in 1937 at a Friends World Conference in Philadelphia to assist in fostering fellowship among Friends. FWCC maintains consultative status with the Economic and Social Council of the United Nations.

The only authority that Quakers accept is the authority of truth. This is why Quakers do not believe in oaths. They believe that truth can be known or experienced by all, and is to be tested experimentally or experientially by whether it can build a better society. This fundamental belief has led to various social testimonies on peace, community, equality, and simplicity. Quakers have worked to oppose war, have provided war relief, ambulance service during wars, and food and other aid after them, have started schools and colleges, have worked to improve conditions in prisons and hospitals, and were active in abolishing slavery. Margaret Fell, wife of George Fox, began Friends work in prisons. The American Friends Service Committee, formed in 1917 during World War I, was given the Nobel Peace Prize for its relief work with refugees.

George Fox's *Journal* recounts that when he was asked to take up leadership in the Commonwealth army he stated: "I told them, I knew from whence all wars arose, even from the lust . . . and that I lived in the virtue of that life and power that took away the occasion of all wars." John Woolman (1720–1772), an American Quaker, first brought up the concern against slavery, in his *Word of Remembrance to the Rich,* and explained his views in his comment that selfishness and greed lay at the root of both slavery and war. "May we look upon our treasures, the furniture of our houses, and our garments, and try whether the seeds of war have nourishment in these our possessions.''

See CHRISTIANITY AND WAR; CONSCIENTIOUS OBJECTION; PACIFISM.

BIBLIOGRAPHY

Brinton, Howard H., *Friends for 300 Years* (New York: Harper & Brothers, 1952).

Faith and Practice (Philadelphia: Philadelphia Yearly Meeting, 1972).

Jones, Rufus, *Faith and Practice of Quakers* (Philadelphia: Philadelphia Yearly Meeting, 1958).

Moulton, Phillips P., ed., *The Journal and Major Essays of John Woolman* (New York: Oxford University Press, 1971).

Sheeran, Michael J., *Beyond Majority Rule* (Philadelphia: Philadelphia Yearly Meeting, 1983).

Trueblood, D. Elton, *The People Called Quakers* (New York: Harper & Row, 1966).

Vipont, Elfrida, *The Story of Quakerism Through Three Centuries* (London: Bannisdale Press, 1960).

Carolyn M. Stephenson

QUARTER, NO, WARS OF. This ancient, although contested, forbidden strategy* informed the enemy that surrender would not be accepted, and that the battle would continue either until no enemy were left alive, or until the attacker was ready to stop. In the Middle Ages, rules were created to control both who and how many it was permissible to slay. If a nation declared a war of no quarter they indicated that everyone, including civilians, might be slain. It was customary if a town refused to surrender on request, that the attacker had the right to rape, plunder, and kill every resident. This was tantamount to no quarter. Franciscus de Victoria* (1485–1546) asked ''whether in a just war it is lawful to kill, at any rate, all of the guilty?'' His answer was that in the heat of battle everyone who resists may be slain. May we continue to kill after the enemy has surrendered? In the case of unbelievers, Victoria stated that it would be expedient to slay everyone, but in the case of war against Christians who had entered the war in good faith, it was not proper to slay any of them after surrender. Since unbelievers were usually presumed to lack good faith, it was customary to slay them all. Such a practice was a form of no quarter. One of the consequences in wars for ideology has been that moderation tended to be absent, since the enemy was presumed to be undeserving of protection by the laws of war.

Custom did not support the thesis that wars of no quarter should be forbidden. Hugo Grotius* (1583–1645) extended the right to kill after surrender, not simply to soldiers who had borne arms, or leaders who had instigated the war, but everyone residing in the enemy territory. Johann Textor (1638–1701) accepted the thesis that every armed enemy could be slain in battle or whenever they were in a position to do harm, but he denied that there was any right to kill soldiers who had surrendered. He urged that a distinction be drawn between those who had entered the war willingly and those who had been forced to fight.

Both Christian Wolff (1679–1754) and Emmerich Vattel* (1714–1767) denied any right to kill after surrender. Almost all agreed, however, that where the enemy had committed "grave breaches" of the laws of war*, reprisals*, equivalent to no quarter, were permitted. If evidence that a law forbidding no quarter existed depended on custom, there was insufficient evidence from which such a law could be inferred.

*General Orders 100** (Articles 60–66) rejected wars of no quarter while still allowing no quarter as a reprisal. *Rules of Land Warfare* (1914)* (Articles 182–183) considered no quarter to be a crime, but still allowed no quarter in reprisal (Article 368). The 1934* version concurred. *The Law of Land Warfare* (1956)* (Article 85) forbade commanders to refuse to take prisoners on the grounds that it might be inconvenient, since such an act would be a war of no quarter. Reprisals were permitted against an enemy that had practiced no quarter, and this reprisal could be no quarter. Article 40 of the Geneva Protocol I of 1977* affirmed that: "It is prohibited to order that there shall be no survivors, to threaten an adversary therewith or to conduct hostilities on this basis." The demand that an enemy accept unconditional surrender would appear to imply a demand for no quarter.

A difficulty in modern warfare is that the magnitude of the weapons causes damage in excess of what the rejection of no quarter is supposed to avoid. Modern weapons do not permit discriminating between combatants and non-combatants*, an essential precondition of avoiding no quarter. Guerrilla wars*, like Vietnam*, were basically fought with no quarter, and My Lai and Son My* illustrated this. Since World War II, civilian casualties* have exceeded military casualties, thus approximating no quarter. Conventional aerial bombing*, even apart from the bombing of Hiroshima and Nagasaki*, has been a form of no quarter, since both the indiscriminateness and scope of damage implies a no quarter situation. The rule came out of a time of chivalry and is, perhaps, long since inapplicable in light of modern weapons and strategies.

See AERIAL WARFARE; CASUALTIES OF WAR; CHILDREN AND WAR; FORBIDDEN STRATEGIES; MASS DESTRUCTION, WEAPONS OF; MUTUAL ASSURED DESTRUCTION (MAD); NUCLEAR DETERRENCE; NUCLEAR WAR; PROPORTIONALITY; RETALIATION, MASSIVE.

BIBLIOGRAPHY

Contamine, Philippe, *War in the Middle Ages* (Oxford: Basil Blackwell, 1985).

Keen, Maurice Hugh, *The Law of War in the Late Middle Ages* (London: Routledge & Kegan Paul, 1965).

"Protocol Additional to the Geneva Conventions of 12 August 1949, and Relating to the Protection of Victims of International Armed Conflicts (Protocol I)," in *American Journal of International Law* 72 (1978).

R

RAYMOND OF PENAFORTE (1176–1275). A Spanish Dominican monk who served as canon of Barcelona (1219) and supported the Inquisition and a crusade against the Moors (1229). Brought to Rome in 1230 by Pope Gregory IX, he worked on the codification of Roman law, was made Bishop of Tarragona in 1235, and served as general of the Dominican order from 1238 to 1240. He stated that there were five elements in a just war: (1) the war must be fought by laypersons—priests were forbidden to bear arms; (2) the aim of the war must be to redress some wrong committed against rights, possessions, or persons; (3) the war must be a last resort; (4) the aim of those who fight must be a genuine desire for peace; and (5) the war must have been authorized by the Roman Catholic Church or by a sovereign prince. Like most writers of the time, he assumed that wars for national defense needed no justification. He defended superior orders* as a sufficient defense for soldiers even when they used incendiaries*, which were otherwise prohibited. He claimed that such weapons were not to be called incendiaries if they were used under superior orders.

See CHRISTIANITY AND WAR; JUST WAR; SUPERIOR ORDERS.
BIBLIOGRAPHY
Keen, Maurice Hugh, *The Laws of War in the Late Middle Ages* (London: Routledge & Kegan Paul, 1965).

RED CROSS DRAFT RULES FOR CIVILIAN PROTECTION. Between 1957 and 1968 the International Red Cross issued drafts designed for the "limitation of the dangers incurred by the civilian population in time of war." The first draft contained twenty articles and was formally approved at the 19th International Conference of the Red Cross in New Delhi in 1957. Although this draft may have had some influence in later efforts to protect civilians in time of war, there was almost no reaction at the time from the governments to whom it was submitted for examination. Articles 14 and 15 proposed the prohibition of the use of incendiary*, chemical*, bacteriological*, and radioactive weapons, and delayed-action weapons like mines*. The draft also contained a new attempt to define when an area qualified as being unfortified, and hence not permissible for bombing.

In 1965 a second draft was issued for the ''Protection of Civilian Populations Against the Dangers of Indiscriminate Warfare,'' and was adopted by the 20th International Conference of the Red Cross, meeting in Vienna. The resolution forbade attacks against civilian populations, with special emphasis upon the use of nuclear* and similar weapons, and urged nations that had not already done so to ratify the Geneva Protocol of 1925* prohibiting the use of ''asphyxiating, poisonous or other gases, all analogous liquids, materials or devices, and bacteriological methods of warfare.'' The same request was contained in Resolution 23, adopted by the international conference on human rights meeting in Tehran on May 12, 1968. These weapons, however, were standard in the arsenals of the major nations, and they were unwilling to relinquish their use on the mere grounds of reducing collateral damage*.

See BIOLOGICAL/CHEMICAL WARFARE; GENEVA CONVENTION, 1949; INCENDIARIES; MINES; NUCLEAR WAR; RED CROSS, RED CRESCENT, RED LION AND SUN.

RED CROSS, RED CRESCENT, RED LION AND SUN. The Red Cross was founded in 1863 by Henry Dunant, a Swiss citizen who had become determined to set up a way to ease war damage and suffering of the kind he saw on the battlefield at Solferino (1859). Dismayed then that none of the armies maintained an organized or humane system for the care of the wounded and dying during or after the battle, he, with some colleagues, summoned a diplomatic conference in Geneva* in 1864, to formally adopt principles whose purpose was to ensure such care, while taking a neutral posture toward any given conflict. His organization, which adopted the name International Committee for the Red Cross in 1875, has traditionally had a Swiss staff and directorate, and an international mission to serve wherever conflicts existed. In the fifty years between its founding and the onset of World War I, national societies of the Red Cross sprang up around the world. In 1919 these were formed into a federation: The League of Red Cross Societies. To this day there remain two interconnected but functionally distinct parts of the organization: (1) the International Committee of the Red Cross, based in Geneva and still largely under the control of Swiss nationals, and (2) the various National Societies of the Red Cross, each chartered by its home government and engaged in relief efforts at home and/or overseas. Historical events, notably the Crusades*, meant that in some nations the red cross emblem called to mind bitter enmities and wars, which led to the adoption of alternative emblems—the Red Crescent in Moslem nations (beginning in Turkey in 1876), and the Red Lion and Sun (beginning in Iran in 1922). Since 1949, Israel has failed more than once to receive recognition for a red star.

The Red Cross played a central role in the formulation of the modern international law of war. The founders of the Red Cross were among the first to conceive of the idea of the Convention, a meeting of governmental and non-governmental officials from many nations to discuss and agree on terms for a multilateral treaty for the international regulation of war. There was little precedent for such supranational decision making when the first planning conference was held in Geneva (1863). Less than a hundred years after that first meeting, the model had matured enough to allow the formation of the United Nations, though even since the creation of the UN, Red Cross Geneva Conventions have continued to meet to modify the international law of humanitarian relief. The Red Cross/Red Crescent established many of the standards relating to the treatment of the injured and dying, to prisoners of war, and to neutrals and noncombatants, now written into international law. This formulation of an international law of humanitarian aid has had a counterpart—the formulation of an international law of armed combat, codified first at St. Petersberg* in 1868, and subsequently at the Hague*. The Red Cross was concerned with, though not the only instigator of, the Hague Conventions between 1899 and 1907, because they, too, raise humanitarian questions. Since 1977 some attempts have been made by the International Red Cross to combine the Hague and Geneva laws, and the protection of human rights, into a single body of humanitarian law.

The first Geneva Conference to codify the care of the wounded and sick, in 1863, was followed a year later by the convention to finalize an agreement for land warfare. Within a few years, the work of the sixteen founding nations had been endorsed by governments all over the world. At The Hague in 1899, the 1864 convention was extended to sailors and the shipwrecked. In 1906 and 1907, these two Conventions were further refined, but it took the experiences of World War I to force action on a major flaw: the lack of terms relating to prisoners of war (POWs). At Geneva, in 1928–1929, the nations formulated agreements about prisoners' rights. World War II prompted the next major revision, in 1949. To the traditional areas of Red Cross concern, the wounded, sick, and dying, and prisoners of war, was added a new concern: for civilians caught up in the combat. The 1949 Geneva Conventions created detailed new codes of behavior in all areas. Meeting again in Geneva in 1977, delegates were responding once more to defects revealed in recent wars, by making agreements to protect combatants, even when not in uniform, and to deny protection to mercenary troops. The decisions made in 1977, which were prompted by the need for standards appropriate to wars of liberation*, proved controversial, and fifteen years later these protocols had been adopted by fewer than ten national governments.

The Genocide* convention, also a product of the events of World War II, was a UN document, agreed to in 1948. In the years since 1945, the Hague rules of engagement have also been altered and added to several times, to deal with the challenges posed by new military technology. These modifications have generally been quite widely accepted.

For decades now, the Red Cross has maintained peacetime, as well as wartime functions. The International Committee of the Red Cross has taken on the task of visiting those imprisoned for political crimes in nations around the world.

The national societies are agents in the relief of natural disasters, which can range in scale from a fire in a single house, to major floods and earthquakes. In addition to hosting the conventions and drafting the language ultimately adopted by national governments around the world, the Red Cross, both the international society and the national societies of Red Cross, Red Crescent, and Red Lion and Sun, have been constantly in the field with agents to implement the rules that have been adopted. These rules have applied to all disasters, whether natural or man-made. Agents work on the basis of a small number of principles, the first of which is neutrality. No matter what the conflict, or who the participants, the ICRC and the national societies remain neutral. Ambiguities can arise from time to time, because for a national society to exist, it must be chartered by its home government. The second principle is that the Red Cross works collaboratively with others to provide aid, while still respecting sovereignty. The third principle is that the agents work primarily in the emergency phase of a disaster, leaving both disaster prevention, and reconstruction to national governments. The fourth principle is that Red Cross aid is provided free of charge, and without distinctions as to race, religion, nationality, social condition, or political opinion.

When faced, as it often is, with complex and contradictory situations, the organization's first goal is to maximize the access of Red Cross agents to distressed people. The ICRC and the national societies frequently encounter prisoners, civilians, and others in conditions that are in violation of the Geneva conventions, but given a choice about making a challenge to such conditions and losing the right to continue to visit, the Red Cross has usually chosen access. Each national society has its own distinct history. The Red Cross in the United States, spurred on by Clara Barton, managed finally to persuade the government to ratify the Geneva Conventions in 1882. Barton, a heroine of the U.S. Civil War, had founded an entity that quickly became one of the largest national societies. On U.S. soil, aid has rarely been used for those wounded in warfare, but natural disasters abound. In the aftermath of the Russian revolution, the ICRC committed itself to the maintenance of continuity in the new country, holding a conference of Red Cross Societies of Neutral Countries in 1918, and recognizing the Soviet Red Cross. In African countries in recent decades the Red Cross and Red Crescent have worked both in domestic humanitarian challenges and in wartime.

See GENEVA CONVENTIONS, 1864, 1868, 1906, 1929, 1949; GENEVA PROTOCOLS, 1977.

BIBLIOGRAPHY
Forsythe, David P., *Humanitarian Politics: The International Committee of the Red Cross* (Baltimore, Md.: Johns Hopkins University Press, 1977).
Kalshoven, Frits, *Constraints on the Waging of War* (Geneva: International Committee of the Red Cross, 1987).
Prior, Elizabeth B., *Clara Barton: Professional Angel* (Philadelphia: University of Pennsylvania Press, 1987).

Helena Meyer-Knapp

RELIGION AND WAR. *See* AUGUSTINE, ST.; BUDDHISM AND WAR; CALVIN, JOHN; CHAPLAINCY, HISTORY OF IN THE UNITED STATES; CHRISTIANITY AND WAR; CONSCIENTIOUS OBJECTION; DAY, DOROTHY; DODGE, DAVID LOW; GANDHI, MOHANDAS; HENNACY, AMMON; HINDUISM AND WAR; HOLY WARS; ISLAM AND WAR; JOHN OF SALISBURY; JUDAISM AND WAR; JUST WAR; KING, MARTIN LUTHER, JR.; LUTHER, MARTIN; MUSTE, ABRAHAM JOHANNES; PACIFISM; PEACE OF GOD; RAYMOND OF PENAFORTE; ROYDEN, MAUDE; TAOISM AND WAR; VICTORIA, FRANCISCUS DE.

REPRISALS. The United States Department of the Army field manual (FM 27-10), *The Law of Land Warfare**, defines reprisal as follows:

Reprisals are acts of retaliation in the form of conduct which would otherwise be unlawful, resorted to by one belligerent against enemy personnel or property for acts of warfare committed by the other belligerent in violation of the law of war, for the purpose of enforcing future compliance with the recognized laws of civilized warfare. (Paragraph 497 a, p. 177)

Defining "reprisal" in terms of retaliation is not very helpful, since the latter word is roughly synonymous with reprisal, and itself is in need of definition. But aside from that, FM 27-10 provides a good starting point for understanding what reprisals are and whether such acts are permitted legally and ethically. According to this definition, there are four elements in a typical act of reprisal:

1. The first party to a war has committed an unlawful (immoral) act or series of acts
2. There is every indication that the act or acts in #1 will continue
3. The second party (the victim) responds to these acts with acts that are similarly illegal or immoral (or would be considered so in other circumstances)
4. The response act is motivated by a desire to deter the first party's future unlawful (immoral) acts and not by revenge or similar motive

Optimally, the second party can support its act of reprisal with an explanation of its actions. It can identify what it has done publicly or through diplomatic channels as reprisal and, perhaps, indicate that it will desist when its enemy does the same.

FM 27-10's own analysis of when reprisals are not permitted follows closely the two Geneva Conventions of 1949* concerned with the treatment of prisoners* and civilians: "Reprisals against the persons or property of prisoners of war, including the wounded and sick, and protected civilians are forbidden" (497c). Forbidden as well is "The taking of hostages*" (497g). These and other hedges against reprisal reflect the realization that most such acts are not aimed at the original wrongdoer. Otherwise, reprisal might be thought of as an act of punishment aimed at deterring future wrongdoing.

But in view of these hedges, what kinds of reprisals are permitted? Some flexibility is allowable according to FM 27-10, in that the acts "of reprisal need not conform to those complained of by the injured party" (497e). Indeed, they had better not since the complaints that tempt victim nations to practice reprisal frequently have to do with killing prisoners, the wounded, and the like—the very kind of acts forbidden under any circumstances by the Geneva Convention and FM 27-10.

Regretfully, FM 27-10 (and the Geneva Convention) is not of much help here. It says that "reprisals may still be visited on enemy troops who have not yet fallen into the hands of the forces making the reprisal" (497c). But what specifically can be done to enemy troops that would constitute reprisal? Simply attacking them vigorously in accordance with the laws of land warfare is not enough. Such attacks might well be harmful, but since they are not illegal or usually immoral they cannot constitute acts of reprisal. FM 27-10 suggests that acts using otherwise illegal weaponry* would be acceptable, but does not give examples of such weapons. Would use of irregularly shaped or expanding bullets* be acceptable? Glass-filled shells? Poison gas? It is not clear. The reader is left with the impression that the U.S. Army does not want to engage in reprisals, but is loathe to admit as much.

There are at least two closely related problems with the Army's policy that leads almost inevitably to this conclusion. One is that responding to illegal and immoral acts by "using otherwise illegal weaponry" probably means first use* of these weapons. If poison gas were the weapon of choice for a reprisal, the law being violated would be one against just such use. The Hague* Convention of 1899, for example, does not explicitly and absolutely forbid the use of poison gas. Rather, it seems to forbid first use only. But if the reprisal, in fact, represents a first use, the enemy could very well not see the act for what it is, but instead as an escalation of the horrors of war. This points to the second problem. Even if the use of poison gas were announced as an act of reprisal, the enemy would likely respond with a further escalation. It would itself be tempted to use poison gas or, perhaps, to respond in kind by employing still another illegal weapon. In short, the kind of reprisal recommended in FM 27-10 is likely to backfire rather than achieve its deterrence purposes.

There is another problem with reprisal—one that applies to all of its forms. Reprisal tends to blur the distinction between the original wrongdoer and the victim. The nation contemplating reprisal thus needs to ask itself whether it is worth losing the high moral ground it would hold by not responding with a reprisal.

Overall, then, reprisal does not seem to be a very promising practice. It could be argued that reprisals are justifiable where the enemy is killing prisoners on a massive scale. Not to practice reprisal, so the argument might go, is to default on the duty the victim nation has to those of its own personnel who are still in enemy hands and, presumably, might not be alive much longer. But it needs to be asked in response just how many enemy prisoners would the nation engaged in reprisal have to kill? A token number would make little, if any, difference. Would the killing have to be massive in response to the massive killing? It seems almost inconceivable that nations falling in the liberal-democratic tradition could bring themselves to engage in such practices.

If the practice of reprisal is justifiable at all it would be in those situations where military necessity* demands it, as when an enemy uses poison gas and gains a military advantage by doing so. Even here there are hedges. It would not have been proper for the Coalition Forces in the 1990 Gulf War* to have used poison gas even if their outmatched foe had used such weaponry and thereby gained some local advantage by doing so. It is only in a desperate war of equals when one nation starts using such weapons that the other might be forced to respond in kind.

See FORBIDDEN STRATEGIES; FORBIDDEN WEAPONS; JUST WAR; MASS DESTRUCTION, WEAPONS OF; MUTUAL ASSURED DESTRUCTION (MAD); NUCLEAR WAR; RETALIATION, MASSIVE.

BIBLIOGRAPHY

Army, Department of the, *The Law of Land Warfare* (FM 27-10) (Washington, D.C.: U.S. Government Printing Office, 1956).

Christopher, Paul, *The Ethics of War and Peace: An Introduction to Legal and Moral Issues* (Englewood Cliffs, N.J.: Prentice Hall, 1994), Chaps. 10 and 11.

Geneva Convention, Geneva, June 17, 1925, "Protocol for the Prohibition of Poisonous Gases and Bacteriological Methods of Warfare," in Leon Friedman, ed., *The Law of War* (New York: Random House, 1972), 454–56.

Hague IV, 3 The Hague, July 29, 1899 "Prohibiting Use of Gases," in Leon Friedman, ed., *The Law of War* (New York: Random House, 1972), p. 249–50.

Nicholas G. Fotion

RETALIATION, MASSIVE. Massive retaliation is the name of a specific nuclear weapons policy adopted by the United States in the 1950s, as well as the name for a more general approach to the use of nuclear weapons represented by that specific policy. Massive retaliation as a military policy became possible only with the advent of nuclear weapons. The key to understanding massive retaliation is recognizing the unique capacities of nuclear weapons in comparison with conventional weapons. Nuclear weapons are so powerful that a nation with a modest number of nuclear warheads and the means of delivering them has the capacity to destroy its opponent's society, its social infrastructure, and a large portion of its population. Such societal destruction would be the outcome of massive retaliation. In order to deter its opponent's aggression*, a nation with such a capacity could threaten to impose societal destruction in retaliation for such aggression. The threat would be that even minor military aggression with conventional forces would be met with a massive nuclear counterattack. Massive retaliation is primarily a policy of making such a threat, hence it is primarily a policy of nuclear deterrence*, rather than a policy of using nuclear weapons in a nuclear war.

There were several factors that made such a policy attractive to the United States in the mid-1950s, in the early phase of the Cold War* with the Soviet Union. First, the United States had just been involved in a costly conventional war fighting Communist aggression on the Korean* peninsula, and the feeling was that something had to be done to avoid such a war in the future. Second, the nuclear forces needed to threaten massive retaliation were much cheaper than the conventional forces needed to deter aggression. Nuclear weapons provided much more "bang for the buck." Third, the United States at that time had a high level of nuclear superiority over the Soviet Union. In light of these factors, it became appealing to rely on nuclear forces rather than conventional forces to deter aggression. Early in the Eisenhower administration, the policy of massive retaliation was proclaimed by the president's secretary of state, John Foster Dulles. Should Communist nations engage in aggression anywhere in the world, even relatively minor conventional aggression, the United States threatened to destroy Soviet society. But the policy had its critics, and they grew louder as the decade wore on. Most of the criticism focused on the policy's effectiveness as a form of deterrence, but some of the criticism was clearly moral in nature. The moral criticism is our main concern, but to understand it clearly, one needs first to consider the criticism of the policy's effectiveness.

The main criticism was that massive retaliation was not an effective deterrent policy because the threat was not credible. Threats cannot effectively deter if they are not credible, that is, if the party threatened does not believe that it is likely that the threatener would carry out the threats. Children understand this at a young age, and much ineffective discipline is due to parents' failure to make credible the threats of punishment they announce to their children. The reason that the United States' threat of massive retaliation seemed incredible was that the execution of such a threat would likely be met by Soviet nuclear retaliation against U.S. society. After all, once Soviet society had been destroyed, the Soviet Union would have nothing left to lose by a full nuclear counterattack. Would Soviet leaders believe that a U.S. president would order an attack whose consequence might well be that U.S. cities would themselves come under nuclear attack? Because it was unlikely that they would, it was unlikely that the threat of massive retaliation was an effective deterrent. (Some strategists suggested, half seriously, that the way to remedy the credibility problem was to build what was called a doomsday machine, which would allow computers to make the decision to retaliate.)

Of course, part of what made massive retaliation appealing was U.S. nuclear superiority, which made it less likely that the Soviet Union would have the capacity to counterattack. But the margin of superiority shrank as the 1950s progressed, so that the credibility criticism grew stronger. What the critics recommended instead was graduated deterrence, that is, threatening not massive nuclear retaliation, but retaliation (whether nuclear or conventional) proportional to the aggression to which it was a response. This was thought to be a more credible form of deterrence, because proportional retaliation would be unlikely to lead to a Soviet counterattack on U.S. cities.

What about the morality of massive retaliation? Is it a morally justifiable policy? The most appropriate standpoint from which to consider this question is that of just war* theory, the approach developed over centuries to deal with the moral issues involved in the use of military force. There is no doubt that in just war terms the execution of a threat of massive retaliation would not be morally justifiable. Just war theory requires, under the conditions of *jus in bello* (the use of force in war), that the use of force be both discriminate and proportionate*. Discriminate force is force directed only at military targets, while proportionate force is force whose use does not cause harm that is out of proportion to the value of the military goal achieved. Massive retaliation would violate both of these conditions: The nuclear warheads would be targeted on cities of innocent civilians, and the amount of harm done would far exceed the value of avenging some relatively minor act of conventional aggression.

The interesting question is whether massive retaliation understood as a policy of deterrence, rather than a policy of using the weapons in war, is morally justifiable. Is it morally permissible to make a threat to do something morally impermissible, if one is never likely to have to execute the threat? If the threat works and no aggression occurs, good is done (the aggression is avoided) and no one is harmed. Much of the debate over the moral justifiability of nuclear deterrence in general, of which the debate over the moral justifiability of massive retaliation is a specific instance, turns on this issue. It is a matter of considerable controversy. On one side are those who argue that threats of massive retaliation are not morally permissible, because the just war requirements are that one may not *intend* to use force in a way which is not discriminate or proportionate, and the threat of massive retaliation involves such an impermissible intention. It is true that if the threat works, the intention will never be carried out, and no one will actually be harmed. Nonetheless, many argue, the threat involves an impermissible intention, and so is itself impermissible. And, of course, the threatener cannot guarantee that the threat will work, and so cannot guarantee that the threat will not be executed.

One response to this line of argument is that the threat of massive retaliation could be a bluff, and so not involve an intention actually to retaliate. But this is a weak response, in part because if the policy is a bluff, it is unlikely to be effective. A stronger response on the part of the moral defenders of threats of massive retaliation is simply to deny that the mere intention to engage in the indiscriminate or unproportionate use of military force is itself, short of doing the deed, morally wrong. In this view, the threat by itself cannot be morally wrong, because the purpose of making the threat is to insure that it will not have to be carried out. Indeed, if the threat is effective, there is little likelihood that it would ever have to be executed. The threat does only good, no harm, or, at most, but a small risk of harm. As a result, the threat satisfies the just war conditions that the use of force be discriminate and proportionate: There is little or no harm done to innocent civilians, because there is little or no harm done at all.

One might think that the topic of massive retaliation is of historical interest only, as is the Cold War in the context of which the policy was adopted. But this would be a mistake. Since the Cold War has ended, nuclear proliferation* has become a more pressing problem. When nations acquire nuclear weapons, they may well have, for a time at least, overwhelming nuclear superiority in comparison with their regional opponents. Under such circumstances, it would be tempting for them to adopt a policy of massive retaliation. Such a choice seems to have been made by North Korea, which was suspected to have nuclear weapons. In 1994, North Korea threatened that, should there be aggression on the part of its neighbor South Korea, it would turn the South Korean capital Seoul into "a sea of fire."

See CASUALTIES OF WAR; FIRST STRIKE/SECOND STRIKE; HOLO-CAUST, THE; HOSTAGES; INTENTIONALITY AND DOUBLE EFFECT; MILITARY NECESSITY; MUTUAL ASSURED DESTRUCTION (MAD); NUCLEAR DETERRENCE; NUCLEAR WAR; REPRISALS.

BIBLIOGRAPHY
Freedman, Lawrence, *The Evolution of Nuclear Strategy* (New York: St. Martin's, 1981).
George, Alexander, and Richard Smoke, *Deterrence in American Foreign Policy: Theory and Practice* (New York: Columbia University Press, 1974).
Kenny, Anthony, *The Logic of Deterrence* (Chicago: University of Chicago Press, 1985).

Steven Lee

ROUSSEAU, JEAN-JACQUES (1712–1778). French philosopher Rousseau's ideas about war and peace are scattered throughout his writings on politics and education. Although these ideas are not developed systematically, it is possible to identify some general themes. Rousseau argues that humanity is naturally peaceful, that greedy princes cause war, and that submission to an absolute ruler is slavery, not peace. True peace may be pursued through civic education or through an international confederation of states. Rousseau explicitly opposes the ideas of English philosopher Thomas Hobbes* (1588–1679), who argues that humanity is naturally warlike and that an absolute state can enforce peace.

In *Discourse on the Origin of Inequality* (1755), Rousseau describes the gradual slide of humanity from its natural state of peace to the state of perpetual war in which it lives today. As individuals recognize the convenience of living in groups, they begin to compare themselves to one another, and social classes begin to develop. Claiming to serve the interests of all, the rich entice the poor to form political communities, thus institutionalizing an unequal social structure. Domination and violence become necessary to maintain this social structure. People follow orders to harm others because they believe it will help them climb the social ladder.

In his summary and critique of the Abbé de Saint Pierre's *Project for Perpetual Peace* (1758), Rousseau applies these ideas to states in his contemporary

Europe. In these states, the power of princes is extended when they subjugate or annihilate neighboring states. In order to gather resources to conduct foreign wars, princes are continually at war with their own citizens, confiscating their lives and property in the name of the public interest. Blinded by ambition, princes cannot see the advantages of peace. Therefore, they are unlikely to be interested in the Abbé's excellent proposal for a confederation of states analogous to today's United Nations. They are also unlikely to accept the view Rousseau advanced in "On Political Economy" (1755) that a general will—the desire to act as a group—can develop on the level of world society.

For Rousseau, the development of a general will can be encouraged through education. In *Considerations on the Government of Poland* (1771), Rousseau suggests that the best means of civil defense is a patriotic state that pursues domestic justice rather than international power. Such a state will have no reason to attack or be attacked. To create such a state, its children should receive universal public civic education and learn to place patriotism above ambition. For peace education in typical avaricious European states, Rousseau recommends in *Emile* (1762) that children be educated to feel kinship with all humanity. Adolescents, for example, should be exposed to scenes that arouse their pity, introduced to literature that brings historical characters to life, and required to participate in community service.

See CAUSES OF WAR; HUMAN NATURE AND WAR; NATIONALISM; PATRIOTISM; PEACE RESEARCH AND PEACE STUDIES.

BIBLIOGRAPHY

Roosevelt, Grace G., *Reading Rousseau in the Nuclear Age* (Philadelphia: Temple University Press, 1990).

Rousseau, Jean-Jacques, *The Political Writings of Jean-Jacques Rousseau,* 2 vols., C. E. Vaughan, ed. (New York: Wiley, 1962).

Laura Duhan Kaplan

ROYDEN, MAUDE (1876–1956). The first woman priest in the Church of England (1921), where she preached a nondenominational socialism and pacifism. She attended Oxford University from 1896 to 1899 and received a degree in history and went to London as a social worker in 1899, but ill health forced her to retire in 1901. In 1903 she was the first woman appointed as an extension lecturer at Oxford.

In 1908 she campaigned for the vote for women; served on the national council of the National Union of Women's Suffrage Societies, 1912–1914; lobbied in the House of Commons for the suffrage cause; and served as the editor of the suffragette paper, *The Common Cause.* Out of this involvement she became active in the antiwar movement and aligned herself with the pacifists* against the patriots* in the suffrage movement. She participated in a retreat in December 1914 to consider the response of Christians to war. Out of this retreat the Fellowship of Reconciliation (FOR) was formed. In 1915 she published her first pacifist pamphlet, *The Great Adventure,* which called for nonviolent direct action against the government.

During 1914–1917 she spoke widely for the FOR and on one occasion her caravan was burned and she and her compatriots were threatened with death. She stopped the project, feeling that it was counterproductive to create so much anger. She maintained that while women were not essentially antimilitarist, that militarism* was essentially antifeminist. She commented that ''women can do no greater service to the world than to increase healthy skepticism of violence as a method of imposing ideals.'' In 1920 she promoted the idea of the League of Nations and she delivered a sermon on this at the conference of the International Alliance for Women's Suffrage in Geneva in June 1920. Her remarks were delivered from Calvin's pulpit, from which John Knox had stated that to allow women to speak in church was a ''monster in nature, contumely to God and most repugnant to His will and ordinance.'' She aroused particular anger when she suggested that we apply the Sermon on the Mount to feed children* starving in Austria because of the Allied blockade and Russian children who were not being fed because their country was Bolshevik.

When the Japanese invaded Manchuria she asked for women volunteers who would go to Manchuria to be human barricades against the Japanese invasion by lying on the ground at the border. It is not known if she had any candidates, but in 1932 she made another appeal and had 800 volunteers, but by the time she got the group organized the war was over. In 1930 with Dick Sheppard and Herbert Gray she advocated the formation of a Peace Army. On the eve of World War II, however, she changed her mind along with A. A. Milne and C. E. M. Joad and supported the war.

See ADDAMS, JANE; CHILDREN AND WAR; CHILDREN'S RIGHTS IN WAR; CHRISTIANITY AND WAR; DAY, DOROTHY; FEMINISM AND WAR; PACIFISM.

BIBLIOGRAPHY

Mitchell, David, *Women on the Warpath: The Story of the Women of the First World War* (London: Jonathan Cape, 1966).

Moorehead, Caroline, *Troublesome People: The Warriors of Pacifism* (Bethesda, Md.: Adler & Adler, 1987).

Wiltshire, Anne, *Most Dangerous Women: Feminist Peace Campaigners of the Great War* (London: Pandora Press, 1985).

RULES OF LAND WARFARE, 1914, 1934, 1944. *General Orders 100** was revised under a new title in 1914 and issued under the signature of Major General W. W. Witherspoon, chief of staff of the War Department. The task of writing this manual was given to Colonel Edwin F. Glenn of the Army War College, with the understanding that he would take account of new international agreements to which the United States had been a party, including some of the declarations of The Hague* and Geneva*, the Spanish-American War, and new weapons and strategies. The appendix of this new manual, however, listed only the following as binding on the United States: one Geneva convention of 1906, six Hague conventions of 1907, and one Hague declaration prohibiting the discharge of projectiles and explosives from balloons. No mention was made of the declaration of St. Petersburg*, which had banned explosive bullets weighing less than 400 grams, or the Brussels* declaration banning the use of poisons and bacteriologicals. Colonel Glenn stated in the preface that "the accompanying *Rules of Land Warfare* have been prepared for the use of officers of the land forces of the United States," and he noted further that "everything vital contained in *General Orders 100* . . . has been incorporated in this manual." Glenn noted that he had consulted both the British manual written by Professor L. Oppenheim and the book *La Guerre Russo-Japonaise* by Professor Nagao Ariga.

The new manual was prompted, especially, by new weapons and strategies to which the old manual did not speak, which cast new light on the old prohibitions against attacks on unfortified places and civilians. The Hague declaration of 1899* had forbidden weapons that would cause "superfluous injury," while the 1907 Hague convention had forbidden weapons that would cause "unnecessary suffering." Although the United States was a signatory to the declaration prohibiting dropping explosives from balloons, it was not a signatory to the declaration prohibiting the use of projectiles containing asphyxiating or deleterious gases, nor the declaration prohibiting expanding bullets*, and the new manual took note of these by supporting the ban against dropping projectiles from balloons while rejecting the other two declarations. The new manual embraced the Geneva convention of 1906 for the amelioration of the condition of the wounded and sick, and it included those Hague conventions dealing with the general topics concerning the opening of hostilities, the laws and customs of war* on land, the convention respecting the rights of neutral nations, the limits on bombardments by naval forces, the convention with respect to the laying of automatic submarine mines*, and a table of ratification to the second Hague Congress of 1907.

Article 1 affirmed that "the conduct of war is regulated by certain well-established and recognized rules that are usually designated as 'the laws of war.' " Article 9 explained that these limits were conditioned by three principles: (1) whatever acts are militarily necessary* must not be prohibited; (2) whatever is not militarily required is forbidden (the principle of humanity); and (3) chivalry, which required fairness and mutual respect. These same three principles remained in all manual revisions to the present. The task was to determine whether there were any militarily necessary acts that were at the same time forbidden by humanity and chivalry. With respect to forbidden weapons*, this manual rejected explosive bullets while accepting expanding ones, and it rejected the use of poisons (Article 13), but insisted that gases and chemicals were not poisons. Articles 432–440 set limits to the use of automatic mines in an effort to protect neutral shipping, and Article 368 named waging a war of no quarter* to be a war crime*.

The problems associated with the bombing of unfortified cities proved to be difficult to explain. On the one hand, Hague Resolution 25 was cited to the effect that "the attack or bombardment by whatever means, of towns, villages, dwellings, or buildings which are undefended is prohibited" (Article 212), and on the other hand in article 217 an "American Rule" allowed such bombing where it would be militarily advantageous. Articles 366–368 protected individual soldiers from punishment for war crimes when they were following superior orders*. Extensive rules for the care of prisoners* were cited as derived from Geneva conventions of 1906. This was the manual with which the United States entered World War I, and since we were not a signatory to the prohibitions against gas and noxious chemicals we joined the British and French in using gas weapons. Commitment to laws of war reached a plateau at this time. No subsequent edition of the manual was able to accept so many conventions of international congresses. At the time there was a fear that any revision of the laws of war would undermine confidence in the League of Nations.

In spite of vast increases in the explosive power of new weapons accompanied by an inability to discriminate combatants from noncombatants*, few changes appeared in the manual in the 1934 edition. While dumdum bullets were not mentioned by name, the list of banned bullets included those with a "scoring of the surface or filing off the ends," which were, in effect, dumdum bullets. In the sections on forbidden weapons*, Article 34 stated that no prohibition existed against the use of explosives in artillery shells, mines*, torpedoes*, or hand grenades, although the manual did forbid "lances with barbed heads, irregular shaped bullets, and projectiles filled with glass." Like the 1914 version, the 1934 edition banned poisons but accepted gases, chemicals, and incendiaries* (Article 29). In 1944, the treatment of the issue of superior orders was revised (Article 345) to provide that individual soldiers might be prosecuted for obeying orders that violated the laws of war, although superior orders might be taken into consideration as limiting culpability. The sections on the care of prisoners were considerably expanded in line with the 1929 Geneva Conventions, the one area where the military manuals generally adopted the recommendations of the international congresses.

See BIOLOGICAL/CHEMICAL WARFARE; FORBIDDEN STRATEGIES; FORBIDDEN WEAPONS; SUPERIOR ORDERS.

BIBLIOGRAPHY
Rules of Land Warfare (Washington, D.C.: U.S. Government Printing Office, 1914).
Rules of Land Warfare (Washington, D.C.: U.S. Government Printing Office, 1934). Printed as Vol. 2 of the *Basic Field Manual: Military Law.*
Rules of Land Warfare (Washington, D.C.: U.S. Government Printing Office, 1947), FM 27-10, *Basic Field Manual.* This includes Change No. 1, altering Article 345.1 on superior orders.

RUSES OF WAR. Ever since Sun Tzu (c. 500 B.C.) insisted that all warfare was based on deception, debate has continued over whether there should be limits to the ways one could deceive the enemy. Article 50 of *The Law of Land Warfare** (1956) affirmed that ruses were legitimate as long as they did not

involve treachery, but also added that "the line of demarcation between legitimate ruses and forbidden acts of perfidy is sometimes indistinct." The Annex
to Hague* Convention 4, Article 24 of October 18, 1907, was cited in support.
As instances of illegitimate ruses the following were named: deliberate lying
that involves a breach of faith or when there is a moral obligation to speak the
truth; feigning surrender so as to secure an advantage; broadcasting falsely that
an armistice has been signed or the war ended; improperly using the flag of
truce, military insignia, the uniform of the enemy, or the badges of the Red
Cross, Red Shield, Red Crescent*, and so forth; using a hospital as a military
post; using a hospital train to transport arms or troops; or using an airplane
marked with the hospital insignia for aggressive* purposes.

Legitimate ruses included: surprise; ambush; feigning attack or retreat; pretending to have a force larger or smaller than actually the case; transmitting
false or misleading radio or telephone messages; issuing bogus orders as if from
the enemy commander; pretending to communicate with nonexistent troops; using spies*; moving landmarks, street signs, and such; erecting dummy tanks,
planes, and mines*; engaging in psychological warfare activities; and removing
identification from uniforms.

Article 50 stated that the line between what was permitted and what was
forbidden was "sometimes indistinct." Since deliberate lying was both permitted and forbidden depending on whether there was a "moral obligation to speak
the truth," the problem was to determine when, if ever, such a moral obligation
existed. Furthermore, Article 50 concluded that "treacherous or perfidious conduct in war was forbidden because it destroyed the basis for a restoration of
peace short of the complete annihilation of one belligerent by the other." In the
light of what is permitted in war, evidence needs to be provided to show that
using napalm, fragmentation bombs*, or nuclear* bombs indiscriminately on
civilians does not destroy the basis for a restoration of peace.

In addition, the roles of the intelligence agencies* of the various nations
impinge seriously on the conventional meaning of perfidy and make it difficult
to separate legitimate from illegitimate ruses. The *United States Marine Corps
Law of War Course Deskbook* noted as legitimate ruses: the Allied deceptive
measures to convince the Germans that the D Day, June 6, 1944 landing would
be at Pas de Calais rather than Normandy; the "demonstration landing" July
24, 1944, causing the Japanese commander to shift his forces to Tinian Town
while the 4th Marine Division landed almost unopposed at Uishi Airfield; operation BOLO, January 2, 1967, where USAF F-4 fighters lured North Vietnamese MiG planes into a dogfight by posing electronically as bomb-laden F-105s,
with a result of shooting down 6 MiGs. Even the traditional prohibition against
wearing the uniform or insignia of the enemy issued by The Hague, Article 23,
is interpreted by *The Law of Land Warfare,* Article 54, as applying only to
"improper use." Since The Hague declared all use to be a violation, there would
appear to be no proper use. Even the ban on the use of flags of truce is qualified
by the term "surreptitiously" (Article 53). All that remains clearly forbidden is

for armed soldiers to wear the uniform or insignia of the Red Cross or the United Nations and to use them to cloak acts of hostility. To do so would constitute perfidy.

See FORBIDDEN STRATEGIES; FORBIDDEN WEAPONS; INTELLI-GENCE AGENCIES, U.S.; *THE LAW OF LAND WARFARE;* SPIES; WAR CRIMES.

BIBLIOGRAPHY

Betts, Richard, *Surprise Attack* (Washington, D.C.: Brookings Institution, 1982).

Department of the Army Field Manual FM 27-10, *The Law of Land Warfare* (Washington, D.C.: U.S. Government Printing Office, 1956).

Knorr, Klaus, and Patrick Morgan, eds., *Strategic Military Surprise: Incentives and Opportunities* (New Brunswick, N.J.: Transaction Books, 1983).

United States Marine Corps Law of War Course Deskbook, prepared by Law of War Reserve Augmentation Unit (Quantico, Va.: U.S. Marine Corps University, 1990), 132–35.

S

SABRA AND SHATILLA MASSACRE, 1982. After the 1970 civil war in Jordan, the Palestine Liberation Organization (PLO) relocated to Lebanon, recruiting fighters from Palestinian refugee camps. Its presence altered the balance of power among Lebanon's sects, and in 1975 the PLO was drawn into a civil war against the Maronite community, whose military strength was centered in the Phalangist militia. PLO advances against the Phalangists led to Syrian intervention in 1976 to restore the status quo.

Diplomatic gains by the PLO during 1979–1981 caused concern within Israel's Likud government, headed by Menachem Begin. With his Defense Minister Ariel Sharon he planned to crush the PLO militarily and draw Lebanon into a peace treaty with Israel. On June 6, 1982, the Israeli Defense Force (IDF) invaded Lebanon, bombarding refugee camps in southern Lebanon with heavy artillery before moving against PLO forces in West Beruit. It beseiged West Beruit for two months before the United States intervened with a plan to evacuate PLO fighters from Lebanon. This occurred under the auspices of a multinational force on August 21, sent to oversee the evacuation and protect Palestinian refugees who had been left behind. But the multinational force left by early September, claiming its mission was accomplished.

Lebanon's new president, Bashir Gemayel, was reluctant to rush into a peace treaty with Israel, but on September 12 he agreed to Israel's request that Phalangist forces eliminate the 2,000 "terrorists" who Israelis claimed were still in the refugee camps. On September 14, Gemayel was killed in a powerful explosion at the Phalangist headquarters in East Beruit, it being uncertain who was responsible. A day later, the IDF moved into West Beruit in violation of the evacuation agreement. Sharon authorized entry of what were presumed to be members of Gemayel's Lebanese Forces (a Phalangist milita) and Saad Haddad's South Lebanon Army into the Sabra and Shatilla refugee camps, home to 30,000 Palestinians and some Lebanese. The camps were completely sealed off by Israeli tanks. When the militiamen entered on Thursday evening, September

SABRA AND SHATILLA MASSACRE, 1982

16, the only resistance they encountered was from a few lightly armed young boys.

For the next thirty-eight hours, aided by Israeli flares at night, the militiamen raped, tortured, mutilated, and massacred civilians. IDF personnel, including General Amos Yaron, IDF commander in Beirut, were stationed on the rooftop of a seven-story building 200 meters from Shatilla, with a clear view of the camps below. Also, there were members of the Phalangist intelligence who had radio communication with militiamen on the ground. By Friday morning, evidence that a massacre was taking place was communicated to Israeli Chief of Staff Raphael Eitan, but he approved a request that the Phalangists remain in the camps until 5:00 A.M., Saturday. The militiamen finally left the camps at 8:00 A.M.

The exact number killed is not certain. On September 22, the International Red Cross* gave a figure of 2,400, but the militiamen had buried some bodies before evacuating, and sources among both Phalangists and Palestinians claimed that at least 3,000 people were killed or unaccounted for. Among the dead, none could be identified as members of any PLO military unit.

The massacre* was a wild suspension of law and morality, and the interesting normative questions concern the scope and degree of responsibility. The killers entered the camps at the behest of Israeli officials who were certainly aware of Phalangist hostility toward Palestinians—Phalangists had previously massacred Palestinians when the Tel Az-Zater refugee camp was taken in 1976, and Bashir Gemayel had repeatedly described the Palestinians as "a people too many" in Lebanon. An Israeli commission of inquiry ridiculed the claim that a massacre was not forseen by Israeli officials, especially after Gemayel's assassination*, and concluded that "indirect responsibility" rested on the shoulders of Sharon, Eitan, IDF commanders, Foreign Minister Yitzhak Shamir, and Prime Minister Begin. Presumably, the qualifier "indirect" was based on the assumption that Israeli soldiers did not actually do the killing. Yet, allowing the revenge-seeking Lebanese Forces into the camps under the fiction that they would clean out "terrorists" suggests complicity, if not outright instigation. In other circumstances, those responsible—directly or indirectly—would have been convicted of war crimes*.

But Israel was the victor in the Lebanon war, and memories are often short. Within a few years, Shamir was Israel's Prime Minister, Eitan was a Knesset member, General Yaron was military attaché to the Israeli Embassy in Washington, and Israel's agricultural minister, Ariel Sharon, carried *chutzpah* to remarkable heights in a *New York Times* op-ed piece entitled "It's Past Time to Crush the Terrorist Monster."

See AGGRESSIVE VERSUS DEFENSIVE WAR; COMBATANT-NONCOMBATANT DISTINCTION; FORBIDDEN STRATEGIES; MASSACRES; NATIONALISM.

BIBLIOGRAPHY
Ang, Swee Chai, *From Beruit to Jerusalem* (London: Grafton Books, 1989).
Hirst, David, *The Gun and the Olive Branch,* 2d ed. (London: Faber & Faber, 1984).
Kapeliouk, Amnon, *Sabra and Shatila: Inquiry into a Massacre* (Belmont, Mass.: AAUG Inc., 1984).
Randal, Jonathan, *Going All the Way* (New York: Random House, 1984).
Sharon, Ariel, "It's Past Time to Crush the Terrorist Monster," *New York Times,* September 20, 1986.

Tomis Kapitan

ST. PETERSBURG DECLARATION. In December 1868 at the invitation of the Imperial Cabinet of Russia, an international military commission was gathered "in order to consider the desirability of forbidding the use of certain projectiles in time of war." The intent of the deliberations was to fix "technical limits within which the necessities of war ought to yield to the demands of humanity." The conclusion was prefaced by the following assumptions: (1) the calamities of war should be alleviated as much as possible, (2) the only legitimate aim in war should be to weaken the military force of an enemy with the smallest amount of death and destruction, (3) to accomplish this, the aim should be to disable rather than to kill the enemy, (4) this aim would be exceeded by the use of arms that needlessly aggravate suffering or that make death inevitable, and (5) the employment of such arms would, thus, be contrary to the laws of humanity. The major proposal was expressed in a brief statement: "Therefore, the parties to the Declaration agree to renounce, in case of war, any projectile which weighs less than 400 grams, which is explosive, fulminating or inflammable."

The declaration affirmed that its signatories were bound only in wars between nations that had acceded, and such obligation would cease when any nonsignatory nation joined a signatory as an ally. Seventeen nations were present and became signatories: Great Britain, Austria-Hungary, Bavaria, Belgium, Denmark, France, Greece, Italy, The Netherlands, Persia, Portugal, Prussia and the North German Confederation, Russia, Sweden, Switzerland, Turkey, and Wurttemburg. The United States has still not signed this declaration.

See BULLETS, EXPANDING; FORBIDDEN WEAPONS; INCENDIARIES.
BIBLIOGRAPHY
Friedman, Leon, ed., *The Law of War,* vol. 1 (New York: Random House, 1972), 192.

SEXUAL HARASSMENT. *See* FEMINISM AND WAR; HOMOSEXUALITY; MILITARY TRAINING, BASIC; TAILHOOK; WOMEN IN THE MILITARY.

SHIMODA CASE. The only official attempt to determine the legality of using nuclear weapons was in Japan. On December 7, 1963, the District Court of Tokyo issued its decision on behalf of five Japanese persons who had filed to recover damages from the Japanese government for injuries as a result of the bombings of Hiroshima and Nagasaki*. The claim of the plaintiffs was based on the argument that the dropping of the bombs was a violation of the laws of war*, that the act violated municipal law, that the government of Japan had waived the claims of the plaintiffs by reason of Article 19a of the Treaty of Peace of 1951, and that the government of Japan was, thus, obligated to pay the damages. The Japanese court concluded that the United States had violated international law in dropping the bombs, that the plaintiffs were entitled to damages, and that the government of Japan had blocked such satisfaction in court. Neither side exercised its right to appeal to a higher court. The plaintiffs were satisfied that the United States had been found guilty of a war crime*. The Japanese government, while persuaded that the United States had violated international law, had no intention of paying the damages.

The case rested on the belief that international law forbade the use of gas and noxious chemicals, the deliberate bombing of civilian centers, and the causing of unnecessary suffering when no military necessity* was at stake. The primary argument was that the bombing was unwarranted by any appeal to military necessity. Furthermore, the case rejected the common thesis that the lack of a specific prohibition against the use of atomic weapons meant that their use was legal (see Martens Clause*). The court further rejected the U.S. argument that the bombing speeded the Japanese surrender and thus saved lives. The case also raised the question as to how to treat UN Resolution 1653, which had asserted that the use of nuclear weapons was contrary to the spirit and the letter of the aims of the United Nations.

See FORBIDDEN WEAPONS; HIROSHIMA AND NAGASAKI; MASS DESTRUCTION, WEAPONS OF; NUCLEAR WAR; SURRENDER, UN-CONDITIONAL.

BIBLIOGRAPHY

Falk, Richard A., ''The Shimoda Case: A Legal Appraisal of the Atomic Attacks upon Hiroshima and Nagasaki,'' *American Journal of International Law* (October 1965).

Friedman, Leon, ed., *Laws of War,* vol. 2 (New York: Random House, 1971), 1,688ff.

SHINING PATH (SENDERO LUMINOSO). The movement began in the late 1960s at the National University at San Cristobal of Huamanga in Ayacucho, a colonial-era provincial capital high in the Andes, 230 miles southeast of Lima, Peru. Its founder, Abimael Guzman Reynoso, was a philosophy professor at the National University and a leader in the pro-Chinese faction within Peru's Communist Party. He is called ''President Gonzalo'' by his followers. In 1970 he and his followers took the name of ''Shining Path of José Carlos Mariategul,'' the founder of the Peruvian Communist Party in the 1920s. The aim has been to destroy the existing Peruvian politics and economy with an Indian-based peasant regime inspired, in part, by Mao Tse-tung's* cultural revolution in

China. In rural areas it developed ties with the cocoa growers, whom it claims to protect.

The Shining Path guerrillas* controlled the Upper Huallaga Valley where Peru's cocoa leaf is grown. The Peruvian military was less than enthusiastic about fighting the drug trade from which they profited. In 1978 Sendoro went underground, and on May 17, 1980 launched its first attack on a rural polling station, burning all the ballot boxes. In 1991 it was believed to have up to 5,000 followers, including ethnic Indians as well as middle- and upper-class Peruvian youth. Guzman was distrustful of Soviet and Cuban revisionism, denouncing Deng Xiaoping in favor of the "Gang of Four," calling Fidel Castro a "choir boy," and naming Libya's Muammar el-Qaddafi a "fake." The group enforces a strict moral code banning smoking, drinking, and drug use. Like most national liberation* groups it eschews the need to wear uniforms of identity. Some historians of Sendoro suggest that the recent terrorist* strategy was largely a response to military and police brutality, others claim differently. The group illustrates the difficulties faced in applying laws of war* to those who choose not to be limited by such laws, primarily in the matter of clear identification by uniform.

In April 1992, by a military coup, Peru's twelve-year-old democracy was overthrown and in October 1992 Guzman was captured and sentenced to life in prison. In April 1993, he was transferred to an underground concrete cell at a naval base in Calleo, a port city near Lima. Although the United States would be unlikely to support Guzman, support of the existing military dictator seemed counterproductive, since it would give support to the arguments of Shining Path spokespersons that the United States was on the side of colonialism.

See GUERRILLA WAR; LAWS OF WAR; TERRORISM.

BIBLIOGRAPHY

The Shining Path After Guzman: The Threat and the International Response, Hearing Before the Subcommittee on Western Hemisphere Affairs of the Committee on Foreign Affairs, H.R., 102nd Cong., 2d sess., September 23, 1992 (Washington, D.C.: U.S. Government Printing Office, 1992).

The Threat of the Shining Path to Democracy in Peru, Hearings Before the Subcommittee on Western Hemisphere Affairs of the Committee on Foreign Affairs, H.R., 102nd Cong. 2d sess., March 11 and 12, 1992 (Washington, D.C.: U.S. Government Printing Office, 1992).

SHIPWRECKED SAILORS. On October 20, 1868, the second Red Cross* conference was called in Geneva to extend the same protection for sailors at sea as had been provided for soldiers on land in the Red Cross conventions of August 22, 1864. It was recognized that conflict at sea posed some special problems. Article 6, for example, provided that the passengers and crews of sinking ships should be rescued and that the ships that did this rescue assumed neutral status until they had delivered their victims to a safe port.

On October 18, 1907, The Hague* issued a "Convention for the Adaptation to Maritime Warfare of the Principles of the Geneva Convention of August 22, 1864.'' (Hague 10). The Geneva convention* in question had been issued on July 6, 1906, and provided ''For the Amelioration of the Condition of the Wounded and Sick in Armies in the Field.'' The primary emphasis in The Hague convention was on the treatment of the ''wounded, sick or shipwrecked.'' Hospital ships were to be protected, respected, and not captured for the duration of the war, provided that such ships were not used for any later aggression. Ships that carried the wounded or sick were to be protected from attack until they had delivered their cargo to a neutral port. While signatories could denounce the convention, such denunciation could not take effect for one year. Also on October 18, 1907, The Hague issued Hague 11, ''Restrictions with Regard to the Right of Capture in Naval War.'' It attempted to harmonize certain conflicting practices among nations with respect to peaceful commerce. It urged the inviolability of the postal service, the right of fishing, and the protection of vessels on religious, scientific, or philanthropic missions. It urged that the crews of merchant ships not be made prisoners of war*, provided that they supplied a written promise not to serve on an enemy ship while the war lasted. The United States was not a signatory. Also on October 18, 1907, Hague 13 was issued, entitled ''Rights and Duties of Neutral Powers in Naval War.'' Although the United States was not a signatory, the Senate consented to ratify it on April 17, 1908, provided that Article 23 was deleted. Article 23 provided that a neutral power may allow prize ships to enter its ports and sequester them pending a decision of a prize court.

On February 6, 1922, in Washington, D.C., a ''Treaty in Relation to the Use of Submarines and Noxious Gases in Warfare'' was issued. Nine nations, including the United States, were signatories. The treaty emphasized that merchant ships must give permission to be searched before such search can be undertaken, that such ships must not be attacked unless they refuse such search, and if attacked, the attacker must not destroy the ship until the crew and passengers have first been placed in safety. Since submarines were unable to comply with these rules, the treaty merely urged that submarines not be used as ''commerce destroyers.'' The same principle was affirmed in a *Proces-Verbal,* ''Relating to the Rules of Submarine Warfare,'' in London, November 6, 1936.

On August 12, 1949, Geneva Convention 2* for the ''Amelioration of Wounded, Sick and Shipwrecked Members of the Armed Forces at Sea,'' was issued. It asserted that sailors or parachutists* who had landed in the sea were to be rescued. The sick or wounded were to be cared for, and the ship that did so was to be assured hospital status. Article 15 noted, for example, that once a ship took sick or wounded aboard it could take no further part in the operations of war, and Article 16 stated that once such a prisoner was returned to his home, he could take no further part in that war for its duration. Article 18 required that the belligerent search for and rescue all shipwrecked sailors. Article 28 provided that, should fighting occur on a warship, the sick bays on that ship were to be ''protected.'' Article 62 provided that any party may denounce the convention, but it may not do so during a conflict. The United States ratified this convention, with reservations, on July 6, 1955. All further requirements concerning the care of prisoners followed those for land warfare. All restrictions concerning strategies and weapons were drawn from the appropriate Army manual, which is currently *The Law of Land Warfare** (1956 with the 1976 revisions).

See GENEVA CONVENTION, 1868, 1906; HAGUE, THE, CONGRESSES; LAWS OF WAR; MINES; TORPEDOES.

BIBLIOGRAPHY

"Convention for the Amelioration of the Condition of Wounded, Sick, and Shipwrecked Members of the Armed Forces at Sea," in Burns H. Weston, Richard A. Falk, and Anthony D'Amato, eds., *Basic Documents in International Law and World Order* (St. Paul, Minn.: West Publishing Company, 1980), 105–9.

Friedman, Leon, ed., *The Laws of War,* vol. 1 (New York: Random House, 1971).

Treaties Governing Land Warfare, Department of the Army Pamphlet 27-1 (Washington, D.C.: Department of the Army, December 1956).

SIEGE WARFARE. Now recognized to be one of the oldest forms of total war. In battlefield warfare sharp distinctions are made between professional soldiers/warriors and the civilian population. In siege the lives of civilians and their willingness to resist become the central target. In earlier centuries sieges were directed at fortified cities, or at the castles of local nobility, or at fortresses built by invaders to protect their occupying troops. If siege threatened, inhabitants and supplies from the surrounding countryside were gathered inside the fortifications, and the attacking army took up positions outside the walls. By tradition, formal declaration of the onset of siege was signalled by the firing of a shell or missile. The weapons of choice for the defender were dense defensive structures—the fortress walls of ancient times and the coastal bunkers and antiaircraft guns of the modern era—combined with monitoring of the periphery. Thick and high stone walls were manned by people whose tasks were first to keep vigil for signs of attempts to break in, for example by using tunnels and ladders, and secondly to use, sparingly, the arrows, rocks, and other weapons that drove back the would-be attackers. The weapons of choice for attackers were human subterfuge—spies* and ruses* for finding ways to breach the walls, and projectiles—artillery and missiles—that could deliver explosives and fire within the fortifications. The first rockets were designed centuries ago in medieval China for use in siege warfare. A famous case of subterfuge is what we call the Trojan Horse, the wooden horse built by the Greeks, that allowed them to get inside the walls of Troy.

In Europe, stone fortresses lost their value as defensive structures only with the modernization of artillery technology in the late 18th century. By the late 19th century, in a modern manifestation of siege, it became feasible to try to cut off an entire nation from raw materials and access to export markets, using the large-scale naval blockade. The embargo, enforced by military means, has been used with some frequency in this century. It is an ideal strategy for nations wishing to take collaborative action, without exacting excessive costs on any among their allies. The suffering imposed on the civilians of the embargoed nation is not easily measured, because governments on neither side in the conflict have any interest in making such suffering evident. Often such embargoes come to an end, as did the sieges in medieval times, without the use of any explosive force. A settlement can be imposed on a nation starved of resources, or trade begins to find ways around the embargo, and those who imposed it withdraw their demands. Even in this modified form, the embargo contains within it one of the key ingredients of total war—it makes no distinction between civilian and soldier, attacking all indiscriminately.

Defense against siege depended on imposing a rationing system to extend resources as long as possible, the distribution system being designed first to protect the lives of the soldiers, and only secondarily to protect civilians. Defenders also had to block attempts by the besiegers to breach the fortifications, attacking those who got near to or crossed the walls, and rebuilding where there had been physical damage to the defenses. Those pressing the siege had their strategy shaped by the same two key factors—the extent of the resources inside, and the challenge of when and how to breach the walls. Besieging armies faced a choice between the boredom of waiting until those inside were exhausted (and it was known to be hard to keep those waiting from deserting), and attempting a breach, which put troops at the risk of dangerous attacks from well-protected defensive forces. In medieval times European garrison troops threatened any who had the temerity to come too close with archers' bows, and with boiling oil poured down from the ramparts. Attacker and defender shared an interest in preventing those inside the walls from leaving. Attackers kept the population inside as long as possible to maximize the drain on the resources, and to increase the chances that suffering might cause dissent among the defenders, forcing their surrender. Defenders kept the population intact, despite the resultant resource drain, because community solidarity was central to the capacity to resist. These questions arise also in modern forms of siege. During World War II, though some English children were evacuated across the Atlantic, most went no farther than rural areas and the adult population of London prided itself on its willingness to withstand the fears and privations of the bombing.

For the duration of the siege the two armies were kept apart physically, and ethical choices revolved around how to keep morale high and prevent desertions. Cities sometimes would beg that civilians be allowed to leave, and there are tales of atrocities towards those leaving, though there are also tales of chivalry and compassion. Fortresses faced, finally, a choice between surrender on terms, or defeat by storm. The classic sign of surrender was the transfer of the keys of the city. Surrender negotiations would determine how long residents would have to pack, and how much they could take as they left. Negotiations settled whether a ransom must be paid. At times the garrison would arrange surrender terms for itself, leaving the civilian population liable to attack by storm. Once an attacking army had wrought enough damage to fatally weaken the fortress, it could demand a surrender *en règle* (in accordance with rules of procedure, including protection of those who surrendered from capricious actions). If the demand was refused, then those attacking were under no further obligation to protect lives and possessions, after a successful assault. At that juncture the besieged citizens could be taken into slavery, city women knew they had no protection at all, and the attacking soldiers were rewarded by being given the right to loot. Rape and pillage*, with no quarter* given, were commonly wrought against those whose cities were overthrown by siege and assault. Moslem armies were normally allowed only three days of looting and pillage. Troops from European nations had less fixed rules, though even they were let loose only after a limit had been set.

For Europeans, the oldest story of siege warfare is Homer's narrative of Troy, described in *The Iliad* (c. 850 B.C.) While not confirmed directly by archaeological evidence, the events described exemplify the characteristics of a classic siege: (1) the war was long and drawn-out, not a battle completed within a few days, but rather a struggle that lasted years; (2) at times the Greeks were weakened by their unwillingness to stay away from home any longer, at others the Trojans were weakened by shortage of reserves and resources, and by the desertion of their allies; (3) victory came, finally, from subterfuge—the infiltration of the horse—not from a simple assault on the walls; and (4) the city was leveled and much of the population massacred*, or taken into slavery. While Homer's narrative concentrates primarily on the men in both camps, plays about the same events, written by Aeschylus (525–456 B.C.) and Euripides (484–406 B.C.), give a prominent place to the impact of the siege on the women. Siege, because it is total war and because it occurs around and in the midst of communities and settlements, demands of women resilience and courage comparable to what it demands of men. The Crusades, which took place between the 11th and 14th centuries, pitted European invaders against Egyptians and Turks in the Eastern Mediterranean. Europeans, claiming the right to ''protect'' their Holy City, attacked numerous cities on the route between Constantinople and Jerusalem. One of the most famous sieges, at Acre, lasted from 1189 until 1191, prolonged in part by tensions among the different besieging forces. There were nine crusades in all and, in addition to their other legacies, they left behind numerous crusader castles, visible in the Middle East to this day. The Crusader knights built fortresses as a means of protecting their occupying forces from the hostile native population. The castles of Edward I in Wales served a similar function.

The attack on Atlanta lasted for the month of August, 1864. General Hood, retreating with his Southern troops under an unrelenting attack from General Sherman, managed to hold off the Unionists for a month. As in many a classic siege, Hood used the city to protect his army, and the strategy worked until Sherman cut their lines of communication. Hood's Confederates slipped out of Atlanta on September 1, surviving to fight for another three months. On September 2, Sherman's troops took Atlanta, and wrought just the kind of destruction suffered by cities that are punished for having shielded an army. The devastating fires and human catastrophes were made unforgettable by Margaret Mitchell in *Gone with the Wind*, published in 1936. World War II saw examples of old-style city siege at Leningrad, and also examples of the kind of siege now much more commonplace—attack on an entire nation, in this case, Britain. Leningrad was besieged for 900 days. The Nazis cut off the city in August 1941, though at times there reopened, briefly, a perilous route to the east. The encirclement was combined with bombardment; the population was locked in and threatened almost daily, and yet the surrounding troops were unable to bring about a surrender. Narratives of the period detail the lengths to which the city-dwellers were willing to go, eating only a little, and only occasionally, enduring severe shortages of heat in the Russian winter, and a lack of medical supplies, staying to fight on even when they had a chance to leave. The Nazis finally abandoned their siege in January 1944.

The Germans employed three different kinds of siege strategy against Britain. The Battle of Britain (August–October 1940), resembled an attempt to scale the walls of a fortress, using aircraft, and it failed because a combination of early warning systems, antiaircraft gunners, and RAF planes turned back those German fliers who, breaching the walls, managed to cross the Channel. The Battle of the Atlantic, waged by German submarine forces against supply ships crossing the Atlantic, was an attempt to embargo Britain. Lastly, the strategic bombing campaigns, first the Blitz and then, at the end of the war, the V1 and V2 rocket attacks, were attempts to weaken the infrastructure of "fortress Britain" so that its citizens could no longer summon the will to resist.

The war by the allied United Nations forces against Iraq* began in 1990 with the imposition of a total embargo, enforced by military means, on all traffic (except fleeing foreign nationals) in and out of Iraq. Imposed in September 1990, the embargo was the first strategy employed to persuade Iraq to restore Kuwaiti sovereignty. The Iraqi forces deployed in Kuwait and southern Iraq had adopted positions equivalent to fortress defenses, but Iraq quickly agreed to withdraw from Kuwait after those lines were devastated by a frontal assault by allied forces. The explosive combat lasted less than six weeks in the winter of 1991, but the embargo remained in effect for years, while the UN led a program to search out and destroy remaining Iraqi weapons of mass destruction*. The searching of vessels at sea by the U.S. military only ended in August 1994, and even then the embargo remained in effect on all but the transport of food and medical supplies.

See COMBATANT-NONCOMBATANT DISTINCTION; HUMANITARIAN INTERVENTION; INNOCENTS; MASSACRES; TOTAL WAR.

BIBLIOGRAPHY

Duffy, Christopher, *Siege Warfare* (London: Routledge & Kegan Paul, 1979, 1985).

Meyer-Knapp, Helena, *Nuclear Siege to Nuclear Ceasefire* (Ann Arbor, Mich.: University of Michigan Press, 1990).

Watson, Bruce Allen, *Sieges: A Comparative Study* (Westport, Conn.: Praeger, 1993).
Helena Meyer-Knapp

SON MY/MY LAI. Volume 1, Chapter 12, of the Findings and Recommendations of the Peers Commission Report stated:

During the period 16–19 March 1968, US Army troops of [Task Force] TF Barker, 11th Brigade, Americal Division, massacred a large number of noncombatants in two hamlets of Son My Village, Quang Ngai Province, Republic of Vietnam. The precise number of Vietnamese killed cannot be determined but was at least 175 and may exceed 400.

General William C. Westmoreland had sent a message to the troops stating: "Congratulations to officers and men of C-1-20 for outstanding action." This action was first brought to light in a letter written March 29, 1969, to the Secretary of the Army and the Chief of Staff by Ronald L. Ridenhour, a Vietnam veteran, in which he presented evidence that he had gathered on his own that "something very black indeed" had occurred in what was called the village of "Pinkville" (My Lai). On April 23, the case was officially given to the inspector general with instructions to make a full investigation. On August 4, General Westmoreland ordered the inspector general to turn the matter over to the Criminal Investigation Division for investigation. On November 13, the first brief story by Seymour Hersh was printed in thirty newspapers, and on November 20, a second story with eyewitness accounts and black-and-white photographs appeared. On November 24, Westmoreland ordered Lieutenant General William R. Peers to conduct an inquiry. On December 13, Secretary of Defense Melvin R. Laird announced that any present or former serviceman discovered to have had any role in the killing at My Lai would be brought to trial.

A joint memorandum of November 26, 1969, from the secretary of the Army and the chief of staff, U.S. Army, directed Peers to find the answers to two questions: (1) were the Army investigations to date adequate? and (2) had there been a suppression or withholding of material information by persons involved? Peers conducted the investigation with a committee of over ninety staff members, and submitted a four-volume report to the secretary of the Army and the chief of staff on March 14, 1970. This report was kept secret for more than four years until November 1974, when the secretary of the Army authorized publication of Volumes 1 and 3. The report listed thirty individuals who were involved in criminal omissions and commissions, but by the time the report was published, only Lieutenant William Calley had been held to full account. The cases against twelve of the thirty were dismissed before trial. Charges were also brought against an additional nine persons not listed in the report. The report attributed military training* deficiencies as a cause for what the soldiers had done, a matter that remained to be corrected, and found that the Army investigation had been woefully inadequate.

The Peers Report considered what it named to be the significant factors that contributed to the My Lai tragedy. These included, but were not limited to, the following: (1) The orders issued to T.F. Barker were vague, failed to emphasize the combatant-noncombatant distinction*, and left the impression that the attack would be only on soldiers. (2) T.F. Barker had some men who had been "law violators and hoodlums in civilian life." Added to this was the general practice of referring to the Vietnamese as "gooks" or "slants" as if they were not quite human. The report referred to this as a "dangerously permissive attitude." (3) The casualties* suffered in previous battles from mines* and boobytraps and the fact that they had not encountered identifiable enemy forces had affected morale and had led to frustration and the wish to kill. Previous battles had resulted in a very low ratio of captured weapons to persons killed (1 for every 10 slain). The fact that the ratio at My Lai was 1 for every 40 slain should have prompted some questions. (4) Many soldiers testified that competition existed between groups as to who could bring in the largest casualty list, and many felt that they were being ordered to take no prisoners (*see* Quarter, No, Wars of) and to leave no one alive. (5) T.F. Barker had a lack of sufficient staff and a lack of any clear executive officer. (6) Lieutenant Colonel Frank A. Barker, Jr. did not have a close relationship with his company commanders, leading to a void in communication. (7) It was general policy to consider the area as a free fire zone. This meant in simple language that everyone in the area could be killed. (8) The soldiers believed it to be a "hotbed" of enemy strength. The Peers Report summed up with the comment:

It became apparent that if on the day before the Son My operation only one of the leaders at platoon, company, task force, or brigade level had foreseen and voiced an objection to the prospect of killing noncombatants, or had mentioned the problem of noncombatants in their preoperational orders and instructions, or if adequate restraining orders had been issued early on the following day, the Son My tragedy might have been averted altogether.

Attached as an enclosure to the findings was a list of thirty persons who knew of the My Lai massacre and who, in one way or other, failed to make any official report. The list included two Generals, four Colonels, two Lieutenant Colonels, three Majors, eight Captains, one First Lieutenant, five Second Lieutenants, one Sergeant, and one SP 5. Included in the list was one chaplain. The only person tried and found guilty was Lieutenant William Calley. He was convicted on March 29, 1971, and sentenced to life imprisonment on March 31, although the sentence was reduced to twenty years by the Third Army commander on August 20. On February 16, 1973, the Court of Military Review upheld the twenty-year sentence, and on December 21, 1973, the Court of Military Appeals upheld the conviction. On April 16, 1974, Secretary of War Howard H. Callaway reduced the sentence to ten years. On September 29, 1974, the conviction was overturned by District Judge Elliott, and on November 9, 1974, Calley was released on bond. On September 10, 1975, the U.S. Court of Appeals for the Fifth Circuit reversed the decision of District Judge Elliott, but since so few days remained of the original sentence, Calley was set free on parole.

See CRIMES AGAINST HUMANITY; FORBIDDEN STRATEGIES; FORBIDDEN WEAPONS; MILITARY JARGON; MILITARY TRAINING, BASIC; PROPAGANDA; VIETNAM WAR; WAR CRIMES; WINTER SOLDIER INVESTIGATION.

BIBLIOGRAPHY

Court Martial Reports, Holdings and Decisions of the Courts of Military Review and the United States Court of Military Appeals, vol. 46 (1971–1973), 1138.

Goldstein, Joseph, Burke Marshall, and Jack Schwartz, eds., *The My Lai Cover-Up: Beyond the Reach of the Law, The Peers Commission Report* (New York: Free Press, 1976).

Hammer, Richard, *The Court-Martial of Lt. Calley* (New York: Coward, McCann & Geoghegan, 1971).

Melman, Seymour, ed., *In the Name of America* (Annandale, Va.: Turnpike Press, 1968).

Sack, John, *Lieutenant Calley: His Own Story* (New York: Viking, 1970).

SPANISH-AMERICAN WAR. *See GENERAL ORDERS 100;* PHILIPPINES WAR CRIMES TRIALS.

SPIES. The traditionally negative attitude toward spies arose in part out of the age of chivalry, when knights eschewed those who worked by stealth. As late as the 19th century, German philosopher Johann G. Fichte (1762–1814) condemned the use of snipers who fired on their opponents from secret hiding places. Spies were commonly used during the American Civil War, and although the use of spies was considered legitimate, the punishment for captured spies was worse than for conventional soldiers in order to deter the practice. *General Orders 100** portrayed the spy as without redeeming qualities, and spies were punishable by hanging, whether or not they had been successful. The exchange of spies was different from that of ordinary prisoners. *Rules of Land Warfare* (1914)* defined the spy as one who acted clandestinely and in a disguise; however, soldiers in uniform were not spies, even if clandestine. No change appeared in the 1934 and the 1956 versions of the Army manual. The current U.S. Army manual, *The Law of Land Warfare,* notes the ambiguities implicit in determining when a person is "lurking" about a place significantly enough to be considered a threat to national security. A spy is defined as a person who secretly, in disguise or under false pretense, seeks information with the intention of communicating it to the enemy. The manual affirms that The Hague* convention considered the use of spies to be legal. The operations of military intelligence make it evident that the practice of spying has official sanction, and is now referred to as legal, though covert, intelligence activity.

See FORBIDDEN STRATEGIES; INTELLIGENCE AGENCIES, U.S.; PRISONERS OF WAR.

BIBLIOGRAPHY
Bakeless, John, *Spies of the Confederacy* (New York: J. B. Lippincott, 1970).
Singer, Kurt, and Jane Sherrod, *Spies for Democracy* (Minneapolis, Minn.: T. S. Denison, 1960).

STOCKHOLM/ROTHSKILDE WAR CRIMES TRIALS. The distinguished historian of war, Quincy Wright, considered that six questions needed to be answered before the Vietnam War* could be put in legal or moral perspective: (1) Was the war a civil war such that the United States was guilty of aggression in its invasion? (2) Did the proposed elections of 1965 (the Geneva Accords) intend an election with no prerequisite that there be conditions favorable to a free election? (3) Was the North an aggressor? (4) Did the Gulf of Tonkin* resolution of Congress of August 1, 1964, authorize the president to send troops? (5) Did the United States have legal commitments to come to the aid of South Vietnam? (6) Were the U.S. reprisals against the North in violation of international law? Wright concluded that none of the American presumptions was valid. General Telford Taylor pointed out in his *Nuremberg and Vietnam: An American Tragedy* that the Vietnam War symbolized the difficulty of identifying laws of war*, crimes of war*, or crimes against the peace*. Vietnam illustrated the gulf between what military policy permitted and what Nuremberg* had forbidden. It showed, also, what moral crises are created when a war of ideology is undertaken, and it revealed that even a democratic country like America could be led astray by moral crusaders.

In the text of one of the reports of the Fulbright Committee on Foreign Relations, with regard to the massive bombing of North Vietnam, Robert Biles observed that the objectives the United States gave for the bombing included: to make North Vietnam pay a high price for supporting the war, to break the will of North Vietnam, and to raise American and South Vietnamese morale. These ends required using civilians as hostages*. The committee noted that none of the U.S. aims was ever accomplished, and that the results were the needless killing of great numbers of North Vietnamese civilians, the loss of many American lives, and a serious loss of the moral standing of America in the world. American war strategies in Vietnam were given ambiguous titles, such as "Search and Destroy," the "Phoenix Program," and "harassment and interdiction," which concealed the fact that they were designed to make deliberate and indiscriminate war on civilians.

Two unofficial trials were conducted in an effort to assign blame for the U.S. role in Vietnam. The Democratic Republic of North Vietnam (DRVN) conducted a commission for the investigation of "U.S. Imperialist War Crimes in Vietnam." Since the commission was from North Vietnam it was in no legal position to get those it charged before its court. The other, more famous, of these unofficial efforts were the trials conducted in Stockholm, Sweden and Rothskilde, Denmark, initiated by two philosophers, Bertrand Russell of Great Britain and Jean-Paul Sartre of France. Initial efforts were made to hold the trials in Great Britain or France, but neither country would allow visas for those who needed to come. By invitation, the first hearings were conducted in Stockholm.

The hearings considered two questions: (1) Did the United States, Australia, New Zealand, and South Korea commit acts of international aggression according to international law? and (2) Had there been bombardments of targets of a purely civilian nature, and on what scale did these bombings occur? In support of the contention that the four nations had participated in prohibited acts of war, the tribunal followed the precedent of Nuremberg and cited the following kinds of evidence: (1) the Paris Peace Pact* had outlawed war, (2) Article 2 of the UN Charter had reaffirmed the Paris Pact, (3) Article 6 of the Nuremberg charter identified aggressive war* as in violation of treaties, (4) the UN resolution of December 1960 obligated members not to wage aggressive war, and (5) the Geneva Accords had forbidden any invasion of Vietnam by American troops.

Utilizing these documents as the bases for crimes against the peace*, the Stockholm tribunal ruled unanimously that the United States had been guilty of aggressive war. With respect to the charge that the United States had waged deliberate war against civilians, the tribunal appealed to The Hague* convention of October 18, 1907, which had established, sufficiently for use at Nuremberg, that belligerents did not have unlimited choice of the means to injure the enemy. Article 23 of that convention had prohibited weapons that caused "unnecessary suffering." Article 25 forbade attacks on undefended towns, and Article 27 forbade the bombardment of hospitals, churches, schools, museums, and historical monuments. The tribunal also cited Article 6 of the statutes of the Nuremberg tribunal, which had classified the bombing of civilian targets as a crime, as had Article 18 of the Geneva convention (1949). The Stockholm tribunal even cited the U.S. Army manual, *The Law of Land Warfare** in its support. Based on the testimony at the trials all four nations, by unanimous decision, were found guilty as charged.

From November 30 through December 1, 1967, the tribunal met in Rothskilde, Denmark. At these second sessions the tribunal considered the following charges: (1) Japan, Thailand, and the Philippines had been accomplices in the acts of aggression committed by the United States, (2) weapons were used that were forbidden by the laws of war, (3) prisoners of war* were maltreated, (4) the war was illegally extended into Laos, and (5) the charge of genocide* could be leveled against the United States as far as the aim of killing Communists was concerned. In its verdict, the tribunal concluded unanimously that the governments of Thailand and the Philippines were guilty as charged. The government of Japan was ruled guilty of complicity by a vote of 8 to 3, and the United States was ruled guilty of genocide, crimes against humanity, the use of forbidden weapons*, and the maltreatment of prisoners of war by a unanimous vote.

See AERIAL WARFARE; FORBIDDEN STRATEGIES; FORBIDDEN WEAPONS; MILITARY JARGON; PROPAGANDA; SON MY/MY LAI; VIETNAM WAR; WINTER SOLDIER INVESTIGATION.

BIBLIOGRAPHY
"Bombing as a Policy Tool in Vietnam Effectiveness," a staff study based on the Pentagon Papers, prepared for the U.S. Senate Committee on Foreign Relations, Study 5 (October 12, 1972), 1.
Citizens Committee of Inquiry, *The Dellums Committee Hearings on War Crimes in Vietnam* (New York: Random House, 1972).
Cookson, John, and Judith Nottingham, *A Survey of Chemical and Biological Warfare* (London: Sheed and Ward, 1969).
Duffett, John, ed., *Against the Crime of Silence: Proceedings of the International War Crimes Tribunal* (New York: Simon & Schuster, 1968).
Thomas, Ann Van Wynen, and A. J. Thomas, Jr., *Legal Limits on the Use of Chemical and Biological Weapons* (Dallas, Tex.: Southern Methodist University Press, 1970).

STRATEGIC DEFENSE INITIATIVE (SDI). The name given in 1983 by the Reagan administration to the research and development effort to examine the feasibility of defending the United States against an attack by ballistic missiles armed with nuclear warheads. The United States has done research and development of technologies relevant to defense against ballistic missiles since the late 1950s but the names and emphasis given to this effort have varied. The original name of ballistic missile defense (BMD) was replaced by antiballistic missiles (ABM) in the late 1960s. The Reagan administration gave missile defense research a high priority and renamed the program, but SDI became popularly known as Star Wars because the exotic, space-based weaponry envisioned resembled that in the *Star Wars* films. In May 1993, Secretary of Defense Les Aspin announced that the organization responsible for this effort would have its name changed from the Strategic Defense Initiative Organization (SDIO) to the Ballistic Missile Defense Organization (BMDO).

Evaluation of defenses against ballistic missiles armed with nuclear warheads involves strategic, scientific, technological, and political, as well as ethical considerations. No one has experience with a large-scale nuclear war*, but the enormous destructive potential of the thousands of currently deployed nuclear weapons implies that any defense would need to be nearly perfect to prevent unprecedented destruction. Imperfect defenses could, however, be very useful against a small-scale attack such as an accidental* or unauthorized launch of a few missiles. Therefore, it is important to keep in mind what capabilities the defense system is intended to have. The strategic considerations involve assessments of the capabilities of missiles deployed by potential adversaries and of the evolution of weapons development. The political considerations involve judgments of the intentions of potential adversaries and of the likely effectiveness of political and diplomatic means of reducing the threat of attack. Scientific and technological assessments of technologies that might contribute to a defense and to offensive countermeasures are important in estimating the capabilities and cost of a defense system.

The emphasis given to missile defense by the United States has been influ-

enced by scientific and technological developments and by the perceived threat
from the Soviet Union. Work to try to upgrade antiaircraft missiles to ABM
missiles began in the late 1950s, when relations between the United States and
the Soviet Union were very contentious. The 1962 Cuban Missile Crisis* emphasized how vulnerable the United States was to a missile attack. By the late
1960s, missile defense had developed to the point that the United States proposed to deploy a defense. The ensuing debate about whether and what type of
defense to deploy was commonly known as the ABM debate.

The substantial opposition from scientists to the ABM system developed in
the late 1960s was based on technical judgments about its likely ineffectiveness
and the destabilizing effects of countermeasures to it. There was also considerable public opposition when it became apparent that defending cities would
involve placing nuclear-armed ABM interceptors in the suburbs. ABM proponents emphasized the Communist threat and argued that any ABM defense was
better than no defense. ABM defense was also promoted by private corporations
and government labs working on relevant technologies. As it became clear that
an ABM system could not protect the U.S. population from a large-scale Soviet
attack, ABM proponents changed the emphasis to defending against a small-
scale attack from China. In 1969, the Nixon administration announced the Safeguard ABM system, which was intended to protect missiles that could be used
to retaliate against an attacker. The Safeguard system barely passed the U.S.
Senate on a 50-50 vote, with Vice-President Spiro Agnew casting the tie-
breaking vote. This system was deployed in Grand Forks, North Dakota but was
deactivated in 1976.

Another factor that influenced decisions about ABM systems was the Nixon
administration's detente policy toward the Soviet Union. Two products of detente were the SALT I and ABM treaties signed in 1972. These treaties attempted to limit the nuclear arms race by limiting both the number of offensive
weapons and ABM defenses. The rationale for limiting defenses was that it
would not be possible to limit offensive weapons if ABM defenses were being
deployed, because such defenses could be overcome by increasing offensive
capability.

By the early 1980s, hopes for detente had faded. There was growing distrust
of the Soviet Union, which was characterized as the "Evil Empire" in anti-
Communist rhetoric. In addition, the SALT treaties had clearly failed to limit
the number of offensive nuclear weapons. The Reagan administration argued
that the arms control process that produced the SALT and ABM treaties had
put the United States at a disadvantage and, in any case, that the Soviets were
violating these treaties. Its strident anti-Soviet rhetoric and the renewed offensive
arms race alarmed many people and was an important impetus for the nuclear
freeze movement. The Reagan administration's response to the nuclear freeze
movement was the surprising announcement at the end of Reagan's March 23,
1983, speech that it was initiating a high-profile effort on missile defense intended to render nuclear weapons "impotent and obsolete."

The SDI program was enthusiastically welcomed by long-time proponents of missile defense, but generated enormous controversy from its inception. Over $30 billion was spent on SDI from 1983 to 1993, but important questions remained about what technologies could and should be used and what the goal of the defensive system should be. There was also a continuing controversy about ABM treaty constraints on missile defense research. The end of the Cold War* and the disintegration of the Soviet Union have changed the strategic situation profoundly. The 1993 reorientation of missile defense research and development toward defenses against shorter-range, nonnuclear missiles such as the Scuds used by Iraq in the 1991 Gulf War reduced the attention on strategic missile defense, without producing a consensus on how to proceed.

Proponents of missile defense often argue that the only way to decide whether defense is worthwhile is to build the best defense one can and see how well it works. Critics respond that it is not possible to test the defense under conditions that realistically simulate a large-scale nuclear attack. Furthermore, one cannot assume that the offensive threat is static; a determined adversary would try to develop countermeasures to whatever defense is developed. Nuclear weapons could also be delivered by cruise missiles or other means against which the defense is ineffective. Another complication is that the decision to engage scientific and technical resources to develop missile defenses may preclude other technological initiatives that might be more productive and may also doom political and diplomatic efforts to reduce nuclear arsenals.

Ethical issues associated with development of missile defenses involve not only the desired goal but also the likely effects of a large-scale research and development effort on defenses. An ideal missile defense, in which defensive weapons destroy only missiles and do not harm people, is very appealing on ethical grounds. President Reagan's March 23, 1983, speech illustrated this appeal by posing the rhetorical question. ''What if free people could live secure in the knowledge that their security did not rest upon the threat of instant U.S. retaliation to deter a Soviet attack; that we could intercept and destroy strategic ballistic missiles before they reached our own soil or that of our allies?'' Unfortunately, it is difficult, if not impossible, to develop technologies that could allow such an ideal defense to prevent unprecedented death and destruction from a large-scale nuclear attack. In thirty years of offense-defense arms competition, neither the United States nor the Soviet Union ever had sufficient confidence in a defensive system to abandon offensive weapons and just rely on defense. The ethical dilemmas posed by the development of a realistic defensive system are considerable. Simultaneous development of a defensive system along with a substantial offensive capability is likely to be regarded as threatening by a potential adversary. Despite the best intentions, there would be a great temptation in a crisis to use offensive weapons first so that the defensive system would have fewer weapons to deal with. Furthermore, defensive weapons capable of destroying nuclear-armed missiles at long range would themselves have some offensive capability—at least against an opponent's satellites.

A related ethical issue is whether there are better ways to reduce the threat of nuclear attack and better uses for scientific and technological resources than trying to develop missile defense. Missile defense proponents are generally skeptical of political and diplomatic means of dealing with potential adversaries and prefer to rely on weapons technologies (offensive as well as defensive); opponents are equally skeptical of technological solutions and tend to prefer political solutions such as arms control and disarmament. The pitfalls of relying on political and diplomatic means are commonly recognized, but there are as serious, if more obscure, problems with relying only on technology. Developing a missile defense system also involves investigating possible countermeasures to it, so the effort to develop a defense could produce even more threatening offensive weapons. For example, multiple-warhead missiles and antisatellite weapons were developed in part as countermeasures to potential missile defenses and are generally viewed as adding instability to the nuclear arms race. Thus, the commitment to technological solutions may lead to an endless offense-defense weapons technology competition. At the least, one needs to consider whether there are better uses for scientific and technological resources.

Scientists and engineers involved in developing weapons technologies face other ethical dilemmas. Because most of the details of this work are secret (even from members of Congress), people in the program are responsible for evaluating the progress and promise of various technologies. Can these people provide honest evaluations of the technologies they are trying to develop? Charges have been made that some reports of progress in the SDI program were intentionally deceptive. One example that attracted considerable attention involved exaggerated claims of progress with the X-ray laser being developed at Lawrence Livermore Laboratory. Another was revealed in the August 18, 1993, *New York Times* report of charges by former Reagan administration officials that one much-publicized test in 1984 had been rigged and that other data had been faked to deceive the Soviet Union. Apparently, the deception also misled the U.S. Congress. The people who made the charges spoke on condition that they not be identified. This makes it difficult to determine the validity of the charges and illustrates how difficult it is to identify ethical misconduct in the program.

It is uncertain how missile defense research will proceed in the future. Many people expect that this effort will dwindle now that the Cold War is over. However, in 1993 the Army began the Strategic Target System program to launch strategic missile defense test objects from the island of Kauai in Hawaii and was still planning for increased testing at the ABM test range at Kwajalein Atoll in the Marshall Islands. The Department of Defense October 1993 Bottom-Up Review recommended spending $18 billion from 1995 to 1999. It may be left to historians to judge whether SDI fulfilled President Reagan's ''vision of the future which offers hope'' or was another example of what Freeman Dyson characterized as ''technical follies'' associated with weapons development.

See ANTIBALLISTIC MISSILES/STAR WARS; ACCIDENTAL NU-
CLEAR WAR; CIVIL DEFENSE; COLLATERAL DAMAGE; COUNTER-

FORCE VERSUS COUNTERVALUE; FIRST STRIKE/SECOND STRIKE; MASS DESTRUCTION, WEAPONS OF; MUTUAL ASSURED DESTRUCTION (MAD); NUCLEAR PROLIFERATION.

BIBLIOGRAPHY
Boffey, Phillip M., William J. Broad, Leslie H. Gelb, Charles Mohr, and Holcomb B. Noble, *Claiming the Heavens* (New York: Times Books, 1988).
Dyson, Freeman, *Weapons and Hope* (New York: Harper & Row, 1984).
Lakoff, Sanford, and Herbert F. York, *A Shield In Space?* (Berkeley: University of California Press, 1989).
National Academy of Sciences, *Nuclear Arms Control: Background and Issues* (Washington, D.C.: National Academy Press, 1985).
Patel, C. Kumar N., and Nicolaas Bloembergen, "Strategic Defense and Directed-Energy Weapons," *Scientific American* (September 1987), 39–45.
Porro, Jeffrey, ed., *The Nuclear Age Reader* (New York: Alfred Knopf, 1988).
U.S. Congress, Office of Technology Assessment, *Directed Energy Missile Defense in Space: A Background Paper,* OTA-BP-ISC-26 (Washington, D.C.: U.S. Government Printing Office, 1984).
———, *Ballistic Missile Defense Technologies,* OTA-ISC-254 (Washington, D.C.: U.S. Government Printing Office, 1985).
———, *SDI: Technology, Survivability, and Software,* OTA-ISC-353 (Washington, D.C.: U.S. Government Printing Office, 1988).

Michael D. Jones

SUAREZ, FRANCISCO (1548–1617). A Spanish Jesuit theologian and philosopher, a strong supporter of the philosophy of Thomas Aquinas, and a member of the naturalist school who sought for principles of justice in natural law. He was a professor at universities in Segovia, Valladolid, Rome, Alcala, and Salamanca. Like Franciscus de Victoria* (1486–1546), Samuel von Pufendorff (1632–1694), Christian Wolff (1679–1754), and Emmerich Vattel* (1714–1767), he spoke of defensive wars of a preventive nature, a precursor of the modern notion of first strike* capability. Suarez believed that a nation could fire the first shot and still claim to be waging a war of defense. This effectively abolished the time-honored and useful distinction between defensive versus offensive wars, by which aggressor nations were singled out from those transgressed against. He accepted alliances between Christian princes and non-Christian ones, and gave early credence to the premise that evil princes might wage just wars*, or at least that the justice of a war was not dependent upon the ideology of the prince. He insisted that only the most superior rulers had the authority to declare and wage wars. The Pope clearly satisfied this condition. Suarez concluded that any war that was declared without legitimate authority was "contrary not only to charity, but also to justice, even if legitimate cause for it exists."

He agreed with both Franciscus de Victoria and Balthazar Ayala* (1548–1584) that wars to promote religion were unjust. The clerics at Toledo, however, had already decreed that heretics should be punished by war. He agreed with

Victoria that it would be unreasonable to inflict grave harm when the injustice was slight, but neither an objective judge nor a yardstick existed to determine when the harm caused by a war or a strategy was excessive. The Hague congresses* faced the same difficulty when they attempted to explain what was meant by either "superfluous injury" or "unnecessary suffering."

He assumed that superior orders* were to be obeyed, and soldiers who did obey were protected by a mantle of immunity. But generals were equally protected, because they could appeal to military necessity. Although he agreed that it would be just to go to war to help a friendly country, he insisted that the friendly country itself must have been justified in going to war in the first place. If an injured party did not want to go to war on its own behalf, then no other country would be justified in coming to its defense. In one case, however, he allowed that a country might intervene* without an invitation, namely, if the prince forcibly compelled his subjects to practice idolatry. Otherwise, he rejected any open-ended right to intervene on the grounds that to permit this would lead to abuse.

See AYALA, BALTHAZAR; BELLI, PIERINO; BYNKERSCHOEK, COR-NELIUS; GROTIUS, HUGO; VATTEL, EMMERICH DE; VICTORIA, FRAN-CISCUS DE.

BIBLIOGRAPHY

Keen, Maurice Hugh, *The Law of War in the Late Middle Ages* (London: Routledge & Kegan Paul, 1965).

Suarez, Francisco, *The Three Theological Virtues* (Oxford: Clarendon Press, 1944).

SUPERFLUOUS INJURY. *See* COLLATERAL DAMAGE; FORBIDDEN STRATEGIES; FORBIDDEN WEAPONS; MASS DESTRUCTION, WEAP-ONS OF; HAGUE, THE, CONGRESSES; PRISONERS OF WAR; PROPOR-TIONALITY; TOTAL WAR.

SUPERIOR ORDERS. The earliest writings on the subject assumed, as a matter of course, that soldiers were to obey the orders of their superiors. In 1189 John of Salisbury* wrote in his *Policraticus* that there should be no questioning of the authority of the commander's orders. In such matters it was a crime even to blink an eye unless the commander allowed it. John advised the soldier, "If you bid me plunge my sword in my brother's heart or my father's throat, or into the womb of my wife big with child, I will do in full your bidding, though with an unwilling hand." Francisco Suarez* (1548–1617) stated that generals were under no obligation to worry about the orders they gave, and that soldiers who followed orders were exempt from legal or moral blame for doing so. Pierino Belli* (1502–1575) advised that while soldiers ought not to obey unjust orders, they were rarely in a position to know when an unjust order had been given. Balthazar Ayala* (1548–1584) recommended that in a monarchic state the soldier was well advised to follow orders. Emmerich Vattel* (1714–1767) stated that all in authority bound those under them to obey.

Until 1944 the U.S. military manuals presumed that soldiers were obligated to follow superior orders. In anticipation, however, of the war crimes trials (*see* Nuremberg Trials) the Allies expected to conduct after the war, the United States revised its manual such that the plea of superior orders, although mitigating, did not constitute a sufficient defense. The new manual explained:

The fact that the law of war has been violated pursuant to an order of a superior authority, whether military or civil, does not deprive the act in question of its character as a war crime, nor does it constitute a defense in the trial of an accused individual, unless he did not know and could not reasonably have been expected to know that the act ordered was unlawful. (Article 509)

The manual explained that since obeying orders was required of every soldier, any court should take this into consideration, and that soldiers cannot be expected in time of war "to weigh scrupulously the legal merits of the orders received." The manual reminded the reader that war crimes could be committed legally in reprisal*, and that not every nation agreed on the list of war crimes. Some nations might have acceded to a prohibition, but with reservations.

The war crimes trials after the Philippines War*, World War I, World War II, and Vietnam* evidenced not only the degree to which soldiers may be unaware of the existence of certain laws of war*, but also how much disagreement existed as to whether either the notion of military necessity* or the right of reprisal might supersede any putative prohibitions.

See CONTROL COUNCIL LAW NO. 10; LEIPZIG TRIALS; NUREMBERG TRIALS; SHIMODA CASE; SON MY/MY LAI; STOCKHOLM/ROTHSKILDE WAR CRIMES TRIALS; TOKYO TRIALS; WINTER SOLDIER INVESTIGATION.

BIBLIOGRAPHY

Daniel, Aubrey M., "The Defense of Superior Orders," *University of Richmond Law Review* (1973), 477–509.

Dickenson, John, trans., *The Statesman's Book of John of Salisbury* (New York: Russell & Russell, 1963).

Dinstein, Yoram, *The Defense of Superior Orders in International Law* (Leiden: Sitjhoff, 1965).

Manner, George, "The Legal Nature and Punishment of Criminal Acts of Violence Contrary to the Laws of War," *American Journal of International Law* 37 (July 1943).

SURRENDER, UNCONDITIONAL. Since the middle of the 19th century, the demand for unconditional surrender has been seen as militarily expedient, and the argument has been based on the demands of the doctrine of military necessity*. Unconditional surrender was an incidental consequence of the acceptance of the notion of total war*. Carl Clausewitz had argued that the ability of the enemy to wage war in the future required unconditional surrender. This argument emphasized the psychological component in successful victory. No longer was it sufficient to defeat the enemy on the field of battle; now it was necessary to attack and destroy the will of the enemy.

President Franklin Roosevelt found himself in a difficult position during World War II. He believed that discussion of war aims would ignite divisive isolationist-internationalist-militarist-pacifist debates of the kind that had preceded the bombing of Pearl Harbor. Such debate, he feared, would destroy any consensus in favor of the war. Discussion of the postwar aims abroad might divide the Alliance. Were the French and British to reassert their postwar goals, and the Soviets insist on control of Eastern Europe, allied cooperation would have been difficult. Roosevelt believed that the best way to foreclose such debate was to demand unconditional surrender, thus leaving the future ambiguous. Roosevelt may also have been convinced that the difficulties that President Woodrow Wilson had faced at Versailles were exacerbated by his error in articulating clear and unrealistic war aims beforehand and then discovering that he could not get them accepted at the peace conference. Requiring unconditional surrender possessed the advantage of protecting Roosevelt from repeating Wilson's mistake.

The demand for unconditional surrender, however, tends to be unrealistic both politically and militarily. It implies politically that the conquering nation is prepared to take over the conquered people's government, replacing old enemy functionaries with new ones. If nothing else, the demand leaves the conquered nation ignorant of the price of surrender. Victors have traditionally relied on vanquished functionaries to continue in office, and in both Germany and Japan this proved to be the case. Cordell Hull's request for clarification of Roosevelt's policy of surrender could have avoided the Axis fears; however, Roosevelt's reply evaded this request: "Lee surrendered unconditionally to Grant but immediately Grant told him that his officers should take their horses home for the spring plowing. This is the spirit I want to see abroad—but it does not apply to Germany. Germany understands only one kind of language." Unconditional surrender is unrealistic militarily, since it tends to postpone surrender. Joseph Goebbels was reported to have been elated upon hearing of Roosevelt's demand for unconditional surrender, since he expected, correctly as it turned out, that it would stiffen German resistance. General Dwight Eisenhower repeatedly sought clarification from Roosevelt on the conditions for surrender, and cited intelligence reports that the demand for unconditional surrender was a principal reason for German resistance. The same problem had arisen after Mussolini was overthrown by Marshall Badoglio in July 1943. Badoglio initiated secret talks with the Allies, but Roosevelt's intransigence over unconditional surrender prevented the negotiations from succeeding until September, by which time the Germans had deployed large forces across the Alps and occupied the full length of Italy. As a consequence, instead of possibly gaining most of the peninsula without a fight by meeting Badoglio's modest demands in July, the Allies were forced to engage in some of the fiercest combat of the war.

Evidence suggests that Japanese surrender would have come much sooner had it not been for the unconditional demand, which left ambiguous whether the emperor could be retained. Indeed, General Douglas MacArthur wanted to assure the Japanese on this score but Roosevelt prevented this. As it turned out, the Japanese were allowed to keep their emperor so that the unconditional demand was both militarily and politically pointless.

See QUARTER, NO, WARS OF; SIEGE WARFARE; TERMINATION OF WAR.

BIBLIOGRAPHY

Armstrong, Anne, *Unconditional Surrender: The Impact of the Casablanca Policy upon World War II* (New Brunswick, N.J.: Rutgers University Press, 1961).

Clausewitz, Carl L. von, *On War,* Michael Howard and Peter Paret, eds. and trans. (Princeton, N.J.: Princeton University Press, 1976).

Kecskemeti, Paul, *Strategic Surrender* (Stanford, Calif.: Stanford University Press, 1958).

Strozier, Charles, ''The Tragedy of Unconditional Surrender,'' *MHQ: The Quarterly Journal of Military History* 2 (Spring 1990).

Brien Hallett

T

TAILHOOK. ''Tailhook'' became the symbol in 1991 for indecent sexual behavior by U.S. military men. The name belongs to the Tailhook Association, a private organization with a membership made up of U.S. Navy and Marine Corps aviators on active duty, retired and in the Reserve, and of defense contractors. (''Tailhook'' refers to a hook on the tail end of carrier-based aircraft, which catches on an arresting cable and stops the plane upon landing.) The 1991 Tailhook Symposium (or ''convention'' as it was referred to in the press) was a three-day event, held since 1963 at a Las Vegas hotel and supported financially and logistically by the U.S. Navy and various defense contractors. The symposium was a combination of professional meetings relating to naval aviation, recreational events, and socializing. Socializing included, in 1991, behavioral excesses such as drunkenness, indecent exposure, and sexual assault.

While such misconduct had become characteristic of Tailhook conventions in the 1980s, public exposure occurred in 1991 as a result of charges of sexual assault brought by Lieutenant Paula Coughlin, an admiral's aide, who testified that she had been attacked in a hotel hallway and subjected to a male groping activity known as the ''gauntlet.'' In April 1992, an investigation performed by the Naval Investigative Service reported that only a handful of officers could be charged with misconduct, due to a lack of witnesses. Indeed, then-Secretary of the Navy H. Lawrence Garrett III and many high-ranking military officers who attended the Convention stated publicly that they saw no evidence of wrongdoing while there.

These denials brought further charges against the Navy, this time of a cover-up, in light of the fact that by the time the first report was issued, another twenty-six women, including fourteen woman officers, had come forward to attest to sexual assaults. Barbara Pope, assistant secretary of the Navy for manpower and the reserve and the highest-ranking female civilian in the Navy, openly threatened to resign if the Tailhook investigation were not pursued more vigorously. The investigation was turned over from the Navy to the inspector general in the

Department of Defense. Navy Secretary H. Lawrence Garrett resigned in June 1992.

The report of the Defense Department investigation issued in April 1993 was comprehensive: 2,911 interviews of convention attendees were held all over the world by over forty investigators at a cost of approximately $4.5 million. The report found that "117 officers were implicated in one or more incidents of indecent assault, indecent exposure, conduct unbecoming an officer or failure to act in a proper leadership capacity." Indecent behavior ranged from public nudity of various kinds, to public sex acts and showing of pornography, to physical attacks on women. (Some women in attendance at the convention were consensual parties to such activities; others protested and resisted.) The report concluded with a condemnation of senior officers who condoned the misconduct, as well as of the junior officers who perpetrated it. Disciplinary proceedings, along with resignations and retirements, followed the issuance of the report.

The report examined the justifications offered for the Tailhook excesses. One common rationale provided by interviewees was that naval aviators, among the elite of the armed forces, were entitled to behave in any way they wanted in order to "let off steam" and "live for today," especially in light of their recent heroic service during the Gulf War. A second defense was that the Tailhook Symposium was a private gathering, with the goings-on traditionally kept out of the public view. Finally, some interviewees explained aggressive behavior toward women as a response to women's entry into the military, which was causing a decline in morale, loss of job opportunity for males, and changes in the military lifestyle.

The Tailhook scandal forced the U.S. Navy to face the issues surrounding sexual harassment and full integration of women into its ranks. One early response was a full-day "stand-down" for training on sexual harassment for all 750,000 Navy personnel. Another consequence has been more vigorous enforcement of regulations involving sexual offenses. Although not directly related to Tailhook, 1993 policy changes to allow female Navy pilots to fly combat missions and promote the further integration of women into shipboard assignments were seen by many as a way to eliminate women's second-class citizenship in the Navy (see Women in the Military). While there were also reports of post-Tailhook backlash against Navy women, the predominant reaction has been a commitment by the Navy's leadership to return the service to "conduct becoming an officer."

Nevertheless, prosecution of the officers charged with Tailhook offenses provoked considerable controversy. Critics of the Navy argued that dealing with alleged criminal actions through "captain's masts," that is, in-house hearings, resulted in lighter than necessary discipline and a whitewash of the service. In contrast, defenders of the Navy attacked the few Navy court martials that did take place as witch hunts. Certainly, the prosecutions were marred by the failure of key witnesses to make successful identifications of alleged perpetrators.

The Tailhook Symposium was canceled in 1992. It did take place in San Diego in 1993 but the Navy severed all connections with it and warned any aviators planning to attend that they had to take vacation leave to do so. Finally, most senior officers who were in attendance at Tailhook in 1991 received official letters of reprimand for failing to restrain their men in one of the U.S. Navy's least shining moments.

See FEMINISM AND WAR; MILITARY TRAINING, BASIC; WOMEN IN THE MILITARY.

BIBLIOGRAPHY

Inspector General, *Report of Investigation: Tailhook 91—Part 2* (Arlington, Va.: Department of Defense, April 12, 1993).

Ellen Boneparth

TAOISM AND WAR. Three teachings, Confucianism, Taoism, and Buddhism*, have shaped Chinese culture. Each has made a unique contribution and the claim that "Chinese civilization would have been utterly different if the book of Lao Tzu had never been written" is valid for Confucianism and Buddhism as well. Lao Tzu (6th century B.C.) was the founder of Taoism. His major work is the Tao Te Ching. Chuang Tzu (3rd century B.C.) is his best-known follower, whose text bears his name.

Two central Taoist concepts are the Tao and Wu-wei. The Tao is the supreme reality. Man's goal of becoming one with it is achieved through the practice of reflection, contemplation, or meditation in a natural setting if possible and, if not, one that resembles nature as much as possible. One must look inward, concentrate on the inner self, and free oneself from external attractions and distractions. Through such practice the right way of action will become apparent. The Taoist calls that way of acting Wu-wei. Wu-wei does not mean no action but action of a certain type. It is action that does not arouse antagonism, hostility, or opposition. It is action without overacting. It is action characterized by spontaneity and naturalness, untainted by artificiality and convention. Its intent is not to gain, manipulate, control, or dominate. It allows and encourages people and things to pursue their natural course of development. It is not motivated by self-interest and does not seek honor, fortune, fame, or glory for oneself. Its concern is the well-being of all. It is disinterested action, that is, acting without excessive attachment to the results of the action. The Taoist says such action does not give rise to vanity and pride, personal or national. It does not result in acrimony, discord, quarreling, and conflict, but brings about fraternity, harmony, mutuality, and concord.

The person acting in terms of Wu-wei values contentment, serenity, tranquillity, quietude, modesty, honesty, impartiality, mutuality, and cooperation. His or her ideal is a life of simplicity in which the profit motive is discarded, cleverness abandoned, selfishness minimized, and desires reduced. One gives without obligation, and assists without creating dependency. One is motivated by the "three treasures" of compassion, frugality, and not putting oneself forward, rather than the "three evils" of envy, discontent and coveting. It is a life of inner freedom from self-interested inclinations and prejudices and of external freedom from the excessive conventions, rules, regulations, and artificialities of everyday society.

Taoist ethics and its social and political philosophy are correlated. Lao Tzu pictured the ideal society as consisting of many small, independent, self-sufficient villages where everyone knew everyone else and all cared and worked for the common good. Class distinctions were nonexistent. Nature was viewed as beneficent and plenteous. Wealth was equitably distributed so there were no poor or wealthy. People did not demand more than they needed. They acted naturally and spontaneously. Harmony and cooperation were prized. The village was self-administered. Relations with the central government were minimal. The emperor ruled by example much more than by law enforced by a bureaucracy. Through inner purification he would be a model of virtue that his subjects would emulate.

This, briefly, was and continues to be the Taoist outlook. It consisted of an idealistic metaphysic that asserted the reality and priority of the nonmaterial, an ethic that stressed inner purification and the gentle virtues, and a social, economic, and political philosophy of equality, equity, and noninterference. It upheld an optimistic view of man as good when left to himself, unimpeded by social conventions. Nature was viewed as benign, a suitable model for man to follow and was not to be selfishly exploited but carefully nurtured and shared in by all. As a philosophy, Taoism exercised the greatest influence among the highly esteemed literati. In the 3rd and 4th centuries C.E., it became a religion as well, giving it popular appeal without its moral and basic tenets being compromised.

Lao Tzu was concerned about promoting peace and well-being and avoiding wars between contending factions. The Legalists' way was through extensive laws and stern, autocratic rule. The Confucianists' way was through an extensive, enlightened bureaucracy, an upright ruler, and excessive court formalities and ceremonies. In contrast, the Taoists advocated a minimum of government, decentralization of power, and abolishing the bureaucracy and formalities, and a return to living simply and in accord with nature, which is the wu-wei way.

Scholars note that many dynasties owed their stability, prosperity, and peacefulness to Taoist influence, while Taoism contributed to the fall of others. Two early emperors of the Han dynasty (201 B.C.–C.E. 220) ruled by the Taoist principle of wu-wei. Their governing was not extensive, intrusive, or onerous. On the other hand, when the dynasty declined because of corruption, an extensive bureaucracy, and internal struggles, a revolt against the emperor was staged by the Taoist-inspired Yellow Turbans. Dynasties like the Sung (960–1279) granted Taoism official recognition in its middle years. Others, such as the Tang (618–907), were patrons of Taoism, giving it a privileged and semi-official status. Emperors like Wenti, first ruler of the Sui dynasty (581–618), combined Taoism and Confucianism in their way of ruling. Even among rulers primarily

Confucianist, Taoism still made its way felt through the scholarly officials in the bureaucracy who, while outwardly Confucianist, inwardly maintained a Taoist outlook. It led them, upon leaving the government, to retire to their home provinces to paint and write poetry in imitation of the Taoist recluse. Many rulers did the same, even those as late as Chiang Kai-shek and Mao Tse-tung.*

Significantly, Westerners who were born and lived among the Chinese in the early 20th century found them to be pacific in nature and outlook. Pearl Buck wrote in her autobiography that "In old Asia the soldier was given no honor and war was without glory." The soldier was looked down on as being lower than the beggar. People viewed the military profession* with contempt. They neither valued military prowess nor admired the ruthless strong man. Scholars did not eulogize war. Poets like Liang P depicted warfare in terms of its horror and devastation rather than the glory of battle.

There are both ideological and practical reasons for that cultural outlook. Obviously, credit for China's nonmilitancy should be given to Confucianism with its emphasis on reason and compromise and to Buddhism with its ethics of love and compassion. But Taoism should be given its fair share of credit, too. The noted Chinese philosopher Wing-Tsit Chan wrote that both Confucianism and Taoism "oppose the use of force." He added that "the opposition of Taoism to the use of force is well known and the most bitter attack on militarism* is found in Lao Tzu."

See CHRISTIANITY AND WAR; HINDUISM AND WAR; JUDAISM AND WAR; MENCIUS; MO TZU (MO TI); TAOISM AND WAR; TZU, SUN.

BIBLIOGRAPHY
Chan, Wing-Tsit, *A Sourcebook in Chinese Philosophy* (Princeton, N.J.: Princeton University Press, 1963).
Chiu, Milton, *The Tao of Chinese Religion* (Lanham, Md.: University Press of America, 1984).

Donald H. Bishop

TERMINATION OF WAR. The ending of a state of war has traditionally taken place in two phases. The first phase is the cessation of hostilities—ceasefire—which often takes the form of a signed agreement fixing combatants in place and silencing their weapons, though they may remain deployed in the field and fully armed. The second phase is the making of peace, also normally a signed agreement, which specifies the postwar disposition of territories, powers, and resources, and which can spell out terms for reparations, disarmament, and the repatriation of displaced peoples. In contrast to the laws covering declarations of war* (*jus ad bellum*) and laws for the conduct of combat (*jus in bello*), written expositions of laws governing the termination of warfare are almost nonexistent, although traditions in the use of emblems conveyed similar meanings over the centuries. The capture of the commander's banner in battle was taken as a sign of victory on the field. In a siege* war, the leader of a surrendering city was expected to bring out the keys to the gates, and offer them to the victorious besiegers. A white flag was the traditional means of communicating to the enemy that one wished to discuss terms for the cessation of hostilities. The Hague Convention of 1907* codified the tradition of the white flag as the emblem of truce.

Warring parties can agree to temporary or geographically limited ceasefires for tactical reasons. These make it possible to redeploy forces, to break out of deadlocked engagements, and to concentrate on activities or regions that promise to be more fruitful. Accepting victory or defeat on a battlefield is a sign of no more than that the fighting at that particular location has come to an end, at least for the moment. Even armies forced into retreat can gather strength once again, and make preparations to reengage. In modern times, technologically advanced weaponry, the ability to handle extended supply lines, and armies with complex command structures or made up of troops from many countries, have combined in battles that lasted days or weeks and covered huge amounts of terrain. Victory and defeat in a given battle now are rarely clear-cut events.

An enduring ceasefire, or armistice as it is often called, is concerned first with establishing a basis for trusting that, though still armed, neither side will resort again to the use of force. Ceasefire agreements determine how troops remaining in the field are to be deployed, and begin to set up terms for military occupation if there is to be one. They also must establish a manner in which to communicate with distant forces that hostilities have come to an end. A ceasefire agreement can also settle how and when peace talks will commence, and it may begin to lay out terms for the exchange of prisoners*, repatriation of people displaced by the combat, even reparations for war damage. Normally it spells out the consequences for any future outbreaks of violence between combatant forces or against civilians. A ceasefire can come about as a result of negotiation between the warring parties or as a result of a total capitulation by one side or another. Historical evidence indicates that negotiated ceasefires are much more common than capitulations.

Capitulation, total surrender, is the outcome to be expected in a civil war, since one side or another normally wishes to establish uncontested control over the entire terrain. Negotiated settlements, where warring sides agree to negotiate future frontiers, powers, and resources, are the more common outcome in wars between states. After 1945, the United Nations from time to time authorized member nations to use force against each other, and passed resolutions that preset the terms for a ceasefire.

The 20th century offers examples of each kind of ceasefire. As an example of *tactical* ceasefire, the war between the Koreas* ended with an armistice at the 38th parallel in 1953. Though most observers believed at the time that this was a final ceasefire, a prelude to a permanent peace treaty, final peace eluded negotiators despite regular discussions over forty years. Those years saw few fatal military engagements but frequent threats, military maneuvers and a continuation of war-like propaganda* and mutual enmity. The fall of Saigon and the collapse of the government of South Vietnam* in April 1975 offers an example of a complete *capitulation*. In the final weeks of the war, people closely associated with the political leadership or with the military of the collapsing nation fled by the thousands, well aware that once the capital city fell they would have absolutely no basis for negotiating either their own safety or any future dispositions in the country. *Unconditional surrender** was specified by the Allies as one of the requirements for a ceasefire in World War II. Setting stringent terms in such an absolute and public way may have contributed to lengthening the war, because neither Germany nor Japan was willing to contemplate an unconditional complete loss of power to negotiate the postwar settlements. In the end, the Japanese, in keeping the Emperor on his throne, managed to avoid such a surrender. Hitler's suicide and the meeting of Soviet and United States troops at the Elbe river left Nazis with no say over the German future, though other German nationals were given authority even in the years of occupation. As an example of *negotiated ceasefire,* during World War II, in 1940, France negotiated a ceasefire with the Nazi* government after French forces found themselves unable to hold back the invaders. Despite their military weakness, the French were still able to negotiate a division of the country, leaving the Nazis in control of Paris and the north, and a French government, under Marshall Pétain, headquartered in Vichy ruling the southern part of the country, in co-ordination with Germany. A *United Nations settlement* was reached in the war against Iraq*, which began in 1990 with Iraq's invasion of Kuwait and the resultant UN embargo enforced by military means. In 1991, an air and land war lasted for six weeks. A ceasefire in that phase of the war was agreed to only after Iraq announced its willingness to abide by the UN Security Council resolutions on the withdrawal of troops from Kuwait, and the dismantling of weapons of mass destruction*. Iraq's refusal to formally accept Kuwaiti sovereignty kept the embargo in place for years.

Peace treaties, the second phase in the termination of a war, are written after the ending of a war, to redistribute lands, powers, and resources. In going to war, combatants challenge each other's sovereignty over disputed terrain, and it is rare that those challenges are fully resolved until the signing of a peace treaty even though, with the cessation of hostilities, the combatants agree to stop trying to make adjustments to boundaries by the use of force. Establishing sovereignty means, first, the settling of boundary lines. After the onset of colonialism, European claims of sovereignty also frequently entailed discussions of the boundaries of distant territories around the world. The geographical shape of a jurisdiction having been settled, peace treaties have also made dispositions about the nature of the government. These have included placing particular people or parties in power, and depriving those who prosecuted the war of future roles. Treaties have been used to specify which religions it is now acceptable to practice, and the fate of those who attempt to practice another faith. The treaties can also specify where the secular authority resides, which authority may retain an armed force, and who that force is designed to protect. Reparations to the victor for the cost of fighting a war are also commonplace in peace agreements. In earlier times, the right to take slaves and booty from captured territories became the practical means whereby victors collected reparations. One particularly famous case of reparations, those imposed on the Germans at the ending of World War I by the Peace of Versailles in 1919, demanded so much in payments for rebuilding in the war-torn Allied nations that the German economy was seriously undermined for a long period. After World War II, Germany was asked to do much less for the Allies, but for nearly fifty years it continued to make reparations payments to its own citizens, Jews and others, whose families and livelihoods were destroyed during the war.

There is no fixed time allotted to make a peace agreement after the cessation of hostilities. In earlier centuries the commanders could take months getting from the battlefield to the site agreed upon for negotiations. The negotiations can also take a considerable amount of time to complete. The Allies met for five months at Versailles before they signed their agreements with Germany in June 1919. Final agreements over the disposition of the Ottoman Empire were not signed until August 1920. It is also possible for a war to end without a peace treaty ever being signed. This was the case with respect to West Germany after World War II. It was the United Nations that signed the treaties ending that conflict. Nations taken to have collaborated with Germany, Hungary for example, signed treaties in 1947. The treaty with Japan was signed in 1951. By 1948, tensions among members of the UN, prompted by the successes of Communism in Eastern Europe and by the Soviet blockade of Berlin, meant that making Western Germany an ally in the Cold War* was more important to its occupying powers than finishing negotiations to terminate World War II.

Peace treaties may attempt to make final settlements of powers and resources, but they can contain within them the grounds for a future war. Some of the repeated conflicts in the medieval era between France and England, over control of territory we now consider France, were spurred by earlier settlements in which English monarchs ceded to French kings and nobles territories to which they continued to believe they had a hereditary right. Over the centuries, the people in what are now The Netherlands, Belgium, and Luxembourg saw their lands used as bargaining tools in peace treaties between France, Burgundy, and Spain. The local people's failure to achieve independence in any of these treaties played a part in fomenting later conflicts. Peace treaties have also been seen as establishing the legitimacy of claims to sovereignty. European nations, having drawn boundaries around territories they were claiming as colonies, found that in wars among themselves they could trade colonial control, consolidating empires. In the 20th century this colonialism began being tempered by claims that the people in the colonies had rights to self-determination. In the treaties ending World War I, the territories reassigned from the Ottoman Empire were given as ''mandates,'' and after World War II the United Nations developed a listing for each colonial power of the territories to which it needed to offer self-determination. Despite the weakening powers of colonialism, many wars in the

20th century were precipitated by the failure of earlier peace treaties to offer the local population the right to self-determination.

See COLD WAR; DECLARATION OF WAR; SIEGE WARFARE; SURRENDER, UNCONDITIONAL.

BIBLIOGRAPHY

Fromkin, David, *A Peace to End All Peace: Creating the Modern Middle East* (New York: H. Holt, 1989).

Kecskemeti, Paul, *Strategic Surrender: The Politics of Victory and Defeat* (Palo Alto, Calif.: Stanford University Press, 1958).

Meyer-Knapp, Helena, *Nuclear Siege to Nuclear Ceasefire* (Ann Arbor, Mich.: University of Michigan Press, 1990).

Pillar, Paul, *Negotiating Peace: War Termination as a Bargaining Process* (Princeton, N.J.: Princeton University Press, 1983).

Helena Meyer-Knapp

TERRORISM. The strategy of employing violence or the threat of violence to escalate people's fears in order to achieve or keep political power. Terrorism consists of randomly violent attacks on persons or property in order to frighten and coerce a large number of people. The activities of terrorism can include bombing, hijacking (airplanes, trains, buses, and ships), murder, and assassination.

The term was first used during the French Revolution (1789–1799), when tactics of violence and fear were employed to sustain Robespierre's government against its adversaries. Other examples of leaders who used terror to remain in power include Adolf Hitler, Benito Mussolini, Joseph Stalin, and Mao Tsetung*. In many instances the exploiters of terror tactics eventually become victims of terror tactics. A prime example was Robespierre, who died on the guillotine to which he had sentenced so many.

Terrorism is a means that needs to be justified. Ordinarily, terrorist acts are thought to be different from military operations, but that distinction is not always clear. Some military tactics (e.g., firestorm bombing as seen in Tokyo and Dresden in World War II) seemed designed to terrorize entire populations. Guerrilla* warfare further erodes the distinction between military and terrorist acts.

The justification of terrorism can vary. Placing terrorism in a consequentialist means-ends framework leads to two questions: (1) Is terrorism successful? and (2) Is terrorism moral? The assessment of success depends on the goals to be obtained. Objectives by terrorists fighting against those in power include to achieve publicity for the cause, to draw governments into greater repression leading to a general uprising, and/or to create a just social order. Terrorists out of power *have* achieved publicity and *have* drawn governments into being more repressive but have generally *not* brought about the social and political changes they desired. Even if terrorists are able to neutralize their opponents militarily, they and their opponents may not share enough of a moral community to be able to build a society together. If the terrorists' goal is ultimately to create a just social order after a revolution, with whom will they do that, and how? Terrorists need to address two questions: (1) What are the best means for really changing our lives? and (2) With whom will we build a just social order and how? Walzer points out that, if dignity and self-respect are to be the outcomes of armed struggle for human freedom, the struggle cannot consist of terrorist attacks on children*.

The terrorist dehumanizes those whom he attacks. The child who dies when a school bus is bombed is neither the author of nor able to change the governmental policies that the terrorist opposes. The terrorist is treating the victim merely as a means and not as an end in himself. The victim has become a thing to be used in the struggle, but is no longer regarded as a person.

Terrorism tends to justify its means by the value of its ends. Terrorists often claim to hold a higher morality than their opponents. Robespierre, using terror in the political context of the French Revolution, did not call his program the "Reign of Terror" but the "Reign of Terror and Justice." This label provided a flavor of the moral high ground that terrorists seek to occupy. The document, *Minimanual of the Urban Guerrilla,* by Carlos Marighella, adopts a moral tone: "Today to be an assailant or a terrorist is a quality that ennobles any honorable man because it is an act worthy of a revolutionary engaged in armed struggle against the shameful military dictatorship and its monstrosities." He justifies his tactics in terms of the evil nature of his opponent. Marighella writes, "The urban guerrilla's arms are inferior to the enemy's, but from a moral point of view, the urban guerrilla has an undeniable superiority." Alberto Bayo's *150 Questions to a Guerrilla* states that rebels must engage in a "struggle against the injustices which a people suffer." Bayo warns, "Whoever revolts unrighteously reaps nothing but a crushing defeat."

Terrorism has sometimes been linked with a nihilistic world view by such as Albert Camus. From this perspective, the terrorist might argue that since there is no authority for any moral standards, one might as well kill other people if the social arrangement has collapsed or if such acts will further the cause. They ask, "Why assume you need a *reason* to kill?"

A different defense of terrorism would be to argue that if a government does not enhance the liberty of its citizens, then terrorism is a form of feedback that is not the problem but a solution to the problem. In other words, terrorism may be the best option available to redress grievances.

A subcategory is state-sponsored terrorism. This refers to situations in which governments support terrorists logistically and financially, and provide them sanctuary after they have engaged in acts of terror. Historically, the governments that have sponsored terrorism have not, by and large, been democracies. Terrorism is inconsistent with the principles of constitutional democracy, especially regarding the enhancement of personal liberties. It is difficult to see how acts of terror could be a justifiable means to achieve the ends of a democractic state.

See ASSASSINATION; COMBATANT-NONCOMBATANT DISTINC-TION; CRIMES AGAINST HUMANITY; EXECUTION, SUMMARY; FOR-

BIDDEN STRATEGIES; HUMAN RIGHTS; INNOCENTS; MASS
DESTRUCTION, WEAPONS OF; MUTUAL ASSURED DESTRUCTION
(MAD); NUCLEAR WAR; QUARTER, NO, WARS OF; TOTAL WAR.

BIBLIOGRAPHY
Camus, Albert, *The Rebel: An Essay on Man in Revolt* (New York: Alfred A. Knopf,
    1961).
Mallin, Jay, *Terror and Urban Guerrillas: A Study of Tactics and Documents* (Coral
    Gables, Fla.: University of Miami Press, 1971).
Walzer, Michael, *Just and Unjust Wars: A Moral Argument with Historical Illustrations*
    (New York: Basic Books, 1977).

                                                                   David E. Johnson

TOKYO TRIALS. By a special proclamation of January 16, 1946, an international tribunal for the Far East was established by the Allies to prosecute
alleged Japanese war criminals. It appealed to the Cairo Declaration of December 1, 1943, the Declaration of Potsdam of July 26, 1945, the instrument of
surrender of September 2, 1945, and the Moscow* conference of December 26,
1945. The same charges were involved as had been the case at Nuremberg*,
although the size of the tribunal was enlarged from four as at Nuremberg to not
fewer than five nor more than nine. Members were appointed by General Douglas MacArthur, the supreme commander of the Allied powers in the Far East,
from a list submitted by the signatories of the instrument of surrender. The panel
was subsequently increased to eleven, consisting of one member from each of
the following countries: Australia, Canada, China, France, Great Britain, India,
the Netherlands, New Zealand, the Philippines, the USSR, and the United States.
The tribunal sat from May 3, 1946, to November 12, 1948. The United States
was more directly involved in the Tokyo trials than they had been at Nuremberg.
Japan had been occupied, according to the Potsdam agreement, solely by American forces, and MacArthur was the absolute governor of Japan. The procedures
followed were American; for example, the defense had the right of cross-
examination. The more than 46,000 pages of reports were not published as were
those from Nuremberg, although the Tokyo trials lasted far longer than those at
Nuremberg.

   Like the first trial at Nuremberg, the first Tokyo trial prosecuted only those
Japanese whose crimes had not been limited to any specific place and who could
not plead that they were acting under superior orders*. Twenty-five Japanese
were tried with the following resultant sentences: seven were sentenced to hanging, thirteen received life sentences, one received a twenty-year sentence, and
one received a sentence of seven years. As in the case of the Nuremberg trials,
the first Tokyo trial was followed by additional trials of persons whose crimes
had been located in a specific country. The United States conducted ninety-
seven trials in the Philippines of 215 defendants, of whom 195 were convicted,
with ninety-two receiving the death sentence. Trials in China, where Chiang
Kai-shek's Nationalist government gave the United States temporary authority

to conduct war crimes trials, included trials against seventy-five defendants. Sixty-seven were found guilty, with ten death sentences and eight acquittals. On December 28, 1949, a military tribunal of the USSR tried twelve former Japanese servicemen charged with manufacturing and employing bacteriological weapons. Among the specific charges was that a military expedition in 1940 had sent germs of typhoid and cholera and plague-infected fleas to the Chinese region of Nimpo. A similar expedition sent plague-infected fleas to the region of Changteh in 1941, and another in 1942 in Central China sent plague-infected fleas and the germs of typhoid and paratyphoid. The Soviet sentences ranged from two to twenty-five years in prison.

The U.S. Navy conducted trials in the Pacific Islands. Three cases were tried in Kwajalein and forty-four in Guam. A trial in Guam ending in September 1947 found nineteen Japanese guilty of torturing to death eight American prisoners of war (POWs) at Truk using "inhuman experimental use of bacteria, dynamite, and bamboo spears." Captain Hiroshi Iwanami, surgeon and commanding officer of the naval hospital on Truk Atoll, was executed, and the remaining eighteen received sentences ranging from ten years to life imprisonment. America conducted a total of 474 cases with 1,409 defendants, with 1,229 convictions resulting in 163 death sentences.

The British tried Gozawa Sadaichi and nine others in a British court in Singapore. The Right Honorable Earl Mountbatten noted that only those whose sentences were likely to exceed seven years would be tried. Since the British did not recognize either crimes against the peace* or crimes against humanity*, their trials emphasized war crimes*. By the end of the period of the trials, the British had tried 920 persons in 306 trials. Death sentences were carried out on 265 and life imprisonment on fifty-five.

Australia, Canada, and New Zealand all conducted trials of Japanese defendants. In 1944, Australia established its own war crimes commission, which conducted investigations to get information on Japanese war crimes, and by 1945 they had gathered 1,481 suspects for trial. By early March 1948 the Australians had tried almost 800 Japanese for war crimes. These trials marked the end of trials in the Far East.

Canada conducted a few trials in conjunction with other Allies, hampered primarily by Canadian war regulations that allowed only senior officers in command in the Far East to convene military courts. Since Canada had no occupation forces in the Far East, it was unable to convene any trials on its own. New Zealand played a part in the main Tokyo trials, but otherwise accepted the major roles of the United States, Britain, and Australia. The role of the Soviet Union was conditioned by the fact that they did not enter the war in the Far East until August 9, 1945, and they primarily associated themselves with other Allied war crimes trials. The Soviets did, however, create a Russian Extraordinary War Crimes Commission, which tried and convicted Germans as early as December 1943. The Soviets held a trial at Khabarovsk in December 1949, in spite of the recommendation of the Far East commission that all trials be ended by September 30, 1949.

China suffered the largest number of victims from the Japanese, going back to 1937 and continuing up to 1945. In 1943 they created a national office to investigate war crimes, and later a Chinese war crimes commission to conduct trials. By early 1949 the Chinese had tried 883 accused. At this time the Chinese transferred their remaining 260 convicted Japanese war criminals to Tokyo to finish their terms of imprisonment. The Netherlands cooperated with other Allies in trials in the Far East, but, in addition, conducted their own trials in Java, Borneo, Sumatra, Amboina, and the Celebese Islands. By 1950, when the Netherlands transferred all their remaining Japanese prisoners to Sugamo prison, Tokyo, they had tried 1,038, and convicted 969. About 24 percent of those convicted were given the death penalty.

The Philippines did not gain its independence from the United States until July 4, 1946, and consequently participated primarily in the trials in their country conducted by the United States. On January 1, 1947, the U.S. War Crimes Branch in Manila formally closed, and beginning on July 29, 1947, further war crimes trials were conducted under an executive order of President Manuel A. Roxas. The most notorious was the case of thirty-one Japanese in Mindanao accused of cannibalism. By 1949, Philippine courts had tried 169 accused, of whom seventeen received the death sentence, while 182 were freed because of insufficient evidence. With the exception of the Soviets, France conducted the fewest war crimes trials in the Far East, conducting only four trials in Indochina. Of the seven persons tried, five were sentenced to death and the remaining two were imprisoned.

Uneasiness over these trials was worldwide. Writers such as F. B. Schick, Marion Lozier, Alwyn W. Freeman, Erwin Knoll, Richard Minear, and Judith Nies McFadden expressed strong reservations. Even Telford Taylor admitted that the trials failed to establish any definitive precedent. The Nuremberg trials had underemphasized crimes against humanity, while Control Council Law No. 10* had emphasized them without establishing a precedent. Hans Erhard, for example, observed that the only basis for the trials was an agreement of the Allies that was antedated by the offenses it was supposed to prosecute. Furthermore, contrary to international tradition, the judges came solely from the victor nations. The uneasiness was sufficient that only nineteen governments of the United Nations signed in approval of the trials.

Considerable disagreement arose among the counsels of the military tribunal of the Far East. In view of the magnitude of the disagreement, Bruce Blakeny, on behalf of the entire defense counsel, filed a defense appeal to General MacArthur, charging that the trials had been unfair. His list included the following: (1) the prosecution did not present its case fairly; (2) the defendants did not receive a fair trial (Even the chief prosecutor admitted that some innocent persons had been charged.); (3) the tribunal used two sets of rules: one for the prosecution and another for the defense. For example, the prosecution was allowed to use rumor, hearsay, and newspaper reports as evidence. Justices Pal of India, Bernard of France, and Roling of the Netherlands had underscored these malpractices; (4) even the president of the tribunal had expressed doubts that aggressive war* was a crime; (5) the great mass of evidence from defense witnesses was never taken into consideration; (6) in no case did the bare seven-judge majority agree on a sentence. Death had been approved with as few as four votes out of eleven; (7) unlike the Nuremberg trials, where guilt or innocence was declared individually, at the Tokyo trials it was declared *en masse;* and (8) men who had been outspoken opponents of the militarism* of Japan and against the aggression were sentenced along with established supporters. Part of the problem lay in the nature of the charges and the difficulty, given the nature of modern war, in admitting that laws of war existed or that there were limits beyond which armies ought not to go. Part of the legal problem lay in the difficulty of showing that antecedent laws existed, the breaking of which would constitute crimes.

See CASUALITIES OF WAR; CHILDREN AND WAR; COLLATERAL DAMAGE; GENEVA CONVENTION, 1929; HAGUE, THE, CONGRESSES; JUST WAR; LAWS OF WAR; NUREMBERG TRIALS; OKINAWA, MILITARY OCCUPATION OF; PSYCHIC NUMBING; SHIMODA CASE; TOTAL WAR.

BIBLIOGRAPHY
Horowitz, Sol, "The Tokyo Trial," *International Conciliation,* no. 465 (Washington, D.C.: Carnegie Endowment, November, 1950).
Materials on the Trial of Former Servicemen of the Japanese Army Charged with Man-ufacturing and Employing Bacteriological Weapons (Moscow: Foreign Language Publishing House, 1950).
Minear, Richard H., *Victor's Justice: The Tokyo War Crimes Trials* (Princeton, N.J.: Princeton University Press, 1971).
Pal, Radhabinode, *International Military Tribunal for the Far East: Dissential Judgment* (Calcutta: Sanyal Press, 1953).
Piccigallo, Philip R., *The Japanese on Trial* (Austin: University of Texas Press, 1979).
Sleeman, Colin, ed., *Trial of Gozawa Sadaichi and Nine Others* (London: William Hodge & Company, 1948).

TORTURE. The infliction of excruciating physical pain or unbearable psychological torment for such reasons as punishment, extracting confessions and information, or intimidating and instilling terror in others. Commonly practiced in ancient civilizations, including the Greek and Roman, torture became less frequent in Western European legal systems after the end of the Roman Empire, but was widely revived in the 13th century when confession became, along with eyewitness testimony, the means of determining guilt in most of Europe. It was also employed in cases of heresy by the Roman Catholic Church's inquisitions, especially between the 12th and 15th centuries.

By 1800, most European countries had legally abolished the use of torture in trials, having followed the example of England (begun in the 12th century) of instituting rules for admissible circumstantial evidence. Torture reappeared in the 20th century, however, in unexpectedly high proportions. It was widespread first in states that used law as a means of imposing ideology, as in fascist Italy, Nazi* Germany, and the Soviet Union under Stalin. In the latter half of the century its use spread widely in Africa, Asia, and Latin America, and became increasingly an extra-legal means by which governments and wealthy elites suppressed political opposition and waged terrorist* campaigns against civilians (often impoverished peasants) seeking reform. The use of official paramilitary death squads and ''disappearances'' became especially prevalent in Argentina, Chile, El Salvador, and Guatemala.

Torture commonly accompanied warfare, although it was often not as common as outright execution, enslavement, or ransoming of prisoners of war*. The Treaty of Westphalia in 1648 (ending the Thirty Years War) released prisoners without ransom, and is generally regarded as a turning point concerning the treatment of prisoners of war. The notion that prisoners should be quarantined to prevent them from doing harm, but not mistreated, was advanced by Enlightenment thinkers Charles Montesquieu, Jean-Jacques Rousseau*, and Emmerich de Vattel*. By the middle of the 19th century, a body of principles for the treatment of prisoners was generally recognized in the West, for instance, ''Leiber's Code,'' *General Orders 100**, the 1863 product of German-American jurist Frances Lieber*, prohibited torture and became a model for armies in the field. Yet a declaration prepared by an international conference in 1874 at Brussels* was not ratified, and the rules drawn up by international conferences at The Hague* in 1899 and 1907 were widely violated during World War I.

In 1929 the Geneva* Convention Relating to the Treatment of Prisoners of War provided that belligerents must treat prisoners humanely, supply information about them, and permit visits to prisoner camps by representatives of neutral states. Although ratified by France, Germany, Great Britain, and the United States, provisions of the Geneva Convention were extensively violated during World War II. In consequence, and in order to address depredations suffered by civilians, the 1949 Geneva Conventions expressly prohibited the torture of prisoners of war, as well as the deportation of civilians, the taking of hostages*, collective punishment and reprisals, torture of civilians, and outrages upon personal dignity. More than 150 states including the United States became parties to the 1949 convention. In addition, Article 5 of the 1948 UN Universal Declaration of Human Rights expressly prohibits torture and cruel, inhumane, or degrading treatment. In 1966, Part III, Article 7 of the International Covenant on Civil and Political Rights repeated the 1948 and 1949 prohibitions. An international conference sponsored by the Red Cross* in 1977 approved two protocols to the 1949 Geneva Conventions, extending protection against torture to guerrilla* combatants fighting wars of ''self-determination'' or civil wars in which they exercised ''control'' over significant stretches of territory. But only slightly more than half the signatories of the 1949 conventions signed the 1977 protocols, and both the United States and the United Kingdom have not.

Despite extensive protection in international law, there are few mechanisms for enforcing these legal instruments, and little interest on the part of the international community to press for sanctions that might threaten the principles of sovereignty and nonintervention. Thus, paper proscriptions against torture have increased along with its expanded use by states against civilians (often in contravention of their own constitutions). Paradoxically, enemy combatants taken prisoner often receive better treatment than do civilians suspected of disloyalty or perceived as subversives.

The effectiveness of torture was challenged as early as Cicero and Seneca, who claimed that "it forces even the innocent to lie." In the Middle Ages, Augustine* opposed it as immoral for being indiscriminate in imposing pain on persons not known to have committed a crime. Its widespread use in the late 20th century as a means of crushing suspected opposition is especially puzzling given widespread evidence of its counterproductive tendencies, as demonstrated in Argentina and El Salvador. Tragically for their victims, recent studies suggest that despite its ineffectiveness, torture plays an important role in providing dictators and authoritarian regimes with the illusion of power. Although Milgram's infamous shock experiments disproved the common belief that only sadistic or psychotic individuals are capable of torturing, recent research shows that torturers are often beaten themselves and made to become dependent on their trainers. Peters suggests that torture helps to perpetuate a "fabricated political reality," while in *The Body in Pain,* Scarry describes torture as a "grotesque piece of compensatory drama" that has as its purpose "the production of a fantastic illusion of power." Studying Argentina's "dirty war," Graziano claims that some authoritarian regimes require "enemies" to justify their own inhumane forms of domination and, in the absence of external threats, may torture their own citizens to create them.

See BANALITY OF EVIL; CONCENTRATION CAMPS; CRIMES AGAINST HUMANITY; FORBIDDEN STRATEGIES; LAWS OF WAR; PRISONERS OF WAR; TERRORISM.

BIBLIOGRAPHY
Amnesty International, *Torture in the Eighties* (New York: Amnesty International, 1984).
Graziano, Frank, *Divine Violence* (Boulder, Colo.: Westview Press, 1992).
Milgram, Stanley, *Obedience to Authority* (New York: Harper & Row, 1974).
Peters, Edward, *Torture* (Oxford: Basil Blackwood, 1986).
Scarry, Elaine, *The Body in Pain* (New York: Oxford University Press, 1985).
Timerman, Jacobo, *Prisoner Without a Name, Cell Without a Number* (New York: Alfred A. Knopf, 1981).

Robert Paul Churchill

TOTAL WAR. Although the term *total war* was not coined until early in the 20th century, practices associated with total war, particularly the mass slaughter of noncombatants, characterized warfare throughout most of human history. A precursor to the modern concept of total war was the concept of "absolute war,"

introduced by the Prussian general and military theoretician Carl von Clausewitz* in his famous book, *On War,* first published in 1832. Clausewitz was
influenced by the Napoleonic wars of the late 1700s and early 1800s, which
were far more destructive than any other European war during the 150 years
that preceded them. Defining war as "an act of force to compel our enemy to
do our will," Clausewitz argued that "there is no logical limit to the application
of that force" and warned that "To introduce the principle of moderation into
the theory of war itself would always lead to logical absurdity" (Clausewitz
1976 [1832], 75, 77). Historians of war Richard Preston and Sydney Wise wrote
that "the core" of Clausewitz's teaching is that modern wars tend to become
"absolute" and to involve "the full utilization of the moral and material resources of a nation to bring about, by violence, the complete destruction of the
enemy's means and will to resist" (Preston and Wise 1979, 238).

The conception of absolute war attributed to Clausewitz had a powerful influence on later strategists and military officers. Historian Berenice Carroll referred to "succeeding generations of military strategists" who were
"hypnotized" by "his idea of 'absolute' war, in which the complete overthrow,
or even destruction, of the entire enemy nation is the object, and unlimited effort
and violence the means" (Carroll 1968, 23). In an article on "The German
Concept of Total War," sociologist Hans Speier discerned that in the post–
World War I writings of German General Erich Ludendorff ("the military dictator of Germany" between the two world wars) a number of assumptions about
modern warfare reflected the influence of Clausewitz. They included the necessity of extending the fighting to the entire territory of the enemy, rather than
confining it to the battlefield; the need to involve the whole population in the
war effort; the value of propaganda*; and the importance of a strong, central
authority (Speier 1971 [1943], 288).

The actual term *total war* was invented in 1918, when a French essayist, Leon
Daudet wrote a relatively unimportant polemical book, *La Guerre Totale* (*Total
War*). According to Carroll, Daudet's book and its title had been inspired by a
far more important book by another French writer, Alphonse Seché, published
in 1915. Seché's book, *Les Guerres d'Enfer* (*The Hellish Wars*), which Carroll
considered as "the first full appreciation of the subject" of total war, outlined
a vision of future wars derived from a consideration of the early months of
World War I as well as the Napoleonic wars of the 1790s (Carroll 1968, 21).

Seché maintained that an era of total war had begun in August 1793, with
the establishment of mass conscription* and the formation of a large national
army by the French government. The expanded size of the army increased the
extent to which the entire nation was directly involved in the war, and the
increased scale of warfare necessitated extensive mobilization of the economic
resources of the warring nation. Moreover, as the economy became integral to
the war effort, Seché wrote, the "division of forces into combatants and noncombatants*" became "outmoded" (quoted in Carroll 1968, 32). Seché also

emphasized the role of science and industry in making modern wars increasingly destructive.

The involvement of much of the nation in the war and the extremely high level of death and destruction have been emphasized in more recent definitions and analyses. In his pioneering study of 20th-century collective violence, *Twentieth Century Book of the Dead,* Gil Elliot stated that total war is "based on the complete dedication of a nation's energies to producing the means of war, and the readiness of forces in the field to destroy the enemy's men and materials to the completest extent" (Elliot 1972, 7). More recently, Arthur Marwick and his colleagues included the " 'nation in arms,' ideological warfare, horrendous battle casualties*, and the extermination of civilian populations" among the key characteristics of total war (Marwick et al. 1990, 13). The notion of the "nation in arms" refers to the fact, as pointed out by Seché above, that many economic resources of the nation must be dedicated to the war effort. It also implies that the impact of the war will be felt throughout the society, rather than confined to the soldiers or relatively limited sectors of the economy that design and build war materiel.

The ideological nature of total war pointed out by Marwick accounts for the widespread use of propaganda to maintain the morale of soldiers and the support of the civilians by demonizing and/or dehumanizing the enemy. Such vilification of the enemy helps justify another feature of total war—the breakdown of psychological and ethical restraints against deliberate slaughter of both enemy soldiers and enemy civilians. By requiring a high degree of centralization and concentration of governmental authority and power that are antithetical to essential features of democracy, engaging in total war tends to blur the political, military, and moral distinctions between democratic and totalitarian nations (Markusen and Kopf 1995, 76–78).

No recent war, even World Wars I and II, has been completely "total" in the sense that all of the available resources of the combatant nations have been devoted to the conflict or that the destruction of the enemy nation has been complete. During World War II, for example, Germany invested "only" 55 percent of its economic resources in the war effort, and the United States never committed more than 45 percent of its gross national product to the war (Carroll 1968, 11–12). The key distinguishing feature of total warfare, according to Markusen and Kopf, is the assault on civilians, whether as an inadvertent by-product of combat between soldiers (as when distribution of food is disrupted) or as a deliberate policy (as when cities are attacked by incendiary* bombs). They note that the proportion of civilians injured and killed in wars of the 20th century has steadily increased over time: in World War I, only 5 percent of the deaths were civilian; by World War II civilians constituted 66 percent of the deaths; and in wars since the 1970s civilians have accounted for 80 percent or more of the deaths (Markusen and Kopf 1995, 1–2).

See AERIAL WARFARE; BIOLOGICAL/CHEMICAL WARFARE; CHILDREN AND WAR; COLLATERAL DAMAGE; COUNTERFORCE VERSUS

COUNTERVALUE; CRIMES AGAINST HUMANITY; FORBIDDEN STRATEGIES; FORBIDDEN WEAPONS; GENEVA CONVENTIONS, 1929, 1949; HIROSHIMA AND NAGASAKI; HOLOCAUST, THE; INNOCENTS; JUST WAR; MASSACRES; MASS DESTRUCTION, WEAPONS OF; NUCLEAR DETERRENCE; NUCLEAR WAR; PROPORTIONALITY; QUARTER, NO, WARS OF.

BIBLIOGRAPHY

Carroll, Berenice A., *Design for Total War: Arms and Economics in the Third Reich* (The Hague: Mouton, 1968).

Clausewitz, Carl von, *On War,* Michael Howard and Peter Paret, ed. and trans. (Princeton, N.J.: Princeton University Press, 1976).

Elliot, Gil, *Twentieth Century Book of the Dead* (New York: Charles Scribner's Sons, 1972).

Markusen, Eric, and David Kopf, *The Holocaust and Strategic Bombing: Genocide and Total War in the Twentieth Century* (Boulder, Colo.: Westview Press, 1995).

Marwick, Arthur, et al., *War and Change in Twentieth-Century Europe,* Book 5 (Buckingham, England: Open University Press, 1990).

Preston, Richard, and Sydney Wise, *Men in Arms: A History of Warfare and Its Interrelationships with Western Society,* 4th ed. (New York: Holt, Rinehart, & Winston, 1979).

Speier, Hans, ''The Social Types of War,'' in *Social Order and the Risks of War* (Cambridge, Mass.: MIT Press, 1971).

Eric Markusen

TZU, SUN (Sun Wu). Probably lived between the last third of the 6th century B.C. and the middle of the 5th century. He is known for having written a small book named after him, but later titled *The Art of War.* It is likely that he wrote the book partly as a result of his experiences while serving the state of Wu during its attacks on the state of Chu. *Sun Tzu* represents the earliest known book dedicated to military concerns. It is a manual about how a commander is supposed to conduct military operations so as to maximize his chances of success.

One of the two primary themes in *Sun Tzu* is knowledge. According to Sun Tzu, the knowledge a commander has about the enemy, on the one hand, and himself and his people, on the other, are prerequisites for military success. Given his emphasis on knowledge, it is not surprising that Sun Tzu places a high value on espionage (Book 13). He identifies various kinds of spies*. There are local (resident) spies, and ''moles'' such as discontented enemy officials and avaricious enemy concubines. There are also spies who travel among the enemy looking to all the world like fools but who, in fact, are resourceful and brave. In addition, there are so-called converted spies, that is, defectors from the other side. All these spies, and other types as well, present the commander with straightforward information. But another type has the quite different task of spreading disinformation. These spies, belonging to the commander, are given false information, which they hand over to the enemy. The hope is that the enemy will be fooled long enough for the commander to gain real military advantage. Unfortunately for these spies, the likelihood is that it will become apparent sooner or later that the information they are peddling is really disinformation. Their resulting execution makes it clear why Sun Tzu calls these poor souls doomed spies. Whatever the justice of their fate, these and the other spies serve their commander's purpose of creating an asymmetrical relationship between what he and what the enemy commander knows.

Sun Tzu says little directly about self-knowledge, but he implies that the commander who is unaware of his tendencies to become angry, impatient, and careless, and who does not take the time to know his allies and his troops, is not going to fare well. As part of the process of knowing about himself and his people, the commander will develop a variety of virtues including wisdom, credibility (sincerity), courage, benevolence and, at the same time, a policy of strictness in dealing with his troops. A mixture of several of these virtues will make him self-effacing. He will not seek glory, although it may well come to him.

Beyond having knowledge of the enemy, denying the enemy knowledge and also knowing about himself, there is a need for knowledge concerning the weather and the terrain. Knowledge of the weather is especially important when using fire to destroy or harm the enemy (Book 12). Sun Tzu tells us that it is wise to place one's troops windward, and not foolishly in the path of the fire. As to terrain (Book 10) and to types of ground that an army must traverse (Book 11), he identifies their various forms and then advises about military operations with respect to each. Thus Sun Tzu advises moving swiftly to occupy the areas around narrow passes before the enemy does so, and not attempting to block the enemy in ground he labels open. He also advises moving past marshes, mountains, and forests rather than fighting in these difficult settings.

The second primary theme in *Sun Tzu* is control. This theme has two parts: control of one's own people and control of the enemy. One's own people are controlled first by benevolence. Here perhaps Sun Tzu is influenced by Confucius's notion of humanheartedness (jen) although, with Sun Tzu, benevolence or humanheartedness seems to be appropriate only for one's own side—and not for humankind in general. Whatever the source of this concept, Sun Tzu is clear that it is important for the commander to treat his soldiers (and probably his civilian population) fairly. Rewards to the worthy in battle need to be carefully distributed (Book 2). It does not do for the commander to give captured chariots to his friends just because they are his friends. The commander must also make sure his troops are well fed, clothed, housed, and generally cared for. Why? Not simply because of benevolence for its own sake, but because well-treated troops fight better. They also fight better if they are not overindulged. Discipline, applied especially after the troops identify with the commander, must be administered to maintain order, but above all it must be administered fairly. Control over the troops is obtained, then, by a deft use of the carrot and the stick.

But there is more. The commander mystifies his troops and officers (Book

11). Not even his most trusted officers are permitted to understand what he is up to. This mystery, especially when he is successful, creates a sense of awe and thereby enables him to control his people even more successfully.

Controlling one's own people is difficult enough; controlling the enemy is even more so. But it can and must be done. How? In part, by having more knowledge than the enemy. But control over the enemy is also achieved through the use of disinformation that the commander himself spreads. The commander must employ ruses* that, for example, make it appear he is retreating when he is not, is here when he is there, has divided his forces when he has not, is weak when he is not, and is stupid when he is not (Books 5 and 7).

Still, beyond gaining control by controlling information, the commander must also exert his will over the enemy. He moves here and there, always keeping the other side off balance. He does not react, but instead forces the other side to react to him—making it guess where the next blow will strike. Although the commander who follows Sun Tzu's teachings will be unpredictable, some of his general guidelines bring about a certain degree of predictability. If the enemy commander is short-tempered, Sun Tzu says he should be induced to anger (Book 8). If cities are fortified heavily, they should be by-passed and the countryside plundered instead (Book 8). If there are regions or places in the invaded nation prized by the enemy, these are the ones that should be attacked. Fertile territory should also be attacked so that the commander's troops can feed off the land (Book 11).

For Sun Tzu, gaining knowledge and maintaining control over situations where war threatens or where it has already started is important because war, literally, is a life and death matter (Book 1). It was all too obvious to him, given the disunited status of China during his day, that states cannot hope to survive on the good will of their neighbors. Instead, they must prepare for war, and prepare for it not just defensively. Indeed, most of *Sun Tzu* suggests that the fighting should be done on enemy territory. War is costly in men and supplies, but ever more so if the fighting is being done on home territory. So the greater burden of war should be placed on the other side. Nonetheless, even the aggressor* army has heavy burdens, so the aim of a campaign is to finish it as soon as possible. Sun Tzu does not care for protracted war (Book 2). His preference is for the truly brilliant commander who gets his way without even lifting a sword. This commander befuddles and intimidates enemy forces to the point that they submit meekly like sheep (Book 3). The advantage of such policies, of course, is not only that costs and losses are kept to a minimum, but the occupied country is taken over in good condition—lock, stock, and barrel.

It is tempting to ask whether Sun Tzu falls into the just war* tradition that puts limits on war activities for moral or ethical reasons, or into the realist tradition that supposes ethics and war have nothing to do with one another and that, during war, "anything goes." At first blush, the answer seems to be the former. After all, he talks extensively of the commander's virtues (e.g., benevolence) and at one point he even suggests that prisoners* should be treated in a kindly fashion (Book 2). As we have also seen, he prefers to occupy a country without ravaging it. However, when we consider that his talk related to morality is usually couched in terms of the state's self-interest, he can probably be best thought of as a realist in war. He may be an enlightened realist who realizes that kindness rather than cruelty pays off, but still he is a realist.

See JUST WAR; LAWS OF WAR; MILITARY TRAINING, BASIC.

BIBLIOGRAPHY

Clavell, Thomas, ed., *The Art of War* (New York: Dell, 1983).

Cleary, Thomas, ed., *Mastering the Art of War: Zhuge Liang's and Liu Ji's Commentaries on the Classic by Sun Tzu* (Boston and Shaftesbury: Shambala, 1989).

Sun Tzu, *Sun Tzu,* research and reinterpretation by J. H. Huang (New York: Quill, William Morrow, 1993).

Nicholas G. Fotion

U

UNIFORM CODE OF MILITARY JUSTICE **(UCMJ).** Enacted by the U.S. Congress in 1950 to standardize the system of courts and procedures that are used by all branches of the U.S. armed forces to prosecute military personnel for crimes committed during peacetime and wartime. It replaced, but at the same time retained, many of the provisions found in the statutes it succeeded, namely, the Articles for the Government of the Navy and the Articles of War. Acting under the authority of UCMJ Article 36, various U.S. presidents have approved by executive order a Manual for Courts Martial (MCM) to address issues necessary for the orderly administration of military justice not otherwise specifically addressed in the UCMJ. Both the UCMJ and MCM and decisions rendered by military and civilian courts form the fabric of the U.S. military justice system today.

Alleged violations of the UCMJ are prosecuted by court-martial. In serious cases, an accused may appeal his conviction first to a Court of Military Criminal Appeals for the service to which he or she belongs. This court is composed of senior judge advocates who sit as appellate judges to review issues of law and fact that are raised on appeal after a court-martial conviction. All appeals from this court go to the U.S. Court of Appeals for the Armed Services, a five-judge civilian court that normally sits in Washington, D.C. This court must hear all cases ''in which the sentence . . . extends to death'' and ''all cases . . . which the Judge Advocate General orders sent'' to the court. It may hear any other case already reviewed by a Court of Military Criminal Appeals when persuaded by an appellant that it should do so.

The UCMJ has universal application, that is, anyone subject to the UCMJ may be prosecuted for violating the code regardless of where the offense is committed. This provision reflects the fact that U.S. military forces serve both in the United States and overseas and gives military commanders the power to enforce discipline in peacetime and in wartime, at home and abroad. Most people, however, are not subject to the code. In general the UCMJ applies only to ''members of a regular component'' of the U.S. military, members of a reserve component while in training or performing active duty, members of the National Guard who are performing federal service, some retired military personnel, prisoners of war when in the custody of U.S. armed forces, and civilians serving with or accompanying U.S. military forces "in time of war." As such, Americans who have no affiliation with the U.S. military are not subject to the UCMJ and cannot be prosecuted by court-martial. Although Congress did include language in the UCMJ to permit prosecution of civilian dependents who accompany their military sponsors overseas, the U.S. Supreme Court has ruled in a series of celebrated cases that, in peacetime, this jurisdiction is unconstitutional. Moreover, the provision that gives military authorities jurisdiction over civilians serving with or accompanying the armed forces "in time of war" has been interpreted to mean a war declared by Congress.

The UCMJ is divided into twelve subchapters. Subchapter 1, "General Provisions," includes articles that define terms, identify persons subject to the code, establish rules for appointing military attorneys (judge advocates), and require the president to "prescribe procedures for the investigation and disposition of charges, allegations, or information pertaining to the fitness of a military judge or military appellate judge." Subchapter 2 establishes rules for apprehension and restraint. Subchapter 3 contains only one article (Article 15), but is one of the most important sections of the code. Under Article 15, commanders are authorized to use nonjudicial punishment instead of trial by court-martial to discipline military personnel who commit minor UCMJ infractions. Personnel who are offered nonjudicial punishment may reject it and demand trial by court-martial. Those who accept nonjudicial punishment have the right to present a defense to their commander but leave to the commander the decision of whether to impose punishment and, if so, the type and amount of punishment to be imposed. Subchapter 4 establishes three types of court-martial that may be convened to prosecute UCMJ violations (summary, special, and general) and outlines the jurisdiction of each. Subchapter 5 outlines procedures that must be followed to convene a court-martial. In general, articles included in this chapter identify people who may convene courts-martial and describe situations that require the detail of a military judge or counsel. Subchapters 6, 7, and 9 establish rules that affect, respectively, pretrial, trial, and posttrial procedures. Subchapter 10 contains the punitive articles and subchapter 7 establishes rules for sentencing people who are convicted of committing a UCMJ violation. Subchapter 10 contains two broad categories of offenses (murder, manslaughter, rape, robbery, etc.) that are prohibited by the vast majority of the world's legal systems, and military offenses (absence without leave, desertion, disrespect, disobedience, etc.). Subchapter 8 abolishes punishments such as flogging and branding that are now considered cruel and unusual, but otherwise permits the president to establish maximum punishments that can be imposed for violating a punitive article. Subchapter 11, "Miscellaneous Provisions," permits persons who may convene a court-martial to convene a court of inquiry. It also authorizes certain persons to administer oaths and to act as a notary, requires that the UCMJ be taught to all enlisted personnel, provides procedures that military personnel can use to file complaints of wrongdoing against their commander, and provides an administrative remedy that individuals can invoke to obtain compensation when U.S. military personnel wilfully damage or destroy their property or wrongfully take it. Subchapter 12 establishes rules regarding the composition and jurisdiction of the U.S. Court of Appeals for the Armed Services.

See MILITARY TRAINING, BASIC; SUPERIOR ORDERS.

BIBLIOGRAPHY

Kinsella v. Singleton, 361 U.S. 234 (1960).

Moyer, H. E., Jr., *Justice and the Military* (London: Royal Institute of International Affairs, 1972).

Reid v. Covert, 354 U.S. 1 (1957).

Uniform Code of Military Justice, 10 U.S.C. 801–946 (19). The Code has been amended several times, most notably in 1958 (Pub. L. 85-861); 1983 (Pub. L. 98–209); and 1989 (Pub. L. 101–189).

William G. Schmidt and Norman K. Thompson

UNITED NATIONS PEACEMAKING AND PEACEKEEPING. The UN was established on October 24, 1945, by the victors in World War II with its primary purpose, according to its charter, "to maintain international peace and security . . . to bring about by peaceful means the settlement of international disputes or situations which might lead to a breach of the peace." Over the past fifty years the UN has served that objective through a variety of means, commonly called peacemaking and peacekeeping.

While these two means are often interwoven, peacemaking generally involves diplomatic efforts such as negotiation, arbitration, and other nonmilitary means by one of the principal organs of the institution, such as the secretary general. Peacekeeping, on the other hand, traditionally involves the dispatch of uniformed UN personnel under the authority of the Security Council with such tasks as monitoring cease-fire lines, establishing buffer zones between warring parties, or enforcing decisions of the Security Council, frequently combining such efforts with humanitarian operations to relieve civilian suffering.

PEACEMAKING

The UN is not a world government, and its powers are restricted not only by the charter prohibition on interference in the internal affairs of member states, but also by the authority of all five permanent members of the Security Council (China, France, the UK, Russia, and the United States). These five have the power to veto any decision of the Security Council through a negative vote. Despite these limitations, the patient negotiating efforts of the secretary general or his representatives have, on many occasions, ended bloody conflict. For example, in 1949, Undersecretary Ralph Bunche received the Nobel Peace Prize for arranging a truce between the Arab countries and the newly created state of

Israel. The secretary general commonly uses his own so-called "good offices" to provide a respected and acceptable third party in assisting the resolution of disputes between parties who find it difficult to deal directly with each other. Notable among such successes was the arrangement of a cease-fire between Iran and Iraq in 1988, concluding a war that had cost over one million lives. Later the same year the secretary general completed a two-year negotiating effort by arranging a peace settlement between the contending parties in the conflict in El Salvador, which had cost an estimated 75,000 lives. As of 1995, UN negotiators are continuing their four-year efforts to conclude the tragic war in the former Yugoslavia.

In addition to the efforts of the secretary general, the Security Council has often exercised pressure on parties to a dispute to settle their differences by adopting resolutions appealing for an end to the conflict or by exercising additional pressure through such other means as economic embargoes.

PEACEKEEPING

UN peacekeeping is the use of multinational military forces under UN command to provide the international community with a variety of services. The forces are authorized by the Security Council, which specifies their mandate depending on the particular circumstances prevailing in a given situation. The forces are organized by the secretary general, and the troops are contributed by member states with funding provided through financial contributions usually assessed on an obligatory basis.

In the past fifty years, UN peacekeeping forces have operated on every continent except North America. During its early history the preponderance of such activities was concentrated in the Middle East. For many years UN troops maintained a truce between Egypt and Israel until a peace treaty between the two nations obviated their further need. Even today, twenty years after its inception, the UN Disengagement Observer Force supervises a cease-fire between Israel and Syria in the strategically important Golan Heights area. On the island of Cyprus, after thirty years, UN soldiers continue to provide a buffer zone between antagonistic Turk and Greek Cypriot forces.

More recent operations have involved new geographic areas and substantially more difficult tasks than the traditional roles of monitoring cease-fire lines and separating contending parties while efforts continued to resolve their conflicts. Current facts of international life involve the difficulties faced by some countries after the end of the Cold War*, with withdrawal of great power support, weak national institutions, collapsing economies, ethnic strife, partitions, and natural disasters. More traditional military operations are further complicated by the need to strengthen institutions, encourage democratic participation in government, protect human rights, and promote economic and social development.

This new situation has resulted in rapid expansion in both the number of UN peacekeeping operations and the breadth of their responsibilities. In addition to providing a buffer zone between warring parties, UN forces are now required to disarm combatants, quell anarchy, implement political settlements, and guarantee the delivery of humanitarian aid. In its fifty-year history, the UN has mounted thirty-three peacekeeping operations, and as of 1995, has forces involved in seventeen places around the world. Twelve of these were established in the years 1993–1995. All these operations involved about 70,000 troops, with a cost of about $3 billion a year.

The recent growth in the costs and mandates of these forces has led to increased political controversy in the United States. The U.S.-led UN operation in Somalia, which involved the loss of American lives, and the operation in Haiti, also U.S.-led, attracted particular criticism. Under the new Republican congressional leadership, legislation has been introduced to sharply reduce U.S. financial support for peacekeeping and to discourage such operations from engaging in so-called ''nation-building'' programs. This move has been criticized by leading Democrats, who have argued that this would destroy an important foreign policy option that affords a multilateral rather than a unilateral means of dealing with international problems.

See BIOLOGICAL/CHEMICAL WARFARE, UN RESOLUTIONS BANNING; CHILDREN'S RIGHTS IN WAR; GULF WAR (DESERT STORM); HUMANITARIAN INTERVENTION; KOREAN WAR; NUCLEAR PROLIFERATION; NUCLEAR WEAPONS TESTING, UN RESOLUTIONS BANNING; NUCLEAR WEAPONS, UN RESOLUTIONS BANNING MANUFACTURE OR USE; YUGOSLAVIA, WAR CRIMES IN THE FORMER.

BIBLIOGRAPHY

The Blue Helmets (New York: UN Department of Public Information, 1990).

Hall, Brien, ''Blue Helmets, Empty Guns,'' *New York Times Magazine* (February 2, 1994).

Higgins, Roslyn, *UN Peacekeeping,* 4 vols. (London: Oxford University Press, 1969–1981).

Stanley, C. Maxwell, *Managing Global Problems* (Iowa City: University of Iowa Press, 1979).

United Nations Chronicle: UN Peacekeeping Around the World (New York: UN Department of Public Information, 1993).

Urquart, Brian, *Ralph Bunche: An American Life* (New York: Norton, 1993).

William Burnside Buffum

V

VATTEL, EMMERICH DE (1714–1767). Although a defender of natural law, many of Vattel's writings emphasized customs as the bases for laws of war. His works became standard reference works for writers in international law. Vattel shared the widely held view that wars ought to be declared* by the proper authority, although by his time the rise of democratic aspirations had considerably altered the nature and source of such authority. In spite of this, he insisted that no one was excused from declaring war simply because his neighbor had not done so. The rise of nationalism influenced him to conclude that all wars were equally lawful for every nation, hence the distinction between just* and unjust wars disappeared. Unlike Hugo Grotius* (1583–1645), Vattel insisted that citizens were obligated to serve in the army when the prince gave the call to arms. There was no room for a soldier to question superior orders*.

Although he deplored acts that he called "essentially evil and unlawful," he still permitted princes to use whatever force was required to subdue the enemy, and his remarks implied that there were no limits in natural law to allowable force. Although he agreed with Christian Wolff (1679–1754) that it was not allowable to kill those who had surrendered*, he made exceptions in the case of enemies who had committed grave breaches of the laws of war*. In such cases, reprisals* in kind were permitted, although he drew the line at the use of poisons and the practice of perfidy. He classified treacheries by degrees. Poison, for example, was more revolting than assassination*, yet poisoned weapons were less objectionable than poisoning the water supply.

See AYALA, BALTHAZAR; BELLI, PIERINO; BYNKERSCHOEK, CORNELIUS; GENTILI, ALBERICO; GROTIUS, HUGO; SUAREZ, FRANCISCO; VICTORIA, FRANCISCUS DE.

BIBLIOGRAPHY
Vattel, Emmerich de, *The Law of Nations or the Principles of Natural Law* (Washington, D.C.: Carnegie Foundation, 1916).

VICTORIA, FRANCISCUS DE (1480–1546). A professor of theology at the University of Salamanca and the first in a series of writers on what came to be known as international law. Their aim was to determine the source of laws of war. Two options were open: (1) to derive such laws from custom, or (2) derive them from "natural laws." Victoria accepted the Roman Catholic belief that natural reason could discover such laws structured in the nature of things. His arguments were fortified by quotations from scripture and the church fathers, and by the belief that natural laws existed from which laws of war could be derived.

His major work, *On the Indians: Or on the Law of War Made by the Spaniards on the Barbarians,* was published in 1523. He was convinced that the Spanish war against the Indians was unjust; that all men were free under the law of nature; that the Indians were the owners of their lands and goods; and that, as a consequence, the imperial claims of the Spanish monarch were invalid. The children of Spanish-Indian marriages should have the full rights of local citizens, and he denied that either the Pope or any secular prince could claim to have spiritual domination over nonbelievers. The only land that could be claimed by another was land not already owned by anyone. He observed that some so-called "customs of war" were not in accordance with natural law, and he urged, especially, that no war could be justly entered unless reason and persuasion had first been tried.

Victoria considered wars for religion, for the personal glory of the prince, or for the extension of the empire, to be unjust. He rejected the prevailing papal view that good faith need not be kept in wars against heretics and unbelievers. Neither the aim of suppressing nor of spreading a religion were worthy ends of war. Could justice be on both sides of a given war? He answered with reservations. If justice were on both sides in the same war, and this was not precluded, it seemed to follow that injustice would also be on both sides. This followed from the premise that it was unjust to wage war against a nation that had justice on its side. In such cases, Victoria allowed ignorance as an excuse, so that both sides could wage such a war justly. Might citizens refuse to fight in a war where injustice was on their side? He argued that if the subject was convinced of the injustice of the war, then he ought not to serve in it even though his prince commanded him, but since such assurance was rarely possessed by the citizen, Victoria warned subjects that they ran the risk of exposing their state to the enemy, which he considered more serious than fighting a war of doubtful justice.

He distinguished between wars of defense and those of aggression*, although he maintained that both offensive and defensive wars could still qualify as just wars* if they were based on just causes. Once the nation was in war, were there limits to what could justly be done to win the war? He affirmed that, even in wars against the Turks, it was not allowed to kill women and children. He also added that it was not permitted to kill clerics, foreigners, guests, or members of religious orders. Practice did not accord with his claim. He spoke to the issue of proportionality* and observed that if attacking a city might result in great devastation and human slaughter, then such an attack should be forbidden.

See AYALA, BALTHAZAR; BELLI, PIERINO; CHRISTIANITY AND

WAR; GENTILI, ALBERICO; GROTIUS, HUGO; HOLY WAR; SUAREZ, FRANCISCO; VATTEL, EMMERICH DE.
BIBLIOGRAPHY
Beeler, John, *Warfare in Feudal Europe* (Ithaca, N.Y.: Cornell University Press, 1971).
Keen, Maurice Hugh, *The Laws of War in the Late Middle Ages* (London: Routledge & Kegan Paul, 1965).
Victoria, Franciscus de, *On the Indians: Or on the Law of War Made by the Spaniards on the Barbarians* (Washington, D.C.: Carnegie Foundation, 1917).

VIETNAM WAR. The United States' participation in the hostilities in Vietnam during the 1960s and 1970s was rationalized on several premises by successive presidential administrations. The hostilities grew out of France's withdrawal as the colonial power in Indochina in the face of an armed resistance led in Vietnam by a political-military administration that established a seat of government in the city of Hanoi.

In 1954, the Hanoi administration's army defeated the French army in a major battle at Dien Bien Phu, leading to a French military withdrawal from the country. As that occurred, the Vietnamese who had been allied with the French established an administration in Saigon, the seat of France's administration. Internationally sponsored talks were held in Geneva, leading to an agreement that divided the two administrations at an imaginary line at the 17th parallel. The agreement called for national elections to be held in 1956 in order to form a single government for all Vietnam.

The Hanoi administration was left-oriented and had engaged in land reform. The Saigon administration was Western-oriented. President Dwight Eisenhower was concerned that if elections were held in 1956, the winner would be Ho Chi Minh, head of the Hanoi administration. Eisenhower encouraged the Saigon administration to refuse to hold the elections, and as a result those elections were not held.

The end of the electoral option led the Hanoi administration to explore other means to reunite the country. Civil war broke out south of the 17th parallel, initiated by Vietnamese who viewed the Saigon administration as a puppet of the West. These Vietnamese had the support of the Hanoi administration. By 1963 the Kennedy administration sent military advisors to aid the Saigon administration.

In 1964 the Johnson administration decided on the need to bomb targets in the north to convince the Hanoi administration to stop supporting the rebels in the south. For this project, President Johnson desired approval by Congress. At his direction, Johnson's staff in May 1964 drafted a joint resolution for Congress to authorize bombing north of the 17th parallel. At the time, however, there was little prospect that Congress would pass such a resolution.

In July 1964, however, an incident occurred that resulted in Congress giving its approval. On July 30, 1964, naval vessels of the Saigon administration, acting under U.S. advisors, raided two islands in the Gulf of Tonkin*, which lies north of the 17th parallel. Simultaneously, an American destroyer geared for electronic surveillance, the U.S.S. *Maddox,* sailed into the Gulf of Tonkin seeking intelligence information for use in bombing the north.

Following a repetition of raiding by the Saigon navy, torpedo boats of the Hanoi administration approached the U.S.S. *Maddox,* in the apparent belief that it was involved in the raids. The *Maddox* frightened the torpedo boats away, and President Johnson ordered another destroyer, the U.S.S. *C. Turner Joy,* into the area to protect the *Maddox.*

On August 4, the U.S.S. *Maddox* reported to Washington that torpedo boats of the Hanoi administration had fired on it. No one on the U.S.S. *Maddox* had seen any firing, and the ship was not hit, but sonar and radar readings made it appear that torpedoes had been fired. The U.S.S. *C. Turner Joy,* sailing nearby, detected no firing, although it had more sophisticated sonar than the *Maddox.* A U.S. Navy pilot flying above the U.S. vessels that night reported seeing no vessels of the Hanoi administration, no gunfire, and no torpedo* wakes.

The commanders of the *Maddox* and *C. Turner Joy* soon realized that in fact the *Maddox* had not been fired upon. The error apparently occurred because crew members of the *Maddox* mistook sonar reflections of their ship's rudder for torpedoes. The commander sent a new message to Washington to retract the report of a firing.

Despite the retraction, the reported firing gave the Johnson administration an opportunity it could not resist. Secretary of Defense Robert McNamara asked military commanders to double check to find out whether there might in fact have been a firing and, without waiting for an answer, the Defense Department put out a press statement claiming a "deliberate attack" by the Hanoi administration. President Johnson announced that he would order reprisal strikes. "Renewed hostile actions against United States ships on the high seas in the Gulf of Tonkin have today required me," Johnson said in a televised speech, "to order the military forces of the United States to take action in reply." He charged the Hanoi administration with "open aggression."

Johnson then revised his draft congressional resolution for air strikes and sent it to Capitol Hill. He did not tell Congress that the report of a firing on the U.S.S. *Maddox* had been retracted. Congress quickly adopted a joint resolution to authorize bombing above the 17th parallel. In a preamble, the resolution stated, "Whereas naval units of the Communist regime in Vietnam, in violation of the principles of the Charter of the United Nations and of international law, have deliberately and repeatedly attacked United States naval vessels lawfully present in international waters." In an operative paragraph, the resolution approved the president's decision to take "all necessary measures to . . . prevent further aggression." The House passed the resolution 416 to 0, and the Senate voted 88 to 2 in support.

George Ball, who was under-secretary of state at the time, said some years later that President Johnson knew that his information about a firing was flawed, but that he was eager to bomb the north of Vietnam and therefore used the information.

Following passage of the joint resolution, Johnson undertook substantial bombing of the north of Vietnam. In addition, he introduced substantial numbers of U.S. ground troops into the hostilities.

The alleged attack in the Gulf of Tonkin, being a single incident, did not provide a complete explanation for the U.S. involvement in the Vietnam hostilities. The State Department prepared for that purpose a paper headed *Aggression from the North: The Record of North Vietnam's Campaign to Conquer South Viet-Nam.* The paper recited that "a Communist government," meaning the Hanoi administration, "has set out deliberately to conquer a sovereign people in a neighboring state," meaning the area south of the 17th parallel. The paper said that Hanoi's tactic, rather than all-out invasion, was "concealed aggression," meaning the instigation of an insurgency in the south of Vietnam.

The insurgency movement, which called itself the National Liberation Front, was, according to the paper, not a genuine movement but "was formed at Hanoi's order in 1960." Its "principal function," the paper said, was "to create the false impression that the aggression in South Vietnam is an indigenous rebellion against the established government."

To show that the insurgency was northern-directed, the paper said that the insurgency received "many of the weapons and much of the ammunition and other supplies" from the Hanoi administration. The paper depicted the Saigon administration as fighting back in self-defense. As a rationale for the United States' role, the paper said, "the United States has responded to the appeals of the Government of the Republic of Vietnam [Saigon administration] for help in this defense."

A major weakness in the paper's analysis was its assumption that the two sectors of Vietnam were separate states. The demarcation line at the 17th parallel was not an international boundary, and both the Hanoi administration and the Saigon administration considered Vietnam to be a single state.

In 1961 the Vietnamese Communist Party, viewing Vietnam as a single state, referred to the north as a "source of support and a base area of the revolution to liberate the South," and urged the insurgency to increase military efforts against the Saigon administration in rural areas. There was thus substance to the paper's view that the north was intimately involved in the insurgency in the south. The significance of that involvement, however, turned on whether Vietnam was a single state or two separate states.

The 1961 directive, moreover, did not mean that there was not support among southerners for an insurgency against the Saigon administration. Southern members of the Vietnamese Communist Party had asked the party hierarchy to adopt the directive calling for military action against the Saigon administration. In 1960–1961, these southerners viewed military action as necessary, because Ngo Dinh Diem, head of the Saigon administration, was suppressing his leftist opponents, and they feared elimination if they did not attack his administration.

The insurgents, moreover, controlled about half of the rural area south of the 17th parallel and enjoyed considerable support from the population south of the 17th parallel. It was to combat this control by the insurgents that the Central Intelligence Agency, in an effort called Operation Phoenix, instituted a program of assassinating village leaders loyal to the insurgents.

The State Department paper left the impression that the insurgents received nearly all their personnel and equipment from north of the 17th parallel. Regarding personnel, the paper said that between 1959 and 1964, 39,550 combatants moved south to join the insurgency. However, figures cited elsewhere by U.S. government sources indicated that if this figure were true, it would account for only 10 percent of the insurgency's combatants.

Moreover, many of those Vietnamese moving south were originally southerners, having gone north in 1954, after the demarcation line was drawn. The State Department was aware of this phenomenon and argued in the paper that 75 percent of those coming south were natives of the north. However, it cited little evidence for this figure.

Regarding armaments, the insurgency received support from the Hanoi administration. The International Control Commission for Viet Nam, which policed the 1954 Geneva agreement, in 1962 reported "in specific instances" that "armed and unarmed personnel, arms, munitions and other supplies have been sent from the Zone in the North to the Zone in the South." However, most of the insurgents' weapons were manufactured in the south, or were bought or captured from the Saigon administration's army. U.S. Department of Defense figures for 1962–1964 showed that the insurgents captured 12,300 more weapons than they lost to the Saigon army.

The dual explanation for the U.S. involvement was thus the Gulf of Tonkin incident and the State Department's analysis of the hostilities. Both aspects of the explanation revealed considerable factual weakness. The widespread protest in the United States against the war arose both because America was seen as an aggressor and because of the widespread use of historically forbidden weapons, such as incendiaries like napalm and chemicals like Agent Orange, and forbidden strategies such as obliteration bombing of civilian villages.

See AGGRESSIVE VERSUS DEFENSIVE WAR; BIOLOGICAL/CHEMICAL WARFARE; COMBATANT-NONCOMBATANT DISTINCTION; FORBIDDEN STRATEGIES; FORBIDDEN WEAPONS; FRAGMENTATION BOMBS; INCENDIARIES; MASS DESTRUCTION; SON MY/MY LAI; STOCKHOLM/ROTHSKILDE WAR CRIMES TRIALS.

BIBLIOGRAPHY
"Aggression from the North: The Record of North Vietnam's Campaign to Conquer South Viet-Nam." Pub. no. 7839, *Department of State Bulletin* 52 (1965), 404.
Fall, Bernard, *Viet-Nam Witness 1953–66* (New York: Praeger, 1966).
Gettleman, Marvin E., *Vietnam: History, Documents, and Opinions on a Major World Crisis* (Greenwich, Conn.: Fawcett, 1965).

Goulden, Joseph C., *Truth Is the First Casualty: The Gulf of Tonkin Affair—Illusion and Reality* (Chicago: Rand McNally, 1969).

Joint Resolution to Promote the Maintenance of International Peace and Security in Southeast Asia, August 10, 1964, U.S. Congress, *Statutes at Large* 78 (1964), 384.

Lacouture, Jean, "Viet Cong: Who Are They, What Do They Want?" *New Republic,* March 6, 1965, 21.

McNamara, Robert, *In Retrospect: The Tragedy and Lessons of Vietnam* (New York: Random House, 1995).

The Pentagon Papers (Washington, D.C.: U.S. Government Printing Office, 1971).

The Pentagon Papers as Published by the New York Times (New York: Bantam Books, 1971).

"The President's Address," *New York Times,* August 5, 1964, A1, col. 6.

Special Report to the Co-Chairmen of the Geneva Conference on Indo-China, International Commission for Supervision and Control in Vietnam, Saigon, June 2, 1962, Command Paper 1755, in Great Britain, *Parliamentary Papers* (House of Commons and Command), Session 31 October 1961–25 October 1962, vol. 39, p. 7, col. 6.

"Tonkin—Dubious Premise for War," *Los Angeles Times,* April 29, 1985, A1, col. 1.

Turley, William S., *The Second Indochina War: A Short Political and Military History, 1954–1975* (Boulder, Colo.: Westview Press, 1986).

War Experiences Recapitulation Committee of the High-Level Military Institute, People's Army Publishing House, Hanoi, *The Anti-U.S. Resistance War for National Salvation 1954–1975: Military Events,* U.S. Government, Joint Publications Research Service No. 80968, June 3, 1982, 43.

John Quigley

W

WAR CRIMES. The belief that there should be moral limits to permissible war practices is of ancient origin. Thucydides and Cicero spoke of laws of war, from which they inferred crimes of war. The Athenians accused the Spartans of committing needless cruelties in war; Roman historians portrayed the invaders from the North as barbarians; and early Christian writers were convinced that Christian soldiers would wage wars with humanity. Punishment of the vanquished for putative offenses by the victors was all too common. But such victor's justice lacked the element of legality or universality desirable in a genuine war crimes trial. Two preconditions were required: (1) a duly authorized court, and (2) preexisting laws, the breaking of which constituted the crime. The U.S. prosecution of Captain Henry Wirz* for putative war crimes during the Civil War had the semblance of both requirements in *General Orders 100**. Using the same bases, the United States prosecuted a number of its own soldiers for criminal acts during the Philippine* war. An attempt was made after World War I to hold war crimes trials (*see* Leipzig Trials).

Preparation for the war crimes trials after World War II, however, resulted in elaborate specifications of what war crimes were believed to be. The charter of the Nuremberg* international military tribunal, Article 6, defined war crimes as:

violations of the laws or customs of war. Such violations shall include, but not be limited to, murder, ill-treatment or deportation to slave labor or for any other purpose of civilian population of or in occupied territory, murder or ill-treatment of prisoners of war or persons on the seas, killing of hostages, plunder of public or private property, wanton destruction of cities, towns or villages, or devastation not justified by military necessity*.

The current U.S. Army manual, *The Law of Land Warfare**, mentions crimes against the peace* and crimes against humanity*, but deals in detail only with war crimes. The above-listed war crimes had been recognized by Articles 46, 50, 52, and 56 of The Hague* convention of 1907, and by Articles 2, 3, 4, 46, and 51 of the Geneva convention of 1929*, and the U.S. manual refers to these as well, citing Article 6 of the Nuremberg charter. Some scholars argued that The Hague conventions did not apply because of the "general participation" clause, which asserted that the provisions did not apply in wars where nonsignatories were involved, and some of the belligerents were not signatories. The manual also included as war crimes, biological experiments*, wilfully causing great suffering and serious injury to body or health, unlawful confinement, forcing protected persons to labor or armed service, and executions* without fair trial. Further, the manual lists "other types of war crimes" as including the using of forbidden weapons* and forbidden strategies* such as treacherous request for quarter, maltreatment of dead bodies, abuse of flags of truce, firing on undefended localities that are without military significance, soldiers wearing civilian clothing, misuse of the Red Cross* emblem, improper use of privileged buildings for military use, poisoning of wells or streams, pillage*, compelling prisoners* or civilians to perform prohibited labor, killing spies* without trial, and violation of surrender terms. The manual decreed that such offenses would be tried by U.S. courts-martial using the *Uniform Code of Military Justice*ic* rather than the Nuremberg procedure. Paragraph 507 of the U.S. manual stated that "the jurisdiction of United States military tribunals in connection with war crimes is not limited to offenses committed against nationals of the United States," but extends to persons anywhere in the world. Such a policy, however, would generate confusion if all the nations had a similar claim to jurisdiction. At the time that *The Law of Land Warfare* was revised in 1976, the United States did not envision any further international tribunals for the prosecution of such crimes. In 1993, however, the UN Security Council authorized the establishment of a war crimes tribunal for putative offenses in the war in the former Yugoslavia*.

See CONTROL COUNCIL LAW NO. 10; LEIPZIG TRIALS; NUREMBERG TRIALS; PHILIPPINES WAR CRIMES TRIALS; SHIMODA CASE; STOCKHOLM/ROTHSKILDE WAR CRIMES TRIALS; TOKYO TRIALS; WIRZ, CAPTAIN HENRY.

BIBLIOGRAPHY

Appleman, John Alan, *Military Tribunals and International Crimes* (Westport, Conn.: Greenwood Press, 1971).

Falk, Richard A., Gabriel Kolko, and Robert Jay Lifton, *Crimes of War* (New York: Random House, 1971).

Knoll, Erwin, and Judith Nies McFadden, *War Crimes and the American Conscience* (New York: Holt, Rinehart & Winston, 1970).

Manner, George, "The Legal Nature and Punishment of Criminal Acts of Violence Contrary to the Laws of War," *American Journal of International Law* 37 (July 1943).

WAR CRIMES TRIALS. *See* CONTROL COUNCIL LAW NO. 10; IRAQ COMMISSION OF INQUIRY; LEIPZIG TRIALS; PHILIPPINES WAR

CRIMES TRIALS; NUREMBERG TRIALS; SHIMODA CASE; SON MY/MY LAI; STOCKHOLM/ROTHSKILDE WAR CRIMES TRIALS; TOKYO TRIALS; WINTER SOLDIER INVESTIGATION; WIRZ, CAPTAIN HENRY; YUGOSLAVIA, WAR CRIMES IN THE FORMER.

WARISM. The view that war is morally justifiable in principle and often morally justified in fact. There are many ways to express warism: it can be found in warist language including war imagery and metaphor as well as in warist behavior, such as combative personal interaction and assault-style approaches to groups. The central notion is that war can be and often is morally acceptable, largely because it is simply a fact of nature.

In every culture there are basic concepts, assumptions, values, beliefs, and ideas that together form a frame of reference, conceptual scheme, or perspective through which members of the culture experience the world. A conceptual scheme consists of what is taken as given when engaging the world. Such givens are like normative lenses through which reality is conceived.

In modern culture, warism is a dominant outlook, an unconscious fundamental presupposition contributing to the conceptual scheme of the vast majority of people. It seems so obvious to most members of modern culture that war is morally justifiable that they do not realize that they are assuming it; no other way of understanding large-scale human conflict has occurred to them.

Warism can be like racism, sexism, and homophobia: a prejudicial bias built into conceptions and judgments without the knowledge of those presupposing it. Or it can be an explicitly held, openly articulated position on the morality of war deliberately taken as a value judgment. In the former case, the uncritical presumption of warism distorts judgments on conflicts between nations and predisposes warists to take war to be a perfectly natural, normal, and necessary feature of the modern international arena. In the latter case, war can be touted as the only thing the enemy understands, brandished as a threat to help secure the status quo, or carefully defended as necessary for the establishment of justice. In any case, warism misguides our attitudes and institutions to the extent that it overstates the necessity and inevitability of war.

Evidence of modern culture taking war for granted as morally acceptable is manifest in virtually all aspects of life from the obvious cases of politics and popular media to business, education, and even religion. Advertising, television, and school curricula all reflect the dominant outlook. Popular heroes like Rambo, Dirty Harry, and GI Joe swagger with warist bias. Even scholars are considered to be survivors of academic jousting, embattled in verbal attack and rejoinder, warriors fighting for truth, exchanging linguistic blows in efforts to win arguments and defeat rivals. At every level of society, conflict entails fights for superiority.

Students have ample opportunities to learn of the battles, tactics, heroics, and military leadership in the wars that made the current political configuration of the globe. Rarely is mention made of advocates of nonviolence, pacifists*, models of cooperative rather than domineering domestic and foreign policies. Further evidence of the common cultural disposition to consider war morally accepta-ble—even morally required—is the fact that pacifists are much more frequently called upon to defend their views than are those who take war to be a legitimate activity of nations. The war system—the standard operating procedure of nations constantly preparing for, threatening, and undertaking war—is simply taken for granted. The burden of proof rests on anyone who calls it into question.

The widespread, unquestioning acceptance of warism leaves the dominant conceptual framework of culture in place. Having assumed (without realizing it in most cases) that war is morally acceptable, our moral considerations of war turn to questions of the moral acceptability of a particular war or of specific acts within a given war. These are important issues, but focusing on them leaves unchallenged the presumption that war is morally justifiable.

The slow but increasing awareness in dominant culture of racial, ethnic, and gender oppression and the efforts of liberation from within the oppressed groups offer hope that even the most deeply held and least challenged predispositions of life might be questioned, examined, and criticized. Perhaps one day those oppressed by warism may challenge, examine, criticize, and expose this fun-damental feature of dominant culture so that war is no longer taken for granted as natural, moral and inevitable.

See DEMOCRACY AND THE MILITARY; MILITARY-INDUSTRIAL COMPLEX; MILITARY TRAINING, BASIC.

BIBLIOGRAPHY
Cady, Duane L., *From Warism to Pacifism: A Moral Continuum* (Philadelphia: Temple University Press, 1989).
———, ''In Defense of Active Pacifists,'' *Journal of Social Philosophy* 25, no. 2 (Fall 1994).
Smithka, Paula, ''Are Active Pacifists Really Just-Warists in Disguise?'' *Journal of So-cial Philosophy* 23, no. 3 (Winter 1992).

Duane L. Cady

WARNING ZONES AND MILITARY EXCLUSION ON THE HIGH SEAS. It has been almost axiomatic since the days of Hugo Grotius* (1583–1645) that navigation and fishing on the high seas should be free and unimpeded. Nonetheless, in recent years several major maritime nations have claimed the right to declare exclusionary or warning zones on the high seas to serve their military purposes. These claims appear to conflict with the norms now governing the high seas, which have developed from treaties, the practices of nations, and the views of modern jurists. Claims to exclude or limit free navigation can be sustained only if they have no appreciable effect on navigation and no significant effect on the environment or resources of the region. Furthermore, a vessel entering such a zone could not be forcibly removed from the area except by the nation whose flag it flies. If a vessel operating with the support of its flag government is damaged by the military activities of another nation, its owner would be entitled to compensation from the nation causing the damage.

SOVIET MISSILE TESTS

The USSR's first announced broad ocean area missile tests were between January 15 and February 15, 1960. These missiles were launched from the east-central Soviet mainland into a broad area of the central Pacific Ocean. The USSR requested other countries to avoid an area of the high seas of approximately 100,000 square miles for a period of one month.

The USSR used three land-based launch sites for testing its intercontinental ballistic missiles (ICBMs), along with a fleet of submarines for testing sea-launched ballistic missiles (SLBMs) and sea-launched cruise missiles (SLCMs). The usual impact area for the land-based launch sites was just east of the Kamchatka Peninsula. The Soviets also, but less frequently, utilized broad ocean areas in the central Pacific Ocean as impact zones. Between May 1985 and November 1987, for instance, the USSR launched fourteen ballistic missiles in the central Pacific Ocean, warning ships and aircraft to avoid areas as large as 200,000 square nautical miles. (The United States launched forty such missiles in the same time period to areas of the Pacific.)

Although formal protests concerning the Soviet claims to use areas of the high seas for missile testing purposes have been limited, these claims have caused increasing concern. After the USSR's first missile test in the Pacific, portions of the U.S. public called for President Dwight D. Eisenhower to issue a protest on grounds that the tests violated international law*. President Eisenhower responded that such tests were not against international law and that it would be inappropriate to issue a protest because the United States uses the oceans for exactly the same purpose.

U.S. MISSILE TESTS

The United States announced its first missile test on July 8, 1950. These missiles were launched to a point near the Bahamas from Cape Canaveral, Florida. In 1959, launchings to Kwajalein Atoll in the Marshall Islands in the mid-Pacific began from the Vandenberg Air Force and Point Mugu Naval Bases in California. Each test was preceded by public notices requesting mariners and pilots to avoid designated areas for a period of time. Some areas, like the 200-nautical-mile zone around Kwajalein Atoll, are considered permanent warning areas in effect twenty-four hours a day, 365 days of the year.

Currently, Cape Canaveral has launchings to Ascension Island and beyond into broad areas of the Indian Ocean. The California bases (most Vandenberg) continue to launch into Kwajalein and also into broad ocean areas further south into the Pacific. In addition, the U.S. fleet of missile-capable submarines has test launchings, usually from international waters adjacent to either the California or Florida coast, with consequent warning areas around the submarines and the destinations of the launched missiles. Kwajalein Atoll receives the bulk of the U.S. testing because of the extensive tracking facilities located there. Kwajalein typically receives about twenty-five missile "missions" launched from the American mainland each year. The United States is now making increasing use of ocean areas heading south toward Australia and New Zealand.

U.S. NUCLEAR WEAPONS TESTING* PROGRAM

The weapons testing program that has had the most significant effect on the free use of the high seas has been the tests of nuclear bombs. Nuclear testing in the Pacific began on July 1, 1946, when the United States exploded an atom bomb in the middle of Bikini Atoll* in the Marshall Islands. The United States established "danger zones" for all of its Pacific nuclear bomb tests. Approximately 150,000 square nautical miles were included in the danger zone declared for the first nuclear bomb tests. This zone was in effect from the end of June to mid-August 1946.

The next series of tests began in 1948, with a smaller warning area of 30,000 square nautical miles in effect, at first for the calendar year, and then "until further notice." In May 1953, the danger area was extended 135 nautical miles eastward, the area being "dangerous to all ships, aircraft and personnel entering it." During this time, Johnston Atoll (717 nautical miles southwest of Honolulu) was also being used for atomic tests. A danger zone with a radius of 400 nautical miles around the island was established on July 25, 1958, for a month. The final series of tests occurred in 1962 at Johnston and Christmas Atolls. The United States also established during this period an aircraft warning zone extending 700 nautical miles around Johnston at 30,000 feet and above. Both of these zones became effective on April 15, 1962. The last test on Johnston Island took place on November 4, 1962.

UK NUCLEAR BOMB TESTING PROGRAM

Australia declared a danger zone of 6,000 square nautical miles around the Monte Bello Islands for the UK's first nuclear tests in 1952. The UK's first H-bomb tests occurred on Malden and Christmas islands in the spring of 1957, and it announced at that time a 700,000 square nautical mile warning zone would be in effect from March 1 to August 1, 1957. This notice was a "public warning" that the area was "dangerous to shipping and aircraft." British Prime Minister Harold MacMillan said "We do not consider that we are in any breach of international law." The UK vacated Johnston Island and ended its Pacific Ocean testing in December 1958.

FRENCH NUCLEAR BOMB TESTING PROGRAM

The French atmospheric nuclear tests in French Polynesia occurred between 1966 and 1974—a total of forty-one tests. The maritime danger zone extended 150 miles from Moruroa Atoll, with a 500-nautical-mile easterly downwind corridor. The zone for aircraft extended 200 miles beyond the island with a corridor fanning out for 1,000 miles to the east.

The recent French testing program has been conducted undersea. A permanent "prohibited area" exists for aircraft, encompassing 1,650 square nautical miles, as indicated on the Operational Navigational Charts of the area. A surface warning zone is also declared for each test of limited range (approximately thirty miles in radius) and duration. In spite of widespread protests in December 1995, the French continue to test in the South Pacific.

GOVERNING LEGAL PRINCIPLES

All nations appear to agree upon six basic freedoms of the high seas: freedom of navigation, freedom of overflight, freedom to lay submarine cables, freedom to construct artificial islands and other installations permitted under international law, freedom of fishing, and freedom of scientific research. This list is not absolute or complete. The 1982 UN Convention on the Law of the Sea provides for certain exceptions, including policing power with regard to slave trade, piracy, illegal broadcasting, the breaking of submarine cables, and the right of hot pursuit. In addition, Articles 88 and 141 state that the high seas and the seabed below the high seas must be used exclusively for "peaceful purposes."

The text of the convention appears to support the conclusion that, although military activities inconsistent with the UN Charter are prohibited, at least some military activities on the high seas are permissible. Although nations agree on this concept of freedom of the high seas in the abstract, issues arise when limitations on this freedom are claimed on behalf of "national interest" or "national security." Yet no use of the sea is absolute, even though all "reasonable" uses are permitted.

THE OFFICIAL U.S. POSITION

When the United States first articulated its position on high seas weapons tests and their attendant danger zones, it stated that it asserted no sovereignty over these danger zones, and that they were only warning areas, subject to freedom of navigation. The United States has been careful not to claim the right to establish a prohibited or restricted area. In contrast, danger or warning areas on the high seas are predicated on the principle of voluntary compliance. Although this official position has been articulated often by U.S. government lawyers, it may be disingenuous because it tries to draw a line that is difficult to sustain in practice.

THE SOVIET POSITION

The former USSR's analysis of the legal regime governing missile testing on the high seas has been similar to the official U.S. position. When it first announced a broad-ocean-area missile test in the Pacific Ocean on January 8, 1960, it issued a "request" in the interests of navigational safety to all nations to avoid the area. It has continued to issue these announcements prior to each of its Pacific Ocean missile tests, and has sometimes issued announcements immediately following the conclusion of tests reopening the area ahead of the preannounced time.

CONCLUSION

The relativistic and flexible approach may be appropriate in some circumstances for new problems that are just beginning to be examined by the community of nations, but the imprecision of this approach is almost an invitation to conflict. As nations focus on a problem, they develop norms that are specific and understandable in order to promote a stable and predictable world order. Strong protests were registered against atmospheric nuclear bomb tests on the high seas, and all nations have now stopped this practice. One can make a compelling argument that this practice is now contrary to customary international law.

Missile testing on the high seas interferes with other uses of the high seas (such as navigation and fishing) somewhat less and has less of a negative impact on the environment than nuclear bomb tests. Nonetheless, the protests of nations to the high seas nuclear bomb testing and the concerns expressed about recent missile test launches clearly indicate that missile testing on the high seas will continue to be accepted as a legitimate use of the sea only insofar as these tests do not significantly interfere with navigation and fishing.

Attempts to appropriate areas of the oceans for military purposes by declaring exclusionary zones on the high seas are now seen as improper because they do not permit other lawful and necessary maritime activities to continue in these zones. The military powers have tried to avoid this problem by declaring warning zones instead, which are argued to be less intrusive claims. In fact, however, such claims are essentially identical to exclusionary zones, and the military powers have acted as if the vessels of other nations are not entitled to enter such zones. Such warning zones must therefore be viewed with the same degree of suspicion and concern that nations have been expressing toward exclusionary zones. The *Corfu Channel* case stands as a strong precedent that maritime navigational freedoms cannot be interfered with, even to protect security interests, and that compensation must be paid when injuries to persons and property occur. A UK vessel was blown up by a mine in the Corfu channel, which lies between Albania and Greece. The ICJ ruled that Albania knew about these mines and had failed to notify neutral shipping, which had the right of passage. Albania was ordered to pay recompense but refused to do so.

The current state of international law is, therefore, that missile testing on the high seas, and other similar military activities on the oceans, are legitimate only if they do not impede free navigation, interfere with fishing activities, cause any significant harm to the environment, or threaten human settlements. Exclusionary and warning zones that cover large areas or are extended in duration cannot be viewed as acceptable.

See COMBATANT-NONCOMBATANT DISTINCTION; ENVIRONMENTAL ISSUES, POLLUTION AND THE MILITARY; NUCLEAR TESTING IN THE PACIFIC; NUCLEAR WEAPONS TESTING.

BIBLIOGRAPHY

Corfu Channel Case (*UK v. Albania*), 1949 ICJ 4.

Firth, S., *Nuclear Playground* (Honolulu: Haven Press, 1986), 23.

Hayes, P., L. Zaarsky, and W. Bello, *American Lake: Nuclear Peril in the Pacific* (Harmondsworth Middlesex, UK: Penguin Books, 1986), 240.

McDougal, Myres, and Norbert Schlei, "The Hydrogen Bomb Tests in Perspective: Lawful Measures for Security," *Yale Law Journal* 64 (1955), 648.

United Nations Convention on the Law of the Sea, December 10, 1982, Montego Bay, UN Sales No. E.83.V.5 (1983), reprinted in 21 *I.L.M.* 1261 (1982).

Van Dyke, Jon M., "Military Exclusion and Warning Zones on the High Seas," *Marine Policy* (May 1991), 147.

Jon M. Van Dyke

WINTER SOLDIER INVESTIGATION. This unofficial investigation was convened in Detroit, Michigan, on January 31 and February 1–2, 1971 by a group of Vietnam* veterans who had information that Son My* and My Lai were not isolated incidents, but part of an established American policy. During three days of testimony over 100 veterans and sixteen civilians testified to war crimes* they had either committed or witnessed between 1963 and 1971, and the transcript of their testimony ran to over 1,000 pages. Al Hubbard, the executive secretary of the Vietnam Veterans Against the War, summed up the intent: "The purpose of the hearings was not to punish but to preclude the continuance of man's inhumanity to his fellow man." The name "Winter Soldier" was taken from a remark of Thomas Paine about the trials of the "summer soldier and the sunshine patriot."

On April 19–23, 1973, a meeting of the national steering committee of the organization called Vietnam Veterans Against the War/Winter Soldier Organization issued a position paper on amnesty*, which was presented at congressional hearings on the subject in 1974. The amnesty statement demanded universal, unconditional amnesty with no punitive measures for: (1) all military resisters (so-called "deserters") and draft resisters in exile or underground in the United States; (2) all who are or have been in civilian or military prisons because of opposition to the Vietnam War; and (3) the over half-million veterans with less than honorable discharges. The paper argued that since the Vietnam War was illegal, opposition to it should not be a crime. A much-publicized case was that of Captain Howard Levy, who was sentenced to two years in Leavenworth prison for refusing to train Green Berets, because in his own words, he believed that they would be "murdering women and children." At his trial the military judge requested proof that serving in Vietnam would obligate the participants to commit war crimes. While no such evidence was available, the question remained whether the massacres* were an isolated incident or part of standard policy. Members of the Bertrand Russell international war crimes tribunal proposed public forums to be held in the United States following those already held in Stockholm*, Sweden and Rothskilde*, Denmark at which Vietnam veterans could present testimony.

Prior to the creation of the Winter Soldier group, a plan for citizens' commissions to organize hearings had been devised by Tod Ensign and Jeremy Rifkin. A coordinating committee was formed, which included such sponsors as Benjamin Spock, Noam Chomsky, Dick Gregory, Julius Lester, and David Dellinger. The first such commissions were held in Annapolis, Maryland on March 11 and 12, 1970, followed by others in New York City, Boston, Baltimore, Buffalo, Minneapolis, Los Angeles, Philadelphia, Portland, Oregon, and Washington. D.C. The project was supported by Congressman Ronald V. Dellums (D-CA), and as a consequence the material was named the "Dellums Committee Hearings." Testimony was received from hundreds of Vietnam veterans to the effect that no training had ever been given telling them that certain acts of war were criminal. In particular, graduates of military schools reported the near absence of any such instruction in the laws of warfare or the nature of the kinds of crimes identified at the Nuremberg* trials.

See MILITARY EDUCATION; MILITARY TRAINING, BASIC; SON MY/ MY LAI; STOCKHOLM/ROTHSKILDE WAR CRIMES TRIALS; VIETNAM WAR.

BIBLIOGRAPHY

Citizens Commission of Inquiry, eds., *The Dellums Committee Hearings on War Crimes in Vietnam* (New York: Vintage Books, 1972).

Amnesty, Hearings Before the Subcommittee on Courts, Civil Liberties, and the Administration of Justice of the Committee on the Judiciary, H.R., 93rd Cong. 2d sess., March 8, 11, and 13, 1974 (Washington, D.C.: U.S. Government Printing Office, 1974), 788–805.

Legislative Proposals Relating to the War in Southeast Asia, Hearings Before the Committee on Foreign Relations, Senate, 92nd Cong., 1st sess., April 20, 21, 22, and 28; May 3, 11, 12, 13, 25, 26, and 27, 1971 (Washington, D.C.: U.S. Government Printing Office, 1971), 546–52; 568–69; 572–73; 586–87.

Vietnam Veterans Against the War, *The Winter Soldier Investigation: An Inquiry into American War Crimes* (Boston: Beacon Press, 1972).

WIRZ, CAPTAIN HENRY (1822–1865). The commandment of the prisoner-of-war* camp at Andersonville, Georgia, Wirz was executed for putative war crimes* in the management of the camp. Born in Zurich, Switzerland, he emigrated to Kentucky in 1849 and practiced medicine in Milliken's Bend, Louisiana from 1854 to 1861. At the outbreak of the Civil War he enlisted as a private in Company D, 4th Louisiana Battalion. He was promoted the same year to Lieutenant, then captain and assistant adjutant general in 1862, and major and assistant adjutant general in 1863. He was so severely wounded at Seven Pines that his right arm was virtually paralyzed for life. He served briefly as staff officer at Tuscaloosa military prison. General John H. Winder sent him to Europe as a Confederate agent and, on his return, he served as a dispatch bearer until he was assigned, in March 1864, the position of commandant of the Andersonville, Georgia prisoner-of-war camp. The camp was a rough log stockade, initially about sixteen acres and later enlarged to twenty-six acres. Only enlisted men were imprisoned there. The camp had been moved from Richmond, where the large numbers of prisoners seemed a hazard and too great a drain on the local food supply. By the end of 1864, a total of 32,899 had been confined there.

Article 59 of *General Orders 100: Instructions for the Government of Armies of the United States in the Field** (1863) served as the basis for his trial for alleged crimes against prisoners of war in that camp. Article 59 had stated that "a prisoner of war remains answerable for his crimes committed against the captor's army or people, committed before he was captured, and for which he has not been punished by his own authorities." Wirz denied the charges on the grounds that he was under the superior orders* of General John H. Winder, who had denied his requests for improvement in the camp, and furthermore he had been in Europe when Winder had established the camp. Although *General Orders 100* did not speak to the issue of whether following superior orders was a sufficient excuse, the manual did make reference to the care of prisoners. Article 53 stated that medical personnel were not to be considered prisoners of war, although it presumed that such professionals would be allowed to treat the wounded of their own captured soldiers and as such would be in the prisoner-of-war camps; Article 56 assured that prisoners would not be punished by intentional suffering, lack of food, or medical care, although no specific mention was made of hospitals; Article 71 stated that it was forbidden to inflict additional wounds on those already wounded; Article 76 stated that prisoners were to be fed "plain and wholesome food, whenever practicable and treated with humanity"; Article 79 was the only one that spoke specifically to medical care: "Every captured wounded enemy shall be medically treated according to the ability of the medical staff." Wirz was prosecuted and charged with failure to treat the prisoners at Andersonville "according to the ability of the medical staff." Further charges and countercharges were made at the trial to the effect that, in addition, Wirz had been involved in maltreatment of prisoners.

Article 13 of *General Orders 100* provided for the establishment of a military commission to try such cases, and on August 23, 1865, the first such commission was established by President Andrew Johnson to hear charges of murder and conspiracy against eight former Confederates in connection with the operation of the camp at Andersonville. When the Union Army had captured the camp in April 1864, they found that over 13,000 inmates of the camp had been buried in a mass grave, about 40 percent of all prisoners who had been incarcerated there. While reports varied about the exact numbers, there are 12,912 graves at the National Cemetery at Andersonville of soldiers who were said to have died in that prison.

This first military commission consisted of nine officers of the U.S. Army, who ranged in age from 21 to 61 and in rank from lieutenant colonel to Major General Lew Wallace. They met in the Court of Claims in the Capitol. In the initial charge the following were named as confederates with Wirz: John H. Winder, Richard B. Winder, Joseph White, W. S. Winder, R. R. Stevenson, and ''others whose names are unknown.'' The event was documented voluminously, and the court transcript consisted of 815 pages of the *Congressional Record*. Wirz was the only person connected with Confederate prisons to be charged and executed, although Private James W. Duncan, an employee at Andersonville, was arrested when he appeared in the courtroom as a defense witness, convicted of the death of a prisoner on June 8, 1866, and sentenced to fifteen years at hard labor, but escaped eleven months later and was not recaptured. General John H. Winder, to whom Wirz reported and who was chiefly responsible for the abysmal conditions, was formally found guilty in the indictment against Wirz of having conspired to kill prisoners, although he died in 1865 before the judgment of guilt could be handed down. The remaining persons named in the initial charge were dropped from the proceedings, thus casting doubt on the opening charge that Wirz had been part of a conspiracy. The court met from August 23 to October 21, 1865, during which time testimony was heard from 148 witnesses. Witnesses testified 654 times for the prosecution and 279 times for the defense.

Two charges were made against Wirz: (1) he had ''maliciously, wilfully, and traitorously conspired with others (J. H. Winder, R. B. Winder, W. S. Winder, R. R. Stevenson, and Joseph White) to injure the health and to destroy the inmates of Andersonville camp'' and (2) he was guilty of the murder or maltreatment of prisoners in violation of the laws and customs of war. As for the first charge, Wirz did not take over the camp until March 1864, and the camp had been established by W. S. Winder in 1863 while Wirz was still in Europe. Indeed, Colonel Persons fully exonerated Wirz from complicity in the selection of the site, for the overcrowded conditions, and the poor food; Colonel Chandler and two medical doctors said that Wirz was not responsible for the hospital conditions. The charges included contaminated food and water, lack of medicine, attacks by camp dogs, and the shooting of prisoners. Of the many witnesses called, no univocal evidence was ever presented to support the charges against Wirz. In the initial charge the names of Robert E. Lee, Lucius Northrup, and others were included, yet all of them were removed from the list of those charged. Had there been a conspiracy, surely there would have been others charged. With regard to the second charge, that of maltreatment of prisoners, he was charged personally with thirteen occasions of having shot or beaten prisoners or having ordered guards to do so. Such actions constituted murder and/or atrocities laid to his charge. Of the thirteen crimes he was charged with, in no instance was there a name, date, or circumstance stated. In spite of Wirz's plea that he should have been protected under the surrender terms agreed on by Generals William T. Sherman and Joseph E. Johnson, he was declared guilty and hanged on November 12, 1865. Evidence suggests that had General Winder not died in February 1865, he would have been hanged instead of Wirz.

The summary statement for the court by Major General Lew Wallace found Wirz guilty of having conspired with Jefferson Davis, James A. Seddon, Howell Cobb, John H. Winder, Richard B. Winder, Isaiah H. White, W. S. Winder, W. Shelby Reed, R. R. Stevenson, S. P. Moore, Mr. Kerr, hospital steward James Duncan, Wesley W. Turner, Benjamin Harris, and others to violate laws of war* with respect to the treatment of prisoners at Andersonville between March 27, 1864 and April 10, 1865, and that Wirz should be hanged until dead. Two-thirds of the members of the Court concurred. The recommendation was reviewed by Judge Advocate General J. Holt and in his report issued October 31, 1865, he concurred with Major General Wallace that the sentence should be executed. On November 3, 1865 President Andrew Johnson ordered that the execution be carried out, and this was done November 12, 1865.

Many Southerners complained about these military commissions, in part because they had been formed without presidential approval. About 2,000 commission judgments were issued throughout the Reconstruction period. The U.S. Supreme Court never reviewed the legality of the commissions and they ceased to be held after the termination of the Reconstruction laws.

See GENERAL ORDERS 100; PRISONERS OF WAR; WAR CRIMES.

BIBLIOGRAPHY

Laska, Lewis L., and James M. Smith, "Hell and the Devil: Andersonville and the Trial of Captain Henry Wirz, C.S.S., 1865," *Military Law Review* 68 (Spring 1975), 77–132.

"The Trial of Henry Wirz," H. R., *Executive Documents,* vol. 8, no. 23, 40th Cong. 2d sess., December 7, 1867 (Washington, D.C.: U.S. Government Printing Office, 1867–1868), 1–850.

WOMEN IN THE MILITARY. An unpublicized revolution—the integration of significant numbers of U.S. women into the peacetime military—occurred in the 1970s and 1980s. When the all-volunteer military was established in 1973, only 50,000 women, or 2.5 percent, were serving in the armed forces; twenty years later over 200,000 women (11.5 percent of active-duty personnel) were serving. In the 1990s, issues surrounding women in the military such as occupational discrimination, exclusion from combat, and sexual harassment, while surfacing earlier, took center stage. In 1991, the publicity from the Tailhook Convention scandal (*see* Tailhook*) was partly responsible for escalating change as it highlighted women's second-class citizenship in the military. At the same time, the Gulf War* delivered a message about equal performance in that women soldiers functioned effectively on the front lines and were as subject to the perils of war as men.

During the American Revolutionary War, women often joined their husbands behind the lines and occasionally fought in battle. The legendary Molly Pitcher followed her husband to an engagement at Monmouth in 1778, earned her named by carrying water to soldiers in battle and, when her husband fell, took his place as cannoneer. In the Civil War, 60,000 served as nurses, cooks, scouts, couriers, and saboteurs. Women were first officially enlisted during World War I; women recruits (clericals known as Navy "yeomanettes" and Marine Corps "marinettes" as well as nurses in the Army and Navy Nurse Corps) numbered around 34,000. Between 350,000 and 400,000 women served in World War II, again primarily as nurses and clerks, but also as stateside pilots.

The Vietnam War brought the first major breakthrough into nontraditional occupations, with 2,500 women serving in Vietnam in support positions (transportation, supply, communications, and intelligence) as well as in medical and clerical assignments. By the 1991 Gulf War, women were formally assigned to combat support positions as pilots, artillery directors, commanders of prisoner-of-war* camps, and on ship and construction crews; over 40,000 served in both nontraditional and traditional fields.

Distinct occupational segregation has characterized U.S. women's peacetime service, but is beginning to break down. In 1973, 64 percent of enlisted women were in support and administrative skill categories, but by 1993 that percentage dropped to 33 percent. Over the same period, the percentage of all women officers segregated in healthcare positions declined from 72 to 45 percent. The extent of occupational desegregation varied by service; in 1993, 95 percent of U.S. Air Force positions were open to women, as compared to 80 percent in the U.S. Marine Corps. While it was not expected that all military women would seek nontraditional jobs, women soldiers, more than civilians, sought out opportunities in traditionally male fields.

As assignment barriers dropped, so did barriers to advancement. In 1975, Congress ordered that all military academies be opened to women. A 1989 General Accounting Office study found that women at senior grades were being promoted at a rate similar to men, although the absolute numbers were low due to a historically small pool. In 1993, there were twenty-one female generals and admirals on active duty compared to only six a few years earlier. There were no gender differences in the overall proportion of officers (15 percent) to enlisted personnel (85 percent).

The Clinton administration made some ground-breaking appointments of women, most notably, Sheila Widnall as secretary of the Air Force and Roche Lee as assistant secretary of defense for reserve affairs. Nevertheless, with the military down-sizing of the 1990s, both women and men were facing decreasing opportunities for promotion. Several high-level monitoring groups were made accountable for implementation of equal opportunity. In particular, the Defense Advisory Committee on Women in the Service took an active role in investigating conditions for women and proposing policy changes. Yet, despite official commitment to equality, studies revealed that far more women soldiers reported exposure to sexual harassment, for example, than did civilian women.

With demobilization after World War II came a decision by Congress in 1948 to exclude women in the military from future combat. The combat exclusion rule came under attack in the 1970s and 1980s as an obstacle to women's achievement of full equality, both because so many combat-related jobs were consequently closed to women and because promotion to senior ranks was informally linked to service in combat. Under pressure from female members of Congress led by Congresswoman Pat Schroeder (D-CO), a high-ranking member of the House Armed Services Committee, Congress partially repealed the ban in 1991 in order to allow women to fly combat missions, but the military delayed implementation. At that time, Congress also ordered the creation of a commission to study the entire issue and make recommendations to the president.

The fiercely divided Presidential Commission on the Assignment of Women in the Armed Forces reported in November 1992, voting to maintain the bans on land and air combat but agreeing by a close vote to permit women on most Navy combat ships, except submarines. The outgoing Bush administration handed over the issue to the new Clinton team, which took a very different approach, seeking ways to accelerate rather than obstruct integration.

In April 1993, Secretary of Defense Les Aspin ordered the services to implement an order allowing women to fly combat aircraft and to prepare for women on warships. Congressional authority was to be secured in that year's defense appropriations legislation. Aspin also asked the Army and Marine Corps to justify the continuing exclusion of women from ground infantry units. Military reaction to Aspin's order was generally positive, with many servicewomen, younger servicemen, and top brass in the Navy and Air Force applauding the decision. The leadership of the Army and Marine Corps, however, produced a draft policy paper that was very negative regarding assignment of women to potential combat duty. The Defense Department was clearly frustrated by the attempt of these services to resist a change in policy.

Along with the unresolved issue of ground combat for women is the issue of conscription, should the United States ever return to the draft. The Supreme Court held in *Rostker v. Goldberg* in 1981 that women were not subject to the draft because, being excluded from combat, they were not in the ''same situation'' as men. Some observers have argued that opening up combat to women puts them in the same situation and therefore makes them eligible for the draft. Others maintain that, in the unlikely event that the draft is revived, a new draft law need not require either conscription or combat duty for *all* women or for *all* men; exemptions on the basis of gender-neutral categories such as single parenting could be allowed.

A more immediate factor that could retard women's entry into combat-associated jobs was the cost of accommodating them. The Navy estimated that it would cost approximately $500,000 per ship to reconfigure living quarters and to outfit ships with special equipment for women. The logistics of providing for women in the cramped conditions of attack submarines posed the greatest dilemma.

While the possibility of returning to a more restrictive policy on the status of military women is always present, the Clinton administration appeared committed to meeting the challenge of fully integrating women and making the process irreversible. Unlike its policy directives on homosexuality*, the policy on gender equality won support both inside and outside the military. The main concern of servicewomen as well as men was that the "down-sized" post-Cold War military would offer fewer opportunities for advancement.

See FEMINISM AND WAR; TAILHOOK.

BIBLIOGRAPHY

Women's Research and Education Institute, *Women in the Military 1980–1990* (Washington, D.C.: WREI, 1990).

Ellen Boneparth

WORLD WAR I. *See* BIOLOGICAL/CHEMICAL WARFARE; BRITTAIN, VERA; BRUSSELS DECLARATION; CASUALTIES OF WAR; CONSCIENTIOUS OBJECTION; GENEVA CONVENTION, 1906; GERMAN WAR BOOK (USAGES OF WAR ON LAND); HAGUE, THE, CONGRESSES; INCENDIARIES; LEIPZIG TRIALS; MARTENS CLAUSE; PROPAGANDA; *RULES OF LAND WARFARE.*

WORLD WAR II. *See* AERIAL WARFARE; CASUALTIES OF WAR; CHILDREN AND WAR; COLLATERAL DAMAGE; CONTROL COUNCIL LAW NO. 10; COUNTERFORCE VERSUS COUNTERVALUE; FIRST STRIKE/SECOND STRIKE; FORBIDDEN STRATEGIES; FORBIDDEN WEAPONS; GENEVA CONVENTION, 1929; GENOCIDE; HAGUE, THE, CONGRESSES; HIROSHIMA AND NAGASAKI; HOLOCAUST, THE; HUMANITY, CRIMES AGAINST; INCENDIARIES; *THE LAW OF LAND WARFARE;* LONDON AGREEMENT ON WAR CRIMINALS; MOSCOW DECLARATION; NUCLEAR WAR; NUREMBERG TRIALS; PARIS PEACE PACT; PRISONERS OF WAR; REPRISALS; SUPERIOR ORDERS; SURRENDER, UNCONDITIONAL; TOKYO TRIALS; WAR CRIMES.

WOUNDED AND SICK. *See* COMBATANT-NONCOMBATANT DISTINCTION; CHILDREN AND WAR; CONCENTRATION CAMPS; EXECUTION, SUMMARY; FORBIDDEN STRATEGIES; GENEVA CONVENTION, 1864, 1868, 1906, 1929, 1949; HUMANITARIAN INTERVENTION; HUMANITY, CRIMES AGAINST; PRISONERS OF WAR; RED CROSS, RED CRESCENT, RED LION AND SUN; SHIPWRECKED SAILORS.

Y

YUGOSLAVIA, WAR CRIMES IN THE FORMER. The UN estimated that there were at least 250,000 casualties in the conflict in the former Yugoslavia by spring 1994. On August 13, 1992, the UN Security Council asked the member states of the UN to collect data on possible war crimes there, and on October 6, 1992, the Security Council unanimously voted to create a war crimes commission for the former Yugoslavia but did not specify any details. The present World Court was not mandated to handle such trials. On February 22, 1993, after comments and requests from many countries, the Security Council requested the secretary general to submit a proposal for the establishment of a war crimes tribunal for offenders in the former Yugoslavia, and on that same day the Security Council unanimously issued Resolution 808, endorsing such a tribunal. Annexed to the resolution was a proposed statute for an international tribunal, which listed the offenses as the "grave breaches" of the 1949 Geneva* conventions that included violations of the laws of war*, genocide*, and crimes against humanity*. The statute affirmed that the principle of individual responsibility regardless of rank would hold, that the decisions of the tribunal would take precedence over any national courts, and that when the tribunal was functioning in its legal capacity, it would not be subject to control by the Security Council.

The tribunal would consist of three chambers, a prosecutor, and a registry that would serve the chambers and prosecutor. Two of the chambers would be for trial and one for appeals. Three judges would serve in each of the trial chambers, and five judges in the appeals chamber. Member states were invited to submit up to two names to the UN secretary general, who would then submit a list of not fewer than twenty-two nor more than thirty-three to the General Assembly. The assembly would then elect eleven. The judges would serve for four years. The penalties would be limited to imprisonment plus the return of property or proceeds that might have been acquired in the criminal conduct. Imprisonment would be in a state willing to accept the task. The state would be selected by the tribunal from applicants. This tribunal would meet in The Hague, with expenses borne by the regular UN budget in accordance with Article 17 of the UN Charter. On April 8, 1993, the International Court of Justice (ICJ) said that Serbia and Montenegro should take measures to prevent genocide in Bosnia and Herzegovina. The Soviet Judge, Tarassov, demurred and insisted that the same measures should be urged against Bosnia and Herzegovina, since offenses had probably been committed by both sides in the conflict. In the interim before the formal establishment of the tribunal, the fifteen-member ICJ on September 13 expressed grave concern that genocidal acts were continuing. A recent addition to the ICJ was the distinguished international jurist, Hersch Lauterpacht. Although urged by Bosnia and Herzegovina to take more vigorous steps, the court has declined to do so.

From January through September, a five-member commission of experts held sessions under Resolution 780 to analyze possible violations. A trust fund was set up by the secretary general and contributions to it were encouraged. At its fifth session, May 24–25, 1993, the commission voted to send an investigative team to the area of Abcimi/Vitez to inquire into mass killings committed there in April, and to consider testimony from the rapporteur, William J. Fenric of Canada, as well as from alleged war criminals detained by the Croatian authorities. In October 21, 1993, the chairman of the commission, Fritz Kalshoven, was replaced by Cherif Bassiouni of Egypt.

On May 3, 1993, the secretary general of the UN issued a report to establish an international tribunal to prosecute persons who may have been responsible for war crimes in the former Yugoslavia. On May 25, 1993 the UN Security Council unanimously approved this report in Resolution 827, and adopted a statute of the international tribunal. The first meeting of this tribunal was held on November 17, 1993. Eleven judges took their oaths and Ramon Escovar-Salom, attorney general of Venezuela, was appointed the prosecutor. Carl August Fleischhauer, UN legal counsel, stated that the tribunal would have the full support of the Security Council. Nine men and two women were selected. The procedure for arresting people was yet to be invented.

After this commission had made its report on possible breaches, it was to terminate. The commission reported that all defendants had been guilty. Of special concern were violations of the rights of children*. The tribunal reconvened on January 17, 1994, and reported in February 1994 that Escovar-Salom had resigned his post to take a new position in the Venezuelan government. In March 1994 the tribunal reported that Graham Blewitt, of Australia, had been named to serve as chief prosecutor. At this time he had received a ''model indictment,'' prepared by Peter Thompson, working under the auspices of the Minnesota Advocates for Human Rights. The indictment specified twenty-two individuals and charged them each with one count of conspiracy and thirteen counts of committing specific crimes. Claude Jorda of France was appointed judge of the tribunal until September 17, 1997, replacing Germaine Le Foyer de Costil of France, who resigned effective January 1, 1994. Theodoor C. van Boven of the Netherlands was named acting registrar of the tribunal on January 21, 1994.

Along with other states, the United States had worked on a proposal to establish a tribunal. September 22, 1992, the U.S. Department of State presented to the UN Security Council on War Crimes in the Former Yugoslavia the first of seven reports documenting war crimes. The State Department appointed three rapporteurs to conduct the inquiry into violations of the laws of war, crimes against humanity, and genocide: Ambassador Turk from Austria, Ambassador Corell from Sweden, and Mrs. Thune of Norway. They visited the country from September 30 to October 5, 1992, and on February 22, 1993, presented their report to the U.S. Commission on Security and Cooperation in Europe, meeting in Helsinki. This and subsequent reports listed the offenses under the following headings: willful killing, torture of prisoners, abuse of civilians in detention centers, deliberate attacks on noncombatants, wanton devastation and destruction of property, and the mass forcible expulsion and deportation of civilians. The report was titled *Proposal for an International War Crimes Tribunal for the Former Yugoslavia.*

Independently of these Security Council efforts, a Bosnia military court in Sarajevo on March 30, 1993, had condemned to death for war crimes two Serbs who had served with the Serbian Nationalist Army. Both were accused of genocide and rape against Moslems. On February 15, 1994, the German police arrested Dusko Tadic, a Serb, and charged him with participation in genocide, murder, and serious assault. Some German officials recommended that he be turned over to the newly appointed tribunal, but German prosecutors initially claimed that they had authority to try him in Germany. By early 1995 Germany had passed a law allowing his transfer to the tribunal at The Hague. In Denmark a similar action was taken against a Bosnian Muslim accused of atrocities against Croats. Both Germany and Denmark planned to proceed with their trials unless and until the international tribunal might request that the cases be transferred to it.

As a war in which the litigants were of one race, but three religions, the term ''ethnic cleansing'' may be inappropriate for what was happening. Even the religious issue did not account for the conflict, since by 1994, Muslims were fighting against Muslims. Bosnian Serb Muslims, Croatian Roman Catholics, and Eastern Orthodox Serbs had a long history of conflict, and charges of genocide were made on all sides during and following World War II.

See CASUALTIES OF WAR; CHILDREN'S RIGHTS IN WAR; COMBATANT-NONCOMBATANT DISTINCTION; FORBIDDEN STRATEGIES; GENOCIDE; HOSTAGES; INNOCENTS; JUST WAR; TOTAL WAR.

BIBLIOGRAPHY

Congressional Record, vol. 140, February 1, 1994, no. 6; February 2, 1994, no. 7; March 7, 1994, no. 23; March 8, 1994, no. 24; and March 16, 1994, no. 29.

Dedijer, Vladimir, *The Yugoslav Auschwitz and the Vatican* (Buffalo, N.Y.: Prometheus Books, 1992).

Former Yugoslavia: The War Crimes Tribunal: One Year Later, vol. 6, no. 3 (New York: Human Rights Watch/Helsinki, 1994).

Helsinki Watch Releases Eight Cases for War Crimes Tribunal on Former Yugoslavia, vol. 5, no. 12, August 1, 1993 (New York: Helsinki Watch, 1993).

Human Rights in the Former Yugoslav Republic of Macedonia (New York: Human Rights Watch, January 1994).

Implementation of the Helsinki Accords: Prospects for a War Crimes Tribunal for the Former Yugoslavia, Hearing Before the Commission on Security and Cooperation in Europe, 103rd Cong., 1st sess., April 21, 1993 (Washington, D.C.: U.S. Government Printing Office, 1993).

Paris, Edmond, *Genocide in Satellite Croatia: 1941–1945* (Chicago: American Institute for Balkan Affairs, 1961).

Procedural and Evidentiary Issues for the Yugoslav War Crimes Tribunal, vol. 5, no. 15 (New York: Human Rights Watch/Helsinki, 1993).

Report on the International Tribunal to Adjudicate War Crimes Committed in the Former Yugoslavia, Submitted by a Special Task Force of the ABA Section of International Law Practice, July 8, 1993.

U.S. Department of State Dispatch (bi-weekly issues), 1993–1994.

War Crimes in Bosnia-Hercegovina: Bosanski Samac, vol. 6, no. 5 (New York: Human Rights Watch/Helsinki, 1994).

War Crimes in Bosnia-Hercegovina: U.N. Cease-Fire Won't Help Banja Luka, vol. 6, no. 8 (New York: Human Rights Watch/Helsinki, 1994).

Z

ZAGREB RESOLUTION (1971). Issued by the Institute of International Law and titled "Conditions of Application of Humanitarian Rules of Armed Conflict to Hostilities in Which United Nations Forces May Be Engaged." Several international bodies had considered whether the laws of war* applied to UN forces. Among these were the 1954 Hague Intergovernmental Conference, which issued a "Cultural Property Convention" and a resolution recommending that the UN forces involved in military action follow this convention. The Institute of International Law, an unofficial organization, was founded in 1873 with sixty members and sixty associates. All of the members were distinguished international lawyers, and the aim of the institute was to promote the development of international law. In 1965 the institute asked its commission to study the application of laws of war to military operations of the United Nations and regional organizations such as the North Atlantic Treaty Organization (NATO), the South East Treaty Organization (SEATO), and the Warsaw Pact. In 1967 the commission decided to limit its study to UN forces, which it was presumed existed and which might be called upon to engage in armed hostilities. Before this task was undertaken the UN command in Korea in late 1950, the UN Emergency Force in Egypt (1957), and the UN Operation in the Congo (1963) had instructed all forces under their command to observe the provisions of the 1949 Geneva* Convention 3 concerning prisoners of war*.

Article 2 of the Zagreb Resolution recalled the previous resolutions issued by the Institute of International Law pertaining to certain forbidden weapons* and announced that these prohibited weapons would not be used by UN troops. Although these weapons were not named, the UN General Assembly had already issued prohibitions against the use of incendiaries*, fragmentation bombs*, expanding bullets*, gas and noxious chemicals, germ bombs, and nuclear weapons*, none of which is forbidden in the current U.S. Army manual, *The Law of Land Warfare**, with the exception of germ bombs. Thus, the arsenal of UN soldiers would not resemble that of the soldiers of member nations, rather they would be armed like police.

See BIOLOGICAL/CHEMICAL WARFARE; FORBIDDEN STRATEGIES; FORBIDDEN WEAPONS; NUCLEAR WEAPONS, UN RESOLUTIONS BANNING MANUFACTURE OR USE OF.
BIBLIOGRAPHY
Friedman, Leon, ed., *The Laws of War,* vol. 2 (New York: Random House, 1972).

ZONES OF PEACE (ZOP). Perhaps as old as war itself, the idea and practice of ZOP has historically gone through four stages, from sanctuaries, to specific purpose, general purpose, and empowering peace zones.

In the first stage, religious sanctuaries predominated. The ancient Polynesians had a practice of "puuhonua," or place of refuge, where wrongdoers were forgiven. The ancient Israelites had Cities of Refuge and Sabbaths. The Christian world in the Middle Ages knew about the "Truce of God" and the "Peace of God*." Islam* divides the world into a zone of peace (*Dar al-Islam*) and a zone of war (*Dar al Harb*); it also considers the mosques and the shrines as zones of peace in which combatants can take refuge.

In the second stage of their development, ZOPs have evolved into secular and functionally specific territories of peace. In modern history, diplomatic missions (embassies and consular offices) have served as the territorial extensions of the guest in the host country, with a zone of peace immunity. Red Cross* headquarters and vehicles in the midst of combat, countries declaring themselves neutral in times of war, and nuclear weapons free zones (NWFZ) all have one feature in common: for specific times, places, and functions, certain designated territories may be considered as inviolable by the combatants. In recent decades, threats of nuclear war* have led to a movement for NWFZs, which increased from about 250 in 1982 to about 5,000 in 1991. There are already twenty-four countries in the world that have unilaterally declared themselves as NWFZs. There are also five formal NWFZ treaties signed among governments, encompassing Antarctica, Outer Space, Latin America, the International Seabed, and the South Pacific. A UN conference held in 1992 in Colombo also declared the Indian Ocean an NWFZ.

The third stage of development of ZOPs is of more recent origin. The general-purpose zones of peace are often the result of years of peaceful social, economic, cultural, and political cooperation and integration, declared or undeclared. Since the War of 1812, for instance, the U.S.-Canadian border has been a general-purpose ZOP. Since 1945, the European Economic Community (EEC) also has become one such zone for its twelve member-states. Since its establishment in 1967, the Association of South East Asian Nations (ASEAN) has similarly provided a general-purpose framework for peace, security, and cooperation among its six member-states. With the worldwide movement toward regional cooperation and security arrangements, as exemplified by the Conference on Security and Cooperation in Europe (CSCE) and the Asia-Pacific Economic Cooperation (APEC), prospects for general-purpose ZOPs look encouraging.

Following World War II, the idea of peace and neutrality found its greatest advocates among those powers with the most to lose from protracted conflict. The nonaligned movement, launched by Nehru, Sukarno, Nasser, Chou En-lai, and Tito at the Bandung Conference of 1955, sought to avoid the costs of entanglement with the Cold War through a doctrine of neutrality and peaceful coexistence. The moral authority of this movement as well as the worldwide peace movement, however, came from the practice of nonviolent resistance led by such figures as Gandhi*, Martin Luther King, Jr.*, and Bishop Tutu. Although ZOPs need not be fully committed to nonviolence, many proponents of the idea believe in the Gandhian principles of *Satyagraha* and nonviolent resistance against any form of oppression.

In more recent years, the idea of peace zones has been proposed by a number of scholars and activists, including Johan Galtung, Bishop Antonio Fortich, Edna Fuerth Lemle, the Cheju International Council in South Korea, and the Dalai Lama. Johan Galtung has proposed it for Palestine, and Bishop Fortich and his coworkers have, in fact, successfully established a number of peace zones in the Philippines. The Filipino zones of peace are civilian-initiated demilitarized areas created to allow noncombatants to establish homes and economic bases without the fear of becoming caught in the cross-fire between the military and the rebels. The communities define geographic areas where neither rebels nor government forces may enter. Inhabitants practice strict nonviolence, maintain their infrastructure of roads, bridges, and schools, and form peacekeeping forces that monitor the presence of strangers. Edna Lemle has pursued this idea with the British and Argentine governments for a peaceful settlement of the Falkland/Maldive Islands conflict by establishing an autonomous land authority. The Cheju International Council is proposing to turn the island into a zone of peace for the reconciliation of North and South Korea*. Most recently, the Dalai Lama has called for the establishment of a zone of peace based on nonviolence in Tibet within the sovereign territory of the People's Republic of China.

The fourth stage of development of ZOPs, therefore, is of even greater promise. It indicates a deepening and broadening of the concept beyond the often limited acts of governments and toward citizen action and participation in the building of peace zones. It may therefore be called a citizen *empowering* phase, characterized by grassroots movements. About 1,500 communities in Japan, 168 in the United States, 178 in Canada, and 2,000 in Europe have unilaterally declared their localities as nuclear weapons free zones. In this connection, the story of Palau is most instructive. As of 1991, after seven rounds of voting, the people of Palau have refused to give in to U.S. pressures for a change in their constitution, which calls for a nuclear-free zone in that island trust territory.

There is no general agreement on how to define ZOPs. A broad working definition may include some or all of the following elements: (1) a well-defined territory or region in which the parties at dispute commit themselves to nonviolent and pacific settlement of their conflicts by total or partial disarmament and through binding adjudication, arbitration, or mediation procedures, (2) a governing authority consisting of the governments or parties at dispute over that territory under the supervision of the United Nations or other intergovernmental bodies, (3) a land authority for the development of a free economic zone among the members and other interested parties acquiring "peace bonds" with commercial rates of return, and (4) guarantees of the civil and human rights of all citizens regardless of race, color, or creed.

Issues of sovereignty, governance, and surveillance are the main policy problems facing such an enterprise. Sovereignty is perhaps the thorniest issue. The UN Charter recognizes the indivisible sovereignty of its member-states and forbids any direct interference in their internal affairs. However, the traditional notions of indivisible national sovereignty have eroded on both global and local fronts. On the global front, the rights of the international community to intervene in the internal affairs of a sovereign state on humanitarian* or collective security grounds have now been established in international law. The UN Security Council has recently intervened in Somalia, Bosnia, and Cambodia on humanitarian grounds. It also intervened in the Persian Gulf* War on grounds of collective security. On the local front, the rights of municipal governments to determine by popular referenda their own defense policies have received increasing popular recognition. Some municipalities in the United States have established their own offices of Municipal Foreign Policy. The U.S. government, however, considers decisions dealing with defense and foreign policy to be within its own, exclusive jurisdiction. It does not generally recognize any authority for municipal or even state governments in such matters.

National sovereignty has been further undermined, both practically and theoretically, by other developments. Practically, some new telecommunication technologies such as global satellite surveillance, direct broadcast satellites (DBS), electronic cash transfers, and transborder data flows have effectively limited government control of information flows within and outside of their own national borders. The dominant position of the transnational corporations in the world economy has also severely limited the regulatory powers of the national governments with respect to the movements of capital and production centers.

Theoretically, notions of transnational as opposed to national sovereignty provided the basis for the UN Trusteeship over former colonial territories. The concept of trusteeship now can be extended in order to establish ZOPs in situations of protracted conflict such as Kurdistan, Palestine, Kashmir, Bosnia, or Somalia. By resolving protracted conflicts in a peaceful way, clearly all parties win more security. By entering into a common market or establishing a free trade zone, the participating governments and populations win in economic prosperity. By giving autonomy and status to disenfranchised ethnic groups, the entire world wins in the achievement of greater human rights and international harmony. In the case of Kurdistan, for instance, none of the states presently controlling the Kurdish population is willing to grant independence. All of them may be willing, however, to recognize the cultural autonomy of the Kurds under a plan that puts them in control (as members of the UN Board of Trustees) while attracting millions of dollars for a cooperative development of the region.

Even if the issue of sovereignty is resolved satisfactorily, the problem of governance presents the next most important policy dilemma: How to give de facto powers sufficient incentive in the governance of ZOPs in order to elicit their recognition of the de jure status of ZOPs as zones of partial or general disarmament. The answer to this question depends on the functional and spatial scopes of ZOPs. As demonstrated by the examples, the governance problems of each of these types are unique. Holy sites and diplomatic missions (consular offices and embassies) have been historically treated as inviolable zones of peace. One of the latest examples of this was when General Manuel Noriega took refuge in the Vatican Embassy in Panama and could not be captured until he negotiated his surrender to the U.S. authorities.

The NWFZs have either been declared unilaterally or negotiated into treaty agreements among a number of states. The general-purpose ZOPs are best represented by those world regions such as the EEC and ASEAN that have achieved durable peace and security through long-term social, economic, cultural, and political cooperation. The empowering ZOPs are essentially of two kinds, top-down or bottom-up. The top-down variety is best represented by the postwar UN trusteeship system, in which the former colonial powers were put in charge of a territory for the purpose of preparing it for self-government. The bottom-up variety is best represented by citizens' initiatives in North America, Europe, Japan, and Asia-Pacific for the establishment of NWFZs in their own localities. The initiatives by the Cheju Islanders and Falkland Islanders represent yet another popular effort by citizens to turn their land into zones of peace for reconciliation between the parties at conflict, namely North and South Korea and Argentina and Britain, respectively.

Zones of peace in the post–Cold War era provide a new paradigm for international relations. The normative principles of this paradigm call for a ban on weapons of mass destruction* (nuclear*, biological/chemical*, and high-tech "Star Wars*"), pacific settlement of all disputes, development of economic communities, and ultimately a ban on all forms of violence from the face of the earth.

See ENVIRONMENTAL ISSUES, POLLUTION, AND THE MILITARY; HAZARDOUS DUMPING IN PROTECTED MARINE AREAS; NATIONALISM; NUCLEAR WEAPONS TESTING; WARNING ZONES AND MILITARY EXCLUSION ON THE HIGH SEAS.

BIBLIOGRAPHY
Boulding, Elise, "The Zone of Peace Concept in Current Practice: Review and Evaluation," Paper presented at the Inaugural Conference on the Center for Peace Studies, Curtin University and University of West Australia, January 14–16, 1991.
Broadhurst, Arlene, *Nuclear Weapons Free Zones: A Comparative Analysis of Theory and Practice* (Canberra: Peace Research Center, Research School of Pacific Studies, Australian National University, 1988).

Majid Tehranian

ZYKLON B WAR CRIMES TRIAL. Zyklon B, a hydrogen cyanide poison originally developed as a commercial insecticide, was used by the Nazis to exterminate human beings in the gas chambers of the Auschwitz death camp. During 1942 and 1943, nearly twenty tons of the poison was shipped to Auschwitz by the German firm of Tesch and Stabenow for use in several gas chambers, the largest of which could hold 2,000 human beings at one time. Raul Hilberg, who wrote a detailed account of the "extermination industry," estimated that one million people were murdered at Auschwitz (Hilberg 1985, 890–94). The so-called Zyklon B Trial charged three officials of Tesch and Stabenow—including its president and owner, Bruno Tesch—with complicity in the mass murder of Auschwitz inmates (UN War Crimes Commission 1947, 93). The trial took place under the jurisdiction of a British Military Court in the German city of Hamburg from March 1 through March 8, 1946. The prosecution argued, on the basis of affidavits from employees of Tesch and Stabenow and other witnesses, that the defendants, by virtue of their positions in the firm, had been aware that the Zyklon B was used to kill masses of people at Auschwitz. The defense argued that the defendants had no knowledge of that use. Two of the defendants, including Tesch, were found guilty and hanged; one was acquitted. The significance of the trial lies in the fact that individuals who were not directly involved in mass killing, but who supplied the means by which the mass killing could be accomplished, had "made themselves accessories before the fact of that murder." The court "acted on the principle that any civilian who is an accessory to a violation of the laws and customs of war is himself also liable as a war criminal" (UN War Crimes Commission 1947, 101, 103).

See BIOLOGICAL/CHEMICAL WARFARE; CHEMICAL AND BIOLOGICAL EXPERIMENTS ON HUMAN SUBJECTS; CRIMES AGAINST HUMANITY; FINAL SOLUTION; FORBIDDEN STRATEGIES; GENEVA; HOLOCAUST, THE; INNOCENTS; MASSACRES; MEDICAL CASE; NAZISM; NUREMBERG PRINCIPLES; NUREMBERG TRIALS; PSYCHIC NUMBING; TORTURE; TOTAL WAR.

BIBLIOGRAPHY
Hilberg, Raul, *The Destruction of the European Jews,* revised and definitive ed., Vol. 3 (New York; Holmes & Meier, 1985).
UN War Crimes Commission, *Law Reports of the Trials of War Criminals,* Selected and Prepared by the United Nations War Crimes Commission, vol. 1 (London: His Majesty's Stationery Office, 1947).

Eric Markusen

INDEX

Page numbers in **boldface** indicate the location of main entries.

International Tribunal of the Far East. *See* Tokyo Trials
International Tribunal, for Yugoslavia, 496–99
International waters. *See* Law of the Sea Convention
Intervention, 24. *See also* Aggression, attempts to define; Aggressive versus defensive war; First strike/second strike; Humanitarian, intervention; Paris Peace Pact; Reprisals; Retaliation
Intifada, 70, 250–51
IPPNO. *See* International Philosophers for the Prevention of Nuclear Omnicide
Iran-Contra affair, 299
Iran-Iraq War (1980–1988), **240–43**
Iraq Commission of Inquiry, **243–44**
Isaak, Abraham, 3
Islam and war, 28, 154, 210, **244–46**
Israeli Defense Force (IDF), 20, 22, 422
Izard, Walter, 388

Jackson, Gen. T. J. "Stonewall," 65
Jagerstatter, Franz, 101
Jainism, 152, 201
James, St., Declaration (January 1943), **247**, 363
James, William (1842–1910), 59, 61, **247–48**
Jay, Secretary of State John, 236
Jefferson, President Thomas, 64
Jehovah's Witnesses, 79, 98
Jewish casualties, 98. *See also* Holocaust, The
Jihad, 244–46, **249**. *See also* Christianity and War; Holy War; Islam and war
Jingoism, 382. *See also* Military, jargon; Propaganda
Jinnah, Mohamed Ali, 153
Joad, C.E.M., 417
John of Salisbury (1115–1180), 77, **249–50**, 442
Johnson, President Andrew, 13
Johnson, President Lyndon: on intelligence committees, 231; involved in Dominican Republic (1963), 190; on limited war, 276; Tonkin Gulf, 181; Vietnam War, 475–78

Johnston Atoll, 196–97
Joint Chiefs of Staff: CIA, 276; on Bay of Pigs, 37; oppose lifting ban on homosexuals in the military, 212
Jomini, Baron Antoine Henri de, 156
Jonassohn, Kurt, 166
Jones, Rufus, 319
Jorda, Claude, 487
JROTC. *See* Junior Reserve Officers Training Corps
Judaism and war, 208–9, **250–52**
Jung, Carl G., 59
Junger, Ernst, 295
Junior Officers Training Corps (JROTC), 298
jus ad bellum, 18, 22, 252–53, 256–59, 398, 450
jus in bello, 18, 22, 229, 243, 256–59, 398, 450
Justice trial, 106
Just war, 31, 39, 52, 54, 55, 209, 253, **255–59**, 379
Justice, can both sides have?, **252–55**, 473

Kahn, Herman, 339
Kallen, Horace, 199
Kamikaze (divine wind), 210
Kant, Immanuel (1724–1804), 129, 223, **260–62**, 299, 376
Karbala V offensive, 243
Kassebaum Amendment, 237
Katzenbach, Nicholas, 232
Kaufmann, William, 339
Kauravas, 200
Kautilya, 199–200
Kautsky, Karl, 284
Kavka, Gregory, 340
Kedma Mizracha, 251
Kellogg-Briand Peace Pact, **262**. *See also* Paris Peace Pact
Kelman, Herbert, 387
Kennan, George: containment theory, 90; on non-violent defense, 331
Kennedy, President John F., 36, 115; Cuban Missile Crisis, 117–19; intelligence committees, 232; Nuclear, proliferation, 341

ABOUT THE CONTRIBUTORS

DAVID ADAMS is Professor of Psychology at Wesleyan University and holds a permanent post at UNESCO in Paris as senior program specialist in the Culture of Peace Program. He has published widely on the brain mechanisms of aggression, as well as in peace studies. His books on the latter subject include *The American Peace Movements* (1986) and *Psychology for Peace Activists* (1987).

SIDNEY AXINN is Emeritus Professor of Philosophy at Temple University and a Board Member of the *Journal of the History of Ideas*. His publications include *A Moral Military* (1989) and *The Logic of Hope: Extensions of Kant's View of Religion* (1994).

HUGO ADAM BEDAU is Fletcher Professor of Philosophy at Tufts University and former Visiting Professor on the Law Faculty at the University of Westminster, London (1994). His publications include *Death Is Different* (1987) and "Genocide in Vietnam?" in *Boston University Law Review* (May 1973).

DONALD H. BISHOP is Emeritus Professor of Philosophy at Washington State University, where he taught for thirty-two years. He has lectured at Hampton College, Iowa Wesleyan, and Tunghai University, Taiwan. He has received grants from the Society for Higher Education, the American Council of Learned Societies, the Indian Council for Cultural Relations, the Pacific Cultural Foundation, the Chinese Philosophical Association, and the Institute of Global Conflict. In addition to numerous articles, he is the editor of *Indian Thought: An Introduction* (1975), *Thinkers of the Indian Renaissance* (1982 and 1993), and *Chinese Thought: An Introduction* (1985).

ELLEN BONEPARTH is a former Affiliate Professor of Political Science at the University of Hawaii at Hilo, former Dean of the College of Arts and Sciences at that institution, and a Political Officer in the U.S. Foreign Service. She currently resides in Athens, Greece.

JOHN W. BRINSFIELD, Chaplain, Colonel (U.S. Army) is a Special Project Officer at the Office of the Chief of Chaplains in the Pentagon. He is writing a history of the Army Chaplaincy from the end of Vietnam to the end of the Cold War. Previous assignments include serving as an Assistant Professor in the Department of History at West Point.

WILLIAM BURNSIDE BUFFUM is a retired career diplomat with the U.S. Department of State. His former posts include Political Officer, U.S. Embassy, Bonn; Director, Office of UN Political Affairs; Deputy U.S. Representative to the United Nations; U.S. Ambassador to Lebanon; Assistant Secretary of State for International Organizations; and UN Under-Secretary General for Political and General Assembly Affairs.

DUANE L. CADY is Professor of Philosophy at Hamline University. He is the author of *From Warism to Pacifism: A Moral Continuum* (1989); coeditor with Richard Werner of *Just War, Nonviolence and Nuclear Deterrence* (1991); and coeditor with Karen Warren of a special issue of *Hypatia* on ''Feminism and Peace'' (Spring 1994).

MARTIN L. CALHOUN is Senior Research Analyst at the Center for Defense Information in Washington, D.C. His current research has focused on the impact of military activities on human health and safety and the environment.

ROBERT PAUL CHURCHILL is Professor of Philosophy at George Washington University. He recently edited *The Ethics of Liberal Democracy.* He has published articles on militarism, national defense, and nonviolent resistance. His present research is on genocide and crimes against humanity.

JEAN BETHKE ELSHTAIN is Laura Spellman Rockefeller Professor of Ethics at the University of Chicago. She is the author of many books, including *Public Man, Private Woman* (1981), *Women and War* (1987), and *Democracy on Trial* (1995).

KATHY E. FERGUSON is Professor of Political Science and Women's Studies at the University of Hawaii. She specializes in issues of identity, politics, and knowledge. Her books on feminist theory include *The Man Question* (1993) and *Kibbutz Journal* (1995).

NICHOLAS G. FOTION is Professor of Philosophy at Emory University. He is the author of *Military Ethics: Looking Toward the Future* (1990); *Military Ethics: Guidelines for Peace and War,* coauthor with G. Elfstrom (1986); and articles including ''The Gulf War: Cleanly Fought,'' *Bulletin of the Atomic Scientists* (September 1991) and ''Getting Consent from the Troops,'' *Biomedical Ethics Review* (1993).

BARRY L. GAN is Associate Professor of Philosophy and Director of Justice, Peace, and Conflict Studies at St. Bonaventure University. He is the editor of *The Acorn,* a journal featuring articles about the teaching on nonviolence of Mohandas Gandhi and Martin Luther King, Jr.

WILLIAM C. GAY is Chair of the Department of Philosophy at the University of North Carolina. He specializes in literature on nuclear weapons and peace studies as a collaborator with the Institute of Philosophy in Moscow. His publications include *The Nuclear Arms Race* (1987, 1995); co-editor of *On the Eve of the 21st Century: Perspectives of Russian and American Philosophers* (1994); and co-author of *Capitalism with A Human Face? The Quest for A Middle Road in Russian Politics* (1995).

BRIEN HALLETT is Assistant Professor at the University of Hawaii Matsunaga Institute for Peace. His publications include editing and contributing to *Engulfed in War: Just War and the Persian Gulf* (1991).

RON HIRSCHBEIN is Professor of Philosophy and Director of War and Peace Studies at California State University, Chico. He has served as a Visiting Professor in Peace and Conflict Studies for the University of California and as a Visiting Research Philosopher at the Institute on Global Conflict and Cooperation. His publications include *Newest Weapons/Oldest Psychology: The Dialectics of American Nuclear Strategy* (1989, 1991) and numerous articles on international crises.

ROBERT L. HOLMES is Professor of Philosophy at the University of Rochester. His publications include *On War and Morality* (1989) and *Nonviolence in Theory and Practice* (ed.) (1990).

WILLIAM J. HOURIHAN is the U.S. Army Chaplain Branch Historian. He has taught at the University of Massachusetts (Boston) and Northeastern University. His articles have appeared in the *American Neptune, Naval War College Review,* and *Military Chaplains' Review.*

DAVID E. JOHNSON is Professor of Philosophy at the U.S. Naval Academy. He specializes in military ethics and the philosophy of mind. He has been a visiting lecturer at the University of Gothenberg, Sweden, a visiting tutor at St. John's College, Annapolis, and a visiting fellow at the Centre for Peace Studies of the Australian National University.

MICHAEL D. JONES is Associate Physicist at the University of Hawaii. He has done research in high energy physics at Lawrence Laboratory, Argonne National Laboratory, and Fermilab. He helped develop the "UH Perspectives on Nuclear War" course and has published analyses of Star Wars experiments on Kauai and at Kwajalein Atoll. His reports on the Strategic Target System program on Kauai have appeared in the *Bulletin of the Atomic Scientists.*

TOMIS KAPITAN is Associate Professor of Philosophy at Northern Illinois University. He is the editor of *Philosophical Perspectives on the Israeli/Palestinian Conflict,* and "Self-Determination in the Israeli/Palestinian Conflict," in Laurence Bove and Laura Duhan Kaplan (eds.), *In the Eye of the Storm: Philosophy of Peace and Regional Conflict* (1994).

LAURA DUHAN KAPLAN is Assistant Professor of Philosophy and Coordinator of Women's Studies at the University of North Carolina at Charlotte. She is coeditor with Laurence F. Bove of *In the Eye of the Storm: Philosophy of Peace and Regional Conflict* (1994) and the author of numerous essays on feminist peace theory.

GEORGE KENT is Professor of Political Science at the University of Hawaii. He is the author of *The Political Economy of Hunger: The Silent Holocaust* (1984); *War and Children's Survival* (1990); *The Politics of Children's Survival* (1991); *Implementing the Rights of Children in Armed Conflict* (1992); "Analyzing Conflict and Violence," *Peace and Change* (October 1993); and "The Children's Holocaust," *Internet on the Holocaust and Genocide,* no. 28 (Jerusalem, September 1990).

JOHN KULTGEN is Professor of Philosophy at the University of Missouri, Columbia. His publications, especially in the area of nuclear weapons, include *Ethics and Professionalism* (1988) and "Purging Our Nuclear Intentions," *Journal for Peace and Justice Studies* (1993).

DOUGLAS P. LACKEY is Professor of Philosophy at Baruch College and the Graduate Center, City University of New York. His publications include *Moral Principles and Nuclear Weapons* (1984); *The Ethics of War and Peace* (1990); and *Ethics and Strategic Defense* (1990).

STEVEN LEE is Professor of Philosophy at Hobart and William Smith Colleges. He has written extensively about ethical issues raised by nuclear weapons policy and is currently pursuing topics in legal and social philosophy. His major publications include *Morality, Prudence, and Nuclear Weapons* (1993).

ERIC MARKUSEN is Professor of Sociology at Southwest State University, Marshall, Minnesota. He is coauthor with John B. Harris of *Nuclear Weapons and the Threat of Nuclear War* (1986); with Robert Jay Lifton of *The Genocidal Mentality: Nazi Holocaust and Nuclear Threat* (1988); and with David Kopf of *The Holocaust and Strategic Bombing: Genocide and Total War in the Twentieth Century* (1994).

HELENA MEYER-KNAPP has taught at the Evergreen State College, the Graduate School of the Union Institute, the University of Hawaii at Hilo, and in 1994–1995 was a Fellow of the Bunting Institute, Radcliffe College. She has written in the areas of war termination, siege warfare, and ceasefire. Her publications include *Nuclear Siege to Nuclear Ceasefire* (1990).

STEPHEN NATHANSON is Professor of Philosophy at Northeastern University. He is the author of *The Ideal of Nationality* (1986); *An Eye for An Eye?: The Immorality of Punishing by Death* (1987); *Should We Consent to be Governed?* (1992); and *Patriotism, Morality and Peace* (1993).

JOHN QUIGLEY is Professor of Law and Adjunct Professor of Political Science at the Ohio State University. He is the author of *The Ruses for War: American Interventionism Since World War II* (1992) and *Palestine and Israel: A Challenge to Justice* (1990).

C. HAROLD RICKARD is a retired clergyman/missionary to Okinawa and Japan, 1951–1981. He has served as a peace consultant to the National Council of Churches of Christ in the United States and as a regional coordinator of the Peace with Justice program of the United Methodist Church. His publications include ''The Okinawa Land Problem,'' *Japan Christian Quarterly* (Winter 1971) and translator of Shoko Ahagon, *The Island Where People Live* (1989).

JOHN K. ROTH is the Pitzer Professor of Philosophy at Claremont McKenna College. A specialist on Holocaust studies and ethics, he has published more than twenty books, including *Approaches to Auschwitz: The Holocaust and Its Legacy,* with Richard L. Rubenstein (1987); *Different Voices: Women and the Holocaust,* coedited with Carol Rittner (1993). He and Carol Rittner are editors for a Greenwood Press series on Christianity and the Holocaust.

WILLIAM G. SCHMIDT, Lieutenant Colonel (USAF) is Senior Associate Professor of Law and Deputy for Elective Courses, Department of Law, U.S. Air Force Academy. He currently teaches air and space law, comparative legal systems, international law, and law for commanders. He has published and lectured extensively, especially on the international humanitarian law of armed conflict, and teaches that subject both at the Academy and at the International Institute of Humanitarian Law, San Remo, Italy.

KATHRYN R. SCHULTZ is Senior Research Analyst at the Center for Defense Information in Washington, D.C., and a former Herbert Scoville, Jr. Peace Fellow. She specializes in issues of nuclear weapons and European security.

CAROLYN M. STEPHENSON is Associate Professor of Political Science at the University of Hawaii and an authority on peace research and peace education. Her publications include *Alternative Methods for International Security* (1982).

MAJID TEHRANIAN is Professor of Communication, University of Hawaii, and former Director of the Matsunaga Institute for Peace in Hawaii. His most recent book is *Restructuring for World Peace: On the Threshold of the 21st Century* (1992).

NORMAN K. THOMPSON, Major (USAF) is Associate Professor and Course Director of Law, U.S. Air Force Academy. He currently teaches comparative legal systems and law for commanders. His extensive experience in military justice includes serving as Trial Counsel or Defense Counsel in over forty court-martials.

PATRICK R. TOWER, Major (USAF) is Associate Professor of Philosophy, U.S. Air Force Academy. His publications include "A Creedal Code of Ethics for the Profession of Arms," *U.S. Air Force Academy Journal of Professional Military Ethics* (February 1984); "Functionalism and Military Ethics," *JSCOPE Proceedings* (1994); and "Bridging the Gap Between Theory and Practice: What the Philosopher and the Consultant Can Teach Each Other," *Proceedings of the Fifth Annual National Conference on Ethics in America* (1994).

PHYLLIS TURNBULL is Assistant Professor of Political Science at the University of Hawaii at Manoa. Her specialization has been in the implications for cultural politics of the military in Hawaii. She is the author of "Remembering Pearl Harbor: The Semiotics of the *U.S.S. Arizona* Memorial," in Shapiro and Alker, *Territorial Identities and Global Flows* (1994).

JON M. VAN DYKE is Professor of Law at the Richardson School of Law at the University of Hawaii. His publications include "Military Exclusion and Warning Zones on the High Seas" in *Marine Policy* (1991); *Nuclear Activities and the Pacific Islanders* (1984); "Protected Marine Areas and Low-Lying Atolls" in *Ocean and Shore Line Management* (1991); "The Riddle of Establishing Clear and Workable Rules to Govern Armed Conflicts" in *UCLA Pacific Basin Law Journal* (1984); "The Laws of War: Can They Ever Be Enforced?" in the *Center Magazine* (1971).

JAMES C. F. WANG is Professor of Political Science and International Studies at the University of Hawaii, Hilo. His many scholarly interests include the politics of the law of the sea and Asian studies. His publications include *Handbook on Ocean Politics and Law* (1992).

DONALD A. WELLS is Emeritus Professor of Philosophy, University of Hawaii, Hilo, and Adjunct Professor at Southern Oregon State College. His numerous articles include "How Much Can the Just War Justify?" *Journal of Philosophy* (1969). His books include *The War Myth* (1967); *War Crimes and Laws of War* (1984, 1991); and *The Laws of Land Warfare: A Guide to the U.S. Army Manuals* (1992).

KENNETH H. WENKER, Colonel (USAF) (ret.) is Emeritus Professor of Philosophy at the U.S. Air Force Academy and Director of the Rocky Mountain Ethics Center. His publications include "Military Necessity and Morality," in *Military Ethics: Reflections on Principles* (1987); "Just War Pacifism," in *American Catholic University Proceedings* (1983); and "Morality and Military Obedience," in *Air University Review* (July–August 1981).

RICHARD WERNER is John S. Kennedy Professor and Chair of Philosophy at Hamilton College. He specializes in issues of moral realism and the philosophy of war. His publications include "Nuclear Deterrence and the Limits of Moral Theory," *The Monist* (July 1987); and "The Immorality of Nuclear Deterrence," in *Political Realism and International Morality,* Kenneth Kipnis and Diana T. Myers, eds. (1987).

ISBN 0-313-29116-0

EAN

9 780313 291166

90000>

HARDCOVER BAR CODE